Dear Member of the Institute of Noetic Sciences,

This edition of *The Life We Are Given* was printed by special arrangement with Tarcher/Putnam solely for the Institute of Noetic Sciences. It is a great pleasure and honor for us to participate in this publishing project.

When the Institute of Noetic Sciences was founded, we were excited by its vision and promise, and through the years since we have admired and frequently been involved in its work. We have, for example, joined with it through Esalen Institute to sponsor nine annual meetings in Big Sur on the implications of contemporary meditation research, as well as several conferences to explore new directions in parapsychology and the study of consciousness.

No other organization has done more than the Institute of Noetic Sciences to promote research into the mind-body-spirit connection or to encourage new thinking about the interconnectedness of the individual, culture, and the environment. The Institute is a natural ally for us as we develop the theories and practices described in the book. We hope to work with this pioneering organization for many years as we develop a permanent center in the San Francisco Bay Area for Integral Transformative Practice.

With warm regards,

Michael Murphy   George Leonard

OTHER BOOKS BY GEORGE LEONARD:

The Decline of the American Male
(with William Attwood and J. Robert Moskin)

Shoulder the Sky (a novel)

Education and Ecstasy

The Man & Woman Thing, and Other Provocations

The Transformation

The Ultimate Athlete

The Silent Pulse

Adventures in Monogamy

Walking on the Edge of the World

Mastery

OTHER BOOKS BY MICHAEL MURPHY:

Golf in the Kingdom

Jacob Atabet

An End to Ordinary History

The Future of the Body

In the Zone (with Rhea White)

The Life We Are Given

A Long-Term Program for
Realizing the Potential of Body,
Mind, Heart, and Soul

GEORGE LEONARD
and
MICHAEL MURPHY

A JEREMY P. TARCHER/PUTNAM BOOK
published by G. P. PUTNAM'S SONS
New York

Excerpts of five-line poem by Yamaoka Tesshu translated by John Stevens, page 159 of *The Sword of No Sword* by John Stevens © 1984.

A Jeremy P. Tarcher/Putnam Book
Published by G. P. Putnam's Sons
Publishers Since 1838
200 Madison Avenue
New York, NY 10016

Library of Congress Cataloging-in-Publication Data

Leonard, George Burr, date.
    The life we are given: a long-term program for realizing the potential of body, mind, heart, and soul / George Leonard and Michael Murphy.
        p.   cm.
    "A Jeremy P. Tarcher/Putnam Book."
    Includes bibliographical references.
    ISBN 0-87477-853-0
    1. Human potential movement.   2.   Leonard, George Burr, date.
3. Murphy, Michael, date.   I. Murphy, Michael, date.
II. Title.
BF637.H85L46   1995   95-8623 CIP
158'.1—dc20

Book design by Lee Fukui

Illustrations by Sergio Giovine

Printed in the United States of America

10   9   8   7   6   5   4   3   2

This book is printed on acid-free paper. ⊗

We dedicate this book to our fellow teachers in the experimental
Integral Transformative Practice classes of 1992 and 1993:

ANNIE STYRON LEONARD
& ERIK VAN RISWOLD

and to the participants in the class who, through their devotion,
creativity, and perseverance, gave life to these ideas and practices:

Sanford Anderson	Donald Kerson	Tyrone Polastri
Jani Ashmore	Kathie Kertesz	Hollis Polk
Pamela Carrara	Leslie Lauf	Karen Preuss
Dan Carte	Ruth Kissane	Katherine Randolph
Walter Cole	David Lombardi	Andrea Rossman
Scot Combs	Beth McCarthy	Hubert Schmidt
Niki Cronin	Chris McCluney	Robert Sperber
Alan Epstein	Linda Menicucci	Dan Svagerko
Anna Ernstthal	Richard Moran	Sylvia Timbers
Robert Ernstthal	Phillip Moffitt	Janice Uchida
Lacey Fosburgh	Roy Nakashima	Neal Vahle
Irwin Friman	Bruce Nelson	Debra Viall
Charlotte Hatch	John Nicholas	Karen Wilson
James Hatch	Linda Novy	Patrice Winchester
Joan Herz	Bruce Orcutt	Lari Wolf
Linda Jue	Jim Patrick	Mira Zussman
Elizabeth Kelly	Stephen Perelson	

Contents

Joining the Evolutionary Adventure

Like the human heart, the world points beyond itself to something greater and more beautiful than its present condition. That something attracts us all, in different ways, and leads many of us to seek transformation. Does it secretly inform the entire evolutionary adventure? Could it be that the human heart and the world's heart are one in their self-surpassing? We believe that they are. As we grow in love and strength, we become vehicles for the world's growth. We bring new sustenance to our families, new joy to our friends, new light to our places of work. We enhance the physical things around us, and the earth itself.

More and more of us are waking up to this fact. Never before has humankind enjoyed so much knowledge about our evolutionary universe and the ways in which we embody its stupendous adventure. It becomes more and more evident that our own well-being is indissolubly linked to the health of society and our environment. It is possible, now more than ever before, to see that our own growth is rooted in, and furthers, the whole world's advance.

We are fortified in this perception by the emerging story of our universe. It is, we feel, the greatest story of our time, our story of stories, this immense panorama of universal evolution from the incredible birth of space and time to the emergence of human culture. To various degrees, all of us are influenced by it, and each of us can turn to it for inspiration. Through transformative practices of the kind presented in this book, we can share the most fundamental tendencies of the world's unfoldment—to expand, create, and give rise to more conscious forms of life. Like evolution itself, we can bring forth new possibilities for growth, new worlds for further exploration.

We live only part of the life we are given.

M. M.

The story of evolution, as it has been elaborated by modern science, is a new story for the human race. Though a few poets and philosophers had guessed that humans developed from simpler forms of life, the fact of evolution was not widely recognized until Charles Darwin published *On the Origin of Species* in 1859. The deeper implications of this enormous revelation are still dawning on us. Many physicists and biologists, for example, believe that something more than chance and material causes is involved in the universe's awesome journey. The world's advance from atomic particles to consciousness, from inorganic matter to the human awareness of God, is an event that confronts every thinking person, leading many of us to wonder "What is impelling it all? Where is the universe headed? What is the relation between evolution and higher powers? Can the human race advance any further? Can it move closer to God?"

Since the nineteenth century, a compelling answer to these questions has begun to emerge among certain scientists, philosophers, and laypeople. That answer, we believe, will grow in the world's imagination, and it has guided the work described in this book. In simple terms, it can be stated like this: While remaining transcendent to all created things, the divine spirit involved itself in the birth of the material universe. The process that followed, the uneven but inexorable emergence of ever higher organization from matter to life to humankind, is then—at the heart of it—the unfolding of hidden divinity. Evolution follows involution. What was implicit is gradually made explicit, as the spirit within all things progressively manifests itself. In the words of the Indian philosopher Sri Aurobindo, "apparent nature is secret God."

This idea has been developed in different ways by the German philosophers Hegel and Friedrich Schelling; by Henry James, Sr., the father of William and Henry James; by the French philosopher Henri-Louis Bergson; by the Jesuit theologian Teilhard de Chardin; and by twentieth-century thinkers such as Jean Gebser, Alfred North Whitehead, Charles Hartshorne, and Sri Aurobindo. The vision put forth by these and other philosophers reflects intuitions reported by countless people since antiquity that they enjoy a secret contact or kinship with the founding principle of the universe. The recognition of a reality ordinarily hidden but immediately apprehended as our true identity, our immortal soul, our "original face," our secret at-oneness with God is implicit in much Buddhist, Hindu, Platonist, Christian, Jewish, and Islamic thought.

The idea that divinity is present in all things, manifesting itself through the immense adventure of evolution, helps account for the mystery of our great surplus capacities, our yearnings for God, our inextinguishable creativity, our sense of grace in human affairs. It helps explain our quest for self-transcendence and humanity's proliferation of transformative practices.

For it is the case that people in every culture, and in every age, have invented ways to realize their kinship or oneness with divinity. Neanderthals held burial ceremonies, indicating their sense of an afterlife, and Cro-Magnon peoples, more than fifteen thousand years ago, left us cave drawings of shamanic figures. These *Homo sapiens* had developed an awareness of themselves in relation to things beyond. In this awareness, this reach beyond the ordinary world, there occurred an immense evolutionary leap. The universe awakened to its secret soul, its guiding presence and destiny. That awakening has been nurtured ever since through innumerable practices of transformation that have arisen around the globe.

Such practices appeared on earth long ages ago, through shamans such as those depicted in Stone Age cave paintings. These first specialists of human society had extraordinary powers to overcome pain, understand others, and provoke ecstasy in themselves and their fellows. Around fires at night, they led ceremonies with chanting and dance and sometimes with hallucinogens. Through mythic narrative, they reenacted the world's creation and led members of their group through symbolic death and rebirth. In their spirit-body they flew to the gods, descended to the underworld, and remembered their secret identity. These first masters of transformative practice sustained humanity's intuition that mind and flesh can be transformed in the fire of our secret divinity.

Many peoples have preserved the spirit of Stone Age shamanism and have extended our reach into the unseen. On the Indian subcontinent, for example, inspired philosophers have enlarged our spiritual vocabulary, broadened our metaphysial imagination, and invented yogas now practiced in every part of the earth. The Indian witness to our latent divinity is typified by the Katha Upanishad:

> Finer than the fine, greater than the great, the Self hides in the secret heart of the creature . . .
> Seated, he journeys far off, lying down, he goes everywhere. Realizing the bodiless in bodies, the established in things unsettled, the great and omnipresent Self, the wise and steadfast soul grieves no longer.

For more than three thousand years, India has been a laboratory for spiritual exploration, constantly illuminating our capacities for extraordinary life. Through the Hindu and Buddhist traditions that began there, its teachings have spread around the world. Today, its philosophies and practices are enjoying a great renaissance.

Tranformative practices also spread from China and Japan, extending the sense of our secret source into the things of everyday life. China's *feng shui* encourages a reverent sensitivity to dwelling and landscape; its medicine and martial arts incorporate yogic and shamanic lore about the body's potentially luminous anatomy; its decorative arts convey the subtlety and depth of mystic insight. Japan's aikido, its gardening and home-building crafts, its arts of tea ceremony and flower arrangement, bring the illumination of Zen into the simplest things, reminding us that the physical world is suffused with enlightenment.

This diffusion of soul-awakening from the East is complemented today by the rediscovery of Western esoteric traditions. People of many intellectual persuasions have embraced the teachings of cabalistic and Hasidic mysticism, with their emphasis upon the divine splendor, the *zohar*, which shines forth when we live in accordance with God. Sufism has had a similar revival. In both Islam and Judaism there are ways to find holy joy in daily life—around the dinner table, in the wedding bed, at our places of work. In the words of the Talmud and various Sufi writings, a good work, a good marriage, a feast among family and friends, can provide a foretaste of the life to come.

And the words of Christian mystics are being published in record numbers. The early desert fathers, orthodox Greek and Russian saints, medieval mystics such as Hildegarde of Bingen and Meister Eckhart, the Spanish ascetics St. Teresa of Avila and St. John of the Cross, Protestant ecstatics such as Jakob Böhme and George Fox, and other God-intoxicated people of ancient, medieval, and modern Christendom influence us today through their newly translated writings, their vivid examples of holy life, and their imaginative ways of self-transcendence.

To learn is to change. Our destiny is to learn and keep learning for as long as we live.

G. L.

Every sacred tradition is having a generative influence in the global village, stimulating countless people to embrace once esoteric ways of growth. This worldwide event has helped produce a momentous new stage in the development of transformative practice. For today, more than ever before, long-term human change can be understood and guided with the help of science. There are many reasons for this, among them new advances in the understanding of psychodynamics by modern psychology; demonstrations of our capacity for highly specific change in psychoneuroimmunology, sports medicine, biofeedback training, placebo studies, and hypnosis research; new discoveries about the mind's ability to reshape motivations, emotions, and the flesh; and sociologists' demonstrations that each social group nurtures just some of our attributes while neglecting or suppressing others. Never before has there been so much scientifically based knowledge about the transformative capacities of human nature. This knowledge, combined with the lore and inspiration of the sacred traditions, gives the human race an unprecedented opportunity to make a great evolutionary advance. It is possible now, we believe, for humanity to pursue its destiny with more clarity than ever before. To quote the poet Christopher Fry: "Affairs are now soul-size. The enterprise is exploration into God."

Every person on this planet can join the procession of transformative practice that began with our ancient ancestors. That is the guiding idea of this book. The ways of growth described here, which can be adopted by anyone, embrace our many parts. We call them *integral* to signify their inclusion of our entire human nature—body, mind, heart, and soul.

When wisely pursued, such practices bestow countless blessings. If we do not obsess about their results, they make us vehicles of grace and reveal unexpected treasures. In this, they often seem paradoxical. They require time, for example, but frequently make more time available to us: They can slow time down, and open us to the timeless moment from which we have arisen. They require sacrifice, but they restore us. While demanding the relinquishment of established patterns, they open us to new love, new awareness, new energy; what we lose is replaced by new joy, beauty, and strength. They require effort, but come to be effortless. Demanding commitment, they eventually proceed like second nature. They need a persistent will, but after a while flow unimpeded. Whereas they are typically hard to start, they eventually cannot be stopped.

For most of us, integral practices require hard work. But with patience, the initial discomfort they cause turns into an ever-recurring pleasure. Renewing mind and heart, rebuilding the body, restoring the soul, become sources of endless delight.

Because they arise from the same primordial source, transformative practice and the world's evolution have similar patterns. In both, there are periods of stasis—long plateaus of the learning curve—followed by bursts of rapid development. In both, things are sacrificed as something new emerges. In both, new levels or dimensions of functioning take into themselves what went before, giving fuller expression to our latent divinity. And in both, there are times when the process of change itself graduates to a higher level. We are, it seems, involved in such a momentous transition. The discovery of evolution, the marriage of science with the sacred traditions, and the recognition that our entire human nature, including the flesh, can grow in the light of God: all this conspires to make possible transformative practices with unprecedented depth and power. This book, we hope, will open a doorway to such practice for you.

VISION
and
PRACTICE

ONE

A Lifetime's Quest

For years, the two of us had wanted to try out our ideas about the realization of extraordinary human abilities, to see if people with busy lives could change themselves for the better through long-term practice. We had long held a vision of human evolution and the transformation of human societies. Separately and together, we had worked for most of our adult lives inspired by the belief that all of us possess a vast, untapped potential to learn, to love, to feel deeply, to create, and that there are few tragedies so pervasive, so difficult to justify, as the waste of that potential.

Novelist James Agee wrote, "I believe that every human being is potentially capable, within his 'limits,' of fully 'realizing' his potentialities; that this, his being cheated and choked of it, is infinitely the ghastliest, commonest, and most inclusive of all the crimes of which the human world can accuse itself. . . . I know only that murder is being done against nearly every individual on the planet."

We are haunted by Agee's words. They bring to mind the victims of war, famine, and disease, of ignorance, poverty, and injustice. They point to the dogmatism that inhibits thought, numbs the feelings, and twists the perceptions of entire cultures. But the crime of which Agee speaks is not a distant phenomenon, not something "out there." It touches the lives not only of those trapped by injustice or material deprivation, but also of those considered fortunate: our parents and children, our friends and sisters and brothers, ourselves. It is hard to imagine words more heart-wrenching than those of a close friend or relative who at the approach of death is heard to say, "I realize now I've wasted my life." Against the backdrop of the billions of years it took to give us our life and the brief time we have to experience it here, the dimensions of such waste are beyond calculation.

And this isn't just a private matter. It's hard to say how much of the world's neuroses, drug abuse, illness, crime, and general unhappiness can be traced to our failure to develop our God-given abilities. But surely people who are deeply involved in lifelong learning, in practices that encourage community, good health, and a sense of oneness with the spirit of the universe, would be unlikely to sink into the despair, unrest, and cynicism that lead to so many individual and societal ills.

Early in 1992, sustained by our faith in the human potential, we convened an experimental class in what we called Integral Transformative Practice (ITP). The experiment lasted for two years and provided material and inspiration for this book. But it isn't just this one class that informs our words, but rather the gleanings of a long journey, a lifetime's quest.

In Search of the Human Potential

In World War II, George Leonard served as a combat pilot in the South Pacific. During the Korean War, he was an analytical intelligence officer and then an air force magazine editor. This work brought him to *Look* magazine as a senior editor, where he reported on religion, politics, social change, and the Cold War. His experience in covering the Civil Rights Movement, from Little Rock to Ole Miss and Selma, helped shape his feelings about human potential and social change. As a native Southerner, he knew how deeply segregation had penetrated every aspect of Southern life. To witness "unthinkable" changes in a matter of years or months showed him that when the historic moment arrives some sort of transformation is possible and perhaps inevitable.

More than any other subject, education became the focus of Leonard's reportage and writing. He visited scores of schools and hundreds of classrooms preparing award-winning essays and special features on the subject, seeking that magical moment when a child

flings up a hand and says, "I know! I know!" This firsthand experience with education and miseducation led him, in 1964, to embark
on a ten-month-long project to produce a major *Look* essay under
the title, "The Human Potential." It was during this investigation, in
February 1965, that he met Michael Murphy, whose Esalen Institute
had opened in 1962 under the banner, "Human Potentialities."

Murphy and Leonard were introduced at a dinner given by one
of Murphy's friends. They stayed up most of the night talking, discovering that their interests and aspirations made a serendipitous
match. Leonard brought knowledge of social and political movements, behavioral psychology, and brain research, Murphy of humanistic and depth psychology, of Eastern religion and philosophy.
They started a series of conversations and brainstorming sessions
that continue to this day. During one session, still in early 1965, they
found themselves discussing the Civil Rights and Free Speech movements. In the heady spirit of the mid-1960s, Leonard proposed that
there should also be a Human Potential Movement, thus naming a
movement which, in ways neither he nor Murphy imagined at the
time, has touched the lives of millions of people.

Esalen Institute's Early Years

In 1950, Michael Murphy was a Stanford University student when
he took a class with Frederic Spiegelberg, a charismatic professor of
Comparative Religious Studies. Spiegelberg was recently returned
from India where he had encountered the famous sage Ramana Ma-
harishi and the philosopher Sri Aurobindo. His lectures had a profound and lasting influence on Murphy, inspiring him to give up his
pre-med courses and dedicate himself to the study of philosophy and
the practice of meditation. He read widely in religion and psychology, focusing on visions of evolutionary development. In 1956 and
1957, he spent a year and a half at the Aurobindo Ashram in
Pondicherry, India, where he deepened his meditation practice and
confirmed his committment to personal and social transformation.

Murphy's family owned land on California's Big Sur coast, with
redwood canyons, hot mineral springs, high cliffs, and magnificent
outlooks on the Pacific Ocean. With Richard Price, a former Stanford classmate, Murphy started an institute there, which he and
Price named after the Esalen Indians who had lived on the coast. In
its first years, Esalen hosted seminars on Eastern thought and reli-

*Whatever your age, your up-
bringing, or your education,
what you are made of is mostly
unused potential.*

G. L.

gious practice, Christian mysticism, shamanism, psychedelic drugs, humanistic psychology, ecology, and other subjects loosely grouped under the banner of human potentialities and the education of the whole person. Historian Arnold Toynbee, theologian Paul Tillich, psychologists Abraham Maslow, Carl Rogers, Rollo May, and B. F. Skinner, philosophers Alan Watts and Gerald Heard, comparative mythologist Joseph Campbell, gestalt therapist Fritz Perls, family counselor Virginia Satir, creativity researcher Frank Barron, and pioneers of somatic education such as Charlotte Selver and Ida Rolf, among others, led programs at the institute. As time passed, the emphasis in these programs shifted from lecture and discussion to meditative, emotional, and somatic work, from a primarily cognitive approach to what Aldous Huxley called the "nonverbal humanities."

In 1967, Murphy started an Esalen center in San Francisco to reach people in their places of work. Esalen also pioneered holistic approaches to medicine, created a sports center that explored new approaches to sport psychology and physical fitness, and initiated a program of cultural and scientific exchanges to foster better relations between the Soviet Union and America. With grants from the Ford Foundation, the institute worked with professor George Brown to develop curricula for elementary and secondary schools that joined cognitive, affective, and somatic training. Brown called this program "confluent education" to denote its joining of mind, heart, and body, and started a graduate school to promote such education at the University of California, Santa Barbara. From its first years, the institute fostered work for social as well as individual development.

Murphy's experience at Esalen introduced him to many ways of growth derived from Eastern and Western religious disciplines, psychotherapy, somatic education, and other fields. And it confirmed his faith in human tranformative capacities. But this experience taught him, too, that people cannot make healthy and lasting changes without attention to the whole person, without long-term practice, and without solid social support. Programs for growth, he found, can go wrong in many ways.

THE TROUBLE WITH INSTANT ENLIGHTENMENT

In those early days, both of us were impressed with techniques that seemed to transform lives in a weekend. For example, a man might have been holding some dark secret all his life, perhaps a childhood episode of sexual abuse, afraid that if it got out he would be ruined. During an encounter weekend, primed by exercises designed to elicit self-revelation and encouraged by the intimate revelations of others, he would tell all to the group—and the sky wouldn't fall in. Instead, he would be praised and embraced as he wept euphoric tears of relief. Or an aloof woman might take a psychedelic drug under skilled guidance and discover beauty in the most mundane objects while perceiving what is unique and holy in people previously considered quite ordinary.

Some of these transformative experiences were aimed specifically at social reform. In 1967, Leonard and Price Cobbs, a black psychiatrist, began a series of interracial marathon encounters designed to get at the roots of racism. The first of these sessions, called "very likely the toughest encounter session that had ever been convened at Esalen," by Walter Truett Anderson in *The Upstart Spring*, set the format and style for a series of black-white encounter groups that followed over the next two years. The thirty-seven participants met for an introductory session on Friday night. Then at noon on Saturday, they began twenty-four hours of nonstop encounter, with meals brought in and no sleep.

By the time those long, sleepless hours ended, very little had been left unexposed, not the fiercest rage or the most well-disguised resentment, not the most manipulative games or the most subtle prejudice. As each level of prejudice and rage was uncovered, however, it only led to another, deeper level. In the last hours before dawn, a chilly fog rolled in from the Pacific and all hope for a breakthrough seemed lost in despair and desolation.

But sometime after sunrise, there was a shift in the climate, a feeling that something unforeseen would happen. The moment finally came when a simple act of kindness by a black woman to a white woman broke the barriers between the races, and soon the whole room was full of weeping, embracing people. Tears and hugs were common in this setting, but these were made possible only through uncommon stamina and the participants' courage to confront prejudice and rage in themselves. In the searing spotlight of race, these people, many for the first time, had glimpsed the fragile and tragic beauty of existence and their deep connection with others.

It was often like that, not just in the interracial groups but in other short-term, cathartic programs of the time. Many people came out of such experiences with the feeling that they were beginning a new life, that they would never again be the same. And in a way they were right. They could always bring to mind that brief time of awakening, of living in a different world. But when they returned to their old environments, their old ways of life, the memory lost its urgency and the learning ceased. Within a few days or weeks or months, most of them fell back into their old, familiar paterns. The interracial marathons were particularly dramatic, but even here, unless participants continued their practice of interracial understanding, the power of the experience faded.

In a culture intoxicated with promises of the quick fix, instant enlightenment, and easy learning, it was hard to accept one of the most important lessons that came to us out of those powerful but short-term experiences: *Any significant long-term change requires long-term practice, whether that change has to do with learning to play the violin or learning to be a more open, loving person.* We all know people who say they have been permanently changed by experiences of a moment or a day or a weekend. But when you check it out you'll generally discover that those who ended up permanently changed had spent considerable time preparing for their life-changing experience or had continued diligently practicing the new behavior afterward.

The Transformative Power of Long-term Practice

Our attempts to establish transformative programs that lasted longer than a weekend go back a long way. Late in 1965, Murphy started laying plans for a nine-month resident program at Esalen. Leonard and others joined him in formulating a practice for the mind, body, heart, and soul, with a core faculty and many visiting teachers. The curriculum would include not just cognitive training but also what Aldous Huxley called the "nonverbal humanities"—such activities as meditation, creativity training, encounter, movement, sensory awareness, emotional expressiveness, and inner imagery. Residential fellows would complete a project during the nine months of the program, something that would make a contribution to society. The first program began in the fall of 1966, with seventeen fellows, selected from around two hundred applicants.

All of life, especially the part that deals with significant innovation, is full of surprises. Shortly after the program began, Virginia Satir, the noted psychologist chosen as its leader, left for no apparent reason. The program limped along for a while and finally pulled itself together, but could not be termed a success. The 1967 residential program was another thing entirely: a colorful, controversial, and strongly focused experiment in radical human change. Led by Will Schutz, a pioneer in open encounter, the program became a laboratory devoted to pressing the limits of self-revelation. The U.S. space program was then nearing its climax and the twenty-one residential fellows, who sometimes termed themselves "psychonauts," were shooting for the stars of openness and honesty. Rather than trying to establish a regular, long-term practice, this program concentrated on breaking through personal and interpersonal barriers. It had high and low moments, successes and tragedies, and was described in several national media features. In terms of establishing a long-term education for the whole person, however, it was not what we had had in mind.

Our study of the transformative process continued. Leonard's 1968 book, *Education and Ecstasy*, was a manifesto for the transformation of American schooling. In 1970, Leonard resigned from *Look* to write *The Transformation*, a book about the transformation of society and the individual. Other books followed—on the transformation of sports and the body, on the transformation of sexualilty, and in *The Silent Pulse*, on the nature of the transformative process itself.

In 1970, shortly after he left *Look*, Leonard took up the Japanese martial art of aikido. In the twenty-four years since then, there has rarely been a week during which he has not practiced this art. He received his first-degree black belt in 1976, his fourth-degree in 1992. Aikido of Tamalpais, the aikido school he and his partners, Wendy Palmer and Richard Heckler, started in 1976 in Mill Valley, California, has produced dozens of black belts. From shaky beginnings, it has evolved into an *aikidojo* known and visited by aikidoists from many parts of the world.

Far more than a physical self-defense art, aikido has profound philosophical, spiritual, and interpersonal implications. It is through his practice in this art, more than anything else, that Leonard has learned about the ups and down, the long stretches of diligent practice with no apparent improvement, the ecstatic movements that seem to come from nowhere—in short, the enduring joy and transformative power of long-term practice.

From aikido have come nonmartial arts exercises designed to teach new ways of being in the world. Over the years, Leonard has introduced his version of this work, Leonard Energy Training (LET), to some fifty thousand people. The relationship between what we call "mind" and "body" and the potential of both for positive change becomes clear in LET. In 1981 and 1982, as part of an ongoing LET class at Aikido of Tamalpais, Leonard carried on a bodily transformation project that produced some interesting results, including a number of significant bodily alterations. Over a six-month period, for example, a woman experienced the healing of a congenital heart defect. A man in his late thirties increased his height from 5 feet 10 inches to 5 feet 11¼ inches. This transformative work continued with two-month-long, sixteen-hour-day, six-day-week Leonard Energy Training certification programs in 1983, 1984, and 1987 at Esalen Institute.

THE FUTURE OF THE BODY

In 1972, Murphy published *Golf in the Kingdom*, a novel about his encounter with Shivas Irons, a mystical golf professional who made the game a transformative practice. The book prompted people to write Murphy describing their own illuminations in sport. Among the experiences they described were feelings of merging with the environment, uncanny sensations of physical suspension, perceptions marked by superordinary clarity, sensitivity to others that seemed telepathic, and moments of unaccountable joy. Murphy had known that people have metanormal experiences in many walks of life, but hadn't appreciated how diverse these are. A second novel, *Jacob Atabet*, about an artist with a gift for psychophysical transformation, caused more people to send reports of dramatic mind-body changes. As these multiplied, they convinced Murphy that people harbor a wider range of metanormal capacities than is generally thought, and that these are strikingly similar to the extraordinary powers, the "siddhis" and "charisms," produced by Hindu, Buddhist, Christian, and other religious practice.

Murphy's interest in metanormal experience was reinforced by his own practice, which now involved distance running. Guided by Mike Spino, an innovative running coach who brought mental techniques and great emotion to his training, he began to compete in Seniors' races, including marathons. In 1983, he was third in the 1,500 meter race for fifty-year-olds during the National Masters Championships in Houston, running the race in four minutes and thirty-five seconds. In the same year, he won the fifty-and-over bracket in eleven of his thirteen races, at distances ranging from 800 to 10,000 meters. His training at the time, which with Spino included meditation and visualization, gave rise to experiences such as those his correspondents described.

Inspired in part by such experiences and the continuing response to his books, Murphy began to assemble an archive dealing with extraordinary human experiences. He was assisted in this by his wife, Dulce Murphy, and Jim Hickman, both of whom subsequently directed Esalen's Soviet-American exchanges; by Steven Donovan, Esalen's president; by Margaret Livingston, who became the project's principle researcher; and by funding from Esalen. George Leonard participated in this work from its inception, joining discussions of the project's findings and critiquing the conclusions Murphy drew from the archive materials as he wrote *The Future of the Body*.

The Esalen archive contains scientific studies of meditation, hypnosis, biofeedback, mental imagery, spiritual healing, fitness training, somatic education, martial arts, and other potentially transformative activities, as well as descriptions of psychosomatic changes that occur in disorders such as multiple personality and hysterical stigmata. In building this collection, Murphy was influenced by Frederic Myers, who pioneered the study of metanormal capacities and was a principal founder of psychical research, by William James and his *The Varieties of Religious Experience*, and by Abraham Maslow, who studied peak-experience. These and other researchers have created a field of inquiry that can be regarded as a natural history of extraordinary functioning. Murphy and his colleagues followed their example, gathering material from many sources, including Russian scientists they met through Esalen's pioneering Soviet-American Exchanges who were studying "hidden human reserves." The body of information they produced, which grew to more than ten thousand journal articles, monographs, dissertations, and books, provides massive evidence that dramatic alterations of mind and body, whether healthy, pathological, or merely curious, occur in virtually all walks of life.

This collection dramatizes the fact that human beings have extraordinary capacities for change, which operate both creatively and destructively. It also provides evidence that certain activities, or "transformative modalities," such as imagery, catharsis, and self-observation, are involved in most significant alterations of human functioning. Murphy came to believe that these operate in effect as transformative practices, even when they aren't recognized as such. For example, both false pregnancy and the development of weight lifters' physiques are facilitated by sustained emotionally laden imagery. Women with false pregnancy and championship bodybuilders alike typically imagine their somatic changes with great passion and consistency. Such deeply felt imagery is evident as well in effective psychotherapy, somatic education, and other disciplines. It seems that a limited number of such modalities constitute all enduring ways of growth.

At the heart of it, mastery is practice. Mastery is staying on the path.

G. L.

And Murphy was led to three further beliefs. First, every human attribute can give rise to extraordinary versions of itself. In *The Future of the Body*, Murphy chose twelve attributes with which to illustrate this principle: perception of external events, kinesthetic awareness, communication skills, vitality, movement abilities, capacities to influence the environment directly, pain and pleasure, cognition, volition, individuation, love, and bodily processes. All twelve have metanormal expressions among men and women, young and old, in different cultures. Examples of these are presented in later chapters.

Second, most significant human growth results from practices that address the whole person. In *The Future of the Body*, Murphy defines tranformative practice as a complex and coherent set of activities that produces positive changes in a person or group. It is most effective when pursued for its own sake, and when it is *integral*, that is, when it embraces body, mind, heart, and soul.

And third, each of us has more latent capacities than is generally known, many of which resemble the extraordinary powers produced by religious disciplines. Recognition of these helps broaden our understanding of the human potential. It gives us more options for growth. Many are described in *The Future of the Body*, and several of them are discussed in this book.

A TRANSFORMING CRISIS

In 1989, Leonard faced a health crisis. Its resolution gave proof that an integral transformative practice can change the human body for the better. It started early that year when a routine treadmill test indicated a mild blockage in his right coronary artery. His cardiologist told him that it was not life threatening and that, essentially, he should go on with his life and come back in a year. Anyway, the treadmill test might not be right. "We don't like to do an angiogram [a much more accurate but invasive test] until just before the operation."

Leonard didn't take the test results lightly. Both his father and his father's father had died at relatively early ages of heart attacks, and his own younger years as a combat pilot and hard-driving journalist had been marked by high stress and high-fat food in equal quantities. But "come back in a year" and "the operation" surely didn't exhaust all possibilities for dealing with the situation. Leonard contacted his friend Dean Ornish, a physician who was running a study on reversing coronary artery disease by lifestyle changes, without drugs or surgery.

Ornish's study involved twenty-two heart patients in a treatment group and nineteen in a control group, all of whom had shown arterial blockage on angiograms. Members of the control group had continued with their conventional coronary care. Members of the treatment group had committed themselves to an introductory week-long retreat and two four-hour meetings every week for at least a year. At the meetings, also attended by their spouses, they took a forty-five-minute walk followed by fifteen minutes of cool-down exercises, then did yoga, meditation, and mental imagery for an hour. After a vegetarian, very-low-fat dinner, they participated in an hour-long group meeting facilitated by Ornish or staff psychologist Jim Billings during which they aired their feelings. They continued the exercise, yoga, and diet during the other five days of the week.

Ornish had taken on a tough one. The plaque that blocks blood flow to the heart isn't just a coating on the inside of the coronary arteries, like the gunk that lines old pipes. It comes from changes within the walls themselves. White blood cells congregate, fibrous tissue forms, cholesterol and other debris accumulates, and the walls thicken and bulge inward. No wonder the medical establishment had long believed that, while this complex process could be slowed or possibly stopped, it could never be reversed. Some of the people in the treatment group had been advised to have bypass operations. Now they were not even to take cholesterol-lowering drugs.

Leonard met with Ornish, who showed him slides of some of the patients' angiograms and PET (positron emission tomography) scans, showing significant reductions in arterial blockages. Ornish suggested that Leonard get a PET scan, which provides a noninvasive way of accurately measuring blood flow to all parts of the heart. When this test corroborated the results of the treadmill test, Ornish invited Leonard and his wife, Annie Styron Leonard, to join their treatment group, not as members of the study but rather as participant-observers.

Thirteen months after his first PET scan, Leonard went back to the same facility for another. Beyond all his expectation, it showed up as completely normal. By then, the first year results for all members of the treatment group were in and most of them were quite good. Ornish reported the results in detail at the annual scientific meetings of the American Heart Association and in the medical journal *Lancet* and other medical journals. Now there was no way the medical establishment could ignore the evidence. The National Institutes of Health made a large grant—enough to keep the program going until all the participants had completed four years.

Actually, the Ornish program was even better than the scientific studies, by their very nature, could show. For example, arteries that were completely blocked were ruled out of the study from the beginning. No one would have dreamed that these arteries would begin to open—which in some cases is exactly what happened. Openings of completely blocked arteries couldn't be reported in the study. On his walks with members of the treatment group, Leonard also heard compelling firsthand accounts of positive changes in many aspects of the participants' lives—gout cured, eyesight and hearing sharpened, digestion improved, breathing difficulties cleared up. Even more significant, perhaps, were dramatic shifts in the participants' psychological attitudes. Ornish often said he was more interested in opening hearts than opening arteries, and there was no question but that hearts were opened.

From the outside, one is tempted to suppose that the very-low-fat diet is the chief factor in reversing heart disease. But statistical studies suggest that it is the combination of all four main elements—exercise, stress reduction, diet, and support groups—that does the good work. Those in the program would agree. But if pushed to pick one of the four that is finally the most important, they might well name the support groups and the general sense of community. Leonard's experience with the Ornish group deepened an understanding of the power of the group process that began with those explosive groups at Esalen in the 1960s.

The Ornish program was not perfect; a few of the participants who didn't participate wholeheartedly didn't show reduction in arterial blockage. But there was a strong statistical correlation between adherence and success in reversing heart disease. In other words, those who followed the program the most diligently got the best results, and vice versa. Ornish's work was particularly heartening to us, not only because of its immediate personal and social value, but because it dramatically demonstrated the power of what Leonard and Murphy were calling Integral Transformative Practice (ITP).

> It was *integral* in that it dealt with the body (diet, exercise, yoga), mind (reading and discussions of articles and book excerpts on relevant subjects), heart (group process, community activities), and soul (meditation, imaging, yoga).

> It was *transformative* in that it aimed at positive change in body and being, in this case a transformation that was generally deemed impossible.

> It was a *practice* in that it involved long-term, regular, disciplined activities which, above and beyond any specific external rewards, were of value in and of themselves. Members of the Ornish treatment group often said that even if their hearts were perfectly okay they would continue with the program because the quality of their lives improved. Leonard got word of his normal PET scan after only thirteen months on the program, but he didn't quit the group. He stayed on for two and a half years, until he began the Integral Transformative Practice class that informs this book and that owes much to Dean Ornish and the brave men and women who have gone against the prevailing wisdom and have prevailed.

Guidelines for Long-term Transformation

By the middle of 1991, Leonard's book on long-term practice, *Mastery*, was in the bookstores and Murphy's *The Future of the Body* was about to be published. Murphy had been writing it for seven years, after immersing himself in the Esalen archives for eight years before that. His research as well as our own experiences with transformative disciplines had confirmed our belief that all humans possess great capacities for growth, and that these are nurtured best by integral practice. The prospect of such a practice for people with demanding work and family commitments had great appeal for us, and we began laying plans for an experimental class in Integral Transformative Practice, that would put our ideas to the test.

We didn't have all the answers as we prepared to begin the project in January 1992, but we were willing to learn from experience, to correct mistakes. And above all else, we were unwilling to get locked in doctrine and dogma. Still, from our years of experience we had drawn certain basic principles for the enterprise of human transformation, principles that would guide us in leading the class and which continue to guide us today. Among them are the following:

Lasting transformation requires long-term practice. We have already touched upon this essential principle and will return to it more than once in subsequent pages. Leonard's book, *Mastery*, a required text for members of the ITP class, shows how quick-fix thinking has vitiated modern life and argues that any profound learning requires long stretches of dedicated practice with no seeming progress. Only now are we beginning to realize that those people we consider masters are generally marked by their willingness not only to endure the plateaus of the learning curve but to love the process itself, to find satisfaction in diligent, long-term practice for its own sake as well as for the gains it brings.

The most effective transformative practices involve the whole person—body, mind, heart, and soul. The idea of the whole person goes back at least to the ancient Greeks. Most Greek thought, in fact, was informed by a sense of the wholeness of things, a sense sometimes quite lost in the increasingly specialized, fragmented modern West. Mind has been cut away from body, the mental from the material realm. In most of our current education, mind is enshrined, body often neglected, heart ignored, and soul assigned to other venues. Our concept of *integral* sees body, mind, heart, and soul as separate windows to an underlying wholeness. For us, the body can be a wise teacher, a royal road to the subconscious, a mirror of the emotions, and a holy companion of the soul. Recent research in psychoneuroimmunology identifes specific mechanisms through which thought and feeling directly affect what we call body and vice versa. To attempt high spiritual experience without the wise counsel of mind, body, and heart can create the kind of imbalance that leads to spiritual tyranny. For us, in short, the key is *balance.*

Transformative practices in this age are best guided by several mentors rather than a single, all-powerful guru. As the putative embodiment of some remote human possibility, the guru holds great appeal for many seekers. But it is almost impossible for a person who is considered superior to others, or even perfect, to get the rich and honest feedback needed for balanced practice, for the correction of wrong turns, and finally for sanity itself.

We have had ample opportunity since the mid-1960s to witness the swift rise and catastrophic fall of several originally appealing but finally destructive guru-led practices. Clearly, human life has at times been enlightened and enriched by great teachers who have been considered avatars by their followers. But this is a bad time for gurus and cults. We believed strongly in multiple mentors relating somewhat in the manner of a college faculty, with a feeling of collegiality. To this end, we enlisted two additional teachers, Annie Styron Leonard and Erik Van Riswold, both of them aikido black belts and experienced workshop leaders. Each of the four of us would lead classes, assist one another, and provide invaluable feedback.

Though practitioners at times must surrender creatively to mentors, community, and transformative agencies beyond ordinary functioning, the final authority always remains with the individual. A certain surrender, a certain relinquishment of dubious certainties, of old patterns of thought, feeling, and action, is necessary for any profound learning. To question every statement of a teacher or habitually sabotage group efforts in the name of personal independence can be a tedious, finally trivial exercise in ego. Still, we strongly believe that the final authority resides with the individual practitioner. For the teacher or the group to tell the practitioner what he or she is feeling constitutes tyranny. Practitioners' experiences are valid for them. Teachers and community are very important for transformation, but transformed thoughts, feelings, and actions arise at the deepest level of individual being and are the responsibility of the individual.

In transformative practice, there is also surrender to agencies beyond ordinary functioning, to God or the spirit of the universe. Sometimes, it seems, we must give up our knowing for a higher knowing. The grace that brings seemingly unearned gifts often surpasses our powers of understanding. But even in this ultimate surrender, in which we might experience ourselves and the universe as one, we invoke balance and individual responsibility.

The Path that Never Ends

A notice for the Integral Transformative Practice class appeared in the January–June 1992 Esalen Catalog, distributed in the fall of 1991.

Announcements also went out to the people on George Leonard's mailing lists. Applicants began coming in for the ITP group that would begin on January 4, 1992—far more than we could accommodate. For the people we accepted, and for us, the months to come would bring life changes, large and small, and in that sense, something new and different. But in a more fundamental sense, we viewed ITP merely as an extension of a path that reaches back to the beginning of time and stretches out to a measureless future. In the East, it is said that any true practice puts us on a journey during which, for every mile we travel toward the destination, the destination is two miles farther away. We were ready to embark on such a journey.

Beginning January 4, 1992
An Ongoing Workshop
Sponsored Jointly by Esalen Institute
and Aikido of Tamalpais

George Leonard, Michael Murphy,
Annie Styron Leonard & Erik Riswold

In his new book, *The Future of the Body* (to be published in May 1992 by Tarcher), Michael Murphy raises the possibility that by gathering data from many fields — including medical science, anthropology, sport, the arts, psychical research, and comparative religious studies — we can identify extraordinary versions of most, if not all, our basic attributes. Murphy's research has shown that the most reliable path toward the realization of these extraordinary attributes involves regular, disciplined practice. He defines a transformative practice as a coherent set of activities designed to produce positive changes in a person or group. For a practice to be integral as well, it must aim to cultivate the physical, vital, cognitive, volitional, affective, and transpersonal dimensions of human functioning in an integrated way.

Beginning Saturday, January 4, 1992, Esalen Institute and Aikido of Tamalpais will jointly sponsor a weekly two-hour workshop devoted to the development of integral transformative practice. The workshop will be held at the Aikido of Tamalpais studio in Mill Valley, California, and will relate Murphy's findings to the practice of Leonard Energy Training (LET) and other mind-body disciplines. LET is a integral transformative practice inspired by the martial art of aikido.

Through LET and other practices, participants in the workshop will have the chance to explore personal development in the twelve aspects of human functioning outlined in *The Future of the Body*: perception of external events, somatic awareness, communication abilities, vitality, movement abilities, capacities to manipulate the environment directly, feelings of pain and pleasure, cognition, volition, sense of self, love, and bodily structure. Participants will be offered the opportunity to engage in an extended bodily transformation experiment (see George Leonard, *The Silent Pulse*, Dutton, 1986, p. 159ff), and there will be discussion of the applications of integral transformative practice to society at large.

Recommended reading: Murphy, *The Future of the Body* (Tarcher, in press), Leonard, *The Silent Pulse* (Dutton), *The Transformation* (Tarcher), and *Mastery* (Dutton).

The notice for the class as it appeared in the
January–June 1992 catalog of the Esalen Institute.

TWO

A Householder's Path

The Hindus have a term for it: "householder's path," a spiritual practice not for full-time practitioners but for those who have family and job obligations. In this sense, the thirty-six people who met for the first class in Integral Transformative Practice (ITP) on Saturday, January 4, 1992, were householders. They were a journalist and an attorney, a pediatrician and a playwright, a product designer and a landscape architect, a financial manager and a veterinarian, a psychotherapist and a photographer. They were successful people who ranged in age from twenty-eight to seventy-eight; the kind of people who were willing to take on something new and adventurous.

We had selected our thirty-six participants from sixty applicants. We had made it clear during interviews with each of them that the class would be based on an educational rather than a therapeutic model, and we chose people who were in better than average physical and psychological health. There's no question that healing is transformational—often powerfully so—and we were by no means ruling out the healing possibilities of the practice. But we wanted to be sure that our applicants would be willing to work toward the realization of extraordinary states *beyond* what is considered ordinary good health.

For eleven months, this group (Cycle 92) would meet every Saturday from 8:45 to 10:45 A.M. at the Aikido of Tamalpais studio in

Mill Valley, California, a 2,000-square-foot, second-story loft with exposed rafters and large windows through which the morning sunlight streamed. A second group (Cycle 93) would meet for ten months in 1993. Members of both groups would also attend occasional evening meetings at participants' or teachers' homes to discuss their readings and would take part in one overnight stay at a retreat center in the country during the 1992 cycle and two in 1993.

A chilly, crystal-clear day added to the undercurrent of excitement that marked our first meeting. After introductions and some necessary business, which included signing the legal release forms required of everyone who participates in a marital arts studio, George Leonard made a brief talk, starting out by joking that their mission was "to go where no man or woman has gone before." Actually, he went on to say, much of what they would do might seem quite ordinary. We knew that among the people gathered there for the first class were several teachers of human development, and we figured that most of them, as well as we four ITP teachers, could undoubtedly lead the class in exercises that would provide spectacular, gee-whiz experiences in short order. But we felt that some exercises give only the illusion of significant change and can even interfere with lasting, long-term transformation. We held a strong belief in the transformative power—and the sacredness—of life's quiet virtues, including intellectual curiosity and integrity, a sense of the spiritual, unconditional love, healthy exercise, and devotion to practice. We were in it for the long run.

"Yes, we're going to have a good time," Leonard said. "We're going to have fun. But more important is learning to enjoy regular practice, finding satisfaction in the unembellished beauty of the commonplace, and learning to love the plateau, the periods when you seem to be making no progress, just as much as you love the inevitable spurts of learning and change."

He went on to tell the group that the teachers were hoping

1. to work toward creating an integral transformative practice, one that is appropriate for the current American lifestyle;

2. through this practice, to offer every participant the opportunity to enjoy increased centeredness, health, and growth in body, mind, heart, and soul; and

3. to experiment with transformations of the body and of all human faculties, from the ordinary to the extraordinary or metanormal.

Throughout our first meeting and during subsequent meetings as well, we stressed the fact that our fundamental purpose was to create a *practice*; that is, a nontrivial activity undertaken on a regular basis primarily for its own sake. Our practice would be *integral* in that it would involve and seek to integrate body, mind, heart, and soul. It would be *transformative* in that it would aim toward positive, long-term personal change. We would experiment with transformations of body/mind/heart/soul that would range from the easily explainable to the extraordinary. In this experiment, we would all make written affirmations of desired transformations and keep careful records of the results. As mentioned in the previous chapter, Leonard had used affirmations in his 1991–92 bodily transformation projects with good results. We explained to the ITP participants that, for the sake of the study, we would ask them to make affirmations in four categories:

1. *Normal.* This affirmation would specify some measurable physical change that could be realized through normal means. A person with a waistline of 33 inches, for example, might want to take two inches off his or her waist, in which case the affirmation would be, "My waist measures 31 inches." This affirmation could probably be realized through diligent attention to diet and exercise. There would be no mystery about the outcome. We asked participants to make their first affirmation in terms of bodily changes that could be easily measured, not because we were emphasizing the body over the other factors in integral practice but simply to make the results of this particular affirmation as objective as possible.

2. *Exceptional.* This affirmation would involve some change in body, mind, heart, or soul that might not defy conventional scientific explanation but would be an exception to what is generally considered normal. As it turned out, for example, one fifty-nine-year-old man in Cycle 92, an avid sports participant, made the following Af-

Affirming the Transformation of Body and Psyche

firmation Two: "I have sufficient mobility, strength, and range of motion in my left arm, shoulder, and back so that I can serve a tennis ball in the 100-mph range and pitch a baseball in the low 80s." At the time he made the affirmation, limited mobility and strength in his left shoulder plus occasional back pain had reduced the speed of his tennis serve to the 60-mph range and his baseball pitching to the 40-mph range. By the end of Cycle 92, on November 21, he was serving a tennis ball in the 90-mph range and throwing a baseball in the 70-mph range—not quite what he affirmed but still, it seemed to us, exceptional.

3. *Metanormal.* In *The Future of the Body*, Michael Murphy defines extraordinary or metanormal functioning as "human functioning that in some respect radically surpasses the functioning typical of most people living today." The metanormal, as we see it, would be difficult to explain in conventional scientific terms. To put the distinction in perspective in purely physical terms: If a thirty-five-year-old person, 5 feet 6 inches tall and in good physical shape, increased in height by half an inch or even three-quarters of an inch, such an increase might be explained in terms of improved posture and would fall in the normal range (Affirmation One). An increase of an inch might still submit to conventional explanation but would be exceptional (Affirmation Two). An increase in height of two inches or more would be metanormal (Affirmation Three). Here let us say that we were by no means urging people to increase their height. We're using this example simply because it clearly delineates the differences among Affirmations One, Two, and Three. Most metanormal functioning, as we see it, involves a significant change in state, a qualitative rather than quantitative change. And most of the metanormal affirmations in our experimental classes turned out to aim for positive change not in the body but in the mind, heart, and soul.

4. *Overall good health.* The last affirmation was the same for everyone: "My entire being is balanced, vital, and healthy." We considered Affirmation Four the most important of all in that it would provide a mitigating influence on the other three. We did not want a participant to achieve any affirmation through unbalanced, undesirable change. For example, we would not want anyone to grow in height by two inches at the expense of stability in the joints and ribs,

nor would we want anyone to achieve out-of-the-body travel at the expense of mental stability. Good health was our overriding concern. Affirmation Four also served as a measure of Integral Transformative Practice itself. Any viable practice, it seemed to us, should increase balance, vitality, and general health.

We were well aware that this study of integral transformation could by no means qualify as a rigorous scientific experiment. There was no control group. And there were far too many and too many *different* types of variables. Still, we believed it would be valuable to keep careful and complete records of our results to learn how the participants' adherence to various elements of the practice correlated with their success in realizing their affirmations. We predicted, for one thing, that there would be a strong correlation between participants' overall adherence and their success in achieving their affirmations; in other words, those who followed the practice most closely would get the best results. To guide us in analyzing the statistics, we enlisted the help of Stephen Sparler, who had compiled and analyzed statistics for Dean Ornish's experiment in reversing heart disease.

Guided by the Integral

Beginning with the first class meeting, we stressed the importance not only of balance within each of the four aspects of our practice—body, mind, heart, and soul—but also among the four. We believe that these four aspects represent different manifestations of a single and fundamental *identity* that is unique for each individual, the uniqueness of which is revealed in your DNA, fingerprints, voiceprint, brain wave pattern, scent, handwriting, your very way of moving and being. Your identity, in fact, manifests itself in every aspect of your life. To change one of these aspects is, to some degree, to change all. To ingore or downgrade one is to create an unbalanced practice, an unbalanced life. To think of one as opposed to another—the "unruly, lustful" body as a threat to the "logical, judicious" mind, to give a familiar example—is to falsely blame human nature for what actually springs from cultural limitation. Today we are learning that body and mind mirror each other, sometimes with exquisite fidelity.

Guided by a deep respect for the integral, we did the best we could to address every aspect of being. A typical class might begin with a session of "staying current," during which anyone with a pressing emotional problem could express it openly to the group and receive support and understanding rather than advice or reassurance. This could be followed by the ITP Kata, a forty-minute-long series of physical, mental, and spiritual exercises that will be described briefly below, then treated fully in chapters 6, 7, and 8. There would likely be discussions of the current reading assignment from *The Future of the Body* or *Mastery*, and the class would almost always include an exercise from Leonard Energy Training (LET). Several of the most important of these are described in chapter 11.

Briefly, LET leads practitioners into a change of context which creates a transformational possibility. In "Taking the Hit as a Gift," for example (see page 152), a partner sneaks up behind you and grabs your wrist with a shout. This represents any unexpected blow in your life, from losing a valued heirloom to losing your job or worse. In dealing with your startled reaction, you learn to avoid fighting back reflexively, denying your feelings, or falling in the victim's role. Instead, you learn to experience and acknowledge your upset by paying attention to the bodily sensations it causes. After that, you can change the context of the situation, experiencing the hit as a gift of energy that can empower you to deal with this particular blow—with energy left over for further positive life changes.

Some classes involved working directly with our affirmations, most notably through a process called "Focused Surrender," which combines highly focused imagery with moments of surrender and alignment with God or the universe, as described in chapter 5. We also spent considerable time together in meditation and often broke up into small groups to discuss various aspects of the practice or simply to share feelings without becoming judgmental. As the weeks passed, the group became a community. After each session, most participants adjourned to a nearby cafe to continue the discussions begun in class. More and more of them joined in social groupings. And we became more familiar with the ITP Kata, a single form that touched many points of our practice.

THE ITP KATA

The Japanese word *kata* means simply "form." Our usage in this case is similar to that in the martial arts, where the practitioner performs a series of predetermined moves in a certain sequence. Each move in the ITP Kata is designed to flow naturally into the next, balancing and warming up the body, articulating every major joint, stretching muscles and tendons, relaxing the body, and quieting the mind. These movements lead to a session of induction and imaging followed by ten minutes or more of meditation.

George Leonard started working on the ITP Kapa in August of 1991, five months before the first ITP classes began. He tried it out with various individuals and workshop groups, revising and improving it. He drew on exercises from hatha yoga, the martial arts, modern exercise physiology, Progressive Relaxation, visualization research, and witness meditation.

Many of the movements of the ITP Kata are familiar, but the sequencing is unique, reflecting our belief that one should warm up the body and gently articulate the joints before performing stretching exercises; that the relaxation phase of every stress-relaxation cycle is important; that one should be deeply relaxed before beginning imaging; that meditation is deeper and more satisfying after the body is warm, articulated, stretched, and relaxed than if done cold; and that meditation can serve, to borrow a metaphor from photography, to "print" one's images of positive change.

Knowing that today's householders lead busy lives, Leonard at first tried to hold the Kata to thirty-five minutes, but eventually expanded it to forty minutes. This is the minimum time within which the practitioner can do the full Kata without hurrying, but is by no means a limit. One can expand any part of it.

LONG-TERM COMMITMENTS

The Saturday morning group sessions were important, but made up only a small part of the overall practice. All participants committed themselves to attend meetings regularly and punctually and also to deepen their practice on the days between meetings. They further agreed:

—to maintain their individual autonomy and authority while committing themselves to the group in vision and practice, thus creating a powerful field of group intentionality that could aid and abet positive, healthy transformations of individual body, mind, heart, and soul.

—to do the ITP Kata at least five times a week.

—to do at least three hours of aerobic exercise every week in increments of at least thirty minutes. In addition, they agreed to do whatever flexibility, strength, balance, coordination, concentration, and relaxation exercises would be necessary to realize their affirmations.

—to be conscious of everything they ate and to consider the many benefits of a diet low in fat and high in fiber. This meant, first of all, no unconscious snacking. It meant reading food labels. It meant eating deliberately, with full awareness of the contents, texture, smell, and taste of everything eaten.

—to read all written material assigned by the teachers and, commensurate with their own best judgment, seek to integrate it into their practice.

—to stay current in their relationships with teachers and fellow participants and to take care of emotional needs in appropriate and healthy ways.

—to include their affirmations in their Kata and to seek in all appropriate and healthy ways to manifest those affirmations in body and being.

RELINQUISHING THE QUICK FIX

Considering the busy lives that class members led, attendance was remarkably good. A few people dropped out. Some felt there was too much interpersonal work. Some felt there was not enough. Others left because of changes in residence or job. During the first couple of months, we replaced the drop-outs, six in all, from our waiting list. The twenty-seven remaining participants, plus the six we added, finished Cycle 92.

The most insidious and powerful enemy of our practice and, it seemed to us, of all long-term endeavors, was modern industrial culture itself, with its relentless celebration of immediate gratification. Amid the din of quick-fix appeals, it is difficult to learn about the efficacy and enduring joys of regular, long-lasting practice. To keep our consumerist economy afloat, it seems, people have to buy goods and services that they often don't need and sometimes don't really want. Television commercials glorify immediate gratification, showing life as an endless series of climactic moments with no lead-in or follow-through. The disproportionate number of climactic moments on TV is matched by our nation's disproportionate use of illegal drugs that produce immediate highs or oblivion. But we are hooked on legal drugs as well, with their promise of "fast, temporary relief," and we are served by a medical system that features quickie doctor appointments culminating in prescriptions for drugs or surgery, with little or no advice on long-term lifestyle changes that can prevent or reverse many medical problems.

The essence of boredom is to find yourself in the obsessive search for novelty.

G. L.

The quick fix is evident in many places: in socially approved gambling, in fast-weight-loss diets, in thrill-a-minute movie and television dramas, in audio tapes that "teach you" while you sleep, in how-to books that offer management skills in a minute and total fitness in a half-hour a week, in weekend management seminars that promise you an "action item" you can use in your office on Monday with no practice at all, in bottom-line management itself, in the whole credit-card economy.

And in self-development programs as well—those that shoot for catharsis, self-knowledge, and transcendence, all in a weekend, or even in a day. But we shouldn't consider this unusual in the least; all of us who have participated wholeheartedly in our society have become addicted to some extent to the quick fix. Perhaps the most significant discontent we encountered in ITP came from those who had participated in a number of big-bang weekend seminars and who urged us to push more strenuously for high moments rather than long-term practice. While the course in its unfoldment did occasion its share of catharsis, self-knowledge, and transcendence, we resisted the temptation to forego our long-term emphasis and push for a series of climactic moments. Gradually, most of us settled into our practice. There was a certain amount of grumbling about having to do the Kata at least five times a week. But then some people began reporting that it was getting harder *not* to do it than to do it.

The Fruits of Long-term Practice

Cycle 92 class members made their affirmations on February 15, 1992. After writing all four affirmations, they signed and dated their papers, then filled out a "Record of Body Transformation" form. They copied their affirmations onto this form, precisely as written. This was followed by a description of the current condition addressed by each affirmation. A space was left blank for a description of each condition as of November 21, 1992, to be filled in at that time. The Record of Body Transformation forms were copied, with one copy going to the participant and one kept on file by the teachers.

On Saturday, November 21, the target date for the 1992 affirmations, all thirty-three participants who completed Cycle 92 filled out their Record of Body Transformation forms, describing the condition addressed by their affirmations as it was on that day. Then, comparing their present condition with what it had been on February 15, they rated the amount of positive change on a scale of from 0 to 10. If, to use a simple physical example, a person affirmed he would reduce his waistline by two inches and ended up reducing it by only one inch, he would give himself a rating of 5. Some affirmations, however, did not lend themselves to such purely objective measures. We spent considerable time over three class sessions preparing participants to rate all affirmations with integrity, avoiding either positive or negative bias. Comparing the participants' ratings with our own measurements and other observations, we concluded that they were as reliable as any self-ratings could be, probably better than most of those that are commonly used in epidemiological studies. On the same day, participants also completed an ITP Adherence Questionnaire, their third that year, and an Evaluation Form. The Adherence Questionnaire was designed primarily to determine how faithfully participants had fulfilled their commitments to the class and to learn how their adherence to the program correlated with their success in realizing their affirmations.

The most striking finding involved the strong statistical correlationship ($p = .0002$) between adherence to the program and progress made toward realizing affirmations. This correlation jumped out at us, suggesting strongly that the people who followed the practice faithfully were likely to be the ones who successfully transformed body and being. The statistical analysis helped us evaluate our work, but it was the personal success stories that brought us the most insight.

To take one case, a thirty-nine-year-old psychologist made the following Affirmation Three: "My will is in tune with the Divine Will of the universe. There are no obstructions. All things flow to me and through me: love, health, wealth, success, and creativity." As to her condition at the time she made the affirmation, she wrote, "I am frequently in conflict over finances, writing ability, and my relationships with [a former teacher]." At the end of the year, she wrote, "This has been my most startling result. My financial situation has tripled as a result of my not plotting how it would resolve. My most serious interpersonal conflict has completely resolved from its state. . . . There has been an almost total shift in my attitude. From former attempts to 'make' things happen to an acceptance of whatever is presented and an acceptance of whatever I am feeling. I truly feel more flowing and internally without the former obstacles that caused me sadness. I no longer feel stuck."

The Story Continues

During the two and a half months between Cycle 92 and Cycle 93, we pondered the first year's lessons. We had reasons to believe we were on the right track, encouraged by the fact that those who most faithfully followed the program generally got the best results. We were also heartened by the participants' generally positive evaluations. In rating the elements of the program as to importance in enhancing their practice and value in their lives, participants gave top billing to the ITP Kata, the Leonard Energy Training (LET) exercises, the affirmations, and the readings in *The Future of the Body*—all of which we considered basic to the project.

We decided to stick with the basics in 1993. Rather than trying to intensify the practice or to load the classes with exercises that yield immediate, sometimes spectacular results, we proceeded even more slowly and patiently than in 1992, making sure, for example, that everyone thoroughly understood the affirmation process before making their affirmations, even if that involved considerable repetition.

Once again, our deliberate pace occasioned a certain amount of grumbling. From the outset, we had espoused nonauthoritarian leadership and free expression, and our participants were, for the most part, mature professionals with no qualms about speaking out. (Thirteen participants from Cycle 92 continued through the Cycle 93 training.) Now a small but vocal minority began asking for an "Advanced ITP" or an "ITP II." We listened and talked the matter over but essentially hewed to the idea of long-term, patient practice.

A Strong Finish

The ITP class was built on a vision of continuing human evolution, including the possibility of dramatic transformations through long-term practice. Yet we grounded our most ambitious aspirations in the particulars of the body. For our 1993 training, seeking a purely objective measure, we replaced the "Exceptional" category for Affirmation Two with the most particular of measures: percent of body fat. The new Affirmation Two was the same for everybody: "My percent of body fat is significantly less than it was on March 27, 1993, and my lean body mass is equal to or greater than it was on March 27, 1993."

We selected percent of body fat as a measure not only because we could get objective measurements but also because of the clear relationship between a low percentage of fat and overall good health. We were impressed by recent studies showing conclusively that maintaining or increasing muscle mass and reducing fat could increase vitality and delay or prevent many negative effects of aging, as well as reducing susceptability to numerous diseases. In a time of rapidly rising health costs, this matter has serious socioeconomic implications. We made it clear to the class that we were interested in health, not weight loss per se. We were aware of that peculiar set of mind that equates any desire for a healthy, well-toned body with "narcissism"—a vestige, perhaps, of an old puritanism, of our lingering denigration of the body. For us, there are many body types, all of them sacred. We consider the body a reflection of one's essence, co-equal with mind, heart, and soul. Its health and vitality is not a trivial matter.

To calculate before-and-after body fat percentages, an experienced physiologist, Terri Merritt, made skin-fold measurements for all participants on March 27, then again on November 13. The results were encouraging. Between March 27 and November 20, the percent body fat of the thirty class members dropped by an average of 12.60 percent. (As it turned out, the four teachers averaged exactly the same reduction: 12.60 percent.)

The results on the other three affirmations were also encouraging. Participants filled out two questionnaires during the 1993 Cycle. Results from the final questionnaire (November 20, 1993) were used for statistical analysis. Thirty participants finished the 1993 Cycle and completed the questionnaire. The average scores for progress made toward realizing affirmations, on a scale of from 0 to 10, are presented here, as compared with scores from Cycle 92. (The Cycle 93 scores for Affirmation Two are not comparable. In 1992, as previously noted, Affirmation Two was "Exceptional" on a scale of 0 to 10. In 1993, it was percentage change in body fat. Also note that the "Average of affirmations" is an average of all the individual figures, not an average of the averages):

	Cycle 92	Cycle 93
Affirmation 1	5.67	6.30
Affirmation 2	4.30	-12.60%
Affirmation 3	4.53	6.67
Affirmation 4	6.58	8.30
Average of affirmations	5.30 (av. of all 4)	7.09 (av. of 1, 3, and 4)

In Appendix B, you'll find a complete set of Cycle 93 statistics along with a detailed analysis. Here we'll note only four points of interest:

1. Success on realizing Affirmation Four ("My entire body is balanced, vital, and healthy") was remarkably high and correlated to a statistically signficant extent to participants' adherence to every important aspect of Integral Transformative Practice.

2. Success on Affirmation Two (having to do with reduction of percent of body fat) correlated to a statistically signficant degree only to the amount of aerobic exercise a week and class attendance. This doesn't mean that factors such as diet and strength training were not important, but it does highlight the importance of aerobic exercise.

3. We found that consciousness, awareness, and focused attention related strongly to success in achieving affirmations. For example, participants' *awareness* of what they ate showed up as even more significant in their success in achieving affirmations than did *what* they ate.

4. Success for achieving Affirmation Three ("metanormal") is even higher than that for Affirmation One ("normal") and shows no statistically significant correlation to any adherence factor. This might be explained by the fact that the class members' metanormal affirmations included many that were not objective and thus easier to rate incorrectly. But a close examination of the results as reflected in the participants' prior and post states and behavior leads us to believe that this was not a major factor. The metanormal process, as we came to know it, often involved intentionality and what we might call grace, and was not always amenable to reductive explanation.

Even in the case of the purely objective affirmations, intentionality alone sometimes might have played a part. For example, one thirty-seven-year-old man reduced his percent of body fat from 11.1 to 8.3 (a 25.3 percent reduction) while making no change in his exercise regimen and actually falling prey to a craving for oil, consuming large amounts of french-fried potatoes over the last two months of Cycle 93. We couldn't be sure that such dramatic bodily changes as his could be attributed solely to participation in the class and all that it entailed rather than to specific adherence factors. We suspected, however, that this was indeed the case. In the end, we were left with a healthy respect for long-term practice and for the power, and the mystery, of the affirmation process.

Cataracts, a Loving Heart, and a Mass Murder

Again, it was not so much the statistics as the participants' stories of their transformations that convinced us of the program's value. From the beginning, we had told class members that if they had any affirmations they considered too personal to make public they should write them on a separate sheet of paper. A number of people told us of great successes with these private affirmations—which never appeared in the statistics. Other stories also escaped the statistical net. There was, for example, the story of Charlotte Hatch's eyes.

Charlotte Hatch's grandfather on her mother's side had practically gone blind from cataracts. That was before the operation was available. Her mother was operated on for cataracts in her forties, as were each of her three older sisters. "Have you got your cataracts yet, Charlotte?" her mother began asking her when she turned forty. At first she could say no with a clear conscience, but at forty-two, when she found she did have them, she didn't want to admit it. "No, not yet," she would say. Then she would change the subject. Finally, she began telling the truth. "All of you girls got my genes," her mother lamented. "Not one of you with eyes like your father's."

In January 1992, at age forty-five, Charlotte entered the Integral Transformative Practice class. For one of her affirmations, she chose to reverse her heredity: "I intend to see that the following circumstances have occurred by November 21, 1992: The lenses of my eyes are clear.... My eyesight is improving daily."

As instructed by the teachers, Charlotte went to her HMO for an eye exam to get a baseline for the experiment. When she told the doctor what she was doing, he was unimpressed. The cataracts, he told her, were not yet very large, but were right in the middle of the lens, and thus were sure to obscure her vision. An operation loomed in her future.

Despite her doubts, Charlotte participated fully throughout Cycle 92. When November came, however, she couldn't bring herself to go back for another exam. So she simply left her Record of Body Transformations for that affirmation blank.

Charlotte signed on for Cycle 93 and left any mention of her eyes out of her new affirmations. But from force of habit more than anything else, she continued doing the cataract imaging and induction. In the fall of 1993, she found herself needing a pair of prescription sunglasses but having no up-to-date prescription. Reluctantly, bracing herself for bad news, she returned to her HMO. But the doctor completed the exam without saying a word about her cataracts.

"*Don't I have them?*" Charlotte asked.

"No. Your left eye is totally clear, and there's a tiny deposit at about 10:30 in your right eye. But it's not big enough to be called a cataract."

Practice is a seedbed of miracles.

M. M.

The affirmations made by members of the ITP class were not limited to the physical. They also included wished-for transformations of mind and heart. For example, a highly successful criminal lawyer affirmed, "My heart is open. I radiate love to all people." On March 27 he wrote, "[My heart is] currently about one-half open." On November 20 he reported, "This affirmation was chosen as a last ditch effort to save my disintegrating marriage. I devoted a great deal of energy, attention, and effort to saving this relationship, including: economic, psychological [effort], meditation, and just devoting my time to [it]. The results are that we are still together with a greater understanding and love for each other. Comparing where I was on March 27 and now, the score is a 10. . . ."

The improvement in balance, vitality, and health covered by Affirmation Four showed up in the ITP participants' increased ability to deal with the stresses of life—nowhere more dramatically than in the case of Karen Wilson, who played an important role in dealing with a mass shooting that made headlines all over the world. At 3:00 P.M. on July 1, 1993, a fifty-five-year-old former client with two semi-automatic pistols strapped to his suspenders, another pistol in one hand and a bag of ammunition in the other, walked into the offices of the law firm of Pettit and Martin on the thirty-fourth floor of 101 California Street in San Francisco. He moved from office to office, from floor to floor, shooting people as he went, killing eight and wounding six before killing himself. On the thirty-sixth floor, Karen and a group of her fellow workers barricaded themselves in the personnel department offices.

"We knew the killer was at large," Karen told us. "We wondered if he was coming to get us."

Karen, who served as Pettit and Martin's personnel manager, had been doing Integral Transformative Practice for five months when the massacre occurred. She characterized herself as a high-strung person, but said that her practice had given her "a center, something with which to stabilize myself." When the killer's location was uncertain, she had a chance to see how she and her fellow workers reacted.

"There were people around me who panicked. A couple of attorneys were close to hysteria. But I never panicked. Not to say I didn't react, but I just knew I had a center. I could see how calm I was. I started doing things like calling around to other offices finding out where people were, what they knew, and getting information flowing. It was more form than substance, but it was calming to people because they thought I was doing something. A lot of them came up to me afterward and said they really appreciated the fact that I had kept my head and tried to do something useful.

"Having my practice also helped me get through the aftermath. It was traumatic and people were very upset. Those of us in management were called upon to do a lot more work, longer hours. Having the practice was invaluable. It gave me something to go back to, no matter what happened. It changed my life."

THE ENDURING JOYS OF PRACTICE

Since earliest childhood, we have been told we must practice in order to achieve our goals. This has led us to assume that practice is merely a means, not an end in itself, and indeed that much of what we do in life is of value only for what we will get out of it sometime later. In our ITP classes, we have certain goals—our affirmations, for example—and practice makes it possible to achieve them. But that is only part of the equation. We don't just practice to achieve our goals, we have goals in order to enhance our practice, for we regard practice as having great value in itself.

As might be expected, there was some resistance to a regular practice on the part of almost every participant. Resistance to any significant change, whether it be for the worse or for the better, is a natural tendency of all living organisms, and this often ignored aspect of existence will be treated at length in the next chapter. Some participants never overcame that resistance. A few dropped out. As the weeks stretched into months, however, most of us experienced an ever-increasing richness in our practice. If at first we resisted doing the Kata, finally the moment came when a day without it seemed incomplete. For some participants it was the sense of community, the feeling of being joined with others in a meaningful enterprise, that seemed most rich. For some it was the creation of a calm core, a center of stability in the midst of the ups and downs, the vicissitudes that mark life in the electronic age. For most of us there was the tingling, fully alive feeling that comes from good health in the broadest sense: the health of body, mind, heart, and soul. And for all of us there was the vision that first brought us together: the awe-some knowledge that the universe is embarked on an enormous journey of evolution and that each of us has a chance to make a positive contribution—no matter how small, how incremental—to that journey. It is, after all, the accretion of minute changes that ultimately powers the most startling evolutionary leaps.

When Cycle 93 ended on November 27, 1993, we stepped back to assess the results and implications of the study we had conducted and to write this book. Integral Transformative Practice, as we see it, is a work in progress, which will continue to develop. Still, we feel that what we learned from the class, added to the learnings of our two lifetimes, provides the guidance necessary to specify a practice now, one that not only will enhance individual lives but also will be of significant social value.

We have received much encouragement in our work, none more welcome than the response of class participants when the teachers stepped back. Dismayed with the idea that the class might end, a core group formed to keep it going. As of this writing, Cycle 3, as the group chose to call it, is growing in number and commitment. In the pages that follow, we offer you instructions for joining them and us in our quest. You can form your own group or do the practice alone; ITP is a portable discipline. Becoming consciously involved in your own evolution and that of your culture can begin with something as simple as taking your first step on a path of practice—as you'll see in the next chapter.

A

TRANSFORMATIVE

PRACTICE

for

OUR TIME

THREE

Stepping on the Path

To begin any strong practice is to turn the pages of your life to a new chapter. Eastern wisdom sees practice, first of all, as a path (*tao* in Chinese, *do* in Japanese). For every mile you travel on such a path (if your practice is a profound one), the destination is two miles farther away. And would you really want it any other way? Think about it. The more you know, the more there is to know. By your very knowing, you help create more knowing. The knowing gets richer, more fascinating for as long as you live. The more you create, the more you can create. The more you love, the more you can love. A profound practice never ends.

In the Buddhist tradition, a practice is viewed sometimes as a path, sometimes as a stream. The metaphor of the stream invites you to imagine a strong but gentle current that is already there to speed your journey. Just to enter such a stream makes you a different person. Even if you should go back to shore, you would feel its power. You might enter the stream then return to shore many times, but if you keep practicing you're finally there for good—in the stream, on the path. Just to consider getting started expands your vision and lifts your spirit. Taking the all-important first step with a sincere heart can be a sort of enlightenment. It presages an evolutionary adventure, and offers inner peace. It is momentous, and it is nothing special.

Many fine practices, many paths, exist. In the words of the thirteenth century sage Wu-Men, "The Great Way has no gate. There are a thousand paths to it." Many, many activities can be considered practices—meditation, yoga, bodybuilding, mountaineering, devotional religion, various forms of service to others. Americans once spoke reverently about the *practice* of medicine or law, and these professions are indeed practices if they are undertaken for their own sake as well as for extrinsic rewards, for the fascination and service they provide, as an expression of the practitioners' inner essence. But if that practice is only a collection of clients, a way of making money and gaining prestige, then it is not truly a practice.

Even something as commonplace as gardening can be a practice if done for the sheer love of it, as an expression of the gardener's soul. It is a practice to garden with care for every shoot, every bud. It is a practice to develop a communion with everything in your garden, so that your roses, for example, are treated not as mere objects to be manipulated and used but as honored guests at the banquet of your life, so that eventually they will come to have the special look of flowers that are looked at with love.

But if you garden merely to impress the neighbors or win prizes with your roses, then, in the deepest sense, such gardening is not a practice. Paradoxically, the person who gardens as a practice, for the love of it, is probably the one who will impress the neighbors and win prizes.

The Social Value of ITP

Integral Transformative Practice, as we have pointed out, is designed for people with busy lives. Unlike most practices, it aims to involve and integrate body, mind, heart, and soul. It is based on a vision of evolutionary transcendence and offers the possibility of positive changes in many aspects of your being. We also feel that it has significant social value. For one thing, the practice of ITP has greatly improved the overall health of the great majority of those who have undertaken it. Good health, it seems to us, is intrinsically valuable. But in today's economic and social climate, there's more to it than that. Without a significant shift toward a healthier way of life among its citizens, every advanced industrial nation now faces a fast-growing and perhaps unbearable strain on its health care system, no matter what system it adopts. Drugs and medical technology have produced marvels of healing and life support, but have also produced an exponential rise in health care costs and have, in many cases, prolonged suffering in life's final stages. The only solution, as experts in the health care field have long acknowledged, lies in changing the way we live. *In terms of social responsibility, the pursuit of good health is a moral act.*

The health care situation, however, only highlights the destructiveness of our prevailing way of life with its emphasis on immediate gratification, short-term planning, and the quick fix. The biblical admonition that "Where there is no vision the people perish" might have an unfashionably apocalyptic ring to it, and the ancient Eastern belief voiced by aikido founder Morihei Ueshiba that "Without practice a nation goes to ruin" might sound extravagant. But in the absence of vision and practice, our values—even our ability to talk about values—wither away. In the kingdom of the quick fix, the individual is most valued for her ability to consume. "The one who dies with the most toys wins" becomes an unexamined cultural affirmation, and the noble individualism that once occupied a central place in the vision of the West devolves from "I am" to "I want," creating a climate of selfishness and self-indulgence.

We believe that any long-term practice which encourages community and individual autonomy while aiming at the realization of positive human potential can be a healthy antidote to a frenetic, scattered, quick-fix way of life. We believe that people on a householder's path, people who combine their practice with job and family rather than remaining in isolation, can make a significant positive impact on their communities and on the world at large.

It is not our purpose to argue that this particular practice is the best or the only one. We have said that many fine teachings can come your way, and we feel the choice is up to you. If you keep your vision clear, you can discover rich possibilities in many practices. As the nineteenth century sword master, Yamaoka Tesshu, wrote of his own practice of swordsmanship:

> *Do not think that*
> *This is all there is.*
> *More and more*
> *Wonderful teachings exist*
> *The sword is unfathomable.*

Whatever practice calls to you, answer that call wholeheartedly and generously. In Goethe's words, "Whatever you can do, or dream you can, begin it. Boldness has genius, power, and magic in it." If you

choose Integral Transformative Practice, here is the heart of it—
eight personal commitments adapted from the commitments followed
in the 1992–93 ITP classes:

Beginning Your Practice

If the practice and vision described in this book do call to you, then
it is time for you to begin. *You don't have to wait until you have learned
to do every part of the practice before beginning it.* If a child waited to
speak in full, grammatically correct sentences before beginning to
talk, he or she would never talk. Learning the practice is part of the
practice—and the learning never ends.

The Eight ITP Commitments

1. I take full responsibility for my practice and for all transformations of my body and being that flow from it. While
   respecting my teachers and fellow practitioners, I fully
   understand that I am the final authority.

2. I seek to join in community with other ITP practitioners.
   While maintaining my individual autonomy and authority, I commit myself to my ITP community in vision and
   practice. I understand that just two people can make a
   community. I also know that I can create a community
   through electronic networks, or even practice alone, bol-
   stered by the greater ITP community. [See chapter 13.]

3. I do the ITP Kata at least five times a week. I understand
   that, time permitting, I can lengthen any part of the Kata,
   and that extended periods of meditation at the end of the
   Kata and at other times of the day are recommended. [See
   chapters 6, 7, and 8.]

4. I accomplish at least two hours of aerobic exercise every
   week in increments of no less than twenty minutes.
   (Three hours a week in increments of no less than thirty
   minutes are recommended.) Three sessions of strength

Try to find at least one other person to join you. Form a group if possible. But bear in mind that ITP can be done alone. Workshops on Integral Transformative Practice are being held at Esalen and other places, and we are planning a Center for Transformative Practice in the San Francisco area. But now that this book is available, workshops are not necessary to introduce you to the practice of ITP. All the necessary information is included here. An instructional videotape by George Leonard could make it easy to learn the Kata (see Appendix A for ordering instructions). Again, however, this is not necessary; the ITP Kata can be learned from this book.

Indeed, Integral Transformative Practice as we see it requires a minimum of special equipment. You'll need good walking or run-

training a week are also recommended, but there is no commitment on this. [See chapter 9.]

5. I am conscious of everything I eat. I am aware of the many benefits of a diet low in fat and high in fiber. [See chapter 10.]

6. I develop my intellectual powers by reading, writing, and discussion. I thoughtfully consider the visions and the readings set forth in chapter 12 and, commensurate with my own best judgment, seek to integrate cognitive understanding into my practice.

7. I open my heart to others in love and service. I stay current in expressing my feelings to those close to me and take care of my emotional needs in appropriate and healthy ways, seeking counsel when needed. [See chapter 13.]

8. For each six- to twelve-month period, I make at least one affirmation having to do with significant positive change in my own being. I also make the following affirmation: "My entire being is balanced, vital, and healthy." I include my affirmations during transformative imaging in my Kata and seek in appropriate and healthy ways to realize those affirmations. [See chapters 4 and 5.]

ning shoes—but these are essential for good health in any case. (We also invite all those who, for various reasons, are unable to run or walk or who face other physical challenges to join in this practice by doing whatever parts of it are possible for you.) You'll need certain books—but these can be shared with fellow practitioners or obtained at libraries. Access to a health club might enhance your practice, but lack of such access need not keep you from practicing. One of our greatest hopes, in fact, is to further our vision of transformative practice for all people, regardless of physical or financial status.

Travel Tips

The way to begin a practice is simply to begin. Don't wait for a change in the climate or a sign in the sky. Don't put it off until you "have more time"; most of us are probably already sacrificing many hours to that life-devouring device in the TV room or other forms of passive "entertainment," time that could easily be reclaimed. To get started, just step on the path.

So you don't yet know exactly how to do the ITP Kata? Do the parts you can do. Do the best you can do. It doesn't have to be perfect. You'll get better. Same thing with aerobic exercise. If you've been living a sedentary life, begin slowly and consciously. Starting out too fast is the commonest reason people stop exercising. *Remember, this is not a quick fix. Be patient. You're in this practice for the long haul.* Our consumerist society has effectively demoted, if not suspended, patience. The literature of the East, however, is loaded with sword master-and-apprentice stories that mythologize patience as the virtue of virtues. All have the same general drift. A young man learns about a master of the sword who lives in a far province. After a long and difficult journey, he presents himself at the master's door and asks to become his student. The master closes the door in the young man's face. Every day thereafter, the young man comes to sit on the master's doorstep, simply waiting. A year passes, and the master grudgingly starts letting the young man do chores around the house—chop wood, carry water. Months go by, maybe years. One morning, without warning, the master attacks the young man from behind and whacks him on the shoulder with a bamboo sword. The master has begun to teach alertness. At length, the master gives his apprentice his own sword and continues teaching him the art of

A certain naivete is prerequisite to all learning. A certain optimism is prerequisite to all action.

G. L.

using it. All along, the apprentice has been learning the essence of every profound practice: patience.

But you don't have to find a sword master to teach you patience. A few months from now, if you've simply been patient and practiced diligently, you'll be surprised and delighted when you recognize how much you've improved. In some elements of your practice, nutrition, for example, it might be easier to make a change all at once rather than in small increments. Bear in mind that your taste for fat is acquired and can be retrained. You might try switching immediately to a low-fat, high-fiber diet, then waiting patiently for your body to adjust. After two or three months, food prepared with what seems little fat will probably strike you as quite delicious. But here, as in other aspects of your practice, don't be rigid. Eating should be a happy experience. If now and then you slip, so be it.

The other elements of your practice will gather force with the development of your attention and intentionality. How do you become more intellectually interested and focused? Practice. How do you become a more loving, caring, emotionally expressive person? Practice. How do you develop a sense of community and social service? Practice.

It's not that these various activities stand out as separate, time-consuming chores. In ITP, at best, the various elements naturally blend and become part of your daily life, informing and adding meaning to all you do. *You might discover, as did some of our class members, that you have more extra time after beginning this practice than before.*

The Efficacy of Long-term Practice

Top-level performance in any profound skill fills us with awe. To hear a master violinist in concert, for example, leads us to assume that such talent must be inborn, a gift from God. The primacy of talent in achieving mastery, in fact, has been assumed for centuries. Recent research, however, has shown that long-term focused practice, rather than talent, holds the master key to top performance in almost every field. This recent research is surveyed in a long article in the August 1994 *American Psychologist* by psychologists K. Anders Ericsson and Neil Charness.

In a study of violinists at respected music academies, Dr. Ericsson found that the top-rated violinists had practiced an average of about 10,000 hours by age twenty, the second-level violinists had practiced some 7,500 hours, and the lowest level violinists had practiced about 5,000 hours.

Ericsson and Charness show that even skills thought to be purely innate can be learned through practice. Perhaps the best example of a seemingly God-given ability is perfect pitch: the ability to correctly name each of the musical tones with no reference from a tuning fork or other instrument. Only one out of every ten thousand people possess this marvelous skill. Experiments show, however, that, with practice, any normal child between three and six can develop perfect pitch. The children, in fact, *prefer* to learn perfect pitch rather than relative pitch, which is the ability to recognize the relationship between pitches.

Focused long-term practice can accomplish miracles in many fields. Take short-term memory. Almost every psychology textbook repeats the "fact" that short-term memory is limited to around seven bits of information—the length of a local phone number. Dr. Ericsson and his associates, however, have used long-term practice with college students to shatter this putative memory barrier in spectacular fashion. After fifty hours of practice, four of the students could correctly repeat up to 20 digits after a single hearing. Another student, a business major not particularly talented in mathematics, practiced for four hundred hours and was then able to remember 102 random digits after only one hearing.

Practice can clearly improve physical performance, but the extent of this improvement is illuminating. The 1904 Olympic Gold Medalist in the marathon, for example, couldn't qualify for this year's Boston Marathon, an event for which thousands of amateur runners are now qualified. We could try to explain this disparity in terms of better nutrition, coaching, and equipment, but these factors pale against the fact that even topflight runners at the turn of the century trained for only a few months preceding the event. Runners today train all year long, every year.

Long-term physical practice, Ericsson and Charness point out, changes not only the body's performance abilities but also its shape and its very physiology, not only growing hundreds of miles of new capillaries but even changing the proportion of different types of muscle cells. Practicing activities that require quick, explosive muscle power creates more fast-twitch muscle cells. Practicing endurance activities creates more slow-twitch muscle cells.

Obviously, we aren't focusing integral practice on attaining perfect pitch, remembering random digits, or running marathons, but the effect of practice on these activities applies to almost all human learning and change. We believe that every human individual is unique, one of a kind, and that each of us is born with a genius that will manifest itself in wonderfully unique ways. There are geniuses of love and of service to others, geniuses of spiritual radiance and understanding, geniuses of extraordinary and as yet undefined abilities that will light the way to the next step in our evolution. But none of these capacities can be realized without practice.

THE INEVITABLE HUMAN RESISTANCE TO CHANGE— AND HOW TO HANDLE IT

There's one more thing. Somewhere down the road, say three or four months from the time you begin, you might feel a strong and inexplicable urge to stop practicing. This generally occurs just when your practice is going very well, just when you're beginning to change in a noticeably positive way.

Don't be alarmed. Every one of us resists significant change, no matter whether its for the worse or for the better. Our body, brain, and behavior have a built-in tendency to stay the same within rather narrow limits and to snap back when changed—and it's a very good thing they do. Just think about it: If your body temperature moved up or down by 10 percent, you'd be in big trouble. Same thing with your blood-sugar level and with many other functions in your body. This condition of equilibrium, this resistance to change, is called homeostasis. It characterizes all self-regulating systems, from a bacterium to a frog to a human individual to a family to an organization to a whole culture. And it applies to psychological states and behavior as well as to physical functioning.

A simple example of homeostasis may be found in your home heating system. The thermostat on the wall senses the room temperature. When the temperature on a winter's day drops below the level you've set, the thermostat sends an electrical signal that turns the heater on. The heater completes the loop by sending heat to the room in which the thermostat is located. When the room temperature reaches the level you've set, the thermostat sends an electrical signal back to the heater, turning it off, thus maintaining homeostasis.

Keeping a room at the right temperature takes only one feedback loop. Keeping even the simplest single-celled organism alive takes thousands. And maintaining a human being in a state of homeostasis takes trillions of interweaving electrochemical signals pulsing in the brain, rushing along nerve fibers, coursing through the bloodstream.

One example: Each of us has about 150,000 tiny thermostats in the form of nerve endings close to the surface of the skin that are sensitive to the loss of heat from our bodies, and another 16,000 or so a little deeper in the skin, which can alert us to the entry of heat from hot objects. An even more sensitive thermostat resides in the hypothalamus at the base of the brain, close to branches of the main artery that brings blood from the heart to the head. This thermostat can pick up tiny changes of temperature in the blood. When you start getting cold, these thermostats signal the sweat glands, pores, and small blood vessels near the surface of the body to close down. Glandular activity and muscle tension increase to the point of shivering in order to produce more heat. And your senses send a clear message to keep moving, to put on more clothes, to cuddle closer to someone, to seek shelter, to build a fire.

Homeostasis in social groups brings additional feedback loops into play. Families stay stable by means of instruction, exhortation, punishment, privileges, gifts, favors, signs of approval and affection, and by means of extremely subtle body language and facial expressions. Social groups larger than the family add different kinds of feedback systems. A national culture, for example, is held together by the legislative process, law enforcement, education, the popular arts, sports and games, economic rewards that favor certain kinds of activity, and by a complex web of mores, prestige markers, celebrity role modeling, and style that relies largely on the media as a national nervous system. And though we might think that our culture is mad for the new, the predominant function of all this—as with the feedback loops in your body—is the survival of things as they are.

The problem is, homeostasis works to keep things as they are even if they aren't very good. Let's say, for instance, that for the last twenty years—ever since high school, in fact—you've been almost entirely sedentary. Now most of your friends are working out, and you figure that if you can't beat the fitness revolution, you'll join it. Buying the tights and running shoes is fun, and so are the first few steps as you start jogging on the high school track near your house. Then, about a third of the way around the first lap, something terrible happens. Maybe you're suddenly sick to your stomach. Maybe you're dizzy. Maybe there's a strange, panicky feeling in your chest. Maybe you're going to die.

No, you're not going to die. What's more, the particular sensations you're feeling probably aren't significant in themselves. What you're really getting is a homeostatic alarm signal—bells clanging, lights flashing. WARNING! WARNING! SIGNIFICANT CHANGES IN RESPIRATION, HEART RATE, METABOLISM. WHATEVER YOU'RE DOING, STOP DOING IT IMMEDIATELY.

Homeostasis, remember, doesn't distinguish between what you would call change for the better and change for the worse. It resists *all* change. After twenty years without exercise, your body regards a sedentary style of life as "normal," while the beginning of a change for the better is interpreted as a threat. So you walk slowly back to your car, figuring you'll look around for some other revolution to join.

No need here to count the ways that organizations and cultures resist change and backslide when change does occur. Just let it be said that the resistance is generally proportionate to the size and speed of the change, not to whether the change is a favorable or unfavorable one. If an organization or cultural reform meets tremendous resistance, it is because it's either a tremendously bad idea or a tremendously good idea. Trivial change, bureaucratic meddling, is much easier to accept, and that's one reason why you see so much of it. In the same way, the talkier forms of psychotherapy are acceptable, at least to some degree, perhaps because they sometimes change nothing very much except the patient's ability to talk about his or her problems. But none of this is meant to condemn homeostasis. We want our minds and bodies and organizations to hold together. We want our pay check to arrive on schedule. In order to survive, we need stability.

Still, change does occur—in individuals, families, organizations, and whole cultures. Homeostats are reset, though the process might well cause a certain amount of anxiety, pain, and upset. The questions are: How do you deal with homeostasis? How do you make change for the better easier? How do you make it last?

*Your resistance to change
is likely to reach its peak
when significant change is
imminent.*

G. L.

These questions rise to great importance when you embark on a path of practice. Your whole life obviously will change, and thus you'll have to deal with homeostasis. Realizing significantly more of your potential in almost anything can change you in many ways. And however much you enjoy and profit from the change, you'll probably meet up with homeostasis sooner or later. You might experience homeostatic alarm signals in the form of physical or psychological symptoms. You might unknowingly sabotage your own best efforts. You might get resistance from family, friends, and coworkers. Ultimately, you'll have to decide if you really want to spend the time and effort it takes to get on and stay on the path. If you do, here are five guidelines adapted from *Mastery* that might help.

Be aware of the way homeostasis works. This might be the most important of all. Expect resistance and backlash. Realize that when the alarm bells start ringing it doesn't necessarily mean you're sick or crazy or lazy or that you've made a bad decision in embarking on an evolutionary journey. In fact, you might take these signals as an indication that your life is definitely changing—just what you've wanted. Of course, it might be that you've started something that's not right for you. Only you can decide. But, in any case, don't panic and give up at the first sign of trouble.

You might also expect resistance from friends and family and coworkers. (Homeostasis applies to social systems as well as individuals.) Say you used to struggle out of bed at 7:30 and barely drag yourself to work at 9:00. Now that you're practicing ITP, you're up at 6:00 to do the Kata, then a three-mile run, and you're in the office, charged with energy, before 9:00. You might figure that your coworkers would be overjoyed, but don't be too sure. And when you get home, still full of energy, do you think your family will welcome the change? Maybe. Bear in mind that a whole system has to change when any part of it changes. So don't be surprised if some of the people you love start covertly or overtly trying to undermine your practice. It's not that they wish you harm. It's just homeostasis at work.

Be willing to negotiate with your resistance to change. When and if you should run into resistance, don't back off and don't bull your way through. Negotiation is the ticket to successful long-term change. The long-distance runner, working for a faster time on a measured course, negotiates with homeostasis using pain not as an adversary but as the best possible guide to performance. The ITP practitioner keeps his or her eyes and ears open for signs of dissatisfaction or dislocation, but doesn't stop practicing. Better to play the edge of discontent, the inevitable escort of transformation.

The fine art of playing the edge involves a willingness to take one step back for every two forward, sometimes vice versa. It also demands a determination to keep pushing, but not without awareness. Simply turning off your awareness to the warnings deprives you of guidance and risks damaging the system. Simply pushing your way through, despite the warning signals, increases the possibility of eventually backsliding.

You can never be sure exactly where the resistance will pop up. A feeling of anxiety? Psychosomatic complaints? A tendency toward self-sabotage? Squabbles with family, friends, or fellow workers? None of the above? Stay alert. Be prepared for serious negotiations.

Develop a support system. You can do it alone, but it helps a great deal to have other people with whom you can share the joys and perils of the change you're making. The best support system would involve people who have gone through or are going through a similar process, people who can tell their own stories of change and listen to yours, people who will brace you up when you start to backslide and encourage you when you don't. The path of practice, fortunately, generally fosters social groupings. In his seminal book, *Homo Ludens: A Study of the Play Element in Culture*, Johan Huizinga comments upon the tendency of sports and games to bring people together. The play community, he points out, is likely to continue after the game is over, inspired by "the feeling of being 'apart together' in an exceptional situation, of sharing something important, of mutually withdrawing from the rest of the world and rejecting the usual norms." The same can be said about many other pursuits—arts and crafts, hunting, fishing, yoga, Zen, the professions, and most certainly the practice of integral transformation.

And what if your quest is a lonely one? What if you can find no fellow voyagers on your path? At the least, you can let the people close to you know what you're doing and ask for their support.

Follow a regular practice. People embarking on any kind of change can gain stability and comfort through practicing some worthwhile activity on a more or less regular basis, not so much for the sake

In the master's secret mirror, there is an image of the newest student in class, eager for knowledge, willing to play the fool.

                     G. L.

of achieving an external goal as simply for its own sake. A traveler on the path of integral transformation is again fortunate, for practice in this sense (as we've said more than once) is the foundation of the path itself. Practice is a habit, and any regular practice provides a sort of underlying homeostasis, a stable base during the instability of change.

Dedicate yourself to lifelong learning. We tend to forget that learning is much more than book learning. To learn is to change. Education is a process that changes the learner. It doesn't have to end at college graduation or at age forty or sixty or eighty, and the best learning of all involves learning how to learn—that is, to change. The lifelong learner is essentially one who has learned to deal with homeostasis, simply because he or she is doing it all the time. Lifelong learning is the special province of those who have a profound practice, those who travel the path that never ends.

MIRACLES, LUCK, AND PRACTICE

There's a popular teaching that flies the banner, "Expect Miracles." And why not? Life itself is a miracle: We are here on this wondrous planet. Children are born. We know joy and sorrow. The grass keeps growing. And there are many more miracles to come. If cosmology and biology teach us anything, it is that we live in a transformative universe. Nevertheless, if ITP were to fly a banner, it would be a different one: "Expect nothing. Be ready for anything." Beyond expectations, beyond miracles, beyond good fortune, there is practice.

And there is a paradox: For those who practice diligently, for those who practice because they love to practice, seeming miracles become commonplace. The story goes that Ben Hogan, one of the greatest golfers of all time, was questioned by a reporter after winning a major tournament.

"How is it," the reporter asked, "that under pressure you're able to hit so many miraculous shots?"

After reflecting on the question, Hogan answered: "I guess I'm just lucky."

"But Mr. Hogan," the reporter said, "you practice more than any golfer who ever lived."

"Well," Hogan said. "The more I practice, the luckier I get."

❁

FOUR

The Powers of Affirmation

On the path of Integral Transformative Practice, our affirmations are clear, straightforward statements of positive change in body, being, and performance. They represent a firm contract with ourselves. They focus our best conscious efforts on transformation while seeking to enlist powers beyond our conscious understanding. They are written in the present tense to describe conditions as you intend them to be at some specified time in the future.

To take an example: Say you're a person who is often too busy or preoccupied to consider other people's feelings. You want to develop more empathy. Your affirmation could be "I enjoy a profound empathy for other people that sometimes appears to be telepathic." Present tense. It would not be, "I will develop my powers of empathy" or "I intend to be a more empathic person" or "To be more empathic."

By employing the present tense, the affirmation, "I enjoy a profound empathy for other people that sometimes appears to be telepathic," might seem to deny reality. Yes, right now, in the life you lead, you are by no means an empathic person. But your affirmation is not a denial of that reality. Rather, it is an instrument for creating a parallel, present-tense reality in your consciousness, a precondition for the affirmation work we use in ITP.

This consciousness of yours is nothing you can touch or photo-graph or measure with any known instrument, but it is nonetheless real. It exists in the universe. It is organized. It produces results. Your job is to create the condition of being an empathic person in the realm of your consciousness. This may be accomplished through language (repeating the affirmation silently or aloud), imaging (creating a strong image of yourself as an empathic person, one who listens wholeheartedly), and emotion (feeling what another feels). In this example, some part of the change can be accomplished simply through practicing being empathic with loved ones, acquaintances, or strangers—even if that practice seems at first pro forma. It's also important to open yourself to the magic of grace, that mysterious, seemingly unearned mediation that often comes when least expected (see chapter 5). But whether the mediation is practical and easily understandable or metanormal and mysterious, the concentrated intentionality triggered by the affirmation process is central.

Later in this chapter, we list guidelines for making your affirmations, and at the end of the next chapter, we describe exercises –designed to trigger your unrealized transformative powers. But first, let us simply explain how the affirmations are to be written. We recommend that you not rush. Make notes. Think about your affirmations for a couple of weeks or more. Do they really fit your desires? Do you really want to commit yourself to these particular affirmations.

When you're ready, get a sheet of lined, letter-sized paper. Using a pen, write on the top: "I, [your first and last names], intend to see that the following circumstances have occurred by [a date six to twelve months from now]:" Skip a line and write your affirmations, numbering them. We recommend that you make no more than four affirmations for any period, with this last affirmation: "My entire being is balanced, vital, and healthy." We would not want any affirmation to be realized at the cost of balance, vitality, and health.

After writing the affirmations, read them carefully, then sign and date them. A sample is shown here. This is a composite, based on experiences of participants in our class.

When you have finished your affirmations, make a copy for a friend to keep, if you wish, in case you should lose your copy. Then put the original in a convenient, safe place. Take it out to reread if you should become confused about the exact langauge, but don't ob-

SAMPLE AFFIRMATION SHEET

I, Jane Doe, intend to see that the following circumstances have occurred by September 1, 1996:

1. I enjoy a profound empathy for people that at times appears to be telepathic.

2. At work, I operate in the "flow" all day, working in a state of harmony with my employees and customers.

3. I experience illuminations in which I feel a oneness with all of existence.

4. My entire being is balanced, vital, and healthy.

Signed, Jane Doe
OCTOBER 1, 1995

sess about it. No need to reread your affirmations every day. They're there in your life.

Though you'll be working with your affirmations throughout the affirmation period, this is all the writing you have to do: your affirmations are made. But we recommend that on the same day you make them you also make a written record of your present condition in the areas covered by the affirmations. A record for those affirmations might read as follows on page 56.

Here again, you might want to make a copy for a friend. Keep the original of this record with your affirmation sheet. On the due date you've picked for your affirmations, make the appropriate measurements if you have affirmed changes in your body and performance, evaluate your progress in realizing those affirmations that don't lend themselves to objective measurements, and again make a written record. This record might read as follows on page 57.

SAMPLE RECORD OF STATES OF BEING ON THE DAY AFFIRMATIONS ARE WRITTEN

1. I have been told by family members and fellow workers that I sometimes don't take their feelings into consideration. I am aware that I put getting things done above the feelings of others. Part of this, I'm sure, is because my powers of empathy are poor. I've never given high priority to tuning-in to others' feelings. But I have had experiences that could be telepathic. On rare occasions, I have anticipated exactly what another person was going to say.

2. At work, I am currently in the "flow" about an hour a day on the average. For me, "flow' is a state in which everything goes easily and my mind doesn't wander. In this state, I effortlessly stay focused on the task at hand. I don't feel hurried or harassed, and I experience a sense of synchrony with my employees and customers.

3. I have read about mystical experiences that bring a sense of oneness with everything. On two or three occasions, I have had a vague sense of this, but never to the degree expressed in the books I have read.

4. I feel my energy is too "forward." I tend to get ahead of myself. My vitality is good most of the time, but I sometimes have low energy at midday and early in the afternoon. I use coffee at lunch for an energy lift. I suffer moderate headaches at my forehead and temples once or twice a week. In general I consider myself quite healthy.

Signed, Jane Doe
OCTOBER 1, 1995

SAMPLE RECORD OF STATES OF BEING ON THE DAY AFFIRMATIONS COME DUE

1. My empathy has greatly improved. This gives me and the people I'm with great pleasure. I attribute this mostly to practice. I have practiced tuning-in to others' feelings and have been delighted with my progress. As for telepathic powers—nothing new to report on this front.

2. As of this date, I am in the flow almost all day, with only short periods of time being the exception. Rather than compartmentalizing my day, which I believe was based on habit and fear, I surrendered that control. I replaced it with faith in the universe, new skills, and a centered confidence in myself.

3. On June 17, on a soft, sunny late afternoon, while sitting on a grassy hill near my house, I felt an unexplainable well-being and remembered my affirmation to experience the mystical state. Focusing my attention on a tree across the valley below me, I said to myself, "I am one with all I perceive." In an instant, my state of well-being deepened into a joy I had never experienced before, and I was overwhelmed by a sense that I was one with everything I saw, every rock and tree and blade of grass. Everything they say about the mystical state is true. It brings a peace and joy that passes understanding.

4. Much improvement! I rarely have headaches now, and I've stopped using coffee. My energy feels more balanced. Being in the flow state so much, I'm not ahead of myself nearly as much as I used to be.

Signed, Jane Doe
SEPTEMBER 1, 1996

After your first cycle of affirmations is finished, you might make a new set. But don't hurry. Take a few days, or weeks, to decide what's good for you and what you really want.

But what if you have experienced little or no success on a certain affirmation? If you wish, you can simply include it in your new set of affirmations, wording it the same way or rewording it so as to better express your intention. Several members of our ITP class who stayed with the project for two years made identical or similar affirmations for the second year, with good results.

Body and mind reflect and influence each other with amazing fidelity.

G. L.

For example, Tyrone Polastri, a forty-six-year-old marketing consultant with a special interest in sports, affirmed a 50 percent increase in body strength for 1992. Due to a broken left elbow and serious personal problems, he made little progress that year. In 1993, he affirmed a 30 percent increase in body strength. He was tested in ten different exercises (bench press, biceps curl, leg press, etc.) as to the maximum weight he could move at the beginning of the class, then again at the end. During this period, he did strength training for sixty minutes three times a week; however, he missed eight weeks of training. As it turned out, his strength increased an overall 88 percent. Particularly significant is the fact that improvement showed up even in muscles not included in his training program. Since he was concentrating on upper body strength, for example, he did no leg press exercises and did not change his bicycling activity from that of previous years. Yet his leg strength increased by 140 percent.

QUESTIONS TO ASK YOURSELF BEFORE MAKING YOUR AFFIRMATIONS

Does the affirmation really represent a change in me rather than in the external world? Affirmations as used in Integral Transformative Practice are not magical. They are statements of an intention to change your own functioning in a positive way, not to make the external world play tricks for you. We were dumbfounded when one 1992 participant asked if, in the metanormal category, he could affirm that he had won the California Lottery—twice. "That would be metanormal, wouldn't it?" Then there was the woman who wanted to affirm that her business would net her $150,000. This, too, was inappropriate. But by increasing the amount of time she was in the flow state or developing her intuition or becoming more balanced and centered, she might well contribute to the financial success of her business. In every case, we asked participants to affirm positive changes in their own functioning rather than in the external results of that functioning.

Am I getting ahead of myself? A twenty-nine-year-old financial manager and neophyte golfer made this affirmation in 1992: "I play par golf consistently, and my drives are, on average, 200 yards long." This woman, whose drives then averaged 125 yards, was actually a long way from par. Closing the gap over a ten-month period was not beyond the realm of the possible. And her affirmation did involve her own functioning rather than outside forces. Still, we found it questionable. The process as well as the result is important. To drastically foreshorten or entirely bypass the journey of mastery is to forfeit much of the richness of life.

> A Journal of Practice
>
> *You can simply record the ITP activities you complete each day along with the state of your awareness during each activity. If you wish, you can also note your thoughts, reflections, emotions, and sensations. Such a record is most valuable during an affirmation period.*

George Leonard started in aikido as a raw beginner at age forty-seven and was awarded his first degree black belt five years and three months later. To have magically attained black belt rank in a few months time would have been to miss out on many joyous and poignant moments and to violate an essential rhythm of practice.

Still, this is a matter of degree. We would not want to discourage practitioners from speeding and enhancing improvements of their functioning. Learning involves short, spectacular spurts as well as long stretches on the plateau, and affirmations can shorten the plateaus without breaking the rhythm of practice. One person in the class, a competitive Masters' Class runner, had been trying for years to reduce his waistline in order to increase his speed and endurance. In 1992, he affirmed reducing his waist by one and a quarter inches. His chief device for realizing this affirmation was an especially vivid and persistent image of a "girdle of fire" around his waist whenever he was running. In just three months, with the girdle of fire image, his waist was smaller by two full inches—this without any changes in his diet or exercise regimen. This person was by no means bypassing his practice, having been a serious and disciplined runner for over twenty years. But despite all his prior training, such a sudden spurt of improvement in physical conditioning testifies to the generally unrecognized powers of affirmation and imaging.

When we see the body as a structure of heavy meat and bones, all we can do is cut it or drug it or otherwise manipulate it from the outside. But when we create a picture more consonant with modern physics and see the body as elegant, ethereal fields of waves joined in innumerable feedback circuits, then we realize that thoughts and feelings can set off sympathetic vibrations in it. The deeper vibrations connected with the power we have called "intentionality" can produce transformations in weeks, days, or perhaps even minutes.

And how about the woman golfer who wanted to shoot par? Her record of affirmations at the end of the years tells the story: "I do not play par golf (surprise!). My drives now range between 150 and 175 yards. Generally my game is more consistent, and I'm hitting it straight down the middle more often."

Our advice? Don't be greedy, but also don't be timid.

Is the change a healthy one? The word "health" shares ancestry with "heal," "whole," and "holy" and should serve as a watchword not only in making your affirmations but throughout your practice. Bear in mind that transformation can be negative and destructive as well as positive and constructive. Attention to good health is of the essence. We consider the affirmation, "My entire being is balanced, vital, and healthy," as a gold standard and safety net for all the others. At the same time, we feel it wise to examine each affirmation of its own in terms of good health. You would not want to develop massive upper-body muscles to the detriment of a balanced body. You would not want to develop the ability to take out-of-body journeys at the expense of mental stability. Even at best, transformation can involve destruction: the breakdown of old patterns in the creation of the new. Consider the overall health of body, mind, soul, and heart before making your affirmations. If at any time during the process you should feel your health is being threatened, you can always slow down or pull back.

In the 1993 Cycle, Hollis Polk, a thirty-five-year-old real estate broker, affirmed that she was 5 foot 4 inches tall. At that time, she was 5 foot 1¼ inches. To realize her affirmation, she would have to grow two and a quarter inches. We urged her to reconsider, but she was dead set on 5 foot 4. After two months, she reported she had grown three-quarters of an inch, but was suffering pains in her ribs and joints. At this point, she agreed to back off. By the end of the class, she had grown between an inch and an inch and a quarter, with no ill effects.

Good health is the bottom line, and in this matter it is also important—as we will point out more than once in this book—not to neglect what mainstream medicine has to offer. Take your flu shots, if indicated. Make prompt and intelligent use of the exquisite diagnostic instrumentalities and healing capabilities developed by our science. This practice aims to integrate worlds that some people foolishly attempt to separate.

How will this change affect others in my life? Say you affirm a significant increase in your personal autonomy, your ability to control your own destiny. Say the affirmation is fully realized. Previously you'd been very dependent on other people. Now you're making decisions for yourself and generally operating more effectively. Do you think family and fellow workers will be overjoyed? Well, maybe. Before making your affirmations, consider the likely effects on the people around you. Discuss your plans with those you work with and those you care for.

Do I really want this change? Am I prepared to live with it? There's an old saying: "Be careful what you ask for. You might get it." Are you really the kind of person who is willing to be taller or enjoy abundant energy or express your love openly and freely or get in touch with self-existent delight or manifest metanormal capabilities? Are you the kind of person who is willing to realize your latent powers? Are you willing to live with a fuller expression of beauty and creativity?

Sometimes we have to look deep inside to know how fearful we are of our own potentialities. This fear has roots in society's tireless efforts, covert and overt, to shape us within the boundaries of "normality," which in a mass society too often devolve toward the lowest common denominator. During his years of writing on the subject of education, George Leonard discovered that educators are sometimes even more threatened by exceptionally high abilities than by exceptionally low abilities in their students. One student in Virginia, for example, took home a programmed course in geometry and finished a semester's work in one long weekend. This left the teacher with the daunting question: What can I do with him the rest of this semester? And, if he should continue at this rate, how about the semester after that? If this mental transformation is threatening,

Ultimately, human intentionality is the most powerful evolutionary force on this planet.

G. L.

how much more threatening are transformations of body, heart, and spirit?

To become consciously involved in an enterprise that may presage further human evolution takes courage and a sense of adventure. As in all high adventure, there are risks and no certainty of success. But regular, disciplined practice builds a base camp of security and support. No matter how high you climb, your practice is always there, waiting for you. If you wish, you can photocopy this form (adapted from the Record of Affirmations form used by members of our experimental class) and use it to record your own success in realizing your affirmations. We strongly recommend that your final affirmation, in every case, should be "My entire being is balanced, vital, and healthy."

INTEGRAL TRANSFORMATIVE PRACTICE
RECORD OF AFFIRMATION

Affirmation 1   (Write affirmation here)

Description of the condition addressed by Affirmation 1 as of date affirmation is written. Note dates of measurements or tests if other than present date.

Description of the condition addressed by Affirmation 1 as of date affirmation is due. Note dates of measurements or tests if other than this date.

Your evaluation of change on a scale of 0 to 10. _____

(Write affirmation here)   **Affirmation 2**

Description of the condition addressed by Affirmation 2 as of date affirmation is written. Note dates of measurements or tests if other than present date.

Description of the condition addressed by Affirmation 2 as of date affirmation is due. Note dates of measurements or tests if other than this date.

Your evaluation of change on a scale of 0 to 10. _____

(Write affirmation here)   **Affirmation 3**

Description of the condition addressed by Affirmation 3 as of date affirmation is written. Note dates of measurements or tests if other than present date.

Description of the condition addressed by Affirmation 3 as of date affirmation is due. Note dates of measurements or tests if other than date affirmation is due.

Affirmation 4   (Write affirmation here)

Description of the condition addressed by Affirmation 4 as of date affirmation is written. Note dates of mesaurements or tests if other than present date.

Description of the condition addressed by Affirmation 4 as of date affirmation is due. Note dates of measurements or tests if other than date affirmation is due.

Your evaluation of change on a scale of 0 to 10. _____

FIVE

Catching the Winds of Grace: More on Affirmations

"The winds of grace are always blowing," the Indian mystic Ramakrishna said. "But we have to raise our sails." Through grace we are granted such priceless gifts as self-transcending love, joy, and peace as well as those extraordinary capacities that lift us above the commonplace. With grace, all comes to us as if freely given rather than earned, spontaneously revealed rather than attained.

Every enduring religious tradition recognizes this feature of human experience. Many traditions see a personal God as the gift giver, but this is not always the case. Zen, for example, has no doctrine of an external god. Still, "Buddha-Nature" is analogous to the grace of a personal deity in that, as Zen patriarch Dogen tells us, it is "always and everywhere present," everlastingly available, endlessly responsive to our aspirations for new life.

In terms of the evolutionary vision that informs this book, the infinite possibilities of the Divine Spirit were *involved* in the universe from the very beginning. Evolution is the process through which these hidden possibilities are revealed. Extraordinary life often emerges as a gift rather than as the product of striving, because it is already there.

Here is a paradox: Grace seems freely given, involving surrender more than struggle. At the same time, dedicated, long-term practice seems to predispose us to its gifts. The same paradox inhabits the matter of prayer, which is similar to affirmation in that it involves consciousness and intentionality. In his book, *Healing Words*, Larry Dossey surveys numerous studies of prayer in healing. Such studies suggest that *petition prayer*, in which one asks for specific outcomes, is not quite as efficacious in the healing process as is *prayerfulness*, in which one surrenders to the greater mystery and aligns oneself with God, as reflected in the simple prayer, "Thy will, not mine, be done."

Through our experiments with affirmations, we have learned that our students generally best realize their affirmations by practicing what we call Focused Surrender. This practice combines strongly imaging a desired outcome in the present tense, as if it already was happening or had happened, then totally surrendering to grace. Thus, to the extent that the affirmation process is analogous to prayer, Focused Surrender combines petition prayer with prayerfulness.

George Leonard coined the term Focused Surrender while working on *The Silent Pulse*. He noted that every episode of grace or "perfect rhythm" described in the book involved the unlikely marriage of trying and not trying, of zeroing-in and letting go. It appeared that both focused intentionality and the surrender of ego were necessary for experiencing existence at such a fundamental level and creating what often appeared miraculous. It was at the moment of surrender, after intense concentration during these episodes, that grace became manifest. From 1973 through 1975, for example, a researcher named Duane Elgin conducted a remarkable series of exercises at Stanford Research Institute, attempting to influence a sensitive, heavily shielded magnetometer by his intentionality alone. The magnetometer measures changes in a magnetic field and records these changes on a moving sheet of paper.

The first few exercises generally followed the same course. Elgin would sit or stand a few feet from the magnetometer, where he could see the recording device, and would focus all the force of his will on the instrument, trying to influence it and thus make the needle move. He would continue this concentrated effort for twenty to thirty minutes, watching the needle tracing an almost straight line—

but with no results. Finally, exhausted and exasperated, he would say to himself, "I give up." At that moment, the needle would start indicating a change in the magnetic field. These changes were by no means insignificant. In some of Elgin's exercises, the needle went entirely off the scale; to get such results by normal means would take a force estimated to be one thousand times stronger than that of the earth's magnetic field. Nor did physical distance lessen Elgin's effectiveness. In one instance, he was able to affect the magnetometer strongly from his home several miles away.

Later, Elgin learned to refine his technique. "I'd spend twenty to thirty minutes doing the best I could to establish a sense of rapport and connectedness with the instrument, and with great will and concentration I would coalesce that sense of connectedness into a field of palpable energy. I'd feel myself coming into the magnetic field and pulsing it to respond. Then, when there would be a moment of total surrender, the response would occur."

There's no question but that ego has great power, but it also has limitations. If we entertain the notion that the universe somehow already contains all information, all possibilities, and that each of us is a context of the universe from a particular point of view, then we might say that to create a sharply focused, vivid image of what we are seeking serves to "tune" our being to that precise possibility. But that's not enough. The striving, the ego still gets in the way. When we surrender, relinquishing the ego with its limitations, we open the way for grace: news from the universe, a direct connection with the divine.

However we explain it, Focused Surrender has served in our bodily transformation exercises since 1981 as our most effective process for realizing affirmations. Focused Surrender exercises, can be used in a number of variations. We start with this basic exercise.

Focused Surrender

Find a carpeted or matted space where you won't be disturbed. Lie on your back with your feet about as far apart as your shoulders and your arms out a few inches from your sides, palms up. Close your eyes and breathe deeply, letting the incoming breath expand your abdomen as well as your chest. Feel the surface beneath you. Shift slightly, as if you are nestling deeper into this surface.

Now send a beam of awareness through your body, searching out any area of tension. Wherever you find tension, let it melt away, as if it is sinking into the surface beneath you then into the earth. After completing this process of relaxation, you will spend a few minutes on a special kind of breathing that will require your concentration—and your surrender.

Start by taking a deep breath through your nostrils, with your mouth gently closed, being sure to let your abdomen expand. After you have inhaled fully, part your lips slightly and *consciously* blow the air out. But do it noiseleessly, as if you are blowing a small ball of cotton away from you. Continue blowing the air out consciously until you have fully exhaled. Then gently close your lips and simply wait, fully relaxed, expecting nothing. This is your moment of surrender. The incoming breath will enter your nostrils of its own accord. You need do nothing at all. If you are in a complete state of surrender, *the precise moment of inhalation will come as a slight surprise*. After the inhalation has filled you, open your lips slightly and repeat the cycle, consciously exhaling, then closing your lips and waiting for the spontaneous inhalation.

In this process, you are joining the voluntary with the involuntary, the willed with the spontaneous, the conscious with the unconscious. In the timeless pause between the willed exhalation and the spontaneous inhalation, you can begin to experience that state of egoless not-doing that is the very essence of creation and grace. Continue with this mode of breathing for a few minutes, then let your breath return to normal.

Now place your left hand, palm down, on your abdomen. With eyes still closed, bring to mind one of your affirmations. Say it aloud several times. Then create a mental image of yourself and your life as it would be were the affirmation already realized. Make it real in your consciousness. Flesh out that reality with as many feelings as you can. As soon as the realized affirmation becomes vividly present in your consciousness, let your left hand rise a few inches above your abdomen. Let it float there as if suspended, with no effort on your part. Focus intently on the image, holding it in your mind with all your will. Concentrate!

When you can no longer hold the image in place, simply *give up* and let your hand fall to your abdomen. Lie there in a state of grateful acceptance of whatever may be, with a feeling of total surrender, a sense of alignment with the divine spirit or with the universe itself.

Whenever you're ready, repeat the exercise. There's a good

chance the image will become more vivid with repetition. It might well be that your left hand will begin to rise spontaneously, with no conscious effort on your part, accurately signaling the presence of a vivid image in your consciousness.

When you choose to end the exercise, remove your left hand from your abdomen and put it on the floor a few inches out from your left side, palm up. Lie there in a state of acceptance for a while, then deepen your breathing. Move your body around gently with increased awareness of the surface beneath you. Stretch your arms and legs and, if you feel like it, yawn. Then open your eyes and sit up.

At best, concentration transcends effort.

G. L.

THE VOID OF SILENCE

For this variation, you'll need some instrument which, after being struck, will continue to resonate, the sound gradually fading away. A well-tempered bell or going or chime will serve the purpose. If a piano is available, use a note in the lower register, with the sustain pedal down. An electric guitar can be set so that a note, once struck, will gradually fade away. An extra person, one not participating in the exercise, is required to sound the tone. This variation is appropriate for use with groups, even very large groups.

Start with the relaxation and breathing processes used in the basic Focused Surrender exercise. *Before* bringing an affirmation to mind, place your left hand on your abdomen. The extra person will sound the tone. When you hear it, let your left hand rise a few inches above your abdomen and float there as if sustained by the tone. Follow the sound of the tone as it descends into silence. Use all your powers of concentration as it becomes fainter and fainter. Let it take you down into the void of silence, the nothingness out of which all things arise. When at last, despite your best efforts, you can no longer hear the sound, surrender completely and let your left hand fall to your abdomen. Lie there doing nothing, thinking nothing, simply experiencing a state of total surrender. When the hands of everyone doing the exercise have fallen to their abdomens, the extra person will sound another tone. Repeat the process several times.

Now, leaving your left hand on your abdomen, bring one of your affirmations to mind. Repeat it silently several times. The extra person will then sound the tone. As soon as you hear it, let your left hand float up as before. At the same time, let your affirmation become vivid and real in your consciousness, as if fully realized. Hold this image with concentrated focus until you've descended into the creative void and can no longer hear the tone. (Concentrate on the image; the sound will serve to take you down into the void.) Then let your hand drop to your abdomen and *give up* your affirmation. Surrender completely. Lie there in a state of acceptance and alignment with the universe.

The extra person will sound the tone at least seven times. Then he or she will tell you to place your left hand on the floor and return to the world of ordinary consciousness, as in the basic exercise.

CHANTING YOUR AFFIRMATION

This exercise can be done alone but is especially effective with a group. Find a place where you can speak aloud without disturbing anyone or feeling self-conscious. Start by sitting as you might sit in meditation, on a cushion on the floor or in a straight-backed chair, hands on your knees. Check your posture, which should have a feeling of groundedness, uprightness, and openness. Close your eyes and send awareness through your body, locating and relaxing the tense places. Choose one of your affirmations. With your eyes still closed, take three deep breaths, then say the affirmation in a clear and resonant voice and with strong intentionality. Take another breath and say it again. Continue for at least ten minutes—more if you wish.

A strong image of your affirmation as if already realized might come to your consciousness during this exercise, but this isn't necessary. Here, the power of words is what counts. At first, the words will have clear cognitive meaning. If meaning later becomes secondary to sound and if the sound of your voice is more like music than talk, be willing to let this happen. This exercise tends to gain transformative power with the length of time you can keep it going. You might find it rewarding to continue for quite a long while.

When you finish, whether alone or with a group, remain seated while taking three deep breaths. Then lie on the floor on your back with feet about shoulder-width apart and arms a few inches out from your sides, hands palm up. Simply lie there in a state of acceptance, thanksgiving, and alignment with the universe. Take your time reentering your workaday life.

As If

Focused Surrender has proven to be a powerful modality for transformation, but there are others. Sometimes the best ways of realizing affirmations are the simplest. As you go about your daily life, for example you might simply act *as if* an affirmation has already been realized. Say you affirmed being open and loving at all times. Just ask yourself, "What does it feel like to be an open and loving person at all times? How does an open and loving person act?" You don't have to wait. You can start out immediately being and acting as if you are that person.

This doesn't imply denial. Yes, you know that you haven't achieved constant openness and lovingness yet. You slip. You fall. But that doesn't keep you from starting again. Which brings us back to the foundation of all enduring transformation: *practice*. How do you become an open and loving person? You practice.

On matters of physical change—becoming stronger or faster for example—you obviously can't start by literally acting as if you are, say, 30 percent stronger. But you can immediately start acting as if you're the *kind of person* who is 30 percent stronger or faster. You can ask yourself what it would be like if you were 30 percent stronger. How would you stand and walk? How would you approach people? How would your self-image change? How would your body feel? By repeatedly exploring these *as if* conditions mentally and emotionally, you can set the essential personal context for the change that's underway.

And keep in mind that while seeming miracles might happen through grace, the best context for both grace and miracles involves sincere, diligent practice.

Affirmation Checkpoints

In the hurry and worry of daily life, it's easy to neglect what we most desire. A community of practice—even one other committed person—can help us stay on the path. Still, we forget. The electronic clamor that surrounds us, the unrelenting seductiveness of "entertainment," the hypnotic pull of sheer busy-ness all conspire against the awareness that furthers transformation.

To remind yourself of your affirmations (and of your overall practice as well), select two or three checkpoints in your house or workplace. Pick places you are sure to pass on a typical day—the door to your bathroom or kitchen, a staircase, the front or back entrance. To help catch your attention, you might mark your checkpoints. (The brightly colored paste-on circles available at office supply stores make good markers.) Eventually, you might become so accustomed to these markings that you no longer notice them. In that case, change the colors of the markings. Change the location of the checkpoints themselves.

Every time you pass one of these reminders, say an affirmation silently or aloud. Bring an image of the affirmation to mind. Act as if in some way it is aleady realized. Perhaps the words, the image, the *as if* state of being will stay with you for more than a short while as you carry on with your daily life. Traveling a householder's path, it might not be easy but it is possible to integrate your practice in some significant manner with your responsibilities to job and family. Affirmation checkpoints can jump-start the process that produces such a fusion.

A Possibility to be Realized

But it's not just our affirmations, or even our practice, that we forget. We become numb to wonder, rarely considering the fact that each of us is unique in all of space and all of time. We become forgetful, even of our own existence. Here is a possibility to be realized: Through the active consideration of transforming ourselves, of becoming consciously involved in our own evolution, we can reawaken to the miracle of existence. Through simple strategies and patient, diligent practice, we can reclaim the feeling of wonder we held so carelessly between our hands on summer days when we were very young.

The ITP Kata:
The Tao of Practice

The Japanese word *kata* (kah-tah) means "form." Our usage here is similar to that in the martial arts, where the practitioner performs a series of predetermined moves. The ITP Kata was designed by George Leonard to be performed in forty minutes, each element blending into the next without a sense of haste. You can trace its lineage to hatha yoga, the martial arts, modern exercise physiology, Progressive Relaxation, visualization research, and witness meditation. It offers practitioners the following benefits:

Balances and centers the body and psyche

Provides a generalized warm-up, speeding the heartbeat, increasing the flow of blood and sending an infusion of heat to all parts of the body

Articulates practically every joint in the body, enhancing the lubrication of the synovial joints (those such as the shoulder or knee, which are surrounded by capsules filled with synovial fluid)

Makes available a comprehensive course of stretches, increasing flexibility in all major muscle groups

Includes three essential strength exercises

Provides a full set of Progressive Relaxation exercises, in which muscle groups are tightened then allowed to relax deeply

Presents numerous opportunities for deep, rhythmic breathing

Includes a period devoted to transformational imaging during which the powers of intentionality can be applied to making positive changes in body and psyche

Concludes with ten minutes of meditation

While the ITP Kata can be performed in forty minutes without hurrying, parts of it may be extended for as long as the practitioner desires. This is especially true of the last two sections (transformational imaging and meditation). Participants in our experimental classes committed themselves to doing the Kata at least five times a week, and we consider this one of the commitments for full participation in the Integral Transformative Practice program. Many practitioners have found it best to do the Kata in the morning for the relaxing, centering and energizing effect it would have on their whole day.

The ITP Kata embodies the definition of practice itself; that is, an activity which, *for all its benefits*, is done on a regular basis primarily for its own sake, because it is the path upon which you walk. The Kata can be practiced in a group or alone. Group practice gathers power from sharing rhythm and intentionality with others. But even when practicing in solitude, you can be reasonably sure that other people are going through the same sequence of movements and experiences, thus creating a community, whether visible or invisible.

Like many of our participants, you might at first find it a bit frustrating to learn some of the movements and perform them in such a way that they flow smoothly, one into the other. But this practice does not demand the skill of a martial artist or dancer; most people achieve a degree of proficiency after only a few sessions. A few weeks after starting to do the Kata, you, like some of our participants, might encounter a reluctance to continue your practice. This is perfectly natural, a manifestation of the resistance to any significant change in your life, whether for ill or for good, the homeostasis that we have discussed in chapter 3. But if you simply persist, you will in all likelihood arrive at the day when it is easier to do the Kata than not to do it. That, in any case, has been the experience of most of our participants. At the end of our first year's training, participants filled out evaluation forms. The two first items were: "(1) Rank the following ITP elements in order of importance in enhancing your ITP practice," and "(2). Rank the same ITP elements as to their value in your life." All the major elements of the ITP practice were listed. In both cases, participants ranked the Kata second, just below affirmations.

You'll need no special equipment to do the ITP Kata, only a carpeted floor or mat and loose clothing or perhaps an outdoor setting, a soft surface covered with a blanket or mat. Start slowly and use common sense. Don't push any of the stretches to the point of strain or pain. If any exercise seems too strenuous, do it easily at first or even partially. For guidance, tune into your own sensations and feelings. In performing the Kata, think in terms of months or years, not days or weeks. To shift from short-term to long-term thinking and acting is to gain what might well be the most important lesson this training has to offer. An outline of the ITP Kata is presented on the next page, followed by detailed descriptions of each step, with illustrations where needed.

BALANCE AND CENTER—GRACE

The ITP Kata, Step by Step

The word GRACE serves here as an acronym, a sort of pilot's check list for balancing and centering. Start in an upright stance, without shoes, feet shoulder-width apart, eyes open and soft. Spend a few seconds on each letter of the word:

G–Ground Imagine what it would be like if your feet and legs extended down through the surface beneath you and deep into the earth. Feel your weight shifting downward. Let your knees bend ever so slightly. Be aware of the loving embrace of gravity. Consider your profound connection with this planet and, through that, your connection with the entire universe.

R–Relax Breathe deeply. Exhale all the way. Let all your face muscles relax completely. Feel your shoulders melting downward. Release

THE ITP KATA IN OUTLINE

Balance & Center—GRACE

The Water Series
    1. Drill for water, 4 left, 4 right
    2. Pump water, 6
    3. Fountain, 6
    4. Finger spray, 4
    5. Half windmill, 4 (left, right, left, right)
    6. Rowing, 10 left, 10 right, with reach and shake

Articulation
    7. Shoulder rotation, 4 forward, 4 back
    8. Head rotation, 4 each of 3 variations
    9. Arm swing, 12
    10. Pelvic rotation, 4 left, 4 right
    11. Knee rotation, 4 left, 4 right

Floor Series
    12. Hip joint rotation, 8
    13. Quad tightening, 6 x 6"
    14. Foot rotation, 4 counterclockwise, 4 clockwise
    15. Hamstring stretch
    16. Hip stretch
    17. Quad stretch
    18. Back stretch
    19. Spinal Curl
    20. Curl-up, 5 x 10"
    21. Elongation stretch, 2
    22. Groin stretch

Mini-Yoga
    23. Sun salutation, 2
    24. Spinal twist (left & right)
    25. Deep relaxation

Transformational Imaging

Ten-Minute Meditation

the tension in your chest, your abdomen, your back, your pelvic area, your legs. Feel a warming, melting sensation moving down your entire body, your hands becoming warm and heavy, the soles of your feet warming the surface beneath them and that surface warming the soles of your feet.

A–Aware Let yourself become keenly aware of your surroundings: the objects in the enclosed space you are inhabiting, the outdoor world you can see through the window—the condition of the sky, the wind moving the leaves, the infusion of light. Sense the air that caresses every inch of your body. Let there be eyes all over you, in your back as well as front—the small of your back, the back of your neck, the back of your knees. Tune in to every sound and every smell and also to every sensation that has no commonly accepted name. Let all that you can sense become a part of you. What would it be like if a stone owned some measure of consciousness? Affirm your kinship with the material world. Consider the possibility of other, coexistent worlds now invisible to your senses.

C–Center Touch your abdomen about an inch below your navel. Here, in the center of your belly, is the body's center of mass. By focusing your attention on this point, whether in stillness or in motion, you can achieve the calmness that empowers and the power that contributes to good in the world. Breathe deeply, letting your abdomen expand. Ask yourself this question: "Am I willing to get in touch with and use my own best and truest power?"

E–Energize Hold your arms open in front of you with your hands wide open. Imagine energy—high voltage electricity, for example—shooting from your outspread fingertips. With knees slightly bent, shift your body around, sensing this energy inhabiting every part of you. Check to see if this energy is equal and even—right and left, back and front, top and bottom. Move around the room in this energized, balanced, centered, relaxed state. Then return to your original position.

The Water Series

1. DRILL FOR WATER

Place your feet wider apart—separated by about two to three feet. Imagine a wheel mounted horizontally directly in front of you. Its diameter is the same as the space between your feet, and it has a crank handle on top near the edge. Grasp this imaginary handle with both hands and begin turning the wheel, as if you were drilling for water deep in the earth. Bend your knees and shift your body from side to side as you drill. Keep your trunk upright. Don't bend your upper body. The side to side motion is accomplished entirely by your legs. Keep your feet in full contact with the surface beneath you, as if they were sinking into it. Turn the large wheel counterclockwise four times, then clockwise four times. Breathe deeply during this exercise. Become aware of your heart beginning to beat faster. Proceed directly and smoothly into the next exercise.

2. PUMP WATER

Continue to stand with feet apart. Clasp your hands in front of you and raise them above your head, taking in a very large breath as you do so. Lean back slightly and look up at your hands. Then let grav-

1. Drill for water   *2. Pump water*

ity take your upper body forward and into a deep bend, so that your hands are between your legs, exhaling heartily with this pumping motion. It's important to leave your knees bent and to be gentle with your lower back during the next movement, in which you uncurl your upper body, bringing it to the previous upright, leaned back position. As in all of these exercises, keep your feet firmly connected to the floor surface; don't let your toes or heels rise. After six full pumping motions, go directly into the next exercise, continuing the rhythmic breathing. If you're having trouble with your lower back, skip this exercise.

3. Fountain

Exhaling strongly, reach straight down as if to scoop up a large amount of water, bringing your hands together just in front of your feet. Bend your knees as much as you can without strain as you reach down. Don't overdo it. Bear in mind that this can be a strenuous exercise. Start rising toward an upright position, inhaling deeply. Bring the backs of your hands together as they pass your chest on the way up, then rotate them so that the palms are pressed together as they

3. Fountain

pass your face, then so that the backs are again touching as they reach high above your head. All this occurs in a smooth, continuous motion. Swing your hands out to the sides and down, making an imaginary fountain as you once again reach down to scoop up water, exhaling as you do so. Reach down six times. On the last repetition, stop your arms' downward motion when they are straight out to the sides, and go directly into the next exercise.

4. FINGER SPRAY

With hands extended straight out to the sides, clench and unclench your fist, as if spraying water from the tips of your fingers. Do this rather slowly four times, attending to the articulation of all ten fingers.

5. HALF WINDMILL

Place your right hand on your hip. Bring your left hand out to the side, watching it swing up over your head and down in a wide arc to

4. Finger spray   *5. Half windmill*

the right of your body, bending your upper body to the right as you do so. Inhale as your hand rises and exhale as it descends. Reverse the positions of the hands, this time bending to the left, for a total of four repetitions.

6. ROWING

Place the toe of your left foot about fifteen inches behind the heel of your right foot and turn the left foot out at a forty-five-degree angle as you prepare to rock steadily forward and back with your entire lower body. As you rock forward, your right knee should bend slightly as the left leg straightens. When you rock back, the right leg straightens as the left leg bends. The upper body stays upright or *slightly* forward during the entire exercise. Both feet remain firmly on the ground.

Curl your fingers into a loose fist, with the backs of your hands forward. As you rock forward, swing your arms forward. As you rock back return your arms to your sides.

6. Rowing

Check your balance. If you find yourself unbalanced in any way, forward or back, left or right, make the necessary adjustments. As you continue this rowing motion, focus awareness on your center. Let your center initiate and lead each motion. Have it be the source of a deep, soft power like that of a wave moving onto the beach, then subsiding.

After you have completed ten forward and back motions with the right foot forward, bring the left foot forward to the usual side-by-side stance. With a large incoming breath, reach high above your head with both hands as if to cup a piece of the sky in your hands. Bring your gently clasped hands down to your center while exhaling and shake your clasped hands so vigorously that you vibrate all over. Let this vibration shake any tension out of your body.

Now release your hands and repeat the rowing exercise ten times with your left foot forward, followed by another reach and shake.

Articulation   7. SHOULDER ROTATION

With your arms hanging by your sides, roll your shoulders forward four times, then backward four times. Keep your hands alive and energized while doing so.

7. Shoulder rotation   *8. Head rotation*

8. HEAD ROTATION

Turn your head left then right for a total of four stretches. Then tilt your head first left then right, as if trying to touch ears to shoulders, for four stretches. Continue by bringing chin to chest then back to the upright position for four streches. These exercises should be done carefully and consciously. Sense the articulation of the cervical vertebrae *from the inside*. Make no sudden or extreme movements. Don't try to tilt your head far back.

9. ARM SWING

Standing upright with feet planted firmly in a wide stance, begin a vigorous rotary movement, turning hips, trunk, and head first right, then left. Let your arms hang as limp as pieces of wet spaghetti during this exercise. Centrifugal force will cause them to swing out during rotation and slap against your body when you start to turn the other way. Let your shoulders relax. Be aware of your center. Make sure your feet don't rise from the ground. Do a total of twelve moves.

9. Arm swing

10. PELVIC ROTATION

Maintaining a deeply rooted wide stance, place your hands on your hips, bend your knees, and, in the manner of a belly dancer, rotate your pelvic area in a strong horizontal circle, four times left, then four times right.

11. KNEE ROTATION

Bring your feet together. With the palms of both hands, gently hold your knees together while rotating them in a horizontal circle to the left. Try to keep your feet flat on the floor during this movement, thus articulating the ankle joints. After four rotations to the left, press your knees gently back. Complete the execise with four rotations to the right. Again press the knees back.

The Floor Series

12. HIP JOINT ROTATION

Sit on the floor with your legs extended in front of you, your feet about eighteen inches apart. Support your upper body with your arms if need be. Turn your feet out as far as possible, then in as far as possible for a total of eight moves. Feel the rotation in your hip joints.

10. *Pelvic rotation*   11. *Knee rotation*   12. *Hip joint rotation*

13. Quad Tightening

Continue sitting on the floor with legs extended straight in front of you and feet together. Now take a deep breath and press your knees down as hard as you can for six seconds. Then totally relax, exhaling fully. Repeat six times, pressing your knees down *into* the surface beneath them. In this, as in all other exercises that stress the muscles, put full attention on the relaxation phase as well as on the stress phase.

14. Foot Rotation

Lie on your back and draw your knees up with feet flat on the floor. Lift your left leg and grasp it beneath the knee with both hands. Rotate your left foot four times counterclockwise and four times clockwise, moving your toes as you do so. Continue working with your left leg for the next three exercises.

15. Hamstring Stretch

Still lying on your back with knees up and feet flat on the floor, lift your left leg, straighten it completely, grasp it beneath the knee with both hands and draw it back as far as you can without pain. Some very flexible people will be able to draw it back far enough to grasp the foot or ankle, but the important thing is keeping the leg straight at the knee rather than seeing how far back you can draw it. Hold this stretch for twenty seconds. Go directly into the next exercise. The next period for relaxation comes after the Quad Stretch (#17).

13. Quad tightening   *14. Foot rotation*   *15. Hamstring stretch*

16. Hip Stretch

Begin again lying on your back with knees up and feet flat on the floor. Cross your right ankle over your left leg. Lift the left leg and grasp it beneath the knee, drawing it back so as to put a rotary stretch on your right hip joint. Hold for twelve seconds. Move directly into the next exercise.

17. Quad Stretch

Roll over on your right side. Reach down behind you, grasp your left ankle with your left hand and pull it toward your buttocks. This will stretch your left quadriceps, the muscles on the front of your upper leg. (You can use your right hand to cradle your head.) Hold the stretch for twelve seconds. Relax fully.

Now go back to *Foot Rotation* and repeat exercises 14 through 17 with your right leg. Again relax.

18. Back Stretch

Lying on your back, draw the knees up, slide both arms beneath them and hug them to you, lifting your head so it comes down to or even in between the knees. Hold this stretch for sixteen seconds.

16. Hip stretch   *17. Quad stretch*   *18. Back stretch*

19. SPINAL CURL

Leave your knees up, feet flat on the floor, hands palms down a few inches out from your sides. Start curling your pelvis up, lifting the tailbone off the floor. Inhaling while you do so, lift each vertebra off the floor, one after the other, starting with the lowest, until you are balanced on your feet, head, shoulder blades, and arms. Tighten your buttocks and hold for a count of twelve. Exhaling, lower your vertebrae to the floor, one after the other, in reverse order, then relax.

20. CURL-UP

Lie on your back, knees drawn up, feet flat on the floor. If you haven't done much in the way of abdominal exercises, cross your arms over your lower chest. If your abdomen is already toned to some extent, grasp the back of your right hand with your left hand and place the back of your left hand on your forehead. Now suck in your abdomen and press the small of your back down tight against the floor, bringing your pubic bone as close to your lower ribs as you can. Then inhale and gently curl up your head and shoulders until your shoulder blades come up off the floor, and maybe a little higher. Hold for a count of ten, then slowly lower your shoulders and head to the floor while exhaling. As an alternative, you can pulse upward slightly ten times in rhythm with your count before lowering shoulders and head.

It's most important to keep the small of your back against the floor throughout the exercise. If the back should begin to arch, it means you're tiring and should stop.

19. Spinal curl　　　　　*20. Curl-up*

This exercise is very important since it strengths the muscles that function as back stabilizers. Be sure to start slowly. Repeat for a total of five times. If you can do so without feeling significant muscular effort, it probably means you aren't doing the exercise right. Try raising your upper body a little higher off the floor.

21. ELONGATION STRETCH

Take a few moments to relax. Then stretch both arms out along the floor above your head. Take a deep breath and try to lengthen your body, extending your hands and arms in one direction and your feet and legs in the opposite direction. Open your mouth wide and yawn if you wish. Then relax completely. Inhale and stretch again, and this time, as you exhale, curl up into a sitting position and go straight into the next exercise. (If you're having back problems, don't try to curl straight up. Instead, turn on your side and use your arms and hands to help you rise to a sitting position. Remember to use common sense and take care of your own particular needs on all these exercises.)

22. GROIN STRETCH

From a sitting position, grasp your ankles and draw them back as close to your groin as you comfortably can, pressing the soles of your feet together. Lean forward and press your knees toward the floor with your elbows. Hold the stretch for twelve seconds. Then gently release the stretch and come to a standing position for the next exercise.

21. Elongation stretch   *22. Groin stretch*

23. Sun Salutation   **Mini Yoga**

Yoga is among the most ancient of tranformative practices, with roots perhaps in Stone Age shamanism. The word itself comes from the Sanskrit "yoke," meaning to bring together, to make whole. Yoga is not a religion but a means for making one whole. The physical aspect of yogic practice that involves stretches and postures is called hatha yoga, and is unsurpassed in balancing the muscle groups; if you stretch forward, for example, you'll also stretch backward.

The sun salutation is a sort of yoga anthology, putting together a coherent series of essential yogic postures. It is best performed not by rote but with full consciousness as a salute to the sun, to nature, to the strange and wondrous universe in which we live.

1. Stand tall with feet together and inhale deeply, expanding first the lower abdomen, then the lower chest, then the upper chest. Exhale, then press your palms together in front of your chest, touching the area of the heart with the back of your thumbs.

2. Inhale. Lock your thumbs and extend your hands out in front of you. Watch your hands as you raise them high above your head. With knees slightly bent, lean backward from your hips as far as is comfortable.

3. Exhale and fold slowly forward from your waist until your hands are either touching the floor just outside your feet or hanging in a relaxed manner.

4. Inhale. Bend your knees and place your palms firmly alongside your feet. Leaving your right foot between your hands, extend your left foot far back and place your left knee on the floor. Bring your right knee up to your chest and look up.

5. Exhale and extend your right foot back to meet the left, leaving your hands where they are. Push your buttocks up to make a triangle with the floor. Look at your feet and lower your heels toward the floor.

6. Begin to inhale. Lower your knees, chest, and chin to the floor, leaving your pelvis raised. Keep your palms beneath your shoulders, your elbows in close to your body.

7. Continue to inhale. Lower your pelvis to the floor and let your head and shoulder curl upward like a cobra ready to strike. Look up.

8. Exhale and push yourself up in the triangle again as in posture five.

9. Inhale and swing your left foot forward between your hands. This leaves your right foot stretched back with the right knee on the floor. Your left knee is up against your chest. Look up as in posture four.

10. Exhale. Swing your right foot forward until it is next to the left foot between your hands. Straighten your knees while keeping your arms and hands down, on or near the floor. Don't strain.

11. Inhale. Lock your thumbs and unfold your body slowly and consciously to a standing position. Look up at your hands as you keep bending backward as far as is comfortable.

12. Exhale. Slowly and consciously bring your palms together in front of your chest, the backs of the thumbs touching the heart area.

Put your feet about shoulder-width apart, take a deep breath, and relax for a moment before repeating the sun salutation exercise. Then lie flat on your back in the relaxation position—eyes closed, feet about shoulder-width apart, hands out a few inches from your sides, palms up—and become aware of your heartbeat slowing.

#1　　　#2　　　#3　　　#4

23. Sun salutation

#5

#6

#7   #8

23. Sun salutation (cont.)

#9   #10   #11   #12

24. SPINAL TWIST

Lying on your back, extend your arms straight out to the sides, palms up. Draw your knees up, feet flat on the floor, and take a deep breath. Cross your right leg over the left and let both knees swing to the right, turning your head and upper body toward the left as you exhale. Hold this position for twelve seconds, then reverse the procedure.

25. DEEP RELAXATION

Before beginning, make sure you're comfortably and warmly dressed and that no bright lights are shining in your eyes. For the first few times, it would be best to have someone read the following instructions aloud in a clear, soothing voice, pausing where there are three dots. Or you might record the instructions, then play them back. (For information on ordering a video tape of the ITP Kata, see Appendix A.)

"Lie comfortably on your back in the relaxation position, eyes closed. Become aware of the rhythmic rise and fall of your chest and abdomen as you breathe. Let the floor support you. . . . In the next series of exercises, you'll be tensing then relaxing certain muscles. When tensing a particular muscle, do the best you can to leave the rest of your body completely relaxed. In some of these exercises you'll be lifting your legs or arms a few inches off the floor as you tense them. When you hear the signal to let them drop, release them completely, as if a string has been cut from a puppet. You'll be exhaling on each relaxation. . . .

"Start by focusing your attention on the center of your abdo-

24. Spinal twist

men. . . . Now let your attention travel down to your right leg. Extend it out along the floor. Take a deep breath and lift your leg a few inches off the floor, tightening its muscles from the toes to the hip. Hold it. Hold it. . . . Exhale and let it drop. Roll your leg gently from side to side and relax it comletely. . . . Now send your attention to your left leg. Extend it out along the floor. Take a deep breath and lift it a few inches, tensing all its muscles from the toes to the hip. . . . Tight, tight, tight. . . . Let it drop. Roll it gently from side to side and relax it completely. . . .

"Attention on your right arm and hand. Extend your arm out along the floor, tensing the muscles. Splay out the fingers, take a deep breath, make a fist, and raise your arm a few inches off the floor, tightening it all the way up to the shoulders. . . . Hold it. Tight, tight. . . . Let it drop. Roll it gently from side to side and relax your arm and hand completely. . . . Attention on your left arm and hand. Extend your left arm out along the floor, tensing the muscles. Splay out the fingers, take a deep breath, make a fist, and raise your arm a few inches off the floor, tightening it all the way up to the shoulders. . . . Hold it. Tight, tight. . . . Let it drop. Roll it gently from side to side and relax your arm and hand completely. . . .

"Attention now to your pelvis and buttocks. Take a deep breath and tighten your pelvis and buttocks. . . . Hold it a little longer. . . . Exhale and relax your pelvis and buttocks completely. Roll your lower body gently from side to side and relax completely. . . .

"Now with a big incoming breath, puff up your abdomen like a large balloon. . . . Make it a little larger. . . . Open your mouth and let the air *rush* out. . . .

"With an even larger incoming breath, puff up your chest like an even larger balloon. . . . Larger. . . . Open your mouth and let the air *rush* out. . . .

"Attention to your shoulders. With a deep inhalation, raise and tighten your shoulders. Curl them foward, as if around your chest. Pull them far back, hard against the floor. . . . Release your breath and relax your shoulders completely, working them down toward your feet. . . .

"Roll your head gently from side to side. . . . Bringing your head to the center, relax your neck and throat completely. . . .

"Open your mouth wide. Take in a big breath. Move your jaw around, releasing all the tension. Yawn if you wish. . . . Relax your mouth and jaw completely. . . .

"Puff out your cheeks.... Suck in your cheeks.... Relax your cheeks.

"Tighten your face. Make it tiny. Squeeze all the facial muscles together. Bring everything in close to your nose.... Relax your face. Feel all the muscles in your face relaxing completely....

"Raise your eyebrows and wrinkle your forehead.... Relax your eyebrows and forehead....

"Now we're going to take an interior journey through your body, relaxing any subtle tensions without moving. We'll start the journey by focusing attention on your center. Let that attention move down to your legs, your feet, your toes. Relax your big toes, your second toes, your third, fourth, and fifth toes. . . . Relax the soles of your feet and the tops of your feet. Relax your ankles, your lower legs, and your upper legs.... Let your attention now turn to your arms, hands, and fingers. Relax your thumbs, your index fingers, your third, fourth and fifth fingers. Relax the palms of your hands and the backs of your hands.... Relax your wrists, your lower arms, and your upper arms. Relax your shoulders. Let the tension melt away.... Attention now to your buttocks and pelvis. Relax completely. Let all the tension melt away.... And now your abdomen. Relax all the muscles and all the organs of your abdomen.... Relax your diaphram. Relax your chest, your heart, your lungs.... Once again, relax your shoulders. Relax them completely, from the inside.... Relax your lower back, your middle back, your upper back. Relax your throat, your jaw, your tongue. Relax your cheeks, your temples, your ears, your eyes, your eyelids. Relax your forehead, your scalp, the back of your neck.... Relax all your body. Become a pure witness. Experience your body in complete relaxation.... Now become aware of your breath as it flows in and flows out with no effort on your part. Don't try to control it. Just witness it.... Become aware of any thoughts that might be floating through your mind. Just observe them.... Now take this opportunity to become aware of the peace and joy of existence itelf, the invisible connections that join us with all beings, with all of the universe, with the miracle of the life we are given."

At this point, you're ready for the final two stages of the ITP Kata, Transformational Imaging and Induction, and Witness Meditation. A separate chapter will be devoted to each of these.

SEVEN

The ITP Kata:
Transformational Imaging

In this section of the Kata, we use mental imagery to foster positive changes of body, mind, heart, and soul. This practice gives you a chance to strengthen your affirmations, but you need not limit yourself. Here you can work to improve *any* aspect of your physical and psychological functioning. Before describing this set of exercises, though, we will say a few words about the transformative power of mental images.

All of us have experienced the influence of imagery upon our body, emotions, and impulses. If, for example, we constantly see ourself losing a game, we are more likely to lose that game than we would be if we had a positive attitude toward it. If we habitually dwell upon people's shortcomings, we are less likely to respect them than we would be if we focused on their virtues and strengths. If we carry a persistent image that we have some undiscovered disease, we will probably dampen our mood and might even depress our immune system.

This is not a new insight. It has long been thought that powerful pictures in the mind produce lasting changes of psyche and soma. Doctors of Greek and Roman antiquity, for example, believed that images and feelings actually moved in the blood, directly affecting emotions and physical functioning. According to a famous Hippocratic maxim, imagination and bodily processes "tread in a ring," constantly influencing one another. This belief was generally held in Europe until the late seventeenth century. One Renaissance doctor, for example, wrote that imagination "marks and deformes, nay, sometimes kills Embryos in the womb, hastens Births, or causes Abortions." In *Approved Directions for Health* (1612), William Vaughan declared that the physician "must invent and devise some spiritual pageant to fortify and help the imaginative faculty, which is corrupted and depraved; yea, he must endeavor to deceive and imprint another conceit, whether it be wise or foolish, in the patient's braine, thereby to put out all former phantasies." These words reflect the general opinion of the day that mental process is profoundly connected with bodily process.

Eastern cultures hold a similar view. India's Ayurvedic medicine advocates spiritual practices—as well as herbal and other physical agencies—to improve one's psychological and physical functioning. Chinese healing practice, which was deeply influenced by the integral worldview of Taoist yoga, enlists the mind in its approach to health. In both China and India, for more than two thousand years, philosophers and healers have viewed human nature as a single hierarchical structure in which mind and body are profoundly joined.

From the late 1600s until recent decades, however, this holistic understanding was largely displaced in the West. The French philosopher René Descartes argued that mind and body operate on parallel tracks, in different domains of existence, so that mind "has no need of place, and is not dependent on any material thing." This view came to dominate Western science and supported the mechanistic medicine of the eighteenth and nineteenth centuries (which was influenced by the discovery that much of our somatic functioning can be understood in terms of hydraulics and engineering principles). The study of human nature was compartmentalized, the body being assigned to anatomists and physiologists, the mind to philosophers and psychologists. The unified psychophysiology of ancient Greece, the Renaissance, and Eastern cultures was replaced by a science that separated psychological from somatic sickness. This attitude led many physicians and lay people to devalue the mind's role in healing and contributed to psychologists' neglect of imagery's transformative power.

But things change. In the twentieth century, and especially since the 1960s, researchers have discovered new links between mind and the flesh and are returning to a holistic view of human nature. Imagery has become a legitimate object of study by experimental psychologists and is used with increasing frequency by psychotherapists, sport psychologists, and others to foster healing, performance, and growth. The view that mind and body form an integral entity is respectable among scientists again. Indeed, many connections between the two are understood better than ever.

Laboratory tests have shown, for example, that the immune system can be strengthened (or weakened) by images, attitudes, and emotions. Many agencies of such influence have been identified, among them molecules called opioid peptides secreted by the brain and other organs that attach to specific receptor sites throughout the body. Numerous studies have shown that these molecules cause alterations of mood, pain, and pleasure and that they influence the immune system. The immune system in turn affects the nervous system through glandular secretions. Many *two-way* paths among the nervous, endocrine, and immune systems have been discovered, and it has been shown that all of these can be directly affected by our thoughts and feelings. The cumulative results of such research confirm the ancient belief that mind and body constantly interact, influencing each other for better or worse. Greek, Indian, Chinese, and Renaissance doctors were right when they said that thoughts are intimately involved with feelings and the flesh.

As the study of imagery's power develops, researchers are increasingly impressed with its specificity. It has been shown, for example, that elaborate marks, which appear spontaneously on the bodies of certain people, dramatize signficant emotional issues. These marks, sometimes called "hysterical stigmata," are caused in large part by vivid mental process. For instance, a woman described in the British medical journal *Lancet* by physician Robert Moody exhibited a bruise that resembled an elaborately carved death's head on a walking stick her father had used to beat her. This bruise, according to Moody, arose spontaneously, without external manipulation, during a psychotherapy session. The huge number of cells and the complexity of physiological processes involved in such marks have

caused researchers to marvel at the body's capacity for specific alter-
ation and its responsiveness to highly charged imagery.

The effects of placebos also dramatize the exactitude with
which mind can affect the body. Studies at hospitals, medical schools,
and drug companies show that dummy treatments such as sugar
pills relieve many kinds of affliction, produce toxic side effects
(when they are expected to), and catalyze dramatic changes of mood
and behavior. The alterations produced by placebos, which in
them-selves have no specific effects, have convinced medical people
that human beings can alter their functioning without external devices. Even though they are inert substances or nothing more than
sugar pills, placebos have been used to relieve angina pectoris, allergies, seasickness, anxiety, postoperative pain, warts, asthma, arthri-
tis, depression, sleep disorders, obesity, and many other afflictions.
Dummy treatments have caused intoxication, euphoria, blurred vision, dizziness, increased libido, lumbar pain, heart palpitations,
and serenity among people who expected such reactions. Expectations of particular results, in conjunction with accompanying
rehearsals of them (which may be unconscious), produce the expected outcomes.

Consider the implications of these placebo effects. If, for example, they produce relief from allergies—which can be highly resistant to standard therapies—what does this tell us about the powers
of mind in the body? Allergies involve interactions among trillions
of cells and virtually all of the body's organs; getting rid of them requires precise alterations of the nervous, hormonal, and immune
systems. That men and women do in fact get rid of them simply because they believe in a sugar pill has caused medical people to marvel at our abilities for self-transformation. Placebo effects have
forced researchers to see that the mind can touch *just the right tissues*
and shift the functioning of *just the right cells* involved in the change,
rebalancing the body all the while as it breaks its familiar patterns.
Indeed, to relieve an allergy through mental imagery can be considered a supreme athletic feat. Such feats suggest that we harbor possibilities for change that we have hardly tapped yet.

Well-established scientific research on placebo effects, hysterical stigmata, and other prodigies of psychosomatic change show that
sustained mental imagery can induce positive (as well as negative) alterations of thought, feeling, and the flesh. In the sections that fol-

low, we give specific instructions for the use of such imagery to foster creative changes of body, mind, heart, and soul.

Imaging in the Kata

Back to the ITP Kata. You've just finished a session of deep relaxation. You're lying on your back, feet shoulder-width apart, hands on the floor a few inches from your sides, palms up. Inhaling deeply, swing your arms out from your sides and around in a wide arc until they are above your head on the floor. Exhaling, bring your hands from above your head down the front of your body, palms toward your feet, as if you are pushing a wave of energy from above your head all the way past your feet. Your hands don't touch your body; with practice, however, you'll probably learn to feel what might be called an energy wave, not just on the front of your body but all the way through it. As you create each wave, you might say, "My entire being is balanced, vital, and healthy," silently or aloud. You can use any affirmation you wish with this exercise, or none at all. The basic idea here is overall health, vitality, and balance.

After creating several waves, you can move on to any part of your body you wish, using imaging (as will be described in the examples below) as an aid to provide preventive maintenance, repair defective functioning, or produce positive bodily changes ranging from what is considered normal to what would be considered extraordinary. Feel free to include any positive bodily changes you desire.

We recommend that, as is the case with affirmations, you employ positive statements expressed in the present tense for whatever words you use in helping create your images. This is by no means to deny the reality of any undesirable or unwanted prevailing condition. Yes, the undesirable condition does exist in the material realm. Your job is to bring the condition that you intend to realize into sharp, positive, present-tense focus in your consciousness.

What if you are a person who doesn't easily create images? Do the exercises anyway. Keep practicing. Don't expect immediate results; you're in this practice for the long term. And don't be discouraged if your image lacks clarity and sharp focus. Even a glimmering of yourself as you wish to be can bring effective results. Still, you may be surprised to find that your imaging ability improves with practice. Also bear in mind that images don't have to be visual. Some people tend to create kinesthetic images, feeling images, which can be powerful and effective. You might well be able to *feel* the way it would be if you had, say, a relaxed, supple, erect posture. Some people have auditory imagery. Others have images of smell and taste.

But a word of caution: In the healing funtion, Integral Transformative Practice is not meant to supplant mainstream medical science. An integral practice is not exclusive; it reaches out to the best of all that is available. Our medical science has developed many effective techniques, especially in diagnosis, the treatment of trauma and infection, and the development of life support technology. Members of our ITP groups were urged to use good judgment and common sense in dealing with undesirable bodily conditions, to use ITP if need be as a *complement* to mainstream, Eastern, or alternative methods. In many cases, ITP seemed greatly to enhance the effects of mainstream medical treatments already underway. Bear in mind that any decision to transform body, mind, spirit, or heart is your responsibility.

Here are a few sample exercises for this section of the Kata. Unless otherwise noted, all are done while lying down. Note that in this practice every imaging exercise invokes the body, whether or not you are imaging a purely physical transformation. Our experience has shown that by somehow grounding every image in the marvelous physical entity we call a body, we significantly increase the effectiveness of the exercise. We also recommend that you take a moment after each imaging exercise to lie still in an attitude of acceptance, thankfulness, and alignment with God or the universe.

To help improve vision. Rub your hands together briskly until the palms are warm. Cup your palms over your closed eyes to exclude all light and let your eyes relax completely. Take a few moments to gently massage your closed eyes with the pads of your fingers. Then cup your hands a few inches *above* your closed eyes and begin a stroking or massaging motion, as if the heat or other energy from your hands is somehow moving or otherwise affecting not only the suface but also the interior of the eyes. If at first you don't feel any effect in the eyes themselves—a sort of warmth, pressure, "magnetism," or presence—simply continue the exercise. Chances are you'll feel it after a few days' practice.

At the same time, begin to create a vivid mental image of your eyes as totally healthy and your vision as extremely sharp. Mentally,

The galaxies exist in you, not printed as mere images within your skull, but in your every cell, your every atom.

G. L.

see the visible world as bright, sparkling, and crystal clear. If you're imaging not just normal but metanormal telescopic vision, create an image of a small bird in a distant tree. Note the color of its plumage, the precise shape of its bill, the sharp lines that delineate its eyes. Track the bird as it flits from one branch to another. See if you can pick out individual feathers.

If you wish to use words with mental images and the stroking motion of your hands, here are some samples: "My vision is crystal clear and my eyes are balanced, vital, and healthy." "The lenses of my eyes are clear, perfectly shaped, and completely healthy." "The aqueous fluid in my lenses is pure and clear and circulating healthily." In every case, use words that feel right to you. Go with the ones that touch your heart.

To help prevent or reverse coronary artery disease. Rub your hands vigorously together. Place your left hand on your heart and your right hand on your left hand. Physically massage your heart area with a feeling of love and caring for your heart. Slide your right hand down to your *hara* or physical center, about an inch or so below your navel; leave it there as a strong connection between your center of feeling (the heart) and your center of action and intuition (the *hara*). Lift your left hand a few inches above your body and begin a stroking motion with the intentionality of "touching" your physical heart. With practice, just as in the case of your eyes, you'll probably be able to feel the sensation of your hand's energy in your heart itself.

Aware now of your heart's approximate shape and size, begin to image it as balanced, vital, healthy, and fully alive with radiant energy. "My entire heart is balanced, vital, and healthy." "My heart is pulsing in perfect rhythm." Then image or "feel" your heart's arteries. (If you wish, use a picture from an anatomy book as a model for your image.) Begin to create an image of your arteries as open, supple, and healthy. Repeat those words if you so desire while continuing the stroking motion of your left hand: "My heart's arteries are open, supple, and healthy." Use any words that feel right for you or no words at all, just a sharp, clear visual or feeling image of your coronary arteries as strongly pumping life-giving blood to all areas of your heart.

Slide your right hand up over your heart area and your left hand down to your belly. Repeat the above induction, this time reversing the two hands' roles. Be sure to "feel" all of the heart, including the top, bottom, and back, and all the arteries.

To help open your heart to others, to be a more loving person. Bring your left hand to your heart center and place your right hand over the left. Ask yourself, "What would it be like if I were a more loving person?" Begin to create an image of yourself as open-hearted and loving, a person who experiences deep compassion for others. Imagine meeting a person with whom you have been less than compassionate and loving. Bring an image of this person to your mind. Create a vivid mental and emotional experience of opening your heart to her or him. Tune-in to the present-tense feelings in your body as you do so. How does your body feel when you approach someone in this open-hearted manner? What are the particular qualities of the feeling? Explore different images. Try taking a deep breath and physically opening your arms wide, expanding your rib cage, making your heart available to others. Stay with it. Pick a vision that brings a thrill to your body, a feeling of the many possibilities that open up when you open your heart to someone previously unloved. Expand this feeling to encompass all of humanity.

To help reshape your body. Start by focusing strongly on the part of your physical body you want to change. Stroke your hands over it, increasing the awareness in that part. Bear in mind that energy follows attention. Sense the additional energy now localized in the body part given extra attention. Let's say you want to reduce your waistline. Here you might follow the example of the ITP practitioner who reduced his waist measurements by two inches in three months by imagining a "girdle of fire" around his middle (see chapter 4). In his case, the image became an obsession, vivid in his consciousness not just while doing the Kata but during many of his waking hours. Successful transformation is almost always closely related to the practitioner's ability to produce and hold a vivid, positive, present-tense image—then, at times, to surrender to grace. It's also important that you choose an imaging and induction procedure that's right for you, one that expresses your own personal being.

To help improve physical performance. Say your best time for a 10K race is forty-two minutes, and you've made an affirmation to run that distance in thirty-eight minutes. Place your hand over your *hara* and your left hand over your right hand. Now bring to mind the race itself. Make everything vivid and present: the wind on your face as you're warming up, the tingling, fully alive feeling that goes along with removing your warm-up garb and standing at the starting line, the exuberant burst of energy at the starter's gun. Pick specific moments in the race: the feeling of power as you surge uphill, the release and joy of flying downhill, and finally the sense of triumph as you reach the finish line in thirty-eight minutes or less.

Or, if you wish, you might focus your awareness on the cellular level, imaging your red blood cells absorbing oxygen more efficiently than usual. Combine this visualization with several deep breaths, giving your red cells a chance to practice in the material realm what you are experiencing in the mental realm.

To increase your creativity. Start with the assumption that creatvity is a natural human state and that, potentially, your ability to create, to put together the stuff of existence in novel ways, is limitless. Place your left hand, palm down, on your *hara*. Place your right hand on your upper chest. Breathe so that your left hand rises and falls with each breath while the right hand remains motionless. Once you've established this deep belly breathing, place your hands on the floor, palms up, a few inches out from your sides. Allow the breath to enter through your nostrils and travel downward as if to fill the abdomen. Exhale consciously through the mouth until your lungs are as empty as is comfortably possible. At this point of emptiness, as in Focused Surrender (Chapter 5), simply close your mouth. The incoming breath arises spontaneously. The precise moment of its coming is unexpected, a delightful little surprise. When the incoming breath has again traveled downward as if to fill the belly, open your mouth and exhale consciously. Repeat the cycle several times.

This simple breathing technique shows the subtle, crucial relationship between what is willed and what is spontaneous, between the conscious and the subconscious. Magda Proskauer, a master of breathing techniques, has called the brief interval between outgoing and incoming breath the "creative pause." During this moment of pure, unwilled being, you can experience the impulse of creation that arises, unbidden, from the depths of each of us.

Continue this mode of breathing. Now, elbows out to the sides, touch your forehead gently with the tips of your fingers while you are consciously exhaling. When the incoming breath spontaneously comes in through your nostrils, let your arms open wide in synchrony with the incoming breath. It is as if you are breathing in the whole universe. During your conscious exhalation, bring your arms together, until your fingertips gently touch your throat. Again open your arms in synchrony with the incoming breath. Repeat this cycle, touching your heart, solar plexis, *hara*, and pubis in turn, thus invoking bodily centers that are sometimes associated with thought, expressiveness, feeling, power, intuitive action, and generation.

Now lie in the relaxation position, hands palm up by your sides, and bring to mind some creative project. See and feel yourself operating with effortless, joyful creativity. Experience the delight of making new connections, of gaining insights that seem to come from the creative void, from "nowhere." Experience the fun of creative work with others. Consider the creative possibilities in every life, not just in art and "creative writing" and the like but in management, in love and sex, in gardening, entertaining, and household chores. Think of the creativity latent in every moment of time.

Finish this exercise, as with every imaging exercise, in an attitude of acceptance, thanksgiving, and alignment with God or the universe.

We offer these samples simply to trigger your creativity. We believe that you can find a uniquely personal imaging procedure for any transformation of your body and psyche you sincerely desire. Our experience has shown us that such procedures are highly effective in most cases.

It's possible that you'll experience quick changes for the better but don't expect immediate results. Learning and change tend to take place in irregular spurts of progress separated by long periods on the plateau, with no apparent gain. But the plateau represents the esssential topography of all human development. Even quick changes must be followed by diligent practice if they are to be permanent. Keep practicing diligently and you can be reasonably sure the gains will eventually come.

The ITP Kata concludes in the next chapter.

EIGHT

The ITP Kata: Meditation

We now move to the Kata's last exercise, a ten-minute period of meditation. By "meditation" we mean the disciplined observation of thoughts, feelings, impulses, and sensations, as well as the spontaneous turning of heart and mind toward a Presence beyond the ordinary self. This practice, which combines self-observation with what is sometimes called "contemplative prayer," helps practitioners contact new depths of being, awareness, and delight.

The American philosopher William James described the transformative power of meditation and prayer. The further limits of human nature, he wrote

> plunge into an altogether other dimension of existence from the sensible and merely "understandable" world. Name it the mystical region, or the supernatural region, whichever you choose. So far as our ideal impulses originate in this region (and most of them do originate in it, for we find them possessing us in a way for which we cannot articulately account), we belong to it in a more intimate sense than that in which we belong to the visible world, for we belong in the most intimate sense wherever our ideals belong. Yet the unseen region in question is not merely ideal, for it produces effects in this world. When we commune with it, work is actually done upon our finite personality, for we are turned into new men, and consequences in the way of conduct follow in the natural world upon our regenerative change.

A New Buoyancy and Sense of Freedom

In the ITP Kata, meditation begins as soon as you have finished imaging and induction. Assume a sitting position with back straight, on a floor cushion with your legs crossed, or in a chair. An erect sitting posture, either on a cushion that elevates your seat from the ground or in a straight-backed chair, will help you remain alert for the exercise to follow. It will also help prevent the muscular soreness that poor posture causes. If during the exercise you find yourself slumping, straighten your spine and rebalance yourself. During meditation, a good physical attitude facilitates a good psychological attitude. An alert but relaxed posture tends to produce an alertly poised state of mind. In this, the body and the inner life mirror one another.

Place your attention a few feet in front of you. Do not stare or strain to concentrate. Instead, maintain a relaxed focus, as if you were gazing at a gentle stream. This style of attention, this soft downward look, is not as fatiguing as staring. It also helps to keep your mind from drifting. You can, however, meditate with eyes closed, but, if you do, you might have a tendency to drift into sleep. Meditation with eyes open will help you stay relaxed but alert.

When your posture is comfortable, let your belly expand. Make sure that your breath is not confined to your chest. Full, relaxed respiration, in which both the lower and upper abdomen are involved, is more conductive to meditation than constricted breathing, which typically causes or is caused by anxiety. Anchor your attention in the rise and fall of your breath. Focus on your lower abdomen and return to it whenever your mind wanders.

As your posture, gaze, and respiration join to form a state of alert relaxation, remain calmly present to your stream of consciousness, to both its familiar and unfamiliar patterns. Do not judge yourself, for in meditation of this kind there is no "good" or "bad." At this stage of practice, you are simply deepening your self-awareness, whatever it brings to light. You are getting more intimate with yourself. You are gently exercising new control of your mind and exploring new depths of your body and soul. Here are some questions meditation beginners typically ask.

What do you do if you can't escape a repetitive thought or particular mood?
If an object of awareness won't pass, simply study it and let it unfold. If it is a relatively familiar set of thoughts or feelings, you can note new subtleties and nuances in it. No two moods or mental pictures are exactly the same, even when they seem to be. Your inner life is

endlessly mutable, and your most familiar patterns of consciousness nearly always contain something new. Wait for that newness to reveal itself. It might show you something important. One of our students, for example, was obsessed by a childhood fall from a tree. In meditation, she found herself focusing—again and again—on the smell and feel, the shock, and the pain of her accident, which had happened some twenty years before. For several weeks in which the memory dominated her meditation, she witnessed more and more details of the tree, of her sweater and jeans, of her emotions as she looked at the leaves around her, of her grip on the slippery branches. Then, suddenly, she experienced it all in a new way, from another vantage point. Now she looked down on her fall, as if she were the sky itself. All at once, her fright was gone. The fall even had the feel of flight. From then on, the memory didn't haunt her meditation. More importantly, she felt a new liberation in the rest of her life. Her consciousness had expanded, it seems, so that it could embrace her memories of the accident—and life in general—with new security.

Disciplined self-observation can yield results analogous to those of our student. If you remain calmly present to a presistent image or mood, you might see an old trauma in a new light, discover new qualities in a familiar situation, or find new solutions to a pressing problem.

Does the relinquishment of thoughts interfere with creative thinking? Don't we risk losing a bright idea if we let it go? No. Experience teaches us that creative insights persist. As writers, we have learned that good ideas come back when formal meditation is done. If an idea is worth remembering, you will remember it.

What do you do about physical discomfort? Straighten your back, rebalance yourself, and relax. If the discomfort persists, sit through it. One of meditation's great lessons is that pain can be released through calm awareness of it. There is a profound analogy here to those problems in life that are dealt with best by embracing them without avoidance.

What do you do with your hands? They can be placed on your knees, as they are in many Indian yogas, or cupped in your lap with your thumbs touching, as they are in most Zen practice. Either way is fine. Experiment, then stick with one method so that you can deepen your concentration without physical distraction.

Why does one need to sit still? Because physical stillness facilitates mental stillness, and the complex set of physiological changes called the "relaxation response" (see p. 114). Eventually, the centered poise produced by sitting meditation can be taken into every activity of everyday life. Meditation in action is a primary goal of integral practice.

Can one repeat a word, a mantra, to help focus attention? Yes. Mental repetition of a phrase has long been used in meditation as a concentration device. You can experiment with a word or short sentence to see if it helps focus your mind. But to repeat: Once you have settled on a concentration method that works, whether it is focusing on your breath, a mantra, or your stream of consciousness, stick with it. Moving from one technique to another can distract you from the deeper rewards of meditation.

Sometimes meditation gives rise to strange experiences. How should they be dealt with? Many an unusual experience is reported by meditators, among them distortions of body image, perceptions of "auras," sensations of rising from the ground, and auditions of sounds with no apparent physical causes. Remain calmly present to such experiences, as if they are ordinary thoughts and feelings. By staying centered, you will let them reveal whatever lessons they can teach. They are a natural by-product of sustained meditation practice and might be first glimpses of metanormal abilities. If they persist, there are two ways to handle them: first, simply let them go until they subside entirely; and second, let them unfold to reveal a latent capacity. Using the second approach, one of our students cultivated the perception of auras that her meditation triggered. Such perceptions were uncomfortable at first, but eventually became a source of information and pleasure.

How do we know if we are becoming enlightened? We do not use the term "enlightenment" in our ITP programs, partly because it is used in different and sometimes confusing ways, and partly because we emphasize practice itself rather than specific outcomes. If by "enlightenment" you simply mean the greater goods of meditation, those will come by degrees, often unexpectedly, especially if you do not compulsively strive for them.

Some books about personal growth talk about a higher, truer, or deeper being beyond one's ordinary sense of self. Does meditation help us discover it? Meditation deepens an awareness that transcends your ordinary functioning. As you continue meditating, you realize that you are more than any idea or mental picture, more than any emotion, more than any impulse, more than any bodily process, more than any pattern of experience with which you typically identify. That something more, you will find, brings an unshakable security, freedom, and delight. You might experience it as a boundless space, or unbroken essence, that connects you with everything. From it, you can realize new mastery of mind and body.

This depth beyond ordinary feeling and thought is given different names by sages and philosophers and is characterized in different ways in the various sacred traditions. But however it is described and no matter how it blossoms, it produces a new buoyancy and unity with the world at large.

The deeper being that meditation brings is its own reward. It is also helpful—and we believe necessary—for the practical success of integral discipline. That is the case because its regenerative freedom helps cushion the readjustments and restructurings of body and mind required for significant change. Its all-encompassing embrace helps sustain a radical renewal of our entire organism. Because it transcends our particular parts, it helps us rise above the many obstacles to growth we encounter.

"A SPECIAL DRAFT UPON THE UNSEEN"

In the course of meditation, many people experience a gratitude for life that impels them to commune with a higher power. In contemplative traditions that do not bear witness to a personal divinity, the devotional urge is expressed in prayerful chanting, either silent or vocal, as in Zen Buddhism and Indian Vedanta. The sense of blessedness that deep meditation bestows turns the heart toward the source of things. Meditation naturally turns to that source, asking for nothing more than loving contact with it.

Frederic Myers, a principal founder of modern psychical research and pioneering personality theorist, believed that in prayer we intensify a process that is always happening in us. He wrote in *Human Personality and Its Survival of Bodily Death:*

I have spoken of it as a fluctuation in the intensity of the draft which each man's life makes upon the Unseen. I have urged that while our life is maintained by continual inflow from the World-Soul, that inflow may vary in abundance or energy in correspondence with variations in the attitude of our minds. . . . The supplication of the Lourdes pilgrims, the adoring contemplation of the Christian Scientists, the inward concentration of the self-suggesters, the trustful anticipation of the hypnotized subject—all these are mere shades of the same mood of mind—of the mountain-moving faith which can in actual fact draw fresh life from the Infinite.

Each of us can draw upon the Unseen for transformations beyond the purview of mainstream science. Some members of our classes, for example, have experienced remissions from afflictions that many doctors think are incurable. But although science cannot explain such remissions (and other kinds of extraordinary experience described in this book), there is a growing body of research that supports anecdotal reports of such changes produced by transformative practices. By 1993, for example, more than 1,400 studies published in reputable journals had shown that meditation can have many desirable outcomes. In their monograph, *The Physical and Psychological Effects of Meditation*, Michael Murphy, Steven Donovan, and Margaret Livingston published a review of such studies, which have shown that meditation can help to:

lower resting heart rate;

reduce both systolic and diastolic blood pressure (including systolic reductions of 25 mm Hg or more);

produce significant changes in cortical activity, among them increased frequency and amplitude of alpha waves (8–12 cycles per second), strong bursts of theta waves (4–8 cycles per second), and the synchronization of alpha waves between brain hemispheres, all of which indicate that meditators experience a state of alert relaxation and perhaps increased brain efficiency;

increase respiratory efficiency while the meditator is sitting and also while engaged in strenuous activity;

reduce muscle tension;

reduce blood lactate concentrations associated with anxiety and high blood pressure;

increase skin resistance, which indicates a lowering of anxiety and stress;

increase salivary translucence, while decreasing salivary proteins and bacteria, all of which helps to prevent tooth cavities;

reduce chronic pain;

heighten visual sensitivity, auditory acuity, and the discrimination of musical tones;

improve reaction time and responsive motor skills;

improve the ability to make visual and kinesthetic discriminations in spite of misleading stimuli from the environment (an ability that is correlated with independence of judgment and a strong sense of body and self);

improve concentration;

increase empathy for other people;

reduce anxiety;

help relieve addictions;

improve memory and general intelligence;

increase equanimity;

promote feelings of pleasure and ecstasy;

increase energy and healthy excitement; and

increase dream recall.

These benefits come without the meditator striving for them. They are among the graces of transformative practice. But along with these, meditation can have negative outcomes for certain people. Some psychologists have reported, for example, that it can intensify obsessiveness, divert attention from genuine problems, and contribute to feelings of depression. That is why we have insisted that members of our ITP classes take care of their emotional needs in appropriate ways, seeking counsel when needed.

That meditation can have negative, as well as positive, results has long been noted in the contemplative literature. The path to enlightenment is "sharp as the razor's edge," reads the Katha Upanishad, one of India's most revered scriptures. Though the rewards of meditation can be great, they do not come without disciplined self-knowledge. That is why we have placed meditation within the context of integral practice, which emphasizes the long-term development of health, self-awareness, and balance.

A GREAT RETURN ON YOUR INVESTMENT

Practiced properly, meditation is a richly efficient means of self-transformation. Like a good business deal or scientific theory, it produces great returns on investment of time and energy. Economically, it enhances many of our inborn capacities. In this respect, it resembles imagery practice and other transformative modalities that draw upon various human endowments to produce several fruitful results at once.

Herbert Benson, a physician who has pioneered research on the relations of mind and body, invented the term "relaxation response" to represent the integrated changes produced by contemplative activity. With other researchers, he has emphasized the fact that meditation produces multiple benefits by activating the parasympathetic nervous system, which mediates the slowing of heart rate and respiration, reduction of muscle tension, and other components of relaxation. Meditation *economically* produces many good results because it triggers a coordinated response of our whole organism. We emphasize this observation because it applies as well to other integrated changes produced by transformative practices. Creative work and athletic discipline, for example, facilitate a condition that resembles certain inherited behaviors of animals in the wild. Like hunting (or hunted) animals, many artists and athletes exhibit a trancelike focus of attention, an indifference to discomfort and pain, and a remarkable forgetting of difficulty. The deep concentration, analgesia, and selective amnesia that characterize creative absorption is analogous to—and may be derived from—the freezing and stalking behaviors, freedom from pain, and blindness to adversity that is evident among hunting animals. Like the relaxation response, creative absorption economically enlists many psychosomatic processes.

And a similar enlistment of inborn tendencies is evident in sport and the martial arts when a contest stimulates heart rate, adrenaline flow, and strong bursts of energy. The fight-or-flight response, like the relaxation response and creative absorption, is part of our common human endowment, and can be enlisted for transformative activity. It, too, operates synergistically and can facilitate the development of mind and flesh.

In *The Future of the Body*, Michael Murphy suggests that all transformative modalities have some of this "all-at-once" character, by which they produce creative change in a coordinated manner. Imagery practice can give rise to metanormal powers and consciousness by the recruitment of many somatic processes. Through such recruitment, countless cells are somehow enlisted by mental images so that *as an integrated whole* they support extraordinary functioning. Similarly, the repetition of affirmations, sustained expectation of success, focused intention, surrender to ego-transcending powers, and other transformative acts can trigger complex changes in us. All programs for healing and growth depend upon such responses, and integral practice is no exception. Drawing upon the wisdom inherent in religious and other transformative disciplines, we have incorporated activities with an "all-at-once" character into the program described in this book.

Lasting Benefits

Our Kata ends with meditation, but in a fundamental sense it is not finished then. Two years of ITP classes have taught us that this set of exercises often produces an afterglow. Typically, its results spill into one's everyday activities. The ongoing effects of repeated affirmations, the pleasure of exercised muscles and ligaments, the multiple benefits of imagery and meditation last longer than the Kata itself. That is the ultimate reward of this forty-minute practice.

The Taoist saying "meditation in action is a hundred, a thousand, a million times greater than meditation in repose" reflects the aim of integral discipline. The exercises described here are meant to join meditation with action in every part of our lives. New freshness of perception, increased empathy for others, alert relaxation, enhanced sensory-motor skills, and other improvements of mind and body have been evident in members of our classes, as they have been in the contemplative traditions and scientific studies of meditation.

NINE

✺

The Exercise Factor

The strong relationship between regular physical exercise and good health has been established beyond all doubt. Reports of scientific studies on what exercise can do for you appear frequently in the popular press. The benefits are many and varied, and we'll list them later in this chapter. In Integral Transformative Practice, however, we prefer to view vigorous physical movement not as a mechanical process that yields so many benefits for so much effort expended, but rather as a fundamental expression of our embodiment, essential to our practice precisely because it is valuable *for its own sake*. In ITP, we repeat this phrase, "for its own sake," like a prayer or incantation.

In this culture, as we have pointed out, we are relentlessly urged to do one thing only for the sake of something else—some goal, some reward, something not here, not now: something in the future. Early in life, we are urged to study hard so that we'll get good grades. We're told to get good grades so that we'll graduate from high school and get into college, so that we'll get a good job. We're told to get a good job so that we can buy a house and a car. We spend our lives stretched on an iron rack of contingencies. Clearly, contingencies are important. Goals are important. But the real juice of life is to be found not nearly so much in the products of our efforts as in the process of living itself, in how it feels to be alive.

We were born, it seems to us, with a God-given right to move vigorously, gracefully, and joyfully. Our being so often robbed of this right constitutes a major tragedy of our civilization, one that can be traced in large part to the denigration of the body common to most civilized societies as well as to the mind-body split that has dominated Western thought for some three hundred years. In this milieu, the body has been considered an object, an instrument, a brute machine of gratification and procreation. At the height of the Victorian period, in fact, members of polite society often seemed to vacate the body entirely, making it a topic to be rarely considered or mentioned. Now we are beginning to reinhabit our bodies, beginning to see this most extraordinary of entities for what it is.

Far from being a mere machine, the human body is the most advanced material realization we've encountered of the divine potential hidden in the early, inchoate universe. Each body is all time remembered. In its dancing quanta of radiation, its elementary particles, its atoms and ions, its simple and complex molecules, its cells and organelles and organs, its bone and marrow and muscle and sinew, we can read the story of cosmic evolution, that chronicle of exquisite joinings and hairbreadth escapes, which has created a consciousness capable of knowing itself.

To live is to move. Even when seemingly motionless in sleep, the body is incessantly moving. We share a silent pulsing of heart, blood vessels, glands, diaphragm, lungs—the busy intercourse among a hundred trillion cells—with many other organisms. When we consciously move through space, we can't help but affirm what is both unique and universal about our species.

Our Commitment to Exercise

We ask that everyone involved in Integral Transformative Practice accomplish a minimum of two hours of aerobic exercise every week in increments of at least twenty minutes each. The word *aerobic* means "using air to live." During aerobic exercise, the rate at which oxygen reaches the muscles keeps pace with the rate at which it is used. Thus, the muscles operate without having to dip into their reserves of sugar and fat, as is the case with *anaerobic* exercise. In aerobic exercise, you are breathing more deeply and rapidly than while at rest but can still carry on a conversation.

This aerobic exercise commitment can be fulfilled simply by taking vigorous twenty-minute walks six times a week. For greater benefits, we recommend even more, say, three hours of aerobic exercise in increments of at least thirty minutes each. In addition, we highly recommend three sessions of strength training a week. Whatever exercise you do, we urge you to exercise with full awareness. Don't read, watch television, or daydream. Our experience shows that by keeping your mind focused on what you are doing, you can greatly increase the intrinsic pleasure of vigorous movement, as well as the benefits you receive.

To Walk, to Run, to be Human

Walking is one of the most commonplace of human activities. It is also a great wonder—stately, graceful, and efficient, an essential mark of being human. The journey of our lineage toward the large brain, culture and consciousness took a decisive and irreversible turn with the evolutionary gamble of the upright stance and unique bipedal walking of our hominid ancestors. We are so accustomed to it that we are unaware of how marvelous walking is. To see this form of movement as if for the first time, use a lens that turns things upside down or (if you're willing to look a little foolish) lean over so that your head is upside down. From this perspective, a group of people walking toward you, especially in bathing suits on a beach, reveals an amazingly supple, undulating movement, an easy, liquid flow of energy unlike that of any other creature.

To take two brisk hour-long or four thirty-minute or six twenty-minute walks every week would fulfill your ITP aerobic exercise commitment, yield proven health benefits, and help build the foundation for possible transformations—and do all this with a minimal risk of injury. Does this mean you should walk merely to gain benefits, to fulfill your commitment? Better, we think, that you walk primarily for the joy of it. Walk to experience the upright stance, the flow of motion through space and time. Walk with full awareness of your legs and arms swinging freely in perfect counterpoise. Walk with a spring in your steps. Walk with shoulders, neck, chest, and abdomen relaxed. Be aware of the back as well as the front of your body. Give special attention to your physical center, a point an inch or so beneath the navel. Imagine your center moving powerfully and effortlessly through space. Take deep breaths. *Be sure to walk vigor- ously.* A casual stroll doesn't qualify as aerobic exercise.

Whenever possible, walk out of doors rather than on an indoor treadmill, satisfying the innate human desire to explore the world, to discover new vistas. Seek out hills to climb. Wear a loaded backpack to develop added leg strength—or to carry supplies for a picnic. Don't be limited to the minimum ITP commitment. Take extended hikes, gradually increasing the distance. Walk instead of using your car whenever possible. It's possible, but difficult, to walk too much.

Running ups the ante, adding possibilities and risks. When we walk, one foot is always earthbound, but when we run, we leave the ground. The earth becomes our drum, and the rhythm of our drum- ming feet presages the quickened pulse of heart and blood. The face flushes, and we feel the rush of air on cheeks and forehead. Breath- ing deepens. We experience the beginnings of a familiar exultation along with a touch of fear, a momentary catch in the breath. It is a feeling of vertiginous anticipation and delicious dread akin to the first awareness of sexual arousal. Running, we can no longer deny our animal nature. At the same time, we are uniquely human, for no other animal runs as we do.

Running in our singular upright stance confronts us with a seeming contradiction: the human runner is relatively slow and the energy cost of running (oxygen consumption per unit of body weight per unit of distance) is about twice as high for humans as for most other mammals. Yet, in a long chase, a well-conditioned runner can catch a horse, deer, wildebeest, zebra, kangaroo, or pronghorn antelope. This is due not only to the intelligence and fierce determi- nation of our species but also to our unsurpassed ability to dissipate heat, along with the ability to load up on carbohydrates and the vir- tuosity of our breathing. To run long distances, especially with a partner or a group, is to summon our primal past: the profusion of healthy sweat, the lusty breaths, the glory of distance traveled, the shouts of triumph as the prey is overtaken. Some people these days call running a fad or even an addiction, a form of narcissism. But to call running a fad makes as much sense as to call thinking a fad. En- durance running is an essential human activity that preceded ab- stract thought and helped make it possible.

Still, there are risks. The chances of falling or of spraining an ankle or twisting a knee increase as we shift from a walk to a run.

Walking downhill, quickly become weightless. Walking uphill, slowly become your strength.

M. M.

Even more prevalent and troublesome are the persistent, often tricky overuse injuries that can bring debilitating pain and dysfunction to cartilage, tendon, ligament, and joint. Overuse is compounded by the long-term repetitive motion that runners often fall into—the same stride, the same joint movement, the same pounding impact. There's a dangerously hypnotic quality that accompanies running long distances at a steady pace and stride. To avoid overuse and repetitive motion injury, we recommend awareness, variety, and playfulness.

Shine an interior spotlight of awareness on parts of your physique that are subject to undue strain. See if you can relieve that strain by making subtle adjustments in the way you're moving. In some cases, just relaxing the arms can release the rigidity of your stride and increase its grace and efficiency. Check for tension everywhere in the body. There are few sights more dismaying than that of runners with high shoulders and rigid necks and jaws, stamping all this tension into body and psyche with every stride. The secret of power, whatever your sport, lies in relaxation. Every muscle except those being used specifically for locomotion at any given moment should be quite relaxed. Whether running primarily for health and fitness, speed, endurance, or transformation, the runner's first discipline involves releasing tightness, especially of the face, neck, shoulders, chest, and diaphram.

It's also important not to get locked into an unvarying, mechanical motion. Change the length and bounce of your stride. Alternate longer-than-usual with shorter-than-usual strides. Or take an especially long stride, a leap, every third step. Or try skipping. (Don't laugh. Skipping may be better than jogging for aerobic conditioning, while leading to fewer injuries.) If you should find yourself running on a smooth, straight, unobstructed path, try running backward, an essential practice for defensive backs in football. Or try running sideways, crossing the feet alternately, scissors style.

Vary your speed. It was once thought that aerobics meant attaining a certain target heart rate and holding it steady for thirty minutes or more. In recent years, however, researchers have found that varying your heart rate doesn't rob you of aerobic benefits. As it turns out, periodic as well as continuous exercise holds great value; it's all right to stop for a while during a run—or a walk—and stretch for relaxation or just enjoy the view.

Don't confine yourself to the same route on every run. Venture into new territory. Take routes you've never tried before, especially those that lead up and down hills. Work out a steeplechase, a sort of runner's obstacle course, with ditches to leap, walls to run on or jump over, trees and bushes to dodge. But start cautiously. After years of running steadily on smooth, predictable surfaces, you'll need time to reawaken your coordination.

Above all, use your imagination. If you're training for a competitive run, you're pretty well committed to an essentially linear activity. But there's also nonlinear running. With a frisbee, a friend, and an open field, for example, you can easily devise a sport that will yield twenty or more delightful minutes of aerobics. Start twenty or thirty paces apart and launch the frisbee in your friend's general direction, then start running at a comfortable pace in such a way as to maintain about the same distance between the two of you. Keep moving as the frisbee sails back and forth, varying your pace as necessary to catch the flying disk. Similar sports can be devised using anything from a tennis ball to a football. The parabolic curve of a ball in flight adds another element to your running. By catching it, you make visible your intuitive knowledge of the laws of physics. Many ball sports that involve running—tennis, volleyball, racquetball, squash, basketball—can also be made aerobic by switching from a competitive to a collaborative mode, the idea being to keep the ball in play as much as possible and to run at a moderate rate most of the time.

No matter how moderate, though, there's still that lingering chance of overuse and repetitive motion injuries for those who run long distances. To minimize the risk, choose good-fitting, high-quality running shoes and replace them often. (Running shoes lose their tread and their resilience much more quickly than do auto tires.) Run on natural surfaces, on the good earth itself, as much as possible, or on composition tracks. If you must run on city streets, look for asphalt surfaces. Keep your body flexible, but bear in mind that it's not necessary to stretch just before running. In fact, it's not a good idea to stretch while the muscles are cold and subject to injury. Better start with a few minutes warm-up along with the articulation of the body's joints—just what you get in the ITP Kata. Stretching *after* a run is better than stretching cold.

After all of this has been said, there's still one big constraint: Those of us with heavy body builds might consider taking up something other than running as our main long-term mode of aerobic exercise. Even easy jogging sends a heavy impact to the joints. Your feet, ankles, and knees take a jolt of several times your body weight with each stride. Almost everyone can enjoy the exhilaration of running, but a light or medium body build is generally prerequisite to choosing running as your main, long-term mode of aerobic conditioning. And bear in mind that brisk walking offers most of the health benefits of running with few of the risks.

Practice mentally for physical activities. Practice physically for mental activities.

G. L.

The Varieties of Aerobic Experience

If we have given what seems a disproportionate amount of space to aerobic running, it's simply because that primal activity presents us with a disproportionate number of both risks and possibilities and thus demands discussion. There are many other ways of fulfilling your weekly aerobic commitment.

Swimming is an ideal conditioning sport, especially for people of medium and heavy build. It works all of your body. It doesn't subject your shins and joints to the pounding of the running sports. In the weightless, sensuous environment of water, in fact, you have your very best chance of getting fit without getting hurt. The down side of this virtual weightlessness is that, in not stressing the bones, swimming doesn't build bone tissue as the the weight-bearing sports do. Then too, there are the problems of finding a conveniently located pool and overcoming the boredom of swimming laps, the latter of which can be remedied by creating aerobic water games. Even better, you might learn to love the cool, wet, solitary world of the swimmer, even when cruising back and forth from one end of a pool to the other.

Gliding across the earth on a bicycle at the pleasant speed of 12 to 15 mph on softly spinning wheels as both passenger and motor, you can get aerobics along with a sense of freedom. Not only can you travel much farther than a runner in a given period, you can do so without the pounding motion that stresses sinews and joints. The worst biking injuries come from falling off or, worst yet, being struck by another, larger vehicle. Wear your helmet! Pain in the neck and shoulders, lower back, wrists, knees, and feet—to name a few sites—generally are caused by improper alignment with the machine. Check with an expert or a knowledgeable friend to adjust seat and handlebar height and angle.

Then you have rowing, cross-country skiing, skating, skate-blading, and the fruit of whatever fitness technology comes next. Given sufficient imagination and will, aerobic activities are there for the finding. You can jump rope, bounce on a trampoline, shadow box. You can take aerobic classes. You can dance aerobically and thus participate in one of the most primal of activities: There are cultures with no permanent dwelling places, no tool or weapon other than the stick and stone, no clothing other than the loin cloth, no plastic art, but there are no human cultures without music and dance. You can create martial arts routines that are aerobic in nature. And if it's in your nature, you can make an even more primal activity, sexual intercourse, the basis of an aerobic workout. Any happily vigorous activity that uses several muscle groups, especially those long muscles that attach to the pelvic girdle, will grant you the gift of sweat and lusty breathing.

If all else fails, you have the aerobic machines that allow you to keep moving while not getting anywhere. Actually, there's a certain value in treadmills, stationary bicycles, and step machines, in that they allow you precise control of your workouts with a minimal risk of injury. In Integral Transformative Practice, however, we ask that even when using stationary indoor machines you exercise with full awareness rather than reading or watching television. Our experience has clearly shown that energy follows attention, that staying aware of your breath, the articulation of your joints, and the contraction and relaxation of sinew and muscle can significantly improve the quality of your exercise. Most of all, we ask that you do your aerobic exercise primarily for the joy of it. The benefits will come. Here's a list of some of them:

Healthily enlarged and strengthened heart muscle

Increased cardiac output

Lower resting heart rate

Increased blood and hemoglobin levels

Increased venous return

Increased maximum oxygen uptake

Improved circulation

Decreased blood pressure

Greater bone mass

Decreased degeneration of joints and ligaments

Increased muscular strength

Improved reaction time

Increased ability to utilize fats and carbohydrates

Decreased body fat

Increased "good cholesterol" (HDL); less "bad cholesterol" (LDL)

Improved mobilization of lactic acid

Improved hormonal balance

Increased bloodclot-dissolving enzymes

Strengthened immune system

Reduction in coronary heart disease

Improved resistance to cancer

Improved mental functioning and psychological health

In our own experimental work, as noted earlier, the 12.60 percent average reduction in body fat among our 1993 ITP class correlated strongly with the time students spent doing aerobic exercise. Still, with all this, there are negative possibilities. Exercise can produce or contribute to overcompetitiveness, excessive fatigue from overtraining, preoccupation with diet, obsession with body image, neglect of job or family, general self-centeredness, and physical injuries. As in any form of self-cultivation, physical training calls for intelligence, balance, and good judgment in order to produce good results.

MUSCLES VS. AGING

Our strong recommendation that you add three sessions of strength training to your weekly exercise schedule gains urgency from recent research showing the close relationship between muscle mass and strength on the one hand and quality of life on the other, especially as it concerns aging. The practice of ITP, as we've stated earlier, should be available to as many people as possible, regardless of physical or financial status. We also believe that there should be no upper-age limit; aging is a process that involves every one of us. And, as it turns out, muscle strength and mass are crucially important factors as we travel toward the culmination of the life we are given. In their 1991 book, *Biomarkers*, William J. Evans, Ph.D., and Irwin H. Rosenberg, M.D., list ten "biomarkers" of aging and show how all ten can be favorably altered, thus alleviating most of the debility that accompanies old age. They are:

1. Your Muscle Mass

2. Your Strength

3. Your Basal Metabolic Rate (BMR)

4. Your Body Fat Percentage

5. Your Aerobic Capacity

6. Your Body's Blood-Sugar Tolerance

7. Your Cholesterol/HDL Ratio

8. Your Blood Pressure

9. Your Bone Density

10. Your Body's Ability to Regulate Its Internal Temperature

Of these ten, according to Evans and Rosenberg, muscle mass and strength are primary. They write that a high ratio of muscle to fat in the body,

> causes the metabolism to rise, meaning you can more easily burn body fat and alter your body composition even further in favor of beneficial muscle tissue;

> increase your aerobic capacity—and the health of your whole cardiovascular system—because you have more working muscles consuming oxygen;

triggers muscle to use more insulin, thus greatly reducing the chances you'll ever develop diabetes;

helps maintain higher levels of the beneficial HDL cholesterol in your blood.

But can this simple prescription—bigger and stronger muscles—really alter the aging picture, as Evans and Rosenberg claim? We're all familiar with the studies on aging, the books, the articles, all showing the seemingly inevitable, irreversible decline in abilities that comes with the passing years. Aerobic ability, for example, seems to fall off at a rate of some 8 to 10 percent for every ten years after age twenty. On average, we lose almost seven pounds of muscle every decade. From age twenty to around age seventy, we lose nearly 30 percent of our muscle cells. Our basal metabolic rate—the ability to transform food into energy and build tissue—declines by an estimated 2 percent a decade starting at age twenty. And so it goes, a dismal picture of degeneration and decay.

We're not going to say that the studies are wrong per se. But they are terribly misleading. What they measure in most cases is a cross section of our population *as it is now*—that is to say, a population that becomes increasingly sedentary as it ages. Even the longitudinal studies, those that follow the same group of people over a number of years, fail by and large to consider the exercise regimen of the people they follow.

"Most of the decline in physical functioning is caused not by aging but by lack of exercise," says William Evans, who serves as head of the Noll Laboratory for Human Performance Research at Pennsylvania State University. "Once we leave school, most of us spend less time exercising, for obvious reasons—family, job, lack of opportunity. Or we think we *shouldn't* exercise *because* we're getting older. So what we have is a self-fulfilling prophecy; we get weak and frail and assume it's because we're getting old. This just isn't true. We compared young men who underwent endurance training with men between forty-five and sixty years old who had the same training and found that aerobic capacity and percentage of body fat is related to the time spent exercising—not to age. In this study, age did not predict anything."

How about muscular strength and size? It's an old truism in

physical conditioning that strength falls off rapidly with the years and that even if the muscles of the elderly can be made a bit stronger, they can't be made larger.

Wrong again. Walter Frontera, M.D., Ph.D., then at the Human Nutrition Research Center on Aging at Tufts University at Boston, took twelve men between the ages of sixty and seventy-two and put them through a course of rather intense weight lifting, three days a week for twelve weeks, concentrating on the quadriceps and hamstrings (the front and back thigh muscles). The result surprised even the most optimistic exercise enthusiasts. The strength of the men's quadriceps more than doubled and that of the hamstrings tripled, with an average *daily* gain of 3.3 percent and 6.5 percent respectively. The real shocker was that the men's muscles had grown an average of 12 percent.

What about even older people? Also at Tufts, Maria A. Fiatarone, M.D., put ten men and women between eighty-seven and ninety-six years of age, living in a chronic-care hospital, through a similar training regimen. After only *eight* weeks, their leg muscle strength almost tripled and their thigh muscles bulked up by more than 10 percent. The researchers concluded that, contrary to all conventional wisdom on the subject, *muscle growth in people ranging from sixty to ninety-six years old was as great as could be expected in young people doing the same amount of exercise.*

Integral Transformative Practice is not an antiaging program. It is a practice for achieving the transformative potential of all people, whatever their age, gender, or background. Still, we feel this evidence of adaptability and resilience in the very old can serve as an inspiration to us all, an invitation to live fully and physically, whatever our age. The evidence shows that it's neither necessary nor wise to let your muscles wither away with the passing of the years.

BUILDING AND MAINTAINING MUSCLES

Muscle strength and size is maintained or increased by working the muscles against strong resistance. This is most often accomplished by using Nautilus-type machines, lifting free weights, or working against the weight of your own body. Joining a gym or health club is ideal. Machines are generally safer as well as more muscle-specific and conducive to good form than are free weights, especially for beginners. Guidance from experienced trainers, always important, should be available at the beginning of your participation and at regular intervals thereafter. *Again, exercise with full awareness.* This is especially important in strength training. In Arnold Schwarzenegger's words, "A pump when I picture the muscle I want is worth ten with my mind drifting."

With free weights, it's even more important that you have some hands-on guidance at the start. Neither books nor video tapes, no matter how well done, can give you the kind of feedback about form that will get you the best results and help you avoid injury. Books and tapes, though, do become quite useful *after* some personal guidance. With your own free weights, you can work out at home, avoiding the cost and inconvenience of going to a gym.

What if you have neither free weights or access to a gym? You still don't have to let your muscles languish. Note that the ITP Kata itself offers a certain amount of strength training (see chapter 6). The Fountain requires the half squat, one of the best ways of working the muscles of the legs and buttocks. For strength training, try doing not just the six that are required for the Kata but ten or twenty—however many you're capable of. Then rest for one to two minutes and repeat. Same thing with the Curl-Ups, which strengthen the all-important abdominal muscles. The Sun Salutation exercises several muscle groups, notably the lower back muscles. The Quad Tightening offers isometric exercise for the quadriceps. By adding just three more of these self-loaded exercises, you can maintain or increase the strength and size of the most essential muscle groups:

Push-ups. With your hands and toes on the floor and arms and legs straight, lower your chest to the floor, bending the elbows, keeping the body straight. Then push up from the floor and back to the starting position. If this is too hard, leave your knees on the floor when pushing up. If even this is too hard, start with wall push-ups, leaning toward a wall with arms extended, then bending and extending the arms. If the standard push-up is too easy, elevate the legs by placing your feet on a sturdy stool or chair. Move slowly and smoothly up and down, and keep going until you can no longer rise from the floor. Rest for one to two minutes, then repeat the exercise.

The athlete that dwells in each of us is more than an abstract ideal. It is a living presence that can change the way we feel and live.

G. L.

Dips. Place two sturdy chairs (that won't move when you do this exercise) far enough apart so that you can sit on the edge of one and place your feet on the edge of the other. Put your hands, palms down with arms straight, on the chair you're sitting in. Slide your buttocks off the edge of the chair and lower your body as far as you comfortably can by bending your arms. Return to the straight-arm position. Do as many dips as you can slowly and smoothly. Rest for one to two minutes, then repeat the exercise.

Chin-ups. This rather strenuous exercise should be approached respectfully. If possible, start with a firmly secured horizontal bar that you can barely grasp while standing flat-footed. With hands about shoulder-width apart and palms forward, grasp the bar firmly. Using a jumping motion to get you started, pull yourself upward until the level of your chin is slightly higher than that of the bar. Hang there for about five seconds, then slowly lower yourself. Check to see if you can pull up without resorting to a jumping motion. If so, do as many chin-ups as you can, rest for a minute or two, then repeat. If you can't chin-up without jumping, continue using the jump-and-hang method, lowering yourself slowly each time. Do as many of these as you can, rest, and repeat.

As in all exercises, make sure that you have warmed up with fairly vigorous movements before beginning. A reminder: it's not necessary to stretch just before exercising, but it is important to stay flexible at all times by stretching at least five times a week. The ITP Kata provides such stretches and warms you up before the stretches begin. Never stretch strenuously without warming up first. If you wish to make stretching a part of your exercise routine, it's best to stretch *after* exercising. Strenuous stretching with a cold body can cause injuries. Again—start slowly. Pay attention to the needs of your body. Use common sense.

THE ULTIMATE PHYSICAL TRAINER

Most of all, don't forget to appreciate the miracle of the human body in motion. No matter what its present state of conditioning, this body is the culmination of an incredible evolutionary journey, the repository of the experience of aeons, the harbinger of inconceivable adventures yet to come. We have suggested that you be sensible, take prudent precautions. We also know that life itself is risk, always has been, and always will be. Therefore, we respect your right to cross boundaries, to surpass limits, to take with a clear heart and mind the inevitable risks of transformation. The precautions are there to further the adventure, the strenuous training to further the joy. The ultimate physical trainer is not the man or woman with the clipboard, but the delight that resides in your own body, waiting patiently for you to summon it forth.

TEN

Food for Transformation

So much has been written on what we should or shouldn't eat that we hesitate to add even one more line on this subject. Note the almost prurient gleam in the eyes of those around the table when someone reveals that he or she has embarked on a new diet. Consider how many dinner parties have been entirely devoted not just to eating but to talking about eating. And why not? Food is as basic as anything in our lives. We imagine our hunting and gathering forebears sitting around the campfire late into the night discussing the day's harvest of plants in its every particular and spinning ravenous fantasies about the results of the next successful hunt. Food is life. Before words, there is hunger, the crying need for nutrition, a word that comes from "nurse," close kin to "nourish," which takes us back to the Latin *nutrix*, "to nurse," the Sanskrit *snauti*, "she drips, gives milk," and the Greek *naein*, "to flow."

But food is more than sustenance. It is the centerpiece of our holiest ceremonies, the primary instrument of bonding among family, friends, and tribe. It is a marker of status and class, an emblem of national and ethnic heritage, the stuff of sensual pleasure and primal disgust, a medium that delights our aesthetic sense and tempts us with addiction, a nourishing friend, an unrelenting saboteur. For most of human history and for a significant proportion of the world's population today, the problem has been too little food. In the advanced nations today, the problem is too much.

And not just too much food, but the wrong kind. Our current high-fat, high-cholesterol, salty, sugary diet represents, in fact, a radical and unsuccessful experiment in human adaptation. We evolved our bodies in the hunting and gathering life. Researcher S. Boyd Eaton's analysis of 153 species of wild plant foods eaten by hunting and gathering African Bushmen shows the average protein and fiber content to be much higher than in our plant foods. Hunter-gatherer sodium consumption is estimated at 690 milligrams daily, as compared to between 2,000 and 7,000 for present-day Americans. The fat content of the Bushmen's diet was 21 percent (with a high ratio of polyunsaturates), compared to our 40 or so percent. The question: can an organism evolved to eat a low-fat diet safely adapt to a diet of 40 percent of more of fat? The answer: no. The evidence comes from many sources, none more graphic than the fate of people in places such as Singapore who shifted from a low- to a high-fat diet in a very short period of time, only to see an explosive increase in the incidence of obesity, cancer, and heart disease. A steady high-fat diet, we feel, insults the body our species has evolved, not only threatening our health but dulling our minds and dragging down our spirits.

Still, we prescribe no specific diet, nor do we push for weight loss. In fact, we explicitly oppose the whole idea of "dieting." We do, however, recommend that everyone eat a healthy, balanced, low-fat diet. The ITP commitment on the subject of food is quite simple: *"We are conscious of everything we eat. We bear in mind the many benefits of a diet low in fat and high in fiber."* To be conscious means to pay attention, to be mindful, as you choose or prepare food and as you eat, and that you stay mindful of the aftereffects of the food eaten.

In both the 1992 and 1993 ITP classes, we offered participants information on the benefits of a low-fat diet, and in the 1993 class we measured the change in percentage of the participants' bodies composed of fat. This was done by means of caliper skin-fold tests on March 27, 1993, and again on November 13, 1993. After the first caliper test, eight class members and three of the teachers joined a health club for strength training. All of these people showed significant reductions in percent body fat, but so did many others who engaged in no strength training at all. What correlated best with reduced body fat, as it turned out, was the time spent doing aerobic exercise. During the seven-and-a-half-month period between March 27 and November 13, twenty-seven of the thirty ITP participants showed reductions in body fat. The class as a whole lost 122 pounds of fat and gained 66 pounds of lean body mass for an average fat loss of 12.6 percent and an average muscle gain of 2 percent, a notable achievement considering the fact that most class members were already in rather good shape. By and large, this bodily change was accomplished without the agonizing effort, the sense of deprivation, that goes along with dieting.

We have a genius for overlooking openings to extraordinary life.

M. M.

We chose loss in percentage of body fat as an affirmation in 1993 because it would give us a purely objective measurement of the program's effectiveness and also because a body with a low ratio of fat to muscle is such a crucial factor in overall health and vitality—as demonstrated clearly in the recent research by Dr. William Evans and others (see chapter 9). Though overall weight loss was not particularly encouraged, some participants lost significant amounts of weight, almost, it seems, despite themselves. Simply by being conscious of what they were eating, many participants found their nutritional preferences gradually shifting away from foods high in fat. It's important here to stress that, far from pushing participants to change their diets, we simply provided information on the benefits of a diet low in fat while gently reminding them now and then to be aware of what they were eating. The caliper skin-fold tests during the 1993 training served as an additional motivation. Photocopies of low-fat recipes and other dietary information were passed out at intervals throughout the training period, but only one full class session in each of the two years was devoted to nutrition. These classes, presented by Annie Styron Leonard, were especially well received. They included personal, practical advice on how to shift to a healthy, low-fat way of eating—and to enjoy it. Here are excerpts from her 1993 presentation:

Since last year, when I spoke to some of you about reducing the fat in your diet, I've noticed more and more fat-free foods in the supermarkets and special low-fat dishes on restaurant menus. There must be a lot of people out there asking for fat-free food, because big companies like Kraft and Conagra are making fat-free cheese,

An Informal Talk on Nutrition

mayonnaise, salad dressings, sour cream, and cottage cheese. Even bakeries are making delicious fat-free muffins these days. I would like to credit Drs. Dean Ornish and Shirley Brown for much of the information I've gathered for my presentation. Dr. Ornish in his books *Reversing Heart Disease* (1990) and *Eat More, Weigh Less* (1993) as well as many other writers and researchers give convincing arguments in favor of a low-fat diet. There have been many studies that show that by reducing fat you can significantly reduce the risk of developing degenerative diseases such as high blood pressure, clogged coronary arteries, stroke, osteoporosis, diabetes, gallstones, and probably even cancer of the colon, breast, and prostate.

Lowering your intake of calories and fat also reduces the production of free radicals, molecules that damage your cells, speed up aging, and contribute to the diseases I just mentioned as well as others such as cataracts. They also impair the function of your immune system. Your body produces these free radicals as a by-product of normal metabolism and also in response to sunlight, X rays, air pollution, and your diet. A low-fat, healthy diet is low in oxidants that cause your body to produce free radicals and high in oxygen-absorbing foods such as broccoli that help your body remove free radicals.

Our ancestors had to battle with a heavy assault of microbes, which tended to overcome them before old age, but the ones who survived lived virtually free of the diseases we have today. Atherosclerotic heart disease and stroke, obesity, diabetes, hypertension, lung cancer, colon cancer, and several other "diseases of civilization"—even dental cavities—were rare. Were our ancestors primarily vegetarians? Many anthropologists think so. As Ornish reminds us, our teeth are designed primarily for plant-based foods, and our intestinal tract is long to allow for the slow digestion of high-fiber plant foods, rather than the short digestive tract needed to process meat and dispose of the resulting toxic wastes quickly. Why does high-fiber food help to reduce the incidence of colon cancer? One reason is that it shortens the time it takes to digest animal products so that the toxic wastes remain in your colon for less time.

How about breast cancer? In Japan and other countries where the consumption of animal fat is much lower than here it's quite rare—but not because Japanese genes are different. When Japanese women move to the United States and start consuming a high-fat diet, they develop breast cancer at about the same rate as Americans—an astounding 400 percent higher than in Japan.

It's important to remember that we're interested in reduction of body fat, not weight loss. So if I want to succeed in this I would first of all eat foods that have only 10 percent of the calories from fat, such as fruits, vegetables, nonfat dairy products, rice, beans, and whole grains. This means no complicated diets, no weight-loss regimens that, according to a recent panel of experts convened by the National Institutes of Health Nutrition Coordinating Committee, "do more harm than good." They found that when people diet, "there is a strong tendency to regain weight, with as much as two-thirds of the weight loss regained within one year of completing the program and almost all by five years."

And above all, stay away from fasting or quick weight-loss protein diet meals. When you fast or deprive the body of food, it interprets this as stress and immediately goes into action to deposit fat while decreasing the utilization of stored fat. You might lose weight, but you are mostly burning muscle tissue, not fat. This process is well explained by Covert Bailey in his paperback book *Fit or Fat.*

Whenever I used to diet, which since high school was many times, I counted calories. I did it so much I knew by heart how many calories there were in everything I ate. But I didn't know that all calories aren't the same. A fat calorie is not the same as a calorie from protein or carbohydrate in the way it's metabolized by the body. Fat has more than twice as many calories per gram as either protein or carbohydrate. It takes very little energy to store fat in the body. When you eat 100 calories of fat, your body only expends 2.5 calories to store all of it as body fat, whereas your body must spend 23 calories—almost ten times as much—to convert 100 calories of dietary protein or carbohydrate into body fat.

Instead of counting calories, you can simply eat fruits, vegetables, beans, legumes, and grains as often and as much as you want until you're no longer hungry—but not stuffed. Also, you can eat nonfat dairy products and many nonfat or very-low-fat commercially available products. The foods you want to avoid completely are fatty fish and fatty meat. Other foods to either avoid or eat in small amounts are lean meats without the skin, lean fish (yes, there is a big difference between salmon and snapper), oils, avocados, olives, nuts and seeds, sugar and simple sugar derivatives, and any commercially available product with more than 2 grams of fat per serving.

Some of you may be thinking, Don't we need fat in order to stay healthy? Yes, we do. It's not that fat is "bad," it's just that we eat too much of it. As it is now, the average person consumes at least 112 grams a day of fat (mostly saturated). Yet, the average person needs to consume less than 14 grams of fat a day to meet the daily requirements of essential fatty acids. What I'd like to do is offer you some ideas for lowering the amount of fat you consume and leave it up to you to decide what's appropriate for your body. Obviously, someone who has coronary artery disease or a history of it in the family needs to be more concerned about fat and cholesterol in his or her diet than someone who doesn't.

Here's how Ornish sums it up:

> Each gram of fat you eat has more than twice as many calories as each gram of carbohydrate.
>
> Each of those fat calories is harder to burn off than the same amount of calories from carbohydrates.
>
> Dietary fat is easily converted into body fat, whereas very little of the complex carbohydrates in your diet are converted into body fat.
>
> Saturated fat increases your blood cholesterol level.
>
> While some oils are higher in saturated fat than others, all oils contain some saturated fat, and all oils are 100 percent fat. Even olive oil contains 14 percent saturated fat.

When George and I started eating a low-fat diet, I became anxious and depressed. Even though I had cooked with olive oil in sparing amounts and we didn't eat red meat, only chicken or fish, and considered ourselves healthy eaters, the change from low-fat to 10-percent-fat tasty meals seemed impossible to achieve. Added to that, we thought we wouldn't be able to eat out any more— something both of us enjoyed very much. So, I equated fun with fat. But gradually, through talking to other people, reading cookbooks, and experimenting, things started to improve. And perhaps most important, we both began to lose our taste for fat and to enjoy fresh, simple foods that weren't hyped up with excessive seasonings, cream, oil, and cheese.

Many restaurants (not the heat 'em and eat 'em places) are glad to grill fish with no oil and give you steamed vegetables and a baked potato. After all, it's not the potato that makes you fat, it's the sour cream, bacon bits, and butter that do. We can even go to Chinese restaurants and order steamed vegetarian pot stickers and deluxe steamed vegetables with rice and enjoy ourselves tremendously. I learned to dip my fork in the salad dressing I'd ordered on the side at a restaurant and then spear the greens to get the taste of dressing.

On the cooking side, it was the little tricks and tips I picked up from other people, such as how to substitute wine and water or vegetable stock for oil, that made all the difference for me. Also, egg whites, which are all protein with no cholesterol or fat, can actually be a good fat substitute. I learned how to use concentrated apple juice instead of sugar, and that Grape-Nuts and oatmeal held together with bananas make a tasty pie crust. From Zen chef Mark Hall, I got a hollandaise sauce made of orange juice, curry powder, and nonfat yogurt that's great on asparagus. You can make a delicious hummus seasoned with salsa and lemon juices and serve it with nonfat saltines or chips. One of my favorite company desserts is angel food cake with fresh strawberries and nonfat frozen yogurt. One of our most frequent meals is pasta with two salsas and lots of fresh garlic, topped with a dusting of asiago cheese. Fast, healthy, and delicious.

For fiber and protein, I usually have a batch of soup in the refrigerator waiting to be heated for lunch or for a simple supper of soup, bread, and salad. There's a very good fifteen-bean cajun soup available now in the supermarket. *The Greens Cookbook* has a wonderful black bean chili which I make without the oil and serve over soft polenta, topped with a dollop of nonfat sour cream or yoghurt.

One question people often ask is: "How do you get enough protein on a vegetarian diet?" First, too much protein, like too little protein, can be harmful. Animals on high-protein diets die sooner than those given the same number of calories but with less protein. Too much protein can also lead to bone demineralization and osteoporosis. And in animal studies, even a low-fat diet that is high in protein can promote the formation of coronary artery blockage.

Protein is formed from building blocks called amino acids—twenty-two of them. Your body can make thirteen. The other nine are called "essential amino acids," since they have to be supplied in the diet. The amino acids that come from plant foods are exactly the same as those that come from animal foods. When you eat protein, whether from a lamb chop or from lentils and rice, that protein is converted into the necessary amino acid building blocks. You don't have to be a nutrition expert to combine foods for a low-fat, complete protein. *Just remember to eat any grains and any legumes anytime during the same day.* It's that simple. Some examples of complete protein dishes are: rice and beans, bean burritos, tofu with rice, pasta and chickpeas, black-eyed peas and rice, or lentils and whole-grain bread.

Other ways to make a complete protein are to combine any grains or legumes with nonfat dairy: oatmeal with milk or yogurt, whole wheat pancakes made with egg whites and nonfat milk, or black bean vegetarian chili topped with nonfat sour cream. I used to consider myself a pretty good cook—I could produce dishes from cookbooks very well. But now I experiment and even come up with something original once in a while. I always read recipes with the thought, "Would this be good even without the fat?"

In cooking low-fat food there's one indispensible kitchen item: the Teflon frying pan. I have a large one with a cover and a medium-sized one, both of which I treat lovingly and with which I'd never use anything but a plastic or wooden utensil for stirring. I keep them covered so they don't get scratched. And one tip for sautéing things. I put a few drops of extra-virgin olive oil in the pan because it's tastier, more olivey, and then wipe it out with a paper towel before adding my ingredients.

Which brings me to: **Read the Label.** Manufacturers are required to list ingredients in descending order of quantity contained in each package. This will give you some idea of the amount of fat as well as other things such as whole wheat flour, sugar, and bran in a product. As you may know, new labels began appearing on foods in 1993. This marked an important step in standardizing definitions such as "low-fat," "light" or "lite," "healthy," "low cholesterol," etcetera, to reduce confusion in shopping. Unfortunately, these guidelines are based on a diet consisting of 30 percent of calories from fat, which may give many the erroneous idea that a 30 percent fat diet is acceptable. Dean Ornish's successful program in reversing heart disease recommends a diet consisting of 10 percent calories from fat, but the AMA and most doctors claim no one will follow such a diet. This untested assumption plus pressure from the meat and dairy industries explains the 30 percent figure. Of course, as long as doctors keep saying people won't eat less than 30 percent fat, they probably won't. Twenty percent would be much better.

There are two more things you shouldn't forget. First, in order to reduce my body fat, I have to raise the thermostat, the metabolic setting of my body, to burn the fat more quickly and reduce the stores in those fat vaults I have in my body. This is best accomplished by a regular aerobic exercise program that ideally includes muscle building. Muscle needs more calories to function than does fat. More muscles mean a more active metabolism.

Second, I will use my creativity to image ways of reducing fat in my body. Create your own "girdle of fire." Act *as if* your fat is melting away.

Friends often ask me, "Do you eat just 10 percent fat?" I truthfully answer, "Usually." And then sheepishly I confess to my fondness for and indulgence in oatmeal chocolate chip cookies. So now and then I splurge on the biggest, best one there is. But usually I treat myself to fruit and yogurt or maybe some nonfat ice cream.

In addition to just feeling healthy, I like the awareness and heightened consciousness that paying attention to what I eat brings me. George and I eat dinner with candles and music. We have a connecting ritual before we begin. I cherish the pure magnificence of fruits and vegetables when they're in season—the color, the flavor, the texture—knowing that when I eat, I'm being nurtured and helped to grow. I've found that good very-low-fat food, prepared simply, is truly something to enjoy and be grateful for.

The Fruits of Conscious Eating

In this manner, we sang the praises of low-fat, conscious eating, offering it as a happy possibility, but making no dietary demands. Still, almost all the participants were affected to some degree. Asked at the end of the 1993 cycle to rate the healthfulness of their diet on a scale of 0 to 10, especially in terms of avoiding a high-fat content, they came up with a respectable average of 7.10. While the many benefits of a diet low in fat were presented merely as something to bear in mind, being conscious of everything eaten was a definite commitment, and the participants' adherence to this commitment was reflected in the extremely high average response of 8.83 to the following question: "Over the last seven days, how conscious have you been of what you have eaten on a scale of zero to 10,

*Metanormal capacities typi-
cally emerge from normal
abilities that have been developed through life-encompassing
practice.*

                    M. M.

with 0 being totally unconscious and 10 being totally conscious?"

Both the healthfulness of the participants' diet, and their consciousness of what they ate turned out to have a strong statistical relationship to their success in achieving Affirmation Four, "My entire body is balanced, vital, and healthy." Of the two, however, only the response involving consciousness was also related in a statistically significant way with their success in achieving Affirmations One (normal), Three, (metanormal), and Four ("balanced, vital, and healthy") *combined*. Surprisingly, neither of the questions regarding food correlated to a statistically significant degree to Affirmation Two (the participants' success in reducing their percentage of body fat). Only two factors (as noted earlier) could be significantly related to that affirmation: the average number of minutes of aerobic exercise a week and regularity of class attendance (see Appendix B).

Statistics can be useful, but are not the last word; we know of several people in the program whose success in reducing percentage of body fat must have had some relation with low-fat eating. The fact that most of our participants were quite fit to start out with was another factor in this equation. Low-fat eating would probably have a significant impact on reducing the percentage of body fat of any group whose members were overweight. Even then, however, aerobic exercise would doubtless play a major role.

WEIGHT LOSS AS A SIDE EFFECT

Though overall weight loss was not particularly encouraged, some class members lost significant amounts of weight, almost it seemed, despite themselves. The most striking case was that of Karen Wilson, whose experience during a mass shooting at her law firm was described in chapter 2. Karen turned to conscious, low-fat eating when she first signed on for Cycle 93, two months before the class began in February 1993. At that time, she weighed 138 at a height of 5 foot 5. When the class ended on November 28 she weighed 108.

"Interestingly enough," Karen explained, "my goal was not to lose weight. It was to lose body fat and to get healthy. That was the one thought in my mind all the time. I was really conscious of what I ate. I've had moments of unconsciously eating things, but I'm just more aware of every thing I eat. It's not to say I don't sometimes make conscious choices to eat things that are not good for me—like I ate a lot of fudge at Christmas time. But it was a conscious choice, and I used to do kind of mindless eating, nervous eating, snacking on something when I wasn't particularly hungry. My whole relationship to food is something I think is permanently changed due to this class."

At first, Karen found giving up fat hard but soon began enjoying her new way of eating. "A perfect example is, this morning I went to breakfast with a friend and she had eggs Benedict, and looking at that hollandaise sauce on her plate was almost too much for me. It looked terrible. I know how hollandaise sauce tastes. It's just too rich. I can't eat things like that anymore. I have no desire to eat things like that. You change in what appeals to you—what sounds good, what looks good."

Karen followed the program faithfully, doing the Kata five times a week, rarely missing her aerobic exercise. Losing thirty pounds, she insisted, was "really effortless."

A Fundamental Expression of our Embodiment

Five months after the end of ITP Cycle 93, in May 1994, the Harvard School of Public Health, with two other health organizations, released a new dietary guide—not so much a low-fat diet as a low-*animal*-fat diet, with emphasis on grains, beans, olive oil, cheese, and fish. All saturated fats are cast as villains, especially, red meat, the largest source of saturated fat in our diet. Red meat is linked here not only with increased risk of heart disease but also colon cancer, and perhaps other cancers as well.

Drawn from the food habits of Crete, Greece, and southern Italy, where chronic disease rates are low and life expectancies are high, this "Mediterranean diet" has obvious appeal and goes to show that, as long as people have choices as to what they can eat, there may never be a final word on this subject. Still, we feel you can't go wrong by reducing your intake of fat and increasing vegetables, legumes, and fruits. We are less concerned with the precise content of your diet than with quality of your food consciousness.

Finally, how we eat, just as is the case with how we exercise, stands as a fundamental expression of our embodiment and is thus important to our practice, not merely for the benefits it might bring but *for its own sake*. To eat with full awareness turns us toward a diet that is both good and good for us. It rejoins us with the matrix of our existence and can inspire us with thanksgiving for the everyday wonder of food, the everlasting miracle of the life we are given.

ELEVEN

The Body as Teacher

There is a profound wisdom in the body, in the pulsing of the blood, the rhythm of the breath, the turning of the joints. Once we are aware of its subtle power, the body becomes a sensitive antenna for tuning into nature and other people. It can serve as a metaphor for every human thought, emotion, and action. It is the royal road to the unconscious. It is a small, handy model of the universe. All the books, computers, and electronic networks in the world contain only a miniscule fraction of the information it takes to create one human body.

It is also a master teacher. In our ITP practice, we offer exercises that call upon this teacher not only to show us how to live a more balanced, vital, and healthy life but also to point the way toward the next stage of human evolution. As previously pointed out, we see body, mind, heart, and soul as coequal manifestations of the human essence. But where deep down human change is concerned, there is no more effective teacher than the body. In a culture that has traditionally downgraded the flesh and routinely characterized it as a threat to the workings of the mind, such a statement might seem strange. But far from opposing the mind, the body reflects and is reflected by it with amazing fidelity.

Our posture, for example, stands as one of the most comprehensive statements we can make about ourselves. To stand more erectly is to change our relationship with the world. When energy is out of balance in the body there is probably some corresponding imbalance in the psyche. Witness the spiritual seekers who are so much "in their heads," so unfeeling in the remainder of their bodies, that they have lost connection with the real world. Such seekers, giggling approvingly at their guru's every pronouncement (no matter how foolish) and totally out of touch with his machinations (no matter how self-serving), make the guru's inflation and subsequent downfall possible. By increasing bodily awareness, by tuning in to the fascinating information the body is continually broadcasting to mind, heart, and soul, we can increase awareness of the world through every domain of our existence and create a harmonious relationship between our many parts. We can also follow the body's guidance in developing new ways of dealing with everyday problems and, beyond that, in developing extraordinary capacities.

The following exercises are drawn from Leonard Energy Training (LET), a discipline inspired by the sophisticated martial art of aikido, along with Western psychology and physical theory. In this chapter, we present a selection of LET exercises. They are not designed to be done on a daily or weekly basis but rather to be experienced once, then repeated whenever desired. In them, you will practice new ways of being in the world and perhaps discover remarkable capabilities you didn't know you had.

Balancing and Centering

This essential exercise, an amplification of the GRACE checklist that begins the ITP Kata (see chapter 6), aims not at achieving perfect balance but rather discovering just how you are off balance in every particular. With practice, you can bring your bodily balance into a more harmonious state that will be reflected in every aspect of your life.

Balanced means simply that the weight and energy of the body is distributed evenly, right and left, forward and back, all the way from the head to the toes. *Centered* means that body awareness is focused primarily in the center of the abdomen rather than, say, the head or shoulders, and also that movement is initiated from that center.

For most of us top-heavy, forward-pushing Westerners, something as simple as focusing our attention on the abdomen can bring extraordinary results. During a moment of crisis, for example, just touching yourself lightly at a point on the abdomen an inch or two below the navel can alter your attitude and your ability to deal with whatever situation you face.

Try this: Stand normally and draw your attention to the top of your body by tapping yourself a couple of times on the forehead. Then have a partner push you from behind at the shoulder blades just hard enough to make you lose your balance and take a step forward. Next, stand exactly the same way and draw your attention to your center by tapping yourself a couple of times about an inch or two below the navel. Then have your partner push you with exactly the same force as before. Most people find they are more stable with their attention on their centers.

And not just physically. To go into a tense, adversarial situation with body awareness concentrated in head, shoulders, and upper chest is almost certain to produce a different outcome than would be the case if you went into the same situation with attention on the abdomen. The former is more likely to lead to a heated, ineffectual exchange of words and an escalation of the conflict, while the latter tends to bring calm confidence and the power to effect a satisfactory resolution. Again, this might seem strange to those who are not accustomed to dealing with bodily awareness, but the difference in outcome is striking. Try it for yourself.

Eastern martial arts have long stressed the practice of being balanced and centered and the influence of the physical on the psychological. Note the correspondence between a person's physical stance and his or her performance in various nonphysical activities. In our experience, a person who habitually stands and walks with head and shoulders thrust forward is also likely to get ahead of himself or herself in thinking and talking, even in something as cerebral as authoring a technical paper. Such a person tends to come to conclusions without adequate background and backup material. The match between the physical and the cerebral is often uncanny. Correcting your stance through long-term practice, as we have said, can have a powerful effect on every aspect of your life.

You'll need someone to read the following instructions while one or more people go through the balancing and centering procedure. Read slowly and clearly, pausing for a while wherever there are ellipses:

"Please stand with your feet slightly farther apart than your shoulders, eyes open, knees not locked and not bent, trunk upright, arms relaxed by your sides. . . . Now take the fingers of your right hand and touch them to a spot an inch or two below your navel. Press firmly, toward the center of your abdomen. . . . Now drop your right hand to your side. . . . Let yourself breathe normally. Let the breath move downward through your body as if it were going directly to your center. Let your abdomen expand with the incoming breath, from the center outward to the front, to the rear, to the sides of the pelvis, to the floor of the pelvis. . . .

"As your breathing continues in a relaxed manner, lift your arms in front of you, with the wrists limp. Shake your hands so hard that your whole body vibrates. . . . Now lower your arms to your sides. As soon as they touch your legs, let them start rising very slowly, directly in front of you, as if you were standing up to your neck in warm, salty water and your arms were floating to the surface. As the arms rise, lower your body by bending the knees slightly. Let the hands hang loosely, palms down, just as they would if floating in warm water. Keep the trunk upright. When your arms reach the horizontal, put the palms forward into the position you would use if gently pushing a beach ball on the surface of the water. Shoulders relaxed. Sweep the arms from left to right and right to left as if you could sense or 'see' things around you through your open palms. . . .

"Now shake out your hands and repeat the process. . . . Lower your arms to your sides and let them float up again. As the arms rise, the body slightly lowers. Knees bent very slightly, trunk upright. Now put the palms forward and sweep your arms from side to side as if sensing the world through your palms. . . .

"All right. Drop your hands, and this time leave them hanging by your sides naturally, in a totally relaxed manner. . . . Please close your eyes. Knees not locked and not bent. Check to see if your weight is balanced evenly between your right and left foot. Shift your weight very slightly from side to side, fine-tuning your balance. . . . Now check to see if your weight is balanced evenly between the heels and balls of your feet. . . . Knees not locked and not bent. . . . Please leave your eyes closed and shift to a more comfortable position any time you wish. . . . Now move your head forward and backward to find the point at which it can be balanced upright on your spine with the least muscular effort. Be sensitive, as if you were fine-tuning a distant station on your radio. . . .

"Take a moment to relax your jaw . . . your tongue . . . your eyelids . . . the muscles around your eyes . . . your forehead, temples, scalp . . . the back of your neck. . . .

"Now, with a sharp intake of breath, raise and tighten your shoulders. . . . As you exhale, let your shoulders drop and relax completely. They are not slumping forward but melting straight downward, like soft, warm butter. With each outgoing breath, let them melt a little farther. . . . Let that same melting sensation move down your shoulder blades . . . your arms . . . your rib cage . . . down to your diaphragm. . . . Let all your internal organs rest, relax, soften. . . . And now the lower pelvic region: let that relax, too. Release all tension. With each outgoing breath, let go a bit more. . . . Let the melting, relaxing sensation move down your legs to your feet. . . . Feel your feet warming the floor and the floor warming your feet. Sense the secure embrace of gravity that holds you to the earth and holds the earth to you. . . .

"Now consider the back half of your body. What if you could sense what is behind you? What would that be like? What if you had sensors, or 'eyes,' in the small of your back? . . . At the back of your neck? . . . At the back of your knees? . . . With your eyes closed, can you get the general *feeling* of what is behind you? . . .

"Now send a beam of awareness throughout your entire body, seeking out any area that might be tense or rigid or numb. Illuminate that area, focus on it. Sometimes awareness alone takes care of these problems. . . .

"Once more, concentrate on your breathing. . . . Be aware of the rhythm. . . . Now, in rhythm with one of the incoming breaths, let your eyes open. Don't look at any one thing in particular, just let the world come in. We call this the soft-eyed configuration, seeing the periphery just as well as what is directly in front of you. . . . With eyes soft, walk around slowly, maintaining the relaxed and balanced state you've achieved. . . . Let your physical center be your center of awareness. . . . See if things look and feel different to you after this exercise."

As you go through the rest of the day, you might re-create the centering and balancing process at various times. After practice, it takes only a few seconds. Bear in mind that the body can be considered a metaphor for everything else. Your relationships, your work, your fitness activities, your entire life can be centered and balanced.

There are endless ways to turn an impulse into an exercise.

M. M.

If you should be knocked off center in one way or another, there is always the possibility—if you can stay aware—of returning to the balanced and centered condition at an even deeper level.

THE POWER OF RELAXATION: A CHANGE OF CONTEXT

This exercise, derived from the art of aikido, demonstrates the extraordinary human power made possible through a change of context. The word *context* comes from two Latin roots: *con*, with or together, and *textere*, to weave (as in *textile*). In this light, a context is not a passive container for your experience but rather an active process. When you change the way you weave your experience together, some sort of transformation may well occur.

Start by standing and extending one arm to a horizontal position. Either arm will do, but let's say it's the left arm this time. The hand should be open with the fingers spread and the thumb pointing straight up. Have a partner stand at the left of your arm and bend it at the elbow by pressing *up* at your wrist and *down* at your elbow. Don't resist. Note that this exercise involves bending the arm at the elbow, not the shoulder.

The power of relaxation

Now that your partner has practiced bending your arm without any resistance on your part, you'll try two radically different ways of making your arm strong and resilient. After each of these, your partner will attempt to bend your arm at the elbow, adding force gradually. Your partner should not add so much force that a struggle ensues. Bear in mind that this is not a contest but a *comparison* of two different ways of being powerful. The point is to see how much effort is required to keep the arm straight under pressure.

The first way. Hold your arm rigidly straight. Use your muscles to keep your arm from being bent. Have your partner gradually apply force in an attempt to bend your arm. Your arm might bend or it might not. In either case, note how much effort you exerted in the process. Perhaps even more important, note how you feel about this experience.

The change of context. Take a balanced and centered stance and let your arm rise to the same horizontal position as before. This time, sense the aliveness of your arm and the energy flowing from your shoulder to your fingertips. Now visualize or feel your arm as part of a powerful laser beam that starts an infinite distance behind you, then extends through your arm and out past your fingertips, through any walls or other objects in front of you, across the horizon and to the ends of the universe. This beam is larger than your arm, and your arm is a part of it. Your arm is not rigid or tense. In fact, it is quite relaxed. But remember that being relaxed is not being limp. Your arm is full of life and energy. Assume that if anyone tried to bend your arm, the beam would become even more powerful and penetrating, and your arm, without effort, would become more powerful.

Now have your partner gradually apply exactly the same amount of force as before—or perhaps even more—in an attempt to bend your arm. Note how much effort you expended in this case. How do you feel about this experience? The overwhelming majority of people who have tried this exercise find the second way, the "energy arm," significantly more powerful and resilient than the first way, the "resistance arm." Electromyographic measurements of the electrical activity in the muscles indicate that this subjective judgment is correct. The energy arm might give a little, but is far less likely to collapse than the resistance arm.

The implications for physical performance are obvious: relaxation is essential to the full expression of power. And if we take the body as a metaphor for other aspects of our lives, the implications are even more significant. Just think what kind of world it would be if we all realized we could be powerful in everything we do without being rigid and resistant. Take the force on your arm as any problem in your life, then note that in resisting it you were fighting *against* the pressure to bend your arm, and thus were giving power to the problem. In changing context, you focused on your own power by concentrating on your center, while extending your attention *beyond* the problem in sending a beam to the ends of the universe. Try using this change of context in dealing with every problem, physical or nonphysical, that you encounter.

Taking the Hit as a Gift

Rarely have we received guidance on dealing with life's sudden hits, those misfortunes that come without warning. This exercise will allow you to experience an effective way of dealing with them. More than that, it will show you how to *gain* energy from negative happenings, how to turn a hit into a gift, perhaps even a life-transforming experience.

Unexpected blows come in many varieties, from the merely bothersome to the profound. Say you own an antique gold watch handed down from a grandparent, a watch you intend to bequeath to one of your grandchildren. One day, on a boat, you take the watch out to show to a friend; it slips from your hand and drops into deep water. Or say you and your spouse are driving to a wedding along a lonely road, running a little late. Suddenly there is a loud sound and your car lurches to a halt; a tire has blown out. Or say you've worked long and hard to complete a report for your supervisor. You give it to her on Friday afternoon. On Monday morning, she walks into your office holding the report. You smile inwardly, anticipating praise. She throws it on your desk: "This is chaos. It makes no sense at all." Or say your spouse comes home one day wearing a strange, pained expression. "I haven't had the nerve to tell you before, but I have to tell you now that I've been having an affair with your best friend."

Our most common responses to such unfortunate happenings tend to make things worse:

Immediate counterattack. Fighting back reflexively. "Whad'ya mean 'chaos'? This is a damned good report!" Or you might get out of the disabled car and kick the offending tire. Such responses generally only strengthen and solidify the problem.

Whining, playing the victim's role. "Oh no! Not *again!* Why do things like this always happen to me?" The victim's role is not only unattractive, it's self-defeating, inviting misfortune without redemption, forfeiting all chances of an eventual positive outcome.

Denial. "This doesn't bother me. I can handle it. I don't feel a thing." While it's tempting to steel yourself against the vicissitudes of life, to turn off or control your feelings, this path is a particularly dangerous one. If you practice turning off your feelings long enough, you might get too good at it. You might become so insensitive that you honestly don't have the faintest idea that, for instance, you're hurting your young daughter's feelings by laughing at one of her sincere questions; you have to be aware of your own feelings to be aware of others' feelings. What's more, as numerous studies

Taking the hit as a gift

suggest, blocked emotions can be unhealthy for the heart and the rest of the body.

There are better ways. We propose a response to sudden hits that involves fully experiencing and acknowledging strong feelings and using the energy of those feelings to handle the situation at hand—with plenty of power left over for further good works. In the following exercise, you'll have your partner create a representation of a sudden hit by sneaking up behind you, grabbing your wrist, and shouting. You need only enough impact to make you jump, to lose your center. So let your partner know how jumpy you are; maybe you'll need only a very mild startle to do the job.

Start by standing with feet about as far apart as the width of your shoulders, eyes open and soft. Balance and center. When you're ready, let your arms swing out from the sides of your body to a forty-five-degree angle. This is your partner's signal to walk up stealthily behind you and grab either your right or left wrist with both of his or her hands while simultaneously giving a shout. The grab should be sudden and firm, but *should not pull you off balance in any direction.* Your partner should continue to hold your wrist firmly while you process the experience.

Be totally aware of how the sudden hit affected you. Speaking aloud in a clear voice, describe exactly what is going on within you. Specify exactly where in your body each feeling or sensation is located. Don't look at your partner as you speak. Resist the temptation to point the finger of your free hand at different parts of your body. Use words only and be as specific as possible. For example: "When you grabbed me, I jumped and blinked both eyes. My heart seemed to jump up into my throat. Now my throat feels a little dry. I can feel the pressure of your hands on my right wrist. My left shoulder is a little high. My abdomen feels tight. My breathing is shallower than usual."

Keep speaking until you have nothing more to say. At this point, you might note that most of the conditions you've described have melted away. Many people discover that merely becoming aware of an imbalance tends to correct it.

The second part of the exercise requires a change of context. Consider the fact that this sudden shock, by startling you and knocking you off center, has *added energy* to your body and your psyche. In acknowledging and specifying your feelings, you've avoided fighting back reflexively, whining about your fate, or denying your feelings. Your adrenal glands have shot a hormonal cocktail into your bloodstream. As a result of being startled, your entire nervous system has come to the alert. You've been shaken out of whatever lethargy might have previously held you in check. Now you can choose what positive uses you wish to make of the extra energy that is yours to use.

Take a series of deep breaths. Move up and down rhythmically by bending and unbending your knees. Become aware of the extra energy you now possess. Even the tight grip on your wrist is giving you energy. Begin moving around with a feeling of power. Your partner may be having trouble holding you. In any case, ask your partner to release your wrist and walk around the room expansively, arms open. Ask yourself if you have more energy now than when you started the exercise.

Being grabbed by the wrist is not, of course, the same as being confronted by some unexpected blow in your life. But this exercise guides you toward an alternative way of dealing with sudden hits of many types and many degrees of severity. Say your supervisor throws your report on your desk and says, "This is chaos!" You might try not shouting back, "What do you mean, 'chaos'? This is a damned good report. What's more " That might well make matters worse. Don't whine and complain; playing the victim is, in many ways, a losing game. Most of all, don't deny your feelings. Say to yourself, for example, "Boy, I felt that like a blow to the solar plexis. My mouth feels dry. I feel something like anger throbbing at my temples and in the back of my head." Or, if you know your supervisor well enough and have established a certain openness in the expression of feelings, you might even speak your feelings aloud. Just *your* feelings. Don't try to lay blame on the supervisor. Then consider the possibility that this sudden blow has given you the energy with which you and your supervisor, working together, can come up with an even better report. And note how energized you feel. This extra energy can be put to use in many ways.

The particulars of responding to each sudden hit vary, but the pattern is always the same: Fully experience and acknowledge your feelings by localizing them in your body. Be aware of the infusion of extra energy caused by the hit. Put this energy to use for some positive purpose.

Even from misfortune, great power can flow into you.
G. L.

BLENDING: AN ALTERNATIVE WAY OF DEALING WITH VERBAL ATTACKS

"What do you do when somebody pushes you?"

George Leonard has asked this question to various groups, totaling some fifty thousand individuals. In every case, the first answer has been, "Push back." This response to an attack, whether physical or verbal, is deeply ingrained in present-day cultures; Leonard has heard "Push back" in several languages. The problem is, such a response leads to a very limited number of outcomes—win, lose, or stalemate—none of which is ideal. If you win, someone else loses. Losing doesn't feel very good. And a stalemate is a big waste of time. The exercise described here introduces you to a change of context, an alternative response to a verbal attack that greatly multiplies your options.

A note of caution and clarification. We are not teaching physical self-defense here. Blending with physical attacks, a skill most highly developed in the art of aikido, takes months or years to learn. Verbal blending also takes practice to perfect, but it can be used from the very beginning. In this exercise, you'll have an opportunity to get the *feel* of blending through bodily movement under pressure. This

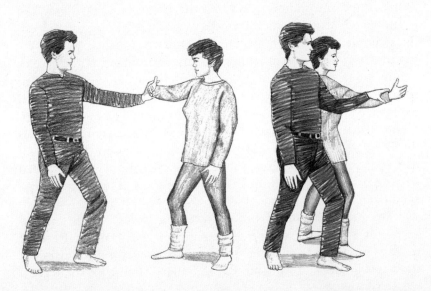

Blending

physical experience will teach you the principles of verbal blending in a more immediate and dramatic fashion than would be possible using words alone.

To do the exercise, you'll need a partner to play the part of an attacker. Start by standing with your right foot about eight to ten inches directly in front of the left. Your left foot is turned out to the left at a forty-five-degree angle. Both feet are planted firmly on the ground. You and the person playing the part of the attacker are standing a few feet apart, facing one another.

Extend your right arm straight out directly in front of you, toward your attacker, with fist clenched, thumb up. Now bend your right arm until the forearm is at a ninety-degree angle to the upper arm, level and directly in front of you. Your attacker then comes forward, grasps your right wrist with his or her left hand and pushes directly toward you. Push back. Don't overdo the struggle that ensues from this "push–push back" mode of dealing with an attack. Just push back long enough to get the feel of it. Recall an episode of verbal sparring in your life when push-push back was the guiding rule. Note its similarity to this physical struggle.

The attacker releases your wrist and steps back. Take the same stance and arm position as before, but this time, instead of making a fist, leave your right hand open. Briefly balance and center. Feel the energy flowing through your arm and out of your fingers. Once again, the attacker comes toward you, grasps your right wrist with his or her left hand and pushes directly toward you. Don't push back. Instead, move slightly toward the attacker and turn to the left, rotating in place as the attacker takes one or two more steps forward, until you are facing in the same direction as the attacker, keeping your arm and hand alive and full of energy. At this point, both of you stop so that you can experience your new situation.

What has happened? You might say that the attack has been diffused or simply that you and your attacker are now lined up in the same direction. But the important point is that you are now seeing the situation from your attacker's viewpoint—*without losing your own.* Consider how different this feels compared to the situation when you were facing your attacker, struggling to push back harder than he or she was pushing you. Note that by blending, you've given yourself a few moments to decide on how to further deal with the attack. Also note that you now have many options rather than just win, lose, or stalemate. From this position, it's easy to break from your attacker's grasp and take leave of the situation or to embrace the attacker or to turn the attack to a new direction or even to strike a winning blow. Blending is not a passive act. It is not "giving in." It is seeing the situation from the attacker's viewpoint, then acting appropriately, bearing in mind that a blend makes reconciliation not only possible but likely.

In the martial arts, the blend stands as an extremely powerful move. Verbally, it is perhaps even more powerful, not only diffusing the force of an attack but often leading to harmonious agreement. As an example, let's say a futurist has made a speech about a visionary school of the twenty-first century where much of the teaching is accomplished through advanced technology. During the question period, an aggressive young man launches a verbal attack. Here we compare two ways of responding:

1. *Push–push back. Aggressive young man rises to his feet with a wicked grin.* "That was a nice little scenario you gave us, but like most futurism it's totally impractical. Where would you get the money to pay for all that technology?"

"Well—" *Speaker pauses, then responds with lofty sarcasm.* "I guess we'd get it where we get all those generous funds we currently devote to our younger generation. Seriously, we could fund a great deal of advanced technology with the money we now spend dealing with the human failures produced by present antiquated educational methods."

"Just a minute! Not so fast!" *Aggressive young man's voice rises.* "The kind of computer power needed for your scenario would cost at least $100,000 for each school and would call for a level of artificial intelligence that doesn't now exist. I have to disagree with you. Your scenario is totally unrealistic."

Speaker tries to control anger. "I assume you're not familiar with the work of Ned Morosco at Massachusetts Institute of Technology. He's already working with prototypes that can do just about everything I've outlined. In any case, what's keeping us from a better future isn't lack of money. It's lack of vision. If the nay-sayers take over, we just as well give it up. Next question."

The aggressive young man shakes his head with derision as he sits down. The speaker has "won" but doesn't feel very good. The audience has had its interest piqued by the interchange, but some of its members are embarrassed and a few feel bad for the young man.

2. *Blending.* *Aggressive young man rises to his feet with a wicked grin.* "That was a nice little scenario you gave us, but like most futurism it's totally impractical. Where would you get the money to pay for all that technology?"

Speaker nods thoughtfully. "That's a good question. I worry about that myself. What you're saying is that new technology is very expensive."

"Yeah, right. And not only that, the computer capability you're talking about doesn't exist yet—and we're not even near getting there."

"Yes, that's true too. I hear what you're saying."

"But, you know—" (*Young man no longer seems aggressive.*) "You know, computers keep getting cheaper all the time. And the increase in memory capacity and speed is exponential."

"Right. I've heard that a generation in computer technology is now defined as two and a half or three years."

"Well, maybe it could happen—if we had the will to do it."

"Right. If we had the will. I really appreciate your comments." *The young man smiles as he takes his seat.*

The first interchange is purely imaginary; it never happened. The second took place during a lecture on education by George Leonard at a large western university. Blending doesn't always work this neatly, with the attacker coming over to the blender's side—*but it often does.* During a book promotion tour, one of the authors went on a radio show as the guest of a man known as the most abrasive talk show host in New York. The program began with a particularly virulent attack, impuning the author's character and painting him as a threat to society. After an hour of blending, the situation couldn't have been more different. Near the end of the show—with the producer in the control room tearing at his hair in frustration—the host and the author were talking with genuine warmth and understanding. The host ended the show by reading the last page of the author's book, with feeling. People who heard the program characterized the shift in the host's attitude as "unbelievable," "miraculous." It was not that he had been manipulated. He had been truly heard and understood, and from that he was able to reveal a deeper, truer persona than the one required for contentious commercialism.

We have said more than once that long-term change takes long-term practice, but if there is an exception to prove the rule, blending might qualify. Though it takes practice to master the art, even unskilled blending rather than pushing back can produce an immediate change in outcome. But there are some provisos and guidelines:

> Blending is presented here as an option, not a one-size-fits-all solution. There are some situations best dealt with through grappling. In a sense, blending is *too* powerful. To use it invariably with your spouse and children, for example, can drive them crazy. ("Mom, will you *stop* blending with me all the time?") And then there are some attacks so destructive, so evil, if you will, that they must be quickly struck down. But even in the worst situations, even in war, it's good to be able to view the situation from the attacker's viewpoint.

> For a blend to be successful, you should be psychologically balanced and centered, and this means being physically balanced and centered. It's very hard if not impossible to blend if your energy is concentrated in your head and upper chest. To remind yourself to stay balanced and centered while blending, touch your physical center.

> Blending doesn't work if done insincerely, just as a strategy. You must come around wholeheartedly to view the situation from the attacker's viewpoint. Again, this doesn't mean giving up your viewpoint. As you start to blend verbally, imagine turning all the way around physically to the attacker's viewpoint rather than turning only part of the way.

Continue practicing this exercise to get the feeling of wholehearted blending. Do it left-handed as well as right-handed. When you feel familiar with the physical exercise, add a verbal attack to the physical. Have your partner verbally attack some position you hold at the same time he or she grasps your wrist and pushes. Blend verbally as you turn. Continue blending verbally as you stand viewing the situation physically from your attacker's viewpoint.

We are by no means suggesting that you do anything to provoke a real-life confrontation just so you can check out the blending option. But if by chance you are attacked verbally, give it a try.

The Crystalline State

This exercise offers you an opportunity to perceive the world with the vivid here and now clarity common to many mystical and other exalted experiences. In the crystalline state, there is no expectation nor any prejudgment. Concentration on the past and future gives way to primary focus on the present. Action taken while in the crystalline state is not *considered* action but rather *appropriate* action. When fully achieved, this state permits awareness of what might be called the perfect rhythm that always exists at the heart of your being. Awareness of this rhythm can come upon you spontaneously. It can arise during meditation. Most people have experienced a few moments or hours or even days during which it seems that nothing can go wrong, that all things are somehow connected, that what is most commonplace is also most wonderous. No set of instructions can guarantee that you will arrive at such a state. The following procedure is offered merely as a guide. Your own intentionality is the key ingredient.

Sit comfortably, either in meditation position on a cushion on the floor or in a straight-backed chair. Balance and center. Using soft

The Crystalline State

vision, create an imaginary ball about the size of a volleyball between your hands. Hold the ball gently. Sense its surface by moving your hands slightly together in a rhythmic manner. Let the ball become real in your imagination. Check if you can *feel* where its surface begins as you move your hands in and out.

Continuing to palpate the ball, think of your most pressing personal problem. *Put this problem in the ball.* Focus your eyes on the problem. Let it take its own shape and texture and color. What does the problem look like now? Does it move? What part of the ball does it occupy?

Ask yourself whether you're willing to give up that problem for the next twenty or thirty minutes (or for however long you want to extend the period). Are you willing to let go of the problem completely for at least this long? Assure yourself that you can get it back when the exercise is finished, if you so desire. (Your problems are important aspects of your ego. In this case, in fact, this particular problem might be said to represent your ego.)

Now, if you're really willing to give up your problem for this next period of time, press the ball with the problem in it down into the floor. Let it sink into the earth. The earth will serve as a bank; you can always recover the problem later.

Shake out your hands. Balance and center. Again create a ball between your hands. The ball is as pure and clear as a crystal. Focus your eyes on its center, allowing the background to go out of focus. Continue "feeling" the ball by moving your hands slightly in and out. You might find it hard to stay focused on "nothing," but keep bringing your focus back to that central point. Continue this practice for about five minutes.

During this period, consider that the crystalline state, now represented by the ball, contains no expectations and no prejudgment. It exists in the vibrancy of the present moment. In this state, what you experience is neither "good" nor "bad," neither "successful" nor "unsuccessful." It just *is*. You experience the world as a young child would: as if for the first time.

After five minutes or so of concentration have passed, ask yourself, "Am I willing to live during this next period of time entirely in the present, without expectation or prejudgment? If the answer that comes from your heart is no, throw the ball away and, if you so desire, take back your problem from the earth. If your heart's answer is yes, however, press the ball into your body at the point of your physical center. This act represents your induction into the crystalline state. Feel the ball expand inside you and spread to fill your whole being.

In the crystalline state now, rise and walk around, experiencing familiar things as if for the first time—a chair, a table, a painting, a flower, a tree. Approach each experience without expectation or prejudgment. Go to a mirror and look at yourself from the intense clarity of the present moment. Maybe you can arrange to meet a friend, a loved one, or a stranger while in this state. If so, there need be nothing out of the ordinary about your external appearance and actions; the crystalline state entails *appropriate* action, and it is appropriate to meet another person in a relaxed and natural manner. Your own experience during the meeting, however, could well be transformed, and this transformation might reveal itself in the essential quality of the relationship. For example, having dropped at least a portion of the dubious armor of prejudgment, you might feel a certain compassion and understanding rather than suspicion or dismissal, thus opening a new level of dialogue.

Whenever you wish, you can return to the state we consider "normal." Remember that your pressing personal problem is still there for you to retrieve and return to your consciousness, if you so desire. The crystalline state is an *alternative* mode of being. To offer it is not to denigrate other modes. The point is that to be able to move into the crystalline state at will, eventually without the induction procedure presented here, is to enjoy the possibility of a richer, more fascinating, more humane life.

TUNING-IN

This exercise and the two that follow offer you the possibility of sampling metanormal sensing. This one requires a partner. You and your partner sit facing each other in the meditation position on cushions or in straight-backed chairs, so close that your knees touch. Both you and your partner should balance and center, then go into the crystalline state. Place your hands on your knees, palms up, and have your partner place his or her hands, palms down, into yours. Both of you now close your eyes.

At this point, simply assume that your partner's bodily states are known to you at some deep level, and that, in fact, you can feel in *your* body every bodily state your partner feels. Let your body be a sensitive antenna that is tuned-in to your partner's body. Wait a few minutes, then, if you feel a tightness in your own neck, say aloud to your partner, "There's a tightness in your neck. See if you can relax it." Keep tuning-in. If you should feel your neck relaxing, say aloud, "Good, your neck is relaxing now." Keep tuning-in by mentally scanning your own body for anything out of the ordinary. Report anything you feel to your partner as if the condition exists in his or her body.

After all possible corrections have been made, start working on *positive* change, on creating a sense of glowing awareness and aliveness in your partner's body. Again, use feelings in your own body as a guide. For example, "Your head feels full of life and energy, but the aliveness seems to stop at your neck, leaving your body rather numb. See if you can let the energy flow downward from your head into your body." Keep tuning-in. When you feel a change in your own body, report it as a change in your partner's body. "Good. Now the energy has flowed through your neck as far as your heart. See if you can let it flow downward and fill your whole body."

Continue giving instructions in this manner until your own body feels relaxed, alive, and glowing. Then, along with your partner, take a few deep breaths, shift your weight, stretch, and open your eyes. Compare notes. Which of your instructions were on target? Which were meaningful and useful? Now change roles and repeat the exercise.

TOUCHING THE WORLD

The primary purpose of this exercise is to make it possible for you to sense a new connectedness with the world. Start by doing it at a location from which you can see a tree or shrub. Briefly balance and center yourself. Bear in mind that in an expanding universe every point can serve as its center. Look in the general direction of the tree with soft eyes, then let your eyes focus on a particular leaf. With the index finger extended, let your left hand rise and point directly at that leaf. The arm and shoulder should be relaxed. Your assumption here is that some aspect of your finger in some way actually *touches* the leaf. Perhaps you can visualize a beam of some sort of energy extending from the fingertip to the leaf, or perhaps you can experience the finger itself somehow transcending space to *touch* the leaf. The idea is to assume mutual influence; by your act of intention, you are to some extent influencing the leaf and the leaf is influencing you.

While your finger is *touching* the leaf, continue to be aware of your own center as the center of the universe. The leaf is also part of the universe that extends out from your center. During this exercise, due to the vector of interest expressed by your intentionality, that particular leaf is given a special significance. After approximately five minutes, let your eyes go soft and swing your hand in a small arc a few degress to either side of the leaf. Can you feel an increased sensitivity at the fingertip every time it *touches* the leaf?

Now drop your arm, shake out both hands, check your balance and center, and repeat the *touching* procedure with the same leaf. This time, if you can get a strong feeling of the leaf while moving your finger in the soft-eyed state, try the same thing with your eyes closed. If this is successful, try moving your finger even farther off the target, and check if you can find the leaf without opening your eyes.

At first, you might find it easier to establish contact with living things, but the exercise can be applied to any part of the world to which you are willing to give significance—clocks, paintings, the moon and stars. One LET student reported touching a hummingbird at a feeder, feeling the shape of its body, its pulsing throat, the vibration of its wings.

A Synchronization Process

This process is presented as an example of large-group activity that is carried on at our classes and workshops. Suitable for groups of sixteen to one hundred or more people, this process offers the possibility of achieving the metanormal connectedness that can exist between human individuals. It requires an unobstructed indoor space large enough for free movement among all participants. As a guideline, a space that seats one hundred people will work for about forty people.

The leader begins by asking the participants to clear the floor of all extraneous objects, then to spread out and stand facing him or her so that they can turn all the way around, arms extended, without touching or just barely touching anyone else. Participants are led through the balancing and centering procedures. They are then

asked to walk swiftly and at random around the room, always moving toward the empty spaces, letting those ever-changing spaces attract them. Soft eyes make it possible to do this, even at a rather fast
pace, without colliding with anyone else.

When the group is thoroughly mixed, the leader asks everyone
to stop, close eyes, and recheck balance and center. "Leaving your
eyes closed," the leader says, "turn in place twice to the left . . . now
twice to the right. . . . Let your hands float up as if in warm, salty
water, then put the palms forward as if pushing a beach ball on the
surface of the water. Now walk slowly, eyes closed, sensing your way
through the palms of your hands, until you find a partner. Take
hands with your partner, leaving eyes closed and remaining silent,
and get to know her or him by what you sense through your hands."

Generally, a few people in these groups are unable to find partners with their eyes closed. The leader and assistants help them get
together.

"In a moment," the leader continues, "I'm going to clap my
hands. When I do, open your eyes and immediately close them
again. Take a quick snapshot of your partner, in which you get only
the essense of his or her face and form. Let this image, this energy
essence, dissolve within you. Let it become part of you."

Two or three minutes later, the leader continues: "Now open
your eyes and watch this demonstration with soft eyes." He walks
around the room, stride for stride, with an assistant or one of the
participants—shoulder to shoulder, arms linked. "Walk this way
with your partner, assuming that the two of you are a single energy
field, greater than the sum of its individual parts. Soft eyes. Keep
walking until your movements are completely synchronized."

For three or four minutes, the couples walk around the room.
The leader reminds them to consider themselves a single energy
field. Then he asks them to gather. He passes out sheets of paper,
one to each couple. The written material on all of the papers is the
same excerpt from some well-written prose work. He tells them to
spread out to the edges of the room and sit facing outward, each couple close together. He asks that they read aloud, synchronizing their
words with their partners' words—but not with the words of the
other couples. The leader suggests that the participants read not for
meaning but just for rhythm, and that they assume, again, that they
are one with their partners. When they come to the end of the page,
they are to start over from the beginning.

Soon there is a pleasant hum throughout the room as the couples read aloud, each couple at its own speed and rhythm. During this part of the process, the breathing of most of the couples becomes synchronized.

After five minutes or so, the leader tells the couples to leave the sheets of paper where they are sitting and begin the synchronized walking again. After the walking-reading cycle is repeated, the couples are asked to sit facing each other, knees touching. Each couple then makes a single large crystalline ball between them; four hands hold and palpate the ball. The leader reminds them of the qualities of the crystalline state. He asks the participants to focus their eyes on the center of the ball, then raise it to eye level.

"Please keep your eyes focused on the center of the ball. This will mean that your partner's face will look out of focus to you. Just keep trying to hold your focus on the center of the ball. . . . Assume that this crystalline ball resonates only to one frequency. In this case, we're going to assume it's tuned to a frequency that represents a resonance common to the two of you, a key frequency in the new unified energy field. When I clap my hands, I ask that you look directly at your partner's eyes *through* the crystalline ball. Let your eyes meet through the ball, on a single, clear, resonant frequency."

The leader claps his hands, and the partners look directly into each other's eyes for two or three minutes. The leader then asks that they crush the ball out of existence between their hands, bringing their four hands together in a firm grasp, and that they rise to a standing position.

"In a moment, I'm going to ask that you silently bid your partner good-bye. Though you'll be physically separated, you'll still be joined in some significant manner. The assumption is that you'll be connected at all times with your partner for as long as this process lasts. You'll always know exactly where your partner is—without looking, without even thinking about it.

"I'm going to ask that you start the random, soft-eyed walk that you did at the beginning of this process. Then, when I clap my hands, stop, let your hands float up to the scanning position and rotate in place, scanning for your partner. Don't *look* for your partner. Keep your vision soft. Assume that you are somehow connected with your partner at all times, without thought. When you sense this connection through your hands or in any other way, zero-in and stop, facing your partner wherever he or she may be in the room."

The random walk begins. When the leader feels that the group is thoroughly mixed, he claps his hand, the participants stop, rotate in place, and zero-in on their partners. This is repeated twice, still with eyes open and soft, as a practice for what is to come.

The partners are then asked to go through the same procedure with eyes barely open, so that they can see only the feet of nearby people. This too, is repeated twice.

Finally, they are asked to walk around with eyes barely open, then, at the sound of the leader's hand clap, to close their eyes tightly and leave them closed as they zero-in on their partners. Scanning for partners takes place, in this case, *with eyes completely closed*. When the partners have had a few moments to zero-in, the leader asks that they open their eyes and, if necessary, correct their alignment. The closed-eye practice is repeated at least three times. The group then gathers informally for a discussion of the process.

We have found this process to give reliably good results. For example, thirty-three people participated in a Synchronization Process during our ITP class of June 25, 1993. We had the participants attempt to locate their partners with eyes closed three times. Only one person failed all three times. Four participants located their partner one of the three attempts, fourteen got direct hits two out of the three attempts, and fourteen found their partners with eyes closed all three times. We considered the possibility that some people were peeking, but close observation showed this not to be the case. Participants have often found their partners even when other people blocked their view. And there have been cases when a participant accurately pinpointed his or her partner's location even though the partner had left the room during the process without notifying anyone.

Results in exercises such as these add to a growing body of evidence that modes of sensing exist that are generally not acknowledged in our culture. We believe that our capacities in areas ranging from what we term normal to what we term metanormal are vastly greater than commonly assumed, and that by cultivating them we can enrich our lives.

TWELVE

✤

The Marriage of
Theory and Practice

All those engaged in a serious calling—whether scientist or nurse, artist or contemplative—are strengthened in that calling by a sustainable philosophy that supports their work. Their practice is enhanced if they know why they must learn certain skills, why they must cultivate particular virtues, and how the elements of their practice fit together. Our classes have emphatically taught us that this holds true for integral practice. No one can endure the resistance from self and others, the doubts, the frustrations, the inevitable ups and downs of long-term discipline without a good set of reasons for doing so.

The need for a basis in theory becomes clear when the practitioners of an integral discipline have to make course corrections. The principles that guide our work have enabled us to assess the effectiveness of our programs and the progress of class members. They have helped us improve certain exercises and invent better ways to make our program effective. There is an analogy here with science in that our theory of integral transformation has been tested by the experience of class members, while, at the same time, members' experience has been guided by theory. Both our theory and our practice have developed from their mutual give and take.

Some Fundamental Principles Underlying Integral Practice

A philosophy is comprised of several principles. Here are some that underlie the integral practice described in this book:

- Most of us realize just a fraction of our human potential. We live only part of the life we are given.

- The culture we inhabit reinforces only some of our latent capacities while neglecting or suppressing others. In the contemporary West, for example, there is great support for high-level athletic development but relatively little for advanced meditation and the metanormal capacities it evokes.

- Most, if not all, human attributes can give rise to extraordinary versions of themselves, either spontaneously or through transformative practice. This is the case for perception of external events, somatic awareness, communication skills, vitality, movement abilities, capacities to manipulate the environment directly, feelings of pain and pleasure, cognition, volition, sense of self, love, and bodily structures.

- Extraordinary attributes, when seen as a whole, point toward a more powerful and luminous human nature, even a new type of physical embodiment in which the flesh will be suffused with new joy, beauty, and power.

- Extraordinary attributes frequently seem to be given rather than earned, and often arise fully formed from a dimension beyond ordinary functioning. Furthermore, their appearance sometimes appears to be mediated by supernormal agencies or processes (which in Christian terms are called the "graces of God," in Buddhism the "workings of Buddha-nature," in Taoism the "way of the Tao").

- A widespread realization of extraordinary attributes might lead to an epochal evolutionary turn analogous to the rise of life from inorganic matter and of humankind from its hominid ancestors.

- However, evolution meanders more than it progresses. This is an adventurous universe, in which each advance can be viewed in retrospect as a perilous journey, a close call with failure. Humankind's further advance is not guaranteed nor is the progress of any individual.

- To last, extraordinary attributes must be cultivated. For a many-sided realization of extraordinary attributes, for *integral transformation*, we need a practice that embraces body, mind, heart, and soul.

- Enduring transformative practices are comprised of several identifiable activities, or *transformative modalities*, such as disciplined self-observation, visualization of desired capacities (see chapter 7), focused surrender to emergent capacities (see chapter 5), and elicitation of the "relaxation response" (see chapter 8). Integral practices incorporate these modalities to produce a balanced development of our entire nature.

- There is an "all-at-once" quality about these transformative modalities. Like a good business deal or scientific theory, they yield great returns on investment of time and energy (see chapter 8).

- These modalities operate in everyday life to some extent, whether or not we are engaged in a formal practice. All of us, for example, are consciously guided—or unconsciously driven—by images of things we desire, and in most transformative practices such imagery is used to facilitate specific physical or psychological changes (see chapter 7). We all occasionally experience the emotional catharsis that is fundamental to many psychotherapeutic and religious disciplines, and we all sometimes practice self-observation. In other words, *all of us practice on a daily basis, albeit in a fragmented, largely unconscious manner.* Integral practice of the kind we propose in this book aims to make our fragmented practices conscious, creative, and coherent and harness them for health and growth.

- There is a powerful resonance between body, heart, mind, and soul. All levels and dimensions of human nature respond to one another, and a change in one typically facilitates a corresponding change in another, as when mental images and affirmations affect the body. This resonance exists because all manifest things arise from a common source, which is "involved" in the stuff of the universe (see below).

- To last and to be successful, integral practice must be engaged primarily for its own sake, without obsession with ends and results. Its practitioners do best when they learn to enjoy the long plateaus of the learning curve. Preoccupation with goals can cause a compulsive striving that blinds us to the emergence of unexpected goods and that inhibits the workings of grace.

- Both the theory and practice of integral transformation are still developing and require a mutual give and take. They are works in progress, requiring course corrections. Like science, they involve continual discovery.

- One reason that transformative practices require course corrections is that they can produce unbalanced development, inhibiting certain capacities while promoting others in a way that subverts lasting growth. They also can give rise to powers that serve destructive motives and therefore need to be monitored by peers and mentors.

- All human attributes depend upon one another, either directly or indirectly. For example, disciplined self-observation requires a certain measure of courage; sustained meditation requires physical stamina; the control of autonomic processes requires kinesthetic sensitivity. Integral practice addresses this aspect of human nature by embracing all aspects of body, mind, heart, and soul.

- The grace-laden nature of extraordinary attributes, and the sublimity, power, and beauty they reveal, strongly suggest that evolution on earth is an unfoldment of a prior "involution," "descent," or "implication" of that sublimity, power, and beauty in the stuff of the universe. In other words, the world's primary tendency is to manifest great goods that are hidden in it. That tendency inclines us toward extraordinary life, which can best be realized through integral practices. We develop this idea in the section that follows.

Involution-Evolution Cosmologists tell us that our world began as some sort of seed, no larger perhaps than a needle point. There was a moment, they say, just the barest instant of time, when from that seed there arose enough energy to create everything in our universe. This stupendous beginning had no atoms, no elements as we know them now, and yet it contained in potentia the billions of galaxies, the millions of species on earth, the human mind and heart. From this womb of our world would come giant red stars and lovers' tears, supernovae and Bach choral masses, animal life and the ecstasy of saints. In that exploding seed was the potential for pain and glory, cruelty and redeeming grace. Our heart tells us that something more than chance was involved. A guiding spirit, an awareness, was secretly there from the start.

For things could have gone wrong at many points in our world's journey. At the very beginning, in that first instant of time, if the density of the budding universe were not what it was, all of creation would have collapsed. In the words of one astrophysicist, that density required "an adjustment not of one part in a thousand, not of one in a trillion, but of one part in infinity." At one point in the evolution of the early universe, had there not been a preponderance of matter over antimatter, the first particle collisions would have yielded nothing but energy. There would have been no stars or planets, no human heart, just radiating particles for aeons to come.

These first narrow escapes were the first of many that have marked the evolutionary journey. For life, for humanity, for self-awareness to exist, the universe has had to win a cosmic lottery—not once, but again and again and again. Let us look at another close call: the genesis of heavy elements, from which our bodies and the earth are made. The creation of carbon and oxygen involved such complexity that astrophysicist Fred Hoyle said it looks like "a put-up job." Reflecting upon the positioning of nuclear resonances that made the two elements possible, Hoyle wrote, "A commonsense interpretation of the facts suggests that a superintellect has monkeyed with physics . . . and that in nature there are no blind forces worth speaking about." Mathematician Paul Davies used another metaphor: If you had dials for setting the initial conditions of creation and could use them to set the values needed to ultimately produce life, you would find that virtually all their settings would make the universe uninhabitable. The odds against all of them being so precisely positioned by chance, randomly, without any design or any designer, are astronomically high.

Reflecting upon the stupendous cosmic coincidences and the multibillion-year defiance of odds that evolution exhibits, we sense

The body is all time remembered.

M. M.

that a purpose, a telos, calls the universe toward a greater existence. And we find such a calling in us. There is a profound affinity between the world's advance and our capacity for transformation, between the emergence of consciousness from the inorganic world and the emergence of new life in us. This affinity has led many thinkers to propose that the universe's evolution is the unfolding of a spirit, or divinity, involved in inconscient matter and energy, a divinity that presses to manifest itself more fully in the course of time. This intuition, this vision, has been developed in various ways from the beginning of the nineteenth century.

Since about 1800, a striking number of the world's most prominent philosophers have proposed that the emergence of higher organization and higher qualities—in individuals, societies, and the world at large—is made possible by their secret existence, or immanence, in nature. The German philosopher Hegel, for example, proposed that *Geist* (the supreme Spirit) gradually reveals itself through the long dialectic of history, recovering its fundamental completeness as one aspect of itself after another is subsumed in a higher fulfillment. In *The Phenomenology of the Spirit* (1807), he traced this process through various stages of human history, from the slave of antiquity who struggled successfully against nature's difficulties to the modern intellectual's embrace of reason's highest principles, in an attempt to show how successive forms of consciousness preserve and lift up the forms that precede them.

Henry James, Sr., the father of William and Henry James, also viewed the world as an unfoldment of spirit. He was led to this view in part by the scientist-philosopher Emanuel Swedenborg. In his metaphysical treatise *Substance and Shadow* (1863), the elder James wrote: "...according to Swedenborg, God creates us or gives us being only by thoroughly incarnating Himself in our nature; but inasmuch as this descent of the creator to creaturely limitations...involves the strictest inversion of the creative perfection...so it must necessarily provoke a corresponding ascending movement." For James, the inorganic, animal, and human realms press to manifest the divinity that is latent in them. "Whatsoever creates a thing," he wrote, "gives it being, *in*-volves the thing. The Creator involves the creature; the creature *e*-volves the Creator."

Some fifty years later, the Indian mystic and philosopher Sri Aurobindo articulated a vision of involution-evolution that resembles

that of James. In his philosophical work *The Life Divine*, Aurobindo
wrote:

> ...if evolution is the progressive manifestation by Nature of that
> which slept or worked in her, involved, it is also the overt realiza-
> tion of that which she secretly is. We cannot, then, bid her pause at
> a given stage of her evolution, nor have we the right to condemn
> with the religionist as perverse or with the rationalist as a disease or
> hallucination any intention she may evince or effort she may make
> to go beyond. If it be true that Spirit is involved in Matter and ap-
> parent Nature is secret God, then the manifestation of the divine in
> himself and the realization of God within and without are the high-
> est and most legitimate aim possible to man upon earth.

There are significant differences between their philosophies, but
both Aurobindo and James saw universal evolution arising from a
previous involution of spirit in nature. James's biographer Frederic
Young wrote: "To read Aurobindo's masterpiece, *The Life Divine*, is,
to one who has read the senior James's works, to experience an inde-
scribable feeling that Aurobindo and James must have corresponded
and conversed with each other; so much spiritual kinship is there between the philosophies of these two thinkers!" Both the Indian and
American philosophers regarded "apparent Nature" to be "secret
God," and saw divinity emerging more fully through the uneven but
inexorable evolution of the universe. Like other thinkers since the
early nineteenth century, they "temporalized the great chain of being,"
to use historian Arthur Lovejoy's phrase, conceiving the world's hierarchy of inorganic, animal, and human forms "not as the inventory
but as the program of nature."

Until notions of progress and the fact of evolution became
prominent in the West, visions of human betterment were usually
embedded in worldviews that regarded the world to be a static or cy-
clincal existence to which time adds nothing new. In Lovejoy's
words, the conception of the Chain of Being (the hierarchy of the
manifest world, including matter, life, and humankind) was in accord
with the Solomonic dictum that there is not—and never will be—
anything new under the sun. But human visions change. Hegel, the
elder James, and Aurobindo represent an historic shift of perspective
by many thinkers from the view that the world is static to a belief
that it is moving, however haphazardly, toward higher levels of exis-

tence. According to these philosophers, our growth as individuals is inextricably linked with the world's growth. Spirit progressively manifests through us *and* through the world's evolution. By the unfoldment of our latent capacities, we *and* the world share the ongoing manifestation of the divinity latent in nature.

For thinkers such as Hegel and Aurobindo, however, divinity also *exceeds* the manifest world. Its immanence, or "involution," does not limit its eternal and infinite existence. In this respect, such thinkers agree with mystics and philosophers East and West who did not know about evolution but who believed that the ultimate source of things was both immanent in and transcendent to the universe. In the words of the Isha Upanishad, one of India's oldest scriptures: "That moves, and That moves not. That is far, and the same is near. That is within all things, and That is outside all things." That this vision has been wedded to both evolutionary and nonevolutionary worldviews shows its lasting appeal to the philosophical imagination, and its resonance with an intuition prevalent in many times and cultures. The idea that divinity is involved in the world while at the same time retaining its timeless and unlimited existence reflects a realization, reported by countless people since antiquity, that we enjoy a secret alliance or identity with the founding principle of this universe. Such realization may be fleeting or lasting, spontaneous or the product of religious practice, but it is an enduring feature of human life. The seers of virtually every sacred tradition have expressed it through stories, epigrams, and philosophical doctrines. For example:

- In a famous Hindu religious parable, a lost tiger cub is raised by sheep, perceiving itself to be one of them until another tiger makes it look at its reflection in a river. We typically identify with those around us, the parable implies, forgetting that we are essentially one with God.

- A well-known Zen *koan* asks: "Before your parents were born, what is your original face?" This line suggests that we have an essential subjectivity or personhood that transcends birth and death.

- The Platonic doctrines of *anamnesis*, or "recollection" of the divine ideas underlying sense impressions, is based upon the belief that humans have immortal souls that communed with those ideas before assuming a mortal body.

• Plotinus, the great mystic-philosopher of Roman antiquity, wrote: "God is outside of none, present unperceived to all; we break away from Him or rather from ourselves; what we turn from we cannot reach; astray ourselves, we cannot go in search of another; a child distraught will not recognize its father; to find ourselves is to know our source." The image of homecoming in this passage is expressed by the German poet Novalis in his famous line *immer nach hause*, "always homeward" to our source.

• The medieval Christian priest Meister Eckehart wrote: "The knower and the known are one. Simple people imagine that they should see God, as if He stood there and they here. This is not so. God and I, we are one in knowledge." And Saint Catherine of Genoa claimed: "My Me is God, nor do I recognize any other Me except my God Himself."

• In similar fashion, the Sufi Bayazid of Bistun exclaimed: "I went from God to God, until they cried from me in me, 'O thou I'!"

These words from Hindu, Buddhist, Platonist, Christian, and Islamic sources express the enduring realization, shared by countless people since the beginnings of recorded history, of a being ordinarily hidden but immediately recognized as our true identity (a tiger among sheep), our original face, our immortal soul, our ultimate home, our shared knowing with God, our oneness with "all the Gods." In the light of such realization, it is natural to see the world either as a stage for the individual soul's return to its source, or (as did Hegel, Aurobindo, and James) as a universal evolutionary process manifesting its secret divinity. The involution-evolution idea economically and beautifully reflects the spiritual realizations of men and women who have lived in different times and many parts of the earth. But it does more than that. This intuition, this vision, helps account for many aspects of human life, and it provides support for the principles underlying integral practice. For example:

The universe is in the business of delivering up the unpredictable.

G. L.

- It gives us a theoretical basis for understanding why every human attribute can give rise to extraordinary versions of itself. If we are secretly allied with the source of the universe, we must share its all-encompassing power. We are capable of radical transformation, and can realize metanormal capacities, because that is our predisposition.

- It helps us understand our yearnings for God. If the entire universe presses to manifest its hidden divinity, then we share that impetus, which often expresses itself as a desire for the ego-surpassing love, the self-existent delight, the oneness with spirit inherent in our deepest nature.

- It helps explain humankind's inextinguishable creativity. If all the world is essentially an infinitely creative spirit, creativity must be accessible to every man, woman, and child.

- The best things in life often seem to be given rather than earned, spontaneously revealed rather than produced by deliberate effort (though practice sets the stage for most of them). This sense of grace in human affairs, which is shared by people in every land, is understandable if life's highest goods are involved in the world, waiting for the right conditions to manifest.

- At the same time, the involution-evolution idea helps us understand the transformative power of deliberate practice and the effectiveness of its essential modalities. Imagery, meditation, and focused surrender work best by aligning us with aspects of the divinity that is latent in us.

- It gives us a compelling reason for the resonance between human volition, imagery, emotion, and flesh through which psychosomatic changes appear to be mediated. If all our parts come from a common source, they must be profoundly connected. Our cells, feelings, and thoughts resonate with each other because they are parts of the same omnipresent reality. Body responds to mind, and mind to body, because they arise from the same ever-present origin.

- For all of the reasons just noted, the involution-evolution idea helps us understand the effectiveness of practices that embrace the whole person, that is, for *integral* practices. We say more about this in the section that follows.

A transformative practice, as we use the term in this book, is a coherent and complex set of activities that produces positive changes in an individual or group. The transformative practices which have endured longest, and which have produced the greatest changes in their practitioners, have typically embraced the whole person. The psychophysical rituals of shamanism, which open the shaman to life's multidimensional splendor; the ethical, somatic, cognitive, and spiritual family of disciplines described in Patanjali's yoga sutras; the rich ways of Zen, which have deeply influenced Japanese arts, morals, work, and play; the offering of everyday life to God in Hasidism, Sufism, and much Christian practice all embrace body, mind, heart, and soul. Each of them is an integral practice.

Such disciplines have endured for many reasons, among them these:

- They orient their practitioners toward the greater life that is latent in all our traits and virtues, all our attributes.

- They creatively use "all-at-once" responses such as the relaxation response (see chapter 8), as well as transformative modalities such as imagery and focused surrender that produce many positive outcomes at once, in a coordinated fashion.

- They help prevent the negative activities caused by parts of one's nature that more limited practices leave neglected (see chapters 13 and 14).

All human virtues and attributes, and all transformative methods, depend to some extent on one another. To develop awareness, for example, we need a certain measure of courage; to achieve strong control of autonomic processes, we need a yielding sensitivity to our body; to develop a powerful will, we must sometimes adapt to particular circumstances. Furthermore, the cultivation of one attribute often benefits others. Spiritual illuminations sometimes happen in sports, for example, even to athletes who don't seek or expect them; while conversely, some contemplatives exhibit amazing physical abilities in conjunction with mystical experiences. Such capacities and experiences emerge in clusters because all our attributes, whether ordinary or extraordinary, are intertwined with one another.

No virtue, no attribute, no transformative method stands alone. That is the case even though (1) extraordinary capacities can exist

Some Reflections on Integral Practice

side by side with psychological and physical deficiencies; (2) different physiological systems, though interdependent, operate with considerable autonomy; and (3) much human activity is affected by dissociated volitions, attitudes, memories, and emotions. Though all our parts have a certain degree of independence, they affect one another directly or indirectly. That is why enduring transformative practices address the whole person.

We cannot escape our many-sidedness. One way or another, each dimension of our complex nature lays claim to its fulfillment. By honoring the diverse claims within us, many-sided disciplines have proved their worth through the long course of human history. Today, we have the opportunity to develop such disciplines by incorporating insights and methods from all the sacred traditions, from modern psychology and medical science, and from other fields. Elaborating this thought in *The Future of the Body*, Michael Murphy wrote:

"Among the advantages we enjoy today in creating integral practices is the proliferation of disciplines for cognitive, emotional, and bodily development. General semantics, linguistics, and related disciplines, most of them influenced directly or indirectly by the analytic philosophy that has flourished in British and American universities, give us new understanding of mental process. Never before have the foibles of thought, the good and bad habits of mind, the means of clear intellectual activity, been so thoroughly examined. . . . transformative practice needs the lessons such disciplines offer. The education of emotions, too, has developed in recent times. Modern depth psychology has increased our understanding of repressed or dissociated feelings, unconscious motivations, and psychodynamics in general, while offering new approaches to health and exceptional functioning. By their insights into the effects of unconscious volitions, and by their discoveries about culture's formative influence on each person's makeup, the human sciences complement the transpersonal perspectives embedded in the religious traditions. Since Freud, the modern West has produced a yoga of the emotions that can support other transformative disciplines. Contemporary psychotherapy, and the affective education it informs, give us many ways to cultivate our relationships, volitions, and feelings to enhance integral practices.

"At the same time, medical science, contemporary sports, and somatic education give us the basis for a physical training with un-precedented variety, richness, and robustness. Never before have so many athletic abilities been cultivated, nor have so many people tried to stretch their physical limits in so many ways, nor has human physiology been so thoroughly understood. Modern sports and the attendant fields of sports medicine and sports psychology constitute a vast laboratory for bodily transformation. Discoveries by athletes and their trainers of optimal methods for superior performance; the growing lore among somatic educators about sensory, kinesthetic, and motor skills training; and the developing insights about bodily functioning provided by medical science can assist any practice oriented toward metanormal embodiment. The cognitive, affective, and physical aspects of human functioning, in short, can be improved by numerous discoveries that few, if any previous cultures enjoyed. These discoveries and the transformative disciplines they inform could comprise a yoga of yogas, as it were, to embrace our many capacities."

Both spontaneously and through transformative practice, a new evolutionary domain is rising in the human species.

M. M.

READINGS THAT CAN ENHANCE YOUR PRACTICE

During our ITP courses, class members explored these and other ideas supporting integral practice. They did this mainly through reading assignments, regularly scheduled seminars, and informal discussions. This exploration was a shared undertaking, in which leaders and participants alike developed their understanding of the theories and disciplines involved. We (Leonard and Murphy) deepened our appreciation of certain previously held principles. For example, we were confirmed in our sense that the appearance of metanormal capacities is hard to predict and that their development requires a surrender to processes beyond normal consciousness. But we were also surprised by some of the things we learned. We were sobered, for example, by the extent to which transformative practice can alter *every* part of our lives. Integral practice, we found, can be more integral than one first imagines. It can challenge intimate relationships, vocational commitments, and our most fundamental patterns of thought, emotion, and bodily functioning. While most of our guiding principles have stood through numerous tests, giving us an anchor for practice, some have been refined or discarded.

So how can the reader make a marriage of theory and integral practice? How do you establish a cognitive track within your own discipline? Here are some first suggestions.

Establish a reading list, starting with Michael Murphy's *The Future of the Body* and George Leonard's *Mastery*, which together with this book present an overview of ideas and practices related to integral transformation. If the *Future of the Body* is too long for you, read Parts One and Three, using Part Two and the appendices for further reading. *Mastery* is shorter and elaborates several principles and observations that are presented here. These two books will give you both practical suggestions about integral discipline and a general theory of human transformation. We also recommend the books listed in Appendix C.

All of these books and articles can contribute to your thinking about integral transformation. None of them, however, has the final word about the subjects they address. Each represents just part of the world's work-in-progress to understand God, humanity, and our evolving universe. Nevertheless, any one of the readings listed in Appendix C can lead you to further information and to ideas that illumine the life we are given. Most of them cite material you can explore, and several have useful bibliographies. Through reading and group discussions, you can begin with one or more of them and fan out to others. Such inquiry leads to new fields of knowledge, and will almost certainly open up new kinds of experience. Our ITP classes have shown us that intellectual activity is a doorway to more than the intellect itself.

For example, we read that meditation can reveal a being that underlies ordinary feeling and thought and that connects us profoundly with others. From then on—as if by magic—such being arises spontaneously, in meetings with friends or talking to someone we deeply love or sitting alone at a restaurant table. An innocent-seeming sentence, just eight or ten simple words, can have tremendous effects upon us. A description of a particular ability, even a mere name for it, can evoke that ability or help us realize that we already have it to some degree. Look for such recognitions in your reading and group discussions. Discovery will lead to further discovery.

Ideas have the power to open us up. They also help us integrate capacities that initially seem strange or threatening. We read, for example, about meditation states in which one experiences "stereophonic" hearing. Learning that some contemplatives cultivate this auditory capacity, we are emboldened to explore it ourselves. Think of some ability that once disturbed you. What led you to value it? What was told to you, or what did you read, that helped you see that it was good? Integral practices sometimes produce potentially creative experiences that at first are disturbing, and for that reason require a mind-set that is favorable to them. Reading books about metanormal experience such as those listed in Appendix C, along with group discussions of them, can help you develop that mind-set. Our conceptual picture of human possibility develops in concord with all our parts. As our *vision* of integral transformation grows, we recognize, and therefore can cultivate, more and more latent capacities. Building a philosophy that embraces an ever wider range of human possibilities will broaden your practice as it broadens your intellect.

As we have pointed out, there is an "all-at-once" quality about certain activities that constitute transformative practice. Like a good business investment or scientific theory, such activities yield strong returns on investment. We repeat that observation here because the cognitive aspects of integral practice have this all-at-once character. A good intellectual grasp of our ITP programs went along with improvements in the emotional and physical functioning of class members. The ancient adage that body, mind, heart, and soul mirror one another has been confirmed by our ITP experience. By embracing the intellect, integral practice enhances *all* our parts.

THIRTEEN

The Magic of Community

In the beginning there was community. When our species, *Homo sapiens*, first emerged in Africa some 150,000 years ago or more, we lived in close-knit hunting and gathering bands numbering around thirty men, women, and children. It was to this way of life, not farming or urban living, that our bodies evolved. Our bones, musculature, central and peripheral nervous systems, endocrine systems, immune systems, and brains are not significantly different from our Stone Age ancestors. To these people, existence without community was unthinkable, impossible. Banishment meant death.

How can we summon up the *feeling* of community, of oneness with others that made our life? Ancient stones offer testimony on campsites, tools, successful hunts, episodes of violent death. Surviving hunting and gathering bands give clues to a way of living that takes us back to our earliest days. And even now there are moments around the campfire beneath the stars with good friends and good food and drink when that vanished life reappears, immediate in our own consciousness, a life full of talk and laughter, rich in ritual and ceremony, a life of langorous nights and leisurely days interspersed with periods of intense physical challenge and moments of risk and high adventure. As our knowledge of the distant past deepens, we realize that it was not only building or working that shaped our bodies

*An education devoid of the
ecstatic moment is the mere
shadow of education.*

G. L.

and brains, for our primitive ancestors had no permanent dwelling places, no jobs. We were also born to art, to music and dance, to a vital feeling for what we now inadequately term the spiritual realm, a consciousness of the variety, immediacy, and beauty of the unseen. Permeating all this was the intricate web of relationships that held us close in the love and nurturance of those we walked with, ate with, slept with. To say "human being" is to invoke community.

With the development of agriculture, the social unit expanded from the small hunting and gathering band to the tribe, the chiefdomship, the city-state, the nation-state; from a group of thirty or so men, women, and chidlren to groups of hundreds, thousands, millions. To these larger groups we gave allegiance and derived a sense of identity and belonging. But still there was our primal, biological need for smaller communities made up of people we could know and touch. This need was fulfilled through clubs organized around work, play, and politics, through clans, secret societies, church groups, the neighborhood, the extended family.

In today's rootless, restless, fragmented society, the bonds of community are badly frayed and sometimes ripped apart. Young people's innate need for community expresses itself through loyalty to street gangs. Adults who have moved far from their families and don't know their neighbors adopt a media community. With no Mrs. Green down the street to relate with or gossip about, many of us follow the intimate doings of Madonna, Michael Jackson, Demi Moore. Print tabloids spawn tabloid TV. But this one-way relationship with a shadow play of celebrities is intrinsically unsatisfying. Too often in our lives today, real community is lacking, a need unfulfilled.

The destructive effects of this isolation along with the healing and transformative powers of community has begun to show up in scientific studies. In his pioneering program of heart disease reversal without drugs or surgery, Dr. Dean Ornish worked with the premise that isolation is a major factor in sickness and that the support groups in his program are a major factor in the transformations of coronary arteries (see chapter 2). Another researcher, Dr. David Spiegel of Stanford University, conducted a study of eighty-six women with metastatic breast cancer. The study was designed to test the alleviation of pain. Fifty of the women—the treatment group— were randomly assigned to meet in support groups for an hour once a week. A control group of thirty-six women did not meet in support groups. All the women in the study received standard medical treatment. After a year, the women in the treatment group showed a significant alleviation of their pain.

Then came a surprise. Four years after the study began, all the women in the control group had died from this devastating disease while one-third of the women in the treatment group were still alive. As it turned out, the women in the treatment group lived an average of eighteen months longer than those in the control group—the only difference between the two groups being the creation of a community that met *only one hour once a week*. Other recent studies show similar results.

The longing for community is universal. A 1993 Lou Harris and Associates survey asked a national sample of people what was the most important thing in their life. More than half (56 percent) of those interviewed said that relationships with friends and family were the most important. This was followed by religious faith (21 percent), doing something to make the world a better place (12 percent), career fulfillment (5 percent), and monetary success (5 percent).

Our own Integral Transformative Practice class offered us the opportunity to witness the singular power of community. Cycle 93 participants were asked to rate twelve aspects of the program in terms of their importance in enhancing their practice. "ITP community" ranked third, just behind "Affirmations" and "Kata," just in front of "LET Exercises." For many of the participants, the community had even greater importance. Most of them adjourned to a nearby cafe for socializing on a regular basis following the Saturday classes. On their own, they organized evening meetings at members' homes to meditate, practice the Kata, discuss readings, or just get together. After we stopped leading classes in order to concentrate on evaluating our results and writing this book, a group of participants continued the program on their own, holding a full schedule of classes and off-site meetings.

There is something magical about any intense, tightly knit group of people working together and playing together, a feeling of being in the world while at the same time being apart from it, *apart together*. We believe that even those of us who have not experienced that magic hear its distant music, feel its ancient call. A transformative community is a nearly indispensable launching pad for transformation. Such a community can create the context and the confidence for a transforming journey.

How Culture Shapes the Body and Being

In recent decades, anthropologists have shown that many human attributes, which biologists used to think were inherited, are in fact culturally conditioned. Smiling, frowning, and other facial expressions have been proven to differ fundamentally from culture to culture. Sociologist David Efron found that assimilated Jews and Italians in New York City gesture differently than do their unassimilated counterparts. In a worldwide survey of postural habits, Gordon Hewes showed that we sit, kneel, stand, and recline in ways that are socially determined. It's now clearly established that human posture, physique, motor habits, and body image, as well as emotions and thought patterns, are culturally shaped. Think for a moment about the manner in which your body and mind have been influenced by others. Where did your habitual gestures come from? Whose laughter does yours resemble? Consider your food preferences, your style of dress, the kinds of exercise you like. Chances are that you can identify a particular person or group that led you to them.

Even our spiritual experiences are shaped by culture. Religious scholar Steven Katz edited a collection of essays, *Mysticism and Philosophical Analysis*, which presses home the fact that different traditions give rise to different kinds of contemplative realization. None of our experiences are immune to social influence. The most independent people are shaped by their acquaintances, friends, family, and by the institutions to which they belong.

We emphasize this observation because the cultures we inhabit either help or hinder the development of particular attributes. Men and women in America today, for example, have a better chance to develop scientific skills than they have to become contemplative adepts, while in village India most people find more support for contemplation than for scientific activity. Generally speaking, *human capacities develop most fully in cultures that prize them.* Because Renaissance Florence celebrated art, it produced some of history's greatest artists. Because Americans love sports, America produces great athletes. Appreciating this fact of human life, educators and religious teachers have built institutions specifically designed to support the attributes they deemed to be important. Saint Paul and Saint Peter formed communities to nurture Christian virtues. To foster the experiences they valued, the Buddha founded a *sangha* (fellowship), Plato the Academy, Aristotle the Lyceum, Saint Benedict his monastery. The university was developed in the late Middle Ages to support the kinds of learning the Church generally shunned. Today, we need to develop social structures to nurture integral practice. That is what we had in mind when we started our ITP classes.

Think of your own attempts to cultivate new capacities. Have you been frustrated by lack of support? How many times have your programs for growth failed because you didn't have friends or mentors to help you? Contemporary society encourages us in countless ways toward a life of distraction. Advertisers invite us to consume things we don't need—or even want—through television, magazines, and uninvited mailings. With the proliferation of telephones, much leisure time is filled with unsolicited conversation. To establish disciplines of any type, we have to counteract many distractions of modern life, and this is particularly true if we undertake long-term transformative practices. For the kinds of growth described in this book, we need healthy group support. Here are some ways to establish communities for integral practice.

The Transforming Alchemy of Listening

First, a support group can consist of two people. Our own experience has taught us that one partner can decisively improve your practice. A single ally can bring new perspectives to your difficulties, give helpful counsel, and lift your spirits through sympathetic listening. He or she can challenge you when inertia holds you back and provide encouragement when the going is tough. Sharing the ups and downs of long-term practice can produce a lasting solidarity. Lasting friendship is perhaps the greatest blessing that such discipline brings us. Those of us who have joined with colleagues in a significant work appreciate the depth of enjoyment this sort of collaboration brings. It is one of life's greatest pleasures.

We suggest that you find a friend who shares your commitment to integral practice. Set regular meeting times with her or him to explore the problems you're having. Schedule periods for meditation, physical exercise, affirmations, and philosophical inquiry. Check each other's progress. Provide challenge and needed support. As time goes on, you'll both learn from and teach one another.

But the sharing of practice, of course, needn't be limited to a single friend. Winning sports teams, excited classrooms, creative religious communities, and other kinds of inspired group have fostered accomplishments ranging from the healing of chronic afflictions to historic advances in science and religious understanding. Many are the cohorts that have facilitated extraordinary functioning. Roger Bannister, for example, broke the four-minute barrier in the mile, a feat once thought impossible, through his concerted effort with two running partners, Chris Chataway and Chris Brasher. The three men trained together for many months, and carefully planned their racing strategies. During their historic race, which took place in Britain during 1954, Brasher paced the first two laps and Chataway the third, putting Bannister in a position from which he sprinted to his record-setting time of 3:59:4. "We had done it—the three of us!" Bannister wrote. "We shared a place where no man had ventured—secure for all time, however fast men might run miles in the future. We had done it where we wanted, when we wanted, how we wanted!" Scientific advances, too, are frequently made by mutually supportive groups. In *The Double Helix*, James Watson chronicled his discovery with Francis Crick of DNA. Reading the book, one senses the mutual stimulation the two biologists experienced as they made their historic breakthrough.

To foster integral practice, you can create a group that provides the stimulation that highly motivated athletic and scientific teams enjoy. At our Saturday meetings and at the midweek meetings arranged by teachers and participants, there was typically a marked excitement and sense of homecoming. Both ITP cycles produced a self-generating sense of momentum. You can form a similar group and create the same kind of excitement.

Begin by setting regular meeting times, including sessions to meditate, share matters of the heart, study philosophy, and do physical exercise. It's important, we believe, that you include activities that nurture body, mind, heart, and soul. Play is important. Lend imagination to your strength and aerobic work, to your mutual counseling, to your intellectual exchanges. Join spontaneity and steadfastness.

To nurture self-awareness and general psychological health, participants can begin by sharing their concerns with fellow participants. Trust has to be built for intimate sharing, and nothing builds it faster than a sympathetic ear. That is the case because we are likely to feel invalidated if, upon revealing something that's troubling us, we get immediate reassurance or advice. So deeply ingrained are these modes of response that even the psychologically sophisticated in our groups sometime had to be reminded not to leap in to reassure or analyze or fix things. In group support sessions, we urged our participants to reveal themselves through feelings rather than opinions or judgments. And we urged those listening to be fully present, willing to hear the speaker out. Reassurances or advice might be given later—best of all when asked for.

Empathic listening builds a climate that helps group members reveal themselves. Through self-revelation in an atmosphere of trust, we learn to accept attributes we had not recognized or fully appreciated. We get new perspectives on our habitual patterns of feeling and thought and new foundations for work on ourselves. Through the growing self-acceptance that is encouraged by the presence of empathic listeners, our wounds can be healed and our capacities developed more freely. Many of the more extraordinary human capacities wither away simply through the self-censorship that springs from fear of ridicule—or worse.

We can conceive of a future without high-rises. But a humanity without music and love is not just inconceivable; it is impossible.

G. L.

That this fear is not without foundation is illustrated by the story of a woman (not a member of the ITP group) who had a powerful mystical experience while doing houshold chores. It was a beautiful day. Gazing out of a window at trees and birds and sky while washing dishes, she fell into a contemplative mood. Suddenly she was struck by the powerful certainty that, in essence, we are all one. This certainty—one which holds an honored place in the most revered spiritual traditions—filled her with a happiness she had never known, and she hurried to tell her husband what she was experiencing. Far from sharing her joy, he became deeply disturbed. After a couple of days during which she maintained her faith in the validity of her experience, he insisted she see a psychiatrist. At this point, realizing that what she had experienced had no safe place in the culture in which she lived, she told the psychiatrist that she guessed we weren't all one after all. She returned to her workaday life, exorcised of the extraordinary, cured of her joy, and filled with a lingering sadness over a new certainty: that she would never let herself have such an experience again.

What happened to this woman was extreme, but the self-censorship of experiences such as hers is extremely common. Even in our ITP group, among people who were dedicating themselves to the realization of human potential, we found it difficult at first to elicit verbal expression of their extraordinary experiences. It took time to develop the trust that would allow material on the fringes of consciousness and beyond the bounds of cultural consensus to be given voice. And it took the presence of empathic listeners:

—listeners who are interested and who really care about others,

—listeners who are willing to forego ego and the need to spout opinions,

—listeners who seek neither to add to nor to take away from what is being said,

—listeners who are patient and willing to withhold judgment for a while,

—listeners who can say, "Yes, I really hear you"—and mean it.

There is a transforming alchemy in such listening.

As intimacy and mutual acceptance in your group increase, participants are more and more likely to enjoy the give and take of ideas as well as experiences. Intellectual embarrassments will fade and curiosity will develop. New ideas arise from integral practice and can be tested in group discussions. Encourage inquiry. Encourage debate. Listen! Excitement about the vision of integral transformation will grow and can be fed by readings such as those proposed in Appendix C.

THE DANGERS OF CHARISMA

But a warning. Though we need communities to support practice, such communities can become destructive. They can diminish as well as facilitate their participants' autonomy, growth, and fulfillment. For example, many groups that are dedicated to personal growth are founded or taken over by a dominant individual who undermines the well-being of its members. Think of Jonestown or the Branch Davidians of Waco, Texas. Jim Jones and David Koresh, the leaders of those communities, did not have peers who could check their destructive influence. Exalted rhetoric, charisma, even spiritual gifts by themselves do not guarantee a leader's goodness. There is reason to be suspicious of gurus who take charge of a person's entire life. In our ITP classes, the four leaders gave one another helpful criticism. *And we listened carefully to feedback from group partic-*

ipants. To deal with the complexities of integral practice, we need multiple mentors. No one today, we believe, can guide someone in all dimensions of human growth.

But even leaderless communities can hinder their members' development. Contemplative retreats, for example, sometimes attract people who don't relate happily to others and reinforce members' isolation by divorcing them from creative human contact. Therapeutically oriented groups sometimes rationalize self-indulgence as psychic liberation or promote excessive confrontation among its participants in the name of openness and honesty. Practice groups of many persuasions stifle intellectual growth by punishing divergent thought.

When communities celebrate some virtues at the expense of others, or when they support narrow beliefs, they limit possibilities for growth. And when they are strengthened in such activities by genuine advances they facilitate among their members, they can become powerful obstacles to integral transformation. While producing a few good outcomes, some practice groups stand in the way of their members' well-rounded development.

Most of us need communities to nurture transformative practice, but we have to make sure they genuinely serve us. While accepting the support and challenges they give us, we need not be limited by them. The final authority in any transformative practice is the individual practitioner.

The Transformative Power of Love

Early in the twentieth century, Sigmund Freud conceived his principle of Eros, a tendency of all things animal and vegetable to join in larger entities, so that life might be prolonged and brought into higher development. At the beginning of time, in a universe made only of hydrogen and helium and intense energy, there was nothing we would call "life." Yet something akin to Freud's erotic principle, some inexorable tendency toward joining, toward the creation of form and complexity, seemed to have been operating.

The universe also involves destructive and dissolution—what Freud called Thanatos—and repulsion as well as attraction. But within the galaxies attraction predominates. The electron, it seems, "wants" to mate with the proton. The hydrogen atom "wants" to join the oxygen atom. The strong nuclear force binds the nucleus in exquisite strength and closeness. And gravity, the weakest of the four major forces in the universe, is entirely attraction, holding all others in its enormous embrace.

In the face of its long history of meandering, of extinctions and close calls, the stuff of the universe reveals its desire to join, to make more complex, highly ordered entities. The poet Dante said it another way: "Love is what moves the sun and the stars." We believe that a community is nothing if it doesn't foster love, an unconditional love that accepts us for what we are while moving us toward the higher good. Pronouncements, books, and statistics pale beside its transformative power.

Love something and watch it blossom.

M. M.

Changing the World by Changing Your Own Heart

We have suggested that cosmic evolution as we know it, from the big bang to the present moment, is finally an expression of Eros, of love. If this is so, how then can we doubt that love stands as the highest and most fundamental human impulse? In integral practice, we feel that love can be expressed in service to others, not just to friends and family and fellow practitioners but also to those in the larger community. We understand that there are many practical reasons for this expression. To serve others accrues to benign self-interest. It exalts us in the world's eyes. It produces positive publicity for our commercial enterprises. It makes us feel good. Those who serve others in love and kindness enjoy better health and live longer.

All this is well and good and not to be denigrated or dismissed. But we believe that there is an even higher possibility in aspiring to serve others in love and kindness, not even for the sake of transformation, but simply because that is a true expression of who we are, a fundamental condition of the path upon which we walk. Love doesn't have to wait for its recipients to be worthy of it. We can love others as they are. The world doesn't have to justify itself for us. We can love the world as it is. "If I love the world as it is," writes the novelist Petru Dumitriu, "I am already changing it: a first fragment of the world has been changed, and that is my own heart."

Perhaps all transformation begins with such a change of heart.

FOURTEEN

The Ultimate Adventure

When the Berlin Wall came down in November 1989 and the entire Eastern Bloc began cracking apart like ice in a thaw, many expert observers found themselves struggling to conceal their astonishment. Just a few years earlier, most would have rated the probability of such a shift in the foreseeable future as close to zero. In hindsight, however, we can see that the process was underway before 1989. The Wall had been coming down for a long time before men and women, East and West, began hammering and ripping it apart.

Today another process is underway throughout much of the world, a grassroots understanding that spirit and body are joined, that mind can somehow influence matter, that lives can radically change, that the further evolution of humankind is possible. The evidence of this process is all around us, in books that come out of nowhere to top the national bestseller lists, in polls on spiritual matters, in sometimes sensational images in the popular media of angels among us, of contacts with alien civilizations.

Some might say that these are merely symptoms of end-of-the-millenium anxieties. And yet we meet with physicists who see similarities between certain implications of quantum mechanics and the great spiritual traditions, with electronic engineers who invoke connections between the mental and the material. We find more and more people, including some scientists, willing to entertain the notion that our science itself, wondrous as it is, has not yet adequately addressed every significant realm of the knowable. Again and again, in different guises, in words and metaphors that often seem to clash, in forms both trivial and profound, the same essential understanding quietly spreads around the world: The reductive, purely materialistic interpretation of reality is not the whole picture. Unfathomed possibilities exist in consciousness and the flesh. Our evolution has not reached a dead end. Despite our frailties and flaws and the seemingly overwhelming horrors of the time, the human species has immense possibilities for advance.

The program we have described in this book has proven to be of significant value to most of those who have participated in it, with extraordinary outcomes for some. There's no doubt in our minds that a regular, long-term practice which involves body, mind, heart, and soul, and which aims at good health and the cultivation of our untapped potenials, can enhance individual lives and contribute to the social good. There are some who would say, "Yes, but you can never get many people to devote themselves to a long-term practice." But how are we to know unless we try?

In the transformations that emerge from an integral practice, the matter of social support is particularly important. It is difficult even to discuss such transformations if everyone around us stands ready to prejudge and invalidate. On the other hand, there is the danger of cultic pressure to see things that don't exist. The nonauthoritarian program we have championed in these pages, along with objective reality checks wherever possible, can help us safely past this pitfall. We feel that as the number of people engaged in the quest for transformation increases, the number of successes will increase even faster. If a significant minority of a society's people consciously and constructively engage in such a quest, we could see something new on this planet: one of those events that cannot be adequately predicted by what has gone before.

DANGERS AND DIFFICULTIES ON THE PATH

But make no mistake. Transformation is not automatic nor is it "easy." In several preceding chapters, we've described problems that arise during integral practice. We have said, for example, that affirmations must be chosen with care and creatively refined or abandoned in the light of unfolding experience. We've noted certain dangers of physical exercise and have urged patient sensitivity to the body's messages during aerobic sports, strength training, and performance of the ITP Kata. We've counseled avoidance of dietary extremes. We've reviewed certain ways in which groups hinder as well as further our development. And we've emphasized the resistance to change, the necessary homeostasis that all of us encounter during any long-term effort to change. To repeat: there can be difficulty in virtually any aspect of transformative discipline.

But the degree of such difficulty varies from person to person. Some people find immediate pleasure in physical training, while others do not. Some easily adopt a healthful diet, while others feel deprived. The joys of meditation come naturally to certain people but not to everyone. As you take up an integral practice, it is useful to remember that some parts of it will come easily, but that some might not. And beyond that, the path of transformation might entail pain you don't want or expect.

PITFALLS AND PROMISES

Any significant shift in consciousness, in how we perceive the world, can be disorienting. Sometimes, simply by relaxing their shoulders during the balancing and centering exercise described in chapter 6, people who have been almost entirely out of touch with their bodies will become aware of bodily sensations they haven't felt since childhood. Even something as gentle and benign as this can cause temporary dizziness or trembling. And powerful experiences of union with the divine or of the oneness of existence can prove much more troubling. This is especially true of people who are not firmly grounded in their bodies or of people with a history of mental illness.

Studies of such experiences have been published in recent years. We refer you, for example, to *The Kundalini Experience: Psychosis or Transcendence?* (Integral Publishing 1987) by psychiatrist Lee Sannella, who has studied so-called "spiritual emergencies" for more than twenty years. In this book, Sannella describes similarities between these crises and the kundalini experience of Indian yoga, during which energy seems to rush from the base of the spine to the top of the head, and lists several articles and books on the subject. Such literature teaches us that transformative discipline can sweep us beyond our familiar patterns into states we don't expect or desire. Such discipline is adventure, and all adventures have risks. It involves sacrifice, through which parts of us die. That is why we emphasize balance and centering during all phases of integral practice, and why we recommend companions and group support when you accept its challenge.

But there is an opposite danger. Transformative practice can reinforce limiting traits and thus hinder integral development. Rather than sweeping us beyond ourselves, it can help solidify our limitations. For example, meditation can—by its very success—lead people who have difficulty relating with others into social withdrawal. Contemplative bliss can provide a defense against the challenges of personal relationship and the adventures of the greater world.

Physical regimens, too, can be obstacles to growth. Some people become obsessively self-centered through running, weight lifting, or other body-enhancing regimens. The world today is filled with fit, well-toned people who have constricted emotional, intellectual, and spiritual lives. Psychological work can also be limiting when, for example, it rationalizes impulse-ridden behavior as the release of repressed emotion or an expression of authenticity, or when it fosters one trait (such as honest self-expression) at the expense of others (such as empathy and kindness).

Transformative practice can also reinforce limiting beliefs. Most of us know someone who, in the passion of his or her recent spiritual experience, has become fanatical about a particular guru, teaching, or cult. Countless people have tightened their lives around a limited set of ideas or a dogmatic teacher. But a passionate life doesn't have to be narrowed in this way. Our practice can be deep while our personal autonomy grows. We can be faithful to our path while pursuing intellectual discovery.

And a practice can subvert many-sided development by emphasizing certain virtues over others. Every culture, organization, and family does this. Think of your own upbringing, your workplace, your community. In these millieus, which virtues have taken precedence? Honesty over kindness? Courage over love? Or vice versa? Have you been shaped by these preferences? In our view, integral practice requires a recognition that all virtues, like all aspects of practice and human growth, are largely interdependent. It's difficult, if not impossible, to cultivate deep feeling for others without both sensitivity and the courage to face pain, without both strength and tenderness. It's hard to meditate for long without both tenacity and yielding, one-pointedness and the capacity for surrender. For integral practice, many virtues are needed.

You can even limit yourself to some degree by realizing authentic, but partial, kinds of extraordinary functioning. Particular traits, beliefs, and virtues can be given too much prominence, or even destructive sway in one's life by a genuine, but partial, experience of the transcendent. Some people, for example, have been led by a powerful mystical experience to perceive ordinary life as ugly, meaningless, or empty, and have thus been stimulated to believe that the world is incapable of significant transformation. Their genuine spiritual realization lends credence to a limited belief about human possibility and supports their cultivation of just some of the traits and virtues required for integral development. To come full circle on this, we can even imagine the idea of the integral, of fully balanced practice, becoming rigid and dogmatic. There are obviously geniuses of the mind who, without fully developing the body, have made great contributions. The same is true in other aspects of our being. And there are obviously times in the lives of all of us when we have stressed one part of our development at the expense of others for a good cause with good results. We strongly believe in the ancient celebration of the whole person and feel that integral practice generally provides the smoothest journey on the path of transformation. But we feel it's even more important to allow for benign human eccentricity and to avoid dogma, whatever form it takes.

Metanormal experience can produce ego inflation. Every sacred tradition warns against grandiosity following illumination. The enormous energies released by encounters with higher powers can cause imbalance in someone who lacks self-awareness. Even spiritual teachers aren't immune to this problem; witness the tragedies of contemporary religious communities such as Rajneeshpuram, which was led into various excesses by the excesses of its founder Rajneesh. Among the safeguards against such inflation are the monitoring of practioners by mentors and friends; the monitoring of mentors by fellow mentors and the community of practice; the celebration of humor in transformative practice; the cultivation of self-understanding; and reminders about the dangers of spiritual grandiosity drawn from religion and modern psychology. Contact with ego-surpassing powers isn't all goodness and light. If we are not balanced and centered, it can cause mental and emotional instability. If we lack healthy relationships, it can foster excessive withdrawal from others. If it fires our passion for perfection, it can contribute to unhealthy obsessions with diet, physical exercise, and cleanliness.

Such difficulties are sometimes loosely characterized as features or products of the human "shadow." This term, as it is commonly used today, was made famous by the psychiatrist Carl Jung and refers in a catch-all way to the unexamined darkness of human nature. The shadow harbors great energies and impulses that can express themselves in negative ways but also, if acknowledged and integrated, can serve as rich sources of creative power. We conclude this chapter by invoking the metaphor the shadow contains. There are dark places to cross in the journey of transformation, but they might contain priceless treasures. When you come to them, stay centered, stay aware, stay in touch with those who support you. Above all, stay on the path.

ADVENTURES IN EVOLUTION

If we have bent over backward in stressing the possible difficulties of transformative practice, it's simply due to our strong feelings about the epidemic of self-help books that promise easy learning, instant enlightenment, total fitness in a few minutes a week, executive wisdom in a minute. But we would be less than forthcoming if we failed to tell you about some of the joys that come through practice.

First, a surprise: If you begin practicing fully and wholeheartedly, you're likely to feel better, much better, in as little as two or three weeks. Make no mistake, this isn't a permanent change; only long-term practice can bring that. Nor will this first flush of joy come to you nearly so soon should you try to ease your way into the practice. The way you eat provides a clear example. If you make gradual changes in your diet, you'll feel deprived without gaining the benefits of good nutrition. If you go all the way right from the beginning, however, you might still feel deprived, but you'll enjoy that sparkling sense of aliveness that comes from eating fresh vegetables, fruits, and carbohydrates with full awareness—and you'll get over the feeling of deprivation and start liking the new diet more quickly than otherwise would be the case. The same thing is true of the rest of your practice. Dedicating yourself wholeheartedly to all of your commitments, whatever your level of expertise, gives you an early taste of the joys of practice. In a culture that relentlessly distracts us with "entertainment" and mere busy-ness, the very reliability and regularity—the discipline—can lend stability, purposefulness, and a deep inner satisfaction to your life.

That's only the beginning. As the weeks and months pass and you overcome your resistance to changing for the better, your practice becomes both easier and richer. Possibilities not dreamed of come into focus. As your senses become keener, your thoughts clearer, you may realize that your evolutionary journey has already begun. Your daily practice, your meditation and imaging, your readings, and your interactions with fellow practitioners have made the world a more fascinating place. You find that sometimes you can apprehend the subtle energy that streams from tree to tree in a forest or from person to person in a crowded room. There is a singing in the swaying of boughs on a breezy day, and all the natural world begins to glow with new and vivid colors. Your empathy for others has increased. As never before, you share thoughts and feelings with friends and lovers—an artful intimacy. More and more, you perceive all of existence as closely joined.

At times, you are amazed at your vitality. For the most part, you need less sleep than before and work more easily and efficiently, flowing from one task to another with little effort. In sports and martial arts, you often find you can anticipate the moves of a competitor, as if you are dancing, moving together. Even something as simple as walking—the turning of your joints, the soft rush of air on your face and hands—brings unanticipated pleasure. You experiment with certain alterations of muscle, bone, and blood and discover your body to be not as obdurate as you might have imagined. You still get occasional head colds and other ills of our species but are amazed at your healing powers.

You may find it significant that the adventures you are engaged in, unlike many other adventures (those, for example, that involve long-distance, high-speed travel and the intrusion into remote locales and cultures), don't poison the biosphere, damage the environment, or exploit other people. And there is no foreseeable end to these explorations.

We can invent things never before seen, ask questions never before asked, and seek answers from out beyond the stars. Unlike computers, we can fall in love.

G. L.

A Renewed Sense of Aliveness, A Love that Asks Nothing in Return

Life has one ultimate message: "Yes!" repeated in infinite number and variety.

G. L.

Throughout our practice, we have taken care to remind ourselves of the stupendous miracle of existence, the ultimate value of every life. We have celebrated our connectedness with all living things and with the stuff of the inorganic world. We have viewed every step in the cosmic journey, from the birth of the universe to the ever-flowing present moment, as our genealogy, and have experienced ourselves as a part of, not apart from, all that we behold or ever could behold. Many who have practiced with us have found the aliveness that has come from our practice to be transformative in and of itself.

To awaken can be painful, for it opens us to a poignant awareness of the pervasive waste of life around us and in us. But the eventual rewards are great. We no longer need horrors to jolt us awake. To see a sunrise is enough. To look into a friend's or lover's eyes, to truly *see* another human being, is enough. To hear a distant strain of music, or a child's laughter, is enough. With this awakening, this renewed aliveness, there generally comes a love for others, a love that asks nothing in return. Such love doesn't imply the denial of evil; the world is a dangerous place and awakening also means being aware of those dangers and standing ready to take centered action to confront wrong when necessary. But the ego-transcending love remains, and it spreads in concentric circles like ripples on a pond, kindling similar feelings in more of those it touches than we might imagine.

There are many powerful forces in the world, and some of them—cynicism, greed, ethnic hatred, heedless ambition, armies, and huge, impersonal organizations, to name a few— have a particular power to destroy. But a love that asks nothing in return is perhaps even more powerful, for it seeks to create, not destroy. Only a long series of close calls has given us this life. Again and again, over aeons of time, often against long odds, Eros has finally won the day. Are we willing to consider the possibility of a society in which love prevails?

The Divine Potential of the Species

We believe that by the very nature of things, each of us carries a spark of divinity in every cell and that we have the potential to manifest powers of body, mind, heart, and soul beyond our present ability to imagine. We believe that a society could find no better primary intention, no more appropriate compass course for its programs and policies, than the realization of every citizen's positive potential. We mean the potential inherent in every aspect of our lives, from the most commonplace to the most extraordinary, the hidden capabilities that wait to be summoned forth, not just in the mind but also in the body, heart, and soul. Such a compass course might create clarity where there is now confusion and bring the human psyche into harmony with nature and the cosmos. At best, it could open the way to the ultimate adventure, during which much of what has been metanormal would become normal, and some who read these pages would be privileged to share the next stage in the world's unfolding splendor.

APPENDIX A

Further Resources for Practice

As this book goes to press, we are producing a new videotape, *The Tao of Practice,* and exploring the possibility of furthering the work described in this book through a Center for Transformative Practice.

In *The Tao of Practice* videotape, George Leonard offers detailed instruction on certain sections of the ITP Kata, then leads the viewer through a full Kata.

The kind of center we are considering might bear a superficial resemblance to a health club, in that it would be open from early morning to evening, seven days a week. It would have a staff of carefully chosen teachers, and would be available to people of all ages, with daily classes in meditation, mental imagery, volitional training, physical movement, strength and aerobic exercise, interpersonal relations, and other transformative disciplines.

Such a facility might also present seminars and lectures on topics related to personal and social transformation. Participants could choose from any of a number of programs, enjoying the option of designing their own practice, emphasizing the kinds of change they might desire. There could be special tracks for those who would like to make commitments and affirmations toward personal transformation. Intensive short-term programs could be offered people from out of town who wish to spend a week or two developing a personal

ITP program they can take home with them. Ideally, a center of this sort would promote the simultaneous pursuit of theory, practice, and research related to the development of the whole person. It would constitute a new kind of social institution, a learning organization for the body, mind, heart, and soul, designed for long-term transformation without cult or dogma.

For information on *The Tao of Practice* videotape or on our plans for the development of a center, write to ITP, P.O. Box 609, Mill Valley, CA 94942.

Statistical Summary: Cycle 93

Two questionnaires were filled out by participants during the 1993 Cycle. Results from the final questionnaire (November 20, 1993) were used for statistical anlaysis. Thirty participants finished the 1993 Cycle and completed the questionnaire.

The mean scores for progress made toward realizing affirmations, on a scale of from 0 to 10, are presented here, as compared with scores from the 1992 Cycle (standard deviations in parentheses):

	Cycle 92	Cycle 93
Affirmation 1	5.67 (3.00)	6.30 (3.16)
Affirmation 2[1]	4.30 (3.06)	-12.60% (11.28)
Affirmation 3	4.53 (2.76)	6.67 (3.20)
Affirmation 4	6.58 (2.32)	8.30 (1.26)
Average of affirmations	5.30 (1.53) (av. of all 4)	7.09 (1.65) (av. of 1, 3, and 4)

1 The scores for Affirmation 2 are not comparable. In 1992, Affirmation 2 was "exceptional" on a scale of 0 to 10. In 1993, it was percent change in body fat.

Selected items from the questionnaire of November 20, 1993, followed by mean scores (underlined) and standard deviations (italicized):

On average, how many times a week have you done the Kata since learning it? 3.95 *1.21*

How vivid and well focused is your induction and imaging during the Kata, on a scale of 0 to 10, with 0 being not vivid and focused at all and 10 being extremely vivid and completely focused? 6.50 *2.30*

On the average, how many minutes of aerobic exercise have you done per week since beginning this program? 243.53 minutes *121.37*

On the average, how many times a week have you done strength training over the last six months? 2.46 *1.83*

Over the last seven days, how conscious have you been of what you have eaten, on a scale of 0 to 10, with 0 being totally unconscious and 10 being totally conscious? 8.83 *1.51*

On a scale of 0 to 10, how would you rate the healthfulness of the diet you have followed over the last six months, especially in terms of avoiding a high fat content? 7.10 *2.63*

On a scale of 0 to 10, how well do you understand the theory behind Integral Transformative Practice and bodily transformation? 8.23 *1.74*

On a scale of 0 to 10, how faithfully have you completed your reading assignments? 6.73 *2.18*

On a scale of 0 to 10, how promptly and fully have you stayed current with teachers and fellow participants in letting them know any significant feelings and considerations that would affect your participation in the class? 8.17 *1.62*

On a scale of 0 to 10, how well satisfied are you with your relationship with the teachers of the ITP class? 8.47 *1.41*

. . . with your fellow participants? 8.40 *1.52*

. . . with your family? 7.60 *2.79*

. . . with your friends? 8.73 *1.17*

Overall, on a scale of 0 to 10, how successful do you feel you have been in following your commitments? 7.23 *1.81*

Absences during Cycle 93. <u>4.87</u> *2.80*

(From July 3, 1993, midterm questionnaire.) On a scale of 0 to 10, how confident are you that if you fulfill your commitments to the class you will realize your affirmations by November 20, 1993? <u>7.52</u> *1.70*

A computer analysis of the correlations between participants' answers to these questions and their success in achieving their affirmations shows statistically significant relationships as listed below. The questions are presented in condensed form. The symbol *r* stands for the correlation coefficient; the larger the *r* figure, the greater the correlation between the participants' answers and their success in achieving the affirmation. (A perfect correlation would be 1.0, but that would be practically impossible.) The *p* rating has to do with probability. The lower the *p* rating, the less probability that the correlation is due to chance. Any *p* rating of less than .05 is considered statistically significant. We are listing only the correlations that proved to be statistically significant.

Affirmation 1

How focused Kata imaging ($r=.381$, $p=.038$)
Strength training av. times/week last six months ($r=.379$, $p=.039$)
Faithfully completed reading ($r=.407$, $p=.026$)
How successful follow commitments ($r=.486$, $p=.006$)

Affirmation 2

(regarding percentage change in body fat)
Aerobic exercise minutes/week ($r=-.514$, $p=.004$)
Absences ($r=.437$, $p=.016$)

Affirmation 3

(metanormal)
No statistically significant correlations

Affirmation 4

(balanced, vital, and healthy)
How focused Kata imaging ($r=.492$, $p=.006$)
Aerobic exercise minutes/week ($r=.593$, $p=.0006$)
How conscious of what eaten ($r=.533$, $p=.002$)
Healthfulness of diet ($r=.541$, $p=.002$)
Understand theoretical underpinnings ($r=.392$, $p=.032$)

Staying current with significant feelings (r=.632, p=.0002)
Satisfied relationships with participants (r=.402, p=.028)
Satisfied relationships with friends (r=.521, p=.003)
How successful follow commitments (r=.420, p=.021)

Average of Affirmations 1, 3, and 4

How focused Kata imaging (r=.395, p=.031)
How conscious of what eaten (r=.386, p=.035)
How successful follow commitments (r=.401, p=.028)

In considering these figures, bear in mind that correlation does not prove a casual relationship. In other words, a p of .028 doesn't mean that successfully following commitments had a rather good probability of *causing* participants to successfully realize Affirmations 1, 3, and 4. Cause might well be involved, but all that is proved here is a statistically significant *relationship* between successfully following commitments and realizing Affirmations 1, 3, and 4 as averaged.

This study involves certain limitations. The participants do not represent a random sample but were selected from applicants who were willing and able to pay $85 a month for the program. Nor was there a control group against which to compare results. Also bear in mind that while some answers to the questionnaires and rating of success in achieving affirmations were based on objective data, others were subjective. As stated in chapter 2, the teachers spent much time preparing participants to rate nonobjective affirmations with total integrity, avoiding either positive or negative bias. Comparing the participants' ratings against our own observations, we concluded that they were as reliable as any self-ratings could be. Despite the limitations, we believe the above correlations and probabilities can be helpful in suggesting certain tendencies that emerge from this practice.

The Authors' Comments on the Statistical Relationship Between Adherence to the Program and Success in Achieving Affirmations

In these comments, we use the condensed form of the items on the participant questionnaire. The full versions are carried near the beginning of this appendix.

We anticipated a connection between participants' adherence to the program and their success in realizing their affirmations. This relationship showed up in the correlation between "How successful follow commitments" and Affirmations 1 and 4, as well as the average of Affirmations 1, 3, and 4. In the 1992 Cycle, the number of times a week participants did the ITP Kata (which we consider a good marker of adherence) showed up as statistically significant as related to success in achieving Affirmation 4 and the average of all affirmations. In the 1993 Cycle, however, "Kata times per week" did not show up as statistically significant in relation to any affirmation.

Participants' consciousness, awareness, and powers of focused attention—all of which might go under the headings of "mind" and "soul"—proved especially significant in this study. Note that "How focused Kata imaging" showed up as statistically significant as related to success in achieving Affirmations 1, 4, and the average of 1, 3 and 4, while the number of times a week participants performed the Kata did not appear. "How conscious of what eaten" showed up in relation to Affirmation 4 and in the average of Affirmations 1, 3, and 4, while "Healthfulness of diet" showed up only in relation to Affirmation 4. The only three items that showed statistically significant relationships to success in achieving Affirmations 1, 3, and 4 as averaged were "How focused Kata imaging," "How conscious of what eaten," and "How successful follow commitments."

Affirmation 2 involved a purely objective measure, the percentage of reduction of body fat. An experienced exercise physiologist took caliper skin-fold measurements on March 27, 1993, then again on November 13, 1993, to determine the changes for each individual and as an average for the thirty participants. The average turned out to be a loss of 12.60 percent. The only items that related in a statistically significant way to success in achieving this loss of percentage of body fat were "Aerobic exercise minutes/week" and attendance at the Saturday morning class.

We are impressed by the strong correlation between aerobic exercise and loss of body fat and somewhat surprised by the lack of statistically significant relationships between this loss and both strength training and diet. Six participants and three teachers engaged in regular programs of strength training at a health club during 1993, and all of them showed significant losses in percentage of body fat. Certain participants adopted very-low-fat diets (see chapter 10), and they, too, showed significant body fat loss. The lack of statistically significant correlations involving these factors does not negate their importance. The strong correlation involving aerobic exercise might be at least partially accounted for by the fact that while ITP participants were committed to only three hours a week of aerobics, they averaged over four hours a week, creating a wide range of scores, which might make statistical significance easier to come by. Still, there is no question that regular aerobic exercise is an important factor, perhaps the most important factor, in a healthy reduction of body fat.

We see the correlation between number of absences and success in reducing body fat (an average loss of 12.6 percent body fat) as another suggestion of the importance of adherence to the program. Note that the correlation between body fat and absences is significantly positive in that when absences go up, body fat goes up (r=.437, p=.016). However the correlation between aerobic exercise and body fat is significantly negative, in that when exercise goes up, body fat goes down (r=-.514, p=.004).

Even though participants reported an average success of 6.67 on a scale of 0 to 10 in achieving Affirmation 3, there are no statistically significant correlations that involve this affirmation except as it figures in the average of Affirmations 1, 3, and 4. Perhaps the subjective nature of many of these affirmations made them hard to rate accurately. But this, we believe, is only part of the story. Our experience has shown us that when we deal with the realm of the metanormal, we sometimes encounter steep and unexpected inflections in the learning curve. Some of the changes simply defy analysis, and we must at least consider the possibility of grace, of extraordinary capacities that come to us as freely given rather than earned, spontaneously revealed rather than attained. Anomalies appear even with the purely objective Affirmation 2. Take the case, for example, of the participant who showed a 24.3 percent loss in body fat along with a 5.5 pound gain in lean body mass despite the fact that he changed his physical regimen not at all during the 1993 Cycle and adopted a diet high in fat two months before the second calipers measurement. We can speculate that there will always be mysteries beyond the reach of analysis. At the same time, we believe we can profit by studying these mysteries, searching for lawfulness in their operations.

We consider this statistical study preliminary and intend to refine our methods for defining and understanding what might be referred to as grace. We urge others to join in this search. We continue to assume that, as Ramakrishna said, "The winds of grace are always blowing. But we have to raise our sails." We continue to believe that a long-term integral, transformative practice is the best way to raise our sails.

In this regard, the correlations with Affirmation 4 are most encouraging. These correlations, in effect, draw a fairly complete profile of a long-term transformative practice, one that integrates body, mind, heart, and soul. "How focused Kata imaging" involves the mind and the soul, as does "How conscious of what eaten." Aerobic exercise and healthfulness of diet involve the body. "Understand theoretical underpinnings" brings the mind into play. Staying current with feelings and having satisfying personal relationships implicates the heart. And successfully following commitments speaks to a dedication to long-term practice itself, the measure of any successful, lasting transformation.

Selected Readings

Every one of the books listed here relates in some way to the ideas and practices we have discussed. Some were written for a popular audience; others are more difficult. Some are historically important in the development of thinking about human nature, the world, and the divine, while others will eventually be replaced by more up-to-date accounts of particular discoveries, theories, or fields of inquiry. A few are currently out of print but can be found in libraries as well as stores that sell used books. All of them, we believe, will broaden your understanding of the principles supporting Integral Transformative Practice.

We recommend that you follow your own first interests in approaching this list. One book will suggest another, so you can begin with any one of them and go on to others. Many have useful bibliographies.

Sri Aurobindo. *The Life Divine*. The Sri Aurobindo Ashram, Pondicherry, India, 1981. This is the main philosophic work of the Indian philosopher noted in the preface and in chapters 1 and 12. In it, the "involution-evolution" perspective is presented with great richness and scope.

Philosophy

Frederick Copleston. *A History of Philosophy* (three volumes). Doubleday Image Books, 1985. An authoritative, widely acclaimed reference work on Western philosophy from the pre-Socratics to Sartre.

The Encyclopedia of Philosophy (four volumes). Macmillan Reprint Edition, 1972. Essays on a huge range of philosophies, ideas, and philosophers by leading authorities on the subjects addressed.

David Ray Griffin. *God and Religion in the Postmodern World.* State University of New York Press, 1989. This book includes a lucid description of Alfred North Whitehead's central philosophic ideas, which resonate strongly with the "involution-evolution" perspective.

Satprem. *Sri Aurobindo, or the Adventure of Consciousness.* India Library Society, 1964. An account of Sri Aurobindo's spiritual life, with vivid descriptions of the philosopher's metanormal experiences.

Ken Wilber. *Sex, Ecology, Spirituality: The Spirit of Evolution.* Shambhala Publications Inc., 1995. A sweeping review and critique of scientific, religious, and philosophic visions regarding universal and human evolution.

The History of Religious Thought and Practice

Karen Armstrong. *The History of God: The Four-Thousand Year Quest of Judaism, Christianity, and Islam.* Alfred A. Knopf Inc., 1993.

Huston Smith. *The World's Religions.* Harper/SanFrancisco, 1991. A lucid, authoritative introduction to the world's religions by one of the world's leading scholars of comparative religious studies.

Philip Novak. *The World's Wisdom.* Harper/SanFrancisco, 1994. A beautifully organized collection of sacred texts from Hinduism, Buddhism, Confucianism, Taoism, Judaism, Christianity, Islam, and the primal religions.

Larry Dossey, M.D. *Healing Words.* Harper San Francisco, 1993. A survey of studies on the power of prayer, with insightful commentary by a pioneer in the interface between the scientific and the spiritual.

Hoyt L. Edge, Robert L. Morris, John Palmer, and Joseph H. Rush. *Foundations of Parapsychology: Exploring the Boundaries of Human Capability.* Routledge & Kegan Paul, 1986. A highly authoritative and comprehensive review of parapsychology and psychical research.

Caryle Hirshberg and Marc Ian Barasch. *Remarkable Recovery.* Riverhead Books, 1995. A well-informed, well-written report on the extraordinary transformations involved in what medical science calls "spontaneous remission."

William James. *Essays in Psychical Research.* Harvard University Press, 1986. These still-illuminating essays in many cases go beyond the standard thinking in contemporary parapsychology.

William James. *The Varieties of Religious Experience.* Random House Inc., 1902 and 1993. A comparative study of religious experience by America's most prominent psychologist-philosopher. James combines a deep appreciation of religious experience with critical distance from theological and philosophic interpretations of them. His approach, like that of Frederic Myers and Abraham Maslow (see below), constitutes a "natural history" of extraordinary functioning and exemplifies the open-minded but discriminating attitude we need in order to understand the complexities of integral transformation.

Abraham Maslow. *Toward a Psychology of Being.* Second Edition. Van Nostrand, 1968. *The Farther Reaches of Human Nature.* Viking Compass, 1971. Two collections of essays about our possibilities for further development. Maslow was a founder of humanistic and transpersonal psychology, and, like William James, helped broaden psychology's embrace of extraordinary human functioning.

Frederic Myers. *Human Personality, and Its Survival of Bodily Death.* Longmans, Green, 1903 and 1954. A comprehensive, richly detailed account of pathological, normal, and metanormal phenom-

Studies of Metanormal Experience

ena that reveal latent powers of mind and body. Myers invented the word "telepathy," was a principal founder of psychical research, and strongly influenced William James, Carl Jung, and other leading students of human nature. For further information about paranormal phenomena, see Edmund Gurney: *Phantasms of the Living,* Scholars' Facsimiles & Reprints, 1970. Gurney was a colleague of Myers and a pioneer of psychical research.

Herbert Thurston, S. J. *The Physical Phenomena of Mysticism.* Burns Oates, 1952.

Cosmology

Paul Davies. *The Mind of God.* Simon & Schuster, 1992. A popular exploration of the mysteries inherent in the laws of mathematics and physics, by a respected mathematical physicist.

George Greenstein. *The Symbiotic Universe.* William Morrow & Co. Inc., 1988. A description of apparent coincidences in the development of the universe without which life would never have developed.

Michio Kaku. *Hyperspace: A Scientific Odyssey Through Parallel Universes, Time Warps, and the 10th Dimension.* Oxford University Press, 1994. An illuminating primer on physical theory, culminating in speculations on higher-dimensional space–time concepts that might someday unify all of nature's fundamental forces into one comprehensive theory.

Joseph Silk. *The Big Bang* (revised edition). W. H. Freeman, and Co. 1989. An account of standard thinking about the universe's birth and early origins.

Evolutionary Theory

David Deamer and Gail Fleischauer. *Origins of Life: The Central Concepts.* Jones & Bartlett Publishers Inc., 1994. A comprehensive review of research discoveries and current theory regarding life's origins.

Monroe Strickberger (editor). *Evolution.* Jones & Bartlett Publishers Inc., 1990. A good overview of the progression of our scientific understanding of life's evolution on earth.

Jonathon Weiner. *The Beak of the Finch.* Alfred A. Knopf Inc., 1994. A delightful book showing that, under certain conditions, biological evolution can move much faster than Darwin—or anyone else—believed possible.

Peter Farb. *Humankind.* Houghton Mifflin Co., 1978. A wide-ranging popular account of discoveries in modern anthropology.

Robert Jurmain, Harry Nelson, and Williams A. Turnbaugh. *Understanding Physical Anthropology and Archeology.* West Publishing Co., 1987. A standard college text that combines physical anthropology with archeology.

Roger Lewin. *In the Age of Mankind.* Smithsonian Institution Press, 1988. A Smithsonian book of human evolution in a beautifully illustrated coffee-table format.

Anthropology and Pre-Civilized Human History

J. Benthall and Ted Polhemus (editors). *The Body As a Medium of Expression.* Allen, Lane & Dutton, 1975. Ted Polhemus (editor). *The Body Reader: Social Aspects of the Human Body.* Pantheon Books, 1978. Collections of essays about the interplay of cultural norms, institutions, and bodily functioning. These essays reveal the pervasiveness of social influences on our carriage, gestures, facial expressions, body image, somatic structure, health, and exercise patterns.

Pierre Bourdieu: *Distinction: A Social Critique of the Judgement of Taste.* Harvard University Press, 1984. Studies of cultural influences (primarily French) on fashion, lifestyle, class tastes, body image, status, sense of entitlement, permitted pleasures, and other aspects of human life.

Sociological and Anthropological Studies of Culture's Influence on Individual Development

Mary Douglas. *Purity and Danger: An Analysis of Concepts of Pollution and Taboo.* Penguin Books, 1970. Case-studies and analyses of society's influence on our concepts of cleanliness, dirtiness, and acceptable physical activity. Douglas helped pioneer the study of the body's cultural shaping.

Stephen Katz (editor). *Mysticism and Philosophical Analysis.* Oxford University Press, 1978. Stephen Katz (editor). *Mysticism and Religious Traditions.* Oxford University Press, 1983. Essays arguing that our religious philosophies, which are culturally shaped, determine the kind of religious experience we have. Katz maintains that mystical experience, like all other human experience, is molded by our socially acquired beliefs.

General Health   William Evans, Ph.D., and Irwin H. Rosenberg, M.D. *Biomarkers.* Simon & Schuster, 1991. Ostensibly about controlling the ill effects of aging, this book makes powerful arguments for the benefits of aerobic and strength exercise at every stage of life.

Dean Ornish, M.D. *Dr. Dean Ornish's Program for Reversing Heart Disease.* Random House Inc., 1990. Designed as a guide to reversing or preventing heart disease, this landmark book also serves as a reliable guide to the general good health of mind, body, heart, and soul for everyone.

About the Authors

GEORGE LEONARD, a pioneer in the field of human potential, is author of ten books, including *The Transformation, Education and Ecstasy, The Ultimate Athlete,* and *Mastery.* During his seventeen years as senior editor for *Look* magazine, he won an unprecedented number of national awards for education writing, and during the 1980s produced annual *Ultimate Fitness* sections for *Esquire,* as well as numerous articles on a wide variety of subjects in such magazines as *Esquire, Harper's, Atlantic, New York, Saturday Review,* and *The Nation.*

Leonard holds a fourth-degree black belt in aikido, and is co-owner of a martial arts school in Mill Valley, California. He is founder of Leonard Energy Training (LET), a transformative practice inspired by aikido, which he has introduced to some 50,000 people in the U.S. and abroad. He is a past-president of the Association for Humanistic Psychology, and is currently vice-chairman of the Board of Esalen Institute.

MICHAEL MURPHY founded Esalen Institute (with Richard Price) in 1962 and helped start Esalen's Russian-American Exchange Program. Through this work, he helped create a new style of citizens' diplomacy that increased understanding between the two superpowers at a historic moment. Murphy currently serves as chairman of the Board of the Esalen Institute.

Murphy is the author of three novels, *Golf in the Kingdom, Jacob Atabet,* and *An End to Ordinary History,* in addition to two works of nonfiction, *In the Zone: Transcendent Experience in Sport* (co-authored with Rhea White), and *The Future of the Body.* A lifelong athlete, Murphy has been a dedicated senior runner since the early 1970s.

Discover More of Yourself
with Inner Work Books

The following Inner Work Books are part of a series that explores psyche and spirit through writing, visualization, ritual, and imagination.

The Artist's Way: A Spiritual Path to Higher Creativity   BY JULIA CAMERON

At a Journal Workshop (revised edition): *Writing to Access the Power of the Unconscious and Evoke Cretive Ability*   BY IRA PROGOFF, PH.D.

Ending the Struggle Against Yourself: A Workbook for Developing Deep Confidence and Self-Acceptance   BY STAN TAUBMAN, D.S.W.

The Family Patterns Workbook: Breaking Free of Your Past and Creating a Life of Your Own   BY CAROLYN FOSTER

Following Your Path: Using Myths, Symbols, and Images to Explore Your Inner Life   BY ALEXANDRA COLLINS DICKERMAN

The Inner Child Workbook: What to Do with Your Past When It Just Won't Go Away   BY CATHRYN TAYLOR, M.F.C.C.

A Journey Through Your Childhood: A Write-in Guide for Reliving Your Past, Clarifying Your Present, and Charting Your Future   BY CHRISTOPHER BIFFLE

Pain and Possibility: Writing Your Way Through Personal Crisis BY GABRIELE RICO

The Path of the Everyday Hero: Drawing on the Power of Myth to Meet Life's Most Important Challenges   BY LORNA CATFORD, PH.D., AND MICHAEL RAY, PH.D.

Personal Mythology: Using Ritual, Dreams, and Imagination to Discover Your Inner Story   BY DAVID FEINSTEIN, PH.D., AND STANLEY KRIPPNER, PH.D.

The Possible Human: A Course in Extending Your Physical, Mental, and Creative Abilities   BY JEAN HOUSTON

The Search for the Beloved: Journeys in Mythology and Sacred Psychology   BY JEAN HOUSTON

Smart Love: A Codependence Recovery Program Based on Relationship Addiction Support Groups   BY JODY HAYES

A Time to Heal Workbook: Stepping-stones to Recovery for Adult Children of Alcoholics   BY TIMMEN L. CERMAK, M.D., AND JACQUES RUTZKY, M.F.C.C.

True Partners: A Workbook for Building a Lasting Intimate Relationship   BY TINA B. TESSINA, PH.D., AND RILEY K. SMITH, M.A.

Your Mythic Journey: Finding Meaning in Your Life Through Writing and Storytelling   BY SAM KEEN AND ANNE VALLEY-FOX

To Order call 1-800-788-6262 or send your order to:
Jeremy P. Tarcher, Inc.
Mail Order Department
The Putnam Berkley Group, Inc.
P.O. Box 12289,
Newark, N.J. 07101-5289

For Canadian orders:
P.O. Box 2500, Postal Station 'A'
Toronto, Ontario, M5W 2X8

_____	The Artist's Way	0-87477-694-5	$12.95
_____	At a Journal Workshop	0-87477-638-4	$15.95
_____	Ending the Struggle Against Yourself	0-87477-763-1	$14.95
_____	The Family Patterns Workbook	0-87477-711-9	$13.95
_____	Following Your Path	0-87477-687-2	$14.95
_____	The Inner Child Workbook	0-87477-635-X	$12.95
_____	A Journey Through Your Childhood	0-87477-499-3	$12.95
_____	Pain and Possibility	0-87477-571-X	$12.95
_____	The Path of the Everyday Hero	0-87477-630-9	$13.95
_____	Personal Mythology	0-87477-484-5	$12.95
_____	The Possible Human	0-87477-218-4	$13.95
_____	The Search for the Beloved	0-87477-476-4	$13.95
_____	Smart Love	0-87477-472-1	$ 9.95
_____	A Time to Heal Workbook	0-87477-745-3	$14.95
_____	True Partners	0-87477-727-5	$13.95
_____	Your Mythic Journey	0-87477-543-4	$ 9.95

Subtotal $_____
Shipping and handling* $_____
Sales tax (CA, NJ, NY, PA, VA) $_____
Total amount due $_____

Payable in U.S. funds (no cash orders accepted). $15.00 minimum for credit card orders.

*Shipping and handling: $2.50 for one book, $0.75 for each additional book, not to exceed $6.25.

Enclosed is my ☐ check ☐ money order

Please charge my ☐ Visa ☐ MasterCard ☐ American Express

Card #_____ Expiration date _____

Signature as on credit card _____

Daytime phone number _____

Name _____

Address _____

City_____ State _____ Zip _____

Please allow six weeks for delivery. Prices subject to change without notice.

Source key IWB

What's New with This Edition

Teach Yourself ANSI C++ in 21 Days, Premier Edition, is a new edition of the international bestseller, *Teach Yourself C++ in 21 Days*. This Premier Edition offers more than just 21 days of learning ANSI/ISO C++.

Major changes throughout this edition have been made to reflect the latest ANSI/ISO C++ draft standard. In addition, seven new lessons, referred to as "Bonus Days," have been added to provide you with additional information for creating more sophisticated programs. The Bonus Day lessons are not required reading in order for you to learn to program in C++. As a matter of fact, on the very first day you will write a simple C++ program.

On Bonus Day 22, "Advanced C++ Features," you learn to use a collection of specialized ANSI C++ tools that many programmers don't even realize exist. These tools are not essential for every C++ programmer to know but are indispensable in many circumstances.

Bonus Day 23, "More About Streams," covers some of the more advanced streams programming techniques. After completing this lesson, you will have all you need to create new manipulators for the stream classes you learn to create on Day 16. You will also learn a great deal about other streams programming techniques that space would not allow us to cover on Day 16.

On Bonus Day 24, "Object-Oriented Design," you learn more about this important subject. Without object-oriented design techniques, C++ is "just another C" with few advantages over its predecessor. This lesson helps you think in a way that builds on the object-oriented design paradigm.

Bonus Days 25 and 26, "Data Structures" and "Simple Sorting and Searching Algorithms," respectively, introduce you to the inner sanctum of computer science. On these two days you learn how to solve several common categories of problems.

"Common Mistakes and Basic Debugging," on Bonus Day 27, is designed to help you avoid some of the common mistakes that many beginning programmers make. Not all errors can be avoided, but with this lesson you should more quickly recognize many errors by their categories and more quickly find their solutions.

The final day of the bonus week, "What's Next?," gives you some insight on where to turn when you run into a question that this book doesn't seem to answer. It also provides the resources you need to further improve your C++ programming skills.

teach
yourself
ANSI C++

in 21 days,
Premier Edition

teach yourself
ANSI C++
in 21 days, Premier Edition

Jesse Liberty
J. Mark Hord

PUBLISHING

201 West 103rd Street
Indianapolis, Indiana 46290

Copyright © 1996 by Sams Publishing

PREMIER EDITION

International Standard Book Number: 0-672-30887-6

Library of Congress Catalog Card Number: 95-72920

99 98 97 96   4   3   2   1

Interpretation of the printing code: the rightmost double-digit number is the year of the book's printing; the rightmost single-digit, the number of the book's printing. For example, a printing code of 96-1 shows that the first printing of the book occurred in 1996.

Composed in Agaramond and MCPdigital by Macmillan Computer Publishing

Printed in the United States of America

Publisher and President	Richard K. Swadley
Acquisitions Manager	Greg Wiegand
Development Manager	Dean Miller
Managing Editor	Cindy Morrow
Marketing Manager	Gregg Bushyeager

Acquisitions Editor
Bradley L. Jones

Development Editor
Anthony Amico

Production Editor
Ryan Rader

Copy Editors
Howard Jones
Marla Reece

Technical Reviewer
Justin Bell
John W. Charlesworth

Editorial Coordinator
Bill Whitmer

Technical Edit Coordinator
Lynette Quinn

Formatter
Frank Sinclair

Editorial Assistants
Sharon Cox
Andi Richter
Rhonda Tinch-Mize

Cover Designer
Tim Amrhein

Book Designer
Gary Adair

Copy Writer
Peter Fuller

Production Team Supervisor
Brad Chinn

Production
Mary Ann Abramson,
Mona Brown, Georgiana Briggs,
Michael Brummitt, Jeanne Clark,
Terri Edwards, George Hamlin,
Sonya Hart, Mike Henry,
Ayanna Lacey, Kevin Laseau,
Paula Lowell, Donna Martin,
Casey Price, Nancy Price,
Brian-Kent Proffitt, Beth Rago,
SA Springer, Tim Taylor,
Andrew Stone, Mark Walchle
Todd Wente, Colleen Williams

Overview

Contents

Acknowledgments

I would like to acknowledge the many people who contributed to this book, both directly and indirectly. First and foremost, Stacey and Robin Liberty, whose support, encouragement, and patience made it possible. Also, Mike Kraley, Ed Belove, and Patrick Johnson, who create an intellectual atmosphere at the Interchange Online Network, which makes it a gas to come to work every day, and the many, many developers at Ziff from whom I learned whatever it is I know about C++.

I must particularly acknowledge those who taught me how to program, Skip Gilbrech and David McCune, and those who taught me C++, including Steve Rogers and especially Steven Zagieboylo. Others who contributed directly or indirectly to this book include Scott Boag, David Bogartz, Gene Broadway, Drew and Al Carlson, Frank Childs, Jim Culbert, Fran Daniels, Thomas Dobbing, James Efstratiou, June Goldstein, Basha Goldstein-Weiss, Michael Griffin, David Heath, Eric Helliwell, Gisele and Ed Herlihy, Mushtaq Khalique, Matt Kingman, Steve Leland, Sangam Pant, Mike Rothman, Michael Smith, Frank Tino, Seth Weiss, Donovan White, Mark Woodbury, and Alan Zeitchek. Special thanks go to Wayne Wylupski and Steven Zagieboylo.

Programming is as much a business and creative experience as it is a technical one, and I must therefore acknowledge Tom Hottenstein, Jay Leve, David Rollert, David Shnaider, and Robert Spielvogel. I also want to thank the many people at Sams Publishing who worked so hard to create this book. If any of what I've written is especially clear, it is thanks to the editors.

Finally, I'd like to thank Mrs. Kalish, who taught my sixth-grade class how to do binary arithmetic in 1965, when neither she nor we knew why.

—*Jesse Liberty*

The first people that come to mind are my family. They've been there through thick and thin, shared my enthusiasm and bore the brunt of my frustrations. Praise God for their love and devotion.

Maggie, if I had to do it all again, I'd still say "I do." Timmy, you're everything I could ever want for a son; I'm very proud. Heather, thank you for your kindness and gentle spirit, and for always loving Daddy even when he was cranky. Alicia, though you are small, your love has always been big; you have been a wonderful daughter. Amber, thank you for your gift of joy and fun that helped me keep focus on the things that really matter.

—*J. Mark Hord*

About the Authors

Jesse Liberty

Jesse Liberty has been programming computers professionally for more than 11 years. He is a Software Architect at AT&T Interchange Online Network where he was a founding member of the Software Development Team. He is also president of The Liberty Group, Inc., and a former vice president of Citibank's Development Division. Jesse lives with his wife, Stacey, and his daughter, Robin, in the suburbs of Cambridge, Massachusetts. He can be reached via the Internet at jl@Ichange.com, or as jl on Interchange.

J. Mark Hord

J. Mark Hord is a C++ programmer for Musicam USA. He has worked in the computer industry since his first exposure while enlisted in the U.S. Navy submarine fleet. His experience spans both commercial and defense companies. Mark lives in New Jersey with his wife and four children.

At A Glance

As you prepare for your first week of learning how to program in ANSI C++, you will need a few things: a compiler, an editor, and this book. If you don't have a C++ compiler and an editor, you can still use this book, but you won't get as much out of it as you would if you were to do the exercises.

The best way to learn to program is by writing programs! At the end of each day you will find a quiz and some exercises. Be sure to take the time to answer all the questions and to evaluate your work as objectively as you can. The later lessons build on the lessons in the earlier lessons, so be sure you fully understand the material before moving on.

1

2

3

4

5

6

7

A Note to C Programmers

The material in the first five days will be familiar to you. Be sure to skim the material and to do the exercises, to make sure you are fully up to speed before going on to Day 6. If you have had some exposure to C++ but not object-oriented programming, you might want to skip ahead and skim through Bonus Days 23 and 24 after Day 5. If you're convinced that C++ is simply a "better C" and nothing else, then you'll miss the point altogether. To be a good C++ programmer, you have to break out of the design paradigm used in C programming and start thinking in objects.

Where You Are Going

The first week covers the material you need to get started with programming in general, and with C++ in particular. Day 1, "Getting Started" and Day 2, "The Parts of the Program," introduce you to the basic concepts of programming and program flow. On Day 3, "Variables and Constants," you learn about variables and constants and how to use data in your programs. On Day 4, "Expressions and Statements," you learn how programs branch, based on the data provided and the conditions encountered when the program is running. On Day 5, "Functions," you learn what functions are and how to use them, and on Day 6, "Basic Classes," you learn about classes and objects. Day 7, "More Program Flow," teaches more about program flow, and by the end of the first week, you will be writing real object-oriented programs.

Day 1

Getting Started

Welcome to *Teach Yourself ANSI C++ in 21 Days, Premier Edition*! Today you will get started on your way to becoming a proficient C++ programmer. You'll learn the following topics:

☐ Why C++ is the emerging standard in software development.

☐ The steps to develop a C++ program.

☐ How to enter, compile, and link your first working C++ program.

A Brief History of C++

Computer languages have undergone dramatic evolution since the first electronic computers were built to assist in telemetry calculations during World War II. Early on, programmers worked with the most primitive computer instructions, machine language. These instructions were represented by long strings of ones and zeros. Soon, assemblers were invented to map machine instructions to humanly readable and manageable mnemonics, such as ADD and MOV.

In time, higher-level languages evolved, such as BASIC and COBOL. These enabled people to work with something approximating words and sentences, such as `Let I = 100`. These instructions were translated back into machine language by interpreters and compilers. An interpreter translates a program as it reads it, turning the programmer's program instructions, or *code*, directly into actions. Compilers translate the code into an intermediary form. This step is called *compiling*, and produces an object file. The compiler then invokes a *linker*, which turns the object file into an executable program. Most modern compilers and linkers are designed to work together as a team, and the transition between the two is invisible to the programmer.

Because interpreters read the code as it is written and execute the code on the spot, they are easy for the programmer to work with. Compilers introduce the extra steps of compiling and linking the code, which are inconvenient, but they produce a program that runs faster. When a program is compiled, the time-consuming task of translating the source code into machine language has already been accomplished.

Another advantage of many compiled languages is that you can distribute the executable program to people who don't have the compiler. With an interpretive language, you must have the interpreter to run the program.

For many years, the principal goal of computer programmers was to write short pieces of code that would execute quickly. The program needed to be small because memory was expensive, and it needed to be fast because processing power was also expensive. As computers have become smaller, cheaper, and faster, and as the cost of memory has fallen, these priorities have changed. Today the cost of a programmer's time far outweighs the cost of most of the computers in use by businesses. Well-written, easy to maintain code is at a premium. "Easy to maintain" means that as business requirements change, the program can be extended and enhanced without great expense.

In the 1970s, some programmers at AT&T were working to develop tools that would make their jobs easier. One of the members of that team, Dennis Ritchie, created a new compiled language and called it *C*. C became popular partially because it provided low-level functionality, along with a high-level control structure. A computer language is said to be a *high-level* language if it hides the details of the computer architecture from the programmer and is referred to as a *low-level* language if it does not. Because C did not fit either category well, it became known as a *medium-level* language.

In the late 1980s, more and more computer scientists began to change the way they approached problems, and they began to realize that the languages they were using did not fit well with their new problem-solving paradigm. Yet, because C was so popular, many were unwilling to throw out all the old in order to start solving problems differently. Instead, new versions of C began to appear that were designed with the new paradigm as their measure. Bjarne Stroustrup at AT&T invented one of those new versions of the C language. Mr. Stroustrup's new C language became known as C++.

ANSI/ISO C++

Programming languages, much like human languages, tend to change with time and even diversify into various *dialects*. Programmers have to learn the local version of a particular language wherever they happen to work, only to have to learn a different version at the next job. Employers have to spend time training new programmers for the programming language eccentricities at their company. So it benefits many to strive to standardize computer languages and limit the extent of those differences. These concerns are part of the drive for a single programming language for the United States Department of Defense, which gave birth to the programming language, Ada.

Similar concerns caused a push for the ANSI C standard some years ago. Today, there is an international effort to standardize the C++ language between the American National Standards Institute (ANSI) and the International Standards Organization (ISO) committees. The purpose of this effort, in the words of the draft standard, is "to promote portability, reliability, maintainability, and efficient execution of C++ language programs on a variety of computing systems." Though the ANSI/ISO C++ standard is currently in draft form and not yet approved as final, future changes to the draft should be minor for the most part. In *Teach Yourself ANSI C++ in 21 Days* we attempt to document the C++ language as it is defined in the ANSI/ISO draft at the time of this writing.

WARNING

Because the ANSI/ISO standard is still in a state of change, compiler vendors have not fully implemented it in their products. Compilers implement the draft standard in varying degrees, so shop around. This means that there might be some programs in this book that you cannot use with your compiler.

You can obtain a copy of the latest ANSI/ISO C++ draft and other useful C++ information through the *C++ Virtual Library* World Wide Web (WWW) site at

```
http://info.desy.de/user/projects/C++.html
```

What Is a Program?

The word *program* is used in two ways: to describe individual instructions, or *source code*, created by the programmer; and to describe an entire piece of *executable* software. This distinction can cause enormous confusion, so we will try to distinguish between the source code on one hand, and the executable on the other.

NEW TERM A *program* can be defined either as a set of written instructions created by a programmer or as an executable piece of software.

Source code can be turned into an executable program in two ways: Interpreters translate the source code into computer instructions, and the computer acts on those instructions immediately. Alternatively, compilers translate source code into a program that you can run at a later time. Although interpreters are easier to work with, most serious programming is done with compilers because compiled code runs much faster. C++ is a compiled language.

Sophisticated Tools for Sophisticated Programming

The problems programmers are asked to solve have been changing. Twenty years ago, programs were created to manage large amounts of raw data. The people writing the code and the people using the program were all computer professionals. Today, computers are in use by far more people, and many know very little about how computers and programs work. These people are more interested in using computers to solve their business problems and don't want using the computer to get in the way of doing that.

Ironically, in order to become easier to use for this new audience, programs have become far more sophisticated. Gone are the days when users typed in cryptic commands at esoteric prompts, only to see a stream of raw data. Today's programs use sophisticated *user-friendly interfaces* involving multiple windows, menus, dialog boxes, and all the myriad metaphors with which we've all become familiar. The programs written to support this new approach are far more complex than those written just 10 years ago.

As programming requirements have changed, both languages and the techniques used for writing programs have evolved. Although the complete history is fascinating, the part that concerns us is the transformation from procedural programming to object-oriented programming.

Procedural, Structured, and Object-Oriented Programming

Until recently, programs were thought of as a series of procedures that acted upon data. A procedure, or *function*, was a set of specific computer instructions executed one after the other. The data was quite separate from the procedures, and the trick in programming was to keep track of which functions called which other functions, and what data was changed. It was considered good programming practice to isolate data and the functions or procedures that operated on them. To make sense of this potentially confusing situation, structured programming was created.

NEW TERM A computer *function* or *procedure* is a logical collection of instructions for performing one part of the problem being solved by the computer program. A program is the whole; a procedure or function is one part in that whole.

The principal idea behind structured programming is as simple as the idea of divide and conquer. A computer program can be thought of as consisting of a set of tasks. Any task that is too complex to be described simply is broken down into a set of smaller component tasks, until the tasks are sufficiently small and self-contained so that they can be easily understood.

As an example, computing the average salary of every employee of a company is a rather complex task. You can, however, break it down into these subtasks:

1. Find out what each person earns.
2. Count how many people you have.
3. Total all the salaries.
4. Divide the total by the number of people you have.

Totaling the salaries can, itself, be broken down into more simple tasks:

1. Get each employee's record.
2. Access the salary.
3. Add the salary to the running total.
4. Get the next employee's record.

In turn, obtaining each employee's record can be broken down into simpler steps as well:

1. Open the file of employees.
2. Find the employee's data in the file.
3. Read the data from disk.

Structured programming remains an enormously successful approach for dealing with complex problems. By the late 1980s, however, some of its deficiencies became all too clear.

First, the separation of data from the tasks that manipulate the data became harder and harder to comprehend and maintain. It is natural to think of your data (employee records, for example) and what you can do with your data (sort, edit, and so on) as related ideas.

Second, programmers often had difficulty structuring a program to solve a problem while solving the problem at the same time. It was a classic inability to see the forest for the trees. Instead of solving problems, they often spent their time reinventing new ways to fit the problem to the structure.

The way we are now using computers—with menus and buttons and windows—fosters a more interactive, *event-driven* approach to computer programming. Event-driven means that an event happens (the user presses a button or chooses from a menu), and the program must respond. Programs are becoming increasingly interactive, making it important to design for that kind of functionality.

NEW TERM Old-fashioned programs forced the user to proceed step-by-step through a series of screens. Modern *event-driven* programs present all the choices at once and respond to the user's actions.

Object-oriented programming attempts to respond to these needs, providing techniques for managing enormous complexity, achieving reuse of software components, and coupling data with the tasks that manipulate that data.

The essence of object-oriented programming is to treat data and the procedures that act upon the data as a single *object*—a self-contained entity with an identity and certain characteristics of its own.

C++ and Object-Oriented Programming

C++ fully supports object-oriented programming, including the four pillars of object-oriented development: *encapsulation, data hiding, inheritance,* and *polymorphism*.

Encapsulation and Data Hiding

Encapsulation and data hiding are object-oriented design techniques that programmers can use to make interchangeable software parts. The goal behind these techniques is to build self-contained objects that can be used as parts in a variety of programs. Now, instead of specialized functions and procedures that work on a narrow collection of data, we can build objects that can be used to build larger objects. To accomplish interchangeability, underlying data inside the object must be hidden so that it cannot be accidentally changed in an unexpected way. Another reason for data hiding is to allow programmers to use an object without needing to know all the details about how the object does what it does.

NEW TERM The property of being a self-contained unit is called *encapsulation*. The fact that the encapsulated unit can be used without regard to how it works is called *data hiding*.

When a radio enthusiast builds a radio and needs a volume control, she doesn't create a new volume control from scratch. Instead, she simply pulls a volume control from a shelf in her garage or at the local electronics store. All the properties of the control are encapsulated in the control object; they are not spread out through the circuits. It is not necessary to understand how the volume control works in order to use it effectively; its data is hidden inside its casing.

C++ supports the properties of encapsulation and data hiding through the creation of user-defined types, called *classes*. You'll see how to create classes on Day 6, "Basic Classes." After it is created, a well-defined class acts as a fully encapsulated entity. It is used as a whole unit. The actual inner workings of the class should be hidden; users of a well-defined class do not need to know how the class works. They just need to know how to use it.

Inheritance and Reuse

When the engineers at Acme Motors want to build a new car, they have two choices: They can start from scratch, or they can modify an existing model. Perhaps their Star model is nearly perfect, but they want to add a turbocharger and a six-speed transmission. The chief engineer would prefer not to start from the ground up, but rather to say, "Let's build another Star, but let's add these additional capabilities. We'll call the new model a Quasar." A Quasar is a kind of Star, but one with new features. A Quasar *inherits* all that a Star is and has additional features, as well.

As with other fields of engineering, software engineers have invented a name for the design technique of making new objects from old. They call this design technique *inheritance*. The initial object in this technique is called the *base* object, and the new object is called a *derived* object. The Quasar is derived from the Star, and thus inherits all its qualities, but it can add to them as needed. Inheritance and its application in C++ is discussed on Day 12, "Inheritance" and Day 15, "Advanced Inheritance."

NEW TERM *Inheritance*, in computer science, is the creation of new objects from other objects that are similar. The new object is said to *inherit* all that the original object contains.

The new Quasar might respond differently than a Star does when you press down on the accelerator. The Quasar might engage fuel injection and a turbocharger, while the Star would simply let gasoline into its carburetor. A user, however, does not have to know about these differences; she can just "floor it," and the right thing will happen depending on which car she's driving.

How C++ Evolved

Since Bjarne Stroustrup created C++ less than a decade ago, it has gone from being used by only a handful of developers at AT&T to being the programming language of choice for an estimated one million developers worldwide. It is expected that, by the end of the decade, C++ will be the predominant language for commercial software development.

Although it is true that C++ is a superset of C, and that virtually any legal C program is a legal C++ program, the leap from C to C++ is very significant. C++ benefited from its relationship to C for many years because C programmers could ease into their use of C++. To really get the full benefit of C++, however, many programmers found they had to unlearn much of what they knew and learn a whole new way of conceptualizing and solving programming problems.

Should I Learn C First?

The question inevitably arises: Because C++ is a superset of C, should you learn C first? Stroustrup and most other C++ programmers agree that not only is it unnecessary to learn C first, but it might be advantageous not to do so. This book attempts to meet the needs of people like you, who come to C++ without prior experience of C. In fact, this book assumes no programming experience of any kind.

Preparing to Program

C++, perhaps more than other languages, demands that the programmer design the program before writing it. Trivial problems, such as the ones discussed in the first few lessons of this book, don't require much design. However, complex problems, such as the ones professional programmers are challenged with every day, do require design; and the more thorough the design, the more likely it is that the program will solve the problems it is designed to solve, on time and on budget. A good design also makes for a program that is relatively bug-free and easy to maintain. It has been estimated that fully 90 percent of the cost of software is the combined cost of debugging and maintenance. To the extent that good design can reduce those costs, it can have a significant impact on the bottom-line cost of the project.

The first question you need to ask when preparing to design any program is, "What is the problem I'm trying to solve?" Every program should have a clear, well-articulated goal, and you'll find that even the simplest programs in this book do so.

The second question every good programmer asks is, "Can this be accomplished without resorting to writing custom software?" Reusing an old program, using pen and paper, or buying software off the shelf are often better solutions to a problem than writing something new. The programmer who can offer these alternatives will never suffer from lack of work; finding less expensive solutions to today's problems will always generate new opportunities later.

Assuming you understand the problem, and it requires writing a new program, you are ready to begin your design.

Your Development Environment

This book makes the assumption that your computer has a mode in which you can write directly to the screen, without worrying about a graphical environment such as the ones in Windows or on the Macintosh.

Your compiler might have its own built-in text editor, or you might be using a commercial text editor or word processor that can produce text files. The important thing is that whatever you write your program in, it must save simple, plain-text files with no word processing commands embedded in the text. Examples of safe editors include the Windows Notepad, the DOS Edit command, Brief, Epsilon, EMACS, and vi. Many commercial word processors, such as WordPerfect, Word, and dozens of others, also offer a method for saving simple text files.

The files you create with your editor are called source files, and for C++, they typically are named with the extension .cpp, .cp, or .c. In this book, all source code files are named with the .cpp extension, but check your compiler documentation for what it needs.

NOTE   Most C++ compilers don't care what extension you give your source code, but if you don't specify otherwise, many will use .cpp by default.

Do   **Don't**

DO use a simple text editor to create your source code, or use the built-in editor that comes with your compiler.

DON'T use a word processor that saves special formatting characters. If you do use a word processor, save the file as ASCII text.

DO save your files with the .c, .cp, or .cpp extension.

DO check your documentation for specifics about your compiler and linker to ensure that you know how to compile and link your programs.

Compiling the Source Code

Although the source code in your file may seem cryptic in the beginning, and anyone who doesn't know C++ will struggle to understand what it is for, it is still in what is called *human-readable form*. Your source code file is not an executable program, so you cannot run it like you can your word processor program.

To turn your source code into an executable program, you use a compiler. How you invoke your compiler, and how you tell it where to find your source code, will vary from compiler to compiler; check your documentation.

After your source code is compiled, an object file is produced. This file is often named with the extension .obj. This is still not an executable program, however. To turn this into an executable program, you must run your linker.

Creating an Executable File with the Linker

C++ programs are typically created by linking one or more .obj files with one or more libraries. A *library* is a collection of linkable files that you created, that were supplied with your compiler, or that you purchased separately. All C++ compilers come with a library of useful functions—or procedures—and classes that you can include in your program. A function is a block of code that performs a service, such as adding two numbers or printing to the screen. A class is a collection of data and related functions; we'll be talking about classes a lot, starting on Day 5, "Functions." Libraries are the general-purpose, reusable objects you can use for building more specialized objects. We will be using an ANSI-defined standard set of libraries throughout this book.

NEW TERM   A *library* is a reusable collection of data and functions, typically entire object definitions, that you can use as interchangeable parts in your programs. They are not complete in themselves, and they may have additional parts in them that your program does not use. However, they are provided as general solutions to typical problems that programmers like you have needed to solve in the past.

The steps to create an executable file are as follows:

1. Create a source code file with a .cpp extension.
2. Compile the source code into a file with the .obj extension.
3. Link your .obj file with any needed libraries to produce an executable program.

The Development Cycle

If every program worked the first time you tried it, that would be the complete development cycle: Write the program, compile the source code, link the program, and run it. Unfortunately, almost every program—no matter how trivial—can and will have errors, or *bugs*, in it. Some bugs cause the compile to fail, some cause the link to fail, and some only show up when you run the program.

Whatever the type of bug you find, you must fix it. This involves editing your source code, recompiling and relinking, and then rerunning the program. This cycle is represented in Figure 1.1, which diagrams the steps in the development cycle.

Figure 1.1.

The steps in the development of a C++ program.

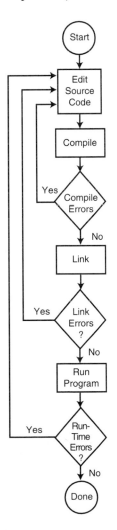

HELLO.CPP: Your First C++ Program

Traditional C programming books begin by writing the words Hello World to the screen, or a variation on that statement. This time-honored tradition is carried on here.

Type the first program directly into your editor, exactly as shown. When you are certain it is correct, save the file, compile it, link it, and run it. It will print the words Hello World to your screen. Don't worry too much about how it works; this is really just to get you comfortable with the development cycle. Every aspect of this program will be covered over the next couple of days.

WARNING

The listings in this book contain line numbers on the left. These numbers are for reference within the book. They should not be typed into your editor. For example, in line 1 of Listing 1.1, you should enter the following:

```
#include <iostream.h>
```

TYPE **Listing 1.1. HELLO.CPP, the Hello World program.**

```
1: #include <iostream.h>
2:
3: void main()
4: {
5:     cout << "Hello World!\n";
6: }
```

Make sure you enter this exactly as shown. The only typing liberty you should take right now is to enter any number of spaces or tabs you prefer before the cout on line 5. Pay careful attention to the special characters. The double less-than arrow symbol (<<) in line 5 is the *redirection symbol*, produced on most keyboards by holding the shift key and pressing the comma key twice. Line 5 ends with a semicolon; don't leave this off!

Also, check to make sure you are following your compiler directions properly. Most compilers link automatically, but check your documentation. If you get errors, look over your code carefully and determine how it is different from Listing 1.1. If you see an error on line 1, such as cannot find file iostream.h, check your compiler documentation for directions on setting up your include path or environment variables. If you receive an error that there is no prototype for main, add the line void main(); just before line 3. You need to add this line to every program in this book before the beginning of the main function. Most compilers don't require this, but a few do.

Your finished program should look like this:

```
1: #include <iostream.h>
2:
3: void main();
4: void main()
5: {
6:     cout <<"Hello World!\n";
7: }
```

Try running hello.exe; it should write the following directly to your screen:

```
Hello World!
```

If so, congratulations! You've just entered, compiled, and run your first C++ program. It might not look like much, but almost every professional C++ programmer started out with this exact program.

Compile Errors

Compile-time errors can occur for any number of reasons. Usually, they are a result of a typo or other inadvertent minor error. Good compilers not only tell you what you did wrong, but they point you to the exact place in your code where you made the mistake. The great ones even suggest a remedy!

You can see this demonstrated by intentionally putting an error into your program. If HELLO.CPP ran smoothly, edit it now and remove the closing brace on line 6. Your program will now look like Listing 1.2.

TYPE　　**Listing 1.2. Demonstration of compiler error.**

```
1: #include <iostream.h>
2:
3: void main()
4: {
5:     cout << "Hello World!\n";
6:
```

Recompile your program and you should see an error that looks similar to the following:

```
Hello.cpp, line 5: Compound statement missing terminating } in function main().
```

This error tells you the file and line number of the problem, and what the problem is (although I admit it is somewhat cryptic). Note that the error message points you to line 5. The compiler wasn't sure whether you intended to put the closing brace before or after the cout statement on line 5. Sometimes the errors just get you to the general vicinity of the problem. If a compiler could perfectly identify every problem, it would fix the code itself.

Summary

After reading this lesson, you should have a good understanding of how C++ evolved and what problems it was designed to solve. You should feel confident that learning C++ is the right choice for anyone interested in programming in the next decade. C++ provides the tools of object-oriented programming and the performance of a systems-level language, which make C++ the development language of choice.

Today you learned how to enter, compile, link, and run your first C++ program, and you learned what the common development cycle is. You also learned a little of what object-oriented programming is all about. You will return to these topics during the next three weeks.

Q&A

Q What is the difference between a text editor and a word processor?

A A text editor produces files with plain text in them. There are no formatting commands or other special symbols that are required by a particular word processor. Text files do not have automatic word wrap, bold print, italics, and so forth.

Q If my compiler has a built-in editor, must I use it?

A Almost all compilers compile code produced by any text editor. The advantages of using the built-in text editor, however, might include the capability to quickly move back and forth between the edit and compile steps of the development cycle. Sophisticated compilers include a fully integrated development environment, allowing the programmer to access help files, edit and compile the code in place, and resolve compile and link errors without ever leaving the environment.

Q Can I ignore warning messages from my compiler?

A Many books hedge on this one, but I'll stake myself to this position: No! Get into the habit, from day one, of treating warning messages as errors. C++ uses the compiler to warn you when you are doing something you might not intend; heed those warnings and do what is required to make them go away.

Q What is compile-time?

A Compile-time is the time when you run your compiler, as opposed to link-time (when you run the linker) or run-time (when you run the program). This is just programmer shorthand to identify the three times when errors usually surface.

Quiz

1. What is the difference between an interpreter and a compiler?
2. How do you compile the source code with your compiler?
3. What does the linker do?
4. What are the steps in the computer program development cycle?

Exercises

1. Look at the following program and try to guess what it does without running it.

```
1:   #include <iostream.h>
2:   void main();// You may not need this line
3:   void main()
4:   {
5:       int x = 5;
6:       int y = 7;
7:       cout << "\n";
8:       cout << "x + y = " << x + y;
9:       cout << "\n";
10:  }
```

2. Type in the program from question one, compile it, and link it. What does it do? Is it what you guessed?

3. Type in the following program and compile it. What error do you receive?

```
1:   include <iostream.h>
2:   void main()
3:   {
4:       cout << "Hello World\n";
5:   }
```

4. Fix the error in the program in exercise 3, and recompile, link, and run it. What does it do?

Day **2**

The Parts of a C++ Program

C++ programs consist of objects, functions, variables, and other component parts. Most of this book is devoted to explaining these parts in depth, but to get a sense of how a program fits together, you must see a complete working program. Today you learn

☐ The parts of a C++ program.

☐ How the parts work together.

☐ What a function is and what it does.

The Parts of a Simple Program

Even the simple program HELLO.CPP from Day 1 had many interesting parts. This section reviews this program in more detail. Listing 2.1 reproduces the original version of HELLO.CPP for your convenience.

Type **Listing 2.1. HELLO.CPP demonstrates the parts of a C++ program.**

```
1: #include <iostream.h>
2:
3: void main()
4: {
5:     cout << "Hello World!\n";
6: }
```

Output   Hello World!

Analysis   On line 1 the file iostream.h is included in the file. The first character is the pound sign or number symbol (#), which is a signal to the preprocessor. Each time you start your compiler, the preprocessor is run. The preprocessor reads through your source code looking for lines that begin with the pound symbol (#) and acts on those lines before the compiler runs.

include is a preprocessor instruction that says, "What follows is a filename; find that file and read it in right here." The angle brackets around the filename tell the preprocessor to look in all the usual places for this file. If your compiler is set up correctly, the angle brackets cause the preprocessor to look for the file iostream.h in the directory that holds all the .h files for your compiler. The file iostream.h (input-output-stream) is used by cout, which assists with writing to the screen. The effect of line 1 is to include the file iostream.h into this program, as if you had typed it in yourself.

New Term   The preprocessor runs before your compiler each time the compiler is invoked; it translates any line that begins with a pound symbol (#) into a special command, getting your code file ready for the compiler.

Line 3 begins the actual program with a function named main(). Every C++ program has a main() function. In general, a function is a block of code that performs one or more actions. Usually functions are invoked or called by other functions, but main() is special. When your program starts, main() is called automatically.

main(), like all functions, must state what kind of value it will return. The return value type for main() in HELLO.CPP is void, which means that this function will not return any value at all. Returning values from functions is discussed in detail on Day 4, "Expressions and Statements."

All functions begin with an opening brace ({) and end with a closing brace (}). The braces for the main() function are on lines 4 and 6. Everything between the opening and closing braces is considered a part of the function.

The meat and potatoes of this program are on line 5. The object cout is used to print a message to the screen. You'll learn about objects in general on Day 6, "Basic Classes," and cout and its related object cin in detail on Day 16, "Streams." These two objects, cout and cin, are used in C++ to print values to the screen.

Use cout in the following manner: Write the word cout followed by the output redirection operator (<<). Whatever follows the output redirection operator is written to the screen. If you want a string of characters to be written, be sure to enclose them in double quotes (") as shown on line 5.

NEW TERM A *text string* is a series of printable characters.

The final two characters, \n, tell cout to put a new line after the words Hello World! This special code is explained in detail when cout is discussed on Day 16.

The main() function ends on line 6 with the closing brace.

A Brief Look at *cout*

On Day 16, "Streams," you will see how to use cout for printing data to the screen. For now, you can use cout without fully understanding how it works. To print a value to the screen, write the word cout, followed by the insertion operator (<<), which you create by typing the less-than character (<) twice. Even though this is two characters, C++ treats it as one.

Follow the insertion character by your data. Listing 2.2 illustrates how this is used. Type in the example exactly as written, but substitute your own name where you see Jesse Liberty (unless your name *is* Jesse Liberty, in which case you can leave it the way it is; it's perfect—but I'm still not splitting royalties!).

TYPE **Listing 2.2. Using cout.**

```
1: // Listing 2.2 using cout
2:
3: #include <iostream.h>
4: void main()
5: {
6:     cout << "Hello there.\n";
7:     cout << "Here is 5: " << 5 << "\n";
8:     cout << "The manipulator endl writes a new line to the screen." << endl;
9:     cout << "Here is a very big number:\t" << 70000 << endl;
10:    cout << "Here is the sum of 8 and 5:\t" << 8+5 << endl;
11:    cout << "Here's a fraction:\t\t" << (float) 5/8 << endl;
12:    cout << "And a very very big number:\t" << (double) 7000 * 7000 << endl;
13:    cout << "Don't forget to replace Jesse Liberty with your name...\n";
14:    cout << "Jesse Liberty is a C++ programmer!\n";
15: }
```

```
Hello there.
Here is 5: 5
The manipulator endl writes a new line to the screen.
Here is a very big number:       70000
Here is the sum of 8 and 5:      13
Here's a fraction:               0.625
And a very very big number:      4.9e+07
Don't forget to replace Jesse Liberty with your name...
Jesse Liberty is a C++ programmer!
```

ANALYSIS On line 3 the statement `#include <iostream.h>` causes the iostream.h file to be added to your source code. This is required if you use `cout` and its related functions.

Line 6 is the simplest use of `cout`, printing a string or series of characters. The symbol `\n` is a special formatting character; it tells `cout` to print a new line character to the screen.

On line 7 three values are passed to `cout`, each separated by the insertion operator. The first value is the string `"Here is 5: "`. Note the space after the colon, which is part of the string. Next the value 5 is passed to the insertion operator, and then the newline character is passed (always in double quotes or single quotes). This causes the line

```
Here is 5: 5
```

to be printed to the screen. Because there is no new line character after the first string, the next value is printed immediately afterwards. This is called *concatenating* the two values.

On line 8 an informative message is printed, and then the *manipulator* `endl` is used. The purpose of `endl` is to write a new line to the screen. (Other uses for `endl` are discussed on Day 16).

On line 9 a new formatting character, `\t`, is introduced. This inserts a tab character and is used on lines 8 through 12 to line up the output. Line 9 shows that not only integers but also long integers can be printed. Line 10 demonstrates that `cout` can do simple addition; the value 8+5 is passed to `cout` but 13 is printed.

On line 11 the value 5/8 is inserted into `cout`. The term `(float)` tells `cout` that you want this value evaluated as a fraction, so a fraction is printed. On line 12 the value 7000 * 7000 is given to `cout`, and the term `(double)` is used to tell `cout` that you want this to be printed using *scientific notation*. All of this will be explained tomorrow when data types are discussed on Day 3, "Variables and Constants."

On line 14 you substituted your name, and the output confirmed that you are indeed a C++ programmer. It must be true if the computer said so!

Comments

When you are writing a program, it is always clear and self-evident what you are trying to do. Funny thing, though—a month later, when you return to the program, it can be quite confusing and unclear. I'm not sure how that confusion creeps into your program, but it's always there.

To fight the onset of confusion and to help others to understand your code, you should use comments. Comments are simply text that is ignored by the compiler but informs the reader of what you are doing at any particular point in your program.

Types of Comments

C++ comments come in two flavors. The double-slash (//) comment, which will be referred to as a *C++-style comment*, tells the compiler to ignore everything that follows this until the end of the line.

The slash-star (/*) comment mark tells the compiler to ignore everything that follows until it finds a star-slash (*/) comment mark. These marks are referred to as *C-style comments*. Every /* must be matched with a closing */.

As you might guess, C-style comments are used in the C language as well, but C++-style comments are not part of the official definition of C.

Many C++ programmers use the C++-style comment most of the time, and reserve C-style comments for blocking out large pieces of a program. You can include C++-style comments within a block that is "commented out" by C-style comments; everything, including the C++-style comments, is ignored between the comment marks.

Using Comments

As a general rule, the overall program should have comments at the beginning, telling you what the program does. Each function should also have comments explaining what the function does and what values it returns. Finally, any statement in your program that is obscure or less than obvious should be commented as well.

Listing 2.3 demonstrates the use of comments, showing that they do not affect the processing of the program or its output.

TYPE   **Listing 2.3. HELP.CPP demonstrates comments.**

```
1: #include <iostream.h>
2:
3: void main()
4: {
5:   /* this is a comment
6:   and it extends until the closing
7:   star-slash comment mark */
```

continues

Listing 2.3. continued

```
8:    cout << "Hello World!\n";
9:    // this comment ends at the end of this line
10:   cout << "That comment ended!";
11:
12:  // double slash comments can be alone on a line
13: /* as can slash-star comments */
14: }
```

 OUTPUT
```
Hello World!
That comment ended!
```

ANALYSIS The comments on lines 5 through 7 are completely ignored by the compiler, as are the comments on lines 9, 12, and 13. The comment on line 9 ended with the end of the line, however; while the comments on lines 5 and 13 required a closing comment mark.

Comments at the Top of Each File

It is a good idea to put a comment block at the top of every file you write. The exact style of this block of comments is a matter of individual taste, but every such header should include at least the following information:

☐ The name of the function or program.

☐ The name of the file.

☐ What the function or program does.

☐ A description of how the program works.

☐ The author's name.

☐ A revision history (notes on each change made).

☐ What compilers, linkers, and other tools were used to make this program.

☐ Additional notes as needed.

For example, the following block of comments might appear at the top of the Hello World program.

```
/************************************************************
Program:      Hello World

File:         Hello.cpp

Function:     Main (complete program listing in this file)

Description:  Prints the words "Hello world" to the screen
```

```
Author:       Jesse Liberty (jl)

Environment:  ANSI C++ Compiler (also compiler and
              operating system specifics should be
              included here)

Notes:        This is an introductory, sample program.

Revisions:    1.00  1/15/95 (jl) First release
              1.01  1/17/95 (jl) Capitalized "World"

*****************************************************************/
```

It is very important that you keep the notes and descriptions up to date. A common problem with headers like this is that they are neglected after their initial creation, and over time they become increasingly misleading. Properly maintained, however, they can be an invaluable guide to the overall program.

The listings in the rest of this book leave off the headings in an attempt to save room. That does not diminish their importance, however; so they will appear in the programs provided at the end of each week. Also, the portion of the comments where I simply have ANSI C++ should contain any specific information about the compiler and operating system under which you developed the code.

A Final Word of Caution About Comments

Comments that state the obvious are less than useful. In fact, they can be counterproductive because the code might change and the programmer might neglect to update the comment. What is obvious to one person can be obscure to another, however; so judgment is required.

The bottom line is that comments should not say *what* is happening; they should say *why* it is happening.

Do	Don't

DO add comments to your code.

DO keep comments up to date.

DO use comments to tell what a section of code does.

DON'T use comments for self-explanatory code.

Functions

Although `main()` is a function, it is an unusual one. Typical functions are called, or *invoked*, during the course of your program. A program is executed line by line, in the order it appears in your source code, until a function is reached. Then the program branches off to execute the function. When the function finishes, it returns control to the line of code immediately following the call to the function.

A good analogy for this is sharpening your pencil. If you are drawing a picture and your pencil breaks, you might stop drawing, go sharpen the pencil, and then return to what you were doing. When a program needs a service performed, it can call a function to perform the service, and then pick up where it was when the function is finished. Listing 2.4 demonstrates this idea.

 Listing 2.4. Demonstrating a call to a function.

```
1:      #include <iostream.h>
2:
3:      // function Demonstration Function
4:      // prints out a useful message
5:      void DemonstrationFunction()
6:      {
7:          cout << "In Demonstration Function\n";
8:      }
9:
10:     // function main - prints out a message, then
11:     // calls DemonstrationFunction, then prints out
12:     // a second message.
13:     void main()
14:     {
15:         cout << "In main\n" ;
16:         DemonstrationFunction();
17:         cout << "Back in main\n";
18:     }
```

```
In main
In Demonstration Function
Back in main
```

ANALYSIS The function `DemonstrationFunction()` is defined on lines 3 through 5. When it is called, it prints a message to the screen and then returns.

2

Line 8 is the beginning of the actual program. On line 10, `main()` prints out a message saying it is in `main()`. After printing the message, line 11 calls `DemonstrationFunction()`. This call causes the commands in `DemonstrationFunction()` to execute. In this case, the entire function consists of the code on line 7, which prints another message. When `DemonstrationFunction()` completes (line 8), it returns to where it was called from. In this case, the program returns to line 17, where `main()` prints its final line.

Using Functions

Functions either return a value, or they return void, meaning they return nothing. A function that adds two integers might return the sum, and thus would be defined to return an integer value. A function that just prints a message has nothing to return and would be declared to return void.

Functions consist of a header and a body. The header consists, in turn, of the return type, the function name, and the parameters to that function. The parameters to a function allow values to be passed into the function. Thus, if the function were to add two numbers, the numbers would be the parameters to the function. The following line is a typical function header:

```
int Sum(int a, int b)
```

A parameter is a declaration of what type of value will be passed in. The actual value passed in by the calling function is called the *argument*. Many programmers use these two terms, *parameters* and *arguments*, as synonyms. Others are careful about the technical distinction. This book uses the terms interchangeably.

The body of a function consists of an opening brace, zero or more statements, and a closing brace. The statements constitute the work of the function. A function can return a value using a `return` statement. This statement also causes the function to exit. If you don't put a `return` statement into your function, it automatically returns void at the end of the function. The value returned must be of the type declared in the function header.

NOTE   Functions are covered in more detail on Day 5, "Functions." The types that can be returned from a function are covered in more detail on Day 3, "Variables and Constants." The information provided today is to present you with an overview because functions are used in almost all of your C++ programs.

Listing 2.5 demonstrates a function that takes two integer parameters and returns an integer value. Don't worry about the syntax or the specifics of how to work with integer values (for example `int x`) for now. That will be covered in detail on Day 3.

TYPE   **Listing 2.5. FUNC.CPP demonstrates a simple function.**

```
1:    #include <iostream.h>
2:    int Add (int x, int y)
3:    {
4:
5:      cout << "In Add(), received " << x << " and " << y << "\n";
6:      return (x+y);
7:    }
8:
9:    void main()
10:   {
11:        cout << "I'm in main()!\n";
12:        int a, b, c;
13:        cout << "Enter two numbers: ";
14:        cin >> a;
15:        cin >> b;
16:        cout << "\nCalling Add()\n";
17:        c=Add(a,b);
18:        cout << "\nBack in main().\n";
19:        cout << "c was set to " << c;
20:        cout << "\nExiting...\n\n";
21:   }
```

OUTPUT
```
I'm in main()!
Enter two numbers: 3 5
Calling Add()
In Add(), received 3 and 5
Back in main().
c was set to 8
Exiting...
```

ANALYSIS   The function Add() is defined on line 2. It takes two integer parameters and returns an integer value. The program itself begins on line 11 where it prints a message. The program prompts the user for two numbers (lines 13 to 15). The user types each number, separated by a space, and then presses Enter. Main() passes the two numbers typed in by the user as arguments to the Add() function on line 17.

Processing branches to the Add() function, which starts on line 2. The parameters a and b are printed and then added together. The result is returned on line 6 and the function returns.

In lines 14 and 15, the cin object is used to obtain a number for the variables a and b, and cout is used to write the values to the screen. Variables and other aspects of this program will be explored in depth in the next few days.

2

Summary

The difficulty in learning a complex subject, such as programming, is that so much of what you learn depends on everything else there is to learn. This lesson introduced the basic parts of a simple C++ program. It also introduced a number of new important terms.

Q&A

Q What does `#include` do?

A This is a directive to the preprocessor, which runs when you call your compiler. This specific directive causes the file named after the word `include` to be read in as if it were typed in at that location in your source code.

Q What is the difference between `//` comments and `/*` style comments?

A The double-slash comments (`//`) "expire" at the end of the line. Slash-star (`/*`) comments are in effect until a closing comment (`*/`). Remember, not even the end of the function terminates a slash-star comment; you must put in the closing comment mark, or you will get a compile-time error.

Q What differentiates a good comment from a bad comment?

A A good comment tells the reader why this particular code is doing whatever it is doing, or explains what a section of code is about to do. A bad comment restates what a particular line of code is doing. Lines of code should be written so that they speak for themselves; reading the line of code should tell you what it is doing without needing a comment.

Quiz

1. What is the difference between the compiler and the preprocessor?
2. Why is the function `main()` special?
3. What are the two types of comments and how do they differ?
4. Can comments be nested?
5. Can comments be longer than one line?

Exercises

1. Write a program that writes I love C++ to the screen.

2. Write the smallest program that can be compiled, linked, and run.

3. **BUG BUSTERS:** Enter this program and compile it. Why does it fail? How can you fix it?

```
1: #include <iostream.h>
2: void main()
3: {
4:     cout << Is there a bug here?";
5: }
```

4. Fix the bug in exercise 3 and recompile, link, and run it.

2

Day 3

Variables and Constants

Programs need a way to store the data they use. Variables and constants offer various ways to represent and manipulate that data.

Today you will learn

- ☐ How to declare and define variables and constants.
- ☐ How to assign values to variables and manipulate those values.
- ☐ How to write the value of a variable to the screen.

What Is a Variable?

In C++, a variable is a place to store information. A variable is a location in your computer's memory in which you can store a value and from which you can later retrieve that value.

Your computer's memory can be viewed as a series of cubbyholes. Each cubbyhole is one of many such holes all lined up. Each cubbyhole—or memory location—is numbered sequentially. These numbers are known as *memory addresses*. A variable reserves one or more cubbyholes in which you can store a value.

Your variable's name (for example, `myVariable`) is a label on one of these cubbyholes so that you can find it easily, without knowing its actual memory address. Figure 3.1 is a schematic representation of this idea. As you can see from the figure, `myVariable` starts at memory address 103. Depending on the size of `myVariable`, it can take up one or more memory addresses.

Figure 3.1.

A schematic representation of memory.

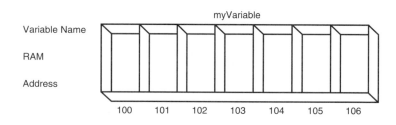

Variable Name

RAM

Address

100   101   102   103   104   105   106

NOTE

RAM is *random access memory*. When you run your program, it is loaded into RAM from the disk file. All variables are created in RAM as well. When programmers talk of memory, it is usually RAM to which they are referring.

Setting Aside Memory

Bits (or *binary digits*) are the smallest pieces of information in computer memory. A bit represents a single binary state (1 or 0). A small collection of bits is called a byte. The number of bits contained by a byte depends on your computer. Some computers have nine bits in a byte, and many have eight. Most of the computers I have worked with use eight-bit bytes to represent a single character. Each bit in a byte carries a weight, just as in other number systems. For instance, the least significant place in the base 10 number system (the one you use every day) is the number of 1s. The next is the number of 10s, the next is the 100s, and so on by powers of 10. In binary, the places carry weights by the power of 2, so the least significant bit (LSB) is the number of 1s, the next place is the number of 2s, the next is the number of 4s, and so on. The most significant bit (MSB) in the byte is the bit that has the highest weight.

When you define a variable in C++, you must tell the compiler what kind of variable it is—for example, integer, character, and so on. This information tells the compiler how much room to set aside and what kind of value you want to store in your variable. As you write programs, you will see how the compiler can help you avoid problems when it knows what type of data is to be stored in a variable.

Each RAM cubbyhole is one byte in size. If the type of variable you create is two bytes in size, it needs two bytes of memory, or two cubbyholes. The type of the variable (for example, integer) tells the compiler how much memory (how many cubbyholes) to set aside for the variable.

Because computers use bits and bytes to represent values, and because memory is measured in bytes, it is important that you understand and are comfortable with these concepts. For a full review of this topic, please read Appendix C, "Binary and Hexadecimal."

NOTE

> Computers do not know about letters, punctuation, or sentences. All they understand are numbers. In fact, all they really know about is whether or not a sufficient amount of electricity is at a particular junction of wires. If so, it is represented internally as a 1; if not, it is represented as a 0. By grouping 1s and 0s, the computer is able to generate patterns that can be interpreted as numbers, and these in turn can be assigned to letters and punctuation.

Size of Integers

On any one computer, each variable type takes up a single unchanging amount of room. That is, an int might be two bytes on one machine and four on another, but on either computer it is always the same, day in and day out.

A char variable (used to hold characters) is most often one byte long. A short int is two bytes on most computers, a long int is usually four bytes, and an int (without the keyword short or long) can be two or four bytes. Listing 3.1 should help you determine the exact size of these and other types on your computer.

NEW TERM A *character* is a single letter, number, or symbol that takes up one byte of memory.

Listing 3.1. Determining the size of variable types on your computer.

```
1:   #include <iostream.h>
2:
3:   void main()
4:   {
5:     cout << "The size of an int is:\t\t"    << sizeof(int)    << " bytes.\n";
6:     cout << "The size of a short int is:\t" << sizeof(short)  << " bytes.\n";
7:     cout << "The size of a long int is:\t"  << sizeof(long)   << " bytes.\n";
8:     cout << "The size of a char is:\t\t"    << sizeof(char)   << " bytes.\n";
9:   cout << "The size of a float is:\t\t"   << sizeof(float)  << " bytes.\n";
10:    cout << "The size of a double is:\t"   << sizeof(double) << " bytes.\n";
11:
12:  }
```

OUTPUT
```
The size of an int is         2 bytes.
The size of a short int is    2 bytes.
The size of a long int is     4 bytes.
The size of a char is         1 bytes.
The size of a float is        4 bytes.
The size of a double is       8 bytes.
```

NOTE

On your computer, the number of bytes presented might be different!

ANALYSIS   Most of Listing 3.1 should be pretty familiar. The one new feature is the use of the `sizeof()` function in lines 5 through 10. `sizeof()` is provided by your compiler, and it tells you the size of the object you pass in as a parameter. When your program is compiled, all the `sizeof()` operations are replaced with the number of bytes that are set aside for the `sizeof()` argument type. For example, on line 5 the keyword `int` is passed into `sizeof()`. Using `sizeof()`, my compiler determined that on my computer, an `int` is equal to a short `int`, which is two bytes.

Signed and Unsigned

In addition, most of these types come in two varieties: signed and unsigned. The idea here is that sometimes you need negative numbers, and sometimes you don't. Integers (short and long) without the word `unsigned` are assumed to be signed. Signed integers are either negative or positive. Unsigned integers are always positive.

Because you have the same number of bytes for both signed and unsigned integers, the largest number you can store in an unsigned integer is twice as big as the largest positive number you can store in a signed integer. An unsigned short integer can handle numbers from 0 to 65,535. Half the numbers represented by a signed short are negative; thus a signed short can only represent numbers from −32,767 to 32,768. Again, if this is confusing, be sure to read Appendix C, "Binary and Hexadecimal."

Fundamental Variable Types

Several other variable types are built into C++. They can be conveniently divided into integer variables (the type discussed so far), floating-point variables, character (including wide character) variables, and bool (short for Boolean) variables.

Floating-point variables have values that can be expressed as fractions; that is, they are real numbers. Character variables hold a single byte and are used for holding the 256 characters and symbols of the ASCII and extended ASCII character sets.

NEW TERM The *ASCII character set* is the set of characters standardized for use on computers. ASCII is an acronym for American Standard Code for Information Interchange. Nearly every computer operating system supports ASCII. The wchar_t char type is a *wide* character type that enables enough storage space to represent international character sets.

With a bool variable, you can represent Boolean information. In computer programming, Boolean is the concept of something being either *true* or *false* (more precisely, true or *not true*). It could represent the concept of on/off or existing/nonexisting. This concept often seems esoteric to beginning programmers, but it will make a lot of sense as you see how it is used in the days to come. Because true or false only requires two values, bools can be represented in cubbyholes that are *less* than a byte in size. On Bonus Day 28, "What's Next," you see how and why you might want to squeeze bools.

The fundamental types of variables used in C++ programs are described in Table 3.1. This table shows the variable type, how much room this book assumes it takes in memory, and what kinds of values can be stored in these variables. The values that can be stored are determined by the size of the variable types, so check your output from Listing 3.1.

Table 3.1. Variable types.

Type	Size	Values
unsigned short int	2 bytes	0 to 65,535
short int	2 bytes	−32,768 to 32,767
unsigned long int	4 bytes	0 to 4,294,967,295
long int	4 bytes	−2,147,483,648 to 2,147,483,647
int	2 bytes	−32,768 to 32,767

continues

Table 3.1. continued

Type	Size	Values
unsigned int	2 bytes	0 to 65,535
char	1 byte	256 character values
wchar_t	2 bytes	65,535 character values
bool	1 byte	true or false
float	4 bytes	1.2e-38 to 3.4e38
double	8 bytes	2.2e-308 to 1.8e308

NOTE The sizes of variables might be different from those shown in Table 3.1, depending on the compiler and the computer you are using. If your computer has the same output as was presented in Listing 3.1, Table 3.1 should apply to your compiler. If your output from Listing 3.1 was different, you should consult your compiler's manual for the values that your variable types can hold.

Defining a Variable

You create, or define, a variable by stating its type, followed by one or more spaces, the variable name, and a semicolon. The variable name can be virtually any combination of letters, but it cannot contain spaces. Legal variable names include x, J23qrsnf, and myAge. Good variable names tell you how the variables are used. Using good names makes it easier to understand the flow of your program. The following statement defines an integer variable called myAge:

```
int myAge;
```

NOTE As a general programming practice, avoid such horrific names as J23qrsnf, and restrict single-letter variable names (such as x or i) to variables that are used only very briefly. Try to use expressive names such as myAge or howMany. Such names are easier to understand three weeks later when you are scratching your head trying to figure out what you meant when you wrote that line of code.

Try this experiment: Guess what these pieces of programs do, based on the first few lines of code:

Example 1

```
voidmain()
{
    unsigned short x;
    unsigned short y;
    unsigned long z;
    z = x * y;
}
```

Example 2

```
voidmain ()
{
    unsigned short Width;
    unsigned short Length;
    unsigned long Area;
    Area = Width * Length;
}
```

Clearly, the second program is easier to understand, and the inconvenience of having to type the longer variable names is more than made up for by how much easier it is to maintain the second program.

Case Sensitivity

C++ is case-sensitive. In other words, uppercase and lowercase letters are considered to be different. A variable named age is different from Age, which is different from AGE.

NOTE   Some compilers allow you to turn case sensitivity off. Don't be tempted to do this; your programs won't work with other compilers, and other C++ programmers will be very confused by your code.

Conventions for naming variables.

There are various conventions for how to name variables, and although it doesn't matter much which method you adopt, it is important to be consistent throughout your program.

Many programmers prefer to use all lowercase letters for their variable names. If the name requires two words (for example, my car), there are two popular conventions: my_car or myCar. The latter form is called *camel notation*, because the capitalization looks something like a hump.

Some people find the underscore character (my_car) to be easier to read; others prefer to avoid the underscore because it is more difficult to type. This book uses camel notation, in which the second and all subsequent words are capitalized: myCar, theQuickBrownFox, and so on.

Many advanced programmers employ a notation style that is often referred to as *Hungarian notation*. The idea behind Hungarian notation is to prefix every variable with a set of characters that describes its type. Integer variables might begin with a lowercase letter i, and longs might begin with a lowercase l. Other notations indicate constants, globals, pointers, and so on. Most of this is much more important in C programming, because C++ supports the creation of user-defined types (see Day 6) and because C++ is strongly typed. Hungarian notation and other coding styles are detailed more on Bonus Day 22, "Coding Styles and Idioms."

Keywords

Some words are reserved by C++, and you cannot use them as variable names. These are *keywords*, and they are used by the compiler to control your program. Keywords include if, while, for, and main. See Appendix B for a complete list of the ANSI C++ keywords.

Do	Don't

DO define a variable by writing the type and then the variable name.

DO use meaningful variable names.

DO remember that C++ is case-sensitive.

DON'T use C++ keywords as variable names.

DO understand the number of bytes each variable type consumes in memory and what values can be stored in variables of that type.

DON'T use unsigned variables for negative numbers.

3

Creating More Than One Variable at a Time

You can create more than one variable of the same type in one statement by writing the type and then the variable names, separated by commas. Here is an example:

```
unsigned int myAge, myWeight;   // two unsigned int variables
long area, width, length;       // three longs
```

As you can see, `myAge` and `myWeight` are each declared as unsigned integer variables. The second line declares three individual long variables named `area`, `width`, and `length`. The type (`long`) is assigned to all the variables. You cannot mix types in one definition statement.

Assigning Values to Your Variables

You assign a value to a variable by using the *assignment operator* (=). Thus, you would assign 5 to `Width` by writing

```
unsigned short Width;
Width = 5;
```

You can combine these steps and *initialize* `Width` when you define it by writing

```
unsigned short Width = 5;
```

Initialization looks very much like assignment, and with integer variables the difference is minor. Later in this lesson, when constants are covered, you will see that some values must be initialized because they cannot be assigned to. The essential difference is that initialization takes place at the moment you create the variable.

Just as you can define more than one variable at a time, you can initialize more than one variable at creation, as in the following example:

```
long width = 5, length = 7;  // create two long variables and initialize them
```

This example initializes the long variable `width` with the value 5 and the long variable `length` to the value 7. You can even mix definitions and initializations of the same type:

```
int myAge = 39, yourAge, hisAge = 40;
```

This example creates three type `int` variables, and it initializes the first and third.

Listing 3.2 shows a complete program, ready to compile, that computes the area of a rectangle and writes the answer to the screen.

3

TYPE | **Listing 3.2. Demonstrating the use of variables.**

```
1:    // Demonstration of variables
2:    #include <iostream.h>
3:
4:    void main()
5:    {
6:        unsigned short int Width = 5, Length; // create two variables,
➥ initialize first
7:        Length = 10; // assign a value to the _uninitialized variable
8:
9:        // create  an unsigned short and initialize with result of multiplying
➥ Width by Length
10:       unsigned short int Area  = Width * Length;
11:
12:       cout << "Width:" << Width << "\n";
13:       cout << "Length: "  << Length << endl;
14:       cout << "Area: " << Area;
15:   }
```

OUTPUT
```
Width: 5
Length: 10
Area: 50
```

ANALYSIS   Line 2 includes the required `include` statement for the `iostream`'s library so that `cout` will work. Line 4 begins the program.

On line 6, `Width` is defined as an unsigned short integer, and its value is initialized to `5`. Another unsigned short integer, `Length`, is also defined, but it's not initialized. On line 7 the value `10` is assigned to `Length`.

On line 10 an unsigned short integer, `Area`, is defined, and it is initialized with the value obtained by multiplying `Width` times `Length`. On lines 12 through 15, the values of the variables are printed to the screen. Note that the special word `endl` creates a new line.

typedef

It can become tedious, repetitious, and (most importantly) error-prone to keep writing `unsigned short int`. C++ enables you to create an alias for this phrase by using the keyword `typedef`, which stands for *type definition*.

In effect, you are creating a synonym, and it is important to distinguish this from creating a new type (which you will do on Day 6, "Basic Classes"). `typedef` is used by writing the keyword `typedef` followed by the existing type and then the new name. For example,

```
typedef unsigned short int USHORT
```

creates the new name USHORT, which you can use anywhere you might have written unsigned short int. Listing 3.3 is a replay of Listing 3.2, using the type definition USHORT rather than unsigned short int.

TYPE   **Listing 3.3. A demonstration of typedef.**

```
1:    // *****************
2:    // Demonstrates typedef keyword
3:    #include <iostream.h>
4:
5:    typedef unsigned short int USHORT;   //typedef defined
6:
7:    voidmain()
8:    {
9:       USHORT  Width = 5;
10:      USHORT Length;
11:      Length = 10;
12:      USHORT Area  = Width * Length;
13:      cout << "Width:" << Width << "\n";
14:      cout << "Length: "  << Length << endl;
15:      cout << "Area: " << Area;
16: }
```

```
Width: 5
Length: 10
Area: 50
```

On line 5, USHORT is defined with a typedef statement as a synonym for unsigned short int. The program is otherwise identical to Listing 3.2, and the output is the same.

Most modern compilers include type definitions for ULONG and USHORT. Many define an unsigned char or wchar_t as a BYTE. If your compiler does not, you might consider placing all your favorites in a header file (.h) and using an include directive in programs where you need them.

Choosing Between *short* and *long*

One source of confusion for new C++ programmers is when to declare a variable to be type long and when to declare it to be type short. The rule, when understood, is fairly straightforward: If there is any chance that the value you'll want to put into your variable will be too big for its type, use a larger type.

As seen in Table 3.1, unsigned short integers (assuming that they are two bytes) can hold a value only up to 65,535. Signed short integers can hold only half that. Although unsigned long integers can hold an extremely large number—4,294,967,295—that is still quite finite.

If you need a larger number, you'll have to go to float or double, and then you lose some precision. Floats and doubles can hold extremely large numbers, but only the first seven or 19 digits are significant on most computers. That means that the number is rounded off after that many digits.

Wrapping Around in Unsigned Integers

The fact that unsigned long integers have a limit to the values they can hold is only rarely a problem, but what happens if you do run out of room?

When an unsigned integer reaches its maximum value, it *wraps around* and starts over, much as a car odometer does. Listing 3.4 shows what happens if you try to put a value that is too large into a short integer.

TYPE

Listing 3.4. Putting a value that is too large in an unsigned integer.

```
1: #include <iostream.h>
2:  void main()
3:  {
4:      unsigned short int smallNumber;
5:      smallNumber = 65535;
6:      cout << "small number:" << smallNumber << endl;
7:      smallNumber++;
8:      cout << "small number:" << smallNumber << endl;
9:      smallNumber++;
10:     cout << "small number:" << smallNumber << endl;
11: }
```

OUTPUT

```
small number: 65535
small number: 0
small number: 1
```

ANALYSIS   On line 4, smallNumber is declared to be an unsigned short int, which on my computer is a two-byte variable, able to hold a value between 0 and 65,535. On line 5 the maximum value is assigned to smallNumber, and it is printed on line 6.

On line 7 smallNumber is *incremented;* that is, 1 is added to it. The symbol for incrementing is ++ (as in the name C++—an incremental increase from C). Thus, the value in smallNumber would be 65,536. But unsigned small integers can't hold a number larger than 65,535, so the value is wrapped around to 0, which is printed on line 8.

On line 9 smallNumber is incremented again, and then its new value, 1, is printed.

Wrapping Around a Signed Integer

A signed integer is different from an unsigned integer in that half of its values are negative. Instead of picturing a traditional car odometer, you might picture one that rotates up for positive numbers and down for negative numbers. One mile from zero is either 1 or −1. When you run out of positive numbers, you run right into the largest negative numbers and then count back down to zero. Listing 3.5 shows what happens when you add one to the maximum positive number in a signed short integer.

TYPE **Listing 3.5. Adding too large a number to a signed integer.**

```
1:   #include <iostream.h>
2:   void main()
3:   {
4:       short int smallNumber;
5:       smallNumber = 32767;
6:       cout << "small number:" << smallNumber << endl;
7:       smallNumber++;
8:       cout << "small number:" << smallNumber << endl;
9:       smallNumber++;
10:      cout << "small number:" << smallNumber << endl;
11:  }
```

OUTPUT
```
small number: 32767
small number: -32768
small number: -32767
```

ANALYSIS On line 4 `smallNumber` is this time declared to be a signed short integer (if you don't explicitly say that it is unsigned, it is assumed to be signed). The program proceeds much as the preceding one, but the output is quite different. To fully understand this output, you must be comfortable with how signed numbers are represented as bits in a two-byte integer. For details, check Appendix C.

The bottom line, however, is that just like an unsigned integer, the signed integer wraps around from its highest positive value to its highest negative value.

Characters

Character variables (type `char`) are typically 1 byte, enough to hold 256 values. A `char` can be interpreted as a small number (0 to 255 for most compilers) or as a member of the ASCII set. Some compilers can even use `char` to represent both positive and negative numbers, so that there is also an `unsigned` version of `char`.

In the ASCII code, the lowercase letter *a* is assigned the value 97. All the lower- and uppercase letters, all the numerals, and all the punctuation marks are assigned a value between 1 and 128. Another 128 marks and symbols are reserved for use by the computer maker, although the IBM extended character set has become something of a standard.

chars and Numbers

When you put a character, for example, 'a', into a char variable, all that is really there is a number between 0 and 255. The compiler knows, however, how to translate back and forth between characters (represented by a single quotation mark and then a letter, numeral, or punctuation mark, followed by a closing single quotation mark) and one of the ASCII values.

The value/letter relationship is arbitrary; there is no particular reason that the lowercase *a* is assigned by the value 97. However, as long as everyone (your keyboard, compiler, and screen) agrees, there is no problem. It is important to realize, however, that there is a big difference between the value 5 and the character '5'. The latter is actually valued at 53, much as the letter 'a' is valued at 97. Listing 3.6 is a program that you can compile to print the character values represented by the numeric values 32 through 127.

 Listing 3.6. Printing characters based on numbers.

```
1:    #include <iostream.h>
2:    void main()
3:    {
4:    for (int i = 32; i<128; i++)
5:         cout << (char) i;
6:    }
```

OUTPUT   !"#$%G'()*+,./0123456789:;<>?@ABCDEFGHIJKLMNOP
_QRSTUVWXYZ[\]^'abcdefghijklmnopqrstuvwxyz<¦>~s

ANALYSIS   This simple program prints the character values for the integers 32 through 127. These are the ASCII values for the printable characters of the ASCII set. Other ASCII values that are not printable include the character number 7, which will make a beeping sound on most computers, and character 13, which is the carriage-return/linefeed pair (equivalent to cout endl or '\n').

Special Printing Characters

The C++ compiler recognizes some special characters for formatting. Table 3.2 shows the most common ones. You put these into your code by typing the backslash (called the escape character), followed by the character. Thus, to put a tab character into your code, you would enter a single quotation mark, the backslash, the letter t, and then a closing single quotation mark:

```
cout << '\n' << '\t' << "<-Return and Tab\n";
```

This example uses two special printing characters, a carriage-return/linefeed (`'\n'`) and a tab character (`'\t'`), to print a message indented from the left on the screen. The special printing characters can be used when printing either to the screen or to a file or other output device.

NEW TERM An *escape character* changes the meaning of the character that follows it. For example, normally the character n means the letter *n*, but when it is escaped by the escape character (\) it means new line.

Table 3.2. The escape characters.

Character	What it means
\n	new line (carriage return and linefeed)
\r	carriage return
\t	horizontal tab
\v	vertical tab
\f	formfeed
\b	backspace
\a	alert
\o*nn*	*nn* is an octal (base 8) value
\x*nnn*	*nnn* is a hexadecimal (base 16) value
\"	double quote
\'	single quote
\0	null character
\?	question mark
\\	backslash

Probably the best way to learn these is to try them out in some of your programs. Some do require a little explanation. For instance, the alert sequence (\a) is used to make a beeping sound from the speaker on most computers. The null sequence (a backslash zero, not an o character) is used extensively in C++ to identify the end of a string of characters. For example, when you wrote

```
cout << "Hello world\n":
```

in the first lesson of this book, the compiler automatically placed an invisible '\0' after your '\n' to let cout know that there were no further characters to display after the '\n' character. In Appendix C you will find a description of other numbering systems that will help you understand the '\o' (lowercase 'o' character, not zero) and '\x' sequences.

Constants

Like variables, constants are data storage locations. Unlike variables (and as the name implies), constants don't change. You must initialize a constant when you create it, and you cannot assign a new value later.

C++ has two types of constants: literal and symbolic.

Literal Constants

A literal constant is a value typed directly into your program wherever it is needed, like so:

```
int myAge = 39;
```

myAge is a variable of type int; 39 is a literal constant. You can't assign a value to 39, and its value can't be changed.

One test of a literal constant is that it can be used on the right side of an equals sign in an assignment but not on the left. In a lot of C++ documentation, you see the term *r-value* used to refer to a literal constant. Table 3.3 provides some literal constant samples.

Table 3.3. Some literal constants

An r-value	What it means
"This is one."	A character string constant
'c'	A character constant
0xf2	A hexadecimal integer constant
3.14	A double constant

Symbolic Constants

A symbolic constant is a constant that is represented by a name, just as a variable is. Unlike a variable, however, after a constant is initialized, its value can't be changed.

If your program has one integer variable named students and another named classes, you could compute how many students you have, given a known number of classes. If you knew there were 15 students per class, the line would look like this:

```
students = classes * 15;
```

NOTE

> * indicates multiplication.

In this example, 15 is a literal constant. Your code would be easier to read, and easier to maintain, if you substituted a symbolic constant for this value:

```
students = classes * studentsPerClass
```

If you later decided to change the number of students in each class, you could do so where you define the constant studentsPerClass without having to make a change every place you use that value!

There are two ways to declare a symbolic constant in C++. The old, traditional, and now obsolete way is with a preprocessor directive, #define.

Defining Constants with #define

To define a constant using the traditional C style, you would enter this:

```
#define studentsPerClass 15
```

Note that studentsPerClass is of no particular type (int, char, and so on). #define does a simple text substitution. Every time the preprocessor sees the word studentsPerClass, it puts in the text 15.

Because the preprocessor runs before the compiler, your compiler never sees your constant; it sees the number 15. On Day 17, "The Preprocessor," you will see #define and some of its other uses.

Defining Constants with const

Although #define works, there is a new and much better way to define constants in C++:

```
const unsigned short int studentsPerClass = 15;
```

This example also declares a symbolic constant named studentsPerClass, but this time studentsPerClass is typed as an unsigned short int. This method has several advantages in making your code easier to maintain, as well as in preventing bugs. The biggest difference is that this constant has a type, and the compiler can enforce that it is used according to its type.

> **NOTE**
>
> Constants cannot be changed while the program is running. If you need to change studentsPerClass, for example, you need to change the code and recompile.

A Word About *volatile*

If a variable is not a constant, it is considered *volatile* (changeable). But there might be times when you want to emphasize a variable's volatility. To do so, C++ has the keyword volatile. You can identify any nonconstant variable as volatile. However, volatility is the default, so all of these statements create volatile variables:

```
int aValue;          // a volatile int variable
volatile int xYZ; // another volatile int
double dValue;       // a volatile double variable
volatile double dvValue; // another volatile double
```

Because volatility is implied, you seldom see variables declared with volatile, and it is not used again in this book. Just think of a volatile variable as the opposite concept of a constant variable.

Do   **Don't**

DON'T use the term int; use short and long to make it clear which size number you intend.

DO watch for numbers overrunning the size of the integer and wrapping around incorrect values.

DO give your variables meaningful names that reflect their use.

DO use constants with meaningful names to identify things that do not change. For instance, instead of 3.1428, declare a constant called pi with that value and use it instead.

DON'T confuse constants with variables. A constant cannot be used to name a value that will be changed in your program.

DON'T use keywords as variable names.

Enumerated Constants

Enumerated constants enable you to create new types and then define variables of those types whose values are restricted to a set of possible values. For example, you can declare COLOR to be an enumeration, and you can define that there are five values for COLOR: RED, BLUE, GREEN, WHITE, and BLACK.

The syntax for enumerated constants is to write the keyword enum, followed by the type name, an open brace, each of the legal values separated by a comma, a closing brace, and a semicolon. Here's an example:

```
enum COLOR { RED, BLUE, GREEN, WHITE, BLACK };
```

This statement performs two tasks:

- ☐ It makes COLOR the name of an enumeration—that is, a new type.
- ☐ It makes RED a symbolic constant with the value 0, BLUE a symbolic constant with the value 1, GREEN a symbolic constant with the value 2, and so on.

Every enumerated constant has an integer value. If you don't specify otherwise, the first constant will have the value 0, and the rest will count up from there. Any one of the constants can be initialized with a particular value, however, and those that are not initialized will count upward from the ones before them. Thus, if you write

```
enum Color { RED=100, BLUE, GREEN=500, WHITE, BLACK~700 };
```

RED will have the value 100, BLUE will have the value 101, GREEN will have the value 500, WHITE will have the value 501, and BLACK will have the value 700.

You can define variables of type COLOR, but they can be assigned only one of the enumerated values (in this case, RED, BLUE, GREEN, WHITE, or BLACK, or else 100, 101, 500, 501, or 700). You can assign any color value to your COLOR variable. In fact, you can assign any integer value, even if it is not a legal color, although a good compiler will issue a warning if you do. It is important to realize that enumerator variables actually are of type unsigned int and that the enumerated constants equate to integer variables. It is, however, very convenient to be able to name these values when working with colors, days of the week, or similar sets of values. Listing 3.7 presents a program that uses an enumerated type.

TYPE **Listing 3.7. A demonstration of enumerated constants.**

```
1:  #include <iostream.h>
2:  void main()
3:  {
```

continues

Listing 3.7. continued

```
4:          enum Days { Sunday, Monday, Tuesday, Wednesday, Thursday, Friday,
➥ Saturday };
5:
6:          Days DayOff;
7:          int x;
8:
9:          cout << "What day would you like off (0-6)? ";
10:         cin  >> x;
11:         DayOff = Days(x);
12:
13:         if (DayOff == Sunday || DayOff == Saturday)
14:               cout << "\nYou're already off on weekends!\n";
15:         else
16:               cout << "\nOkay, I'll put in the vacation day.\n";
17: }
```

OUTPUT
```
'What day would you like off (0-6)?  0
You're already off on weekends!
```

ANALYSIS On line 4 the enumerated constant DAYS is defined with seven values counting upward from 0. The user is prompted for a day on line 8. The chosen value, a number between 0 and 6, is compared on line 11 to the enumerated values for Sunday and Saturday, and action is taken accordingly. The if statement will be covered in more detail on Day 4, "Expressions and Statements."

You cannot type the word Sunday when prompted for a day; the program does not know how to translate the characters in Sunday into one of the enumerated values.

NOTE For this and all the small programs in this book, I've left out all the code you would normally write to deal with what happens when the user types inappropriate data. For example, this program doesn't check—as it would in a real program—to make sure that the user types a number between 0 and 6. This detail has been left out to keep these programs small and simple, and to focus on the issue at hand.

Summary

This lesson has discussed numeric and character variables and constants, which are used by C++ to store data during the execution of your program. Numeric variables are either integral (char, short, and long int), or they are floating point (float and double). Numeric variables can also be signed or unsigned. Although all the types can be of variant sizes among different computers, the type specifies an exact size on any given computer.

You must declare a variable before it can be used, and then you must store the type of data that you've declared correct for that variable. If you put too large a number into an integral variable, it wraps around and produces an incorrect result.

This lesson also reviewed literal and symbolic constants, as well as enumerated constants, and showed two ways to declare a symbolic constant: using #define and using the keyword const.

Q&A

Q If a short int can run out of room and wrap around, why not always use long integers?

A Both short integers and long integers run out of room and wrap around, but a long integer does so with a much larger number. For example, an unsigned short int wraps around after 65,535, whereas an unsigned long int does not wrap around until 4,294,967,295. However, on most machines, a long integer takes up twice as much memory every time you declare one (4 bytes versus 2 bytes), and a program with 100 such variables consumes an extra 200 bytes of RAM. Frankly, this is less of a problem than it used to be, because most personal computers now come with many thousands (if not millions) of bytes of memory. Still, there are applications in which you need to squeeze every bit of performance out of the machine, and the less memory your application uses, the better it performs. A negligible performance improvement in one application is a quantum leap in another.

Q What happens if I assign a number with a decimal to an integer rather than a float?

A Consider the following line of code:

```
int aNumber = 5.4;
```

A good compiler issues a warning, but the assignment is completely legal. The number you've assigned will be truncated into an integer. Thus, if you assign 5.4 to an integer variable, that variable will have the value 5. Information will be lost, however, and if you then try to assign the value in that integer variable to a float variable, the float variable will have only 5.

Q Why not use literal constants? Why go to the trouble of using symbolic constants?

A If you use the value in many places throughout your program, a symbolic constant allows all the values to change just by changing the one definition of the constant. Symbolic constants also speak for themselves. It might be hard to understand why a number is being multiplied by 360, but it's much easier to understand what's going on if the number is being multiplied by degreesInACircle.

Q **What happens if I assign a negative number to an unsigned variable?**

A Consider the following line of code:

```
unsigned int aPositiveNumber = -1;
```

A good compiler will issue a warning, but if the assignment is legal, the negative number will be assessed as a bit pattern and assigned to the variable. The value of that variable will then be interpreted as an unsigned number. Thus, -1, whose bit pattern is 11111111 11111111 (0xFF in hex), will be assessed as the unsigned value 65,535. If this information confuses you, reread Appendix C.

Q **Can I work with C++ without understanding bit patterns, binary arithmetic, and hexadecimal?**

A Yes, but not as effectively as if you do understand these topics. C++ does not do as good a job as some languages at "protecting" you from what the computer is really doing. This is actually a benefit, because it provides you with tremendous power that other languages don't give you. As with any power tool, however, to get the most out of C++, you must understand how it works. Programmers who try to program in C++ without understanding the fundamentals of the binary system often are confused by their results.

Quiz

1. What is the difference between an integral variable and a floating-point variable?
2. What are the differences between an unsigned short int and a long int?
3. What are the advantages of using a symbolic constant rather than a literal?
4. What are the advantages of using the const keyword rather than #define?
5. What makes for a good or bad variable name?
6. Given this enum, what is the value of BLUE?

   ```
   enum COLOR { WHITE, BLACK = 100, RED, BLUE, GREEN = 300 };
   ```

7. Which of the following variable names are good, which are bad, and which are invalid?

   a. Age

   b. !ex

   c. R79J

   d. TotalIncome

   e. __Invalid

Exercises

1. What would be the correct variable type in which to store the following information?

    a. Your age

    b. The area of your backyard

    c. The number of stars in the galaxy

    d. The average rainfall for the month of January

2. Create good variable names for this information.

3. Declare a constant for pi as 3.14159.

4. Declare a float variable and initialize it using your pi constant.

Day **4**

Expressions and Statements

At its heart, a program is a set of commands, executed in sequence. The power in a program comes from its capability to perform different sets of commands based on changing conditions. Today you learn

☐ What statements are.

☐ What blocks are.

☐ What expressions are.

☐ How to branch your code based on conditions.

☐ What truth is, and how to act on it.

Statements

In C++ a statement controls the sequence of execution, evaluates an expression, or does nothing (the null statement). All C++ statements end with a semicolon (;), even the `null` statement, which is just the semicolon and nothing else. Notice that the end of line does not end a statement but the ; does, as in the following:

```
// Here is one, long statement:
cout <<
   3 + 5
 * 9
   << " is the result of a long computation."
   << endl; // <-Statement ends at the ';'
```

One of the most common statements is the following assignment statement:

```
x = a + b;
```

Unlike in algebra, this statement does not mean that x equals a+b. This is read, "Assign the value of the sum of a and b to x," or "Assign to x, a+b." Even though this statement is doing two things, it is one statement and thus has one semicolon. The assignment operator assigns whatever is on the right side to whatever is on the left side.

Another statement that many programmers use is the null statement. A null statement is a statement that does nothing, so it is only an empty line with a ;. It is most often used to cause a delay in processing, as in the following example:

```
for(int I=0; I<10000; I++)
    ; // null statement performed 10000 times
```

On Day 7, the `for` statement will be explained more fully, but for now you only need to know that it is used to perform a step or set of steps a certain number of times. In this example, it perfoms a null statement 10,000 times to cause a delay. You might need a time delay to display a message for a short time on the screen and then clear it after a delay such as this one. This delay method is often used if your computer or compiler has no other way to perform delays.

NEW TERM   A *null statement* is a statement that does nothing.

Whitespace

Whitespace (tabs, spaces, and newlines) is generally ignored in statements. The assignment statement previously discussed could be written as

```
x=a+b;
```

or as

```
x                         =a
+             b           ;
```

Although this last variation is perfectly legal, it is also perfectly foolish. Whitespace can be used to make your programs more readable and easier to maintain, or it can be used to create horrific and indecipherable code. In this, as in all things, C++ provides the power; you supply the judgment.

 Whitespace characters (spaces, tabs, newlines) cannot be seen. If these characters are printed, you see only the white of the paper.

Blocks and Compound Statements

Any place you can put a single statement, you can put a compound statement, also called a *block*. A block begins with an opening brace ({) and ends with a closing brace (}). Although every statement in the block must end with a semicolon, the block itself does not end with a semicolon, as in the following example:

```
{
temp = a;
a = b;
b = temp;
}
```

This block of code acts as one statement and swaps the values in the variables a and b.

Do	Don't

DO use a closing brace any time you have an opening brace.

DO end your statements with a semicolon.

DO use whitespace judiciously to make your code clearer.

Expressions

Anything that evaluates to a value is an expression in C++. Expressions are said to *return* a value. Therefore, 3+2; returns the value 5 and is an expression. All expressions are statements.

The myriad pieces of code that qualify as an expression might surprise you. Here are three examples:

```
3.2                 // returns the value 3.2
PI                  // float const that returns the value 3.14
SecondsPerMinute    // int const that returns 60
```

Assuming that PI is a const equal to 3.14 and SecondsPerMinute is a constant equal to 60, all three of these statements are expressions.

The complicated expression

```
x = a + b;
```

not only adds a and b and assigns the result to x, but it also returns the value of that assignment (the value in x). Thus, this statement is also an expression. Because it is an expression, it can be on the right side of an assignment operator:

```
y = x = a + b;
```

This line is evaluated in the following order:

> Add a to b.
>
> Assign the result of the expression a + b to x.
>
> Assign the result of the assignment expression x = a + b to y.

If a, b, x, and y are all integers, and if a has the value 2 and b has the value 5, both x and y will be assigned the value 7. Listing 4.1 provides an example of some complex expressions and how they are evaluated by the compiler.

TYPE **Listing 4.1. Evaluating complex expressions.**

```
1:    #include <iostream.h>
2:    void main()
3:    {
4:        int a=0, b=0, x=0, y=35;
5:        cout << "a: " << a << " b: " << b;
6:        cout << " x: " << x << " y: " << y << endl;
7:        a = 9;
8:        b = 7;
9:        y = x = a+b;
10:       cout << "a: " << a << " b: " << b;
11:       cout << " x: " << x << "y: " << y << endl;
12:   }
```

OUTPUT
```
a: 0 b: 0 x: 0 y: 35
a: 9 b: 7 x: 16 y: 16
```

ANALYSIS On line 4 the four variables are declared and initialized. Their values are printed on lines 5 and 6. On line 7 a is assigned the value 9. On line 8 b is assigned the value 7. On line 9 the values of a and b are summed, and the result is assigned to x. This expression (x = a+b) evaluates to a value (the sum of a+b), and that value is in turn assigned to y.

Operators

An operator is a symbol that causes the compiler to take an action. Operators act on operands, and in C++ all operands are expressions. In C++ there are several different categories of operators. The following are two such categories:

☐ Assignment operators

☐ Mathematical operators

NOTE

Many of the operators have an alternative notation in case your keyboard does not have the traditional tokens. The tables in this lesson list alterntive tokens parenthetically beside the traditional. You might find it helpful to refer back to Table 1.1 from Day 1 to review the alternative tokens.

Assignment Operator

The assignment operator (=) causes the operand on the left side of the assignment operator to have its value changed to the value on the right side of the assignment operator. The expression

```
x = a + b;
```

assigns the value that is the result of adding a and b to the operand x.

An operand that can legally be on the left side of an assignment operator is called an *l-value*. An operand that can be on the right side is called (you guessed it) an *r-value*.

Constants are r-values. They cannot be l-values. Thus, you can write

```
x = 35;         // ok
```

But you can't legally write

```
35 = x;         // error, not an lvalue!
```

NEW TERM An *l-value* is an operand that can be on the left side of an expression. An *r-value* is an operand that can be on the right side of an expression. Note that all l-values are r-values, but not all r-values are l-values. An example of an r-value that is not an l-value is a literal. Thus, you can write x = 5;, but you cannot write 5 = x;.

Mathematical Operators

There are five mathematical operators: addition (+), subtraction (-), multiplication (*), division (/), and modulus (%).

Addition and subtraction work as you would expect, although subtraction with unsigned integers can lead to surprising results if the result is a negative number. You saw something much like this yesterday, when variable overflow was described. Listing 4.2 shows what happens when you subtract a large unsigned number from a small unsigned number.

TYPE | **Listing 4.2. Subtraction and integer overflow.**

```
1: // Listing 4.2 - demonstrates subtraction and
2: // integer overflow
3: #include <iostream.h>
4:
5: void main()
6: {
7:     unsigned int difference;
8:     unsigned int bigNumber = 100;
9:     unsigned int smallNumber = 50;
10:    difference = bigNumber - smallNumber;
11:    cout << "Difference is: " << difference;
12:    difference = smallNumber - bigNumber;
13:    cout << "\nNow difference is: " << difference;
14: }
```

OUTPUT
```
Difference is: 50
Now difference is: 65486
```

ANALYSIS The subtraction operator is invoked on line 10, and the result is printed on line 11, much as you might expect. The subtraction operator is called again on line 12, but this time a large unsigned number is subtracted from a small unsigned number. The result would be negative, but because it is evaluated (and printed) as an unsigned number, the result is an overflow as described yesterday. This topic is reviewed in detail in Appendix C.

Integer Division and Modulus

Integer division is somewhat different from everyday division. When you divide 21 by 4, the result is a real number (a number with a fraction). Integers don't have fractions, so the *remainder* is lopped off. Therefore, the answer is 5. To get the remainder, you take 21 modulus 4 (21 % 4) and the result is 1. The modulus operator tells you the remainder after an integer division.

Finding the modulus can be very useful. For example, you might want to print a statement on every tenth action. Any number whose remainder is 0 when you modulus divide that number by 10 is an exact multiple of 10. Thus 1 % 10 is 1, 2 % 10 is 2, and so on until 10 % 10, whose result is 0. 11 % 10 is back to 1, and this pattern continues until the next multiple of 10, which is 20. You'll use this technique when looping is discussed on Day 7, "More Program Flow."

WARNING

Many novice C++ programmers inadvertently put a semicolon after their if statements:

```
if(SomeValue < 10);
    SomeValue = 10;
```

What is intended here is to test whether SomeValue is less than 10, and if so to set it to 10, making 10 the minimum value for SomeValue. Running this code snippet will show that SomeValue is *always* set to 10! Why? The if statement terminates with the semicolon (a null statement).

Combining the Assignment and Mathematical Operators

It is not uncommon to want to add a value to a variable, and then to assign the result back into the variable. If you have a variable myAge and you want to increase the value by two, you can write

```
int myAge = 5;
int temp;
temp = myAge + 2;  // add 5 + 2 and put it in temp
myAge = temp;            // put it back in myAge
```

This method, however, is terribly convoluted and wasteful. In C++ you can put the same variable on both sides of the assignment operator, and thus the preceding becomes

```
myAge = myAge + 2;
```

which is much better. In algebra, this expression would be meaningless, but in C++ it is read as, "Add two to the value in myAge and assign the result to myAge."

Even simpler to write, but perhaps a bit harder to read is

```
myAge += 2;
```

The self-assigned addition operator (+=) adds the r-value to the l-value and then reassigns the result into the l-value. This operator is pronounced "plus-equals." The statement would be read "myAge plus-equals two." If myAge had the value 4 to start, it would have 6 after this statement.

There are self-assigned subtraction (-=), division (/=), multiplication (*=), and modulus (%=) operators, as well.

Increment and Decrement

The most common value to add (or subtract) and then reassign into a variable is 1. In C++, increasing a value by one is called incrementing, and decreasing by one is called decrementing. There are special operators to perform these actions.

The increment operator (++) increases the value of the variable by 1, and the decrement operator (--) decreases it by 1. Thus, if you have a variable, C, and you want to increment it, you would use this statement:

```
C++;                    // Start with C and increment it.
```

This statement is equivalent to the more verbose statement

```
C = C + 1;
```

which you learned is also equivalent to the moderately verbose statement

```
C += 1;
```

Prefix and Postfix

Both the increment operator (++) and the decrement operator (--) come in two varieties: prefix and postfix. The prefix variety is written before the variable name (++myAge); the postfix variety is written after (myAge++).

In a simple statement, it doesn't much matter which you use; but in a complex statement, when you are incrementing (or decrementing) a variable and then assigning the result to another variable, it matters very much. The prefix operator is evaluated before the assignment; the postfix is evaluated after. Listing 4.3 shows the use and implications of both types.

TYPE   **Listing 4.3. Prefix and postfix operators.**

```
1:  // Listing 4.3 - demonstrates use of
2:  // prefix and postfix increment and
3:  // decrement operators
4:  #include <iostream.h>
```

```
5:  void main()
6:  {
7:      int myAge = 39;        // initialize two integers
8:      int yourAge = 39;
9:      cout << "I am:\t" << myAge << "\tyears old.\n";
10:     cout << "You are:\t" << yourAge << "\tyears old\n";
11:     myAge++;               // postfix increment
12:     ++yourAge;             // prefix increment
13:     cout << "One year passes...\n";
14:     cout << "I am:\t" << myAge << "\tyears old.\n";
15:     cout << "You are:\t" << yourAge << "\tyears old\n";
16:     cout << "Another year passes\n";
17:     cout << "I am:\t" << myAge++ << "\tyears old.\n";
                   _//note differences
18:     cout << "You are:\t" << ++yourAge << "\tyears old\n";
                   _// between these lines
19:     cout << "Let's print it again.\n";
20:     cout << "I am:\t" << myAge << "\tyears old.\n";
21:     cout << "You are:\t" << yourAge << "\tyears old\n";
22: }
```

OUTPUT
```
I am       39 years old
You are    39 years old
One year passes
I am       40 years old
You are    40 years old
Another year passes
I am       40 years old
You are    41 years old
Let's print it again
I am       41 years old
You are    41 years old
```

ANALYSIS   On lines 7 and 8, two integer variables are declared, and each is initialized with the value 39. Their value is printed on lines 9 and 10.

On line 11 myAge is incremented using the postfix increment operator, and on line 12 yourAge is incremented using the prefix increment operator. The results are printed on lines 14 and 15, and they are identical (both 40).

On line 17 myAge is incremented as part of the printing statement, using the postfix increment operator. Because it is postfix, the increment happens *after* the print, so the value 40 is printed again. In contrast, on line 18 yourAge is incremented using the prefix increment operator. Thus, it is incremented *before* being printed, and the value displays as 41.

Finally, on lines 20 and 21 the values are printed again. Because the increment statement has completed, the value in myAge is now 41, as is the value in yourAge.

Precedence

Is the addition or the multiplication performed first in the following complex statement?

```
x = 5 + 3 * 8;
```

If the addition is performed first, the answer is 8 * 8, or 64. If the multiplication is performed first, the answer is 5 + 24, or 29.

Every operator has a precedence value, and the complete list is shown in Appendix A. Multiplication has higher precedence than addition, and thus the value of the expression is 29.

When two mathematical operators have the same precedence, they are performed in left-to-right order. Thus, in

```
x = 5 + 3 + 8 * 9 + 6 * 4;
```

multiplication is evaluated first, left to right. Therefore, 8*9 = 72, and 6*4 = 24. Now the expression is essentially

```
x = 5 + 3 + 72 + 24;
```

Now the addition, left to right, is 5 + 3 = 8; 8 + 72 = 80; 80 + 24 = 104.

Be careful with this. Some operators, such as assignment, are evaluated in right-to-left order! In any case, what if the precedence order doesn't meet your needs? Consider the following expression:

```
TotalSeconds = NumMinutesToThink + NumMinutesToType * 60;
```

In this expression you do not want to multiply the NumMinutesToType variable by 60 and then add it to NumMinutesToThink. You want to add the two variables to get the total number of minutes, and then you want to multiply that number by 60 to get the total seconds.

In this case, you use parentheses to change the precedence order. Items in parentheses are evaluated at a higher precedence than any of the mathematical operators. So, the following will accomplish what you want:

```
TotalSeconds = (NumMinutesToThink + NumMinutesToType) * 60;
```

Nesting Parentheses

For complex expressions, you might need to nest parentheses one within another. For example, you might need to compute the total seconds and then compute the total number of people who are involved before multiplying seconds times people:

```
TotalPersonSeconds = ( ( (NumMinutesToThink +
                         NumMinutesToType) * 60) *
                  (PeopleInTheOffice + PeopleOnVacation) );
```

This complicated expression is read from the inside out. First, NumMinutesToThink is added to NumMinutesToType because these are in the innermost parentheses. Then this sum is multiplied by 60. Next, PeopleInTheOffice is added to PeopleOnVacation. Finally, the total number of people found is multiplied by the total number of seconds.

This example raises an important, related issue. This expression is easy for a computer to understand but very difficult for a human to read, understand, or modify. Here is the same expression rewritten using some temporary integer variables:

```
TotalMinutes = NumMinutesToThink + NumMinutesToType;
TotalSeconds = TotalMinutes * 60;
TotalPeople = PeopleInTheOffice + PeopleOnVacation;
TotalPersonSeconds = TotalPeople * TotalSeconds;
```

This example takes longer to write and uses more temporary variables than the preceding example, but it is far easier to understand. Add a comment at the top to explain what this code does, and change the 60 to a symbolic constant. You then have code that is easy to understand and maintain.

Do   **Don't**

DO remember that expressions have a value.

DO use the prefix operator (++*variable*) to increment or decrement the variable before it is used in the expression.

DO use the postfix operator (*variable*++) to increment or decrement the variable after it is used.

DO use parentheses to change the order of precedence.

DON'T nest too deeply, because the expression becomes hard to understand and maintain.

The Bitwise Operators

Often you will want to set flags in your objects to keep track of the state of your object. (Is it in AlarmState? Has this been initialized yet? Are you coming or going?)

You can do this with `bool` types, but when you have many flags and storage size is an issue, it is convenient to be able to use the individual bits as flags in a collection. For example, you might want to keep track of a row of on/off switches on a nuclear powerplant control panel. All you need is a single bit for each switch, and you want to be able to treat them all as a group sometimes also (as in "if there is a meltdown, turn off all the switches").

Each byte has eight bits, so in a four-byte `long` you can hold 32 separate flags. A bit is said to be *set* if its value is 1, and *clear* if its value is 0. When you set a bit, you make its value 1, and when you clear it, you make its value 0. (Set and clear are both nouns and verbs.) You can set and clear bits by changing the value of the long, but that can be tedious and confusing.

NOTE

> Appendix C provides valuable additional information about binary and hexidecimal manipulation.

C++ provides bitwise operators that act upon the individual bits. These look like (but are different from) the logical operators, so many novice programmers confuse them. The bitwise operators and their alternatives (if necessary) are presented in Table 4.1.

Table 4.1. The bitwise operators.

symbol	operator
& (bitand)	AND
¦ (bitor)	OR
^ (xor)	exclusive OR
~ (compl)	complement
>>	shift right
<<	shift left

Operator AND

The AND operator (&) is a single ampersand. When you use AND on two bits, the result is 1 if both bits are 1, but 0 if either bit is 0 (or if both are 0). Think of this like so: The result is 1 if bit 1 is set *and* if bit 2 is set.

Operator OR

The second bitwise operator is OR, a single vertical bar (¦). When you OR two bits, the result is 1 if either bit is set or if both are set.

Operator Exclusive OR

The third bitwise operator is exclusive OR (^). When you exclusive OR two bits, the result is 1 if the two bits are different.

The Complement Operator

The complement operator (~) clears every bit in a number that is set and sets every bit that is clear. If the current value of the number is 1010 0011, the complement of that number is 0101 1100.

Shift Operators

The shift right (>>) and shift left (<<) operators are a little confusing because they are exactly the same as the insertion and extraction operators. Trust me on this one; the compiler is able to tell the difference by the context in which the operators are used.

The shift right operator shifts all the bits one position to the right and fills the opening with a zero. So, if the number is 0110 0011, the shift right will make it 0011 0001. The bit on the far right is discarded.

The shift left operator shifts all the bits one position to the left. With the same number, 0110 0011, the shift left will make it 1100 0110.

Setting Bits

When you want to set or clear a particular bit, you use masking operations. If you have a 4-byte flag and you want to set bit 8 to true, you need to OR the flag with the value 128. Why? 128 is 1000 0000 in binary; thus the value of the eighth bit is 128. Whatever the current value of that bit (set or clear), if you OR it with the value 128 you will set that bit and not change any of the other bits. Let's assume that the current value of the 16 bits is 1010 0110 0010 0110. To OR 128 to that value looks like this:

```
9 8765 4321
1010 0110 0010 0110   // bit 8 is clear
¦    0000 0000 1000 0000   // 128
--------------------
1010 0110 1010 0110   // bit 8 is set
```

There are a few things to note. First, as usual, bits are counted from right to left. Second, the value 128 is all zeros except for bit 8, the bit you want to set. Third, the starting number 1010 0110 0010 0110 is left unchanged by the OR operation, except that bit 8 was set. Had bit 8 already been set, it would have remained set, which is what you want.

Clearing Bits

If you want to clear bit 8, you can AND the bit with the complement of 128. The complement of 128 is the number you get when you take the bit pattern of 128 (1000 0000), set every bit that is clear, and clear every bit that is set (0111 1111). When you AND these numbers, the original number is unchanged, except for the eighth bit, which is forced to zero.

```
  1010 0110 1010 0110   // bit 8 is set
& 1111 1111 0111 1111   // ~128
---------------------
  1010 0110 0010 0110   // bit 8 cleared
```

To fully understand this solution, do the math yourself. Each time both bits are 1, write 1 in the answer. If either bit is 0, write 0 in the answer. Compare the answer with the original number. It should be the same except that bit 8 was cleared.

Flipping Bits

Finally, if you want to flip bit 8, no matter what its state, you exclusive OR the number with 128, like so:

```
  1010 0110 1010 0110   // number
^ 0000 0000 1000 0000   // 128
---------------------
  1010 0110 0010 0110   // bit flipped
^ 0000 0000 1000 0000   // 128
---------------------
  1010 0110 1010 0110   // flipped back
```

Fast Math Through the Power of the Bit

Another obscure but powerful use of bit operators is for fast math applications. Assembly language programmers have used binary math for years to improve performance. If your compiler has a good optimizer built in, it will convert a lot of your math operations into some of these equivalents. Let's look at an example. Appendix C has more detail on binary, but for now you'll have to trust me for this example. When you shift left, you raise the number by a power of two with each position shift:

```
x = 2;  // x now contains the bits 0000 0010
x<<1;   // x shifted left 1 bit position now has 0000 0100 or "4"
x<<2;   // x (4) shifted left 2 bit positions now has 0001 0000 or "16"
```

Do **Don't**

DO set bits by using masks and the OR operator.

DO clear bits by using masks and the AND operator.

DO flip bits by using masks and the exclusive OR operator.

The Nature of Truth

Programmers often use Boolean expressions to represent logic in their programs. Boolean expressions are expressions that are either true or false. They are represented by the built-in `bool` data type. However, keep in mind that C++ is an extension of C and has inherited some odd quirks. One of those quirks is that C does not have the `bool` type, so programmers invented various ways to represent `bool` values with integers. A C programmer, therefore, will say that a value of 0 is false and anything that is not false is true. Just keep that in mind in case you run into an old-timer. The methods that C programmers use to represent `bool` values are somewhat varied. The C++ `bool` type should end those variations.

Relational Operators

The relational operators are used to determine whether two numbers are equal, or whether one is greater or less than the other. In ANSI C++, all the relational operators return a `bool` type with the value true or false. The relational operators are presented later in Table 4.2.

If the integer variable `myAge` has the value 41 and the integer variable `yourAge` has the value 40, you can determine whether they are equal by using the relational "equals" operator:

```
myAge == yourAge;  // is the value in myAge the same as in yourAge?
```

This expression evaluates to 0, or false, because the variables are not equal. The expression

```
myAge > yourAge;  // is myAge greater than yourAge?
```

evaluates to 1 or true.

WARNING

Many novice C++ programmers confuse the assignment operator (=) with the equals operator (==). This can create a nasty bug in your program.

There are six relational operators: equals (==), less than (<), greater than (>), less than or equal to (<=), greater than or equal to (>=), and not equals (!=). Notice that the != operator has an alternative (not_eq) for character sets that do not include the exclamation character. Table 4.2 shows each relational operator, its use, and a sample code use.

Table 4.2. The relational operators.

Name	Operator	Example	Evaluates
Equals	==	100 == 50;	false
		50 == 50;	true
Not equal to	!= (not_eq)	100 != 50;	true
		50 != 50;	false
		50 not_eq 50;	false
Greater than	>	100 > 50;	true
		50 > 50;	false
Greater than or equal to	>=	100 >= 50;	true
		50 >= 50;	true
Less than	<	100 < 50;	false
		50 < 50;	false
Less than or equal to	<=	100 <= 50;	false
		50 <= 50;	true

Do	Don't

DO remember that relational operators return a bool value true or false.

DON'T confuse the assignment operator (=) with the equals relational operator (==). This is one of the most common C++ programming mistakes—be on guard for it.

The *if* Statement

Normally, your program flows along line by line in the order in which it appears in your source code. The if statement enables you to test for a condition (such as whether two variables are equal) and branch to different parts of your code depending on the result.

The simplest form of an `if` statement is this:

```
if (expression)
    statement;
```

The *expression* in the parentheses can be any expression at all, but it usually contains one of the relational expressions. If the expression returns a `bool` value of false, the statement that follows it is skipped. If it returns true, the statement that follows it is executed. Consider the following example:

```
if (bigNumber > smallNumber)
    bigNumber = smallNumber;
```

This code compares `bigNumber` and `smallNumber`. If `bigNumber` is larger, the second line sets its value to the value of `smallNumber`.

Because a block of statements surrounded by braces is exactly equivalent to a single statement, the following type of branch can be quite large and powerful:

```
if (expression)
{
    statement1;
    statement2;
    statement3;
}
```

Here's a simple example of this usage:

```
if (bigNumber > smallNumber)
{
    bigNumber = smallNumber;
    cout << "bigNumber: " << bigNumber << "\n";
    cout << "smallNumber: " << smallNumber << "\n";
}
```

This time, if `bigNumber` is larger than `smallNumber`, not only is it set to the value of `smallNumber`, but an informational message is printed. Listing 4.4 shows a fuller example of branching, based on relational operators.

TYPE Listing 4.4. Branching, based on relational operators.

```
1:   // Listing 4.4 - demonstrates if statement
2:   // used with relational operators
3:   #include <iostream.h>
4:   void main()
5:   {
6:       int RedSoxScore, YankeesScore;
7:       cout << "Enter the score for the Red Sox: ";
8:       cin >> RedSoxScore;
9:
10:      cout << "\nEnter the score for the Yankees: ";
11:      cin >> YankeesScore;
```

continues

Listing 4.4. continued

```
12:
13:        cout << "\n";
14:
15:        if (RedSoxScore > YankeesScore)
16:             cout << "Go Sox!\n";
17:
18:        if (RedSoxScore < YankeesScore)
19:        {
20:             cout << "Go Yankees!\n";
21:             cout << "Happy days in New York!\n";
22:        }
23:
24:        if (RedSoxScore == YankeesScore)
25:        {
26:             cout << "A tie? Naah, can't be.\n";
27:             cout << "Give me the real score for the Yanks: ";
28:             cin >> YankeesScore;
29:
30:             if (RedSoxScore > YankeesScore)
31:                  cout << "Knew it! Go Sox!";
32:
33:             if (YankeesScore > RedSoxScore)
34:                  cout << "Knew it! Go Yanks!";
35:
36:             if (YankeesScore == RedSoxScore)
37:                  cout << "Wow, it really was a tie!";
38:        }
39:
40:        cout << "\nThanks for telling me.\n";
41:  }
```

OUTPUT
```
Enter the score for the Yankees: 10
A tie? Naah, can't be
Give me the real score for the Yanks: 8
Knew it! Go Sox!
Thanks for telling me.
```

ANALYSIS This program asks for user input of scores for two baseball teams, which are stored in integer variables. The variables are compared in the if statement on lines 15, 18, and 24.

If one score is higher than the other, an informational message is printed. If the scores are equal, the block of code that begins on line 26 and ends on line 38 is entered. The second score is requested again, and then the scores are compared again.

Note that if the initial Yankees score was higher than the Red Sox score, the if statement on line 15 would evaluate as false, and line 16 would not be invoked. The test on line 18 would evaluate as true, and the statements on lines 20 and 21 would be invoked. Then the if statement on line 24 would be tested, and this would be false (if line 18 was true). Thus, the program would skip the entire block, falling through to line 39.

In this example, getting a true result in one `if` statement does not stop other `if` statements from being tested.

Earlier you learned that the statement inside the `if` test could be something other than a relational test. Here is where the C tradition comes into play. Consider the following:

```
if( x - 400 ) StillBig();
```

If x minus 400 equals 0, the result is considered a Boolean `false`; otherwise, the result is Boolean `true`. In this case, C++ performs an automatic conversion from `int` to `bool` on the result. An `int` 0 is converted to a `bool` `false` and all other `int`s are converted to `bool` `true`.

else

Often you want your program to take one branch if your condition is true, and another if it is false. What you really wanted in Listing 4.4 was to print `Go Sox` if (`RedSoxScore > Yankees`) was true and `Go Yankees` if it was not (barring an illegal tie).

The method shown so far, testing first one condition and then the other, works fine but is a bit cumbersome. The keyword `else` can make for far more readable code:

```
if (expression)
    statement;
else
    statement;
```

Listing 4.5 demonstrates the use of the keyword `else`.

TYPE **Listing 4.5. A Demonstration of the `else` keyword.**

```
1:    // Listing 4.5 - demonstrates if statement
2:    // with else clause
3:    #include <iostream.h>
4:    void main()
5:    {
6:        int firstNumber, secondNumber;
7:        cout << "Please enter a big number: ";
8:        cin >> firstNumber;
9:        cout << "\nPlease enter a smaller number: ";
10:       cin >> secondNumber;
11:       if (firstNumber > secondNumber)
12:            cout << "\nThanks!";
13:       else
14:            cout << "\nOops. The second is bigger!";
15:       cout << "\nThis always prints.\n";
16:   }
```

OUTPUT
```
Please enter a big number: 10
Please enter a smaller number: 12
Oops. The second is bigger!
This always prints.
```

ANALYSIS   The if statement on line 11 is evaluated. If the condition is true, the statement on line 12 is run; if it is false, the statement on line 14 is run. If the else clause on line 13 were removed, the statement on line 14 would run regardless of whether the if statement was true. Remember that the if statement ends after line 12. If the else were not there, line 14 would just be the next line in the program.

Remember that either or both of these statements could be replaced with a block of code in braces.

The *if* Statement

SYNTAX

Form 1

```
if (expression)
    statement;
statement2;
```

If the expression is evaluated as true, the statement is executed and the program continues with the next statement. If the expression is not true, the statement is ignored and the program jumps to the next statement.

Remember that the statement can be a single statement ending with a semicolon or a block enclosed in braces.

Form 2

```
if (expression)
    statement1;
else
    statement2;
statement3;
```

If the expression evaluates true, *statement1* is executed; otherwise, *statement2* is executed. Afterwards, the program continues with the next statement.

Example

```
if (SomeValue < 10)
    cout << "SomeValue is less than 10";

else
    cout << "SomeValue is not less than 10!";
cout << "Done." << endl;
```

Advanced *if* Statements

It is worth noting that any statement can be used in an `if` or `else` clause, even another `if` or `else` statement. Thus, you might see complex `if` statements in the following form:

```
if (expression1)
{
   if (expression2)
      statement1;
   else
   {
      if (expression3)
         statement2;
      else
         statement3;
   }
}
else
   statement4;
```

This cumbersome `if` statement says the following: "If expression1 is true and expression2 is true, execute statement1. If expression1 is true but expression2 is not true, and then if expression3 is true, execute statement2. If expression1 is true but expression2 and expression3 are false, execute statement3. Finally, if expression1 is not true, execute statement4." As you can see, complex `if` statements can be confusing!

Listing 4.6 gives an example of such a complex `if` statement.

TYPE **Listing 4.6. A complex nested `if` statement.**

```
1:   // Listing 4.6 - a complex nested
2:   // if statement
3:   #include <iostream.h>
4:   void main()
5:   {
6:       // Ask for two numbers
7:       // Assign the numbers to bigNumber and littleNumber
8:       // If bigNumber is bigger than littleNumber,
9:       // see if they are evenly divisible
10:      // If they are, see if they are the same number
11:
12:      int firstNumber, secondNumber;
13:      cout << "Enter two numbers.\nFirst: ";
14:      cin >> firstNumber;
15:      cout << "\nSecond: ";
16:      cin >> secondNumber;
17:      cout << "\n\n";
18:
19:      if (firstNumber >= secondNumber)
20:      {
```

continues

Listing 4.6. continued

```
21:        if ( (firstNumber % secondNumber) == 0) // evenly divisible?
22:        {
23:            if (firstNumber == secondNumber)
24:                cout << "They are the same!\n";
25:            else
26:                cout << "They are evenly divisible!\n";
27:        }
28:        else
29:            cout << "They are not evenly divisible!\n";
30:    }
31:    else
32:        cout << "Hey! The second one is larger!\n";
33: }
```

OUTPUT
```
Enter two numbers.
First: 10
Second: 2
They are evenly divisible!
```

ANALYSIS   Two numbers are prompted for and then compared. The first `if` statement, on line 19, checks to ensure that the first number is greater than or equal to the second. If not, the `else` clause on line 31 is executed.

If the first `if` is true, the block of code beginning on line 20 is executed, and the second `if` statement is tested on line 21. This checks to see whether the first number modulo the second number yields no remainder. If so, the numbers are either evenly divisible or equal. The `if` statement on line 23 checks for equality and displays the appropriate message either way.

If the `if` statement on line 21 fails, the `else` statement on line 28 is executed.

Using Braces in Nested *if* Statements

Although it is legal to leave out the braces on `if` statements that are only a single statement, and it is legal to nest `if` statements (such as when writing large nested statements), this can cause enormous confusion. Look at the following example:

```
if (x > y)              // if x is bigger than y
   if (x < z)           // and if x is smaller than z
      x = y;            // then set x to the value in z
```

Remember that whitespace and indentation are a convenience for the programmer; they make no difference to the compiler. It is easy to confuse the logic and inadvertently assign an `else` statement to the wrong `if` statement. Listing 4.7 illustrates this problem.

4

Listing 4.7. A demonstration of using braces for clarification.

`TYPE`

```
1:    // Listing 4.7 - demonstrates why braces
2:    // are important in nested if statements
3:    #include <iostream.h>
4:    void main()
5:    {
6:      int x;
7:      cout << "Enter a number less than 10 or greater than 100: ";
8:      cin >> x;
9:      cout << "\n";
10:
11:     if (x > 10)
12:        if (x > 100)
13:            cout << "More than 100, Thanks!\n";
14:     else                            // not the else intended!
15:        cout << "Less than 10, Thanks!\n";
16:
17:   }
```

`OUTPUT`
```
Enter a number less than 10 or greater than 100: 20
Less than 10, Thanks!
```

`ANALYSIS` The programmer intended to ask for a number less than 10 or greater than 100, check for the correct value, and then print a thank-you note.

If the `if` statement on line 11 evaluates true, the following statement (line 12) is executed. In this case, line 12 executes when the number entered is greater than 10. Line 12 contains an `if` statement also. This `if` statement evaluates true if the number entered is greater than 100. If the number is greater than 100, the statement on line 13 is executed.

If the number entered is less than or equal to 10, the `if` on line 11 evaluates to false. Program control goes to the next line following the `if`—in this case, line 16. If you enter a number less than 10, the output is as follows:

```
Enter a number less than 10 or greater than 100: 9
```

The `else` clause on line 14 was clearly intended to be attached to the `if` statement on line 11, and thus is indented accordingly. Unfortunately, the `else` statement is really attached to the `if` on line 12, and thus this program has a subtle bug.

It is a subtle bug because the compiler will not complain. This is a legal C++ program, but it just doesn't do what was intended. Further, most of the times that the programmer tests this program, it appears to work. As long as a number that is greater than 100 is entered, the program will seem to work just fine.

4

Listing 4.8 fixes the problem by putting in the necessary braces.

TYPE   **Listing 4.8. The proper use of braces with an `if` statement.**

```
1:    // Listing 4.8 - demonstrates proper use of braces
2:    // in nested if statements
3:    #include <iostream.h>
4:    void main()
5:    {
6:      int x;
7:      cout << "Enter a number less than 10 or greater than 100: ";
8:      cin >> x;
9:      cout << "\n";
10:
11:     if (x > 10)
12:     {
13:        if (x > 100)
14:            cout << "More than 100, Thanks!\n";
15:     }
16:     else            // the else intended!
17:        cout << "Less than 10, Thanks!\n";
18:   }
```

OUTPUT   Enter a number less than 10 or greater than 100: 20

ANALYSIS   The braces on lines 12 and 15 make everything between them into one statement, and now the `else` on line 16 applies to the `if` on line 11 as intended.

The user typed 20, so the `if` statement on line 11 is true; however, the `if` statement on line 13 is false, so nothing is printed. It would be better if the programmer put another `else` clause after line 14 so that errors would be caught and a message printed.

NOTE

The programs shown in this book are written to demonstrate the particular issues being discussed. They are kept intentionally simple; there is no attempt to "bulletproof" the code to protect against user error. In professional-quality code, every possible user error is anticipated and handled gracefully. Day 28 includes a listing of books and resources for further reading. If you intend to make programming anything more than a nice hobby, you might want to look into those resources.

Logical Operators

Often you want to ask more than one relational question at a time, such as, "Is it true that x is greater than y, and also true that y is greater than z?" A program might need to determine that both of these conditions are true, or that some other condition is true, in order to take an action.

Imagine a sophisticated alarm system that has this logic: "If the door alarm sounds AND it is after 6 p.m. AND it is NOT a holiday, OR if it is a weekend, then call the police." C++'s three logical operators are used to make this kind of evaluation. These operators and their alternative representations are listed in Table 4.3.

Table 4.3. The logical operators.

Operator	Symbol	Example
AND	&& (and)	`expression1 && expression2`
OR	¦¦ (or)	`expression1 ¦¦ expression2`
NOT	! (not)	`!expression`

Logical AND

A logical AND statement evaluates two expressions, and if both expressions are `true`, the logical AND statement is `true` as well. If it is `true` that you are hungry, AND it is true that you have money, THEN it is `true` that you should buy lunch. Thus,

```
if ( (x == 5) && (y == 5) )
```

or, using the alternative token,

```
if ( (x == 5) and (y == 5) )
```

would evaluate true if both x and y are equal to 5, and it would evaluate false if either one is not equal to 5. Note that both sides must be true for the entire expression to be true.

NOTE
> The logical AND is *two* ampersand (&&) symbols as opposed to the single & operator discussed in the bitwise operators section earlier in this lesson.

Logical OR

A logical OR statement evaluates two expressions. If either one is true, the expression is true. If you have money OR you have a credit card, you can pay the bill. You don't need both money and a credit card; you need only one, although having both would be fine as well. Thus,

```
if ( (x == 5) || (y == 5) )
```

and, alternatively,

```
if ( (x == 5) or (y == 5) )
```

evaluates true if either x or y is equal to 5, or if both are.

NOTE   The logical OR is *two* vertical pipe (||) symbols as opposed to the single vertical pipe (|) bitwise OR.

Logical NOT

This logical operator inverts the expression that follows it; so if the expression that follows it is true, the NOT statement is false. In contrast, if the expression is false, the NOT statement is true. Thus,

```
if ( !(x == 5) )
```

is true only if x is not equal to 5. This is exactly the same as using the not equals (!=) operator:

```
if (x != 5)
```

Relational Precedence

Relational operators and logical operators, being C++ expressions, each return a value depending on the types of the variables. When returned, the values are automatically converted to type bool. If the value returned is a nonzero value, it is converted to true. If the returned value is 0, it is converted to false. If the variables are of type bool, the return value is either true or false. And like all expressions, they have a precedence order (see Appendix A) that determines which relations are evaluated first. This fact is important when determining the value of the following statement:

```
if ( x > 5 && y > 5 || z > 5)
```

It might be that the programmer wanted this expression to evaluate true if both x and y are greater than 5 or if z is greater than 5. On the other hand, the programmer might have wanted this expression to evaluate true only if x is greater than 5 and if it is also true that either y is greater than 5 or z is greater than 5. These two interpretations could be clarified with parentheses:

```
( (x > 5 && y > 5) || z > 5) // first interpretation
```

or

```
( x > 5 && ( y > 5 || z > 5) ) // second interpretation
```

If x is 3, y is 4, and z is 10, the first interpretation is true (z is greater than 5, so ignore x and y). However, the second is false (it isn't true that x is greater than 10 AND that either y or z is as well).

Although precedence determines which relation is evaluated first, parentheses can both change the order and make the statement clearer:

```
if (   (x > 5)   && (y > 5 ||  z > 5) )
```

Using the values from earlier, this statement is false because it is not true that x (3) is greater than 5. The left side of the AND expression is false, and thus the entire statement is false. Remember that an AND statement requires that both sides be true: Something isn't both "good tasting" AND "good for you," if it isn't good tasting.

NOTE
> It is often a good idea to use extra parentheses to clarify what you want to group. Remember that the goal is to write programs that work *and* are easy to read and understand.

More About Truth and Falsehood

In a C++ test expression, a result of zero is converted to a bool false, and any other value is converted to true. Because expressions always have a value, many C++ programmers take advantage of this feature in their if statements. A statement such as

```
if (x)          // if x is true (nonzero)
    x = 0;
```

can be read as "If x has a nonzero value ((x != 0) is true), set x to 0." This is a bit of a cheat; it would be clearer if written out as follows:

```
if (x != 0)     // if x is nonzero
    x = 0;
```

Both statements are legal, but the latter is clearer. It is good programming practice to reserve the former method for true tests of logic, rather than for testing for nonzero values.

These two statements are also equivalent:

```
if (!x)          // if x is 0 (x == 0) is true

if (x == 0)      // if x is zero
```

The second statement, however, is somewhat easier to understand and is more explicit.

Do	Don't

DO put parentheses around your logical tests to make them clearer and to make the precedence explicit.

DO use braces in nested `if` statements to make the `else` statements clearer and to avoid bugs.

DO use the alternative operator representations for software that is to be maintained by an international team of programmers.

DON'T use `if(x)` as a synonym for `if(x != 0)`; the latter is clearer.

DON'T use `if(!x)` as a synonym for `if(x == 0)`; the latter is clearer.

 NOTE

Because C programmers have been defining their own `bool` type for so many years, many C++ compilers have not yet included it as a built-in type. If your compiler does not have `bool`, you can define it with an `enum` or `typedef` making `false=0` and `true=1` to make the examples in this book work.

Conditional (Ternary) Operator

The conditional operator (*expression_test* ? *expression_true* : *expression_false*) is C++'s only *ternary* operator; that is, it is the only operator to take three terms.

The conditional operator takes three expressions and returns a value:

```
(expression1) ? (expression2) : (expression3)
```

4

This line is read as "If *expression1* is true, return the value of *expression2*; otherwise, return the value of *expression3*." Typically, this value would be assigned to a variable.

Listing 4.9 shows an if statement rewritten using the conditional operator.

TYPE **Listing 4.9. A Demonstration of the conditional operator.**

```
1:   // Listing 4.9 - demonstrates the conditional operator
2:   //
3:   #include <iostream.h>
4:   void main()
5:   {
6:       int x, y, z;
7:       cout << "Enter two numbers.\n";
8:       cout << "First: ";
9:       cin >> x;
10:      cout << "\nSecond: ";
11:      cin >> y;
12:      cout << "\n";
13:
14:      if (x > y)
15:          z = x;
16:      else
17:          z = y;
18:
19:      cout << "z: " << z;
20:      cout << "\n";
21:
22:      z = (x > y) ? x : y;
23:
24:      cout << "z: " << z;
25:      cout << "\n";
26:  }
```

OUTPUT
```
Enter two numbers.
First: 5
Second: 8
z: 8
z: 8
```

ANALYSIS Three integer variables are created: x, y, and z. The first two are given values by the user. The if statement on line 14 tests to see which is larger and assigns the larger value to z. This value is printed on line 19.

The conditional operator on line 22 makes the same test and assigns z the larger value. It is read like this: "If x is greater than y, return the value of x; otherwise, return the value of y." The value returned is assigned to z. That value is printed on line 24. As you can see, the conditional statement is a shorter equivalent to the if...else statement.

Summary

This lesson has covered a lot of material. You have learned what C++ statements and expressions are, what C++ operators do, and how C++ if statements work.

You have seen that a block of statements enclosed by a pair of braces can be used anywhere that a single statement can be used.

You have learned that every expression evaluates to a value, and that value can be tested in an if statement or by using the conditional operator. You've also seen how to evaluate multiple statements using the logical operator, how to compare values using the relational operators, and how to assign values using the assignment operator.

You have explored operator precedence. You have seen how parentheses can be used to change the precedence and make precedence explicit and thus easier to manage.

Q&A

Q Why use unnecessary parentheses when precedence determines which operators are acted on first?

A Although it is true that the compiler knows the precedence and that a programmer can look up the precedence order, code that is easy to understand is easier to maintain.

Q If the relational operators always return true or false, why are other values also considered true?

A The relational operators return true or false, but every expression returns a value, and those values can also be evaluated in an if statement. Here's an example:

```
if ( (x = a + b) == 35 )
```

This is a perfectly legal C++ statement. It evaluates to a value even if the sum of a and b is not equal to 35. Also note that x is assigned the value that *is* the sum of a and b in any case. This is known as a side effect because not only is this evaluated as bool true or false here, but x now has the value of a + b, so it can be used elsewhere in the program as a number.

Q What effect do tabs, spaces, and new lines have on the program?

A Tabs, spaces, and new lines (known as whitespace) have no effect on the program, although judicious use of whitespace can make the program easier to read.

Q In a test expression, are negative numbers converted to true or false?

A All nonzero numbers, positive and negative, are converted to true.

Quiz

1. What is an expression?

2. Is x = 5 + 7 an expression? What is its value?

3. What is the value of 201 / 4?

4. What is the value of 201 % 4?

5. If myAge, a, and b are all int variables, what are their values after the following are run:

   ```
   myAge = 39;
   a = myAge++;
   b = ++myAge;
   ```

6. What is the value of 8+2*3?

7. What is the difference between x = 3 and x == 3?

8. Do the following values evaluate to true or false?

   a. 0

   b. 1

   c. -1

   d. x = 0

   e. x == 0 // assume that x has the value of 0

4

Exercises

1. Write a single if statement that examines two integer variables and changes the larger to the smaller, using only one else clause.

2. Examine the following program. Imagine entering three numbers, and write what output you expect.

   ```
   1:   #include <iostream.h>
   2:   void main()
   3:   {
   4:        int a, b, c;
   5:        cout << "Please enter three numbers\n";
   6:        cout << "a: ";
   7:        cin >> a;
   8:        cout << "\nb: ";
   9:        cin >> b;
   10:       cout << "\nc: ";
   11:       cin >> c;
   12:
   13:       if (c == (a-b))
   14:            cout << "a: ";
   15:            cout << a;
   ```

```
16:                 cout << "minus b: ";
17:                 cout << b;
18:                 cout << "equals c: ";
19:                 cout << c << endl;
20:                 if(c > 5)
21:                     cout << "and it is > 5!" << endl;
22:             else
23:                 cout << "a-b does not equal c: " << endl;
24:     }
```

3. Enter the program from exercise 2; compile, link, and run it. Enter the numbers 20, 10, and 50. Did you get the output you expected? Why not?

4. Examine this program and anticipate the output:

```
1:     #include <iostream.h>
2:     void main()
3:     {
4:         int a = 1, b = 1, c;
5:         if (c = (a-b))
6:                 cout << "The value of c is: " << c;
7:     }
```

5. Enter, compile, link, and run the program from exercise 4. What was the output? Why?

Day 5

Functions

Although object-oriented programming has shifted attention away from functions and toward objects, functions nonetheless remain a central component of any program. Today you learn

- ☐ What a function is and what its parts are.
- ☐ How to declare and define functions.
- ☐ How to pass parameters into functions.
- ☐ How to return a value from a function.

What Is a Function?

A function is, in effect, a subprogram that can act on data and return a value. Every C++ program has at least one function, main(). When your program starts, main() is called automatically. main() might call other functions, some of which might call still others.

Each function has its own name, and when that name is encountered, the execution of the program branches to the body of that function. When the function returns, execution resumes on the next line of the calling function. This flow is illustrated in Figure 5.1.

Figure 5.1.

Program flow with function calls.

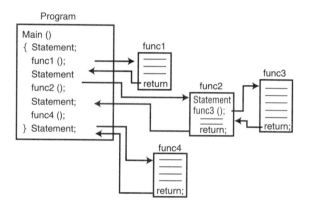

Well-designed functions perform a specific and easily understood task. Complicated tasks should be broken down into multiple functions, and then each can be called in turn. Sometimes a function contains only a single statement, or it might contain several statements. The key is to keep the level of complication low in each function. Dividing the problem into blocks and building larger solutions from the simplified blocks is a key concept in programming.

Functions come in two varieties: user-defined and built-in. Built-in functions are part of your compiler package; they are supplied by the manufacturer for your use. The include files that you have used so far are examples of built-in functions.

Declaring and Defining Functions

Using functions in your program requires that you first declare the function and that you then define the function. The declaration tells the compiler the name, return type, and parameters of the function. The definition tells the compiler how the function works. No function can be called from any other function that hasn't first been declared. The declaration of a function is called its *prototype*.

NEW TERM   *Prototype* is another word for "first," and in this case it means the first time a function is identified in your program. The compiler uses the prototypes for determining how your functions are to be used in your program and making sure that the use is consistent with the use you have defined.

Declaring the Function

You can declare a function in three ways:

☐ Write your prototype into a file, and then use the `#include` directive to include it in your program.

☐ Write the prototype into the file in which your function is used.

☐ Define the function before it is called by any other function. When you do this, the definition acts as its own declaration.

Although you can define the function before using it, and thus avoid the necessity of creating a function prototype, this is not good programming practice for three reasons. First, it is a bad idea to require that functions appear in a file in a particular order. Doing so makes it hard to maintain the program as requirements change.

Second, it is possible that function `A()` needs to be able to call function `B()`, but function `B()` also needs to be able to call function `A()` under some circumstances. It is not possible to define function `A()` before you define function `B()` and also to define function `B()` before you define function `A()`, so at least one of them must be declared in any case.

Third, function prototypes are a good and powerful debugging technique. If your prototype declares that your function takes a particular set of parameters or that it returns a particular type of value, and then your function does not match the prototype, the compiler can flag your error instead of waiting for it to show itself when you run the program.

Function Prototypes

Many of the built-in functions you use have their function prototypes already written in the files you include in your program by using `#include`. For functions you write yourself, you must include the prototype.

The function prototype is a statement, which means that it ends with a semicolon. It consists of the function's return type, name, and parameter list. The parameter list is a list of all the parameters and their types, separated by commas. Figure 5.2 illustrates the parts of the function prototype.

Figure 5.2.

*Parts of a function
prototype.*

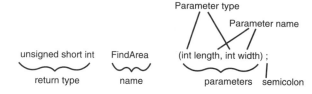

The function prototype and the function definition must agree exactly about the return type, the name, and the parameter list. If they do not agree, you get a compile-time error. Note, however, that the function prototype does not need to contain the names of the parameters, just their types. A prototype that looks like the following line is perfectly legal:

```
long Area(int, int);
```

This prototype declares a function named `Area()` that returns a long and that has two parameters, both integers. Although this is legal, it is not a good idea. Adding parameter names makes your prototype clearer. The same function with named parameters might look like this:

```
long Area(int length, int width);
```

It is now obvious what this function does and what the parameters are.

If a function has no parameters, it can be declared with empty parentheses or with the `void` keyword in place of the parameters list:

```
void DisplayResults(); // Empty parameters list
// can also be declared like this:
// void DisplayResults(void);
```

This book uses the simpler notation of an empty parameters list.

Note that all functions have a return type. If none is explicitly stated, the return type defaults to `int`. Your programs will be easier to understand, however, if you explicitly declare the return type of every function, including `main()`. In fact, some compilers enforce this rule, not allowing you to avoid declaring a return type. Listing 5.1 demonstrates a program that includes a function prototype for the `Area()` function.

TYPE   **Listing 5.1. Declaring, defining, and using functions.**

```
1:    // Listing 5.1 - demonstrates the use of function prototypes
2:
3:    typedef unsigned short USHORT;
4:    typedef unsigned long ULONG;
5:    #include <iostream.h>
6:    ULONG FindArea(USHORT length, USHORT width); //function prototype
7:    void main()
8:    {
```

```
9:      USHORT lengthOfYard;
10:     USHORT widthOfYard;
11:     ULONG areaOfYard;
12:
13:     cout << "\nHow wide (in feet) is your yard? ";
14:     cin >> widthOfYard;
15:     cout << "\nHow long (in feet) is your yard? ";
16:     cin >> lengthOfYard;
17:
18:     areaOfYard= FindArea(lengthOfYard,widthOfYard);
19:
20:     cout << "\nYour yard is ";
21:     cout << areaOfYard;
22:     cout << " square feet\n\n";
23:  }
24:
25:  ULONG FindArea(USHORT l, USHORT w)
26:  {
27:      return l * w;
28:  }
```

OUTPUT
```
How wide is your yard? 100
How long is your yard? 200
Your yard is 20000 square feet
```

ANALYSIS   The prototype for the FindArea() function is on line 6. Compare the prototype with the definition of the function on line 25. Note that the name, the return type, and the parameter types are the same. If they were different, a compiler error would have been generated. In fact, the only required difference is that the function prototype ends with a semicolon and has no body.

Also note that the parameter names in the prototype are length and width, but the parameter names in the definition are l and w. As discussed, the names in the prototype are not used; they are there as information to the programmer. When they are included, they should match the implementation when possible. This is a matter of good programming style and reduces confusion, but it is not required, as you see here.

The arguments are passed into the function in the order in which they are declared and defined, but there is no matching of the names. Had you passed in widthOfYard followed by lengthOfYard, the FindArea() function would have used the value in widthOfYard for length and lengthOfYard for width. The body of the function is always enclosed in braces, even when it consists of only one statement, as in this case.

Defining the Function

The definition of a function consists of the function header and its body. The header is exactly like the function prototype, except that the parameters must be named, and there is no terminating semicolon.

The body of the function is a set of statements enclosed in braces. Figure 5.3 shows the header and body of a function.

Figure 5.3.

The header and body of a function.

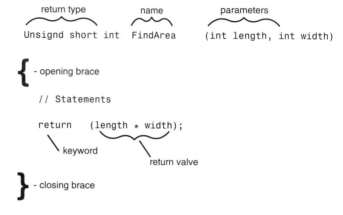

Functions

SYNTAX

Function Prototype

```
return_type function_name ( [type [parameterName]]... );
```

Function Definition

```
return_type function_name ( [type parameterName]...)
{
statements;
}
```

A *function prototype* tells the compiler the return type, name, and parameter list. Functions are not required to have parameters, and if they do, the prototype is not required to list their names—only their types. A prototype always ends with a semicolon (;).

A *function definition* must agree in return type and parameter list with its prototype. It must provide names for all the parameters, and the body of the function definition must be surrounded by braces. All statements within the body of the function must be terminated with semicolons, but the function itself is not ended with a semicolon; it ends with a closing brace.

If the function returns a value, it should end with a return statement; however, return statements can legally appear anywhere in the body of the function.

Every function has a return type. If one is not explicitly designated, the return type will be int. Be sure to give every function an explicit return type. If a function does not return a value, its return type will be void.

5

Function Prototype Examples

```
long FindArea(long length, long width); // returns long, has two parameters
void PrintMessage(int messageNumber); // returns void, has one parameter
int GetChoice();                      // returns int, has no parameters
BadFunction();                        // returns int, has no parameters
```

Function Definition Examples

```
long FindArea(long l, long w)
{
return l * w;
}

void PrintMessage(int whichMsg)
{
    if (whichMsg == 0)
        cout << "Hello.\n";
    if (whichMsg == 1)
        cout << "Goodbye.\n";
    if (whichMsg > 1)
        cout << "I'm confused.\n";
}
```

Execution of Functions

When you call a function, execution begins with the first statement after the opening brace ({). Branching can be accomplished by using the if statement (and related statements that are discussed on Day 7, "More Program Flow"). Functions can also call other functions and can even call themselves (see the section titled "Recursion," later in this lesson).

Local Variables

Not only can you pass variables into the function, but you also can declare variables within the body of the function. This is done using *local variables*, which are so named because they exist only locally within the function itself. When the function returns, the local variables are no longer available.

Local variables are defined like any other variables. The parameters passed into the function are also considered local variables and can be used exactly as if they had been defined within the body of the function. Listing 5.2 is an example of using parameters and locally defined variables within a function.

TYPE   **Listing 5.2. Using local variables and parameters.**

```
1:      #include <iostream.h>
2:
3:      float Convert(float);
4:      void main()
5:      {
6:         float TempFer;
7:         float TempCel;
8:
9:         cout << "Please enter the temperature in Fahrenheit: ";
10:        cin >> TempFer;
11:        TempCel = Convert(TempFer);
12:        cout << "\nHere's the temperature in Celsius: ";
13:        cout << TempCel << endl;
14:     }
15:
16:     float Convert(float TempFer)
17:     {
18:        float TempCel;
19:        TempCel = ((TempFer - 32) * 5) / 9;
20:        return TempCel;
24:     }
```

OUTPUT   Please enter the temperature in Fahrenheit: 212
Here's the temperature in Celsius: 100

Please enter the temperature in Fahrenheit: 32
Here's the temperature in Celsius: 0

Please enter the temperature in Fahrenheit: 85
Here's the temperature in Celsius: 29.4444

ANALYSIS   On lines 6 and 7, two float variables are declared—one to hold the temperature in Fahrenheit and one to hold the temperature in Celsius. The user is prompted to enter a Fahrenheit temperature on line 9, and that value is passed to the function Convert().

Execution jumps to the first line of the function Convert() on line 18, where a local variable, also named TempCel, is declared. Note that this local variable is not the same as the variable TempCel on line 7. This variable exists only within the function Convert(). The value passed as a parameter, TempFer, is also just a local copy of the variable passed in by main().

This function could have named the parameter FerTemp and the local variable CelTemp, and the program would work equally well. You can reenter these names and recompile the program to see this work.

The local function variable TempCel is assigned the value that results from subtracting 32 from the parameter TempFer, multiplying by 5, and then dividing by 9. This value is then returned as the return value of the function, and on line 11 it is assigned to the variable TempCel in the main() function. It is printed on line 12.

The program is run three times. The first time, the value 212 is passed in to ensure that the boiling point of water in degrees Fahrenheit (212) generates the correct answer in degrees Celsius (100). The second test is the freezing point of water. The third test is a random number chosen to generate a fractional result.

As an exercise, try reentering the program with other variable names as illustrated here:

```
1:      #include <iostream.h>
2:
3:      float Convert(float);
4:      void main()
5:      {
6:         float TempFer;
7:         float TempCel;
8:
9:         cout << "Please enter the temperature in Fahrenheit: ";
10:        cin >> TempFer;
11:        TempCel = Convert(TempFer);
12:        cout << "\nHere's the temperature in Celsius: ";
13:        cout << TempCel << endl;
14:     }
15:
16:     float Convert(float Fer)
17:     {
18:        float Cel;
19:        Cel = ((Fer - 32) * 5) / 9;
20:        return Cel;
21:     }
```

You should get the same results.

NEW TERM   A variable has *scope*, which determines how long it is available to your program and where it can be accessed. Variables declared within a block (a collection of statements inside brackets) are scoped to that block; they can be accessed only within that block, and they "go out of existence" when that block ends. Global variables have global scope and are available anywhere within your program.

None of this matters very much if you are careful not to reuse your variable names within any given function.

Global Variables

Variables defined outside of any function have global scope and, thus, are available from any function in the program, including main().

Local variables with the same name as global variables do not change the global variables. A local variable with the same name as a global variable *hides* the global variable, however. If a function has a variable with the same name as a global variable, the name refers to the local variable—not the global—when used within the function. Listing 5.3 illustrates these points.

TYPE **Listing 5.3. A demonstration of global and local variables.**

```
1:    #include <iostream.h>
2:    void myFunction();            // prototype
3:
4:    int x = 5, y = 7;            // global variables
5:    void main()
6:    {
7:
8:        cout << "x from main: " << x << "\n";
9:        cout << "y from main: " << y << "\n\n";
10:       myFunction();
11:       cout << "Back from myFunction!\n\n";
12:       cout << "x from main: " << x << "\n";
13:       cout << "y from main: " << y << "\n";
14:   }
15:
16:   void myFunction()
17:   {
18:       int y = 10;
19:
20:       cout << "x from myFunction: " << x << "\n";
21:       cout << "y from myFunction: " << y << "\n\n";
22:   }
```

OUTPUT
```
x from main: 5
y from main: 7

x from myFunction: 5
y from myFunction: 10

Back from myFunction!

x from main: 5
y from main: 7
```

ANALYSIS This simple program illustrates a few key, and potentially confusing, points about local and global variables. On line 4 two global variables, x and y, are declared. The global variable x is initialized with the value 5, and the global variable y is initialized with the value 7.

On lines 8 and 9 in the function main(), these values are printed to the screen. Note that the function main() defines neither variable; because they are global, they are already available to main().

When myFunction() is called on line 10, program execution passes to line 18, and a local variable, y, is defined and initialized with the value 10. On line 20, myFunction() prints the value of the variable x, and the global variable x is used, just as it was in main(). On line 21, however, when the variable name y is used, the *local* variable y is used, hiding the global variable with the same name.

The function call ends, and control returns to main(), which again prints the values in the global variables. Note that the global variable y was totally unaffected by the value assigned to myFunction()'s local y variable.

Global Variables: A Word of Caution

In C++, global variables are legal, but they are almost never used. C++ grew out of C, and in C, global variables are a dangerous but necessary tool. They are necessary because there are times when the programmer needs to make data available to many functions and does not want to pass that data as a parameter from function to function.

Globals are dangerous because they are shared data, and one function can change a global variable in a way that is invisible to another function. This can and does create bugs that are very difficult to find.

On Day 14 you'll see a powerful alternative to global variables that C++ offers, but that is unavailable in C.

More on Local Variables

Variables declared within the function are said to have local scope. That means, as discussed in the previous section, that they are visible and usable only within the function in which they are defined. In fact, in C++ you can define variables anywhere within the function, not just at its top. The scope of the variable is the block in which it is defined. Thus, if you define a variable inside a set of braces within the function, that variable is available only within that block. Listing 5.4 illustrates this idea.

TYPE   **Listing 5.4. Variables scoped within a block.**

```
1:      // Listing 5.4 - demonstrates variables
2:      // scoped within a block
3:
4:      #include <iostream.h>
5:
6:      void myFunc();
7:
8:      void main()
9:      {
10:         int x = 5;
11:         cout << "\nIn main x is: " << x;
```

continues

Listing 5.4. continued

```
12:
13:        myFunc();
14:
15:        cout << "\nBack in main, x is: " << x;
16:    }
17:
18:    void myFunc()
19:    {
20:
21:        int x = 8;
22:        cout << "\nIn myFunc, local x: " << x;
23:
24:        {
25:            cout << "\nIn block in myFunc, x is: " << x;
26:
27:            int x = 9;
28:
29:            cout << "\nVery local x: " << x;
30:        }
31:
32:        cout << "\nOut of block, in myFunc, x: " << x;
33:    }
```

OUTPUT
```
In main x is 5
In myFunc, local x: 8
In block in myFunc, x is: 8
Very local x: 9
Out of block, in myFunc, x: 8
Back in main, x is 5
```

ANALYSIS This program begins with the initialization of the local variable x on line 10, in main(). The printout on line 11 verifies that x was initialized with the value 5.

MyFunc() is called, and a local variable, also named x, is initialized with the value 8 on line 21. Its value is printed on line 22.

A block is started on line 24, and the variable x from the function is printed again on line 25. A new variable also named x, but local to the block, is created on line 27 and initialized with the value 9.

The value of the newest variable x is printed on line 29. The local block ends on line 30, and the variable created on line 27 goes out of scope and is no longer visible.

When x is printed on line 32, it is the x that was declared on line 21. This x was unaffected by the x that was defined on line 27; its value is still 8.

On line 33 MyFunc() goes out of scope, and its local variable x becomes unavailable. Execution returns to line 15, and the value of the local variable x, which was created on line 10, is printed. It was unaffected by either of the variables defined in MyFunc().

As you've undoubtedly seen by now, this program would be far less confusing if these three variables were given unique names!

Function Statements

There is virtually no limit to the number or types of statements that can be in a function body. Although you can't define another function from within a function, you can call a function, and of course, main() does just that in nearly every C++ program. Functions can even call themselves, which is discussed soon in the section on recursion.

NOTE   Although there is no limit to the size of a function in C++, well-designed functions tend to be small. Many programmers advise keeping your functions short enough to fit on a single screen so that you can see the entire function at one time. This is a rule of thumb, often broken by very good programmers, but a smaller function is easier to understand and maintain.

Each function should carry out a single, easily understood task. If your functions start getting large, look for places where you can divide them into component tasks.

Function Arguments

Function arguments do not all have to be of the same type. It is perfectly reasonable to write a function that takes an integer, two longs, and a character as its arguments.

Any valid C++ expression can be a function argument, including constants, mathematical and logical expressions, and other functions that return a value.

Using Functions as Parameters to Functions

Although it is legal to use a function that returns a value as a parameter to another function, it can make for code that is hard to read and hard to debug.

As an example, suppose you have the functions double(), triple(), square(), and cube(), each of which returns a value. You could write

```
Answer = (double(triple(square(cube(myValue)))));
```

This statement takes a variable, myValue, and passes it as an argument to the function cube(), whose return value is passed as an argument to the function square(), whose return value is in turn passed to triple(), and that return value is passed to double(). The return value of this doubled, tripled, squared, and cubed number is now passed to Answer.

NOTE
> The cube(), square(), triple(), and double() functions in this example are not built-in functions but fictitious functions that might be defined elsewhere in your program.

It is difficult to be certain what this code does (was the value tripled before or after it was squared?), and if the answer is wrong, it will be hard to figure out which function failed.

An alternative is to assign each step to its own intermediate variable:

```
unsigned long myValue = 2;
unsigned long cubed   =  cube(myValue);       // cubed = 8
unsigned long squared = square(cubed);        // squared = 64
unsigned long tripled = triple(squared);      // tripled = 196
unsigned long Answer =  double(tripled);      // Answer = 392
```

Now each intermediate result can be examined, and the order of execution is explicit.

Parameters Are Local Variables

The arguments passed into the function are local to the function. Changes made to the arguments do not affect the values in the calling function. This is known as *passing by value*, which means a local copy of each argument is made in the function. These local copies are treated just like any other local variables. Listing 5.5 illustrates this point.

TYPE   **Listing 5.5. A Demonstration of passing by value.**

```
1:      // Listing 5.5 - demonstrates passing by value
2:
3:      #include <iostream.h>
4:
5:      void swap(int x, int y);
6:
7:      void main()
8:      {
9:        int x = 5, y = 10;
10:
11:       cout << "Main. Before swap, x: " << x << " y: " << y << "\n";
12:       swap(x,y);
```

```
13:            cout << "Main. After swap, x: " << x << " y: " << y << "\n";
14:        }
15:
16:        void swap (int x, int y)
17:        {
18:          int temp;
19:
20:          cout << "Swap. Before swap, x: " << x << " y: " << y << "\n";
21:
22:          temp = x;
23:          x = y;
24:          y = temp;
25:
26:          cout << "Swap. After swap, x: " << x << " y: " << y << "\n";
27:
28:        }
```

OUTPUT
```
Main. Before swap. x: 5 y: 10
Swap. Before swap. x: 5 y: 10
Swap. After swap. x: 10 y: 5
Main. After swap. x: 5 y: 10
```

ANALYSIS This program initializes two variables in main() and then passes them to the swap() function, which appears to swap them. When they are examined again in main(), however, they are unchanged!

The variables are initialized on line 9, and their values are displayed on line 11. swap() is called, and the variables are passed in.

Execution of the program switches to the swap() function, where on line 20 the values are printed again. They are in the same order as they were in main(), as expected. On lines 22 to 24, the values are swapped, and this action is confirmed by the printout on line 26. Indeed, while in the swap() function, the values are swapped.

Execution then returns to line 13, back in main(), where the values are no longer swapped.

As you've figured out, the values passed into the swap() function are passed by value, meaning that copies of the values are made that are local to swap(). These local variables are swapped in lines 22 to 24, but the variables back in main() are unaffected.

On Day 8, "Pointers," and Day 10, "Advanced Functions," you'll see alternatives to passing by value that allow the values in main() to be changed.

Return Values

Functions return a value or return void. void is a signal to the compiler that no value will be returned.

To return a value from a function, write the keyword return followed by the value you want to return. The value might itself be an expression that returns a value, as in the following example:

```
return 5;              // Returns the int value 5
return (x > 5);        // Returns the true or false
return (MyFunction()); // Returns the return value of MyFunction()
```

These are all legal return statements, assuming that the function MyFunction() itself returns a value. The value in the second statement, return (x > 5), is false (or 0) if x is not greater than 5, or it returns true (1). What is returned is the value of the expression, not the value of x.

When the return keyword is encountered, the expression following return is returned as the value of the function. Program execution returns immediately to the calling function, and any statements following the return are not executed.

It is legal to have more than one return statement in a single function. Listing 5.6 illustrates this idea.

TYPE   **Listing 5.6. Multiple return statements.**

```
1:     // Listing 5.6 - demonstrates multiple return
2:     // statements
3:
4:     #include <iostream.h>
5:
6:     int Doubler(int AmountToDouble);
7:
8:     void main()
9:     {
10:
11:        int result = 0;
12:        int input;
13:
14:        cout << "Enter a number between 0 and 10,000 to double: ";
15:        cin >> input;
16:
17:        cout << "\nBefore doubler is called... ";
18:        cout << "\ninput: " << input << " doubled: " << result << "\n";
19:
20:        result = Doubler(input);
21:
22:        cout << "\nBack from Doubler...\n";
23:        cout << "\ninput: " << input << "    doubled: " << result << "\n";
24:
25:
26:     }
27:
28:     int Doubler(int original)
29:     {
```

```
30:          if (original <= 10000)
31:              return original * 2;
32:          else
33:              return -1;
34:          cout << "You can't get here!\n";
35:      }
```

```
Enter a number between 0 and 10,000 to double: 9000
Before doubler is called...
    input: 9000 doubled: 0
Back from doubler...
input: 9000 doubled: 18000

Enter a number between 0 and 10,000 to double: 11000
Before doubler is called...
input: 11000  doubled: 0
Back from doubler...
input: 11000  doubled: -1
```

A number is requested on lines 14 and 15, and it is printed on line 18 along with the local variable result. The function Doubler() is called on line 20, and the input value is passed as a parameter. The result is assigned to the local variable result, and the values are reprinted on lines 22 and 23.

On line 30, in the function Doubler(), the parameter is tested to see whether it is greater than 10,000. If it is not, the function returns twice the original number. If it is greater than 10,000, the function returns -1 as an error value.

The statement on line 34 is never reached because regardless of whether the value is greater than 10,000, the function returns before it gets to line 34, on either line 31 or line 33. A good compiler would warn that this statement cannot be executed, and a good programmer would take it out!

Default Parameters

For every parameter you declare in a function prototype and definition, the calling function must pass in a value. The value passed in must be of the declared type. Thus, if you have a function declared as

```
long myFunction(int);
```

the function must in fact take an integer variable. If the function definition differs or if you fail to pass in an integer, you get a compiler error.

The one exception to this rule is if the function prototype declares a default value for the parameter. A default value is a value to use if none is supplied. The preceding declaration could be rewritten as

```
long myFunction (int x = 50);
```

This prototype says the following: "myFunction() returns a long and takes an integer parameter. If an argument is not supplied, use the default value of 50." Because parameter names are not required in function prototypes, this declaration could have been written as

```
long myFunction (int = 50);
```

The function definition is not changed by declaring a default parameter. The function definition header for this function would be as follows:

```
long myFunction (int x)
```

If the calling function did not include a parameter, the compiler would fill x with the default value of 50. The name of the default parameter in the prototype need not be the same as the name in the function header; the default value is assigned by position, not name.

Any or all of the function's parameters can be assigned default values. The one restriction is this: If any one of the parameters does not have a default value, no previous parameter can have a default value.

If the function prototype looks like

```
long myFunction (int Param1, int Param2, int Param3);
```

you can assign a default value to Param2 only if you have assigned a default value to Param3. You can assign a default value to Param1 only if you've assigned default values to *both* Param2 and Param3. Listing 5.7 demonstrates the use of default values.

TYPE   **Listing 5.7. Default parameter values.**

```
1:   // Listing 5.7 - demonstrates use
2:   // of default parameter values
3:
4:   #include <iostream.h>
5:
6:   int AreaCube(int length, int width = 25, int height = 1);
7:
8:   void main()
9:   {
10:        int length = 100;
11:        int width = 50;
12:        int height = 2;
13:        int area;
14:
15:        area = AreaCube(length, width, height);
16:        cout << "First area equals: " << area << "\n";
17:
18:        area = AreaCube(length, width);
19:        cout << "Second time area equals: " << area << "\n";
20:
21:        area = AreaCube(length);
```

```
22:        cout << "Third time area equals: " << area << "\n";
23:    }
24:
25:    AreaCube(int length, int width, int height)
26:    {
27:
28:        return (length * width * height);
29:    }
```

OUTPUT
First area equals: 10000
Second time area equals: 5000
Third time area equals: 2500

ANALYSIS
On line 6 the AreaCube() prototype specifies that the AreaCube() function takes three integer parameters. The last two have default values.

This function computes the area of the cube whose dimensions are passed in. If no width is passed in, a width of 25 is used and a height of 1 is used. If the width but not the height is passed in, a height of 1 is used. It is not possible to pass in the height without passing in a width.

On lines 10 through 12, the dimensions length, height, and width are initialized, and they are passed to the AreaCube() function on line 15. The values are computed, and the result is printed on line 16.

Execution returns to line 18, where AreaCube() is called again, but with no value for height. The default value is used, and again the dimensions are computed and printed.

Execution returns to line 21, and this time neither the width nor the height is passed in. Execution branches for a third time to line 28. The default values are used. The area is computed and then printed.

5

Do	Don't

DO remember that function parameters act as local variables within the function.

DON'T try to create a default value for a first parameter if there is no default value for the second.

DON'T forget that arguments passed by value cannot affect the variables in the calling function.

DON'T forget that changes to a global variable in one function change that variable for all functions.

Overloading Functions

C++ enables you to create more than one function with the same name. This is called *function overloading*. The functions must differ in their parameter list, with a different type of parameter, a different number of parameters, or both. Here's an example:

```
int myFunction (int, int);
int myFunction (long, long);
int myFunction (long);
```

myFunction() is overloaded with three different parameter lists. The first and second versions differ in the types of the parameters, and the third differs in the number of parameters.

The return types can be the same or different on overloaded functions. However, different return types alone are not sufficient to distinguish between overloaded functions. Two functions with the same name and parameter list but different return types generate a compiler error.

By changing the number or type of the parameters, you can give two or more functions the same function name, and the right one will be called by matching the parameters used. This allows you to create a function that can average integers, doubles, and other values without having to create individual names for each function, such as AverageInts(), AverageDoubles(), and so on.

Suppose you write a function that doubles whatever input you give it. You would like to be able to pass in an int, a long, a float, or a double. Without function overloading, you would have to create four function names:

```
int DoubleInt(int);
long DoubleLong(long);
float DoubleFloat(float);
double DoubleDouble(double);
```

With function overloading, you make this declaration:

```
int Double(int);
long Double(long);
float Double(float);
double Double(double);
```

This is easier to read and easier to use. You don't have to worry about which one to call; you just pass in a variable, and the right function is called automatically. Listing 5.8 illustrates the use of function overloading.

5

TYPE Listing 5.8. Function overloading.

```
1:    // Listing 5.8 - demonstrates
2:    // function overloading
3:
4:    #include <iostream.h>
5:
6:    int Double(int);
7:    long Double(long);
8:    float Double(float);
9:    double Double(double);
10:
11:   void main()
12:   {
13:       int      myInt = 6500;
14:       long     myLong = 65000;
15:       float    myFloat = 6.5;
16:       double   myDouble = 6.5e20;
17:
18:       int      doubledInt;
19:       long     doubledLong;
20:       float    doubledFloat;
21:       double   doubledDouble;
22:
23:       cout << "myInt: " << myInt << "\n";
24:       cout << "myLong: " << myLong << "\n";
25:       cout << "myFloat: " << myFloat << "\n";
26:       cout << "myDouble. " << myDouble << "\n";
27:
28:       doubledInt = Double(myInt);
29:       doubledLong = Double(myLong);
30:       doubledFloat = Double(myFloat);
31:       doubledDouble = Double(myDouble);
32:
33:       cout << "doubledInt: " << doubledInt << "\n";
34:       cout << "doubledLong: " << doubledLong << "\n";
35:       cout << "doubledFloat: " << doubledFloat << "\n";
36:       cout << "doubledDouble: " << doubledDouble << "\n";
37:
38:   }
39:
40:   int Double(int original)
41:   {
42:     cout << "In Double(int)\n";
43:     return 2 * original;
44:   }
45:
46:   long Double(long original)
47:   {
48:     cout << "In Double(long)\n";
49:     return 2 * original;
50:   }
51:
```

continues

Listing 5.8. continued

```
52:  float Double(float original)
53:  {
54:    cout << "In Double(float)\n";
55:    return 2 * original;
56:  }
57:
58:  double Double(double original)
59:  {
60:    cout << "In Double(double)\n";
61:    return 2 * original;
62:  }
```

OUTPUT
```
myInt: 6500
myLong: 65000
myFloat: 6.5
myDouble: 6.5e20
In Double(int)
In Double(long)
In Double(float)
In Double(double)
DoubledInt: 13000
DoubledLong:130000
DoubledFloat:13
DoubledDouble: 13e21
```

ANALYSIS The Double() function is overloaded with int, long, float, and double. The prototypes are on lines 6 through 9, and the definitions are on lines 40 through 62.

In the body of the main program, eight local variables are declared. On lines 13 through 16, four of the values are initialized, and on lines 28 through 31, the other four are assigned the results of passing the first four to the Double() function. Note that when Double() is called, the calling function does not distinguish which one to call; it just passes in an argument, and the correct one is invoked.

The compiler examines the arguments and chooses which of the four Double() functions to call. The output reveals that each of the four was called in turn, as you would expect.

Special Topics

Because functions are so central to programming, a few special topics arise that might be of interest when you confront special problems. Used wisely, inline functions can help you squeak out that last bit of performance. Function recursion is one of those wonderful, esoteric bits of programming, which every once in a while can cut through a thorny problem otherwise not easily solved.

Inline Functions

When you define a function, normally the compiler creates just one set of instructions in memory. When you call the function, execution of the program jumps to those instructions, and when the function returns, execution jumps back to the next line in the calling function. If you call the function 10 times, your program jumps to the same set of instructions each time. This means there is only one copy of the function, not 10.

There is some performance overhead in jumping in and out of functions. It turns out that some functions are very small, just a line or two of code, and some efficiency can be gained if the program can avoid making these jumps just to execute one or two instructions. When programmers speak of efficiency, they usually mean speed: The program runs faster if the function call can be avoided.

If a function is declared with the keyword `inline`, the compiler does not create a real function: It copies the code from the inline function directly into the calling function. No jump is made; it is just as though you had written the statements of the function right into the calling function.

Note that inline functions can bring a heavy cost. If the function is called 10 times, the inline code is copied into the calling functions each of those 10 times. The tiny improvement in speed you might achieve is more than overshadowed by the increase in size of the executable program. Even the speed increase might be illusory for several reasons. First, today's optimizing compilers do a terrific job on their own, and there is almost never a big gain from declaring a function `inline`. Not only that, but the ANSI/ISO standard does not guarantee that all functions given the `inline` keyword will be inlined. Compiler vendors are allowed the freedom in the interest of optimizing code appropriately for the situation. More importantly, the increased size from using `inline` functions brings its own performance cost.

What's the rule of thumb? If you have a small function of one or two statements, it is a candidate for `inline`. When in doubt, though, leave it out. Listing 5.9 demonstrates an inline function.

| TYPE | Listing 5.9. An inline function. |

```
1:    // Listing 5.9 - demonstrates inline functions
2:
3:    #include <iostream.h>
4:
5:    inline int Double(int);
6:
7:    void main()
8:    {
9:      int target;
10:
```

continues

Listing 5.9. continued

```
11:    cout << "Enter a number to work with: ";
12:    cin >> target;
13:    cout << "\n";
14:
15:    target = Double(target);
16:    cout << "Target: " << target << endl;
17:
18:    target = Double(target);
19:    cout << "Target: " << target << endl;
20:
21:
22:    target = Double(target);
23:    cout << "Target: " << target << endl;
24: }
25:
26: int Double(int target)
27: {
28:    return 2*target;
29: }
```

OUTPUT

```
Enter a number to work with: 20
Target: 40
Target: 80
Target: 160
```

ANALYSIS   On line 5 Double() is declared to be an inline function taking an int parameter and returning an int. The declaration is just like any other prototype except that the keyword inline precedes the return value.

This compiles into code that is the same as if you had written

```
target = 2 * target;
```

everywhere you entered

```
target = Double(target);
```

By the time your program executes, the instructions are already in place, compiled into the .OBJ file. This saves a jump in the execution of the code, at the cost of a larger program.

NOTE

> Inline is a *hint* to the compiler that you would like the function to be inlined. The compiler is free to ignore the hint and make a real function call.

Recursion

Besides calling other functions, a function can call itself. This is called *recursion*, and recursion can be direct or indirect. It is direct when a function calls itself; it is indirect recursion when a function calls another function that then calls the first function.

Some problems are most easily solved by recursion, usually those in which you act on data and then act in the same way on the result. Both types of recursion, direct and indirect, come in two varieties: those that eventually end and produce an answer, and those that never end and produce a run-time failure. Programmers think that the latter is quite funny (when it happens to someone else).

It is important to note that when a function calls itself, a new copy of that function is run. The local variables in the second version are independent of the local variables in the first, and they cannot affect one another directly, any more than the local variables in main() can affect the local variables in any function it calls, which was illustrated in Listing 5.4.

To illustrate solving a problem using recursion, consider the Fibonacci series:

1,1,2,3,5,8,13,21,34...

Each number, after the second, is the sum of the two numbers before it. A Fibonacci problem might be to determine what the twelfth number in the series is.

One way to solve this problem is to examine the series carefully. The first two numbers are 1. Each subsequent number is the sum of the previous two numbers. Thus, the seventh number is the sum of the sixth and fifth numbers. More generally, the nth number is the sum of $n - 2$ and $n - 1$, as long as $n > 2$.

Recursive functions need a stop condition. Something must happen to cause the program to stop recursing, or it will never end. In the Fibonacci series, $n < 3$ is a stop condition.

The algorithm to use is this:

1. Ask the user for a position in the series.
2. Call the fib() function with that position, passing in the value that the user entered.
3. The fib() function examines the argument (n). If $n < 3$, it returns 1; otherwise, fib() calls itself (recursively) passing in $n-2$, calls itself again passing in $n-1$, and returns the sum.

If you call fib(1), it returns 1. If you call fib(2), it returns 1. If you call fib(3), it returns the sum of calling fib(2) and fib(1). Because fib(2) returns 1 and fib(1) returns 1, fib(3) returns 2.

If you call fib(4), it returns the sum of calling fib(3) and fib(2). You've seen that fib(3) returns 2 (by calling fib(2) and fib(1)) and that fib(2) returns 1, so fib(4) sums these numbers and returns 3, which is the fourth number in the series.

Taking this one step further, if you call fib(5), it returns the sum of fib(4) and fib(3). You've seen that fib(4) returns 3 and fib(3) returns 2, so the sum returned is 5.

This method is not the most efficient way to solve this problem (in fib(20) the fib() function is called 13,529 times!), but it does work. Be careful: If you feed in too large a number, you'll run out of memory. Every time fib() is called, memory is set aside. When it returns, memory is freed. With recursion, memory continues to be set aside before it is freed, and this system can eat memory very quickly. Listing 5.10 implements the fib() function.

WARNING

When you run Listing 5.10, use a small number (less than 15). Because this uses recursion, it can consume a lot of memory.

Listing 5.10. Recursion using the Fibonacci series.

```
1:     // Listing 5.10 - demonstrates recursion
2:     // Fibonacci find.
3:     // Finds the nth Fibonacci number
4:     // Uses this algorithm: Fib(n) = fib(n-1) + fib(n-2)
5:     // Stop conditions: n = 2 ¦¦ n = 1
6:
7:     #include <iostream.h>
8:
9:     int fib(int n);
10:
11:    void main()
12:    {
13:
14:      int n, answer;
15:      cout << "Enter number to find: ";
16:      cin >> n;
17:
18:      cout << "\n\n";
19:
20:      answer = fib(n);
21:
22:      cout << answer << " is the " << n << "th Fibonacci number\n";
23:
24:    }
25:
26:    int fib (int n)
27:    {
28:      cout << "Processing fib(" << n << ")... ";
```

```
29:
30:       if (n < 3 )
31:       {
32:          cout << "Return 1!\n";
33:          return (1);
34:       }
35:       else
36:       {
37:          cout << "Call fib(" << n-2 << ") and fib(" << n-1 << ").\n";
38:          return( fib(n-2) + fib(n-1));
39:       }
40:    }
```

OUTPUT

```
Enter number to find: 5
Processing fib(5)... Call fib(3) and fib(4).
Processing fib(3)... Call fib(1) and fib(2).
Processing fib(1)... Return 1!
Processing fib(2)... Return 1!
Processing fib(4)... Call fib(2) and fib(3).
Processing fib(2)... Return 1!
Processing fib(3)... Call fib(1) and fib(2).
Processing fib(1)... Return 1!
Processing fib(2)... Return 1!
5 is the 5th Fibonacci number.
```

ANALYSIS The program asks for a number to find on line 15 and assigns that number to n. It then calls fib() with the n. Execution branches to the fib() function where, on line 28, it prints its argument.

The argument n is tested to see whether it equals 1 or 2 on line 30; if so, fib() returns. Otherwise, it returns the sums of the values returned by calling fib() on n-2 and n-1.

In the example, n is 5, so fib(5) is called from main(). Execution jumps to the fib() function, and n is tested for a value less than 3 on line 30. The test fails, so fib(5) returns the sum of the values returned by fib(3) and fib(4). That is, fib() is called on n-2 (5 - 2 = 3) and n-1 (5 - 1 = 4). fib(4) returns 3 and fib(3) returns 2, so the final answer is 5.

Because fib(4) passes in an argument that is not less than 3, fib() is called again, this time with 3 and 2. fib(3) in turn calls fib(2) and fib(1). Finally, the calls to fib(2) and fib(1) both return 1, because these are the stop conditions.

The output traces these calls and the return values. Compile, link, and run this program, entering first 1, then 2, and then 3, building up to 6, and watch the output carefully. Then, just for fun, try the number 20. If you don't run out of memory, it makes quite a show!

Recursion is not used often in C++ programming, but it can be a powerful and elegant tool for certain needs.

5

NOTE

Recursion is a very tricky part of advanced programming. It is presented here because it can be very useful to understand the fundamentals of how it works, but don't worry too much if you don't fully understand all the details.

Summary

This lesson introduced functions. A function is, in effect, a subprogram into which you can pass parameters and from which you can return a value. Every C++ program starts in the main() function, and main() in turn can call other functions.

A function is declared with a function prototype (which describes the return value), the function name, and its parameter types. A function can optionally be declared inline. A function prototype can also declare default variables for one or more of the parameters.

The function definition must match the function prototype in return type, name, and parameter list. Function names can be overloaded by changing the number or type of parameters; the compiler finds the right function based on the argument list.

Local function variables, and the arguments passed into the function, are local to the *block* in which they are declared. Parameters passed by value are copies and cannot affect the value of variables in the calling function.

Q&A

Q Why not make all variables global?

A There was a time when this was exactly how programming was done. As programs became more complex, however, it became very difficult to find bugs in programs because data could be corrupted by any of the functions; global data can be changed anywhere in the program. Years of experience have convinced programmers that data should be kept as local as possible and access to changing that data should be narrowly defined.

Q When should the keyword inline be used in a function prototype?

A If the function is very small—no more than a line or two—and won't be called from many places in your program, it is a candidate for inlining.

Q Why aren't changes to the value of function arguments reflected in the calling function?

A Arguments passed to a function are passed *by value*. That means that the argument in the function is actually a copy of the original value. This concept is explained in depth in the Extra Credit section that follows the Exercises.

Q If arguments are passed by value, what do I do if I need to reflect the changes back in the calling function?

A On Day 8, pointers will be discussed. Use of pointers solves this problem and also provides a way around the limitation of returning only a single value from a function.

Q What happens if I have the following two functions?

```
int Area (int width, int length = 1);
int Area (int size);
```

Will these overload?

A The declarations compile, but if you invoke Area with one parameter, you will receive a compile-time error that says something like this: ambiguity between Area(int, int) and Area(int).

Quiz

1. What are the differences between the function prototype and the function definition?
2. Do the names of parameters have to agree in the prototype, definition, and call to the function?
3. If a function doesn't return a value, how do you declare the function?
4. If you don't declare a return value, what type of return value is assumed?
5. What is a local variable?
6. What is scope?
7. What is recursion?
8. When should you use global variables?
9. What is function overloading?
10. Are different return types alone enough for the compiler to distinguish overloaded functions?

Exercises

1. Write the prototype for a function named Perimeter(), which returns an unsigned long int and takes two parameters, both unsigned short ints.
2. Write the definition of the function Perimeter() as described in question 1. The two parameters represent the length and width of a rectangle. Have the function return the perimeter (twice the length plus twice the width).

3. **BUG BUSTERS:** What is wrong with the function in the following code?

```
#include <iostream.h>
void myFunc(unsigned short int x);
void main()
{
    unsigned short int x, y;
    y = myFunc(x);
    cout << "x: " << x << " y: " << y << "\n";
}

void myFunc(unsigned short int x)
{
    return (4*x);
}
```

4. **BUG BUSTERS:** What is wrong with the function in the following code?

```
#include <iostream.h>
int myFunc(unsigned short int x);
void main()
{
    unsigned short int x, y;
    y = myFunc(x);
    cout << "x: " << x << " y: " << y << "\n";
}

int myFunc(unsigned short int x);
{
    return (4*x);
}
```

5. Write a function that takes two unsigned short integer arguments and returns the result of dividing the first by the second. Do not do the division if the second number is zero, but do return −1.

6. Write a program that asks the user for two numbers and calls the function you wrote in exercise 5. Print the answer, or print an error message if you get −1.

7. Write a program that asks for a number and a power. Write a recursive function that takes the number to the power. Thus, if the number is 2 and the power is 4, the function returns 16.

Extra Credit

If you really feel confident, and you want to dig deeper into functions, plunge into the next sections for more information.

How Functions Work

When you call a function, the code branches to the called function, parameters are passed in, and the body of the function is executed. When the function completes, a value is returned (unless the function returns void), and control returns to the calling function.

How is this task accomplished? How does the code know where to branch to? Where are the variables kept when they are passed in? What happens to variables that are declared in the body of the function? How is the return value passed back out? How does the code know where to resume?

Most introductory books don't try to answer these questions, but without understanding this information, you'll find that programming remains a fuzzy mystery. The explanation requires a brief tangent into a discussion of computer memory.

Levels of Abstraction

One of the principal struggles for new programmers is grappling with the many layers of intellectual abstraction. Computers, of course, are just electronic machines. They don't know about windows and menus, they don't know about programs or instructions, and they don't even know about ones and zeros. All that is really going on is that voltage is being measured at various places on an integrated circuit. Even this is an abstraction: Electricity itself is just an intellectual concept, representing the behavior of subatomic particles.

Few programmers bother much with any level of detail below the idea of values in RAM. After all, you don't need to understand particle physics to drive a car, make toast, or hit a baseball, and you don't need to understand the electronics of a computer to program one.

You do need to understand how memory is organized, however. Without a reasonably strong mental picture of where your variables are when they are created and how values are passed among functions, it will all remain an unmanageable mystery.

Partitioning RAM

When you begin your program, your operating system (such as DOS or Microsoft Windows) sets up various areas of memory based on the requirements of your compiler. As a C++ programmer, you'll often be concerned with the global name space, the free store, the registers, the code space, and the stack.

Global variables are in global name space. You'll learn more about global name space and the free store in coming days, but for now, let's focus on the registers, code space, and stack.

Registers are a special area of memory built right into the Central Processing Unit (or CPU). They take care of internal housekeeping. A lot of what goes on in the registers is beyond the scope of this book, but what we are concerned about is the set of registers responsible for pointing, at any given moment, to the next line of code. These registers, together, are called the *instruction pointer*. It is the job of the instruction pointer to keep track of which line of code is to be executed next.

The code itself is in *code space*, which is the part of memory set aside to hold the binary form of the instructions you created in your program. Each line of source code is translated into a series of instructions, and each of these instructions is at a particular address in memory. The instruction pointer has the address of the next instruction to execute. Figure 5.4 illustrates this idea.

Figure 5.4.

The instruction pointer.

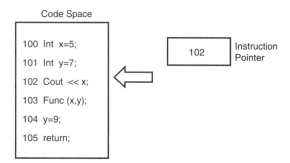

The *stack* is a special area of memory allocated for your program to hold the data required by each of the functions in your program. It is called a stack because it is a last-in first-out queue, much like a stack of dishes at a cafeteria, as shown in Figure 5.5.

Last-in, first-out means that whatever is added to the stack last will be the first thing taken off. A stack is like a stack of coins: If you stack 10 pennies on a tabletop and then take some back, the last three you put on will be the first three you take off.

When data is *pushed* onto the stack, the stack grows; as data is *popped* off the stack, the stack shrinks. Taking the analogy further, it isn't possible to pop a penny off of the stack without first popping off all the pennies placed on after that penny.

A stack of dishes is another common analogy. It is fine as far as it goes, but it is wrong in a fundamental way. A more accurate mental picture is of a series of cubbyholes aligned top to bottom. The top of the stack is whatever cubbyhole the *stack pointer* (which is another register) happens to be pointing to.

Figure 5.5.

A stack.

Each of the cubbyholes has a sequential address, and one of those addresses is kept in the stack pointer register. Everything below that magic address, known as the top of the stack, is considered to be on the stack. Everything above the top of the stack is considered to be off the stack and invalid. Figure 5.6 illustrates this idea.

Figure 5.6.

The stack pointer.

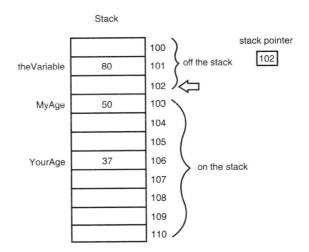

When data is put on the stack, it is placed into a cubbyhole above the stack pointer, and then the stack pointer is moved to the new data. When data is popped off the stack, all that really happens is that the address of the stack pointer is changed by moving it down the stack. Figure 5.7 makes this rule clear.

Figure 5.7.

Moving the stack pointer.

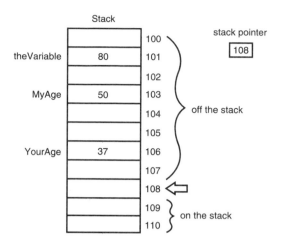

The Stack and Functions

Here's what happens when a program, running on a PC under DOS, branches to a function:

1. The address in the instruction pointer is incremented to the next instruction past the function call. That address is then placed on the stack, and it will be the return address when the function returns.

2. Room is made on the stack for the return type you've declared. On a system with two-byte integers, if the return type is declared to be int, another two bytes are added to the stack, but no value is placed in these bytes.

3. The address of the called function, which is kept in a special area of memory set aside for that purpose, is loaded into the instruction pointer, so the next instruction executed will be in the called function.

4. All the arguments to the function are placed on the stack.

5. The current top of the stack is now noted and is held in a special pointer called the *Stack Frame*. Everything added to the stack from now until the function returns will be considered "local" to the function.

6. The instruction now in the instruction pointer is executed, thus executing the first instruction in the function.

7. Local variables are pushed onto the stack as they are defined.

When the function is ready to return, the return value is placed in the area of the stack reserved at Step 2. The stack is then popped all the way up to the Stack Frame pointer, which effectively throws away all the local variables and the arguments to the function.

5

The return value is popped off the stack and assigned as the value of the function call itself, and the address stashed away in Step 1 is retrieved and put into the instruction pointer. The program thus resumes immediately after the function call, with the value of the function retrieved.

Some of the details of this process change from compiler to compiler, or between computers, but the essential ideas are consistent across environments. In general, when you call a function, the return address and the parameters are put on the stack. During the life of the function, local variables are added to the stack. When the function returns, these are all removed by popping the stack.

In coming days, you'll look at other places in memory that are used to hold data that must persist beyond the life of the function. And, if you choose to keep going into the bonus days, you will see more about stacks.

5

Day 6

Basic Classes

Classes extend the built-in capabilities of C++ to assist you in representing and solving complex, real-world problems. Today you learn

- [ ] What classes and objects are.
- [ ] How to define a new class and create objects of that class.
- [ ] What member functions and member data are.
- [ ] What constructors are and how to use them.

Creating New Types

You've already learned about a number of variable types, including unsigned integers and characters. The type of a variable tells you quite a bit about it. For example, if you declare Height and Width to be unsigned integers, you know that each one can hold a number between 0 and 65,535, assuming an integer is two bytes. That is the meaning of saying they are unsigned integers; trying to hold anything else in these variables causes an error. You can't store your name in an unsigned short integer, and you shouldn't try.

Simply by declaring these variables to be unsigned short integers, you know that it is possible to add Height to Width and to assign that number to another number.

The type of these variables tells you the following information:

☐ Their size in memory

☐ What information they can hold

☐ What actions can be performed on them

More generally, a type is a category. Familiar types include car, house, person, fruit, and shape. In C++, the programmer can create any type needed, and each of these new types can have all the functionality and power of the built-in types.

Why Create a New Type?

Programs are usually written to solve real-world problems, such as keeping track of employee records or simulating the workings of a heating system. Although it is possible to solve complex problems by using programs written with only integers and characters, it is far easier to grapple with large, complex problems if you can create representations of the objects that you are talking about. In other words, simulating the workings of a heating system is easier if you can create variables that represent rooms, heat sensors, thermostats, and boilers. The closer these variables correspond to reality, the easier it is to write the program.

Classes and Members

You make a new type by declaring a class. A class is just a collection of variables—often of different types—combined with a set of related functions. In object-oriented terminology, functions that are included in a class are often referred to as *methods* for that class.

One way to think about a car is as a collection of wheels, doors, seats, windows, and so on. Another way is to think about what a car can do: It can move, speed up, slow down, stop, park, and so on. A class enables you to encapsulate, or bundle, these various parts and various functions into one collection. In other words, a class contains all that is needed to describe what a car is and all that it does. Some programmers call this *active data* because the car class includes not only the data that makes a car, but the actions as well.

Encapsulating everything you know about a car into one class has a number of advantages for a programmer. Everything is in one place, which makes it easy to refer to, copy, and manipulate the data. Likewise, clients of your class—that is, the parts of the program that use your class—can use your object without worrying about what is in it or how it works.

A class can consist of any combination of the variable types and also other class types. The variables in the class are referred to as the member variables or data members. A Car class might have member variables representing the seats, radio type, tires, and so on.

 Member variables, also known as *data members*, are the variables in your class. Member variables are part of your class, just as the wheels and engine are part of your car.

The functions in the class typically manipulate the member variables. They are referred to as member functions or methods of the class. Methods of the Car class might include Start() and Brake(). A Cat class might have data members that represent age and weight; its methods might include Sleep(), Meow(), and ChaseMice().

 Member functions, also known as *methods*, are the functions in your class. Member functions are as much a part of your class as the member variables. They determine what the objects of your class can do.

Declaring a Class

To declare a class, use the class keyword followed by an opening brace, and then list the data members and methods of that class. End the declaration with a closing brace and a semicolon. The declaration of a class called Cat is as follows:

```
class Cat
{
unsigned int   itsAge;
unsigned int   itsWeight;
Meow();
};
```

Declaring this class doesn't allocate memory for a Cat. It just tells the compiler what a Cat is, what data it contains (itsAge and itsWeight), and what it can do (Meow()). It also tells the compiler how big a Cat is—that is, how much room the compiler must set aside for each Cat that you create. In this example, if an integer is two bytes, a Cat is only four bytes in size: itsAge is two bytes, and itsWeight is another two. Meow() takes up no room, because no storage space is set aside for member functions (methods).

Classes Versus Objects

You never pet the definition of a cat; you pet individual cats. You draw a distinction between the idea of a cat, and the particular cat that right now is shedding all over your living room. In the same way, C++ differentiates between the class Cat, which is the idea of a cat, and each individual Cat object. Thus, Frisky is an object of type Cat in the same way in which GrossWeight is a variable of type unsigned int.

 An *object* is an individual instance of a class. When first learning object-oriented design, many programmers confuse the concept of instance/object and classes.

Defining an Object

You define an object of your new type just as you define an integer variable:

```
unsigned int GrossWeight;          // define an unsigned integer
Cat Frisky;                        // define a Cat
```

This code defines a variable called Gross Weight whose type is an unsigned integer. It also defines Frisky, which is an object whose class (or type) is Cat.

Accessing Class Members

After you define an actual Cat object—for example, Frisky—you use the dot operator (.) to access the members of that object. Therefore, to assign 50 to Frisky's Weight member variable, you would write

```
Frisky.Weight = 50;
```

In the same way, to call the Meow() function, you would write

```
Frisky.Meow();
```

When you use a class method, you *call* the method. In this example, you are calling Meow() on Frisky.

Assign to Objects, Not to Classes

In C++, you don't assign values to types, you assign values to variables. For example, you would never write

```
int = 5;                // wrong
```

The compiler would flag this as an error, because you can't assign 5 to an integer. Rather, you must define an integer variable and assign 5 to that variable, as in the following example:

```
int x;            // define x to be an int
x = 5;            // set x's value to 5
```

This is a shorthand way of saying, "Assign five to the variable x, which is of type int." In the same way, you wouldn't write

```
cat.age=5;        // wrong
```

The compiler would flag this as an error, because you can't assign 5 to the age part of a Cat. Rather, you must define a Cat object and assign 5 to that object, as in the following example:

```
Cat Frisky;       // just like int x;
Frisky.age = 5;   // just like x = 5;
```

If It's Not Declared, Your Class Won't Have It

Try this experiment: Walk up to a three-year-old and show her a cat. Then say, "This is Frisky. Frisky knows a trick. Frisky, bark." The child giggles and says, "No, silly, cats can't bark."

If you wrote

```
Cat Frisky;       // make a Cat named Frisky
Frisky.Bark()     // tell Frisky to bark
```

the compiler would say, No, silly, Cats can't bark. (Your compiler's wording may vary.) The compiler knows that Frisky can't bark because the Cat class doesn't have a Bark() function. The compiler wouldn't even let Frisky meow if you didn't define a Meow() function.

Do   **Don't**

DO use the keyword class to declare a class.

DON'T confuse a declaration with a definition. A declaration says what a class is. A definition sets aside memory for an object.

DON'T confuse a class with an object.

DON'T assign values to a class. Assign values to the data members of an object.

DO use the dot operator (.) to access class members and functions.

6

A Word on Naming Conventions

As a programmer, you must name all your member variables, member functions, and classes. As you learned on Day 3, "Variables and Constants," these should be easily understood and meaningful names. `Cat`, `Rectangle`, and `Employee` are good class names. `Meow()`, `ChaseMice()`, and `StopEngine()` are good function names because they tell you what the functions do. Many programmers name the member variables with the prefix `its`, as in `itsAge`, `itsWeight`, and `itsSpeed`. This helps to distinguish member variables from nonmember variables.

C++ is case-sensitive, and all class names should follow the same pattern. That way you never have to check how to spell your class name. (Was it `Rectangle`, `rectangle`, or `RECTANGLE`?) Some programmers like to prefix every class name with a particular letter—for example, `cCat` or `cPerson`—whereas others put the name in all uppercase or all lowercase. The convention that I use is to name all classes with initial-capitalization, as in `Cat` and `Person`.

Similarly, many programmers begin all functions with capital letters and all variables with lowercase letters. Words are usually separated with an underscore (as in `Chase_Mice`) or by capitalizing each word (for example, `ChaseMice` or `DrawCircle`).

The important idea is that you should pick one style and stay with it through each program. Over time, your style will evolve to include not only naming conventions, but also indentation, alignment of braces, and commenting style. On Day 18, we'll discuss coding styles and their importance in more depth.

It's common for software houses to develop programming standards for many style issues. This ensures that all developers can easily read one another's code.

Private Versus Public

Other keywords are used in the declaration of a class. Two of the most important are `public` and `private`.

All members of a class—data and methods—are private by default. Private members can be accessed only within methods of the class itself. Public members can be accessed through any object of the class. This distinction is both important and confusing. To make it a bit clearer, consider an example from earlier in this lesson:

```
class Cat
{
  unsigned int  itsAge;
```

```
    unsigned int  itsWeight;
    Meow();
};
```

In this declaration, itsAge, itsWeight, and Meow() are all private, because all members of a class are private by default. This means that unless you specify otherwise, they are private.

If you write

```
Cat  Boots;
Boots.itsAge=5;          // error! can't access private data!
```

the compiler flags this as an error. In effect, you've said to the compiler, "I'll access itsAge, itsWeight, and Meow() only from within member functions of the Cat class." Yet here you've accessed it from outside a Cat method. Just because Boots is an object of class Cat, that doesn't mean you can access the parts of Boots that are private.

This is a source of endless confusion to new C++ programmers. I can almost hear you yelling, "Hey! I just said Boots is a cat. Why can't Boots access his own age?" The answer is that Boots can, but *you* can't. Boots, in his own methods, can access all his parts—public and private. Even though you've created a Cat, that doesn't mean you can see or change the parts of it that are private.

The way to use Cat so that you can access the data members is

```
class Cat
{
public:
    unsigned int  itsAge;
    unsigned int  itsWeight;
    Meow();
};
```

Now itsAge, itsWeight, and Meow() are all public. Boots.itsAge=5 compiles without a problem.

Listing 6.1 shows the declaration of a Cat class with public member variables.

TYPE **Listing 6.1. Accessing the public members of a simple class.**   **6**

```
1:   // Demonstrates declaration of a class and
2:   // definition of an object of the class,
3:
4:   #include <iostream.h>    // for cout
5:
6:   class Cat                  // declare the class object
7:   {
8:    public:                   // members which follow are public
9:      int itsAge;
10:      int itsWeight;
```

continues

Listing 6.1. continued

```
11:    };
12:
13:
14:    void main()
15:    {
16:        Cat Frisky;
17:        Frisky.itsAge = 5;      // assign to the member variable
18:        cout << "Frisky is a cat who is " ;
19:        cout << Frisky.itsAge << " years old.\n";
20:    }
```

 OUTPUT   Frisky is a cat who is 5 years old.

 ANALYSIS   Line 6 contains the keyword class. This tells the compiler that what follows is a declaration. The name of the new class comes after the keyword class. In this case, it is Cat.

The body of the declaration begins with the opening brace in line 7 and ends with a closing brace and a semicolon in line 11. Line 8 contains the keyword public, which indicates that everything that follows is public until the keyword private or the end of the class declaration.

Lines 9 and 10 contain the declarations of the class members itsAge and itsWeight.

Line 14 begins the main function of the program. Frisky is defined in line 16 as an instance of a Cat—that is, as a Cat object. Frisky's age is set in line 17 to 5. In lines 18 and 19, the itsAge member variable is used to print out a message about Frisky.

> **NOTE**   Try commenting out line 8 (the line that has the word public:) and try to recompile. You will receive an error on line 17, because itsAge no longer has public access. The default for classes is private access.

Make Member Data Private

As a general rule of design, you should keep the member data of a class private. Therefore, you must create public functions known as *accessor methods* to set and get the private member variables. These accessor methods are the member functions that other parts of your program call to get and set your private member variables.

NEW TERM   A *public accessor method* is a class member function used either to read the value of a private class member variable or to set its value.

Why bother with this extra level of indirect access? After all, it is simpler and easier to use the data, instead of working through accessor functions.

Accessor functions enable you to separate the details of how the data is stored from how it is used. This enables you to change how the data is stored without having to rewrite functions that use the data.

If a function that needs to know a Cat's age accesses itsAge directly, that function would need to be rewritten if you, as the author of the Cat class, decided to change how that data is stored. By having the function call GetAge(), your Cat class can easily return the right value no matter how you arrive at the age. The calling function doesn't need to know whether you are storing it as an unsigned integer or a long, or whether you are computing it as needed.

This technique makes your program easier to maintain. It gives your code a longer life because design changes don't make your program obsolete.

Listing 6.2 shows the Cat class modified to include private member data and public accessor methods. Note that this is not an executable listing.

TYPE | **Listing 6.2. A class with accessor methods.**

```
1:        // Cat class declaration
2:        // Data members are private, public accessor methods
3:        // mediate setting and getting the values of the private data
4:
5:    class Cat
6:    {
7:    public:
8:         // public accessors
9:       unsigned int GetAge();
10:      void SetAge(unsigned int Age);
11:
12:      unsigned int GetWeight();
13:      void SetWeight(unsigned int Weight);
14:
15:         // public member functions
16:      Meow();
17:
18:         // private member data
19:   private:
20:      unsigned int  itsAge;
21:      unsigned int  itsWeight;
22:
23:   };
```

6

ANALYSIS This class has five public methods. Lines 9 and 10 contain the accessor methods for `itsAge`. Lines 12 and 13 contain the accessor methods for `itsWeight`. These accessor functions set the member variables and return their values.

The public member function `Meow()` is declared in line 16. `Meow()` is not an accessor function. It doesn't get or set a member variable; it performs another service for the class—printing the word `meow`.

The member variables themselves are declared in lines 20 and 21.

To set Frisky's age, you would pass the value to the `SetAge()` method, as in

```
Cat  Frisky;
Frisky.SetAge(5);     // set Frisky's age using the public accessor
```

Privacy Versus Security

Declaring methods or data private enables the compiler to find programming mistakes before they become bugs. Any programmer worth his consulting fees can find a way around privacy if he wants to. Stroustrup, the inventor of C++ said, "The C++ access control mechanisms provide protection against accident—not against fraud."

The *class* Keyword

SYNTAX The `class` keyword has the following syntax:

```
class class_name
{
   // access control keywords here
   // class variables and methods declared here
};
```

You use the `class` keyword to declare new types. A class is a collection of class member data, which are variables of various types, including other classes. The class also contains class functions (or methods), which are functions used to manipulate the data in the class and to perform other services for the class.

You define objects of the new type in much the same way as you define any variable. State the type (class) and then the variable name (the object). You access the class members and functions by using the dot (.) operator.

You use access control keywords to declare sections of the class as `public` or `private`. The default for access control is `private`. Each keyword changes the access control from that point forward to the end of the class or until the next access control keyword. Class declarations end with a closing brace and a semicolon.

Example 1

```
class Cat
{
public:
unsigned int Age;
unsigned int Weight;
void Meow();
};

Cat  frisky;
Frisky.Age = 8;
Frisky.Weight = 18;
Frisky.Meow();
```

Example 2

```
class Car
{
public:                         // the next five are public

void Start();
void Accelerate();
void Brake();
void SetYear(int year);
int GetYear();

private:                        // the rest is private

int Year;
Char Model [255]
};                              // end of class declaration

Car OldFaithful;                // make an instance of car
int bought;                     // a local variable of type int
OldFaithful.SetYear(84) ;       // assign 84 to the year
bought = OldFaithful.GetYear(); // set bought to 84
OldFaithful.Start();            // call the start method
```

Do	Don't

DO declare member variables as private.

DO use public accessor methods.

DON'T try to use private member variables from outside the class.

DO access private member variables from within class member functions.

6

Implementing Class Methods

As you've seen, an accessor function provides a public interface to the private member data of the class. Each accessor function, along with any other class methods that you declare, must have an implementation. The implementation is called the *function definition*.

A member function definition begins with the name of the class, followed by two colons, the name of the function, and its parameters. Listing 6.3 shows the complete declaration of a simple Cat class and the implementation of its accessor function and one general class member function.

TYPE   **Listing 6.3. Implementing the methods of a simple class.**

```
1:   // Demonstrates declaration of a class and
2:   // definition of class methods,
3:
4:   #include <iostream.h>        // for cout
5:
6:   class Cat                    // begin declaration of the class
7:   {
8:     public:                    // begin public section
9:       int GetAge();            // accessor function
10:      void SetAge (int age);   // accessor function
11:      void Meow();             // general function
12:    private:                   // begin private section
13:      int itsAge;              // member variable
14:   };
15:
16:  // GetAge, Public accessor function
17:  // returns value of itsAge member
18:  int Cat::GetAge()
19:  {
20:     return itsAge;
21:  }
22:
23:  // definition of SetAge, public
24:  // accessor function
25:  // returns sets itsAge member
26:  void Cat::SetAge(int age)
27:  {
28:     // set member variable its age to
29:     // value passed in by parameter age
30:     itsAge = age;
31:  }
32:
33:  // definition of Meow method
34:  // returns: void
35:  // parameters: None
36:  // action: Prints "meow" to screen
37:  void Cat::Meow()
38:  {
```

6

```
39:     cout << "Meow.\n";
40:   }
41:
42:   // create a cat, set its age, have it
43:   // meow, tell us its age, then meow again.
44:   void main()
45:   {
46:     Cat Frisky;
47:     Frisky.SetAge(5);
48:     Frisky.Meow();
49:     cout << "Frisky is a cat who is " ;
50:     cout << Frisky.GetAge() << " years old.\n";
51:     Frisky.Meow();
52:   }
```

OUTPUT
```
Meow.
Frisky is a cat who is 5 years old.
Meow.
```

ANALYSIS   Lines 6 through 14 contain the definition of the Cat class. Line 8 contains the keyword public, which tells the compiler that what follows is a set of public members. Line 9 has the declaration of the public accessor method GetAge(). GetAge() provides access to the private member variable itsAge, which is declared in line 13. Line 10 has the public accessor function SetAge(). SetAge() takes an integer as an argument and sets itsAge to the value of that argument.

Line 11 has the declaration of the class method Meow(). Meow() is not an accessor function. Here it is a general method that prints the word Meow to the screen.

Line 12 begins the private section, which includes only the declaration in line 13 of the private member variable itsAge. The class declaration ends with a closing brace and semicolon in line 14.

Lines 18 to 21 contain the definition of the member function GetAge(). This method takes no parameters; it returns an integer. Note that class methods include the class name followed by two colons and the function name (on line 18). This syntax tells the compiler that the GetAge() function that you are defining here is the one that you declared in the Cat class. With the exception of this header line, the GetAge() function is created like any other function.

The GetAge() function takes only one line; it returns the value in itsAge. Note that the main() function cannot access itsAge because itsAge is private to the Cat class. The main() function has access to the public method GetAge(). Because GetAge() is a member function of the Cat class, it has full access to the itsAge variable. This access enables GetAge() to return the value of itsAge to main().

Line 26 contains the definition of the SetAge() member function. It takes an integer parameter and sets the value of itsAge to the value of that parameter in line 30. Because it is a member of the Cat class, SetAge() has direct access to the member variable itsAge.

6

Line 37 begins the definition, or implementation, of the `Meow()` method of the `Cat` class. It is a one-line function that prints the word `Meow` to the screen followed by a new line. Remember that the `\n` character prints a new line to the screen.

Line 44 begins the body of the program with the familiar `main()` function. In this case, it takes no arguments and returns `void`. In line 46 `main()` declares a `Cat` named `Frisky`. In line 47 the value `5` is assigned to the `itsAge` member variable by way of the `SetAge()` accessor method. Note that the method is called by using the object name (`Frisky`) followed by the member operator (`.`) and the method name (`SetAge()`). In the same way, you can call any of the other methods in a class.

Line 48 calls the `Meow()` member function, and lines 49 and 50 print a message using the `GetAge()` accessor. Line 51 calls `Meow()` again.

Constructors and Destructors

There are two ways to define an integer variable. You can define the variable and then assign a value to it later in the program, as in the following example:

```
int Weight;           // define a variable
...                   // other code here
Weight = 7;           // assign it a value
```

Or you can define the integer and immediately initialize it, as in the following example:

```
int Weight = 7;       // define and initialize to 7
```

Initialization combines the definition of the variable with its initial assignment. Nothing stops you from changing that value later. Initialization ensures that your variable is never without a meaningful value.

How do you initialize the member data of a class? Classes have a special member function called a *constructor*. The constructor can take parameters as needed, but it cannot have a return value—not even void. The constructor is a class method with the same name as the class itself.

NEW TERM   A *constructor* is a special C++ function within a class that constructs an object of that class. A *destructor* is a special C++ function that releases resources for (or destroys) an object of the class. Every data type (including those that are built-in) has at least one constructor. Even if you don't define one in your program, the compiler will create one for you. The same is true with destructors. If you declare a constructor or destructor, the compiler will not generate a default constructor or destructor.

Whenever you declare a constructor, you'll also want to declare a destructor. Just as constructors create and initialize objects of your class, destructors clean up after your object and free any memory you might have allocated. A destructor always has the name of the class preceded by a tilde (~). Destructors take no arguments and have no return value. Therefore, the Cat declaration includes

```
~Cat();
```

Default Constructors and Destructors

If you don't declare a constructor or a destructor, the compiler makes one for you. The default constructor and destructor take no arguments and do nothing.

What good is a constructor that does nothing? In part, it is a matter of form. All objects must be constructed and destructed, and these do-nothing functions are called at the right time. However, to declare an object without passing in parameters, such as

```
Cat Rags;           // Rags gets no parameters
```

you must have a constructor in the form

```
Cat();
```

When you define an object of a class, the constructor is called. If the Cat constructor takes two parameters, you might define a Cat object by writing

```
Cat Frisky (5,7);
```

If the constructor takes one parameter, you would write

```
Cat Frisky (3);
```

For this reason, C++ also enables you to initialize built-in types with a single parameter as if the built-in type has a single-parameter constructor:

```
int Weight (7);    // Same as writing "int Weight = 7;"
```

As a matter of fact, many programmers purposely initialize in this way to be consistent with class constructors.

In the event that the constructor takes no parameters at all, you leave off the parentheses and write

```
Cat Frisky ;
```

Constructors without parameters are an exception to the rule stating that all functions require parentheses, even if they take no parameters. This is why you are able to write

```
Cat Frisky;
```

which is a call to the default constructor. It provides no parameters, and it leaves off the parentheses. You don't have to use the compiler-provided default constructor. You are always free to write your own constructor with no parameters. Even constructors with no parameters can have a function body in which they initialize their objects or do other work.

NOTE

As a matter of form, if you declare a constructor, be sure to declare a destructor, even if your destructor does nothing. Although it is true that the default destructor would work correctly, it doesn't hurt to declare your own. It makes your code clearer.

Listing 6.4 rewrites the Cat class to use a constructor to initialize the Cat object, setting its age to whatever initial age you provide, and it demonstrates where the destructor is called.

TYPE **Listing 6.4. Using constructors and destructors.**

```
1:    // Demonstrates declaration of a constructor and
2:    // destructor for the Cat class
3:
4:    #include <iostream.h>        // for cout
5:
6:    class Cat                    // begin declaration of the class
7:    {
8:     public:                     // begin public section
9:        Cat(int initialAge);     // constructor
10:       ~Cat();                  // destructor
11:       int GetAge();            // accessor function
12:       void SetAge(int age);    // accessor function
13:       void Meow();
14:    private:                    // begin private section
15:       int itsAge;              // member variable
16:    };
17:
18:    // constructor of Cat,
19:    Cat::Cat(int initialAge)
20:    {
21:       itsAge = initialAge;     // Could have written itsAge(initialAge);
22:    }
23:
24:    Cat::~Cat()                  // destructor, takes no action
25:    {
26:    }
27:
28:    // GetAge, Public accessor function
29:    // returns value of itsAge member
30:    int Cat::GetAge()
31:    {
```

6

```
32:     return itsAge;
33: }
34:
35: // Definition of SetAge, public
36: // accessor function
37:
38: void Cat::SetAge(int age)
39: {
40:     // set member variable itsAge to
41:     // value passed in by parameter age
42:     itsAge = age;
43: }
44:
45: // definition of Meow method
46: // returns: void
47: // parameters: None
48: // action: Prints "meow" to screen
49: void Cat::Meow()
50: {
51:     cout << "Meow.\n";
52: }
53:
54: // create a cat, set its age, have it
55  // meow, tell us its age, then meow again.
56: void main()
57: {
58:     Cat Frisky(5);
59:     Frisky.Meow();
60:     cout << "Frisky is a cat who is " ;
61:     cout << Frisky.GetAge() << " years old.\n";
62:     Frisky.Meow();
63:     Frisky.SetAge(7);
64:     cout << "Now Frisky is " ;
65:     cout << Frisky.GetAge() << " years old.\n";
66: }
```

OUTPUT
```
Meow,
Frisky is a cat who is 5 years old.
Meow.
Now Frisky is 7 years old.
```

ANALYSIS Listing 6.4 is similar to 6.3, except that line 9 adds a constructor that takes an integer. Line 10 declares the destructor, which takes no parameters. Destructors never take parameters, and neither constructors nor destructors return a value—not even void.

Lines 19 to 22 show the implementation of the constructor. It is similar to the implementation of the SetAge() accessor function. There is no return value.

Lines 24 to 26 show the implementation of the destructor ~Cat(). This function does nothing, but you must include the definition of the function if you declare it in the class declaration.

6

Line 58 contains the definition of a Cat object, Frisky. The value 5 is passed in to Frisky's constructor. There is no need to call SetAge(), because Frisky was created with the value 5 in its member variable itsAge, as shown in line 61. In line 63, Frisky's itsAge variable is reassigned to 7. Line 65 prints the new value.

Do	Don't

DO use constructors to initialize your objects.

DON'T give constructors or destructors a return value.

DON'T give destructors parameters.

const Member Functions

If you declare a class method const, you are promising that the method won't change the value of any of the members of the class. To declare a class method constant, put the keyword const after the parentheses but before the semicolon. The declaration of the constant member function SomeFunction() takes no arguments and returns void. It looks like this:

```
void SomeFunction() const;
```

Accessor functions are often declared as constant functions by using the const modifier. The Cat class has two accessor functions:

```
void SetAge(int anAge);
int GetAge();
```

SetAge() cannot be const because it changes the member variable itsAge. GetAge(), on the other hand, can and should be const because it doesn't change the object at all. It simply returns the current value of the member variable itsAge. Therefore, the declaration of these functions should be written like this:

```
void SetAge(int anAge);
int GetAge() const;
```

If you declare a function to be const and the implementation of that function changes the object by changing the value of any of its members, the compiler flags it as an error. For example, if you wrote GetAge() in such a way that it kept count of the number of times that the Cat was asked its age, it would generate a compiler error. This is because you would be changing the Cat object by calling this method.

It is good programming practice to declare as many methods to be const as possible. Each time you do, you enable the compiler to catch your errors instead of letting your errors become bugs that show up when your program is running.

Interface Versus Implementation

As you've learned, clients are the parts of the program that create and use objects of your class. You can think of the interface to your class—the class declaration—as a contract with these clients. The contract tells what data your class has available and how your class behaves.

For example, in the Cat class declaration, you create a contract that every Cat has a member variable itsAge that can be initialized in its constructor, assigned to by its SetAge() accessor function, and read by its GetAge() accessor. You also promise that every Cat knows how to Meow().

If you make GetAge() a const function—as you should—the contract also promises that GetAge() won't change the Cat on which it is called.

C++ is *strongly typed*, which means that the compiler enforces these contracts by giving you a compiler when you violate them. Listing 6.5 demonstrates a program that doesn't compile because of violations of these contracts.

WARNING

> Listing 6.5 does not compile!

TYPE **Listing 6.5. A demonstration of violations of the interface.**

```
1:    // Demonstrates compiler errors
2:
3:
4:    #include <iostream.h>          // for cout
5:
6:    class Cat
7:    {
8:      public:
9:        Cat(int initialAge);
10:       ~Cat();
11:       int GetAge() const;         // const accessor function
12:       void SetAge (int age);
13:       void Meow();
14:     private:
15:       int itsAge;
16: };
17:
18:      // constructor of Cat,
19:      Cat::Cat(int initialAge)
20:      {
21:         itsAge = initialAge;
21:         cout << "Cat Constructor\n";
22:      }
23:
```

continues

6

Listing 6.5. continued

```
24:    Cat::~Cat()                    // destructor, takes no action
25:    {
26:       cout << "Cat Destructor\n";
27:    }
28: // GetAge, const function
29: // but we violate const!
30: int Cat::GetAge() const
31: {
32:    return (itsAge++);          // violates const!
33: }
34:
35: // definition of SetAge, public
36: // accessor function
37:
38: void Cat::SetAge(int age)
39: {
40:    // set member variable itsAge to
41:    // value passed in by parameter age
42:    itsAge = age;
43: }
44:
45: // definition of Meow method
46: // returns: void
47: // parameters: None
48: // action: Prints "meow" to screen
49: void Cat::Meow()
50: {
51:    cout << "Meow.\n";
52: }
53:
54: // demonstrate various violations of the
55  // interface, and resulting compiler errors
56: void main()
57: {
58:    Cat Frisky;                 // doesn't match declaration
59:    Frisky.Meow();
60:    Frisky.Bark();              // No, silly, cats can't bark.
61:    Frisky.itsAge = 7;          // itsAge is private
62: }
```

OUTPUT   As it is written, this program doesn't compile. Therefore, there is no output.

ANALYSIS   This program was fun to write because there are so many errors in it.

Line 11 declares GetAge() to be a const accessor function—as it should be. However, in the body of GetAge(), in line 32 the member variable itsAge is incremented. Because this method is declared to be const, it must not change the value of itsAge. Therefore, it is flagged as an error when the program is compiled.

6

In line 13, `Meow()` is not declared `const`. Although this is not an error, it is bad programming practice. A better design takes into account that this method shouldn't change the member variables of `Cat`. Therefore, `Meow()` should be `const`.

Line 58 shows the definition of a `Cat` object: `Frisky`. `Cat`s now have a constructor, which takes an integer as a parameter. This means that you must pass a parameter in. Because there is no parameter in line 58, it is flagged as an error.

Line 60 shows a call to a class method: `Bark()`. `Bark()` was never declared. Therefore, it is illegal.

Line 61 shows `itsAge` being assigned the value `7`. Because `itsAge` is a private data member, it is flagged as an error when the program is compiled.

Why Use the Compiler to Catch Errors?

It would be wonderful to write 100 percent bug-free code, but few programmers have been able to do so. However, what many programmers have done is develop a system to help minimize bugs by catching and fixing them early in the process.

Although compiler errors are infuriating and are the bane of a programmer's existence, they are far better than the alternative. A weakly typed language enables you to violate your contracts without a peep from the compiler, but your program crashes at run-time—when, for example, your boss is watching.

Compile-time errors (errors found while you are compiling) are far better than run-time errors (errors found while you are executing the program). This is because compile-time errors can be found much more reliably. It is possible to run a program many times without going down every possible code path. Thus, a run-time error can hide for quite a while. Compile-time errors are found every time you compile. Thus, they are easier to identify and fix. It is the goal of quality programming to ensure that the code has no run-time bugs. One tried and true technique to accomplish this is to use the compiler to catch your mistakes early in the development process.

6

Where to Put Class Declarations and Method Definitions

Each function that you declare for your class must have a definition. The definition is also called the *function implementation*. Like other functions, the definition of a class method has a function header and a function body.

The definition must be in a file that the compiler can find. Most C++ compilers want that file to end with .C or .CPP. This book uses .CPP, but check your compiler to see what it prefers.

NOTE

> Many compilers assume that files ending with .C are C programs and that C++ program files end with .CPP. You can use any extension, but .CPP minimizes confusion.

You are free to put the declaration in the main source file, but that is not good programming practice. The convention that most programmers adopt is to put the declaration into what is called a header file, usually with the same name but ending in .H, .HP, or .HPP. This book names the header files with .HPP, but check your compiler to see what it prefers.

For example, you put the declaration of the Cat class into a file named CAT.HPP, and you put the definition of the class methods into a file called CAT.CPP. You then attach the header file to the .CPP file by putting the following code at the top of CAT.CPP:

```
#include "Cat.hpp"
```

This tells the compiler to read CAT.HPP into the file, just as if you had typed in its contents at this point. Why bother separating them if you're just going to read them back in? Most of the time, clients of your class don't care about the implementation specifics. Reading the header file tells them everything they need to know; they can ignore the implementation files.

NOTE

> The declaration of a class tells the compiler what the class is, what data it holds, and what functions it has. The declaration of the class is called its *interface* because it tells the user how to interact with the class. The interface is usually stored in an .HPP file, which is referred to as a header file.
>
> The function definition tells the compiler how the function works. The function definition is called the implementation of the class method, and it is kept in a .CPP file. The implementation details of the class are of concern only to the author of the class. Clients of the class (that is, the parts of the program that use the class) don't need to know—and don't care—how the functions are implemented.

Inline Implementation

Just as you can ask the compiler to make a regular function inline, you can make class methods inline. The keyword `inline` appears before the return value. The inline implementation of the `GetWeight()` function, for example, looks like this:

```
inline int Cat::GetWeight()
{
return itsWeight;            // return the Weight data member
}
```

You can also put the definition of a function into the declaration of the class, which automatically makes that function inline, as in the following example:

```
class Cat
{
public:
int GetWeight() { return itsWeight; }    // inline
void SetWeight(int aWeight);
};
```

Note the syntax of the `GetWeight()` definition: The body of the inline function begins immediately after the declaration of the class method; there is no semicolon after the parentheses. Like any function, the definition begins with an opening brace and ends with a closing brace. As usual, whitespace doesn't matter; you could have written the declaration in the following manner:

```
class Cat
{
public:
int GetWeight()
{
return itsWeight;
}                          // inline
void SetWeight(int aWeight);
};
```

Listings 6.6 and 6.7 re-create the `Cat` class, but they put the declaration in CAT.HPP and the implementation of the functions in CAT.CPP. Listing 6.7 also changes the accessor functions and the `Meow()` function to inline.

TYPE Listing 6.6. `Cat` class declaration in CAT.HPP.

```
1:   #include <iostream.h>
2:   class Cat
3:     {
4:   public:
5:     Cat (int initialAge);
6:     ~Cat();
```

continues

Listing 6.6. continued

```
7:    int GetAge() { return itsAge;}          // inline!
8:    void SetAge (int age) { itsAge = age;}  // inline!
9:    void Meow() { cout << "Meow.\n";}       // inline!
10:  private:
11:  int itsAge;
12:  };
```

TYPE   **Listing 6.7. Cat implementation in CAT.CPP.**

```
1:    // Demonstrates inline functions
2:    // and inclusion of header files
3:
4:    #include "cat.hpp"  // be sure to include the header files!
5:
6:
7:    Cat::Cat(int InitialAge)    //constructor
8:    {
9:        itsAge = InitialAge;
10:   }
11:
12:   Cat::~Cat()              //destructor, takes no action
13:   {
14:   }
15:
16:   // Create a cat, set its age, have it
17:   // meow, tell us its age, meow again, then change the age.
18:   void main()
19:   {
20:       Cat Frisky(5);
21:       Frisky.Meow();
22:       cout << "Frisky is a cat who is " ;
23:       cout << Frisky.GetAge() << " years old.\n";
24:       Frisky.Meow();
25:       Frisky.SetAge(7);
26:       cout << "Now Frisky is " ;
27:       cout << Frisky.GetAge() << " years old.\n";
28:   }
```

OUTPUT
```
Meow.
Frisky is a cat who is 5 years old.
Meow.
Now Frisky is 7 years old.
```

ANALYSIS   The code presented in Listing 6.6 and Listing 6.7 is similar to Listing 6.4, except that three of the methods are written inline in the declaration file, and the declaration has been separated into CAT.HPP.

`GetAge()` is declared in line 7 of Listing 6.6, and its inline implementation is provided. Lines 8 and 9 pro-vide more inline functions, but the functionality of these functions is unchanged from the previous "outline" implementations.

Line 4 of Listing 6.7 shows #include `"cat.hpp"`, which brings in the listings from CAT.HPP. IOSTREAM.H, which is needed for `cout`, is included on line 1 of Listing 6.6.

Lines 18 to 28 repeat the `main()` function from Listing 6.4. This shows that making these functions inline doesn't change their performance.

Classes with Other Classes as Member Data

It is not uncommon to build up a complex class by declaring simpler classes and including them in the declaration of the more complicated class. For example, you might declare a wheel class, a motor class, a transmission class, and so forth, and then combine them into a car class. This declares a *has a* relationship. A car has a motor; it has wheels; and it has a transmission.

Consider a second example. A rectangle is composed of lines. A line is defined by two points. A point is defined by an x-coordinate and a y-coordinate. Listing 6.8 shows a complete declaration of a `Rectangle` class, as might appear in RECTANGLE.HPP. Because a rectangle is defined as four lines connecting four points, and each point refers to a coordinate on a graph, you first declare a `Point` class to hold the x,y coordinates of each point. Listing 6.9 shows a complete declaration of both classes.

TYPE   **Listing 6.8. Declaring a complete class.**

```
1:     // Begin Rect.hpp
2:     #include <iostream.h>
3:     class Point      // holds x,y coordinates
4:     {
5:        // no constructor, use default
6:        public:
7:           void SetX(int x) { itsX = x; }
8:           void SetY(int y) { itsY = y; }
9:           int GetX()const { return itsX;}
10:          int GetY()const { return itsY;}
11:       private:
12:          int itsX;
13:          int itsY;
14:    };    // end of Point class declaration
15:
```

continues

6

Listing 6.8. continued

```
16:
17:   class  Rectangle
18:   {
19:      public:
20:          Rectangle (int top, int left, int bottom, int right);
21:          ~Rectangle () {}
22:
23:          int GetTop() const { return itsTop; }
24:          int GetLeft() const { return itsLeft; }
25:          int GetBottom() const { return itsBottom; }
26:          int GetRight() const { return itsRight; }
27:
28:          Point  GetUpperLeft() const { return itsUpperLeft; }
29:          Point  GetLowerLeft() const { return itsLowerLeft; }
30:          Point  GetUpperRight() const { return itsUpperRight; }
31:          Point  GetLowerRight() const { return itsLowerRight; }
32:
33:          void SetUpperLeft(Point Location)   {itsUpperLeft = Location;}
34:          void SetLowerLeft(Point Location)   {itsLowerLeft = Location;}
35:          void SetUpperRight(Point Location)  {itsUpperRight = Location;}
36:          void SetLowerRight(Point Location)  {itsLowerRight = Location;}
37:
38:          void SetTop(int top) { itsTop = top; }
39:          void SetLeft (int left) { itsLeft = left; }
40:          void SetBottom (int bottom) { itsBottom = bottom; }
41:          void SetRight (int right) { itsRight = right; }
42:
43:          int GetArea() const;
44:
45:      private:
46:          Point  itsUpperLeft;
47:          Point  itsUpperRight;
48:          Point  itsLowerLeft;
49:          Point  itsLowerRight;
50:          int    itsTop;
51:          int    itsLeft;
52:          int    itsBottom;
53:          int    itsRight;
54:   };
55:   // end Rect.hpp
```

Listing 6.9. RECT.CPP.

```
1:   // Begin rect.cpp
2:   #include "rect.hpp"
3:   Rectangle::Rectangle(int top, int left, int bottom, int right)
4:   {
5:         itsTop = top;
6:         itsLeft = left;
7:         itsBottom = bottom;
```

```
8:            itsRight = right;
9:
10:           itsUpperLeft.SetX(left);
11:           itsUpperLeft.SetY(top);
12:
13:           itsUpperRight.SetX(right);
14:           itsUpperRight.SetY(top);
15:
16:           itsLowerLeft.SetX(left);
17:           itsLowerLeft.SetY(bottom);
18:
19:           itsLowerRight.SetX(right);
20:           itsLowerRight.SetY(bottom);
21:    }
22:
23:
24:    // compute area of the rectangle by finding corners,
25:    // establish width and height and then multiply
26:    int Rectangle::GetArea() const
27:    {
28:           int Width = itsRight-itsLeft;
29:           int Height = itsTop - itsBottom;
30:           return (Width * Height);
31:    }
32:
33:    void main()
34:    {
35:           //initialize a local Rectangle variable
36:           Rectangle MyRectangle (100, 20, 50, 80 );
37:
38:           int Area = MyRectangle.GetArea();
39:
40:           cout << "Area: " << Area << "\n";
41:           cout << "Upper Left X Coordinate: ";
42:           cout << MyRectangle.GetUpperLeft().GetX();
43:    }
```

OUTPUT
```
Area: 3000
Upper Left X Coordinate: 20
```

ANALYSIS Lines 3 through 14 in Listing 6.8 declare the class Point, which is used to hold a specific x,y coordinate on a graph. As it is written, this program doesn't use Points much. However, other drawing methods require Points.

Within the declaration of the class Point, you declare two member variables (itsX and itsY) on lines 12 and 13. These variables hold the values of the coordinates. As the x-coordinate increases, you move to the right on the graph. As the y-coordinate increases, you move upward on the graph. Other graphs use different systems. Some windowing programs, for example, increase the y-coordinate as you move down in the window.

The Point class uses inline accessor functions to get and set the x and y points declared on lines 7 through 10. Points use the default constructor and destructor. Therefore, you must set their coordinates explicitly.

6

Line 17 begins the declaration of a `Rectangle` class. A `Rectangle` consists of four points that represent the corners of the `Rectangle`.

The constructor for the `Rectangle` (line 20) takes four integers, known as `top`, `left`, `bottom`, and `right`. The four parameters to the constructor are copied into four member variables (see Listing 6.9) and then the four `Points` are established.

In addition to the usual accessor functions, `Rectangle` has a function `GetArea()` declared in line 43. Instead of storing the area as a variable, the `GetArea()` function computes the area on lines 28 through 30 of Listing 6.9. To do this, it computes the width and the height of the rectangle, and then it multiplies these two values.

Getting the x-coordinate of the upper-left corner of the rectangle requires that you access the `UpperLeft` point and ask that point for its `X` value. Because `GetArea()` is a method of `Rectangle`, it can directly access the private data of `Rectangle`, including `itsUpperLeft`. Because `itsUpperLeft` is a `Point` and `Point`'s `itsX` value is private, `GetArea()` cannot directly access this data. Rather, it must use the public accessor function `GetX` to obtain that value.

Line 34 of Listing 6.9 is the beginning of the body of the actual program. Until line 35, no memory has been allocated, and nothing has really happened. The only thing you've done is to tell the compiler how to make a `Point` and how to make a `Rectangle`, in case one is ever needed.

In line 36, you define a `Rectangle` by passing in values for `top`, `left`, `bottom`, and `right`.

In line 38, you make a local variable, `Area`, of type `int`. This variable holds the area of the `Rectangle` that you've created. You initialize `Area` with the value returned by `Rectangle`'s `GetArea()` function.

A client of `Rectangle` could create a `Rectangle` object and get its area without ever looking at the implementation of `GetArea()`.

RECT.HPP is shown in Listing 6.8. Just by looking at the header file, which contains the declaration of the `Rectangle` class, the programmer knows that `GetArea()` returns an `int`. How `GetArea()` does its magic is not of concern to the user of class `Rectangle`. In fact, the author of `Rectangle` could change `GetArea()` without affecting the programs that use the `Rectangle` class.

Structures

A very close cousin to the `class` keyword is the keyword `struct`, which is used to declare a structure. In C++, a structure is exactly like a class, except that its members are public by default. You can declare a structure exactly as you declare a class, and you can give it exactly the same data members and functions. In fact, if you follow the good programming practice of always explicitly declaring the private and public sections of your class, there is no difference whatsoever.

One advantage of struct having a default access of public is that it is good for collections of data elements that are related but do not need full class status. For instance, you might need a thermometer in one of your classes, but you only care about the properties of a thermometer that hold the current value and units of measure. In that case, you might use a struct that has two public members:

```
struct Thermometer {
    double CurrentTemp; // Current reading
    char Units;         // F, C, or K
};
```

Many C++ programmers never use structs and would have declared the Thermometer with a class and two public data members. It's all a matter of preference and offers no great advantage either way. Because classes are more accepted in C++ and entrenched in the way C++ programmers think, use a class whenever in doubt.

Try entering Listing 6.8 again with these changes:

> In line 3, change class Point to struct Point.

> In line 17, change class Rectangle to struct Rectangle.

Now run the program again and compare the output. There should be no change.

Why Two Keywords Do the Same Thing

You're probably wondering why two keywords do the same thing. This is an accident of history. When C++ was developed, it was built as an extension of the C language. C has structures, although C structures don't have class methods. Bjarne Stroustrup, the creator of C++, built upon structs, but he changed the name to class to represent the new, expanded functionality.

6

Do	Don't

DO put your class declaration in an .HPP file and your member functions in a .CPP file.

DO use const whenever you can.

DO understand classes before you move on.

Summary

Today you learned how to create new data types called classes. You learned how to define variables of these new types, which are called objects.

A class has data members, which are variables of various types, including other classes. A class also includes member functions—also known as methods. You use these member functions to manipulate the member data and to perform other services.

Class members—both data and functions—can be public or private. Public members are accessible to any part of your program. Private members are accessible only to the member functions of the class.

It is good programming practice to isolate the interface (or declaration) of the class in a header file. You usually do this in a file with an .HPP extension. The implementation of the class methods is written in a file with a .CPP extension.

Class constructors initialize objects. Class destructors destroy objects and are often used to free memory allocated by methods of the class.

Q&A

Q How big is a class object?

A A class object's size in memory is determined by the sum of the sizes of its member variables. Class methods don't take up room as part of the memory set aside for the object.

Some compilers align variables in memory in such a way that two-byte variables actually consume somewhat more than two bytes. Check your compiler manual to be sure, but at this point there is no reason to be concerned with these details.

Q If I declare a class Cat with a private member itsAge and then define two Cat objects, Frisky and Boots, can Boots access Frisky's itsAge member variable?

A No. While private data is available to the member functions of a class, different instances of the class cannot access each other's data. In other words, Frisky's member functions can access Frisky's data, but not Boots's data. In fact, Frisky is a completely independent cat from Boots, and that is just as it should be.

Q Why shouldn't I make all the member data public?

A Making member data private enables the client of the class to use the data without worrying about how it is stored or computed. For example, if the Cat class has a method GetAge(), clients of the Cat class can ask for the cat's age without knowing or caring whether the cat stores its age in a member variable or computes its age on-the-fly.

Q If using a `const` function to change the class causes a compiler error, why shouldn't I just leave out the word `const` and be sure to avoid errors?

A If your member function logically shouldn't change the class, using the keyword `const` is a good way to enlist the compiler in helping you find silly mistakes. For example, `GetAge()` might have no reason to change the `Cat` class, but your implementation has this line:

```
if (itsAge = 100)
    cout << "Hey! You're 100 years old\n";
```

Declaring `GetAge()` to be `const` causes this code to be flagged as an error. You meant to check whether `itsAge` is equal to 100, but instead you inadvertently assigned 100 to `itsAge`. Because this assignment changes the class, and you said this method would not change the class, the compiler is able to find the error.

This kind of mistake can be hard to find just by scanning the code; the eye often sees only what it expects to see. More importantly, the program might appear to run correctly, but `itsAge` has now been set to a bogus number. This causes problems sooner or later.

Q Is there ever a reason to use a structure in a C++ program?

A Many C++ programmers reserve the `struct` keyword for classes that have no functions. This is a throwback to the old C structures, which could not have functions. Frankly, I find it confusing and poor programming practice. Today's methodless structure might need methods tomorrow. Then you'll be forced either to change the type to `class` or to break your rule and end up with a structure with methods.

Quiz

1. What is the dot operator, and what is it used for?
2. Which sets aside memory, declaration or definition?
3. Is the declaration of a class its interface or its implementation?
4. What is the difference between public and private data members?
5. Can member functions be private?
6. Can member data be public?
7. If you declare two `Cat` objects, can they have different values in their `itsAge` member data?
8. Do class declarations end with a semicolon? Do class method definitions?
9. What would the header look like for a `Cat` function, `Meow`, that takes no parameters and returns `void`?
10. What function is called to initialize a class?

Exercises

1. Write the code that declares a class called `Employee` with these data members: `age`, `YearsOfService`, and `Salary`.

2. Rewrite the `Employee` class to make the data members private, and provide public accessor methods to get and set each of the data members.

3. Write a program with the `Employee` class that makes two `Employees`, sets their age, `YearsOfService`, and `Salary`, and prints their values.

4. Continuing from exercise 3, provide a method of `Employee` that reports how many thousands of dollars the employee earns, rounded to the nearest 1,000.

5. Change the `Employee` class so that you can initialize `age`, `YearsOfService`, and `Salary` when you create the employee.

6. **BUG BUSTERS:** What is wrong with the following declaration?

```
class Square
{
public:
    int Side;
}
```

7. **BUG BUSTERS:** Why isn't the following class declaration very useful?

```
class Cat
{
    int GetAge()const;
private:
    int itsAge;
};
```

8. **BUG BUSTERS:** What three bugs in this code will the compiler find?

```
class  TV
{
public:
    void SetStation(int Station);
    int GetStation() const;
private:
    int itsStation;
};

main()
{
    TV myTV;
    myTV.itsStation = 9;
    TV.SetStation(10);
    TV myOtherTv(2);
}
```

Day **7**

More Program Flow

Programs accomplish most of their work by branching and looping. On Day 4, "Expressions and Statements," you learned how to branch your program using the `if` statement. Today you learn

☐ What loops are and how they are used.

☐ How to build various loops.

☐ An alternative to deeply nested `if`/`else` statements.

Looping

Many programming problems are solved by repeatedly acting on the same data. There are two ways to do this: recursion (discussed on Day 5, "Functions") and iteration. *Iteration* means doing the same thing again and again. The principal method of iteration is the loop.

The Roots of Looping *goto*

In the primitive days of early computer science, programs were nasty, brutish, and short. Loops consisted of a label, some statements, and a jump.

In C++, a label is just a name followed by a colon (:). The label is placed to the left of a legal C++ statement, and a jump is accomplished by writing goto followed by the label name. Listing 7.1 illustrates this.

TYPE   **Listing 7.1. Looping with the keyword** goto.

```
1:      // Listing 7.1
2:      // Looping with goto
3:
4:      #include <iostream.h>
5:
6:      void main()
7:      {
8:              int counter = 0;        // initialize counter
9:      loop:   counter ++;             // top of the loop
10:               cout << "counter: " << counter << "\n";
11:             if (counter < 5)            // test the value
12:                 goto loop;              // jump to the top
13:
14:             cout << "Complete. Counter: " << counter << ".\n";
15:     }
```

OUTPUT
```
counter: 1
counter: 2
counter: 3
counter: 4
counter: 5
Complete. Counter: 5
```

ANALYSIS   On line 8, counter is initialized to zero. The label loop is on line 9, marking the top of the loop. counter is incremented, and its new value is printed. The value of counter is tested on line 11. If it is less than 5, the if statement is true, and the goto statement is executed. This causes program execution to jump back to line 9. The program continues looping until counter is equal to 5, at which time it "falls through" the loop, and the final output is printed.

Why *goto* Is Shunned

goto has received some rotten press lately, and it's well deserved. goto statements can cause a jump to any location in your source code, backward or forward. The indiscriminate use of goto statements has caused tangled, miserable, impossible-to-read programs known as "spaghetti code." Because of this, computer science teachers have spent the past 20 years drumming one lesson into the heads of their students: "Never, ever, use goto! It is evil!"

To avoid the use of goto, more sophisticated, tightly controlled looping commands have been introduced: for, while, and do...while. Using these makes programs that are more easily understood, and goto is generally avoided. However, one might argue that the case has been a bit overstated. As with any tool, carefully used and in the right hands, goto can be a useful construct. Kids, don't try this at home.

The *goto* Statement

Syntax

To use the goto statement, you write goto followed by a label name. This causes an unconditioned jump to the label.

Example

```
if (value > 10)
    goto end;

if (value < 10)
    goto end;

cout << "value is 10!";

end:

cout << "done";
```

WARNING

Use of goto is almost always a sign of bad design. The best advice is to avoid using it. In 10 years of programming, I've only needed it once.

while Loops

A while loop causes your program to repeat a sequence of statements as long as the starting condition remains true. In the example of goto in Listing 7.1, the counter was incremented until it was equal to 5. Listing 7.2 shows the same program rewritten to take advantage of a while loop.

TYPE | **Listing 7.2.** while **loops.**

```
1:    // Listing 7.2
2:    // Looping with while
3:
4:    #include <iostream.h>
5:
6:    void main()
7:    {
8:      int counter = 0;                    // initialize the condition
9:
10:     while(counter < 5)      // test condition still true
11:       {
12:          counter++;                // body of the loop
13:          cout << "counter: " << counter << "\n";
14:       }
15:
16:     cout << "Complete. Counter: " << counter << ".\n";
17:   }
```

OUTPUT
```
counter: 0
counter: 1
counter: 2
counter: 3
counter: 4
counter: 5
Complete. Counter: 5
```

ANALYSIS This simple program demonstrates the fundamentals of the while loop. A condition is tested, and if it is true, the body of the while loop is executed. In this case, the condition tested on line 10 is whether counter is less than 5. If the condition is true, the body of the loop is executed: On line 12 the counter is incremented, and on line 13 the value is printed. When the conditional statement on line 10 fails (when counter is no longer less than 5) the entire body of the while loop (from lines 11 through 14) is skipped. Program execution falls through to line 15.

The *while* Statement

SYNTAX

The while statement performs a statement or a statement block repeatedly as long as a condition is true.

```
while ( condition )
statement;
```

condition is any C++ expression, and statement is any valid C++ statement or block of statements. When condition evaluates to true, the statement is executed, and then the condition is tested again. This continues until the condition tests false, at which time the while loop terminates and execution continues on the first line below the statement.

Example

```
// count to 10
int x = 0;
while (x < 10)
cout << "x: " << x++;
```

More Complicated *while* Statements

The condition tested by a while loop can be as complex as any legal C++ expression. This can include expressions produced using the logical && (and), ¦¦ (or), and ! (not) operators. Listing 7.3 is a somewhat more complicated while statement.

TYPE | **Listing 7.3. Complex while loops.**

```
1:      // Listing 7.3
2:      // Complex while statements
3:
4:      #include <iostream.h>
5:
6:      void main()
7:      {
8:          unsigned short small;
9:          long  large;
10:         const unsigned short MAXSMALL=65535;
11:
12:         cout << "Enter a small number: ";
13:         cin >> small;
14:         cout << "Enter a large number: ";
15:         cin >> large;
16:
17:         cout << "small: " << small << "...";
18:
19:         // for each iteration, test three conditions
20:         while (small < large && large > 0 && small < MAXSMALL)
21:         {
22:           if (small % 5000 == 0)   // write a dot every 5k lines
23:             cout << ".";
24:
25:           small++;
26:
27:           large-=2;
28:         }
29:
30:         cout << "\nSmall: " << small << " Large: " << large << endl;
31:     }
```

7

```
Enter a small number: 2
Enter a large number: 100000
Small:2........
Small:33335 Large: 33334
```

This program is a game. Enter two numbers, one small and one large. The smaller number counts up by ones, the larger number counts down by twos. The goal of the game is to guess when they'll meet.

On lines 12 through 15, the numbers are entered. Line 20 sets up a while loop, which continues only as long as the following three conditions are met:

☐ small is not bigger than large.

☐ large greater than 0.

☐ small doesn't overrun the size of a small integer (MAXSMALL).

If you are having trouble with the while test, you might want to review the operator precedence information in Appendix A.

On line 22 the value in small is calculated modulo 5,000. This does not change the value in small; however, it only returns the value 0 when small is an exact multiple of 5,000. Each time it is, a dot (.) is printed to the screen to show progress. On line 25 small is incremented, and on line 27 large is decremented by 2.

When any of the three conditions in the while loop fail, the loop ends, and execution of the program continues after the while loop's closing brace on line 28.

> The modulus operator (%) and compound conditions were covered on Day 4, "Expressions and Statements."

continue and break

At times, you'll want to return to the top of a while loop before the entire set of statements in the while loop is executed. The continue statement jumps back to the top of the loop.

At other times, you might want to exit the loop before the exit conditions are met. The break statement immediately exits the while loop, and program execution resumes after the closing brace.

Listing 7.4 demonstrates the use of these statements. This time, the game has become more complicated. The user is invited to enter a small number and a large number, a skip number and a target number. The small number is incremented by one, and the large number is decremented by two. The decrement is skipped each time the small number is a multiple of the skip. The game ends if small becomes larger than large. If the large number reaches the target exactly, a statement is printed, and the game stops.

The user's goal is to put in a target number for the large number that stops the game.

TYPE **Listing 7.4.** break **and** continue.

```
1:    // Listing 7.4
2:    // Demonstrates break and continue
3:
4:    #include <iostream.h>
5:
6:    void main()
7:    {
8:        unsigned short small;
9:        long  large;
10:       unsigned long  skip;
11:       unsigned long target;
12:       const unsigned short MAXSMALL=65535;
13:
14:       cout << "Enter a small number: ";
15:       cin >> small;
16:       cout << "Enter a large number: ";
17:       cin >> large;
18:       cout << "Enter a skip number: ";
19:       cin >> skip;
20:       cout << "Enter a target number: ";
21:       cin >> target;
22:
23:       cout << endl;
24:
25:       // set up 3 stop conditions for the loop
26:       while (small < large && large > 0 && small < 65535)
27:       {
28:
29:         small++;
30:
31:          if (small % skip == 0)  // skip the decrement?
32:          {
33:            cout << "skipping on " << small << endl;
34:            continue;
35:          }
36:
37:          if (large == target)    // exact match for the target?
38:          {
39:            cout << "Target reached!";
40:            break;
41:          }
42:
43:          large-=2;
44:       }                        // end of while loop
45:
46:       cout << "\nSmall: " << small << " Large: " << large << endl;
47:    }
```

7

```
Enter a small number: 2
Enter a large number: 20
Enter a skip number: 4
Enter a target number: 6
skipping on 4
skipping on 8
Small: 10 Large: 8
```

ANALYSIS In this play, the user lost; small became larger than large before the target number of 6 was reached.

On line 26 the while conditions are tested. If small continues to be smaller than large, large is larger than 0, and small hasn't overrun the maximum value for a small int, the body of the while loop is entered.

On line 31 the small value is taken modulo the skip value. If small is a multiple of skip, the continue statement is reached and program execution jumps to the top of the loop at line 26. This effectively skips over the test for the target and the decrement of large.

On line 37 target is tested against the value for large. If they are the same, the user has won. A message is printed, and the break statement is reached. This causes an immediate break out of the while loop, and program execution resumes on line 45.

NOTE Both continue and break should be used with caution. They are the next most dangerous commands after goto, for much the same reason. Programs that suddenly change direction are harder to understand, and liberal use of continue and break can render even a small while loop unreadable.

The *continue* Statement

SYNTAX

continue; causes a while or for loop to begin again at the top of the loop.

Example

```
while (condition)
{
    if (condition2)
        continue;
    //statements;
}
```

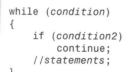

The *break* Statement

break; causes the immediate end of a while or for loop. Execution jumps to the closing brace.

Example

```
while (condition)
{
    if (condition2)
        break;
    // statements;
}
```

The *while (true)* Loop

The condition tested in a while loop can be any valid C++ expression. As long as that condition remains true, the while loop continues. You can create a loop that never ends by using the bool value true for the condition to be tested. Because the condition is always true, the loop never ends, unless a break statement is reached. Listing 7.5 demonstrates counting to 10 using this construct.

TYPE **Listing 7.5.** while (true) **loops.**

```
1:    // Listing 7.5
2:    // Demonstrates a while true loop
3:
4:    #include <iostream.h>
5:
6:    void main()
7:    {
8:      int counter = 0;
9:
10:       while (true)
11:       {
12:          counter++;
13:          if (counter > 10)
14:              break;
15:       }
16:       cout << "Counter: " << counter << "\n";
17:    }
```

OUTPUT   counter: 11

ANALYSIS   On line 10 a while loop is set up with a condition that can never be false. The loop increments the counter variable on line 12, and then on line 13 it tests to see whether counter has gone past 10. If it hasn't, the while loop iterates. If counter is greater than 10, the break on line 14 ends the while loop, and program execution falls through to line 16, where the results are printed.

7

This program works, but it isn't pretty. This is a good example of using the wrong tool for the job. The same thing can be accomplished by putting the test of counter's value where it belongs—in the while condition.

WARNING

Eternal loops such as while(true) can cause your computer to hang if the exit condition is never reached. Use these with caution and test them thoroughly.

C++ gives you many different ways to accomplish the same task. Programmers who have used C or older C++ often use the int value 1 instead of true for the condition. The real trick is picking the right tool for the particular job.

Do   **Don't**

DON'T use the goto statement.

DO use while loops to iterate while a condition is true.

DO exercise caution when using continue and break statements.

DO make sure your loop will eventually end.

---

do...while Loops

It is possible that the body of a while loop never executes. The while statement checks its condition before executing any of its statements, and if the condition evaluates false, the entire body of the while loop is skipped. Listing 7.6 illustrates this.

TYPE | **Listing 7.6. Skipping the body of the while loop.**

```
1:      // Listing 7.6
2:      // Demonstrates skipping the body of
3:      // the while loop when the condition is false.
4:
5:      #include <iostream.h>
```

7

```
6:
7:      void main()
8:      {
9:          int counter;
10:         cout << "How many hellos?: ";
11:         cin >> counter;
12:         while (counter > 0)
13:         {
14:             cout << "Hello!\n";
15:             counter—;
16:         }
17:         cout << "Counter is " << counter;
18:     }
```

OUTPUT

```
How many hellos?: 2
Hello!
Hello!
Counter is 0

How many hellos?: 0
Counter is 0
```

ANALYSIS The user is prompted for a starting value on line 10, which is stored in the integer variable counter. The value of counter is tested on line 12, and decrements in the body of the while loop. The first time through, counter is set to 2, so the body of the while loop runs twice. The second time through, however, the user types in 0. The value of counter is tested on line 12, and the condition is false: counter is not greater than 0. The entire body of the while loop is skipped, and hello is never printed.

What if you want to ensure that hello is always printed at least once? The while loop can't accomplish this because the if condition is tested *before* any printing is done. You can force the issue with an if statement just before entering the while, as shown in the following lines:

```
if (counter < 1)  // force a minimum value
    counter = 1;
```

However, this is what programmers call a "kludge," an ugly and inelegant solution.

The *do...while* Loop

The do...while loop executes the body of the loop before its condition is tested and ensures that the body always executes at least one time. Listing 7.7 demonstrates this program rewritten with a do...while loop.

7

TYPE   **Listing 7.7. A demonstration of the** `do...while` **loop.**

```
1:      // Listing 7.7
2:      // Demonstrates do while
3:
4:      #include <iostream.h>
5:
6:      void main()
7:      {
8:         int counter;
9:         cout << "How many hellos? ";
10:        cin >> counter;
11:        do
12:        {
13:           cout << "Hello\n";
14:           counter—;
15:        } while (counter >0);
16:        cout << "Counter is: " << counter;
17:      }
```

OUTPUT
```
How many hellos?: 2
Hello
Hello
Counter is 0
```

ANALYSIS   The user is prompted for a starting value on line 9, which is stored in the integer variable counter. In the do...while loop, the body of the loop is entered *before* the condition is tested, and therefore it is guaranteed to be acted on at least once. On line 13 the message is printed, on line 14 the counter is decremented, and on line 15 the condition is tested. If the condition evaluates true, execution jumps to the top of the loop on line 13; otherwise, it falls through to line 16.

The continue and break statements work in the do...while loop exactly as they do in the while loop. The only difference between a while loop and a do...while loop is *when* the condition is tested.

The *do...while* Statement

SYNTAX

do...while always performs a statement or statement block at least once and repeats as long as the *condition* is true.

```
do
statement;
while (condition);
```

The *statement* is executed, and then the *condition* is evaluated. If the *condition* is true, the loop is repeated; otherwise, the loop ends. The *statements* and *conditions* are otherwise identical to the while loop.

Example 1

```
// count to 10
int x = 0;
do
    cout << "x: " << x++;
while (x < 10);
```

Example 2

```
// print lowercase alphabet.
char ch = 'a';
do
{
    cout << ch << ' ';
    ch++;
} while ( ch <= 'z' );
```

Do	Don't

DO use do...while when you want to ensure that the loop is executed at least once.

DO use while loops when you want to skip the loop if the condition is false.

DO test all loops to make sure that they do what you expect.

for Loops

When programming while loops, you'll often find yourself setting up a starting condition, testing to see whether the condition is true, and incrementing or otherwise changing a variable each time through the loop. Listing 7.8 demonstrates this.

TYPE **Listing 7.8. The while loop reexamined.**

```
1:    // Listing 7.8
2:    // Looping with while
3:
4:    #include <iostream.h>
5:
6:    void main()
7:    {
8:        int counter = 0;
9:
10:       while(counter < 5)
```

continues

Listing 7.8. continued

```
11:       {
12:            counter++;
13:            cout << "Looping!  ";
14:       }
15:
16:       cout << "\nCounter: " << counter << ".\n";
17:    }
```

OUTPUT
Looping! Looping! Looping! Looping! Looping!
Counter: 5.

ANALYSIS
The condition is set on line 8: counter is initialized to 0. On line 10 counter is tested to see whether it is less than 5. counter is incremented on line 12. On line 13 a simple message is printed, but you can imagine that more important work could be done for each increment of the counter.

A for loop combines the three steps of *initialization, test,* and *increment* into one statement. A for statement consists of the keyword for followed by a pair of parentheses (). Within the parentheses are three statements separated by semicolons (;).

The first statement is the *initialization.* Any legal C++ statement can be put here, but typically this is used to create and initialize a counting variable. The second statement is the *test,* and any legal C++ expression can be used here. This serves the same role as the condition in the while loop. The third statement is the *action.* Typically, a value is incremented or decremented, though any legal C++ statement can be put here. Note that statements one and three can be any legal C++ statement, but the second statement must be an expression—a C++ statement that returns a value. The statement(s) inside the for loop are repeated as long as the second statement in the parentheses is true. Listing 7.9 demonstrates its use.

TYPE **Listing 7.9. Demonstrating the for loop.**

```
1:       // Listing 7.9
2:       // Looping with for
3:
4:       #include <iostream.h>
5:
6:       void main()
7:       {
8:         int counter;
9:         for (counter = 0; counter < 5; counter++)
10:            cout << "Looping! ";
11:
12:          cout << "\nCounter: " << counter << ".\n";
13:       }
```

```
Looping!  Looping!  Looping!  Looping!  Looping!
Counter: 5.
```

The for statement on line 9 combines the initialization of counter, the test that counter is less than 5, and the increment of counter—all into one line. The body of the for statement is on line 10. Of course, a block could be used here as well.

The *for* Statement

SYNTAX

for loops are often used to perform some statement or statement block a specified number of times. A for loop has the following syntax:

```
for (initialization; test; action )
    statement;
```

The *initialization* statement is used to initialize the state of a counter, or to otherwise prepare for the loop. *test* is any C++ expression and is evaluated each time through the loop. If *test* is true, the *action* in the header is executed (typically the counter is incremented) and then the body of the for loop is executed.

Example 1

```
// print hello ten times
for (int i = 0; i<10; i++)
    cout << "Hello! ";
```

Example 2

```
for (int i = 0; i < 10; i++)
{
    cout << "Hello!" << endl;
    cout << "the value of i is: " << i << endl;
}
```

Advanced *for* Loops

for statements are powerful and flexible. The three independent statements (*initialization*, *test*, and *action*) lend themselves to a number of variations.

A for loop works in the following sequence:

1. Performs the operations in the initialization.
2. Evaluates the test condition.
3. If the test condition is true, executes the action statement and the loop.

After each time through the loop, Steps 2 and 3 repeat.

Multiple Initialization and Increments

It is not uncommon to initialize more than one variable, to test a compound logical expression, and to execute more than one statement. The *initialization* and the *action* can be replaced by multiple C++ statements, each separated by a comma. Listing 7.10 demonstrates the initialization and increment of two variables.

TYPE   **Listing 7.10. Multiple statements in `for` loops.**

```
1:  //listing 7.10
2:  // demonstrates multiple statements in
3:  // for loops
4:
5: #include <iostream.h>
6:
7:  void main()
8:  {
9:      for (int i=0, j=0; i<3; i++, j++)
10:          cout << "i: " << i << " j: " << j << endl;
11:  }
```

OUTPUT
```
i: 0   j: 0
i: 1   j: 1
i: 2   j: 2
```

ANALYSIS   On line 9 two variables, i and j, are each initialized with the value 0. The test (i<3) is evaluated, and because it is true, the actions are taken (i and j are incremented). Then the body of the for statement is executed, and the values are printed.

After line 10 completes, the condition is evaluated again, and if it remains true, the actions are repeated (i and j are again incremented) and the body of the loop is executed again. This continues until the test fails, in which case the action statement is *not* executed, and control falls out of the loop.

Null Statements in *for* Loops

Any or all of the statements in a for loop can be null. To accomplish this, use the semicolon to mark where the statement would have been. To create a for loop that acts exactly like a while loop, leave out the first and third statements. Listing 7.11 illustrates this idea.

TYPE   **Listing 7.11. Null statements in `for` loops.**

```
1:      // Listing 7.11
2:      // For loops with null statements
3:
4:      #include <iostream.h>
5:
6:      void main()
```

```
7:    {
8:        int counter = 0;
9:
10:       for( ; counter < 5; )
11:       {
12:           counter++;
13:           cout << "Looping!   ";
14:       }
15:
16:       cout << "\nCounter: " << counter << ".\n";
17:   }
```

OUTPUT

```
Looping!  Looping!  Looping!  Looping!  Looping!
Counter: 5.
```

ANALYSIS You might recognize this as being exactly like the `while` loop illustrated in Listing 7.8! On line 8 the counter variable is initialized. The `for` statement on line 10 does not initialize any values, but it does include a test for counter < 5. There is no increment statement, so this loop behaves exactly as if it had been written as follows:

```
while (counter < 5)
```

Once again, C++ gives you a number of ways to accomplish the same thing. No experienced C++ programmer would use a `for` loop in this way, but it does illustrate the flexibility of the `for` statement. In fact, it is possible, using `break` and `continue`, to create a `for` loop with none of the three statements. Listing 7.12 illustrates how.

TYPE **Listing 7.12. An empty `for` loop statement.**

```
1:    //Listing 7.12 illustrating
2:    //empty for loop statement
3:
4:    #include <iostream.h>
5:
6:    void main()
7:    {
8:        int counter=0;         // initialization
9:        int max;
10:       cout << "How many hellos?";
11:       cin >> max;
12:       for (;;)               // a for loop that doesn't end
13:       {
14:          if (counter < max)        // test
15:          {
16:            cout << "Hello!\n";
17:            counter++;              // increment
18:          }
19:          else
20:              break;
21:       }
22:    }
```

7

```
How many hellos?   3
Hello!
Hello!
Hello!
```

The for loop has now been pushed to its absolute limit. *initialization*, *test*, and *action* have all been taken out of the for statement. The initialization is done on line 8, before the for loop begins. The test is done in a separate if statement on line 14, and if the test succeeds, the action (an increment to counter) is performed on line 17. If the test fails, breaking out of the loop occurs on line 20.

Although this particular program is somewhat absurd, there are times when a for(;;) loop or a while (true) loop is just what you'll want. You'll see an example of a more reasonable use of such loops when switch statements are discussed later today.

Empty *for* Loops

So much can be done in the header of a for statement that at times, you won't need the body to do anything at all. In that case, be sure to put a null statement (;) as the body of the loop. The semicolon can be on the same line as the header, but this is easy to overlook. Listing 7.13 illustrates how this is done.

Listing 7.13. A null statement in a for loop.

```
1:     //Listing 7.13
2:     //Demonstrates null statement
3:     // as body of for loop
4:
5:     #include <iostream.h>
6:     void main()
7:     {
8:        for (int i = 0; i<5; cout << "i: " << i++ << endl)
9:           ;
10:    }
```

```
i: 0
i: 1
i: 2
i: 3
i: 4
```

The for loop on line 8 includes three statements: The initialization statement establishes the counter i and initializes it to 0. The condition statement tests for i<5. The action statement prints the value in i and increments it.

There is nothing left to do in the body of the for loop, so the null statement (;) is used. Note that this is not a well-designed for loop: The action statement is doing far too much. This would be better rewritten as

```
8:          for (int i = 0; i<5; i++)
9:              cout << "i: " << i << endl;
```

Both do exactly the same thing, but this example is easier to understand.

Nested Loops

Loops can be nested, with one loop sitting in the body of another. The inner loop is executed in full for every execution of the outer loop. Listing 7.14 illustrates writing marks into a matrix using nested for loops.

TYPE **Listing 7.14. Nested for loops.**

```
1:    //Listing 7.14
2:    //Illustrates nested for loops
3:
4:    #include <iostream.h>
5:
6:    void main()
7:    {
8:        unsigned int rows, columns;
9:        char theChar;
10:       cout << "How many rows? ";
11:       cin >> rows;
12:       cout << "How many columns? ";
13:       cin >> columns;
14:       cout << "What character? ";
15:       cin >> theChar;
16:       for (int i = 0; i<rows; i++)
17:       {
18:          for (int j = 0; j<columns; j++)
19:              cout << theChar;
20:          cout << "\n";
21:       }
22:    }
```

OUTPUT
```
How many rows? 4
How many columns?  12
What character?  x
xxxxxxxxxxxx
xxxxxxxxxxxx
xxxxxxxxxxxx
xxxxxxxxxxxx
```

7

ANALYSIS The user is prompted for the number of rows and columns and for a character to print. The first for loop, on line 16, initializes a counter (i) to 0, and then the body of the outer for loop is run.

On line 18, which is the first line of the body of the outer for loop, another for loop is established. A second counter (j) is also initialized to 0, and the body of the inner for loop is executed. On line 19 the chosen character is printed, and control returns to the header of the inner for loop. Note that the inner for loop is only one statement (the printing of the character). The condition is tested (j < columns) and if it evaluates true, j is incremented and the next character is printed. This continues until j equals the number of columns.

When the inner for loop fails its test (in this case, after 12 xs are printed) execution falls through to line 20, and a new line is printed. The outer for loop now returns to its header, where *its* condition (i < rows) is tested. If this evaluates true, i is incremented and the body of the loop is executed.

In the second iteration of the outer for loop, the inner for loop is started over. Thus j is reinitialized to 0 and the entire inner loop is run again.

The important idea here is that by using a nested loop, the inner loop is executed for each iteration of the outer loop. Thus, the character is printed columns times for each row.

 NOTE

As an aside, many C++ programmers use the letters i and j as counting variables. This tradition goes all the way back to FORTRAN, in which the letters i, j, k, l, m, and n were the only legal counting variables.

Other programmers prefer to use more descriptive counter variable names, such as Ctr1 and Ctr2. Using i and j in for loop headers should not cause much confusion, however.

Scoping in Loops

Normally scope is obvious, but there are some tricky exceptions when you consider loops. Currently, variables declared within the header of a for or while loop (as in for(int i = 0; i<SomeValue; i++)) are scoped to the for or while loop block alone.

Summing Up Loops

On Day 5, "Functions," you learned how to solve the Fibbonacci series problem using recursion. To briefly review, a Fibbonacci series starts with 1, 1, 2, 3, and all subsequent numbers are the sum of the previous two:

1,1,2,3,5,8,13,21,34...

The *n*th Fibbonacci number is the sum of the *n*-1 and the *n*-2 Fibbonacci number. The problem solved on Day 5 was finding the value of the *n*th Fibbonacci number. This was done with recursion. Listing 7.15 offers a solution using iteration.

Listing 7.15. Solving the *n*th Fibonacci number using iteration.

TYPE

```
1:  // Listing 7.15
2:  // Demonstrates solving the nth
3:  // Fibonacci number using iteration
4:
5:  #include <iostream.h>
6:
7:  typedef unsigned long int ULONG;
8:
9:  ULONG fib(ULONG position);
10:  void main()
11:  {
12:      ULONG answer, position;
13:      cout << "Which position? ";
14:      cin >> position;
15:      cout << "\n";
16:
17:      answer = fib(position);
18:      cout << answer << " is the ";
19:      cout << position << "th Fibonacci number.\n";
20:  }
21:
22:  ULONG fib(ULONG n)
23:  {
24:      ULONG minusTwo=1, minusOne=1, answer=2;
25:
26:      if (n < 3)
27:          return 1;
28:
29:      for (n -= 3; n; n—)
30:      {
31:          minusTwo = minusOne;
32:          minusOne = answer;
33:          answer = minusOne + minusTwo;
34:      }
35:
36:      return answer;
37:  }
```

OUTPUT

```
Which position? 4
3 is the 4th Fibonacci number.
Which position? 5
5 is the 5th Fibonacci number
Which position? 20
6765 is the 20th Fibonacci number
Which position? 100
3314859971 is the 100th Fibonacci number
```

7

ANALYSIS Listing 7.15 solves the Fibonacci series using iteration rather than recursion. This approach is faster and uses less memory than the recursive solution.

On line 13 the user is asked for the position to check. The function fib() is called, which evaluates the position. If it is less than 3, it returns the value 1. Starting with position 3, the function iterates using the following algorithm:

1. Establish the starting position: Fill variable answer with 2, minusTwo with 1 (answer-2) and minusOne with 1 (answer-1). Decrement the position by 3 because the first two numbers are handled by the starting position.

2. For every number, count up the Fibonacci series. This is done by the following steps:

   ☐ Putting the value currently in minusOne into minusTwo.

   ☐ Putting the value currently in answer into minusOne.

   ☐ Adding minusOne and minusTwo and putting the sum in answer.

   ☐ Decrementing n.

3. When n reaches 0, return the answer.

This is exactly how you would solve this problem with pencil and paper. If you were asked for the fifth Fibonacci number, you would write

```
1, 1, 2,
```

and think, "two more to do." You would then add 2+1 and write 3, and think, "one more to find." Finally, you would write 3+2 and the answer would be 5. In effect, you are shifting your attention one number to the right each time through, and decrementing the number remaining to be found.

Note the condition tested on line 29 (n). This is a C++ idiom and is exactly equivalent to n != 0. This for loop relies on the fact that when n reaches 0, it evaluates false, because 0 is false in C++. The for loop header could have been written

```
for (n-=3; n>0; n++)
```

which might have been clearer. However, this idiom is so common in C++ that there is little sense in fighting it.

Compile, link, and run the program source in Listing 7.15 along with the recursive solution offered on Day 5. Try to find position 25 and compare the time it takes each program. Recursion is elegant, but because the function call brings a performance overhead and because it is called so many times, its performance is noticeably slower than iteration. Microcomputers tend to be optimized for the arithmetic operations, so the iterative solution should be blazingly fast.

switch **Statements**

On Day 4 you saw how to write `if` and `if/else` statements. These can become quite confusing when nested too deeply, and C++ offers an alternative. Unlike `if`, which evaluates one value, `switch` statements allow you to branch on any of a number of different values. The general form of the `switch` statement is as follows:

```
switch (expression)
{
case valueOne: statement;
                    break;
case valueTwo: statement;
                    break;
....
case valueN:    statement;
                    break;
default:        statement;
}
```

expression is any legal C++ expression; the *statements* are any legal C++ statements or block of statements. `switch` evaluates expression and compares the result to each of the case values. Note, however, that the evaluation is only for equality; relational operators cannot be used here, nor can Boolean operations.

If one of the `case` values matches the expression, execution jumps to those statements and continues to the end of the `switch` block unless a `break` statement is encountered. If nothing matches, execution branches to the optional `default` statement. If there is no `default` and there is no matching value, execution falls through the `switch` statement, and the statement ends.

NOTE

> It is almost always a good idea to have a `default` case in `switch` statements. If you have no other need for the `default`, use it to test for the supposedly impossible case and print out an error message; this can be a tremendous aid in debugging.

It is important to note that if there is no `break` statement at the end of a `case` statement, execution falls through to the next case. This is sometimes necessary, but usually it is an error. If you decide to let execution fall through, be sure to put a comment indicating that you didn't just forget the break. Listing 7.16 illustrates use of the `switch` statement.

7

TYPE   **Listing 7.16. Demonstrating the switch statement.**

```
1:  //Listing 7.16
2:  // Demonstrates switch statement
3:
4:  #include <iostream.h>
5:
6:  void main()
7:  {
8:    unsigned short int number;
9:    cout << "Enter a number between 1 and 5: ";
10:   cin >> number;
11:   switch (number)
12:   {
13:      case 0:  cout << "Too small, sorry!";
14:               break;
15:      case 5:  cout << "Good job!\n";  // fall through
16:      case 4:  cout << "Nice Pick!\n"; // fall through
17:      case 3:  cout << "Excellent!\n"; // fall through
18:      case 2:  cout << "Masterful!\n"; // fall through
19:      case 1:  cout << "Incredible!\n";
20:               break;
21:      default: cout << "Too large!\n";
22:               break;
23:   }
24:   cout << "\n\n";
25: }
```

OUTPUT
```
Enter a number between 1 and 5:  3
Excellent!
Masterful!
Incredible!

Enter a number between 1 and 5: 8
Too large!
```

ANALYSIS   The user is prompted for a number. That number is given to the switch statement. If the number is 0, the case statement on line 13 matches, the message Too small, sorry! is printed, and the break statement ends the switch. If the value is 5, execution switches to line 15 where a message is printed, and then falls through to line 16 where another message is printed, and so on until hitting the break on line 20.

The net effect of these statements is that for a number between 1 and 5, that many messages are printed. If the value of the number is not 0 through 5, it is assumed to be too large, and the default statement is invoked on line 21.

7

The *switch* Statement

SYNTAX

The switch statement allows for selection of response depending on one of a set of possible values.

```
switch (expression)
{
  case valueOne: statement;
  case valueTwo: statement;
....
  case valueN: statement
  default: statement;
}
```

The switch statement allows for branching on multiple values of *expression*. The *expression* is evaluated and if it matches any of the case values, execution jumps to that line. Execution continues until either the end of the switch statement or a break statement is encountered.

If *expression* does not match any of the case statements, and if there is a default statement, execution switches to the default statement; otherwise, the switch statement ends.

Example 1

```
switch (choice)
{
    case 0:
        cout << "Zero!" << endl;
        break
    case 1:
        cout << "One!" << endl;
        break;
    case 2:
        cout << "Two!" << endl;
    default:
        cout << "Default!" << endl;
}
```

Example 2

```
switch (choice)
{
    case 0:
    case 1:
    case 2:
        cout << "Less than 3!";
        break;
    case 3:
        cout << "Equals 3!";
        break;
    default:
        cout << "greater than 3!";
}
```

7

Using a *switch* Statement with a Menu

Listing 7.17 returns to the for(;;) loop discussed earlier. These loops are also called *forever loops* because they loop forever if a break is not encountered. The forever loop is used to put up a menu, solicit a choice from the user, act on the choice, and then return to the menu. This continues until the user chooses to exit.

Note: Some programmers like to define a new word to make forever loops obvious, as in the following:

```
#define EVER ;;
for (EVER)
{
    // statements...
}
```

Use of #define is covered on Day 17, "The Preprocessor."

NEW TERM   A *forever loop* is a loop that does not have an exit condition. In order to exit the loop a break statement must be used. Forever loops are also known as eternal loops.

TYPE   **Listing 7.17. A forever loop.**

```
1:    //Listing 7.17
2:    //Using a forever loop to manage
3:    //user interaction
4:    #include <iostream.h>
5:
6:    // types & defines
7:
8:    typedef unsigned short int USHORT;
9:
10:   // prototypes
11:   USHORT menu();
12:   void DoTaskOne();
13:   void DoTaskMany(USHORT);
14:
15:   void main()
16:   {
17:
18:       bool exit = FALSE;
19:       for (;;)
20:       {
21:           USHORT choice = menu();
22:           switch(choice)
```

```
23:                    {
24:                        case (1):
25:                            DoTaskOne();
26:                            break;
27:                        case (2):
28:                            DoTaskMany(2);
29:                            break;
30:                        case (3):
31:                            DoTaskMany(3);
32:                            break;
33:                        case (4):
34:                            continue;   // redundant!
35:                            break;
36:                        case (5):
37:                            exit=TRUE;
38:                            break;
39:                        default:
40:                            cout << "Please select again!\n";
41:                            break;
42:                    }            // end switch
43:
44:                    if (exit)
45:                        break;
46:            }                        // end forever
47:    }                                // end main()
48:
49:    USHORT menu()
50:    {
51:        USHORT choice;
52:
53:        cout << " **** Menu ****\n\n";
54:        cout << "(1) Choice one.\n";
55:        cout << "(2) Choice two.\n";
56:        cout << "(3) Choice three.\n";
57:        cout << "(4) Redisplay menu.\n";
58:        cout << "(5) Quit.\n\n";
59:        cout << ": ";
60:        cin >> choice;
61:        return choice;
62:    }
63:
64:    void DoTaskOne()
65:    {
66:        cout << "Task One!\n";
67:    }
68:
69:    void DoTaskMany(USHORT which)
70:    {
71:        if (which == 2)
72:            cout << "Task Two!\n";
73:        else
74:            cout << "Task Three!\n";
75:    }
```

7

OUTPUT

```
**** Menu ****
 (1) Choice one.
 (2) Choice two.
 (3) Choice three.
 (4) Redisplay menu
 (5) Quit.
: 1
Task One!
**** Menu ****
 (1) Choice one.
 (2) Choice two.
 (3) Choice three.
 (4) Redisplay menu
 (5) Quit.
: 3
Task Three!
**** Menu ****
 (1) Choice one.
 (2) Choice two.
 (3) Choice three.
 (4) Redisplay menu
 (5) Quit.
: 5
```

ANALYSIS This program brings together a number of concepts from today and previous days. It also shows a common use of the switch statement. On line 8 typedef is used to create an alias, USHORT, for unsigned short int.

The forever loop begins on line 19. The menu() function is called and prints the menu to the screen and returns the user's selection. The switch statement, which begins on line 22 and ends on line 42, switches on the user's choice.

If the user enters 1, execution jumps to the case 1: statement on line 24. Line 25 switches execution to the DoTaskOne() function, which prints a message and returns. On its return, execution resumes on line 26, where the break ends the switch statement, and execution falls through to line 43. On line 44 the variable exit is evaluated. If it evaluates true, the break on line 45 is executed, and the for(;;) loop ends. However, if it evaluates false, execution resumes at the top of the loop on line 19.

Note that the continue statement on line 34 is redundant. If it were left out and the break statement were encountered, the switch would end, exit would evaluate false, the loop would reiterate, and the menu would be reprinted. The continue does, however, bypass the test of exit.

7

Do	Don't

DO use `switch` statements to avoid deeply nested `if` statements.

DON'T forget `break` at the end of each case unless you want to fall through.

DO carefully document all intentional fall-through cases.

DO put a default case in `switch` statements, if only to detect seemingly impossible situations.

Summary

There are a number of different ways to cause a C++ program to loop. `while` loops check a condition and, if it is true, execute the statements in the body of the loop. `do...while` loops execute the body of the loop and then test the condition. `for` loops initialize a value, and then test an expression. If the expression is true, the final statement in the `for` header is executed as is the body of the loop. Each subsequent time through the loop, the expression is tested again.

The `goto` statement is generally avoided because it causes an unconditional jump to a seemingly arbitrary location in the code and thus makes source code difficult to understand and maintain. `continue` causes `while`, `do...while`, and `for` loops to start over; and `break` causes `while`, `do...while`, `for`, and `switch` statements to end.

Q&A

Q How do you choose between `if/else` and `switch`?

A If there are more than just one or two `else` clauses, and all are testing the same variable, consider using a `switch` statement.

Q How do you choose between `while` and `do...while`?

A If the body of the loop should always execute at least once, consider a `do...while` loop; otherwise, try to use the `while` loop.

7

Q How do you choose between `while` and `for`?

A If you are initializing a counting variable, testing that variable, and incrementing it each time through the loop, consider the `for` loop. If your variable is already initialized and is not incremented on each loop, a `while` loop might be the better choice.

Q How do you choose between recursion and iteration?

A Some problems cry out for recursion, but most problems yield to iteration as well. Put recursion in your back pocket; it might come in handy someday.

Q Is it better to use `while(true)` or `for(;;)`?

A There is no significant difference.

Quiz

1. How do you initialize more than one variable in a `for` loop?
2. Why is `goto` avoided?
3. Is it possible to write a `for` loop with a body that is never executed?
4. Is it possible to nest `while` loops within `for` loops?
5. Is it possible to create a loop that never ends? Give an example.
6. What happens if you create a loop that never ends?

Exercises

1. What is the value of x when the `for` loop completes?
   ```
   int x;
   for (x = 0; x < 100; x++)
   ```
2. Write a nested `for` loop that prints a 10×10 pattern of zeros.
3. Write a `for` statement to count from 100 to 200 by twos.
4. Write a `while` loop to count from 100 to 200 by twos.
5. Write a `do...while` loop to count from 100 to 200 by twos.
6. **BUG BUSTERS:** What is wrong with this code?
   ```
   int counter = 0;
   while (counter < 10)
   {
       cout << "counter: " << counter;
   }
   ```

7. **BUG BUSTERS:** What is wrong with this code?

```
for (int counter = 0; counter < 10; counter++);
cout << counter << " ";
```

8. **BUG BUSTERS:** What is wrong with this code?

```
int counter = 100;
while (counter < 10)
{
    cout << "counter now: " << counter;
    counter—;
}
```

9. **BUG BUSTERS:** What is wrong with this code?

```
cout << "Enter a number between 0 and 5: ";
cin >> theNumber;
switch (theNumber)
{
    case 0:
          doZero();
    case 1:              // fall through
    case 2:              // fall through
    case 3:              // fall through
    case 4:              // fall through
    case 5:
          doOneToFive();
          break;
    default:
          doDefault();
          break;

}
```

WEEK

1

In Review

The listing that follows demonstrates some of the concepts you learned this week. It is provided here to help you review and to give you more practice using the Week 1 concepts.

```
1:      #include <iostream.h>
2:
3:      typedef unsigned short int USHORT;
4:      typedef unsigned long int ULONG;
5:      enum CHOICE { DrawRect = 1, GetArea, GetPerim,
6:                    ChangeDimensions, Quit};
7:
8:      // Rectangle class declaration
9:      class Rectangle
10:     {
11:        public:
12:            // constructors
13:            Rectangle(USHORT width, USHORT height);
14:            ~Rectangle();
```

```
15:
16:            // accessors
17:            USHORT GetHeight() const { return
                         _itsHeight; }
18:            USHORT GetWidth() const { return itsWidth;
                         _}
19:            ULONG GetArea() const { return itsHeight *
                         _itsWidth; }
20:            ULONG GetPerim() const { return 2*itsHeight
                         _+ 2*itsWidth; }
21:            void SetSize(USHORT newWidth, USHORT
                         _newHeight);
22:
23:            // Misc. methods
24:            void DrawShape() const;
25:
26:        private:
27:            USHORT itsWidth;
28:            USHORT itsHeight;
29:        };
30:
31:     // Class method implementations
32:     void Rectangle::SetSize(USHORT newWidth, USHORT newHeight)
33:     {
34:         itsWidth = newWidth;
35:         itsHeight = newHeight;
36:     }
37:
38:
39:     Rectangle::Rectangle(USHORT width, USHORT height)
40:     {
41:         itsWidth = width;
42:         itsHeight = height;
43:     }
44:
45:     Rectangle::~Rectangle() {}
46:
47:     USHORT DoMenu();
48:     void DoDrawRect(Rectangle);
49:     void DoGetArea(Rectangle);
50:     void DoGetPerim(Rectangle);
51:
52:     void main ()
53:     {
54:         // initialize a rectangle to 10,20
55:         Rectangle theRect(30,5);
56:
57:         USHORT choice = DrawRect;
58:         bool fQuit = false;
59:
60:         while (!fQuit)
61:         {
62:             choice = DoMenu();
63:             if (choice < DrawRect ¦¦ choice >  Quit)
64:             {
```

```
65:             cout << "\nInvalid Choice, please try again.\n\n";
66:             continue;
67:         }
68:         switch (choice)
69:         {
70:         case  DrawRect:
71:             DoDrawRect(theRect);
72:             break;
73:         case GetArea:
74:             DoGetArea(theRect);
75:             break;
76:         case GetPerim:
77:             DoGetPerim(theRect);
78:             break;
79:         case ChangeDimensions:
80:             USHORT newLength, newWidth;
81:             cout << "\nNew width: ";
82:             cin >> newWidth;
83:             cout << "New height: ";
84:             cin >> newLength;
85:             theRect.SetSize(newWidth, newLength);
86:             DoDrawRect(theRect);
87:             break;
88:         case Quit:
89:             fQuit = true;
90:             cout << "\nExiting...\n\n";
91:             break;
92:         default:
93:             cout << "Error in choice!\n";
94:             fQuit = true;
95:             break;
96:         }     // end switch
97:     }         // end while
98: }             // end main
99:
100:
101: USHORT DoMenu()
102: {
103:     USHORT choice;
104:         cout << "\n\n    *** Menu *** \n";
105:         cout << "(1) Draw Rectangle\n";
106:         cout << "(2) Area\n";
107:         cout << "(3) Perimeter\n";
108:         cout << "(4) Resize\n";
109:         cout << "(5) Quit\n";
110:
111:     cin >> choice;
112:     return choice;
113: }
114:
115: void DoDrawRect(Rectangle theRect)
116: {
117:     USHORT height = theRect.GetHeight();
118:     USHORT width = theRect.GetWidth();
119:
```

```
120:      for (USHORT i = 0; i<height; i++)
121:      {
122:          for (USHORT j = 0; j< width; j++)
123:              cout << "*";
124:          cout << "\n";
125:      }
126:  }
127:
128:
129:  void DoGetArea(Rectangle theRect)
130:  {
131:      cout << "Area: " <<  theRect.GetArea() << endl;
132:  }
133:
134:  void DoGetPerim(Rectangle theRect)
135:  {
136:      cout << "Perimeter: " <<  theRect.GetPerim() << endl;
137:  }
```

OUTPUT

```
*** Menu ***
 (1) Draw Rectangle
 (2) Area
 (3) Perimeter
 (4) Resize
 (5) Quit
1
****************************
****************************
****************************
****************************
****************************

*** Menu ***
 (1) Draw Rectangle
 (2) Area
 (3) Perimeter
 (4) Resize
 (5) Quit
2
Area: 150

*** Menu ***
 (1) Draw Rectangle
 (2) Area
 (3) Perimeter
 (4) Resize
 (5) Quit
3
Perimeter: 70

*** Menu ***
 (1) Draw Rectangle
 (2) Area
 (3) Perimeter
 (4) Resize
 (5) Quit
```

```
4

New Width: 10
New height: 8
**********
**********
**********
**********
**********
**********
**********
**********

*** Menu ***
 (1) Draw Rectangle
 (2) Area
 (3) Perimeter
 (4) Resize
 (5) Quit
2
Area: 80

*** Menu ***
 (1) Draw Rectangle
 (2) Area
 (3) Perimeter
 (4) Resize
 (5) Quit
3
Perimeter: 36

*** Menu ***
 (1) Draw Rectangle
 (2) Area
 (3) Perimeter
 (4) Resize
 (5) Quit
5
Exiting...
```

ANALYSIS   You should not only be able to enter, compile, link, and run this program, but also understand what it does and how it works, based on the work you did this week.

The first six lines set up the new types and definitions that are used throughout the program.

Lines 8 through 29 declare the Rectangle class. There are public accessor methods for obtaining and setting the width and height of the rectangle, as well as for computing the area and perimeter. Lines 31 through 44 contain the class function definitions that were not declared inline.

The function prototypes for the non-class member functions are on lines 47 through 50, and the program itself begins on line 52. The essence of this program is to generate a rectangle, then to print out a menu offering five options: draw the rectangle, determine its area, determine its perimeter, resize the rectangle, or quit.

A flag is set on line 58, and when that flag is not set to `true`, the menu loop continues. The flag is only set to `true` if the user picks Quit from the menu.

Each of the other choices, with the exception of `ChangeDimensions`, calls out to a function. This makes the `switch` statement cleaner. `ChangeDimensions` *cannot* call out to a function because it must change the dimensions of the rectangle. If the rectangle is passed (by value) to a function such as `DoChangeDimensions()`, the dimensions would be changed on the local copy of the rectangle in `DoChangeDimensions()`, and not on the rectangle in `main()`. On Day 8, "Pointers," and Day 10, "Advanced Functions," you'll learn how to overcome this restriction, but for now the change is made in the `main()` function.

Note how the use of an enumeration makes the `switch` statement much cleaner and easier to understand. Had the `switch` depended on the numeric choices (1 through 5) of the user, you would have to constantly refer back to the description of the menu to see which pick was which.

On line 63, the user's choice is checked to make sure it is in range. If not, an error message is printed and the menu is reprinted. Note that the `switch` statement includes an "impossible" default condition. This is an aid in debugging. If the program is working, that statement can never be reached.

Week In Review

Congratulations! You've completed the first week! Now you can create and understand sophisticated C++ programs. Of course, there's much more to do, and next week starts with one of the most difficult concepts in C++: *pointers*. Don't give up now, you're about to delve deep into the meaning and use of object-oriented programming, virtual functions, and many of the advanced features of this powerful language.

Take a break, bask in the glory of your accomplishment, and then turn the page to start Week 2.

WEEK

2

At A Glance

You have finished the first week of learning how to program in C++. By now, you should feel comfortable entering programs, using your compiler, and thinking about objects, classes, and program flow.

Where You Are Going

Week 2 begins with pointers. Pointers are traditionally a difficult subject for new C++ programmers, but you'll find them explained fully and clearly, and they should not be a stumbling block. Day 9 teaches references, which are a close cousin to pointers. On Day 10 you see how to overload functions, and on Day 11 you learn how to work with arrays and basic collection types. Day 12 introduces inheritance, a fundamental concept in object-oriented programming. Day 13 extends the lessons of Day 12 to discuss multiple inheritance, and Day 14 ends the week with a discussion of static functions and friends.

Day 8

Pointers

One of the most powerful tools available to a C++ programmer is the ability to manipulate computer memory directly by using pointers. Today you learn

☐ What pointers are.

☐ How to declare and use pointers.

☐ What the free store is and how to manipulate memory.

Pointers present two special challenges when learning C++: They can be somewhat confusing, and it isn't immediately obvious why they are needed. This lesson explains how pointers work, step-by-step. You will understand the need for pointers, however, only as the book progresses.

What Is a Pointer?

To understand pointers, you must know a little about computer memory. Computer memory is divided into sequentially numbered memory locations. Each variable is located at a unique location in memory, known as its address. (This is discussed in the "Extra Credit" section following Day 5, "Functions.") Figure 8.1 shows a schematic representation of the storage of an unsigned long integer variable theAge.

Figure 8.1.

A schematic representa-
tion of theAge.

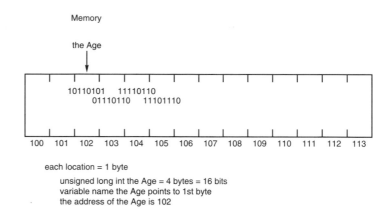

each location = 1 byte
  unsigned long int the Age = 4 bytes = 16 bits
  variable name the Age points to 1st byte
  the address of the Age is 102

NEW TERM A *pointer* is a variable that holds a memory address.

Different computers number this memory using different, complex schemes. Usually
programmers don't need to know the particular address of any given variable because the
compiler handles the details. If you want this information, though, you can use the *address*
of operator (&), which is illustrated in Listing 8.1.

TYPE **Listing 8.1. Finding the address of variables.**

```
1:   // Listing 8.1 Demonstrates address of operator
2:   // and addresses of local variables
3:
4:   #include <iostream.h>
5:
6:   void main()
7:   {
8:      unsigned short shortVar=5;
9:      unsigned long  longVar=65535;
10:     long sVar = -65535;
11:
12:     cout << "shortVar:\t" << shortVar << " Address of shortVar:\t"
        << &shortVar  << "\n";
13:
14:     cout << "longVar:\t"  << longVar  << " Address of longVar:\t"
        << &longVar  << "\n";
15:
16:     cout << "sVar:\t"     << sVar     << " Address of sVar:\t"
        << &sVar     << "\n";
17:
18:  }
```

8

```
shortVar: 5        Address of shortVar: 0x8fc9:fff4
longVar:  65535    Address of longVar:  0x8fc9:fff2
sVar:     -65535   Address of sVar:     0x8fc9:ffee
```

(Your printout may look different.)

ANALYSIS Three variables are declared and initialized: a short in line 8, an unsigned long in line 9, and a long in line 10. Their values and addresses are printed in lines 12 through 16, by using the *address of* operator (&).

The value of shortVar is 5—as expected—and its address is 0x8fc9:fff4 when run on my 80386-based computer. This complicated address is computer-specific and might change slightly each time the program is run. Your results will be different. What doesn't change, however, is that the difference in the first two addresses is two bytes if your computer uses two-byte short integers. The difference between the second and third is four bytes if your computer uses four-byte long integers. Figure 8.2 illustrates how the variables in this program would be stored in memory.

Figure 8.2.
An illustration of variable storage.

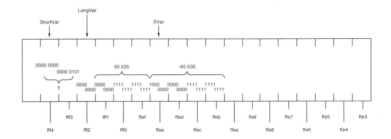

There is no reason why you need to know the actual numeric value of the address of each variable. What you care about is that each one has an address and that the right amount of memory is set aside. You tell the compiler how much memory to allow for your variables by declaring the variable type; the compiler automatically assigns an address for it. For example, a long integer is typically four bytes, meaning that the variable has an address to four bytes of memory.

Storing the Address in a Pointer

Every variable has an address. Even without knowing the specific address of a given variable, you can store that address in a pointer.

For example, suppose that howOld is an integer. To declare a pointer called pAge to hold its address, you would write

```
int *pAge = 0;
```

This declares pAge to be a *pointer to int.* That is, pAge is declared to hold the address of an int.

Note that pAge is a variable like any of the other variables. When you declare an integer variable (type int), it is set up to hold an integer. When you declare a pointer variable, such as pAge, it is set up to hold an address. pAge is just a different type of variable.

In this example, pAge is initialized to 0. A pointer whose value is 0 is called a *null pointer.* All pointers, when they are created, should be initialized to something. If you don't know what you want to assign to the pointer, assign 0. A pointer that is not initialized is called a *wild pointer.* Wild pointers are very dangerous.

NOTE

In the days of C, assigning the value 0 to a pointer did not mean the same thing that it does in C++, and it was considered a dangerous practice to do so. To solve that problem, C programmers would define a constant (traditionally called NULL) with the value ((void *)0) instead and use that constant to NULL pointers. Either method is acceptable. The stdlib header file contains a definition for NULL, so you can use NULL instead of 0 if you prefer.

NOTE

Practice safe computing: Initialize your pointers!

If you do initialize the pointer to 0 (or NULL), you must specifically assign the address of howOld to pAge. Here's an example that shows how to do that:

```
unsigned short int howOld = 50;      // make a variable
unsigned short int * pAge = 0;       // make a pointer
pAge = &howOld;                      // put howOld's address in pAge
```

The first line creates a variable—howOld, whose type is unsigned short int—and initializes it with the value 50. The second line declares pAge to be a pointer of type unsigned short int and initializes it to 0. You know that pAge is a pointer because of the asterisk (*) after the variable type and before the variable name.

The third and final line assigns the address of howOld to the pointer pAge. You can tell that the address of howOld is being assigned because of the *address of* operator (&). If the *address of* operator had not been used, the value of howOld would have been assigned. That might (or might not) have been a valid address.

8

8

At this point, pAge has as its value the address of howOld. howOld, in turn, has the value 50. You could have accomplished this with one fewer steps, as in the following example:

```
unsigned short int howOld = 50;      // make a variable
unsigned short int * pAge = &howOld;  // make pointer to howOld
```

pAge is a pointer that now contains the address of the howOld variable. Using pAge, you can actually determine the value of howOld, which in this case is 50. Accessing howOld by using the pointer pAge is called *indirection* because you are indirectly accessing howOld by means of pAge. Later today you see how to use indirection to access a variable's value.

 Indirection means accessing the value at the address held by a pointer. The pointer provides an indirect way to get the value held at that address.

 NOTE   Pointers can have any name that is legal for other variables. This book follows the convention of naming all pointers with an initial p, as in pAge or pNumber.

The Indirection Operator

The indirection operator (*) is also called the *dereference operator*. When a pointer is dereferenced, the value at the address stored by the pointer is retrieved.

Normal variables provide direct access to their own values. If you create a new variable of type unsigned short int called yourAge and you want to assign the value in howOld to that new variable, you would write

```
unsigned short int yourAge;
yourAge = howOld;
```

A pointer provides indirect access to the value of the variable whose address it stores. To assign the value in howOld to the new variable yourAge by way of the pointer pAge, you would write

```
unsigned short int yourAge;
yourAge = *pAge;
```

The indirection operator (*) in front of the variable pAge means "the value stored at." This assignment says, "Take the value stored at the address in pAge and assign it to yourAge."

NOTE The indirection operator (*) is used in two distinct ways with pointers: declaration and dereference. When a pointer is declared, the star indicates that it is a pointer, not a normal variable, as in the following example:

```
unsigned short * pAge = 0;    // make a pointer to an unsigned
short
```

When the pointer is dereferenced, the indirection operator indicates that the value at the memory location stored in the pointer is to be accessed, rather than the address itself.

```
*pAge = 5;                // assign 5 to the value at pAge
```

Also note that this same character (*) is used as the multiplication operator. The compiler knows which operator to call based on context.

Pointers, Addresses, and Variables

It is important to distinguish between a pointer, the address that the pointer holds, and the value at the address held by the pointer. This is the source of much of the confusion about pointers.

Consider the following code fragment:

```
int theVariable = 5;
int * pPointer = &theVariable ;
```

theVariable is declared to be an integer variable initialized with the value 5. pPointer is declared to be a pointer to an integer; it is initialized with the address of theVariable. pPointer is the pointer. The address that pPointer holds is the address of theVariable. The value at the address that pPointer holds is 5. Figure 8.3 shows a schematic representation of theVariable and pPointer.

Figure 8.3.

A schematic representation of pointers.

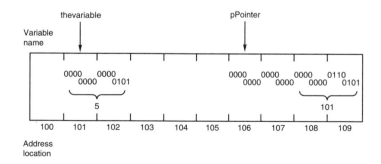

Manipulating Data by Using Pointers

When a pointer is assigned the address of a variable, you can use that pointer to access the data in that variable. Listing 8.2 demonstrates how the address of a local variable is assigned to a pointer and how the pointer manipulates the values in that variable.

TYPE **Listing 8.2. Manipulating data by using pointers.**

```
1:    // Listing 8.2 Using pointers
2:
3:    #include <iostream.h>
4:
5:    typedef unsigned short int USHORT;
6:    void main()
7:    {
8:        USHORT myAge;           // a variable
9:        USHORT * pAge = 0;      // a pointer
10:       myAge = 5;
11:       cout << "myAge: " << myAge << "\n";
12:
13:       pAge = &myAge;          // assign address of myAge to pAge
14:
15:       cout << "*pAge: " << *pAge << "\n\n";
16:
17:       cout << "*pAge = 7\n";
18:
19:       *pAge = 7;              // sets myAge to 7
20:
21:       cout << "*pAge: " << *pAge << "\n";
22:       cout << "myAge: " << myAge << "\n\n";
23:
24:
25:       cout << "myAge = 9\n";
26:
27:       myAge = 9;
28:
29:       cout << "myAge: " << myAge << "\n";
30:       cout << "*pAge: " << *pAge << "\n";
31:
32:    }
```

OUTPUT
```
myAge: 5
*pAge: 5

*pAge = 7
*pAge: 7
myAge: 7

myAge = 9
myAge: 9
*pAge: 9
```

This program declares two variables: an unsigned short myAge and a pointer to pAge (a pointer to the unsigned short myAge). myAge is assigned the value 5 in line 10; this is verified by the printout in line 11.

In line 13 pAge is assigned the address of myAge. In line 15 pAge is dereferenced and printed, showing that the value at the address that pAge stores is the 5 stored in myAge. In line 17 the value 7 is assigned to the variable at the address stored in pAge. This sets myAge to 7, and the printouts in lines 21 through 22 confirm this.

In line 27 the value 9 is assigned to the variable myAge. This value is obtained directly in line 29 and indirectly—by dereferencing pAge—in line 30.

Examining the Address

Pointers enable you to manipulate addresses without ever knowing their real value. After today, you'll take it on faith that when you assign the address of a variable to a pointer, it really has the address of that variable as its value. But just this once, why not check to make sure? Listing 8.3 illustrates this idea.

TYPE **Listing 8.3. Finding out what is stored in pointers.**

```
1:      // Listing 8.3 What is stored in a pointer.
2:
3:      #include <iostream.h>
4:
5:      typedef unsigned short int USHORT;
6:      void main()
7:      {
8:         unsigned short int myAge = 5, yourAge = 10;
9:         unsigned short int * pAge = &myAge;  // a pointer
10:
11:        cout << "myAge:\t" << myAge <<  "\tyourAge:\t" << yourAge << "\n";
12:        cout << "&myAge:\t" << &myAge <<  "\t&yourAge:\t" << &yourAge <<"\n";
13:
14:        cout << "pAge:\t" << pAge << "\n";
15:        cout << "*pAge:\t" << *pAge << "\n";
16:
17:        pAge = &yourAge;          // reassign the pointer
18:
19:        cout << "myAge:\t" << myAge <<  "\tyourAge:\t" << yourAge << "\n";
20:        cout << "&myAge:\t" << &myAge <<  "\t&yourAge:\t" << &yourAge <<"\n";
21:
22:        cout << "pAge:\t" << pAge << "\n";
23:        cout << "*pAge:\t" << *pAge << "\n";
24:
25:        cout << "&pAge:\t" << &pAge << "\n";
26:     }
```

8

```
myAge:          5                yourAge:  10
&myAge:         0xfb3:fff4       &yourAge: 0xfb3:fff2
pAge:           0xfd1:fff4
*pAge:          5
myAge:          5                yourAge:  10
&myAge:         0xfb3:fff4       &yourAge: 0xfb3:fff2
pAge:           0xfd1:fff2
*pAge:          10
&pAge:          0xfd1:fff0
```

(Your output may look different.)

ANALYSIS In line 8 myAge and yourAge are declared to be variables of type unsigned short int. In line 9 pAge is declared to be a pointer to an unsigned short int, and it is initialized with the address of the variable myAge.

Lines 11 and 12 print the values and the addresses of myAge and yourAge. Line 14 prints the contents of pAge, which is the address of myAge. Line 15 prints the result of dereferencing pAge, which prints the value at pAge—the value in myAge, or 5.

This is the essence of pointers. Line 14 shows that pAge stores the address of myAge, and line 15 shows how to get the value stored in myAge by dereferencing the pointer pAge. Make sure that you understand this fully, before you go on. Study the code and look at the output.

In line 17 pAge is reassigned to point to the address of yourAge. The values and addresses are printed again. The output shows that pAge now has the address of the variable yourAge and that dereferencing obtains the value in yourAge.

Line 25 prints the address of pAge itself. Like any variable, it too has an address, and that address can be stored in a pointer. (Assigning the address of a pointer to another pointer is discussed shortly.)

Do	Don't

DO use the indirection operator (*) to access the data stored at the address in a pointer.

DO initialize all pointers either to a valid address or to null (0).

DO remember the difference between the address in a pointer and the value at that address.

Pointers

SYNTAX

To declare a pointer, write the type of the variable or object whose address is stored in the pointer, followed by the pointer operator (*), and the name of the pointer, as in the following example:

```
unsigned short int * pPointer = 0;
```

To assign or initialize a pointer, prepend the name of the variable whose address is being assigned with the *address of* operator (&), as in the following example:

```
unsigned short int theVariable = 5;
unsigned short int * pPointer = & theVariable;
```

To dereference a pointer, prepend the pointer name with the dereference operator (*), as in the following example:

```
unsigned short int theValue = *pPointer
```

Why Would You Use Pointers?

So far, you've seen step-by-step details of assigning a variable's address to a pointer. In practice, though, you would never do this. After all, why bother with a pointer when you already have a variable with access to that value? The only reason for this kind of pointer manipulation of an automatic variable is to demonstrate how pointers work. Now that you are comfortable with the syntax of pointers, you can put them to good use. Pointers are used, most often, for three tasks:

☐ Managing data on the free store.

☐ Accessing class member data and functions.

☐ Passing variables by reference to functions.

The rest of this lesson focuses on managing data on the free store and accessing class member data and functions. Tomorrow you learn about passing variables by reference.

The Stack and the Free Store

In the "Extra Credit" section following the discussion of functions in Day 5, five areas of memory are mentioned:

Global name space
The free store
Registers
Code space
The stack

Local variables are on the stack, along with function parameters. Code is in code space, of course, and global variables are in global name space. The registers are used for internal housekeeping functions, such as keeping track of the top of the stack and the instruction pointer. Just about all remaining memory is given over to the free store, which is sometimes referred to as the *heap*.

The problem with local variables is that they don't persist: When the function returns, the local variables are thrown away. Global variables solve that problem at the cost of unrestricted access throughout the program—which leads to the creation of code that is difficult to understand and maintain. Putting data in the free store solves both of these problems.

You can think of the free store as a massive section of memory in which thousands of sequentially numbered cubbyholes lie waiting for your data. You can't label these cubbyholes, though, as you can with the stack. You must ask for the address of the cubbyhole's hole that you reserve, and then stash that address away in a pointer.

One way to think about this is with an analogy: A friend gives you the 800 number for Acme Mail Order. You go home and program your telephone with that number, and then you throw away the piece of paper with the number on it. If you push the button, a telephone rings somewhere, and Acme Mail Order answers. You don't remember the number, and you don't know where the other telephone is located, but the button gives you access to Acme Mail Order. Acme Mail Order is your data on the free store. You don't know where it is, but you know how to get to it. You access it by using its address—in this case, the telephone number. You don't have to know that number; you just have to put it into a pointer—the button. The pointer gives you access to your data without bothering you with the details.

The stack is cleaned automatically when a function returns. All the local variables go out of scope, and they are removed from the stack. The free store is not cleaned until your program ends, and it is your responsibility to free any memory that you've reserved when you are done with it.

The advantage to the free store is that the memory you reserve remains available until you explicitly free it. If you reserve memory on the free store while in a function, the memory is still available when the function returns.

The advantage of accessing memory in this way, rather than using global variables, is that only functions with access to the pointer have access to the data. This provides a tightly controlled interface to that data, and it eliminates the problem of one function changing that data in unexpected and unanticipated ways.

For this to work, you must be able to create a pointer to an area on the free store and pass that pointer among functions. The following sections describe how to do this.

new

You allocate memory on the free store in C++ by using the new keyword. new is followed by the type of the object that you want to allocate so that the compiler knows how much memory is required. Therefore, new unsigned short int allocates two bytes in the free store, and new long allocates four.

The return value from new is a memory address. It must be assigned to a pointer. To create an unsigned short on the free store, you might write

```
unsigned short int * pPointer;
pPointer = new unsigned short int;
```

You can, of course, initialize the pointer at its creation with

```
unsigned short int * pPointer = new unsigned short int;
```

In either case, pPointer now points to an unsigned short int on the free store. You can use this like any other pointer to a variable and assign a value into that area of memory by writing

```
*pPointer = 72;
```

This means, "Put 72 at the value in pPointer," or "Assign the value 72 to the area on the free store to which pPointer points."

If new cannot create memory on the free store—memory is, after all, a limited resource—it returns the null pointer. You *must* check your pointer for null each time you request new memory.

WARNING

> Each time you allocate memory using the new keyword, you must check to make sure the pointer is not null.

delete

When you are finished with your area of memory, you must call delete on the pointer. delete returns the memory to the free store. Remember that the pointer itself—as opposed to the memory to which it points—is a local variable. When the function in which it is declared returns, that pointer goes out of scope and is lost. The memory allocated with the new is not freed automatically, however. The memory for the new statement becomes unavailable—a situation called a *memory leak*. It's called a memory leak because that memory can't be recovered until the program ends. It is as though the memory has leaked out of your computer.

8

To restore the memory to the free store, you use the keyword delete, as in the following example:

```
delete pPointer;
```

When you delete the pointer, what you are really doing is freeing up the memory whose address is stored in the pointer. You are saying, "Return to the free store the memory that this pointer points to." The pointer is still a pointer, and it can be reassigned. Listing 8.4 demonstrates allocating a variable on the heap, using that variable, and deleting it.

WARNING

When you call delete on a pointer, the memory it points to is freed. Calling delete on that pointer again crashes your program! When you delete a pointer, set it to 0 (null). Calling delete on a null pointer is guaranteed to be safe. Here's an example:

```
Animal *pDag = new Animal;
delete pDog; //frees the memory
   pDog = 0; //sets pointer to null
   //...
delete pDog; //harmless
```

TYPE **Listing 8.4. Allocating, using, and deleting pointers.**

```
1:    // Listing 8.4
2:    // Allocating and deleting a pointer
3:
4:    #include <iostream.h>
5:    void main()
6:    {
7:        int localVariable = 5;
8:        int * pLocal= &localVariable;
9:        int * pHeap = new int;
10:       if (pHeap == 0)
11:         {
12:            cout << "Error! No memory for pHeap!!";
13:            return;
14:         }
15:       *pHeap = 7;
16:       cout << "localVariable: " << localVariable << "\n";
17:       cout << "*pLocal: " << *pLocal << "\n";
18:       cout << "*pHeap: " << *pHeap << "\n";
19:       delete pHeap;
20:       pHeap = new int;
21:       if (pHeap == 0)
22:         {
```

continues

Listing 8.4. continued

```
23:               cout << "Error! No memory for pHeap!!";
24:               return;
25:          }
26:          *pHeap = 9;
27:          cout << "*pHeap: " << *pHeap << "\n";
28:          delete pHeap;
29:     }
```

OUTPUT
```
localVariable: 5
*pLocal: 5
*pHeap: 7
*pHeap: 9
```

ANALYSIS Line 7 declares and initializes a local variable. Line 8 declares and initializes a pointer with the address of the local variable. Line 9 declares another pointer but initializes it with the result obtained from calling new int. This allocates space on the free store for an int. Line 10 verifies that memory was allocated and the pointer is valid (not 0). If no memory can be allocated, the pointer is 0 and an error message is printed.

To keep things simple, this error checking often won't be reproduced in future programs, but you *must* include some sort of error checking in your own programs.

Line 15 assigns the value 7 to the newly allocated memory. Line 16 prints the value of the local variable, and line 17 prints the value pointed to by pLocal. As expected, these are the same. Line 18 prints the value pointed to by pHeap. It shows that the value assigned in line 15 is, in fact, accessible.

In line 19 the memory allocated in line 9 is returned to the free store by a call to delete. This frees the memory and disassociates the pointer from that memory. pHeap is now free to point to other memory. It is reassigned in lines 20 and 26, and line 27 prints the result. Line 28 restores that memory to the free store.

Although line 28 is redundant—the end of the program would have returned that memory—it is a good idea to free this memory explicitly. If the program changes or is extended, it is beneficial to have this step already taken care of.

Memory Leaks

Another way you might inadvertently create a memory leak is by reassigning your pointer before deleting the memory to which it points. Consider this code fragment:

```
1:   unsigned short int * pPointer = new unsigned short int;
2:   *pPointer = 72;
3:   pPointer = new unsigned short int;
4:   *pPointer = 84;
```

Line 1 creates pPointer and assigns it the address of an area on the free store. Line 2 stores the value 72 in that area of memory. Line 3 reassigns pPointer to another area of memory. Line 4 places the value 84 in that area. The original area—in which the value 72 is now held—is unavailable because the pointer to that area of memory has been reassigned. There is no way to access that original area of memory, nor is there any way to free it before the program ends.

The code should have been written like this:

```
1: unsigned short int * pPointer = new unsigned short int;
2: *pPointer = 72;
3: delete pPointer;
4: pPointer = new unsigned short int;
5: *pPointer = 84;
```

Now the memory originally pointed to by pPointer is deleted, and thus freed, in line 4.

NOTE

> For every time in your program that you call new, there must also be a call to delete. It is important to keep track of which pointer owns an area of memory and to ensure that the memory is returned to the free store when you are done with it.

Creating Objects on the Free Store

Just as you can create a pointer to an integer, you can create a pointer to any object. If you have declared an object of type Cat, you can declare a pointer to that class and instantiate a Cat object on the free store, just as you can make one on the stack. The syntax is the same as for integers:

```
Cat *pCat = new Cat;
```

This calls the default constructor—the constructor that takes no parameters. The constructor is called whenever an object is created on the stack or on the free store.

 Free store and *heap* are two terms for the same thing. The heap is a place in memory where your program dynamically requests and receives more memory. Your program must tell the computer when it wants more memory from the heap and when it is finished with the memory. The new keyword is used to request memory from the heap and the keyword delete is used to return memory.

Deleting Objects

When you call `delete` on a pointer to an object on the free store, that object's destructor is called before the memory is released. This gives your class a chance to clean up, just as it does for objects destroyed on the stack. Listing 8.5 illustrates creating and deleting objects on the free store.

TYPE **Listing 8.5. Creating and deleting objects on the free store.**

```
1:    // Listing 8.5
2:    // Creating objects on the free store
3:
4:    #include <iostream.h>
5:
6:    class SimpleCat
7:    {
8:    public:
9:            SimpleCat();
10:           ~SimpleCat();
11:   private:
12:           int itsAge;
13:       };
14:
15:    SimpleCat::SimpleCat()
16:    {
17:           cout << "Constructor called.\n";
18:           itsAge = 1;
19:    }
20:
21:    SimpleCat::~SimpleCat()
22:    {
23:           cout << "Destructor called.\n";
24:    }
25:
26:    void main()
27:    {
28:           cout << "SimpleCat Frisky...\n";
29:           SimpleCat Frisky;
30:           cout << "SimpleCat *pRags = new SimpleCat...\n";
31:           SimpleCat * pRags = new SimpleCat;
32:           cout << "delete pRags...\n";
33:           delete pRags;
34:           cout << "Exiting, watch Frisky go...\n";
35:       }
```

OUTPUT
```
SimpleCat Frisky...
Constructor called.
SimpleCat * pRags = new SimpleCat..
Constructor called.
delete pRags...
Destructor called.
Exiting, watch Frisky go...
Destructor called.
```

ANALYSIS Lines 6 through 13 declare the stripped-down class SimpleCat. Line 9 declares SimpleCat's constructor, and lines 15 through 19 contain its definition. Line 10 declares SimpleCat's destructor, and lines 21 through 24 contain its definition.

In line 29 Frisky is created on the stack, which causes the constructor to be called. In line 31 the SimpleCat pointed to by pRags is created on the heap; the constructor is called again. In line 33, delete is called on pRags, and the destructor is called. When the function ends, Frisky goes out of scope, and the destructor is called.

Accessing Data Members

On Day 6, "Basic Classes," you accessed data members and functions by using the dot (.) operator for Cat objects created locally. To access the Cat object on the free store, you must dereference the pointer and call the dot operator on the object pointed to by the pointer. Therefore, to access the GetAge member function, you would write

```
(*pRags).GetAge();
```

Parentheses around the pointer are used to assure that pRags is dereferenced before GetAge() is accessed.

Because this is cumbersome, C++ provides a shorthand operator for indirect access: the *points-to* operator (->), which is created by typing the hyphen (-) immediately followed by the greater-than symbol (>). C++ treats this as a single symbol. Listing 8.6 demonstrates accessing member variables and functions of objects created on the free store.

TYPE Listing 8.6. Accessing member data of objects on the free store.

```
1:      // Listing 8.6
2:      // Accessing data members of objects on the heap
3:
4:      #include <iostream.h>
5:
6:      class SimpleCat
7:      {
8:      public:
9:          SimpleCat() {itsAge = 2; }
10:         ~SimpleCat() {}
11:         int GetAge() const { return itsAge; }
12:         void SetAge(int age) { itsAge = age; }
13:     private:
14:         int itsAge;
15:     };
16:
17:     void main()
18:     {
```

continues

Listing 8.6. continued

```
19:                    SimpleCat * Frisky = new SimpleCat;
20:                    cout << "Frisky is " << Frisky->GetAge() << " years old\n";
21:                    Frisky->SetAge(5);
22:                    cout << "Frisky is " << Frisky->GetAge() << " years old\n";
23:                    delete Frisky;
24:          }
```

OUTPUT   Frisky is 2 years old
             Frisky is 5 years old

ANALYSIS   In line 19 a SimpleCat object is instantiated on the free store. The default constructor sets its age to 2, and the GetAge() method is called in line 20. Because this is a pointer, the <u>points-to operator (->) is used to access the member data and functions.</u> In line 21, the SetAge() method is called, and GetAge() is accessed again in line 22.

Member Data on the Free Store

One or more of the data members of a class can be a pointer to an object on the free store. The memory can be allocated in the class constructor or in one of its methods, and it can be deleted in its destructor, as Listing 8.7 illustrates.

TYPE   **Listing 8.7. Pointers as member data.**

```
1:    // Listing 8.7
2:    // Pointers as data members
3:
4:      #include <iostream.h>
5:
6:      class SimpleCat
7:      {
8:      public:
9:              SimpleCat();
10:             ~SimpleCat();
11:             int GetAge() const { return *itsAge; }
12:             void SetAge(int age) { *itsAge = age; }
13:
14:             int GetWeight() const { return *itsWeight; }
15:             void setAge(int weight) { *itsWeight = weight; }
16:
17:     private:
18:             int * itsAge;
19:             int * itsWeight;
20:         };
21:
22:         SimpleCat::SimpleCat()
23:         {
24:             itsAge = new int(2);
```

8

```
25:            itsWeight = new int(5);
26:       }
27:
28:       SimpleCat::~SimpleCat()
29:       {
30:            delete itsAge;
31:            delete itsWeight;
32:       }
33:
34:       void main()
35:       {
36:            SimpleCat *Frisky = new SimpleCat;
37:            cout << "Frisky is " << Frisky->GetAge() << " years old\n";
38:            Frisky->SetAge(5);
39:            cout << "Frisky is " << Frisky->GetAge() << " years old\n";
40:            delete Frisky;
41:       }
```

```
Frisky is 2 years old
Frisky is 5 years old
```

The class SimpleCat is declared to have two member variables—both of which are pointers to integers—on lines 18 and 19. The constructor (lines 22 through 26) initializes the pointers to memory on the free store and to the default values.

The destructor (lines 28 through 32) cleans up the allocated memory. Because this is the destructor, there is no point in assigning these pointers to null because they are no longer accessible. This is one of the safe places to break the rule that deleted pointers should be assigned to null, although following the rule doesn't hurt.

The calling function (in this case, main()) is unaware that itsAge and itsWeight are pointers to memory on the free store. main() continues to call GetAge() and SetAge(), and the details of the memory management are hidden in the implementation of the class—as they should be.

When Frisky is deleted in line 40, its destructor is called. The destructor deletes each of its member pointers. If these, in turn, point to objects of other user-defined classes, their destructors are called as well.

The *this* Pointer

Every class member function has a hidden parameter: the this pointer. this points to the individual object. Therefore, in each call to GetAge() or SetAge(), the this pointer for the object is included as a hidden parameter.

It is possible to use the this pointer explicitly, as Listing 8.8 illustrates.

Listing 8.8. Using the this pointer.

```
1:      // Listing 8.8
2:      // Using the this pointer
3:
4:      #include <iostream.h>
5:
6:      class Rectangle
7:      {
8:      public:
9:          Rectangle();
10:         ~Rectangle();
11:         void SetLength(int length) { this->itsLength = length; }
12:         int GetLength() const { return this->itsLength; }
13:
14:         void SetWidth(int width) { itsWidth = width; }
15:         int GetWidth() const { return itsWidth; }
16:
17:     private:
18:         int itsLength;
19:         int itsWidth;
20:     };
21:
22:     Rectangle::Rectangle():
23:     itsWidth(5),
24:     itsLength(10)
25:     {}
26:
27:     Rectangle::~Rectangle()
28:     {}
29:
30:     void main()
31:     {
32:         Rectangle theRect;
33:         cout << "theRect is " << theRect.GetLength() << " feet long.\n";
34:         cout << "theRect is " << theRect.GetWidth() << " feet wide.\n";
35:         theRect.SetLength(20);
36:         theRect.SetWidth(10);
37:         cout << "theRect is " << theRect.GetLength()<< " feet long.\n";
38:         cout << "theRect is " << theRect.GetWidth()<< " feet wide.\n";
39:     }
```

OUTPUT
```
theRect is 10 feet long
theRect is 5 feet long
theRect is 20 feet long
theRect is 10 feet long
```

ANALYSIS The SetLength() and GetLength() accessor functions explicitly use the this pointer to access the member variables of the Rectangle object. The SetWidth and GetWidth accessors do not. There is no difference in their behavior, although the syntax is easier to understand.

If that were all there is to the this pointer, there would be little point in bothering you with it. The this pointer, however, is a pointer; it stores the memory address of an object. As such, it can be a powerful tool.

You'll see a practical use for the this pointer on Day 10, "Advanced Functions," when operator overloading is discussed. For now, your goal is to know about the this pointer and to understand what it is: a pointer to the object itself.

You don't have to worry about creating or deleting the this pointer. The compiler takes care of that.

Stray or Dangling Pointers

One source of bugs that are nasty and difficult to find is stray pointers. A stray pointer is created when you call delete on a pointer—thereby freeing the memory that it points to—and later try to use that pointer again without reassigning it.

It is as though the Acme Mail Order company moved away, and you still pressed the programmed button on your phone. It is possible that nothing terrible happens—a telephone rings in a deserted warehouse. But perhaps the telephone number has been reassigned to a munitions factory, and your call detonates an explosive and blows up your whole city!

In short, be careful not to use a pointer after you have called delete on it. The pointer still points to the old area of memory, but the compiler is free to put other data there; using the pointer can cause your program to crash. Worse, your program might proceed merrily on its way and crash several minutes later. This is called a time bomb, and it is no fun. To be safe, after you delete a pointer, set it to 0. This disarms the pointer.

NOTE

> Stray pointers are often called *wild pointers* or *dangling pointers*.

Listing 8.9 illustrates creating a stray pointer.

TYPE   **Listing 8.9. Creating a stray pointer.**

```
1:     // Listing 8.9
2:     // Demonstrates a stray pointer
3:     typedef unsigned short int USHORT;
4:     #include <iostream.h>
5:
6:     void main()
7:     {
```

continues

Listing 8.9. continued

```
8:          USHORT * pInt = new USHORT;
9:          *pInt = 10;
10:         cout << "*pInt: " << *pInt << endl;
11:         delete pInt;
12:         pInt = 0;
13:         long * pLong = new long;
14:         *pLong = 90000;
15:         cout << "*pLong: " << *pLong << endl;
16:
17:         *pInt = 20;        // uh oh, this was deleted!
18:
19:         cout << "*pInt: " << *pInt  << endl;
20:         cout << "*pLong: " << *pLong  << endl;
21:         delete pLong;
22:     }
```

OUTPUT
```
*pInt:    10
*pLong:   90000
*pInt:    20
*pLong:   65556
```

(Your output may look different.)

ANALYSIS   Line 8 declares pInt to be a pointer to USHORT, and pInt is pointed to newly allocated memory. Line 9 puts the value 10 in that memory, and line 10 prints its value. After the value is printed, delete is called on the pointer. pInt is now a stray, or dangling, pointer because it is not set to 0 or anything else.

Line 13 declares a new pointer, pLong, which is pointed at the memory allocated by new. Line 14 assigns the value 90000 to pLong, and line 15 prints its value.

Line 17 assigns the value 20 to the memory that pInt points to, but pInt no longer points anywhere that is valid. The memory that pInt points to was freed by the call to delete, so assigning a value to that memory is certain disaster.

Line 19 prints the value at pInt. Sure enough, it is 20. Line 20, prints 20, the value at pLong; it has suddenly been changed to 65556. Two questions arise:

☐ How could pLong's value change, given that pLong wasn't touched?

☐ Where did the 20 go when pInt was used in line 17?

As you might guess, these are related questions. When a value was placed at pInt in line 17, the compiler happily placed the value 20 at the memory location that pInt previously pointed to. However, because that memory was freed in line 11, the compiler was free to reassign it. When pLong was created in line 14, it was given pInt's old memory location. (On some computers this might not happen, depending on where in memory these values are stored.)

When the value 20 was assigned to the location that pInt previously pointed to, it wrote over the value pointed to by pLong. This is called "stomping on a pointer." It is often the unfortunate outcome of using a stray pointer.

This is a particularly nasty bug, because the value that changed wasn't associated with the stray pointer. The change to the value at pLong was a side effect of the misuse of pInt. In a large program, this would be very difficult to track down.

Just for fun, here are the details of how 65556 got into that memory address:

1. pInt was pointed at a particular memory location, and the value 10 was assigned.

2. delete was called on pInt, which told the compiler that it could put something else at that location. Then pLong was assigned the same memory location.

3. The value 90000 was assigned to *pLong. The particular computer used in this example stored the four-byte value of 90000 (00 01 5F 90) in byte-swapped order. Therefore, it was stored as 5F 90 00 01.

4. pInt was assigned the value 20 (or 00 14 in hexadecimal notation). Because pInt still pointed to the same address, the first two bytes of pLong were overwritten, leaving 00 14 00 01.

5. The value at pLong was printed, reversing the bytes back to their correct order of 00 01 00 14, which was translated into the DOS value of 65556.

Do   **Don't**

DO use new to create objects on the free store.

DO use delete to destroy objects on the free store and to return their memory.

DON'T forget to balance all new statements with a delete statement.

DON'T forget to assign NULL (0) to all pointers that you call delete on.

DO check the value returned by new.

const Pointers

You can use the keyword const for pointers before the type, after the type, or in both places. For example, all of the following are legal declarations:

```
const int * pOne;
int * const pTwo;
const int * const pThree;
```

pOne is a pointer to a constant integer. The value that is pointed to can't be changed.

pTwo is a constant pointer to an integer. The integer can be changed, but pTwo can't point to anything else.

pThree is a constant pointer to a constant integer. The value that is pointed to can't be changed, and pThree can't be changed to point to anything else.

The trick to keeping this straight is to look to the right of the keyword const to find out what is being declared constant. If the type is to the right of the keyword, it is the value that is constant. If the variable is to the right of the keyword const, it is the pointer variable itself that is constant, as shown by the following commented lines:

```
const int * p1;  // the int pointed to is constant
int * const p2;  // p2 is constant, it can't point to anything else
```

const Pointers and *const* Member Functions

On Day 6 you learned that you can apply the keyword const to a member function. When a function is declared const, the compiler flags as an error any attempt to change data in the object from within that function.

If you declare a pointer to a const object, the only methods that you can call with that pointer are const methods. Listing 8.10 illustrates this.

TYPE   **Listing 8.10. Using pointers to const objects.**

```
1:      // Listing 8.10
2:      // Using pointers with const methods
3:
4:      #include <iostream.h>
5:
6:      class Rectangle
7:      {
8:      public:
9:          Rectangle();
```

```
10:             ~Rectangle();
11:             void SetLength(int length) { itsLength = length; }
12:             int GetLength() const { return itsLength; }
13:
14:             void SetWidth(int width) { itsWidth = width; }
15:             int GetWidth() const { return itsWidth; }
16:
17:         private:
18:             int itsLength;
19:             int itsWidth;
20:         };
21:
22:         Rectangle::Rectangle():
23:         itsWidth(5),
24:         itsLength(10)
25:         {}
26:
27:         Rectangle::~Rectangle()
28:         {}
29:
30:         void main()
31:         {
32:             Rectangle* pRect =  new Rectangle;
33:             const Rectangle * pConstRect = new Rectangle;
34:             Rectangle * const pConstPtr = new Rectangle;
35:
36:             cout << "pRect width: " << pRect->GetWidth() << " feet\n";
37:             cout << "pConstRect width: " << pConstRect->GetWidth() << "
    ➥feet\n";
38:             cout << "pConstPtr width: " << pConstPtr->GetWidth() << " feet\n";
39:
40:             pRect->SetWidth(10);
41:             // pConstRect->SetWidth(10);
42:             pConstPtr->SetWidth(10);
43:
44:             cout << "pRect width: " << pRect->GetWidth() << " feet\n";
45:             cout << "pConstRect width: " << pConstRect->GetWidth() << "
    ➥feet\n";
46:             cout << "pConstPtr width: " << pConstPtr->GetWidth() << " feet\n";
47:         }
```

OUTPUT

```
pRect width:       5 feet
pConstRect width:  5 feet
pConstPtr width:   5 feet
pRect width:       10 feet
pConstRect width:  5 feet
pConstPtr width:   10 feet
```

ANALYSIS Lines 6 through 20 declare Rectangle. Line 15 declares the GetWidth() member method const. Line 32 declares a pointer to Rectangle. Line 33 declares pConstRect, which is a pointer to a constant Rectangle. Line 34 declares pConstPtr, which is a constant pointer to Rectangle.

Lines 36 through 38 print their values.

In line 40 pRect is used to set the width of the rectangle to 10. In line 41 pConstRect would be used, but it was declared to point to a constant rectangle. Therefore, it cannot legally call a non-const member function; it is commented out. In line 42 pConstPtr calls Setwidth(). pConstPtr is declared to be a constant pointer to a rectangle. In other words, the pointer is constant and cannot point to anything else, but the rectangle is not constant.

const this Pointers

When you declare an object to be const, you are in effect declaring that the this pointer is a pointer to a const object. A const this pointer can be used only with const member functions.

Constant objects and constant pointers are discussed again tomorrow in Day 9, "References," when references to constant objects are discussed.

Do	**Don't**

DO protect objects passed by reference with const if they should not be changed.

DO pass by reference when the object can be changed.

DO pass by value when small objects should not be changed.

Summary

Pointers provide a powerful way to access data by indirection. Every variable has an address, which can be obtained using the *address of* operator (&). The address can be stored in a pointer.

Pointers are declared by writing the type of object that they point to, followed by the indirection operator (*) and the name of the pointer. Pointers should be initialized to point to an object or to NULL (0).

You access the value at the address stored in a pointer by using the indirection operator (*). You can declare const pointers (which can't be reassigned to point to other objects) and pointers to const objects (which can't be used to change the objects to which they point).

To create new objects on the free store, you use the new keyword and assign the address that is returned to a pointer. You free that memory by calling the delete keyword on the pointer. delete frees the memory, but it doesn't destroy the pointer. Therefore, you must reassign the pointer after its memory has been freed.

Q&A

Q Why are pointers so important?

A Today you saw how pointers are used to hold the address of objects on the free store, and how they are used to pass arguments by reference. In addition, on Day 13, "Multiple Inheritance," and Day 22, "Advanced C++ Features," you'll see how pointers relate to polymorphism.

Q Why should I bother to declare anything on the free store?

A Objects on the free store persist after the return of a function. Additionally, the ability to store objects on the free store enables you to decide at run-time how many objects you need, instead of having to declare this in advance. This is explored in greater depth tomorrow.

Q Why should I declare an object `const` if it limits what I can do with it?

A As a programmer, you want to enlist the compiler in helping you find bugs. One serious bug that is difficult to find is a function that changes an object in ways that aren't obvious to the calling function. Declaring an object `const` prevents such changes.

Quiz

1. What operator is used to determine the address of a variable?
2. What operator is used to find the value stored at an address held in a pointer?
3. What is a pointer?
4. What is the difference between the address stored in a pointer and the value at that address?
5. What is the difference between the indirection operator and the *address of* operator?
6. What is the difference between `const int * ptrOne` and `int * const ptrTwo`?

Exercises

1. What do these declarations do?
   a. `int * pOne;`
   b. `int vTwo;`
   c. `int * pThree = &vTwo;`
2. If you have an `unsigned short` variable named `yourAge`, how do you declare a pointer to manipulate `yourAge`?

3. Assign the value 50 to the variable yourAge by using the pointer that you declared in exercise 2.

4. Write a small program that declares an integer and a pointer to the integer. Assign the address of the integer to the pointer. Use the pointer to set a value in the integer variable.

5. **BUG BUSTERS:** What is wrong with this code?

```
#include <iostream.h>
void main()
{
    int *pInt;
    *pInt = 9;
    cout << "The value at pInt: " << *pInt;
}
```

6. **BUG BUSTERS:** What is wrong with this code?

```
void main()
{
    int SomeVariable = 5;
    cout << "SomeVariable: " << SomeVariable << "\n";
    int *pVar = & SomeVariable;
    pVar = 9;
    cout << "SomeVariable: " << *pVar << "\n";
}
```

Day **9**

References

On Day 8, "Pointers," you learned how to use pointers to manipulate objects on the free store and how to refer to those objects indirectly. References, the topic of today's lesson, give you almost all the power of pointers but with a much easier syntax. Today you learn

- [ ] What references are.
- [ ] How references differ from pointers.
- [ ] How to create references and use them.
- [ ] What the limitations of references are.
- [ ] How to pass values and objects into and out of functions by reference.

What Is a Reference?

A reference is an alias; when you create a reference, you initialize it with the name of another object, the *target*. From that moment on, the reference acts as an alternative name for the target, and anything you do to the reference is really done to the target.

You create a reference by writing the type of the target object, followed by the reference operator (&), followed by the name of the reference.

Note that the reference operator (&) is the same symbol as the one used for the *address of* operator. However, these are not the same operators, but they are related.

References can use any legal variable name, but this book prefixes all reference names with r. Thus, if you have an integer variable named someInt, you can make a reference to that variable by writing the following:

```
int &rSomeRef = someInt;
```

This is read as "rSomeRef is a reference to integer that is initialized to refer to someInt." Listing 9.1 shows how references are created and used.

Programming is like mathematics: You can only fully understand it by using it. If you try to continue through this very important lesson without doing the examples yourself, you will have a difficult time with the more abstract concepts. Without the foundation of these concepts, you will have difficulty in later lessons that build on these concepts.

TYPE **Listing 9.1. Creating and using references.**

```
1:    //Listing 9.1
2:    // Demonstrating the use of References
3:
4:    #include <iostream.h>
5:
6:    void main()
7:    {
8:        int  intOne;
9:        int &rSomeRef = intOne;
10:
11:       intOne = 5;
12:       cout << "intOne: " << intOne << endl;
13:       cout << "rSomeRef: " << rSomeRef << endl;
14:
15:       rSomeRef = 7;
16:       cout << "intOne: " << intOne << endl;
17:       cout << "rSomeRef: " << rSomeRef << endl;
18:   }
```

```
intOne: 5
rSomeRef: 5
intOne: 7
rSomeRef: 7
```

On line 8, a local int variable, intOne, is declared. On line 9, a reference to an int, rSomeRef, is declared and initialized to refer to intOne. If you declare a reference but don't initialize it, you get a compile-time error. References *must* be initialized.

On line 11 intOne is assigned the value 5. On lines 12 and 13, the values in intOne and rSomeRef are printed and are, of course, the same.

On line 15, 7 is assigned to rSomeRef. Because this is a reference, it is an alias for intOne, and thus the 7 is really assigned to intOne, as shown by the printouts on lines 16 and 17.

Requesting the Address of a Reference

If you ask a reference for its address, it returns the address of its target. That is the nature of references. They are aliases for the target, as demonstrated in Listing 9.2. The similarity with the pointer *address of* (&) operator and the reference declaration operator causes some confusion. Just remember that the reference declaration operator qualifies a variable only on the left side of an assignment operator, while the *address of* operator should only appear qualifying a variable on the right. To illustrate the address operator further, take a look at the following snippet:

```
1: int xYZ = 45;        // An int variable
2: int &anAlias = xYZ; // An alias (reference) for the int variable xYZ
3: int *pInt = &xYZ;    // An int pointer assigned the address of xYZ
4: int *pAlias = &anAlias; // An int pointer assigned the address of anAlias
5:    // Lines 3 and 4 perform exactly the same thing,
6:    // pAlias and pInt now both point to the same value (45)
```

If you think the comments on lines 5 and 6 in the preceding code are incorrect, compile, link, and run the program source in Listing 9.2 to prove it to yourself.

Type **Listing 9.2. Taking the address of a reference.**

```
1:     //Listing 9.2
2:     // Demonstrating the use of References
3:
4:     #include <iostream.h>
5:
6:     void main()
7:     {
8:         int  intOne;
9:         int &rSomeRef = intOne; // An alias (reference) declared for intOne
10:
```

continues

Listing 9.2. continued

```
11:        intOne = 5;
12:        cout << "intOne: " << intOne << endl;
13:        cout << "rSomeRef: " << rSomeRef << endl;
14:
15:        cout << "&intOne: "  << &intOne << endl;
16:        cout << "&rSomeRef: " << &rSomeRef << endl;
17:
18:    }
```

OUTPUT
```
intOne: 5
rSomeRef: 5
&intOne:  0x3500
&rSomeRef: 0x3500
```

ANALYSIS Once again rSomeRef is initialized as a reference to intOne. This time the addresses of the two variables are printed, and they are identical. C++ gives you no way to access the address of the reference itself because it is not meaningful, though it would be if you were using a pointer or other variable. References are initialized when created and always act as a synonym for their respective targets, even when the *address of* operator is applied.

For example, if you have a class called President, you might declare an instance of that class as follows:

```
President  William_Jefferson_Clinton;
```

You might then declare a reference to President and initialize it with this object:

```
President &Bill_Clinton = William_Jefferson_Clinton;
```

There is only one President; both identifiers refer to the same object of the same class. Any action you take on Bill_Clinton is taken on William_Jefferson_Clinton as well.

NOTE
> Be careful to distinguish between the & symbol on line 9 of Listing 9.2, which declares a reference to int named rSomeRef, and the & symbols on lines 15 and 16, which return the addresses of the integer variable intOne and the reference rSomeRef.

Normally, when you use a reference, you do not use the *address of* operator. You simply use the reference as you would use the target variable. This is shown on line 13.

Even experienced C++ programmers, who know the rule that a reference cannot be reassigned and is always an alias for its target, can be confused by what happens when you try to reassign a reference. What appears to be a reassignment turns out to be the assignment of a new value to the target. Listing 9.3 illustrates this fact.

Listing 9.3. Reassigning to a reference.

```
1:     //Listing 9.3
2:     //Reassigning a reference
3:
4:     #include <iostream.h>
5:
6:     void main()
7:     {
8:          int   intOne;
9:          int &rSomeRef = intOne;
10:
11:          intOne = 5;
12:          cout << "intOne:\t" << intOne << endl;
13:          cout << "rSomeRef:\t" << rSomeRef << endl;
14:          cout << "&intOne:\t"  << &intOne << endl;
15:          cout << "&rSomeRef:\t" << &rSomeRef << endl;
16:
17:          int intTwo = 8;
18:          rSomeRef = intTwo;   // not what you think!
19:          cout << "\nintOne:\t" << intOne << endl;
20:          cout << "intTwo:\t" << intTwo << endl;
21:          cout << "rSomeRef:\t" << rSomeRef << endl;
22:          cout << "&intOne:\t"  << &intOne << endl;
23:          cout << "&intTwo:\t"  << &intTwo << endl;
24:          cout << "&rSomeRef:\t" << &rSomeRef << endl;
25:     }
```

```
intOne:                    5
rSomeRef:          5
&intOne:                   0x213e
&rSomeRef:         0x213e

intOne:                    8
intTwo:                    8
rSomeRef:          8
&intOne:                   0x213e
&intTwo:                   0x2130
&rSomeRef:         0x213e
```

ANALYSIS Once again, an integer variable and a reference to an integer are declared on lines 8 and 9. The integer is assigned the value 5 on line 11, and the values and the addresses are printed on lines 12 through 15.

On line 17 a new variable, intTwo, is created and initialized with the value 8. On line 18 the programmer tries to reassign rSomeRef to now be an alias to the variable intTwo, but that is not what happens. What actually happens is that rSomeRef continues to act as an alias for intOne, so this assignment is exactly equivalent to the following:

intOne = intTwo;

Sure enough, when the values of intOne and rSomeRef are printed (lines 19 through 21), they are the same as intTwo. In fact, when the addresses are printed on lines 22 through 24, you see that rSomeRef continues to refer to intOne and not intTwo.

DO use references to create an alias to an object.

DO initialize all references.

DON'T try to reassign a reference.

DON'T confuse the *address of* operator with the reference operator.

What Can Be Referenced?

Any object can be referenced, including user-defined objects. Note that you create a reference to an object, not to a class. You do not write this:

```
int & rIntRef = int;    // wrong
```

You must initialize rIntRef to a particular integer, such as this:

```
int howBig = 200;
int & rIntRef = howBig;
```

In the same way, you don't initialize a reference to a CAT:

```
CAT & rCatRef = CAT;    // wrong
```

You must initialize rCatRef to a particular CAT object:

```
CAT frisky;
CAT & rCatRef = frisky;
```

References to objects are used just like the object itself. Member data and methods are accessed using the normal class member access operator (.). Furthermore, as with the built-in types, the reference acts as an alias to the object. Listing 9.4 illustrates this.

TYPE   **Listing 9.4. References to objects.**

```
1:      // Listing 9.4
2:      // References to class objects
3:
4:      #include <iostream.h>
5:
6:      class SimpleCat
7:      {
8:         public:
9:            SimpleCat (int age, int weight);
10:           ~SimpleCat() {}
```

```
11:            int GetAge() { return itsAge; }
12:            int GetWeight() { return itsWeight; }
13:        private:
14:            int itsAge;
15:            int itsWeight;
16:    };
17:
18:    SimpleCat::SimpleCat(int age, int weight)
19:    {
20:    itsAge = age;
21:    itsWeight = weight;
22:    }
23:
24:    void main()
25:    {
26:        SimpleCat Frisky(5,8);
27:        SimpleCat & rCat = Frisky;
28:
29:        cout << "Frisky is ";
30:        cout << Frisky.GetAge() << " years old. \n";
31:        cout << "And Frisky weighs ";
32:        cout << rCat.GetWeight() << " pounds. \n";
33:    }
```

OUTPUT
```
Frisky is 5 years old.
And Frisky weighs 8 pounds.
```

ANALYSIS   On line 26 Frisky is declared to be a SimpleCat object. On line 27 a SimpleCat reference, rCat, is declared and initialized to refer to Frisky. On lines 30 and 32, the SimpleCat accessor methods are accessed by using first the SimpleCat object and then the SimpleCat reference. Note that the access is identical. Again, the reference is an alias for the actual object.

References

Declare a reference by writing the type, followed by the reference operator (&), followed by the reference name. References must be initialized at the time of creation.

Example 1

```
int hisAge;
int &rAge = hisAge;
```

Example 2

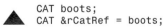
```
CAT boots;
CAT &rCatRef = boots;
```

Null Pointers and Null References

When pointers are not initialized, or when they are deleted, they should be assigned to 0 (often referred to as null). This is not true for references. In fact, a reference cannot be null, and a program with a reference to a null object is considered an invalid program. When a program is invalid, just about anything can happen. It can appear to work, or it can erase all the files on your disk. Both are possible outcomes of an invalid program.

Most compilers support a null object without much complaint, crashing only if you try to use the object in some way. Taking advantage of this, however, is still not a good idea. When you move your program to another machine or compiler, mysterious bugs can develop if you have null objects.

Passing Function Arguments by Reference

On Day 5, "Functions," you learned that functions have two limitations: Arguments are passed by value, and the return statement can return only one value.

Passing values to a function by reference can overcome both of these limitations. In C++, passing by reference is accomplished in two ways: using pointers and using references. The syntax is different, but the net effect is the same: Rather than a copy being created within the scope of the function, the actual original object is passed into the function.

NOTE

> If you read the "Extra Credit" section after Day 5, you learned that functions are passed their parameters on the stack. When a function is passed a value by reference (either using pointers or references), the address of the object is put on the stack, not the entire object.
>
> In fact, on some computers, the address is actually held in a register and nothing is put on the stack. In either case, the compiler now knows how to get to the original object, and changes are made there and not in a copy.

Passing an object by reference allows the function to change the object being referred to.

Recall that Listing 5.5 demonstrated that a call to the swap() function did not affect the values in the calling function. Listing 5.5 is reproduced here as Listing 9.5 for your convenience.

TYPE   **Listing 9.5. A demonstration of passing by value.**

```
1:      //Listing 9.5 Demonstrates passing by value
2:
3:      #include <iostream.h>
4:
5:      void swap(int x, int y);
6:
7:      void main()
8:      {
9:        int x = 5, y = 10;
10:
11:         cout << "Main. Before swap, x: " << x << " y: " << y << "\n";
12:         swap(x,y);
13:         cout << "Main. After swap, x: " << x << " y: " << y << "\n";
14:      }
15:
16:       void swap (int x, int y)
17:       {
18:         int temp;
19:
20:         cout << "Swap. Before swap, x: " << x << " y: " << y << "\n";
21:
22:         temp = x;
23:         x = y;
24:         y = temp;
25:
26:         cout << "Swap. After swap, x: " << x << " y: " << y << "\n";
27:
28:       }
```

OUTPUT
```
Main. Before swap, x: 5 y: 10
Swap. Before swap, x: 5 y: 10
Swap. After swap, x: 10 y: 5
Main. After swap, x: 5 y: 10
```

ANALYSIS   This program initializes two variables in main() and then passes them to the swap() function, which appears to swap them. But when they are examined again in main(), they are unchanged!

The problem here is that x and y are being passed to swap() by value. That is, local copies were made in the function. What you want is to pass x and y by reference.

There are two ways to solve this problem in C++: You can make the parameters of swap() pointers to the original values, or you can pass in references to the original values.

Making *swap()* Work with Pointers

When you pass in a pointer, you pass in the address of the object, and thus the function can manipulate the value at that address. To make swap() change the actual values using pointers, the swap() function should be declared to accept two int pointers. Then, by dereferencing the pointers, the values of x and y are, in fact, swapped. Listing 9.6 demonstrates this idea.

TYPE   **Listing 9.6. Passing by reference using pointers.**

```
1:    //Listing 9.6 Demonstrates passing by reference
2:
3:    #include <iostream.h>
4:
5:    void swap(int *px, int *py);
6:
7:    void main()
8:    {
9:      int x = 5, y = 10;
10:
11:       cout << "Main. Before swap, x: " << x << " y: " << y << "\n";
12:       swap(&x,&y);
13:       cout << "Main. After swap, x: " << x << " y: " << y << "\n";
14:    }
15:
16:    void swap (int *px, int *py)
17:    {
18:      int temp;
19:
20:       cout << "Swap. Before swap, *px: " << *px << " *py: " << *py << "\n";
21:
22:       temp = *px;
23:       *px = *py;
24:       *py = temp;
25:
26:       cout << "Swap. After swap, *px: " << *px << " *py: " << *py << "\n";
27:
28:       }
```

OUTPUT
```
Main. Before swap, x: 5 y: 10
Swap. Before swap, *px: 5 *py: 10
Swap. After swap, *px: 10 *py: 5
Main. After swap, x: 10 y: 5
```

ANALYSIS   Success! On line 5 the prototype of swap() is changed to indicate that its two parameters are pointers to int rather than int variables. When swap() is called on line 12, the addresses of x and y are passed as the arguments.

On line 18 a local variable, temp, is declared in the swap() function. Temp need not be a pointer; it just holds the value of *px (that is, the value of x in the calling function) for the life of the function. After the function returns, temp is no longer needed.

On line 22 temp is assigned the value at px. On line 23 the value at py is assigned to the value at px. On line 24 the value stashed in temp (that is, the original value at px) is put into py.

9

The net effect of this is that the values in the calling function, whose address was passed to swap(), are in fact swapped.

Implementing *swap()* with References

The preceding program works, but the syntax of the swap() function is cumbersome in two ways. First, the repeated need to dereference the pointers within the swap() function makes it error-prone and hard to read. Second, the need to pass the address of the variables in the calling function makes the inner workings of swap() overly apparent to its users.

It is a goal of C++ to prevent the user of a function from worrying about how it works. Passing by pointers puts the burden on the calling function rather than on the called function. Passing by reference places the burden where it belongs, on the function being called. Listing 9.7 rewrites the swap() function, using references.

TYPE   **Listing 9.7. Swap rewritten with references.**

```
1:      //Listing 9.7 Demonstrates passing by reference
2:      // using references!
3:
4:         #include <iostream.h>
5:
6:         void swap(int &rx, int &ry);
7:
8:         void main()
9:         {
10:            int x = 5, y = 10;
11:
12:            cout << "Main. Before swap, x: " << x << " y: " << y << "\n";
13:             swap(x,y);
14:             cout << "Main. After swap, x: " << x << " y: " << y << "\n";
15:         }
16:
17:         void swap (int &rx, int &ry)
18:         {
19:            int temp;
20:
21:             cout << "Swap. Before swap, rx: " << rx << " ry: "
    ➥  << ry << "\n";
22:
23:                 temp = rx;
24:                 rx = ry;
25:                 ry = temp;
26:
27:                 cout << "Swap. After swap, rx: " << rx << " ry: "
    ➥  << ry << "\n";
28:
29:                 }
```

```
Main. Before swap, rx:5 y: 10
Swap. Before swap, rx:5 y:10
Swap. After swap, rx:10 y:5
Main. After swap, rx:10, y:5
```

ANALYSIS Just as in the example with pointers, two variables are declared on line 10, and their values are printed on line 12. On line 13 the swap() function is called, but note that x and y are passed, *not* their addresses. The calling function simply passes the variables.

When swap() is called, program execution jumps to line 17, where the variables are identified as references. Their values are printed on line 21, but note that no special operators are required. These are aliases for the original values, and can be used as such.

On lines 23 through 25, the values are swapped, and then they're printed on line 27. Program execution jumps back to the calling function, and on line 14, the values are printed in main(). Because the parameters to swap() are declared to be references, the values from main() are passed by reference, and thus are changed in main() as well.

References provide the convenience and ease of use of normal variables, with the power and pass-by-reference capability of pointers!

Understanding Function Headers and Prototypes

Listing 9.6 shows swap() using pointers, and Listing 9.7 shows it using references. Using the function that takes references is easier, and the code is easier to read, but how does the calling function know whether the values are passed by reference or by value? As a client (or user) of swap(), the programmer must ensure that swap() in fact changes the parameters.

This is another use for the function prototype. By examining the parameters declared in the prototype, which is typically in a header file along with all the other prototypes, the programmer knows that the values passed into swap() are passed by reference, and thus are swapped properly.

If swap() had been a member function of a class, the class declaration, also available in a header file, would have supplied this information.

In C++, clients of classes and functions rely on the header file to tell all that is needed; it acts as the interface to the class or function. The actual implementation is hidden from the client. This allows the programmer to focus on the problem at hand and to use the class or function without concern for how it works.

When Colonel Roebling built the Brooklyn Bridge, he worried over the details about how the concrete was poured and how the wire for the bridge was manufactured. He was intimately involved in the mechanical and chemical processes required to create his materials. Today, however, engineers make more efficient use of their time by using well-understood building materials, without regard to how their manufacturer produced them.

It is the goal of C++ to allow programmers to rely on well-understood classes and functions without regard to their internal workings. These "component parts" can be assembled to produce a program, in much the same way wires, pipes, clamps, and other parts are assembled to produce buildings and bridges.

In much the same way that an engineer examines the spec sheet for a pipe to determine its load-bearing capacity, volume, fitting size, and so forth, a C++ programmer reads the interface of a function or class to determine what services it provides, what parameters it takes, and what values it returns.

Returning Multiple Values

As discussed previously, functions can only return one value. What if you need to get two values back from a function? One way to solve this problem is to pass two objects into the function by reference. The function can then fill the objects with the correct values. Because passing by reference allows a function to change the original objects, this effectively enables the function to return two pieces of information. This approach bypasses the return value of the function, which can then be reserved for reporting errors.

Once again, this can be done with references or pointers. Listing 9.8 demonstrates a function that returns three values, two as pointer parameters and one as the return value of the function.

Type **Listing 9.8. Returning values with pointers.**

```
1:    //Listing 9.8
2:    // Returning multiple values from a function
3:
4:    #include <iostream.h>
5:
6:    typedef unsigned short USHORT;
7:
8:    short Factor(USHORT, USHORT*, USHORT*);
9:
10:   void main()
11:   {
12:       USHORT number, squared, cubed;
13:       short error;
14:
15:       cout << "Enter a number (0 - 20): ";
16:       cin >> number;
```

continues

Listing 9.8. continued

```
17:
18:         error = Factor(number, &squared, &cubed);
19:
20:         if (!error)
21:         {
22:             cout << "number: " << number << "\n";
23:             cout << "square: " << squared << "\n";
24:             cout << "cubed: "  << cubed   << "\n";
25:         }
26:         else
27:         cout << "Error encountered!!\n";
28:    }
29:
30:    short Factor(USHORT n, USHORT *pSquared, USHORT *pCubed)
31:    {
32:    short value = 0;
33:       if (n > 20)
34:          value = 1;
35:       else
36:       {
37:          *pSquared = n*n;
38:          *pCubed = n*n*n;
39:          value = 0;
41:       }
42:       return value;
43:    }
```

OUTPUT
```
Enter a number (0 - 20): 3
number: 3
square: 9
cubed: 27
```

ANALYSIS On line 12, number, squared, and cubed are defined as USHORTs. number is assigned a value based on user input. This number and the addresses of squared and cubed are passed to the function Factor().

Factor() examines the first parameter, which is passed by value. If it is greater than 20 (the maximum value this function can handle), it sets return Value to a simple error value. Note that the return value from Function() is reserved for either this error value or the value 0, indicating that all went well, and note that the function returns this value on line 42.

The actual values needed, the square and cube of number, are returned not by using the return mechanism, but rather by changing the pointers that were passed into the function.

On lines 37 and 38, the pointers are assigned their return values. On line 39 return Value is assigned a success value. On line 42 return Value is returned.

One improvement to this program might be to declare the following:

```
enum ERROR_VALUE { SUCCESS, FAILURE};
```

Then, rather than returning 0 or 1, the program could return SUCCESS or FAILURE.

Returning Values by Reference

Although Listing 9.8 works, it can be made easier to read and maintain by using references rather than pointers. Listing 9.9 shows the same program rewritten to use references and to incorporate the ERROR enumeration.

TYPE **Listing 9.9. A rewrite of Listing 9.8 using references.**

```
1:    //Listing 9.9
2:    // Returning multiple values from a function
3:    // using references
4:
5:    #include <iostream.h>
6:
7:    typedef unsigned short USHORT;
8:    enum ERR_CODE { SUCCESS, ERROR };
9:
10:    ERR_CODE Factor(USHORT, USHORT&, USHORT&);
11:
12:    void main()
13:    {
14:        USHORT number, squared, cubed;
15:        ERR_CODE result;
16:
17:        cout << "Enter a number (0 - 20): ";
18:        cin >> number;
19:
20:        result = Factor(number, squared, cubed);
21:
22:        if (result == SUCCESS)
23:        {
24:            cout << "number: " << number << "\n";
25:            cout << "square: " << squared << "\n";
26:            cout << "cubed: "  << cubed   << "\n";
27:        }
28:        else
29:        cout << "Error encountered!!\n";
30:    }
31:
32:    ERR_CODE Factor(USHORT n, USHORT &rSquared, USHORT &rCubed)
33:    {
34:        if (n > 20)
35:            return ERROR;    // simple error code
36:        else
37:        {
38:            rSquared = n*n;
39:            rCubed = n*n*n;
40:            return SUCCESS;
41:        }
42:    }
```

Enter a number (0 - 20): 3
number: 3
square: 9
cubed: 27

ANALYSIS Listing 9.9 is identical to 9.8, with two exceptions. The ERR_CODE enumeration makes the error reporting a bit more explicit on lines 35 and 40, as well as the error handling on line 22.

The more significant change, however, is that Factor() is now declared to take references to squared and cubed rather than to pointers. This makes the manipulation of these parameters far simpler and easier to understand.

Passing by Reference for Efficiency

Each time you pass an object into a function by value, a copy of the object is made. Each time you return an object from a function by value, another copy is made.

In the "Extra Credit" section at the end of Day 5, you learned that these objects are copied onto the stack. Doing so takes time and memory. For small objects, such as the built-in integer values, this is a trivial cost.

However, with larger user-created objects the cost is greater. The size of a user-created object on the stack is the sum of each of its member variables. These, in turn, can each be user-created objects, and passing such a massive structure by copying it onto the stack can be very expensive in performance and memory consumption.

There is another cost as well. With the classes you create, each of these temporary copies is created when the compiler calls a special constructor: the copy constructor. Tomorrow, in Day 10, "Advanced Functions," you learn how copy constructors work and how you can make your own. For now, though, it is enough to know that the copy constructor is called each time a temporary copy of the object is put on the stack.

When the temporary object is destroyed, which happens when the function returns, the object's destructor is called. If an object is returned by the function by value, a copy of that object must be made and destroyed as well.

With large objects, these constructor and destructor calls can be expensive in speed and use of memory. To illustrate this idea, Listing 9.10 creates a stripped-down user-created object: SimpleCat. A real object would be larger and more expensive, but this is sufficient to show how often the copy constructor and destructor are called.

Listing 9.10 creates the SimpleCat object and then calls two functions. The first function receives the Cat by value and then returns it by value. The second one receives a pointer to the object, rather than the object itself, and returns a pointer to the object.

TYPE Listing 9.10. Passing objects by reference.

```
1:   //Listing 9.10
2:   // Passing pointers to objects
3:
4:   #include <iostream.h>
5:
6:   class SimpleCat
7:   {
8:   public:
9:           SimpleCat ();                        // constructor
10:          SimpleCat(SimpleCat&);      // copy constructor
11:          ~SimpleCat();                        // destructor
12:   };
13:
14:   SimpleCat::SimpleCat()
15:   {
16:          cout << "Simple Cat Constructor...\n";
17:   }
18:
19:   SimpleCat::SimpleCat(SimpleCat&)
20:   {
21:          cout << "Simple Cat Copy Constructor...\n";
22:   }
23:
24:   SimpleCat::~SimpleCat()
25:   {
26:          cout << "Simple Cat Destructor...\n";
27:   }
28:
29:   SimpleCat FunctionOne (SimpleCat theCat);
30:   SimpleCat* FunctionTwo (SimpleCat *theCat);
31:
32:   void main()
33:   {
34:          cout << "Making a cat...\n";
35:          SimpleCat Frisky;
36:          cout << "Calling FunctionOne...\n";
37:          FunctionOne(Frisky);
38:          cout << "Calling FunctionTwo...\n";
39:          FunctionTwo(&Frisky);
40:   }
41:
42:   // FunctionOne, passes by value
43:   SimpleCat FunctionOne(SimpleCat theCat)
44:   {
45:                  cout << "Function One. Returning...\n";
46:                  return theCat;
47:   }
48:
49:   // FunctionTwo, passes by reference
50:   SimpleCat* FunctionTwo (SimpleCat  *theCat)
51:   {
52:                  cout << "Function Two. Returning...\n";
53:                  return theCat;
54:   }
```

```
 1:  Making a cat...
 2:  Simple Cat Constructor...
 3:  Calling FunctionOne...
 4:  Simple Cat Copy Constructor...
 5:  Function One. Returning...
 6:  Simple Cat Copy Constructor...
 7:  Simple Cat Destructor...
 8:  Simple Cat Destructor...
 9:  Calling FunctionTwo...
10:  Function Two. Returning...
11:  Simple Cat Destructor...
```

NOTE

> Line numbers do not print. They were added to aid in the analysis.

 A very simplified SimpleCat class is declared on lines 6 through 12. The constructor, copy constructor, and destructor all print an informative message so that you can tell when they've been called.

On line 34 main() prints out a message, seen on output line 1. On line 35 a SimpleCat object is instantiated. This causes the constructor to be called, and the output from the constructor is seen on output line 2.

On line 36 main() reports that it is calling FunctionOne, which creates output line 3. Because FunctionOne() is called passing the SimpleCat object by value, a copy of the SimpleCat object is made on the stack as an object local to the called function. This causes the copy constructor to be called, which creates output line 4.

Program execution jumps to line 45 in the called function, which prints an informative message, output line 5. The function then returns, and returns the SimpleCat object by value. This creates yet another copy of the object, calling the copy constructor and producing output line 6.

The return value from FunctionOne() is not assigned to any object, and so the temporary created for the return is thrown away, calling the destructor, which produces output line 7. Because FunctionOne() has ended, its local copy goes out of scope and is destroyed, calling the destructor and producing line 8.

Program execution returns to main(), and FunctionTwo() is called, but the parameter is passed by reference. No copy is produced, so there's no output. FunctionTwo() prints the message that appears as output line 10 and then returns the SimpleCat object, again by reference, which again produces no calls to the constructor or destructor.

Finally, the program ends and Frisky goes out of scope, causing one final call to the destructor and printing output line 11.

The net effect of this is that the call to FunctionOne(), because it passed a SimpleCat by value, produced two calls to the copy constructor and two to the destructor, while the call to FunctionTwo() produced none.

Passing a *const* Pointer

Although passing a pointer to FunctionTwo() is more efficient, it is dangerous. FunctionTwo() is not allowed to change the SimpleCat object it is passed, yet it is given the address of the SimpleCat. This seriously exposes the object to change and defeats the protection offered in passing by value.

Passing by value is like giving a museum a photograph of your masterpiece instead of the real thing. If vandals mark it up, there is no harm done to the original. Passing by reference is like sending your home address to the museum and inviting guests to come over and look at the real thing.

The solution is to pass a const pointer to SimpleCat. Doing so prevents calling any non-const method on SimpleCat, and thus protects the object from change. Listing 9.11 demonstrates this idea.

TYPE **Listing 9.11. Passing const pointers.**

```
1:  //Listing 9.11
2:      // Passing pointers to objects
3:
4:      #include <iostream.h>
5:
6:      class SimpleCat
7:      {
8:      public:
9:          SimpleCat();
10:         SimpleCat(SimpleCat&);
11:         ~SimpleCat();
12:
13:         int GetAge() const { return itsAge; }
14:         void SetAge(int age) { itsAge = age; }
15:
16:     private:
17:         int itsAge;
18:     };
19:
20:     SimpleCat::SimpleCat()
21:     {
22:         cout << "Simple Cat Constructor...\n";
23:         itsAge = 1;
24:     }
25:
```

continues

Listing 9.11. continued

```
26:            SimpleCat::SimpleCat(SimpleCat&)
27:            {
28:                    cout << "Simple Cat Copy Constructor...\n";
29:            }
30:
31:            SimpleCat::~SimpleCat()
32:            {
33:                    cout << "Simple Cat Destructor...\n";
34:            }
35:
36:            const     SimpleCat * const FunctionTwo (const SimpleCat * const
➡                            _theCat);
37:
38:            void main()
39:            {
40:                    cout << "Making a cat...\n";
41:                    SimpleCat Frisky;
42:                    cout << "Frisky is " << Frisky.GetAge() << " years
➡                                        _old\n";
43:                    int age = 5;
44:                    Frisky.SetAge(age);
45:                    cout << "Frisky is " << Frisky.GetAge() << " years
➡                                        _old\n";
46:                    cout << "Calling FunctionTwo...\n";
47:                    FunctionTwo(&Frisky);
48:                    cout << "Frisky is " << Frisky.GetAge() << " years
➡                                        _old\n";
49:            }
50:
51:            // functionTwo, passes a const pointer
52:            const SimpleCat * const FunctionTwo (const SimpleCat *
➡ const theCat)
53:            {
54:                        cout << "Function Two. Returning...\n";
55:                        cout << "Frisky is now " << theCat->GetAge();
56:                        cout << " years old \n";
57:                        // theCat->SetAge(8);    const!
58:                        return theCat;
59:            }
```

OUTPUT
```
Making a cat...
Simple Cat Constructor...
Frisky is 1 years old
Frisky is 5 years old
Calling FunctionTwo
FunctionTwo. Returning...
Frisky is now 5 years old
Frisky is 5 years old
Simple Cat Destructor...
```

9

ANALYSIS SimpleCat has added two accessor functions: GetAge() on line 13, which is a const function, and SetAge() on line 14, which is not. It has also added the member variable itsAge on line 17.

The constructor, copy constructor, and destructor are still defined to print their messages. The copy constructor is never called, however, because the object is passed by reference, so no copies are made. On line 41 an object is created, and its default age is printed on line 42.

On line 44 itsAge is set using the accessor SetAge, and the result is printed on line 45. FunctionOne is not used in this program, but FunctionTwo() is called. FunctionTwo() has changed slightly; the parameter and return value are now declared, on line 36, to take a constant pointer to a constant object and to return a constant pointer to a constant object.

Because the parameter and return value are still passed by reference, no copies are made, and the copy constructor is not called. The pointer in FunctionTwo(), however, is now constant, and thus cannot call the non-const method, SetAge(). If the call to SetAge() on line 57 were not commented out, the program would not compile.

Note that the object created in main() is not constant, and Frisky *can* call SetAge(). The address of this non-constant object is passed to FunctionTwo(), but because FunctionTwo()'s declaration declares the pointer to be a constant pointer, the object is treated as if it were constant!

References as an Alternative

Listing 9.11 solves the problem of making extra copies, and thus saves the calls to the copy constructor and destructor. It uses constant pointers to constant objects, and thereby solves the problem of the function changing the object. It is still somewhat cumbersome, however, because the objects passed to the function are pointers.

Because you know the object is never null, it would be easier to work within the function if a reference were passed in, rather than a pointer. Listing 9.12 illustrates this.

TYPE **Listing 9.12. Passing references to objects.**

```
1: //Listing 9.12
2: // Passing references to objects
3:
4:   #include <iostream.h>
5:
6:   class SimpleCat
7:   {
8:   public:
9:           SimpleCat();
10:           SimpleCat(SimpleCat&);
```

continues

Listing 9.12. continued

```
11:              ~SimpleCat();
12:
13:              int GetAge() const { return itsAge; }
14:              void SetAge(int age) { itsAge = age; }
15:
16:    private:
17:              int itsAge;
18:        };
19:
20:        SimpleCat::SimpleCat()
21:        {
22:              cout << "Simple Cat Constructor...\n";
23:              itsAge = 1;
24:        }
25:
26:        SimpleCat::SimpleCat(SimpleCat&)
27:        {
28:              cout << "Simple Cat Copy Constructor...\n";
29:        }
30:
31:        SimpleCat::~SimpleCat()
32:        {
33:              cout << "Simple Cat Destructor...\n";
34:        }
35:
36:        const     SimpleCat & FunctionTwo (const SimpleCat & theCat);
37:
38:        void main()
39:        {
40:              cout << "Making a cat...\n";
41:              SimpleCat Frisky;
42:              cout << "Frisky is " << Frisky.GetAge() << " years old\n";
43:              int age = 5;
44:              Frisky.SetAge(age);
45:              cout << "Frisky is " << Frisky.GetAge() << " years old\n";
46:              cout << "Calling FunctionTwo...\n";
47:              FunctionTwo(Frisky);
48:              cout << "Frisky is " << Frisky.GetAge() << " years old\n";
49:        }
50:
51:        // functionTwo, passes a ref to a const object
52:        const SimpleCat & FunctionTwo (const SimpleCat & theCat)
53:        {
54:                   cout << "FunctionTwo. Returning...\n";
55:                   cout << "Frisky is now " << theCat.GetAge();
56:                   cout << " years old \n";
57:                   // theCat.SetAge(8);    const!
58:                   return theCat;
59:        }
```

9

OUTPUT
```
Making a cat...
Simple Cat Constructor...
Frisky is 1 years old
Frisky is 5 years old
Calling FunctionTwo
FunctionTwo. Returning...
Frisky is now 5 years old
Frisky is 5 years old
Simple Cat Destructor...
```

ANALYSIS The output is identical to that produced by Listing 9.11. The only significant change is that FunctionTwo() now takes and returns a reference to a constant object. Once again, working with references is somewhat simpler than working with pointers. In addition, the same savings and efficiency, as well as the safety provided by using const, is achieved.

Const References

C++ programmers do not usually differentiate between "constant reference to a SimpleCat object" and "reference to a constant SimpleCat object." References themselves can never be reassigned to refer to another object, so they are always constant. If the keyword const is applied to a reference, it is to make the object to which it is referring constant.

Choosing Between References and Pointers

C++ programmers strongly prefer references over pointers. References are cleaner and easier to use, and they do a better job of hiding information, as you saw in the previous example.

References cannot be reassigned, however. If you need to point first to one object and then another, you must use a pointer. References cannot be null, so if there is any chance that the object in question might be null, you must not use a reference. You must use a pointer.

An example of the latter concern is the operator new. If new cannot allocate memory on the free store, it returns a null pointer. Because a reference can't be null, you must not initialize a reference to this memory until you've checked that it is not null. The following example shows how to handle this:

```
int *pInt = new int;
if (pInt != NULL)
int &rInt = *pInt;
```

In this example, a pointer to int, pInt, is declared and initialized with the memory returned by the operator new. The address in pInt is tested, and if it is not null, pInt is dereferenced. The result of dereferencing an int variable is an int object, and rInt is initialized to refer to that object. Thus, rInt becomes an alias to the int returned by the operator new.

Do	Don't

DO pass parameters by reference whenever possible.

DO return by reference whenever possible.

DON'T use pointers if references will work.

DO use const to protect references and pointers whenever possible.

DON'T return a reference to a local object.

Pointer References

If you want a function to modify a pointer (as opposed to the thing to which it points), you need to pass a pointer reference to the function. Pointer references are particularly useful for very large data objects and enable you to perform "pointer surgery" rather than manipulating the entire object. Look over the version of swap using pointer references in Listing 9.13.

TYPE   **Listing 9.13. swap rewritten with pointer references.**

```
1:    //Listing 9.13 Demonstrates passing by reference
2:     // using pointer references!
3:
4:        #include <iostream.h>
5:
6:        class SomeBigClass {
7:        private:
8:           int itsValue;
7:           // Lots more data in here
8:        public:
8:           SomeBigClass(int Val){ itsValue=Val; }
9:           int Value() { return itsValue; }
10:       };
11:
12:       void swap(SomeBigClass *&prx, SomeBigClass *&pry);
13:
14:       void main()
15:       {
```

```
16:          SomeBigClass C1(5), C2(10);
17:          SomeBigClass *ptrC1 = &C1;
18:          SomeBigClass *ptrC2 = &C2;
19:
20:          cout << "Main. Before swap, C1: "
21:              << ptrC1->Value() << " C2: "
22:              << ptrC2->Value() << "\n";
23:          swap(ptrC1, ptrC2);
24:          cout << "Main. After swap, C1: "
25:              << ptrC1->Value() << " C2: "
26:              << ptrC2->Value() << "\n";
27:      }
28:
29:      void swap (SomeBigClass *&prx, SomeBigClass *&pry)
30:      {
31:          SomeBigClass *temp;
32:
33:          cout << "Swap. Before swap, x: "
34:              << prx->Value() << " y: "
35:              << pry->Value() << "\n";
36:
37:          temp = prx;
38:          prx = pry;
39:          pry = temp;
40:
41:          cout << "Swap. After swap, x: "
42:              << prx->Value() << " y: "
43:              << pry->Value() << "\n";
44:
45:      }
```

OUTPUT

```
Main. Before swap, C1: 5 C2: 10
Swap. Before swap, x: 5 y: 10
Swap. After swap, x: 10 y: 5
Main. After swap, C1: 10 C2: 5
```

ANALYSIS   Lines 6 through 10 declare and define the class SomeBigClass, which could contain a lot of data making it an unwieldy candidate to pass to functions. On line 12, swap() has been changed to take a reference to a pointer to two SomeBigClass objects. Inside main(), two SomeBigClass objects are declared and pointers are assigned to each (lines 16 through 18). Lines 20 through 26 display the SomeBigClass object values before and after they are swapped. But notice that the pointers, and not the objects themselves, are passed to swap(). This makes the function control passing much faster than passing a couple of SomeBigClass objects. Inside swap() (lines 33 to 43), the values are displayed before and after also, just so you can see it as it happens.

Mixing References and Pointers

It is perfectly legal to declare both pointers and references in the same function parameter list, along with objects passed by value. The following is such an example:

```
CAT * SomeFunction (Person &theOwner, House *theHouse, int age);
```

This declaration says that SomeFunction takes three parameters. The first is a reference to a Person object, the second is a pointer to a House object, and the third is an integer. It returns a pointer to a CAT object.

Operator Placement in Declaring Variables

The question of where to put the reference (&) or indirection (*) operator when declaring these variables is a great controversy. You can legally write any of the following:

```
1:   CAT&  rFrisky;
2:   CAT & rFrisky;
3:   CAT  &rFrisky;
```

Whitespace is completely ignored, so anywhere you see a space you can put as many spaces, tabs, and new lines as you like.

Setting aside freedom of expression issues, which is best? Here are the arguments for all three:

The argument for case 1 is that rFrisky is a variable whose name is rFrisky and whose type can be thought of as "reference to CAT object." Thus, as argument 1 goes, the & should be with the type.

The counterargument is that the type is CAT. The & is part of the "declarator," which includes the variable name and the ampersand. More important, having the & near the CAT can lead to the following bug:

```
CAT&  rFrisky, rBoots;
```

Casual examination of this line would lead you to think that both rFrisky and rBoots are references to CAT objects, but you'd be wrong. This really says that rFrisky is a reference to a CAT, and rBoots (despite its name) is not a reference but a plain old CAT variable. This should be rewritten as follows:

```
CAT    &rFrisky, rBoots;
```

9

The answer to this objection is that declarations of references and variables should never be combined like this. Here's the right answer:

```
CAT& rFrisky;
CAT  boots;
```

Finally, many programmers opt out of the argument and go with the middle position, that of putting the & in the middle of the two, as illustrated in case 2.

Of course, everything said so far about the reference operator (&) applies equally well to the indirection operator (*). The important thing is to recognize that reasonable people differ in their perceptions of the one true way. Choose a style that works for you, and be consistent within any one program; clarity is, and remains, the goal.

This book adopts two conventions when declaring references and pointers:

- ☐ Put the ampersand and asterisk in the middle, with a space on either side.

- ☐ Never declare references, pointers, and variables all on the same line.

9

Don't Return a Reference to an Object that Isn't in Scope!

After C++ programmers learn to pass by reference, they have a tendency to go wild. It is possible, however, to overdo it. Remember that a reference is always an alias to some other object. If you pass a reference into or out of a function, be sure to ask yourself, "What is the object I'm aliasing, and will the object still exist every time it's used?"

Listing 9.14 illustrates the danger of returning a reference to an object that no longer exists.

TYPE | **Listing 9.14. Returning a reference to a nonexistent object.**

```
1:      // Listing 9.14
2:      // Returning a reference to an object
3:      // that no longer exists
4:
5:      #include <iostream.h>
6:
7:      class SimpleCat
8:      {
9:      public:
10:           SimpleCat (int age, int weight);
```

continues

Listing 9.14. continued

```
11:              ~SimpleCat() {}
12:              int GetAge() { return itsAge; }
13:              int GetWeight() { return itsWeight; }
14:      private:
15:          int itsAge;
16:          int itsWeight;
17:      };
18:
19:      SimpleCat::SimpleCat(int age, int weight):
20:      itsAge(age), itsWeight(weight) {}
21:
22:      SimpleCat &TheFunction();
23:
24:      void main()
25:      {
26:          SimpleCat &rCat = TheFunction();
27:          int age = rCat.GetAge();
28:          cout << "rCat is " << age << " years old!\n";
29:      }
30:
31:      SimpleCat &TheFunction()
32:      {
33:          SimpleCat Frisky(5,9);
34:          return Frisky;
35:      }
```

 Compile error: Attempting to return a reference to a local object!

 WARNING

> This program won't compile on the Borland compiler. It compiles on Microsoft compilers; however, it should be noted that it is a bad coding practice to return variable references to local function variables.

ANALYSIS On lines 7 through 17, SimpleCat is declared. On line 26 a reference to a SimpleCat is initialized with the results of calling TheFunction(), which is declared on line 22 to return a reference to a SimpleCat.

The body of TheFunction() declares a local object of type SimpleCat and initializes its age and weight. It then returns that local object by reference. Some compilers are smart enough to catch this error and won't let you run the program. Others let you run the program, with unpredictable results.

When TheFunction() returns, the local object, Frisky, is destroyed (painlessly, I assure you). The reference returned by this function is an alias to a nonexistent object, and this is a bad thing.

 9

Returning a Reference to an Object on the Heap

You might be tempted to solve the problem in Listing 9.14 by having TheFunction() create Frisky on the heap. That way, when you return from TheFunction(), Frisky still exists.

The problem with that approach is this: What do you do with the memory allocated for Frisky when you are done with it? Listing 9.15 illustrates this problem.

TYPE **Listing 9.15. Memory leaks.**

```
1:      // Listing 9.15
2:      // Resolving memory leaks
3:      #include <iostream.h>
4:
5:      class SimpleCat
6:      {
7:      public:
8:              SimpleCat (int age, int weight);
9:              ~SimpleCat() {}
10:             int GetAge() { return itsAge; }
11:             int GetWeight() { return itsWeight; }
12:
13:     private:
14:             int itsAge;
15:             int itsWeight;
16:      };
17:
18:      SimpleCat::SimpleCat(int age, int weight):
19:      itsAge(age), itsWeight(weight) {}
20:
21:      SimpleCat & TheFunction();
22:
23:      void main()
24:      {
25:             SimpleCat & rCat = TheFunction();
26:             int age = rCat.GetAge();
27:             cout << "rCat is " << age << " years old!\n";
28:             cout << "&rCat: " << &rCat << endl;
29:             // How do you get rid of that memory?
30:             SimpleCat * pCat = &rCat;
31:             delete pCat;
32:             // Uh oh, rCat now refers to ??
33:      }
34:
35:      SimpleCat &TheFunction()
36:      {
37:             SimpleCat * pFrisky = new SimpleCat(5,9);
38:             cout << "pFrisky: " << pFrisky << endl;
39:             return *pFrisky;
40:      }
```

```
pFrisky:  0x2bf4
rCat is 5 years old
&rCat:    0x2bf4
```

WARNING

This compiles, links, and appears to work. But it is a time bomb waiting to go off.

ANALYSIS The function TheFunction() has been changed so that it no longer returns a reference to a local variable. Memory is allocated on the free store and assigned to a pointer on line 37. The address that pointer holds is printed, and then the pointer is dereferenced and the SimpleCat object is returned by reference.

On line 25 the return of TheFunction() is assigned to a reference to a SimpleCat, and that object is used to obtain the cat's age, which is printed on line 27.

To prove that the reference declared in main() is referring to the object put on the free store in TheFunction(), the *address of* operator is applied to rCat. Sure enough, it displays the address of the object it refers to, and this matches the address of the object on the free store.

So far, so good. But how is that memory freed? You can't call delete on the reference. One clever solution is to create another pointer and initialize it with the address obtained from rCat. This does delete the memory, and plugs the memory leak. One small problem, though: What is rCat referring to after line 31? As stated earlier, a reference must always alias an actual object; if it references a null object (as this does now), the program is invalid.

NOTE

It cannot be overemphasized that a program with a reference to a null object might compile, but it is invalid, and its performance is unpredictable.

There are actually three solutions to this problem. The first is to declare a SimpleCat object on line 25, and to return that cat from TheFunction by value. The second is to go ahead and declare the SimpleCat on the free store in TheFunction(), but have TheFunction() return a pointer to that memory. Then the calling function can delete the pointer when it is done.

The third workable solution, and the right one, is to declare the object in the calling function and then to pass it to TheFunction() by reference.

Who Has the Pointer?

When your program allocates memory on the free store, a pointer is returned. It is imperative that you keep a pointer to that memory, because once the pointer is lost, the memory cannot be deleted and becomes a memory leak.

As you pass this block of memory between functions, someone "owns" the pointer. Typically, the value in the block is passed using references, and the function that created the memory is the one that deletes it. But this is a general rule, not an ironclad one.

It is dangerous for one function to create memory and another to free it, however. Ambiguity about who owns the pointer can lead to one of two problems: forgetting to delete a pointer or deleting it twice. Either one can cause serious problems in your program. It is safer to build your functions so that they delete the memory they create.

If you are writing a function that needs to create memory and then pass it back to the calling function, consider changing your interface. Have the calling function allocate the memory and then pass it into your function by reference. This moves all memory management out of your program and back to the function that is prepared to delete it.

Do	Don't

DO pass parameters by value when you must.

DO return by value when you must.

DON'T pass by reference if the item referred to might go out of scope.

DON'T use references to null objects.

Summary

Today you learned what references are and how they compare to pointers. You saw that references must be initialized to refer to an existing object and cannot be reassigned to refer to anything else. Any action taken on a reference is, in fact, taken on the reference's target object. Proof of this is that taking the address of a reference returns the address of the target.

You saw that passing objects by reference can be more efficient than passing by value. Passing by reference also enables the called function to change the value in the arguments back in the calling function.

You saw that arguments to functions and values returned from functions can be passed by reference, and that this can be implemented with pointers or with references.

You saw how to use const pointers and const references to safely pass values between functions while achieving the efficiency of passing by reference.

Q&A

Q Why have references if pointers can do everything references can?

A References are easier to use and understand. The indirection is hidden, and there is no need to repeatedly dereference the variable.

Q Why have pointers if references are easier?

A References cannot be null, and they cannot be reassigned. Pointers offer greater flexibility, but they are slightly more difficult to use.

Q Why would you ever return by value from a function?

A If the object being returned is local, you must return by value or you are returning a reference to a nonexistent object.

Q Given the danger in returning by reference, why not always return by value?

A There is far greater efficiency in returning by reference. Memory is saved, and the program runs faster.

Quiz

1. What is the difference between a reference and a pointer?
2. When must you use a pointer rather than a reference?
3. What does new return if there is insufficient memory to make your new object?
4. What is a constant reference?
5. What is the difference between passing *by* reference and passing *a* reference?

Exercises

1. Write a program that declares an int, a reference to an int, and a pointer to an int. Use the pointer and the reference to manipulate the value in the int.
2. Write a program that declares a constant pointer to a constant integer. Initialize the pointer to an integer variable, varOne. Assign 6 to varOne. Use the pointer to assign 7 to varOne. Create a second integer variable, varTwo. Reassign the pointer to varTwo.

3. Compile the program in exercise 2. What produces errors? What produces warnings?

4. Write a program that produces a stray pointer.

5. Fix the program from exercise 4.

6. Write a program that produces a memory leak.

7. Fix the program from exercise 6.

8. **BUG BUSTERS:** What is wrong with this program?

```
1:      #include <iostream.h>
2:
3:      class CAT
4:      {
5:          public:
6:              CAT(int age) { itsAge = age; }
7:              ~CAT(){}
8:              int GetAge() const { return itsAge;}
9:          private:
10:             int itsAge;
11:     };
12:
13:     CAT & MakeCat(int age);
14:     void main()
15:     {
16:         int age = 7;
17:         CAT Boots = MakeCat(age);
18:         cout << "Boots is " << Boots.GetAge() << " years old\n";
19:     }
20:
21:     CAT & MakeCat(int age)
22:     {
23:         CAT * pCat = new CAT(age);
24:         return *pCat;
25:     }
```

9. Fix the program from exercise 8.

Day 10

Advanced Functions

On Day 5, "Functions," you learned the fundamentals of working with functions. Now that you know how pointers and references work, you can do more with functions. Today you learn

☐ How to overload member functions.

☐ How to overload operators.

☐ How to write functions to support classes with dynamically allocated variables.

Overloaded Member Functions

On Day 5, you learned how to implement function polymorphism, or function overloading, by writing two or more functions with the same name but with different parameters. Class member functions can be overloaded as well, in much the same way.

The Rectangle class, demonstrated in Listing 10.1, has two DrawShape() functions. One takes no parameters and draws the Rectangle based on the class's current values. The other takes two values, a width and a length, and draws the Rectangle based on those values, ignoring the current class values.

TYPE **Listing 10.1. Overloading member functions.**

```
1:   //Listing 10.1 Overloading class member functions
2:   #include <iostream.h>
3:
4:   typedef unsigned short int USHORT;
5:   enum BOOL { FALSE, TRUE};
6:
7:   // Rectangle class declaration
8:   class Rectangle
9:   {
10:  public:
11:      // constructors
12:      Rectangle(USHORT width, USHORT height);
13:      ~Rectangle(){}
14:
15:      // overloaded class function DrawShape
16:      void DrawShape() const;
17:      void DrawShape(USHORT aWidth, USHORT aHeight) const;
18:
19:  private:
20:      USHORT itsWidth;
21:      USHORT itsHeight;
22:  };
23:
24:  //Constructor implementation
25:  Rectangle::Rectangle(USHORT width, USHORT height)
26:  {
27:      itsWidth = width;
28:      itsHeight = height;
29:  }
30:
31:
32:  // Overloaded DrawShape - takes no values
33:  // Draws based on current class member values
34:  void Rectangle::DrawShape() const
35:  {
36:      DrawShape( itsWidth, itsHeight);
37:  }
38:
39:
40:  // overloaded DrawShape - takes two values
41:  // draws shape based on the parameters
42:  void Rectangle::DrawShape(USHORT width, USHORT height) const
43:  {
44:      for (USHORT i = 0; i<height; i++)
45:      {
46:          for (USHORT j = 0; j< width; j++)
```

10

```
47:          {
48:              cout << "*";
49:          }
50:          cout << "\n";
51:      }
52:  }
53:
54:  // Driver program to demonstrate overloaded functions
55:  void main ()
56:  {
57:      // initialize a rectangle to 30,5
58:      Rectangle theRect(30,5);
59:      cout << "DrawShape(): \n";
60:      theRect.DrawShape();
61:      cout << "\nDrawShape(40,2): \n";
62:      theRect.DrawShape(40,2);
63:  }
```

10

NOTE

This listing passes width and height values to several functions. You should note that sometimes width is passed first and at other times, height is passed first.

OUTPUT

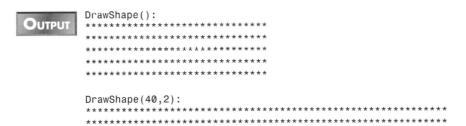

```
DrawShape():
******************************
******************************
******************************
******************************
******************************

DrawShape(40,2):
**********************************************************************
**********************************************************************
```

ANALYSIS Listing 10.1 represents a stripped-down version of the Week in Review project from Week 1. The test for illegal values has been taken out to save room, as have some of the accessor functions. The main program has been stripped down to a simple driver program, rather than a menu.

The important code, however, is on lines 16 and 17, where DrawShape() is overloaded. The implementation for these overloaded class methods is on lines 32 through 52. Note that the version of DrawShape() that takes no parameters simply calls the version that takes two parameters, passing in the current member variables. Try very hard to avoid duplicating code in two functions. Otherwise, keeping them in synch when changes are made to one or the other will be difficult and error-prone.

The driver program on lines 55 through 63 creates a rectangle object and then calls DrawShape(), first passing in no parameters, and then passing in two unsigned short integers.

The compiler decides which method to call based on the number and type of parameters entered. One can imagine a third overloaded function named DrawShape() that takes one dimension and an enumeration for whether it is the width or height, at the user's choice.

Using Default Values

Just as nonclass functions can have one or more default values, so can each member function of a class. The same rules apply for declaring the default values, as illustrated in Listing 10.2.

TYPE **Listing 10.2. Using default values.**

```
1:     //Listing 10.2 Default values in member functions
2:     #include <iostream.h>
3:
4:     typedef unsigned short int USHORT;
5:     enum BOOL { FALSE, TRUE};
6:
7:     // Rectangle class declaration
8:     class Rectangle
9:     {
10:    public:
11:        // constructors
12:        Rectangle(USHORT width, USHORT height);
13:        ~Rectangle(){}
14:        void DrawShape(USHORT aWidth, USHORT aHeight, BOOL UseCurrentVals =
                          _FALSE) const;
15:
16:    private:
17:        USHORT itsWidth;
18:        USHORT itsHeight;
19:    };
20:
21:    //Constructor implementation
22:    Rectangle::Rectangle(USHORT width, USHORT height):
23:    itsWidth(width),        // initializations
24:    itsHeight(height)
25:    {}                      // empty body
26:
27:
28:    // default values used for third parameter
29:    void Rectangle::DrawShape(
30:        USHORT width,
31:        USHORT height,
32:        BOOL UseCurrentValue
33:        ) const
34:    {
35:        int printWidth;
36:        int printHeight;
37:
38:        if (UseCurrentValue == TRUE)
```

```
39:       {
40:           printWidth = itsWidth;        // use current class values
41:           printHeight = itsHeight;
42:       }
43:       else
44:       {
45:           printWidth = width;           // use parameter values
46:           printHeight = height;
47:       }
48:
49:
50:       for (int i = 0;  i<printHeight; i++)
51:       {
52:           for (int j = 0;  j< printWidth; j++)
53:           {
54:               cout << "*";
55:           }
56:           cout << "\n";
57:       }
58:   }
59:
60:   // Driver program to demonstrate overloaded functions
61:   void main ()
62:   {
63:       // initialize a rectangle to 10,20
64:       Rectangle theRect(30,5);
65:       cout << "DrawShape(0,0,TRUE)...\n";
66:       theRect.DrawShape(0,0,TRUE);
67:       cout <<"DrawShape(40,2)...\n";
68:       theRect.DrawShape(40,2);
69:   }
```

OUTPUT

```
DrawShape(0,0,TRUE)...
*****************************
*****************************
*****************************
*****************************
*****************************

DrawShape(40,2)...
**************************************************************
**************************************************************
```

ANALYSIS Listing 10.2 replaces the overloaded DrawShape() function with a single function with default parameters. The function is declared on line 14 to take three parameters. The first two (aWidth and aHeight) are USHORTs, and the third (UseCurrentValue) is a BOOL (TRUE or FALSE) that defaults to FALSE.

NOTE

> Boolean values are those that evaluate to TRUE or FALSE. C++ considers 0 to be false and all other values to be true.

The implementation for this somewhat awkward function begins on line 28. The third parameter, UseCurrentValue, is evaluated. If it is TRUE, the member variables itsWidth and itsHeight are used to set the local variables printWidth and printHeight, respectively.

If UseCurrentValue is FALSE, either because it has defaulted FALSE or is set by the user, the first two parameters are used for setting printWidth and printHeight.

Note that if UseCurrentValue is TRUE, the values of the other two parameters are completely ignored.

Choosing Between Default Values and Overloaded Functions

Listings 10.1 and 10.2 accomplish the same thing, but the overloaded functions in Listing 10.1 are simpler to understand and more natural to use. Also, if a third variation is needed— perhaps the user wants to supply either the width *or* the height, but not both—it is easy to extend the overloaded functions. The default value, however, quickly becomes unusable in complexity as new variations are added.

How do you decide whether to use function overloading or default values? Here's a rule of thumb:

Look to function overloading when

☐ There is no reasonable default value.

☐ You need different algorithms.

☐ You need to support variant types in your parameter list.

The Default Constructor

As discussed on Day 6, "Basic Classes," if you do not explicitly declare a constructor for your class, a default constructor is created that takes no parameters and does nothing. However, you are free to make your own default constructor that takes no arguments but sets up your object as required.

The constructor provided for you is called the default constructor, but by convention so is any other constructor that takes no parameters. This can be a bit confusing, but it is usually clear from context which is meant.

NOTE

> If you make any constructors at all, the default constructor is not made
> by the compiler. So if you want a constructor that takes no parameters,
> and you've created any other constructors, you must make the default
> constructor yourself!

Overloading Constructors

The point of a constructor is to establish the object; for example, the point of a `Rectangle` constructor is to make a rectangle. Before the constructor runs, there is no rectangle, just an area of memory. After the constructor finishes, there is a complete, ready-to-use rectangle object.

Constructors, like all member functions, can be overloaded. The capability to overload constructors is very powerful and very flexible. For example, you might have a rectangle object that has two constructors: The first takes a length and a width, and makes a rectangle of that size. The second takes no values, and makes a default-sized rectangle. Listing 10.3 illustrates this idea.

TYPE **Listing 10.3. Overloading the constructor.**

```
1:     // Listing 10.3
2:     // Overloading constructors
3:
4:     #include <iostream.h>
5:
6:     class Rectangle
7:     {
8:     public:
9:           Rectangle();
10:          Rectangle(int width, int length);
11:          ~Rectangle() {}
12:          int GetWidth() const { return itsWidth; }
13:          int GetLength() const { return itsLength; }
14:     private:
15:          int itsWidth;
16:          int itsLength;
17:     };
18:
19:     Rectangle::Rectangle()
20:     {
21:          itsWidth = 5;
22:          itsLength = 10;
23:     }
```

continues

Listing 10.3. continued

```
24:
25:        Rectangle::Rectangle (int width, int length)
26:        {
27:            itsWidth = width;
28:            itsLength = length;
29:        }
30:
31:        void main()
32:        {
33:            Rectangle Rect1;
34:            cout << "Rect1 width: " << Rect1.GetWidth() << endl;
35:            cout << "Rect1 length: " << Rect1.GetLength() << endl;
36:
37:            int aWidth, aLength;
38:            cout << "Enter a width: ";
39:            cin >> aWidth;
40:            cout << "\nEnter a length: ";
41:            cin >> aLength;
42:
43:            Rectangle Rect2(aWidth, aLength);
44:            cout << "\nRect2 width: " << Rect2.GetWidth() << endl;
45:            cout << "Rect2 length: " << Rect2.GetLength() << endl;
46:        }
```

OUTPUT
```
Rect1 width: 5
Rect1 length: 10
Enter a width: 20
Enter a length: 50
Rect2 width: 20
Rect2 length: 50
```

 The Rectangle class is declared on lines 6 through 17. Two constructors are declared: the default constructor on line 9, and a constructor taking two integer variables.

On line 33, a rectangle is created using the default constructor, and its values are printed on lines 34 through 35. On lines 37 through 41, the user is prompted for a width and length, and the constructor taking two parameters is called on line 43. Finally, the width and height for this rectangle are printed on lines 44 and 45.

The compiler chooses the right constructor just as it does any overloaded function—based on the number and type of the parameters.

Initializing Objects

Until now, you've been setting the member variables of objects in the body of the constructor. Constructors, however, are invoked in two stages: the initialization stage and the body.

10

Most variables can be set in either stage, by initializing in the initialization stage, or by assigning in the body of the constructor. It is cleaner, and often more efficient, to initialize member variables at the initialization stage. The following example shows how to initialize member variables:

```
CAT():          // constructor name and parameters
itsAge(5),      // initialization list
itsWeight(8)
{ }             // body of constructor
```

After the closing parentheses on the constructor's parameter list, write a colon. Then write the name of the member variable and a pair of parentheses. Inside the parentheses, write the expression to be used to initialize that member variable. If there is more than one initialization, separate each one with a comma. Listing 10.4 shows the definition of the constructors from Listing 10.3, with initialization of the member variables rather than assignment.

10

TYPE **Listing 10.4. Initialization of member variables.**

```
1:   Rectangle::Rectangle():
2:        itsWidth(5),
3:        itsLength(10)
4:   {};
5:
6:
7:   Rectangle::Rectangle (int width, int length):
8:        itsWidth(width),
9:        itsLength(length)
10:  {};
```

There are some variables that must be initialized and cannot be assigned to, including references and constants. It is common to have other assignments or action statements in the body of the constructor; however, it is best to use initialization as often as possible.

The Copy Constructor

In addition to providing a default constructor and destructor, the compiler provides a default copy constructor. The copy constructor is called every time a copy of an object is made.

When you pass an object by value, either into a function or as a function's return value, a temporary copy of that object is made. If the object is a user-defined object, the class's copy constructor is called, as you saw yesterday in Listing 9.10.

All copy constructors take one parameter: a reference to an object of the same class. It is a good idea to make the object reference a constant reference, because the constructor does not have to alter the object passed in, as in the following example:

```
CAT(const CAT & theCat);
```

Here the CAT constructor takes a constant reference to an existing CAT object. The goal of the copy constructor is to make a copy of theCAT.

The default copy constructor simply copies each member variable from the object passed as a parameter to the member variables of the new object. This is called a *member-wise* (or *shallow*) copy. Although this is fine for most member variables, it can cause unexpected results for member variables that are pointers to objects on the free store.

NEW TERM   A *shallow* or *member-wise* copy copies the exact values of one object's member variables into another object. Pointers in both objects end up pointing to the same memory. A *deep* copy copies the values allocated on the heap to newly allocated memory.

If the CAT class includes a member variable, itsAge, that points to an integer on the free store, the default copy constructor copies the passed-in CAT's itsAge member variable to the new CAT's itsAge member variable. The two objects now point to the same memory, as illustrated in Figure 10.1.

Figure 10.1.

Using the default copy constructor.

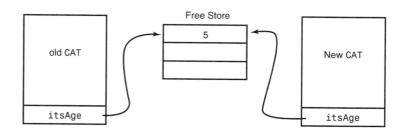

This leads to a disaster when either CAT goes out of scope. As mentioned on Day 8, "Pointers," the job of the destructor is to clean up this memory. If the original CAT's destructor frees this memory and the new CAT is still pointing to the memory, a stray pointer has been created, and the program is in mortal danger. Figure 10.2 illustrates this problem.

The solution to this is to create your own copy constructor and to allocate the memory as required. When the memory is allocated, the old values can be copied into the new memory. This is called a *deep copy*. Listing 10.5 illustrates how to do this.

10

Figure 10.2.

Creating a stray pointer.

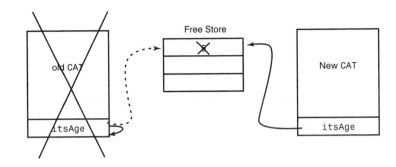

TYPE **Listing 10.5. Copy constructors.**

```
1:    // Listing 10.5
2:    // Copy constructors
3:
4:    #include <iostream.h>
5:
6:    class CAT
7:    {
8:        public:
9:            CAT();                              // default constructor
10:           CAT (const CAT &);      // copy constructor
11:           ~CAT();                             // destructor
12:           int GetAge() const { return *itsAge; }
13:           int GetWeight() const { return *itsWeight; }
14:           void SetAge(int age) { *itsAge = age; }
15:
16:       private:
17:           int *itsAge;
18:           int *itsWeight;
19:   };
20:
21:   CAT::CAT()
22:   {
23:       itsAge = new int;
24:       itsWeight = new int;
25:       *itsAge = 5;
26:       *itsWeight = 9;
27:   }
28:
29:   CAT::CAT(const CAT & rhs)
30:   {
31:       itsAge = new int;
32:       itsWeight = new int;
33:       *itsAge = rhs.GetAge();
34:       *itsWeight = rhs.GetWeight();
35:   }
```

continues

Listing 10.5. continued

```
36:
37:    CAT::~CAT()
38:    {
39:        delete itsAge;
40:        itsAge = 0;
41:        delete itsWeight;
42:        itsWeight = 0;
43:    }
44:
45:    void main()
46:    {
47:        CAT frisky;
48:        cout << "frisky's age: " << frisky.GetAge() << endl;
49:        cout << "Setting frisky to 6...\n";
50:        frisky.SetAge(6);
51:        cout << "Creating boots from frisky\n";
52:        CAT boots(frisky);
53:        cout << "frisky's age: " <<      frisky.GetAge() << endl;
54:        cout << "boots' age: " << boots.GetAge() << endl;
55:        cout << "setting frisky to 7...\n";
56:        frisky.SetAge(7);
57:        cout << "frisky's age: " <<      frisky.GetAge() << endl;
58:        cout << "boot's age: " << boots.GetAge() << endl;
59:    }
```

OUTPUT

```
frisky's age: 5
Setting frisky to 6...
Creating boots from frisky
frisky's age: 6
boots' age:  6
Setting frisky to 7...
frisky's age: 7
boots' age: 6
```

ANALYSIS   On lines 6 through 19, the CAT class is declared. Note that on line 9 a default constructor is declared, and on line 10 a copy constructor is declared.

On lines 17 and 18, two member variables are declared, each as a pointer to an integer. Typically, there would be little reason for a class to store int member variables as pointers, but this was done to illustrate how to manage member variables on the free store.

The default constructor, on lines 21 through 27, allocates room on the free store for two int variables and then assigns values to them.

The copy constructor begins on line 29. Note that the parameter is rhs. It is common to refer to the parameter to a copy constructor as rhs, which stands for *right-hand side*. When you look at the assignments in lines 33 and 34, you'll see that the object passed in as a parameter is on the right-hand side of the equals sign. Here's how it works.

On lines 31 and 32, memory is allocated on the free store. Then, on lines 33 and 34, the value at the new memory location is assigned the values from the existing CAT.

The parameter rhs is a CAT that is passed into the copy constructor as a constant reference. The member function rhs.GetAge() returns the value stored in the memory pointed to by rhs's member variable itsAge. As a CAT object, rhs has all the member variables of any other CAT.

When the copy constructor is called to create a new CAT, an existing CAT is passed in as a parameter. The new CAT can refer to its own member variables directly; however, it must access rhs's member variables using the public accessor methods.

Figure 10.3 diagrams what is happening here. The values pointed to by the existing CAT are copied to the memory allocated for the new CAT.

Figure 10.3.

An illustration of a deep copy.

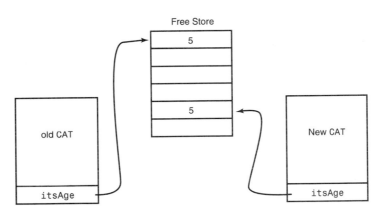

On line 47, a CAT is created, called frisky. frisky's age is printed, and then his age is set to 6 on line 50. On line 52, a new CAT is created, boots, using the copy constructor, and passing in frisky. Had frisky been passed as a parameter to a function, this same call to the copy constructor would have been made by the compiler.

On lines 53 and 54, the ages of both CATs are printed. Sure enough, boots has frisky's age, 6, not the default age of 5. On line 56, frisky's age is set to 7, and then the ages are printed again. This time frisky's age is 7 but boots' age is still 6, demonstrating that they are stored in separate areas of memory.

When the CATs fall out of scope, their destructors are automatically invoked. The implementation of the CAT destructor is shown on lines 37 through 43. delete is called on both pointers, itsAge and itsWeight, returning the allocated memory to the free store. Also, for safety, the pointers are reassigned to NULL.

Operator Overloading

C++ has a number of built-in types, including int, float, char, and so on. Each of these has a number of built-in operators, such as addition (+) and multiplication (*). C++ enables you to add these operators to your own classes as well.

In order to fully explore operator overloading, Listing 10.6 creates a new class, Counter. A Counter object will be used in counting (surprise!) in loops and other applications where a number must be incremented, decremented, or otherwise tracked.

TYPE **Listing 10.6. The Counter class.**

```
1:     // Listing 10.6
2:     // The Counter class
3:
4:     typedef unsigned short  USHORT;
5:     #include <iostream.h>
6:
7:     class Counter
8:     {
9:        public:
10:           Counter();
11:           ~Counter(){}
12:           USHORT GetItsVal()const { return itsVal; }
13:           void SetItsVal(USHORT x) {itsVal = x; }
14:
15:        private:
16:           USHORT itsVal;
17:
18:     };
19:
20:     Counter::Counter():
21:     itsVal(0)
22:     {};
23:
24:     void main()
25:     {
26:        Counter i;
27:        cout << "The value of i is " << i.GetItsVal() << endl;
28:     }
```

OUTPUT The value of i is 0.

ANALYSIS As it stands, this is a pretty useless class. It is defined on lines 7 through 18. Its only member variable is a USHORT. The default constructor, which is declared on line 10 and whose implementation is on line 20, initializes the one member variable, itsVal, to 0.

10

Unlike an honest red-blooded USHORT, the counter object cannot be incremented, decremented, added, assigned, or otherwise manipulated. In exchange for this, it makes printing its value far more difficult!

Writing an Increment Function

Operator overloading restores much of the functionality that has been stripped out of this class. For example, there are two ways to add the capability to increment a Counter object. The first is to write an increment method, as shown in Listing 10.7.

TYPE **Listing 10.7. Adding an increment operator.**

```
1:     // Listing 10.7
2:     // The Counter class
3:
4:     typedef unsigned short   USHORT;
5:     #include <iostream.h>
6:
7:     class Counter
8:     {
9:        public:
10:          Counter();
11:          ~Counter(){}
12:          USHORT GetItsVal()const { return itsVal; }
13:          void SetItsVal(USHORT x) {itsVal = x; }
14:          void Increment() { ++itsVal; }
15:
16:        private:
17:          USHORT itsVal;
18:
19:     };
20:
21:     Counter::Counter():
22:     itsVal(0)
23:     {};
24:
25:     void main()
26:     {
27:        Counter i;
28:        cout << "The value of i is " << i.GetItsVal() << endl;
29:        i.Increment();
30:        cout << "The value of i is " << i.GetItsVal() << endl;
31:     }
```

OUTPUT
```
The value of i is 0
The value of i is 1
```

ANALYSIS Listing 10.7 adds an Increment function, defined on line 14. Although this works, it is cumbersome to use. The program cries out for the capability to add a ++ operator, and of course, this can be done.

Overloading the Prefix Operator

Prefix operators can be overloaded by declaring functions with the form:

returnType operator *op* (*parameters*)

Here, op is the operator to overload. Thus, the ++ operator can be overloaded with the following syntax:

void operator++ ()

Listing 10.8 demonstrates this alternative.

TYPE   **Listing 10.8. Overloading operator++.**

```
1:     // Listing 10.8
2:     // The Counter class
3:
4:     typedef unsigned short   USHORT;
5:     #include <iostream.h>
6:
7:     class Counter
8:     {
9:        public:
10:           Counter();
11:           ~Counter(){}
12:           USHORT GetItsVal()const { return itsVal; }
13:           void SetItsVal(USHORT x) {itsVal = x; }
14:           void Increment() { ++itsVal; }
15:           void operator++ () { ++itsVal; }
16:
17:        private:
18:           USHORT itsVal;
19:
20:     };
21:
22:     Counter::Counter():
23:     itsVal(0)
24:     {};
25:
26:     void main()
27:     {
28:        Counter i;
29:        cout << "The value of i is " << i.GetItsVal() << endl;
30:        i.Increment();
31:        cout << "The value of i is " << i.GetItsVal() << endl;
32:        ++i;
33:        cout << "The value of i is " << i.GetItsVal() << endl;
34:     }
```

OUTPUT
```
The value of i is 0
The value of i is 1
The value of i is 2
```

ANALYSIS On line 15, operator++ is overloaded, and it's used on line 32. This is far closer to the syntax one would expect with the Counter object. At this point, you might consider putting in the extra capabilities for which counter was created in the first place, such as detecting when the counter overruns its maximum size.

There is a significant defect in the way the Increment operator was written, however. If you want to put the counter on the right side of an assignment, it will fail, as in the following example:

```
counter a = ++i;
```

This code intends to create a new counter, a, and then assign to it the value in i after i is incremented. The built-in copy constructor will handle the assignment, but the current Increment operator does not return a Counter object. It returns void. You can't assign a void object to a Counter object. (You can't make something from nothing!)

Returning Types in Overloaded Operator Functions

Clearly, what you want is to return a Counter object so that it can be assigned to another Counter object. Which object should be returned? One approach would be to create a temporary object and return that. Listing 10.9 illustrates this approach.

TYPE **Listing 10.9. Returning a temporary object.**

```
1:    // Listing 10.9
2:    // operator++ returns a temporary object
3:
4:    typedef unsigned short   USHORT;
5:    #include <iostream.h>
6:
7:    class Counter
8:    {
9:       public:
10:          Counter();
11:          ~Counter(){}
12:          USHORT GetItsVal()const { return itsVal; }
13:          void SetItsVal(USHORT x) {itsVal = x; }
14:          void Increment() { ++itsVal; }
15:          Counter operator++ ();
16:
17:       private:
18:          USHORT itsVal;
19:
20:    };
21:
22:    Counter::Counter():
23:    itsVal(0)
24:    {};
```

continues

Listing 10.9. continued

```
25:
26:     Counter Counter::operator++()
27:     {
28:         ++itsVal;
29:         Counter temp;
30:         temp.SetItsVal(itsVal);
31:         return temp;
32:     }
33:
34:     void main()
35:     {
36:         Counter i;
37:         cout << "The value of i is " << i.GetItsVal() << endl;
38:         i.Increment();
39:         cout << "The value of i is " << i.GetItsVal() << endl;
40:         ++i;
41:         cout << "The value of i is " << i.GetItsVal() << endl;
42:         Counter a = ++i;
43:         cout << "The value of a: " << a.GetItsVal();
44:         cout << " and i: " << i.GetItsVal() << endl;
45:     }
```

OUTPUT
```
The value of i is 0
The value of i is 1
The value of i is 2
The value of a: 3 and i: 3
```

ANALYSIS In this version, operator++ has been declared on line 15 to return a Counter object. On line 29, a temporary variable, temp, is created, and its value is set to match that in the current object. That temporary variable is returned and immediately assigned to a on line 42.

Returning Nameless Temporaries

There is really no need to name the temporary object created on line 29. If Counter has a constructor that takes a value, you could simply return the result of that constructor as the return value of the Increment operator. Listing 10.10 illustrates this idea.

TYPE   **Listing 10.10. Returning a nameless temporary object.**

```
1:      // Listing 10.10
2:      // operator++ returns a nameless temporary object
3:
4:      typedef unsigned short  USHORT;
5:      #include <iostream.h>
6:
7:      class Counter
```

```
8:      {
9:         public:
10:            Counter();
11:            Counter(USHORT val);
12:            ~Counter(){}
13:            USHORT GetItsVal()const { return itsVal; }
14:            void SetItsVal(USHORT x) {itsVal = x; }
15:            void Increment() { ++itsVal; }
16:            Counter operator++ ();
17:
18:         private:
19:            USHORT itsVal;
20:
21:      };
22:
23:      Counter::Counter():
24:      itsVal(0)
25:      {}
26:
27:      Counter::Counter(USHORT val):
28:      itsVal(val)
29:      {}
30:
31:      Counter Counter::operator++()
32:      {
33:         ++itsVal;
34:         return Counter (itsVal);
35:      }
36:
37:      void main()
38:      {
39:         Counter i;
40:         cout << "The value of i is " << i.GetItsVal() << endl;
41:         i.Increment();
42:         cout << "The value of i is " << i.GetItsVal() << endl;
43:         ++i;
44:         cout << "The value of i is " << i.GetItsVal() << endl;
45:         Counter a = ++i;
46:         cout << "The value of a: " << a.GetItsVal();
47:         cout << " and i: " << i.GetItsVal() << endl;
48:      }
```

10

OUTPUT
```
The value of i is 0
The value of i is 1
The value of i is 2
The value of a: 3 and i: 3
```

ANALYSIS On line 11, a new constructor is declared that takes a USHORT. The implementation is on lines 27 through 29. It initializes itsVal with the passed-in value.

The implementation of operator++ is now simplified. On line 33, itsVal is incremented. Then, on line 34, a temporary Counter object is created, initialized to the value in itsVal, and returned as the result of the operator++.

This is more elegant, but begs the question, "Why create a temporary object at all?" Remember that each temporary object must be constructed and later destroyed, each one potentially an expensive operation. And the object i already exists and already has the right value, so why not return it?

Using the *this* Pointer

The this pointer, as discussed in Day 9, "References," is passed to the operator++ member function as to all member functions. The this pointer points to i. If it's dereferenced, it returns the object i, which already has the right value in its member variable itsVal. Listing 10.11 illustrates returning the dereferenced this pointer and avoiding the creation of an unneeded temporary object.

TYPE | **Listing 10.11. Returning the this pointer.**

```
1:      // Listing 10.11
2:      // Returning the dereferenced this pointer
3:
4:      typedef unsigned short  USHORT;
5:      #include <iostream.h>
6:
7:      class Counter
8:      {
9:         public:
10:            Counter();
11:            ~Counter(){}
12:            USHORT GetItsVal()const { return itsVal; }
13:            void SetItsVal(USHORT x) {itsVal = x; }
14:            void Increment() { ++itsVal; }
15:            const Counter& operator++ ();
16:
17:         private:
18:            USHORT itsVal;
19:
20:      };
21:
22:      Counter::Counter():
23:      itsVal(0)
24:      {};
25:
26:      const Counter& Counter::operator++()
27:      {
28:          ++itsVal;
29:          return *this;
30:      }
31:
32:      void main()
33:      {
34:          Counter i;
```

10

```
35:          cout << "The value of i is " << i.GetItsVal() << endl;
36:          i.Increment();
37:          cout << "The value of i is " << i.GetItsVal() << endl;
38:          ++i;
39:          cout << "The value of i is " << i.GetItsVal() << endl;
40:          Counter a = ++i;
41:          cout << "The value of a: " << a.GetItsVal();
42:          cout << " and i: " << i.GetItsVal() << endl;
43:      }
```

OUTPUT
```
The value of i is 0
The value of i is 1
The value of i is 2
The value of a: 3 and i: 3
```

ANALYSIS The implementation of operator++, on lines 26 through 30, has been changed to dereference the this pointer and to return the current object. This provides a Counter object to be assigned to a. As discussed earlier, if the Counter object allocates memory, it would be important to override the copy constructor. In this case, the default copy constructor works fine.

Note that the value returned is a Counter reference, thereby avoiding the creation of an extra temporary object. It is a const reference because the value should not be changed by the function using this Counter.

Overloading the Postfix Operator

So far, you've overloaded the prefix operator. What if you want to overload the postfix Increment operator? Here the compiler has a problem: How is it to differentiate between prefix and postfix? By convention, an integer variable is supplied as a parameter to the operator declaration. The parameter's value is ignored; it is just a signal that this is the postfix operator. Listing 10.12 demonstrates the use of both the prefix and the postfix operators.

TYPE   **Listing 10.12. Prefix and postfix operators.**

```
1:      // Listing 10.12
2:      // Returning the dereferenced this pointer
3:
4:      typedef unsigned short  USHORT;
5:      #include <iostream.h>
6:
7:      class Counter
8:      {
9:      public:
10:         Counter();
11:         ~Counter(){}
12:         USHORT GetItsVal()const { return itsVal; }
```

continues

Listing 10.12. continued

```
13:          void SetItsVal(USHORT x) {itsVal = x; }
14:          const Counter& operator++ ();       // prefix
15:          const Counter& operator++ (int); // postfix
16:
17:    private:
18:       USHORT itsVal;
19:
20:    };
21:
22:    Counter::Counter():
23:    itsVal(0)
24:    {}
25:
26:    const Counter& Counter::operator++()
27:    {
28:       ++itsVal;
29:       return *this;
30:    }
31:
32:    const Counter& Counter::operator++(int x)
33:    {
34:       itsVal++;
35:       return *this;
36:    }
37:
38:    void main()
39:    {
40:       Counter i;
41:       cout << "The value of i is " << i.GetItsVal() << endl;
42:       i++;
43:       cout << "The value of i is " << i.GetItsVal() << endl;
44:       ++i;
45:       cout << "The value of i is " << i.GetItsVal() << endl;
46:       Counter a = ++i;
47:       cout << "The value of a: " << a.GetItsVal();
48:       cout << " and i: " << i.GetItsVal() << endl;
49:       a = i++;
50:       cout << "The value of a: " << a.GetItsVal();
51:       cout << " and i: " << i.GetItsVal() << endl;
52:    }
```

OUTPUT

```
The value of i is 0
The value of i is 1
The value of i is 2
The value of a: 3 and i: 3
The value of a: 4 and i: 4
```

ANALYSIS The postfix operator is declared on line 15 and implemented on lines 32 through 36. Note that the call to the prefix operator on line 14 does not include the flag integer (x), but is used with its normal syntax. The postfix operator uses a flag value (x) to signal that it is the postfix and not the prefix. The flag value (x) is never used, however.

10

Operator Overloading Unary Operators

Declare an overloaded operator as you would a function. Use the keyword `operator` followed by the operator to overload. Unary operator functions do not take parameters—with the exception of the postfix increment and decrement, which take an integer as a flag.

NOTE

> The techniques used for overloading `operator++` can be applied to the other unary operators, such as `operator--`.

Example 1

```
const Counter& Counter::operator++ ();
```

Example 2

```
Counter Counter::operator--(int);
```

Do	Don't

DO use a parameter to `operator++` if you want the postfix operator.

DO return a `const` reference to the object from `operator++`.

DON'T create temporary objects as return values from `operator++`.

operator+

The `Increment` operator is a unary operator. It operates on one object only. The addition operator (+) is a binary operator, which involves two objects. How do you implement overloading the + operator for `Count`?

The goal is to be able to declare two `Counter` variables and then add them, as in this example:

```
Counter varOne, varTwo, varThree;
VarThree = VarOne + VarTwo;
```

Once again, you could start by writing a function, `Add()`, that would take a `Counter` as its argument, add the values, and then return a `Counter` with the result. Listing 10.13 illustrates this approach.

Listing 10.13. The `Add()` **function.**

```
1:      // Listing 10.13
2:      // Add function
3:
4:      typedef unsigned short   USHORT;
5:      #include <iostream.h>
6:
7:      class Counter
8:      {
9:      public:
10:         Counter();
11:         Counter(USHORT initialValue);
12:         ~Counter(){}
13:         USHORT GetItsVal()const { return itsVal; }
14:         void SetItsVal(USHORT x) {itsVal = x; }
15:         Counter Add(const Counter &);
16:
17:      private:
18:         USHORT itsVal;
19:
20:      };
21:
22:      Counter::Counter(USHORT initialValue):
23:      itsVal(initialValue)
24:      {}
25:
26:      Counter::Counter():
27:      itsVal(0)
28:      {}
29:
30:      Counter Counter::Add(const Counter & rhs)
31:      {
32:          return Counter(itsVal+ rhs.GetItsVal());
33:      }
34:
35:      void main()
36:      {
37:          Counter varOne(2), varTwo(4), varThree;
38:          varThree = varOne.Add(varTwo);
39:          cout << "varOne: " << varOne.GetItsVal()<< endl;
40:          cout << "varTwo: " << varTwo.GetItsVal() << endl;
41:          cout << "varThree: " << varThree.GetItsVal() << endl;
42:
43:      }
```

OUTPUT
```
varOne: 2
varTwo: 4
varThree: 6
```

ANALYSIS The `Add()` function is declared on line 15. It takes a constant `Counter` reference, which is the number to add to the current object. It returns a `Counter` object, which is the result to be assigned to the left side of the assignment statement, as shown on line 38. That is, `varOne` is the object, `varTwo` is the parameter to the `Add()` function, and the result is assigned to `varThree`.

In order to create varThree without having to initialize a value for it, a default constructor is required. The default constructor initializes itsVal to 0, as shown on lines 26 through 28. Because varOne and varTwo need to be initialized to a nonzero value, another constructor is created, as shown on lines 22 through 24. Another solution to this problem is to provide the default value 0 to the constructor declared on line 11.

Overloading *operator+*

The Add() function itself is shown on lines 30 through 33. It works, but its use is unnatural. Overloading the operator+ would make for a more natural use of the Counter class. Listing 10.14 illustrates this.

TYPE **Listing 10.14.** operator+.

```
1:    // Listing 10.14
2:    //Overload operator plus (+)
3:
4:    typedef unsigned short  USHORT;
5:    #include <iostream.h>
6:
7:    class Counter
8:    {
9:    public:
10:       Counter();
11:       Counter(USHORT initialValue);
12:       ~Counter(){}
13:       USHORT GetItsVal()const { return itsVal; }
14:       void SetItsVal(USHORT x) {itsVal = x; }
15:       Counter operator+ (const Counter &);
16:    private:
17:       USHORT itsVal;
18:    };
19:
20:    Counter::Counter(USHORT initialValue):
21:    itsVal(initialValue)
22:    {}
23:
24:    Counter::Counter():
25:    itsVal(0)
26:    {}
27:
28:    Counter Counter::operator+ (const Counter & rhs)
29:    {
30:        return Counter(itsVal + rhs.GetItsVal());
31:    }
32:
33:    void main()
34:    {
```

continues

Listing 10.14. continued

```
35:      Counter varOne(2), varTwo(4), varThree;
36:      varThree = varOne + varTwo;
37:      cout << "varOne: " << varOne.GetItsVal()<< endl;
38:      cout << "varTwo: " << varTwo.GetItsVal() << endl;
39:      cout << "varThree: " << varThree.GetItsVal() << endl;
40:
41:  }
```

```
varOne: 2
varTwo: 4
varThree: 6
```

ANALYSIS   operator+ is declared on line 15 and defined on lines 28 through 31. Compare these with the declaration and definition of the Add() function in the previous listing; they are nearly identical. The syntax of their use, however, is quite different. It is more natural to say

```
varThree = varOne + varTwo;
```

than it is to say this:

```
varThree = varOne.Add(varTwo);
```

Not a big change, but enough to make the program easier to use and understand.

Operator Overloading: Binary Operators

Binary operators are created in a similar manner to unary operators, except that they do take a parameter. The parameter is a constant reference to an object of the same type.

Example 1

```
Counter Counter::operator+ (const Counter & rhs);
```

Example 2

```
Counter Counter::operator-(const Counter & rhs);
```

Issues in Operator Overloading

Overloaded operators can be member functions, as described in this lesson, or they can be nonmember functions. The latter will be described on Day 14, "Special Classes and Functions," when friend functions are covered.

The only operators that must be class members are the assignment (=), subscript([ ]), function call (( )), and indirection (->) operators.

operator[ ] will be discussed on Day 11, "Arrays." Overloading operator-> will be discussed on Day 14, when smart pointers are covered.

Limitations on Operator Overloading

Operators on built-in types (such as int) cannot be overloaded. The precedence order cannot be changed, and the *arity* of the operator—that is, whether it is unary or binary—cannot be changed. You cannot make up new operators, so you cannot declare a double asterisk (**) to be the "power of" operator.

 The *arity* of an operator is the quality that determines whether it is used for unary or binary operations.

What to Overload

Operator overloading is one of the aspects of C++ that is most overused and abused by new programmers. It is tempting to create new and interesting uses for some of the more obscure operators, but these invariably lead to code that is confusing and difficult to read.

Of course, making the + operator *subtract* and the * operator *add* can be fun, but no professional programmer would do that. The greater danger lies in the well-intentioned but idiosyncratic use of an operator—using + to mean *concatenate a series of letters,* or / to mean *split a string.* There is good reason to consider these uses, but there is even better reason to proceed with caution. Remember, the goal of overloading operators is to increase usability and understanding.

Do	Don't

DO use operator overloading when it will clarify the program.

DON'T create counterintuitive operators.

DO return an object of the class from overloaded operators.

operator=

The fourth and final function that is supplied by the compiler, if you don't specify one, is *operator equals* (operator=()). This operator is called whenever you assign to an object, as in the following example:

```
CAT catOne(5,7);
CAT catTwo(3,4);
// ... other code here
catTwo = catOne;
```

Here, catOne is created and initialized with itsAge equal to 5 and itsWeight equal to 7. catTwo is then created and assigned the values 3 and 4.

After awhile, catTwo is assigned the values in catOne. Two issues are raised here: What happens if itsAge is a pointer, and what happens to the original values in catTwo?

Handling member variables that store their values on the free store was discussed earlier during the examination of the copy constructor. The same issues arise here, as illustrated in Figures 10.1 and 10.2.

C++ programmers differentiate between a shallow or member-wise copy on the one hand, and a deep copy on the other. A shallow copy just copies the members, and both objects end up pointing to the same area on the free store. A deep copy allocates the necessary memory. This is illustrated in Figure 10.3.

There is an added wrinkle with the assignment operator, however. The object catTwo already exists and already has memory allocated. That memory must be deleted if there is to be no memory leak. But what happens if you assign catTwo to itself?

```
catTwo = catTwo;
```

No one is likely to do this on purpose, but the program must be able to handle it. More importantly, it is possible for this to happen by accident when references and dereferenced pointers hide the fact that the assignment is to itself.

If you did not handle this problem carefully, catTwo would delete its memory allocation. Then, when it was ready to copy in the memory from the right-hand side of the assignment, it would have a very big problem: the memory would be gone.

To protect against this, your assignment operator must check to see whether the right side of the assignment operator is the object itself. It does this by examining the this pointer. Listing 10.15 shows a class with an assignment operator.

Listing 10.15. An assignment operator.

```
1:      // Listing 10.15
2:      // Copy constructors
3:
4:      #include <iostream.h>
5:
6:      class CAT
7:      {
8:          public:
9:              CAT();                              // default constructor
10:     // copy constructor and destructor elided!
11:             int GetAge() const { return *itsAge; }
12:             int GetWeight() const { return *itsWeight; }
13:             void SetAge(int age) { *itsAge = age; }
14:             CAT operator=(const CAT &);
15:
16:         private:
17:             int *itsAge;
18:             int *itsWeight;
19:     };
20:
21:     CAT::CAT()
22:     {
23:         itsAge = new int;
24:       itsWeight = new int;
25:       *itsAge = 5;
26:       *itsWeight = 9;
27: }
28:
29:
30: CAT CAT::operator=(const CAT & rhs)
31: {
32:    if (this == &rhs)
33:       return *this;
34:    itsAge = new int;
35:    itsWeight = new int;
36:    *itsAge = rhs.GetAge();
37:    *itsWeight = rhs.GetWeight();
38:    return rhs;
39: }
40:
41:     void main()
42:     {
43:         CAT frisky;
44:         cout << "frisky's age: " << frisky.GetAge() << endl;
45:         cout << "Setting frisky to 6...\n";
46:         frisky.SetAge(6);
47:         CAT whiskers;
48:         cout << "whiskers' age: " << whiskers.GetAge() << endl;
49:         cout << "copying frisky to whiskers...\n";
50:         whiskers = frisky;
51:         cout << "whiskers' age: " << whiskers.GetAge() << endl;
52:     }
```

10

```
frisky's age: 5
Setting frisky to 6...
whisker's age: 5
copying frisky to whiskers...
whisker's age: 6
```

ANALYSIS Listing 10.15 brings back the CAT class and leaves out the copy constructor and destructor to save room. On line 14, the assignment operator is declared, and on lines 30 through 38, it is defined.

On line 32, the current object (the CAT being assigned to) is tested to see whether it is the same as the CAT being assigned. This is done by checking whether the address of rhs is the same as the address stored in the this pointer.

This works fine for single inheritance, but if you are using multiple inheritance, as discussed on Day 13, "Multiple Inheritance," this test will fail. An alternative test is to dereference the this pointer and see if the two objects are the same:

```
if (*this == rhs)
```

Of course, the equality operator (==) can be overloaded as well, allowing you to determine for yourself what it means for your objects to be equal.

Conversion Operators

What happens when you try to assign a variable of a built-in type, such as int or unsigned short, to an object of a user-defined class? Listing 10.16 brings back the Counter class, and attempts to assign a variable of type USHORT to a Counter object.

WARNING

> Listing 10.16 will not compile!

TYPE **Listing 10.16. Attempting to assign a counter to a USHORT.**

```
1:      // Listing 10.16
2:      // This code won't compile!
3:
4:      typedef unsigned short  USHORT;
5:      #include <iostream.h>
6:
7:      class Counter
8:      {
9:         public:
10:           Counter();
11:           ~Counter(){}
```

```
12:                USHORT GetItsVal()const { return itsVal; }
13:                void SetItsVal(USHORT x) {itsVal = x; }
14:           private:
15:                USHORT itsVal;
16:
17:           };
18:
19:       Counter::Counter():
20:       itsVal(0)
21:       {}
22:
23:    void main()
24:    {
25:        USHORT theShort = 5;
26:        Counter theCtr = theShort;
27:        cout << "theCtr: " << theCtr.GetItsVal() << endl;
28:    }
```

Compiler error! Unable to convert USHORT to Counter

ANALYSIS The Counter class declared on lines 7 through 17 has only a default constructor. It declares no particular method for turning a USHORT into a Counter object, so line 26 causes a compile error. The compiler cannot figure out (unless you tell it) that given a USHORT, it should assign that value to the member variable itsVal.

Listing 10.17 corrects this by creating a conversion operator—a constructor that takes a USHORT and produces a Counter object.

TYPE **Listing 10.17. Converting USHORT to Counter.**

```
1:       // Listing 10.17
2:       // Constructor as conversion operator
3:
4:       typedef unsigned short   USHORT;
5:       #include <iostream.h>
6:
7:       class Counter
8:       {
9:          public:
10:             Counter();
11:             Counter(USHORT val);
12:             ~Counter(){}
13:             USHORT GetItsVal()const { return itsVal; }
14:             void SetItsVal(USHORT x) {itsVal = x; }
15:          private:
16:             USHORT itsVal;
17:
18:       };
19:
```

continues

Listing 10.17. continued

```
20:        Counter::Counter():
21:        itsVal(0)
22:        {}
23:
24:     Counter::Counter(USHORT val):
25:     itsVal(val)
26:     {}
27:
28:
29:     void main()
30:     {
31:        USHORT theShort = 5;
32:        Counter theCtr = theShort;
33:        cout << "theCtr: " << theCtr.GetItsVal() << endl;
34:     }
```

OUTPUT   theCtr: 5

ANALYSIS   The important change is on line 11, where the constructor is overloaded to take a USHORT, and on lines 24 through 26, where the constructor is implemented. The effect of this constructor is to create a Counter out of a USHORT.

Given this, the compiler is able to call the constructor that takes a USHORT as its argument. What happens, however, if you try to reverse the assignment with the following lines?

```
1:  Counter theCtr(5);
2:  USHORT theShort = theCtr;
3:  cout << "theShort : " << theShort  << endl;
```

Once again, this generates a compile error. Although the compiler now knows how to create a Counter out of a USHORT, it does not know how to reverse the process.

Operator *unsigned short()*

To solve this and similar problems, C++ provides conversion operators that can be added to your class. This enables your class to specify how to do implicit conversions to built-in types. Listing 10.18 illustrates this. One note, however, is this: Conversion operators do *not* specify a return value, even though they do, in effect, return a converted value.

TYPE   **Listing 10.18. Converting from Counter to unsigned short().**

```
1:  // Listing 10.18
2:  // conversion operator
3:
4:  typedef unsigned short  USHORT;
```

10

```
 5:  #include <iostream.h>
 6:
 7:  class Counter
 8:  {
 9:    public:
10:        Counter();
11:        Counter(USHORT val);
12:        ~Counter(){}
13:        USHORT GetItsVal()const { return itsVal; }
14:        void SetItsVal(USHORT x) {itsVal = x; }
15:        operator unsigned short();
16:    private:
17:        USHORT itsVal;
18:
19:  };
20:
21:  Counter::Counter():
22:  itsVal(0)
23:  {}
24:
25: Counter::Counter(USHORT val):
26: itsVal(val)
27: {}
28:
29: Counter::operator unsigned short ()
30: {
31:     return ( USHORT (itsVal) );
32: }
33:
34: void main()
35: {
36:     Counter ctr(5);
37:     USHORT theShort = ctr;
38:     cout << "theShort: " << theShort << endl;
39: }
```

OUTPUT   theShort: 5

ANALYSIS   On line 15, the conversion operator is declared. Note that it has no return value. The implementation of this function is on lines 29 through 32. Line 31 returns the value of itsVal converted to a USHORT.

Now the compiler knows how to turn USHORTS into Counter objects and vice versa, and they can be assigned to one another freely.

Summary

Today you learned how to overload member functions of your classes. You also learned how to supply default values to functions, how to decide when to use default values, and when to overload.

Overloading class constructors enables you to create flexible classes that can be created from other objects. Initialization of objects happens at the initialization stage of construction and is more efficient than assigning values in the body of the constructor.

The copy constructor and operator= are supplied by the compiler if you don't create your own, but they do a member-wise copy of the class. In classes in which member data includes pointers to the free store, these methods must be overridden so that you allocate memory for the target object.

Almost all C++ operators can be overloaded, though you want to be cautious not to create an operator whose use is counterintuitive. You cannot change the arity (binary versus unary) of operators, nor can you invent new operators.

The this pointer refers to the current object and is an invisible parameter to all member functions. The dereferenced this pointer is often returned by overloaded operators.

Conversion operators enable you to create classes that can be used in expressions that expect a different type of object. They are exceptions to the rule that all functions return an explicit value; like constructors and destructors, they have no return type.

Q&A

Q Why would you ever use default values when you can overload a function?

A It is easier to maintain one function than two, and often easier to understand a function with default parameters than to study the bodies of two functions. Furthermore, updating one of the functions and neglecting to update the second is a common source of bugs.

Q Given the problems with overloaded functions, why not always use default values instead?

A Overloaded functions supply capabilities not available with default variables, such as varying the list of parameters by type rather than just by number.

Q When writing a class constructor, how do you decide what to put in the initialization and what to put in the body of the constructor?

A A simple rule of thumb is to do as much as possible in the initialization phase; that is, initialize all member variables there. Some things, such as computations and print statements, must be in the body of the constructor.

Q Can an overloaded function have a default parameter?

A Yes. There is no reason not to combine these powerful features. One or more of the overloaded functions can have their own default values, following the normal rules for default variables in any function.

10

Q Why are some member functions defined within the class declaration and others are not?

A Defining the implementation of a member function within the declaration makes it inline. Generally, this is done only if the function is extremely simple. Note that you can also make a member function inline by using the keyword `inline`, even if the function is declared outside the class declaration.

Quiz

1. When you overload member functions, in what ways must they differ?
2. What is the difference between a declaration and a definition?
3. When is the copy constructor called?
4. When is the destructor called?
5. How does the copy constructor differ from the assignment operator (=)?
6. What is the `this` pointer?
7. How do you differentiate between overloading the prefix increment and the postfix?
8. Can you overload the `operator+` for short integers?
9. Is it legal in C++ to overload `operator++` so that it decrements a value in your class?
10. What return value must a conversion operator have in its declaration?

Exercises

1. Write a `SimpleCircle` class declaration (without the definition) with one member variable: `itsRadius`. Include a default constructor, a destructor, and accessor methods for radius.
2. Using the class you created in exercise 1, write the implementation of the default constructor, initializing `itsRadius` with the value 5.
3. Using the same class, add a second constructor that takes a value as its parameter and assigns that value to `itsRadius`.
4. Create a prefix and postfix `Increment` operator for your `SimpleCircle` class that increments `itsRadius`.
5. Change `SimpleCircle` to store `itsRadius` on the free store, and fix the existing methods.
6. Provide a copy constructor for `SimpleCircle`.

7. Provide an `operator=` for `SimpleCircle`.

8. Write a program that creates two `SimpleCircle` objects. Use the default constructor on one and instantiate the other with the value 9. Call `Increment` on each and then print their values. Finally, assign the second to the first and print the resulting values.

9. **BUG BUSTERS:** What is wrong with this implementation of the assignment operator?

```
SQUARE SQUARE ::operator=(const SQUARE & rhs)
{
      itsSide = new int;
      *itsSide = rhs.GetSide();
      return *this;
}
```

10. **BUG BUSTERS:** What is wrong with this implementation of operator+?

```
VeryShort  VeryShort::operator+ (const VeryShort& rhs)
{
   itsVal += rhs.GetItsVal();
   return *this;
}
```

Day 11

Arrays

In previous lessons, you declared a single `int`, `char`, or other object. You often want to declare a collection of objects, such as 20 `int`s or a litter of `CAT`s. Today you learn

- [ ] What arrays are and how to declare them.
- [ ] What strings are and how to use character arrays to make them.
- [ ] The relationship between arrays and pointers.
- [ ] How to use pointer arithmetic with arrays.

What Is an Array?

An array is a collection of data storage locations, each of which holds the same type of data. Each storage location is called an *element* of the array.

You declare an array by writing the type, followed by the array name and the subscript. The subscript is the number of elements in the array, surrounded by square brackets. For example, the line

```
long LongArray[25];
```

declares an array named LongArray, which contains 25 long integers. When the compiler sees this declaration, it sets aside enough memory to hold all 25 elements. Because each long integer requires four bytes, this declaration sets aside 100 contiguous bytes of memory, as illustrated in Figure 11.1.

Figure 11.1.

Declaring an array.

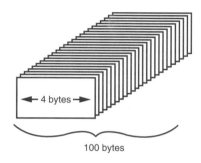

4 bytes

100 bytes

Array Elements

You access each of the array elements by referring to an offset from the array name. Array elements are counted from zero. Therefore, the first array element is arrayName[0]. In the LongArray example, LongArray[0] is the first array element, LongArray[1] the second, and so on.

This can be somewhat confusing. The array SomeArray[3] has three elements. They are SomeArray[0], SomeArray[1], and SomeArray[2]. More generally, SomeArray[n] has *n* elements that are numbered SomeArray[0] through SomeArray[n-1].

Therefore, LongArray[25] is numbered from LongArray[0] through LongArray[24]. Listing 11.1 shows how to declare an array of five integers and fill each with a value.

TYPE | **Listing 11.1. Using an integer array.**

```
1:      //Listing 11.1 - Arrays
2:      #include <iostream.h>
3:
4:      void main()
5:      {
6:         int myArray[5];
7:         for (int i=0; i<5; i++)   // 0-4
8:         {
9:            cout << "Value for myArray[" << i << "]: ";
10:           cin >> myArray[i];
11:        }
12:        for (i = 0; i<5; i++)
13:           cout << i << ": " << myArray[i] << "\n";
14:     }
```

11

OUTPUT
```
Value for myArray[0]:   3
Value for myArray[1]:   6
Value for myArray[2]:   9
Value for myArray[3]:   12
Value for myArray[4]:   15

0: 3
1: 6
2: 9
3: 12
4: 15
```

ANALYSIS Line 6 declares an array called myArray, which holds five integer variables. Line 7 establishes a loop that counts from 0 through 4, which is the proper set of offsets for a five-element array. The user is prompted for a value, and that value is saved at the correct offset into the array.

The first value is saved at myArray[0], the second at myArray[1], and so on. The second for loop prints each value to the screen.

NOTE Arrays count from 0, not from 1. This is the cause of many bugs in programs written by C++ novices. Whenever you use an array, remember that an array with 10 elements counts from ArrayName[0] to ArrayName[9]. There is no ArrayName[10].

11

Writing Past the End of an Array

When you write a value to an element in an array, the compiler computes where to store the value based on the size of each element and the subscript. Suppose that you ask to write over the value at LongArray[5], which is the sixth element. The compiler multiplies the offset (5) by the size of each element—in this case, four bytes. It then moves that many bytes (20) from the beginning of the array and writes the new value at that location.

If you ask to write at LongArray[50], the compiler ignores the fact that there is no such element. It computes how far past the first element it should look (200 bytes) and then writes over whatever is at that location. This can be virtually any data, and writing your new value there might have unpredictable results. If you're lucky, your program will crash immediately. If you're unlucky, you'll get strange results much later in your program, and you'll have a difficult time figuring out what went wrong.

Listing 11.2 shows what happens when you write past the end of an array.

WARNING

> Do not run this program. It might crash your system!

TYPE **Listing 11.2. Writing past the end of an array.**

```
1:      //Listing 11.2
2:      // Demonstrates what happens when you write past the end
3:      // of an array
4:
5:      #include <iostream.h>
6:      void main()
7:      {
8:          // sentinels
9:          long sentinelOne[3];
10:         long TargetArray[25]; // array to fill
11:         long sentinelTwo[3];
12:
13:         for (int i=0; i<3; i++)
14:             sentinelOne[i] = sentinelTwo[i] = 0;
15:
16:         for (i=0; i<25; i++)
17:             TargetArray[i] = 0;
18:
19:         cout << "Test 1: \n";  // test current values (should be 0)
20:         cout << "TargetArray[0]: " << TargetArray[0] << "\n";
21:         cout << "TargetArray[24]: " << TargetArray[24] << "\n\n";
22:
23:         for (i = 0; i<3; i++)
24:         {
25:             cout << "sentinelOne[" << i << "]: " << sentinelOne[i] << "\n";
26:             cout << "sentinelTwo[" << i << "]: " << sentinelTwo[i]<< "\n";
27:         }
28:
29:         cout << "\nAssigning...";
30:         for (i = 0; i<=25; i++)
31:             TargetArray[i] = 20;
32:
33:         cout << "\nTest 2: \n";
34:         cout << "TargetArray[0]: " << TargetArray[0] << "\n";
35:         cout << "TargetArray[24]: " << TargetArray[24] << "\n";
36:         cout << "TargetArray[25]: " << TargetArray[25] << "\n\n";
37:         for (i = 0; i<3; i++)
38:         {
39:             cout << "sentinelOne[" << i << "]: " << sentinelOne[i]<< "\n";
40:             cout << "sentinelTwo[" << i << "]: " << sentinelTwo[i]<< "\n";
41:         }
42:
43:     }
```

11

OUTPUT

```
Test 1:
TargetArray[0]: 0
TargetArray[24]: 0

SentinelOne[0]: 0
SentinelTwo[0]: 0
SentinelOne[1]: 0
SentinelTwo[1]: 0
SentinelOne[2]: 0
SentinelTwo[2]: 0

Assigning...
Test 2:
TargetArray[0]:   20
TargetArray[24]:  20
TargetArray[25]:  20

SentinelOne[0]: 0
SentinelTwo[0]: 20
SentinelOne[1]: 0
SentinelTwo[1]: 0
SentinelOne[2]: 0
SentinelTwo[2]: 0
```

ANALYSIS Lines 9 and 11 declare two arrays of three integers that act as sentinels around TargetArray. These sentinel arrays are initialized with the value 0. If memory is written to beyond the end of TargetArray, the sentinels are likely to be changed. Some compilers count down in memory; others count up. For this reason, the sentinels are placed on both sides of TargetArray.

Lines 19 through 27 confirm the sentinel values in Test 1. On line 31, TargetArray's members are all initialized to the value 20, but the counter counts to TargetArray offset 25, which doesn't exist in TargetArray.

Lines 34 through 36 print TargetArray's values in Test 2. Note that TargetArray[25] is perfectly happy to print the value 20. However, when SentinelOne and SentinelTwo are printed, SentinelTwo[0] reveals that its value has changed. This is because the memory that is 25 elements after TargetArray[0] is the same memory that is at SentinelTwo[0]. When the nonexistent TargetArray[0] is accessed, what is actually accessed is SentinelTwo[0].

This nasty bug can be very hard to find because SentinelTwo[0]'s value is changed in a part of the code that is not writing to SentinelTwo at all.

This code uses "magic numbers," such as 3 for the size of the sentinel arrays and 25 for the size of TargetArray. It is safer to use constants so that when one changes, they all reflect the change.

11

Fence Post Errors

It is so common to write to one number past the end of an array that this bug has its own name. It is called a *fence post error*. This refers to the problem in counting how many fence posts you need for a 10-foot fence if you need one post for every foot. Most people answer 10, but of course you need 11. Figure 11.2 makes this clear.

Figure 11.2.

Fence post errors.

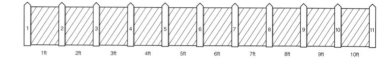

This sort of "off by one" counting can be the bane of any programmer's life. Over time, however, you'll get used to the idea that a 25-element array counts only to element 24, and that everything counts from zero. (Programmers are often confused about why office buildings don't have a floor zero. Indeed, some have been known to push the fourth elevator button when they want to get to the fifth floor.)

NOTE

> Some programmers refer to `ArrayName[0]` as the "zeroth" element. Getting into this habit is a big mistake. If `ArrayName[0]` is the zeroth element, what is `ArrayName[1]`? The first element? If so, when you see `ArrayName[24]`, will you realize that it is not the twenty-fourth element, but rather the twenty-fifth? It is far better to say that `ArrayName[0]` is at offset zero and is the first element.

Initializing Arrays

You can initialize a simple array of built-in types, such as integers and characters, when you first declare the array. After the array name, you put an equal sign (=) and a list of comma-separated values enclosed in braces. For example,

```
int IntegerArray[5] = { 10, 20, 30, 40, 50 };
```

declares `IntegerArray` to be an array of five integers. It assigns `IntegerArray[0]` the value `10`, `IntegerArray[1]` the value `20`, and so on.

If you omit the size of the array, an array just big enough to hold the initialization is created. Therefore, if you write

```
int IntegerArray[] = { 10, 20, 30, 40, 50 };
```

you create exactly the same array as you did in the previous example.

If you need to know the size of the array, you can ask the compiler to compute it for you. For example,

```
const USHORT IntegerArrayLength = sizeof(IntegerArray)/sizeof(IntegerArray[0]);
```

sets the constant USHORT variable IntegerArrayLength to the result obtained from dividing the size of the entire array by the size of each individual entry in the array. That quotient is the number of members in the array.

You cannot initialize more elements than you've declared for the array. Therefore,

```
int IntegerArray[5] = { 10, 20, 30, 40, 50, 60};
```

generates a compiler error because you've declared a five-member array and initialized six values. It is legal, however, to write

```
int IntegerArray[5] = { 10, 20};
```

Although uninitialized array members have no guaranteed value, actually, aggregates will be initialized to 0. If you don't initialize an array member, its value will be set to 0.

Do	Don't

DO let the compiler set the size of initialized arrays.

DON'T write past the end of the array.

DO give arrays meaningful names, as you would with any variable.

DO remember that the first member of the array is at offset zero.

Declaring Arrays

An array can have any legal variable name, but it cannot have the same name as another variable or array within its scope. Therefore, you cannot have an array named myCats[5] and a variable named myCats at the same time.

You can dimension the array size with a const or with an enumeration. Listing 11.3 illustrates this.

TYPE   **Listing 11.3. Using consts and enums in arrays.**

```
1:      // Listing 11.3
2:      // Dimensioning arrays with consts and enumerations
3:
4:      #include <iostream.h>
5:      void main()
6:      {
7:          enum WeekDays { Sun, Mon, Tue, Wed, Thu, Fri, Sat, DaysInWeek };
8:
9:          int ArrayWeek[DaysInWeek] = { 10, 20, 30, 40, 50, 60, 70 };
10:
11:         cout << "The value at Tuesday is: " << ArrayWeek[Tue];
12:     }
```

OUTPUT   The value at Tuesday is: 30

ANALYSIS   Line 7 creates an enumeration called WeekDays. It has eight members. Sunday is automatically initialized to 0, and DaysInWeek is equal to 7.

Line 11 uses the enumerated constant Tue as an offset into the array. Because Tue evaluates to 2, the third element of the array, DaysInWeek[2], is returned and printed on line 11.

Arrays

SYNTAX

To declare an array, write the type of object stored, followed by the name of the array and a subscript with the number of objects to be held in the array.

Example 1

```
int MyIntegerArray[90];
```

Example 2

```
long * ArrayOfPointersToLongs[100];
```

To access members of the array, use the subscript operator.

Example 1

```
int theNinethInteger = MyIntegerArray[8];
```

Example 2

```
long * pLong = ArrayOfPointersToLongs[8]
```

 Arrays count from zero. An array of *n* items is numbered from 0 to *n*-1.

11

Arrays of Objects

Any object, whether built-in or user-defined, can be stored in an array. When you declare the array, you tell the compiler the type of object to store and the number of objects for which to allocate room. The compiler knows how much room is needed for each object based on the class declaration. The class must have a default constructor that takes no arguments so that the objects can be created when the array is defined.

Accessing member data in an array of objects is a two-step process. You identify the member of the array by using the index operator ([ ]), and then you add the member operator (.) to access the particular member variable. Listing 11.4 demonstrates how you would create an array of five CATs.

TYPE **Listing 11.4. Creating an array of objects.**

```
1:     // Listing 11.4 - An array of objects
2:
3:     #include <iostream.h>
4:
5:     class CAT
6:     {
7:        public:
8:            CAT() { itsAge = 1; itsWeight=5; }        // default constructor
9:            ~CAT() {}                                 // destructor
10:           int GetAge() const { return itsAge; }
11:           int GetWeight() const { return itsWeight; }
12:           void SetAge(int age) { itsAge = age; }
13:
14:        private:
15:            int itsAge;
16:            int itsWeight;
17:     };
18:
19:     void main()
20:     {
21:        CAT Litter[5];
22:        int i;
23:        for (i = 0; i < 5; i++)
24:            Litter[i].SetAge(2*i +1);
25:
26:        for (i = 0; i < 5; i++)
27:            cout << "Cat #" << i+1<< ": " << Litter[i].GetAge() << endl;
28:     }
```

OUTPUT
```
cat #1: 1
cat #2: 3
cat #3: 5
cat #4: 7
cat #5: 9
```

ANALYSIS Lines 5 through 17 declare the CAT class. The CAT class must have a default constructor so that CAT objects can be created in an array. Remember that if you create any other constructor, the compiler-supplied default constructor is not created; you must create your own.

The first for loop (lines 23 and 24) sets the age of each of the five CATs in the array. The second for loop (lines 26 and 27) accesses each member of the array and calls GetAge().

Each individual CAT's GetAge() method is called by accessing the member in the array, Litter[i], followed by the dot operator (.) and the member function.

Multidimensional Arrays

It is possible to have arrays of more than one dimension. Each dimension is represented as a subscript in the array. Therefore, a two-dimensional array has two subscripts; a three-dimensional array has three subscripts; and so on. Arrays can have any number of dimensions, although it is likely that most of the arrays you create will be of one or two dimensions.

A good example of a two-dimensional array is a chess board. One dimension represents the eight rows; the other dimension represents the eight columns. Figure 11.3 illustrates this idea.

Figure 11.3.

A chess board and a two-dimensional array.

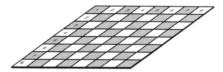

Suppose that you have a class named SQUARE. The declaration of an array named Board that represents it would be

```
SQUARE Board[8][8];
```

You could also represent the same data with a one-dimensional, 64-square array, as in the following example:

```
SQUARE Board[64];
```

This doesn't correspond as closely to the real-world object as the two-dimensional array. When the game begins, the king is located in the fourth position in the first row. Counting from zero, that position corresponds to

```
Board[0][3];
```

assuming that the first subscript corresponds to row, and the second to column. The layout of positions for the entire board is illustrated in Figure 11.3.

Initializing Multidimensional Arrays

You can also initialize multidimensional arrays. You assign the list of values to array elements in order, with the last array subscript changing while each of the former hold steady. Therefore, if you have the following array, the first three elements go into theArray[0]; the next three into theArray[1]; and so on:

```
int theArray[5][3];
```

You initialize this array by writing

```
int theArray[5][3] = { 1,2,3,4,5,6,7,8,9,10,11,12,13,14,15 };
```

For the sake of clarity, you could group the initializations with braces, as in the following example:

```
int theArray[5][3] = {  {1,2,3},
{4,5,6},
{7,8,9},
{10,11,12},
{13,14,15} };
```

The compiler ignores the inner braces, which make it easier to understand how the numbers are distributed.

Each value must be separated by a comma, without regard to the braces. The entire initialization set must be within braces, and it must end with a semicolon.

Listing 11.5 creates a two-dimensional array. The first dimension is the set of numbers from 0 to 5. The second dimension consists of the double of each value in the first dimension.

TYPE | **Listing 11.5. Creating a multidimensional array.**

```
1:      #include <iostream.h>
2:      void main()
3:      {
```

continues

Listing 11.5. continued

```
4:          int SomeArray[5][2] = { {0,0}, {1,2}, {2,4}, {3,6}, {4,8}};
5:          for (int i = 0; i<5; i++)
6:             for (int j=0; j<2; j++)
7:             {
8:                cout << "SomeArray[" << i << "][" << j << "]: ";
9:                cout << SomeArray[i][j]<< endl;
10:            }
11:
12:     }
```

OUTPUT

```
SomeArray[0][0]: 0
SomeArray[0][1]: 0
SomeArray[1][0]: 1
SomeArray[1][1]: 2
SomeArray[2][0]: 2
SomeArray[2][1]: 4
SomeArray[3][0]: 3
SomeArray[3][1]: 6
SomeArray[4][0]: 4
SomeArray[4][1]: 8
```

ANALYSIS Line 4 declares SomeArray to be a two-dimensional array. The first dimension consists of five integers; the second dimension consists of two integers. This creates a 5×2 grid, as Figure 11.4 shows.

Figure 11.4.

A 5×2 array.

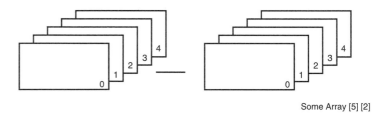

Some Array [5] [2]

The values are initialized in pairs, although they could be computed as well. Lines 5 and 6 create a nested for loop. The outer for loop ticks through each member of the first dimension. For every member in that dimension, the inner for loop ticks through each member of the second dimension. This is consistent with the printout. SomeArray[0][0] is followed by SomeArray[0][1]. The first dimension is incremented only after the second dimension is incremented by 1. Then the second dimension starts over.

A Word About Memory

When you declare an array, you tell the compiler exactly how many objects you expect to store in it. The compiler sets aside memory for all the objects, even if you never use it. This isn't a problem with arrays when you have a good idea of how many objects you'll need. For example, a chess board has 64 squares, and CATs have between one and 10 kittens. When you have no idea how many objects you'll need, however, you must use more advanced data structures.

This book looks at arrays of pointers, arrays built on the free store, and various other collections. Other more advanced data structures that solve large data storage problems are beyond the scope of this book. Two of the great things about programming are that you can always find more things to learn and more books to help you learn them.

Arrays of Pointers

The arrays discussed so far store all their members on the stack. Usually, stack memory is severely limited, whereas free store memory is far larger. It is possible to declare each object on the free store and then to store only a pointer to the object in the array. This dramatically reduces the amount of stack memory used. Listing 11.6 rewrites the array from Listing 11.4, but it stores all the objects on the free store. As an indication of the greater memory that this enables, the array is expanded from 5 to 500, and the name is changed from Litter to Family.

TYPE | **Listing 11.6. Storing an array on the free store.**

```
1:    // Listing 11.6 - An array of pointers to objects
2:
3:    #include <iostream.h>
4:
5:    class CAT
6:    {
7:        public:
8:            CAT() { itsAge = 1; itsWeight=5; }          // default constructor
9:            ~CAT() {}                                    // destructor
10:           int GetAge() const { return itsAge; }
11:           int GetWeight() const { return itsWeight; }
12:           void SetAge(int age) { itsAge = age; }
13:
14:        private:
15:           int itsAge;
16:           int itsWeight;
17:    };
18:
19:    void main()
20:    {
21:        CAT * Family[500];
22:        int i;
23:        CAT * pCat;
24:        for (i = 0; i < 500; i++)
25:        {
```

continues

Listing 11.6. continued

```
26:             pCat = new CAT;
27:             pCat->SetAge(2*i +1);
28:             Family[i] = pCat;
29:         }
30:
31:        for (i = 0; i < 500; i++)
32:            cout << "Cat #" << i+1 << ": " << Family[i]->GetAge() << endl;
33:    }
```

```
Cat #1: 1
Cat #2: 3
Cat #3: 5
...
Cat #499: 997
Cat #500: 999
```

ANALYSIS The CAT object declared on lines 5 through 17 is identical to the CAT object declared in Listing 11.4. This time, however, the array declared on line 21 is named Family, and it is declared to hold 500 pointers to CAT objects.

In the initial loop (lines 24 through 29), 500 new CAT objects are created on the free store, and each one has its age set to twice the index plus one. Therefore, the first CAT is set to 1, the second CAT to 3, the third CAT to 5, and so on. Finally, the pointer is added to the array.

Because the array has been declared to hold pointers, the pointer—rather than the dereferenced value in the pointer—is added to the array.

The second loop (lines 31 and 32) prints each of the values. The pointer is accessed by using the index, Family[i]. That address is then used to access the GetAge() method.

In this example, the array Family and all its pointers are stored on the stack, but the 500 CATs that are created are stored on the free store.

Declaring Arrays on the Free Store

It is possible to put the entire array on the free store, also known as the heap. You do this by calling new and using the subscript operator. The result is a pointer to an area on the free store that holds the array. For example,

```
CAT *Family = new CAT[500];
```

declares Family to be a pointer to the first in an array of 500 CATs. In other words, Family points to (or has the address of) Family[0].

The advantage of using Family in this way is that you can use pointer arithmetic to access each member of Family. For example, you can write the following:

```
CAT *Family = new CAT[500];
CAT *pCat = Family;              //pCat points to Family[0]
pCat->SetAge(10);               // set Family[0] to 10
pCat++;                         // advance to Family[1]
pCat->SetAge(20);               // set Family[1] to 20
```

This declares a new array of 500 CATs and a pointer to point to the start of the array. Using that pointer, the first CAT's SetAge() function is incremented to point to the next CAT, and the second CAT's SetAge() method is then called.

A Pointer to an Array Versus an Array of Pointers

Examine these three declarations:

```
1:   CAT    FamilyOne[500]
2:   CAT *  FamilyTwo[500];
3:   CAT *  FamilyThree = new CAT[500];
```

FamilyOne is an array of 500 CATs. FamilyTwo is an array of 500 pointers to CATs. FamilyThree is a pointer to an array of 500 CATs.

The differences among these three code lines dramatically affect how these arrays operate. What is perhaps even more surprising is that FamilyThree is a variant of FamilyOne but is very different from FamilyTwo.

This raises the thorny issue of how pointers relate to arrays. In the third case, FamilyThree is a pointer to an array. That is, the address in FamilyThree is the address of the first item in that array. This is exactly the case for FamilyOne.

Pointers and Array Names

In C++ an array name is a constant pointer to the first element of the array. Therefore, in the declaration

```
CAT Family[50];
```

Family is a pointer to &Family[0], which is the address of the first element of the array Family.

It is legal to use array names as constant pointers, and vice versa. Therefore, Family + 4 is a legitimate way of accessing the data at Family[4].

The compiler does all the arithmetic when you add to, increment, and decrement pointers. The address accessed when you write Family + 4 isn't four bytes past the address of Family— it is four objects past the address of Family. If each object is four bytes long, Family + 4 is 16 bytes. If each object is a CAT that has four long member variables of four bytes each and two short member variables of two bytes each, each CAT is 20 bytes, and Family + 4 is 80 bytes past the start of the array.

Listing 11.7 illustrates declaring and using an array on the free store.

TYPE   **Listing 11.7. Creating an array by using new.**

```
1:      // Listing 11.7 - An array on the free store
2:
3:      #include <iostream.h>
4:
5:      class CAT
6:      {
7:         public:
8:            CAT() { itsAge = 1; itsWeight=5; }       // default constructor
9:            ~CAT();                                   // destructor
10:           int GetAge() const { return itsAge; }
11:           int GetWeight() const { return itsWeight; }
12:           void SetAge(int age) { itsAge = age; }
13:
14:        private:
15:           int itsAge;
16:           int itsWeight;
17:     };
18:
19:     CAT :: ~CAT()
20:     {
21:        // cout << "Destructor called!\n";
22:     }
23:
24:     void main()
25:     {
26:        CAT * Family = new CAT[500];
27:        int i;
28:        CAT * pCat;
29:        for (i = 0; i < 500; i++)
30:        {
31:           pCat = new CAT;
32:           pCat->SetAge(2*i +1);
33:           Family[i] = *pCat;
34:           delete pCat;
35:        }
36:
37:        for (i = 0; i < 500; i++)
38:           cout << "Cat #" << i+1 << ": " << Family[i].GetAge() << endl;
39:
40:        delete [] Family;
41:
42:     }
```

OUTPUT
```
Cat #1: 1
Cat #2: 3
Cat #3: 5
```

11

```
...
Cat #499: 997
Cat #500: 999
```

 ANALYSIS Line 26 declares the array `Family`, which holds 500 `CAT` objects. The entire array is created on the free store with the call to `new CAT[500]`.

Each `CAT` object added to the array also is created on the free store (line 31). Note, however, that the pointer isn't added to the array this time; the object itself is. This array isn't an array of pointers to `CAT`s. It is an array of `CAT`s.

Deleting Arrays on the Free Store

`Family` is a pointer—a pointer to the array on the free store. When, on line 33, the pointer `pCat` is dereferenced, the `CAT` object itself is stored in the array. (Why not? The array is on the free store.) But `pCat` is used again in the next iteration of the loop. Isn't there a danger that there will now be no pointer to that `CAT` object and a memory leak will be created?

This would be a big problem, except that deleting `Family` returns all the memory set aside for the array. The compiler is smart enough to destroy each object in the array and to return its memory to the free store.

To see this, change the size of the array from 500 to 10 on lines 26, 29, and 36. Then uncomment the `cout` statement on line 21. When line 39 is reached and the array is destroyed, each `CAT` object destructor is called.

When you create an item on the heap by using `new`, you always delete that item and free its memory with `delete`. Similarly, when you create an array by using `new <class>[size]`, you delete that array and free all its memory with `delete[]`. The brackets signal the compiler that this array is being deleted.

If you use only the `delete` keyword without the brackets, it means that only the pointer that identifies the array is deleted, and not the contents of the array! You can prove this to yourself by removing the brackets on line 39. If you edited line 21 so that the destructor prints, you should now see only one `CAT` object destroyed (the one at `Family[0]`). Congratulations! You just created a memory leak.

Do	Don't

DO remember that an array of [n] items is numbered from zero through n-1.

DON'T write or read past the end of an array.

11

> **DON'T** confuse an array of pointers with a pointer to an array.
>
> **DO** use array indexing with pointers that point to arrays.

char Arrays

A string is a series of characters. The only strings you've seen until now have been unnamed string constants used in cout statements, such as the following:

```
cout << "hello world.\n";
```

In C++ a string is an array of chars ending with a NULL character. You can declare and initialize a string just as you would any other array, as in the following example:

```
char Greeting[] = { 'H', 'e', 'l', 'l', 'o', ' ', 'W','o','r','l','d', '\0' };
```

 The last character, '\0', is the same as the value 0 in a char variable, which many C++ functions recognize as the terminator for a string. This special char value is often referred to as the *null character.*

Although the character-by-character approach works, it is difficult to type and permits too many opportunities for error. C++ enables you to use a shorthand form of the previous line of code. It is

```
char Greeting[] = "Hello World";
```

You should note two things about this syntax:

☐ Instead of single-quoted characters separated by commas and surrounded by braces, you have a double-quoted string, no commas, and no braces.

☐ You don't need to add the null character because the compiler adds it for you.

The string Hello World is 12 bytes. Hello is five bytes, the space one, World five, and the null character one.

You can also create uninitialized character arrays. As with all arrays, it is important to ensure that you don't put more into the buffer than there is room for.

Listing 11.8 demonstrates the use of an uninitialized buffer.

TYPE   **Listing 11.8. Filling an array.**

```
1:    //Listing 11.8 char array buffers
2:
```

11

```
3:      #include <iostream.h>
4:
5:      void main()
6:      {
7:         char buffer[80];
8:         cout << "Enter the string: ";
9:         cin >> buffer;
10:        cout << "Here's the buffer:  " << buffer << endl;
11:     }
```

OUTPUT
```
Enter the string: Hello World
Here's the buffer: Hello
```

ANALYSIS On line 7, a buffer is declared to hold 80 characters. This is large enough to hold a 79-character string and a terminating null character.

On line 8, the user is prompted to enter a string, which is entered into the buffer on line 9. It is the syntax of cin to write a terminating null to the buffer after it writes the string.

There are two problems with the program in Listing 11.8. First, if the user enters more than 79 characters, cin writes past the end of the buffer. Second, if the user enters a space, cin thinks that it is the end of the string, and it stops writing to the buffer.

To solve these problems, you must call a special method on cin: get(). cin.get() takes three parameters:

☐ The buffer to fill

☐ The maximum number of characters to get

☐ The delimiter that terminates input

The default delimiter is newline. Listing 11.9 illustrates its use.

TYPE **Listing 11.9. Filling an array.**

```
1:      //Listing 11.9 using cin.get()
2:
3:      #include <iostream.h>
4:
5:      void main()
6:      {
7:         char buffer[80];
8:         cout << "Enter the string: ";
9:         cin.get(buffer, 79);        // get up to 79 or newline
10:        cout << "Here's the buffer:  " << buffer << endl;
11:     }
```

OUTPUT
```
Enter the string: Hello World
Here's the buffer: Hello World
```

ANALYSIS Line 9 calls the method get() of cin. The buffer declared on line 7 is passed in as the first argument. The second argument is the maximum number of characters to get. In this case, it must be 79 to allow for the terminating null character. There is no need to provide a terminating character because the default value of newline is sufficient.

cin and all its variations are covered on Day 16, "Streams," when streams are discussed in depth.

strcpy() and *strncpy()*

C++ inherits from C a library of functions for dealing with strings. Among the many functions provided are two for copying one string into another: strcpy() and strncpy(). strcpy() copies the entire contents of one string into a designated buffer. Listing 11.10 demonstrates its use.

TYPE **Listing 11.10. Using** strcpy().

```
1:   #include <iostream.h>
2:   #include <string.h>
3:   void main()
4:   {
5:       char String1[] = "No man is an island";
6:       char String2[80];
7:
8:       strcpy(String2,String1);
9:
10:      cout << "String1: " << String1 << endl;
11:      cout << "String2: " << String2 << endl;
12:  }
```

OUTPUT
```
String1: No man is an island
String2: No man is an island
```

ANALYSIS The header file string.h is included on line 2. This file contains the prototype of the strcpy() function. strcpy() takes two character arrays—a destination followed by a source. If the source is larger than the destination, strcpy() overwrites past the end of the buffer.

To protect against this, the standard library also includes strncpy(). This variation takes a maximum number of characters to copy. strncpy() copies up to the first null character or the maximum number of characters specified into the destination buffer.

Listing 11.11 illustrates the use of strncpy().

TYPE **Listing 11.11. Using strncpy().**

```
1:    #include <iostream.h>
2:    #include <string.h>
3:    void main()
4:    {
5:        const int MaxLength = 80;
6:        char String1[] = "No man is an island";
7:        char String2[MaxLength+1];
8:
9:
10:       strncpy(String2,String1,MaxLength);
11:
12:       cout << "String1: " << String1 << endl;
13:       cout << "String2: " << String2 << endl;
14:   }
```

OUTPUT
```
String1: No man is an island
String2: No man is an island
```

ANALYSIS On line 10, the call to strcpy() has been changed to a call to strncpy(), which takes a third parameter: the maximum number of characters to copy. The buffer String2 is declared to take MaxLength+1 characters. The extra character is for the null, which both strcpy() and strncpy() automatically add to the end of the string.

String Classes

Most C++ compilers come with a class library that includes a large set of classes for data manipulation. A standard component of a class library is a String class.

C++ inherited the null-terminated string and the library of functions that includes strcpy() from C, but these functions aren't integrated into an object-oriented framework. A String class provides an encapsulated set of data and functions for manipulating that data, as well as accessor functions so that the data itself is hidden from the clients of the String class.

If your compiler doesn't already provide a String class—and perhaps even if it does—you might want to write your own. The remainder of this lesson discusses the design and partial implementation of String classes.

At a minimum, a String class should overcome the basic limitations of character arrays. Like all arrays, character arrays are static. You define how large they are. They always take up that much room in memory even if you don't need it all. Writing past the end of the array is disastrous.

A good String class allocates only as much memory as it needs, and always enough to hold whatever it is given. If it can't allocate enough memory, it should fail gracefully.

Listing 11.12 provides a first approximation of a String class.

TYPE   **Listing 11.12. Using a String class.**

```
1:     //Listing 11.12
2:
3:     #include <iostream.h>
4:     #include <string.h>
5:
6:     // Rudimentary string class
7:     class String
8:     {
9:         public:
10:            // constructors
11:            String();
12:            String(const char *const);
13:            String(const String &);
14:            ~String();
15:
16:            // overloaded operators
17:            char & operator[](unsigned short offset);
18:            char operator[](unsigned short offset) const;
19:            String operator+(const String&);
20:            void operator+=(const String&);
21:            String & operator= (const String &);
22:
23:            // General accessors
24:            unsigned short GetLen()const { return itsLen; }
25:            const char * GetString() const { return itsString; }
26:
27:         private:
28:            String (unsigned short);          // private constructor
29:            char * itsString;
30:            unsigned short itsLen;
31:     };
32:
33:     // default constructor creates string of 0 bytes
34:     String::String()
35:     {
36:        itsString = new char[1];
37:        itsString[0] = '\0';
38:        itsLen=0;
39:     }
40:
41:     // private (helper) constructor, used only by
42:     // class methods for creating a new string of
43:     // required size. Null filled.
44:     String::String(unsigned short len)
45:     {
46:        itsString = new char[len+1];
47:        for (unsigned short i = 0; i<=len; i++)
```

```
48:         itsString[i] = '\0';
49:      itsLen=len;
50:    }
51:
52:    // Converts a character array to a String
53:    String::String(const char * const cString)
54:    {
55:       itsLen = strlen(cString);
56:       itsString = new char[itsLen+1];
57:       for (unsigned short i = 0; i<itsLen; i++)
58:           itsString[i] = cString[i];
59:       itsString[itsLen]='\0';
60:    }
61:
62:    // copy constructor
63:    String::String (const String & rhs)
64:    {
65:       itsLen=rhs.GetLen();
66:       itsString = new char[itsLen+1];
67:       for (unsigned short i = 0; i<itsLen;i++)
68:           itsString[i] = rhs[i];
69:       itsString[itsLen] = '\0';
70:    }
71:
72:    // destructor, frees allocated memory
73:    String::~String ()
74:    {
75:       delete [] itsString;
76:       itsLen = 0;
77:    }
78:
79:    // operator equals, frees existing memory
80:    // then copies string and size
81:    String& String::operator=(const String & rhs)
82:    {
83:       if (this == &rhs)
84:           return *this;
85:       delete [] itsString;
86:       itsLen=rhs.GetLen();
87:       itsString = new char[itsLen+1];
88:       for (unsigned short i = 0; i<itsLen;i++)
89:           itsString[i] = rhs[i];
90:       itsString[itsLen] = '\0';
91:       return *this;
92:    }
93:
94:    //nonconstant offset operator, returns
95:    // reference to character so it can be
96:    // changed!
97:    char & String::operator[](unsigned short offset)
98:    {
99:       if (offset > itsLen)
100:           return itsString[itsLen-1];
101:       else
102:           return itsString[offset];
```

continues

Listing 11.12. continued

```
103:    }
104:
105:    // constant offset operator for use
106:    // on const objects (see copy constructor!)
107:    char String::operator[](unsigned short offset) const
108:    {
109:        if (offset > itsLen)
110:            return itsString[itsLen-1];
111:        else
112:            return itsString[offset];
113:    }
114:
115:    // creates a new string by adding current
116:    // string to rhs
117:    String String::operator+(const String& rhs)
118:    {
119:        unsigned short  totalLen = itsLen + rhs.GetLen();
120:        String temp(totalLen);
121:        for (unsigned short i = 0; i<itsLen; i++)
122:            temp[i] = itsString[i];
123:        for (unsigned short j = 0; j<rhs.GetLen(); j++, i++)
124:            temp[i] = rhs[j];
125:        temp[totalLen]='\0';
126:        return temp;
127:    }
128:
129:    // changes current string, returns nothing
130:    void String::operator+=(const String& rhs)
131:    {
132:        unsigned short rhsLen = rhs.GetLen();
133:        unsigned short totalLen = itsLen + rhsLen;
134:        String  temp(totalLen);
135:        for (unsigned short i = 0; i<itsLen; i++)
136:            temp[i] = itsString[i];
137:        for (unsigned short j = 0; j<rhs.GetLen(); j++, i++)
138:            temp[i] = rhs[i-itsLen];
139:        temp[totalLen]='\0';
140:        *this = temp;
141:    }
142:
143:    void main()
144:    {
145:        String s1("initial test");
146:        cout << "S1:\t" << s1.GetString() << endl;
147:
148:        char * temp = "Hello World";
149:        s1 = temp;
150:        cout << "S1:\t" << s1.GetString() << endl;
151:
152:        char tempTwo[20];
153:        strcpy(tempTwo,"; nice to be here!");
154:        s1 += tempTwo;
155:        cout << "tempTwo:\t" << tempTwo << endl;
156:        cout << "S1:\t" << s1.GetString() << endl;
```

11

```
157:
158:        cout << "S1[4]:\t" << s1[4] << endl;
159:        s1[4]='x';
160:        cout << "S1:\t" << s1.GetString() << endl;
161:
162:        cout << "S1[999]:\t" << s1[999] << endl;
163:
164:        String s2(" Another string");
165:        String s3;
166:        s3 = s1+s2;
167:        cout << "S3:\t" << s3.GetString() << endl;
168:
169:        String s4;
170:        s4 = "Why does this work?";
171:        cout << "S4:\t" << s4.GetString() << endl;
172:    }
```

OUTPUT

```
S1:         initial test
S1:         Hello world
TempTwo;    ;nice to be here!
S1:         Hello world; nice to be here!
S1[4]:      o
S1:         Hello World; nice to be here!
S1[999]     !
S3:         Hello World; nice to be here! Another string
S4:         Why does this work?
```

ANALYSIS   Lines 7 through 31 are the declaration of a simple String class. Lines 11 through 13 contain three constructors: the default constructor, the copy constructor, and a constructor that takes an existing null-terminated (C-style) string.

This String class overloads the offset operator ([ ]), operator plus (+), and operator plus-equals (+=). The offset operator is overloaded twice—once as a constant function returning a char and again as a non-constant function returning a reference to a char.

The non-constant version is used in statements such as

```
SomeString[4]='\x';
```

as seen on line 159. This enables direct access to each of the characters in the string. A reference to the character is returned so that the calling function can manipulate it.

The constant version is used when a constant String object is being accessed, such as in the implementation of the copy constructor (line 63). Note that rhs[i] is accessed, yet rhs is declared as a const String &. It isn't legal to access this object by using a non-constant member function. Therefore, the reference operator must be overloaded with a constant accessor.

If the object being returned is large, you might want to declare the return value to be a constant reference. However, because a char is only one byte, there would be no point in doing that.

The default constructor is implemented on lines 33 through 39. It creates a string whose length is 0. It is the convention of this String class to report its length, not counting the terminating null. This default string contains only a terminating null.

The copy constructor is implemented on lines 63 through 70. It sets the new string's length to that of the existing string—plus one for the terminating null. It copies each character from the existing string to the new string, and it null-terminates the new string.

Lines 52 through 60 implement the constructor that takes an existing C-style string. This constructor is similar to the copy constructor. The length of the existing string is established by a call to the standard String library function strlen().

On line 28, another constructor, String(unsigned short), is declared to be a *private* member function. It is the intent of the designer of this class that no client class ever create a String of arbitrary length. This constructor exists only to help in the internal creation of Strings as required by some special functions. This requirement will be discussed in depth when operator+= is described later in this lesson.

The String(unsigned short) constructor fills every member of its array with the null character. Therefore, the for loop checks for i<=len rather than i<len.

The destructor, implemented on lines 73 through 77, deletes the character string maintained by the class. Be sure to include the brackets in the call to the delete operator, so that every member of the array is deleted, instead of only the first.

The assignment operator first checks whether the right-hand side of the assignment is the same as the left-hand side. If it isn't, the current string is deleted, and the new string is created and copied into place. A reference is returned to facilitate assignments, as in the following line:

```
String1 = String2 = String3;
```

The offset operator is overloaded twice. Rudimentary bounds checking is performed both times. If the user attempts to access a character at a location beyond the end of the array, the last character—that is, len-1—is returned.

Lines 117 through 127 implement operator plus as a concatenation operator. It is convenient to be able to write

```
String3 = String1 + String2;
```

and have String3 be the concatenation of the other two strings. To accomplish this, the operator plus function computes the combined length of the two strings and creates a temporary string temp. This invokes the private constructor, which takes an integer, and creates a string filled with nulls. The nulls are then replaced by the contents of the two strings. The left-hand side string (*this) is copied first, followed by the right-hand side string (rhs).

The first for loop counts through the string on the left-hand side and adds each character to the new string. The second for loop counts through the right-hand side. Note that i continues to count the place for the new string, even as j counts into the rhs string.

Operator plus returns the temp string by value, which is assigned to the string on the left-hand side of the assignment (string1). Operator += operates on the existing string—that is, the left-hand side of the statement String1 += String2. It works just like operator plus, except that the temp value is assigned to the current string (*this = temp) on line 140.

The main() function (lines 143 through 172) acts as a test driver program for this class. Line 145 creates a String object by using the constructor that takes a null-terminated C-style string. Line 146 prints its contents by using the accessor function GetString(). Line 148 creates another C-style string. Line 149 tests the assignment operator, and line 150 prints the results.

Line 152 creates a third C-style string, tempTwo. Line 153 invokes strcpy to fill the buffer with the characters ; nice to be here! Line 154 invokes operator += and concatenates tmpTwo onto the existing string s1. Line 156 prints the results.

On line 158, the fifth character in s1 is accessed and printed. It is assigned a new value on line 159. This invokes the non-constant offset operator ([ ]). Line 160 prints the result, which shows that the actual value has been changed.

Line 162 attempts to access a character beyond the end of the array. The last character of the array is returned, as designed.

Lines 164 through 165 create two more String objects, and line 166 shows the operator plus. Line 167 prints the results.

Line 169 creates a new String object, s4. Line 170 invokes the assignment operator. Line 171 prints the results. You might be thinking, "The assignment operator is defined to take a constant String reference on line 21, but here the program passes in a C-style string. Why is this legal?"

The answer is that the compiler expects a String, but it is given a character array. Therefore, it checks whether it can create a String from what it is given. On line 12, you declared a constructor that creates Strings from character arrays. The compiler creates a temporary String from the character array and passes it to the assignment operator. This is known as *implicit casting*, or *promotion*. If you had not declared (and provided the implementation for) the constructor that takes a character array, this assignment would have generated a compiler error.

Linked Lists and Other Structures

Arrays are much like Tupperware. They are great containers, but they are of a fixed size. If you pick a container that is too large, you waste space in your storage area. If you pick one that is too small, its contents spill all over, and you have a big mess.

One way to solve this problem is with a linked list. A linked list is a data structure that consists of small containers that are designed to fit and that are linked together as needed. The list is not in any specific order physically. The desired order is built logically through the links. The idea is to write a class that holds one object of your data, such as one CAT or one Rectangle, and can point at the next container. You create one container for each object that you need to store, and you chain them together as needed.

The containers are called *nodes*. The first node in the list is called the head, and the last node in the list is called the tail.

Lists come in three fundamental forms. From simplest to most complex, they are as follows:

Singly linked
Doubly linked
Trees

In a singly linked list, each node points to the next one, but not backward. To find a particular node, you start at the top and go from node to node, as in a treasure hunt ("The next node is under the sofa"). A doubly linked list enables you to move backward and forward in the chain. A tree is a complex structure built from nodes, each of which can point in two or three directions. The hierarchical file structure in UNIX and DOS is an example of a tree structure. Figure 11.5 shows these three fundamental structures.

Figure 11.5.

Linked lists.

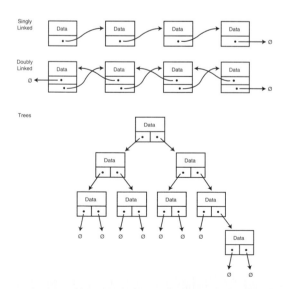

Computer scientists have created even more complex and clever data structures, nearly all of which rely on interconnecting nodes. Listing 11.13 shows how to create and use a simple linked list.

TYPE | Listing 11.13. Implementing a linked list.

```
1:     // Listing 11.13
2:     // Linked list simple implementation
3:
4:     #include <iostream.h>
5:
6:     // object to add to list
7:     class CAT
8:     {
9:     public:
10:        CAT() { itsAge = 1;}
11:        CAT(int age):itsAge(age){}
12:        ~CAT(){};
13:        int GetAge() const { return itsAge; }
14:     private:
15:        int itsAge;
16:     };
17:
18:     // manages list, orders by cat's age!
19:     class Node
20:     {
21:     public:
22:        Node (CAT*);
23:        ~Node();
24:        void SetNext(Node * node) { itsNext = node; }
25:        Node * GetNext() const { return itsNext; }
26:        CAT * GetCat() const { return itsCat; }
27:        void Insert(Node *);
28:        void Display();
29:     private:
30:        CAT *itsCat;
31:        Node * itsNext;
32:     };
33:
34:
35:     Node::Node(CAT* pCat):
36:     itsCat(pCat),
37:     itsNext(0)
38:     {}
39:
40:     Node::~Node()
41:     {
42:        cout << "Deleting node...\n";
43:        delete itsCat;
44:        itsCat = 0;
45:        delete itsNext;
46:        itsNext = 0;
```

continues

Listing 11.13. continued

```
47:        }
48:
49:        // *************************************
50:        // Insert
51:        // Orders cats based on their ages
52:        // Algorithm: If you are last in line, add the cat
53:        // Otherwise, if the new cat is older than you
54:        // and also younger than next in line, insert it after
55:        // this one. Otherwise call insert on the next in line
56:        // *************************************
57:        void Node::Insert(Node* newNode)
58:        {
59:            if (!itsNext)
60:                itsNext = newNode;
61:            else
62:            {
63:                int NextCatsAge = itsNext->GetCat()->GetAge();
64:                int NewAge =  newNode->GetCat()->GetAge();
65:                int ThisNodeAge = itsCat->GetAge();
66:
67:                if (  NewAge > ThisNodeAge && NewAge < NextCatsAge  )
68:                {
69:                    newNode->SetNext(itsNext);
70:                    itsNext = newNode;
71:                }
72:                else
73:                    itsNext->Insert(newNode);
74:            }
75:        }
76:
77:        void Node::Display()
78:        {
79:            if (itsCat->GetAge() > 0)
80:                cout << "My cat is " << itsCat->GetAge() << " years old\n";
81:            if (itsNext)
82:                itsNext->Display();
83:        }
84:
85:        void main()
86:        {
87:
88:            Node *pNode = 0;
89:            CAT * pCat = new CAT(0);
90:            int age;
91:
92:            Node *pHead = new Node(pCat);
93:
94:            while (true)
95:            {
96:                cout << "New Cat's age? (0 to quit): ";
97:                cin >>  age;
98:                if (!age)
99:                    break;
```

```
100:              pCat = new CAT(age);
101:              pNode = new Node(pCat);
102:              pHead->Insert(pNode);
103:          }
104:          pHead->Display();
105:          delete pHead;
106:          cout << "Exiting...\n\n";
107:      }
```

OUTPUT

```
New Cat's age? (0 to quit): 1
New Cat's age? (0 to quit): 9
New Cat's age? (0 to quit): 3
New Cat's age? (0 to quit): 7
New Cat's age? (0 to quit): 2
New Cat's age? (0 to quit): 5
New Cat's age? (0 to quit): 0
My cat is 1 years old
My cat is 2 years old
My cat is 3 years old
My cat is 5 years old
My cat is 7 years old
My cat is 9 years old
Deleting node...
Deleting node...
Deleting node...
Deleting node...
Deleting node...
Deleting node...
Deleting node...
Exiting...
```

ANALYSIS Lines 7 through 16 declare a simplified CAT class. It has two constructors, a default constructor that initializes the member variable itsAge to 1, and a constructor that takes an integer and initializes itsAge to that value.

Lines 18 through 32 declare the class Node. Node is designed specifically to hold a CAT object in a list. Normally, you would hide Node inside a CatList class. It is exposed here to illustrate how linked lists work.

It is possible to make a more generic Node that would hold any kind of object in a list. You'll learn about doing that on Day 14, "Special Classes and Functions," when templates are discussed.

Node's constructor takes a pointer to a CAT object. The copy constructor and assignment operator have been left out to save space. In a real-world application, they would be included.

Three accessor functions are defined. SetNext() sets the member variable itsNext to point to the Node object supplied as its parameter. GetNext() and GetCat() return the appropriate member variables. GetNext() and GetCat() are declared const because they don't change the Node object.

`Insert()` is the most powerful member function in the class. `Insert()` maintains the linked list and adds `Node`s to the list based on the age of the `CAT` that they point to.

The program begins at line 85. The pointer `pNode` is created and initialized to `0`. A dummy `CAT` object is created, and its age is initialized to `0` to ensure that the pointer to the head of the list (`pHead`) is always first.

Beginning on line 94, the user is prompted for an age. If the user presses `0`, this is taken as a signal that no more `CAT` objects are to be created. For all other values, a `CAT` object is created on line 100, and the member variable `itsAge` is set to the supplied value. The `CAT` objects are created on the free store. For each `CAT` created, a `Node` object is created on line 101.

After the `CAT` and `Node` objects are created, the first `Node` in the list is told to insert the newly created `Node`, on line 102.

Note that the program doesn't know—or care—how `Node` is inserted or how the list is maintained. That is entirely up to the `Node` object itself.

The call to `Insert()` causes program execution to jump to line 57. `Insert()` is always called on `pHead` first.

The test on line 59 fails the first time a new `Node` is added. Therefore, `pHead` is pointed at the first new `Node`. In the output, this is the `Node` with a `CAT` whose `itsAge` value was set to `1`.

When the second `CAT` object's `itsAge` variable is set to `9`, `pHead` is called again. This time, its member variable `itsNext` isn't `null`, and the `else` statement on lines 61 to 74 is invoked.

Three local variables (`NextCatsAge`, `NewAge`, and `ThisNodeAge`) are filled with the values of the following:

> The current `Node`'s age: the age of `pHead`'s `CAT` is `0`.
>
> The age of the `CAT` held by the new `Node`: in this case, `9`.
>
> The age of the `CAT` object held by the next node on line: in this case, `1`.

The test on line 67 could have been written as follows:

```
if (  newNode->GetCat()->GetAge() > itsCat->GetAge() && \\
newNode->GetCat()->GetAge()< itsNext->GetCat()->GetAge())
```

This would have eliminated the three temporary variables while creating code that is more confusing and harder to read. Some C++ programmers see this as macho—until they have a bug and can't figure out which one of the values is wrong.

If the new `CAT`'s age is greater than the current `CAT`'s age and less than the next `CAT`'s age, the proper place to insert the new `CAT`'s age is immediately after the current `Node`. In this case, the `if` statement is true. The new `Node` is set to point to what the current `Node` points to, and the current `Node` is set to point to the new `Node`. Figure 11.6 illustrates this.

11

Figure 11.6.

Inserting a Node.

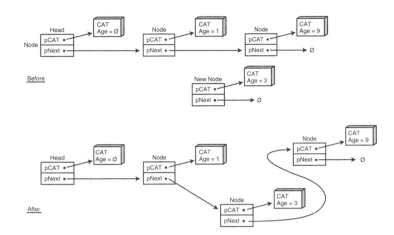

If the test fails, this isn't the proper place to insert the Node, and Insert() is called on the next Node in the list. Note that the current call to Insert() doesn't return until after the recursive call to Insert() returns. Therefore, these calls pile up on the stack. If the list gets too long, it blows the stack and crashes the program. There are other ways to do this that aren't so stack-intensive, but they are beyond the scope of this book.

When the user is finished adding CAT objects, Display() is called on the first Node, pHead. The CAT object's age is displayed if the current Node points to a CAT (pHead does not). Then, if the current Node points to another Node, Display() is called on that Node.

Finally, delete is called on pHead. Because the destructor deletes the pointer to the next Node, delete is called on that Node as well. It walks the entire list, eliminating each Node and freeing the memory of itsCat. Note that the last Node has its member variable itsNext set to zero, and delete is called on that pointer as well. It is always safe to call delete on zero, because it has no effect.

Array Classes

Writing your own Array class has many advantages over using the built-in arrays. For starters, you can prevent array overruns. You might also consider making your array class dynamically sized; at creation, it might have only one member, growing as needed during the course of the program.

You might want to sort or otherwise order the members of the array. There are a number of powerful Array variants you might consider. The following are among the most popular:

- ☐ Ordered collection: Each member is in sorted order.
- ☐ Set: No member appears more than once.

☐ Dictionary: This uses matched pairs in which one value acts as a key to retrieve the other value.

☐ Sparse array: Indices are permitted for a large set, but only those values actually added to the array consume memory. Thus, you can ask for `SparseArray[5]` or `SparseArray[200]`, but it is possible that memory is allocated only for a small number of entries.

☐ Bag: An unordered collection that is added to and retrieved in random order.

By overloading the index operator (`[ ]`), you can turn a linked list into an ordered collection. By excluding duplicates, you can turn a collection into a set. If each object in the list has a pair of matched values, you can use a linked list to build a dictionary or a sparse array. One entire bonus day is dedicated to building more advanced data structures, many of which are based on arrays. Be sure you understand the concepts in this lesson before taking on Day 25.

Summary

Today you learned how to create arrays in C++. An array is a fixed-size collection of objects that are all of the same type.

Arrays don't perform bounds checking. Therefore, it is legal—even if disastrous—to read or write past the end of an array. Arrays count from 0. A common mistake is to write to offset *n* of an array of *n* members.

Arrays can be single-dimensional or multidimensional. In either case, the members of the array can be initialized, as long as the array contains either built-in types, such as int, or objects of a class that has a default constructor.

Arrays and their contents can be on the free store or on the stack. If you delete an array on the free store, remember to use the brackets in the call to delete.

Array names are constant pointers to the first elements of the array. Pointers and arrays use pointer arithmetic to find the next element of an array.

Strings are arrays of characters, or chars. C++ provides special features for managing char arrays, including the capability to initialize them with quoted strings.

Q&A

Q What happens if I write to element 25 in a 24-member array?

A You will write to other memory, with potentially disastrous effects on your program.

Q What is in an uninitialized array element?

A Whatever happens to be in memory at a given time. The results of using this member without assigning a value are unpredictable.

Q Can I combine arrays?

A Yes. With simple arrays, you can use pointers to combine them into a new, larger array. With strings, you can use some of the built-in functions, such as strcat, to combine strings.

Q Why should I create a linked list if an array will work?

A An array must have a fixed size, whereas a linked list can be sized dynamically at runtime.

Q Why would I ever use built-in arrays if I can make a better array class?

A Built-in arrays are quick and easy to use.

Q Must a String class use a char * to hold the contents of the string?

A No. It can use any memory storage the designer thinks is best.

Quiz

1. What are the first and last elements in SomeArray[25]?
2. How do you declare a multidimensional array?
3. Initialize the members of the array in question 2.
4. How many elements are in the array SomeArray[10][5][20]?
5. What is the maximum number of elements that you can add to a linked list?
6. Can you use subscript notation on a linked list?
7. What is the last character in the string "Brad is a nice guy."?

Exercises

1. Declare a two-dimensional array that represents a tic-tac-toe game board.

2. Write the code that initializes all the elements in the array you created in exercise 1 to the value 0.

3. Write the declaration for a Node class that holds unsigned short integers.

4. **BUG BUSTERS:** What is wrong with this code fragment?

```
unsigned short SomeArray[5][4];
for (int i = 0; i<4; i++)
    for (int j = 0; j<5; j++)
        SomeArray[i][j] = i+j;
```

5. **BUG BUSTERS:** What is wrong with this code fragment?

```
unsigned short SomeArray[5][4];
for (int i = 0; i<=5; i++)
    for (int j = 0; j<=4; j++)
        SomeArray[i][j] = 0;
```

Day 12

Inheritance

Cognitive scientists (who study the way humans think) have taught us that it is a fundamental aspect of human intelligence to seek out, recognize, and categorize objects in order to see them in ever more simple basic terms. We build hierarchies, matrices, networks, and other categorizations to explain and understand the ways in which things interact. C++ attempts to capture this in inheritance hierarchies. Today you learn

- ☐ What inheritance is.
- ☐ How to derive one class from another.
- ☐ What protected access is and how to use it.
- ☐ What virtual functions are.

What Is Inheritance?

What is a dog? When you look at your pet, what do you see? A biologist sees a network of interacting organs; a physicist sees atoms and forces at work; and a taxonomist sees a representative of the species *canine domesticus*.

It is that last assessment that interests us at the moment. A dog is a kind of canine; a canine is a kind of mammal; and so forth. Taxonomists divide the world of living things into kingdom, phylum, class, order, family, genus, and species.

This hierarchy establishes an *is-a* relationship. A dog *is-a* canine. You see this relationship everywhere: A Toyota *is-a* car, which *is-a* vehicle. A sundae *is-a* dessert, which *is-a* food.

In C++, you say that something *is-a* something else to identify a specialization relationship. That is, a car *is-a* special kind of vehicle. I keep using the term *is-a* so that you start to think of it as a single-word description of real-world models. The *is-a* relationship is the core concept of inheritance, and it is important that you begin to think using that terminology as you start to code the relationships that can be represented in C++.

Inheritance and Derivation

The concept "dog inherits from mammal," means that a dog automatically gets all the features of a mammal. Because it is a mammal, you know that it has warm blood and it breathes air; all mammals are warm-blooded and breathe air by definition. The concept of a dog adds the idea of barking, wagging its tail, and so on to that definition. You can further divide dogs into hunting dogs and terriers, and you can divide terriers into Yorkshire Terriers, Dandie Dinmont Terriers, and so on.

A Yorkshire Terrier *is-a* terrier, therefore it *is-a* dog, therefore a mammal, therefore an animal, and therefore a living thing. This hierarchy is represented in Figure 12.1.

C++ attempts to represent these relationships by enabling you to define classes that *derive* from one another. Derivation is a way of expressing the *is-a* relationship. You derive a new class, Dog, from the class Mammal. You don't have to state explicitly that dogs move, because they *inherit* that trait from Mammal.

A class that adds new functionality to an existing class is said to *derive* from that original class. The original class is said to be the new class's *base class*.

If the Dog class derives from the Mammal class, then Mammal is a base class of Dog. Derived classes are *supersets* of their base classes. Just as dog adds certain features to the idea of a mammal, the Dog class adds certain methods or data to the Mammal class.

Typically, a base class has more than one derived class. Just as dogs, cats, and horses are all mammals, their classes would all derive from the Mammal class.

12

Figure 12.1.

Hierarchy of animals.

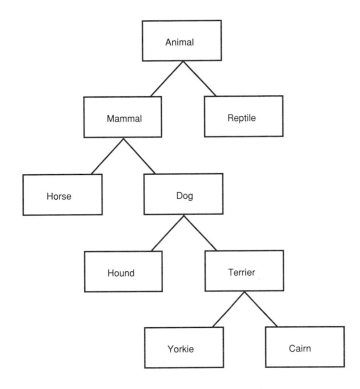

The Animal Kingdom

To facilitate the discussion of derivation and inheritance, this lesson focuses on the relationships among a number of classes representing animals. You can imagine that you have been asked to design a children's game—a simulation of a farm.

In time you can develop a whole set of farm animals, including horses, cows, dogs, cats, sheep, and so on. You create methods for these classes so that they can act in the ways that the child might expect, but for now you'll *stub-out* each method with a simple print statement.

Stubbing-out a function means you'll write only enough to show that the function is called, leaving the details for later when you have more time. Please feel free to extend the minimal code provided in this lesson to enable the animals to act more realistically.

The Syntax of Derivation

When you declare a class, you can indicate what class it derives from by writing a colon after the class name, the type of derivation (public, protected, or private), and the class from which it derives. The following is an example.

12

```
class Dog : public Mammal
```

The type of derivation is discussed later in this lesson. In general, you usually use `public`, which is what you use for now in this lesson.

The class from which you derive must have been declared earlier, or you get a compiler error. Listing 12.1 illustrates how to declare a `Dog` class that is derived from a `Mammal` class.

Type | **Listing 12.1. Simple inheritance.**

```
1:      //Listing 12.1 Simple inheritance
2:
3:      #include <iostream.h>
4:      enum BREED { YORKIE, CAIRN, DANDIE, SHETLAND, DOBERMAN, LAB };
5:
6:      class Mammal
7:      {
8:      public:
9:          // constructors
10:         Mammal();
11:         ~Mammal();
12:
13:         //accessors
14:         int GetAge()const;
15:         void SetAge(int);
16:         int GetWeight() const;
17:         void SetWeight();
18:
19:         //Other methods
20:         void Speak();
21:         void Sleep();
22:
23:
24:     protected:
25:         int itsAge;
26:         int itsWeight;
27:     };
28:
29:     class Dog : public Mammal
30:     {
31:     public:
32:
33:         // Constructors
34:         Dog();
35:         ~Dog();
36:
37:         // Accessors
38:         BREED GetBreed() const;
39:         void SetBreed(BREED);
40:
41:         // Other methods
42:         // WagTail();
43:         // BegForFood();
```

12

```
44:
45:    protected:
46:       BREED itsBreed;
47:    };
```

OUTPUT
This program has no output because it is only a set of class declarations without their implementations. Nonetheless, there is much to see here.

ANALYSIS
On lines 6 through 27, the Mammal class is declared. Note that in this example, Mammal does not derive from any other class. In the real world, mammals do derive; that is, a mammal *is-an* animal. Reality is far too complex to capture all of it, so every C++ hierarchy is an arbitrary representation of the data available. The trick of a good design is to represent the areas that you care about in a way that maps back reasonably close to the real-world objects.

The hierarchy has to begin somewhere; this program begins with Mammal. Because of this decision, some member variables that might properly belong in a higher base class are now represented here. For example, certainly all animals have an age and weight, so if Mammal derived from Animal, you might expect to inherit those attributes. As it is, the attributes appear in the Mammal class.

To keep the program reasonably simple and manageable, only six methods have been put in the Mammal class—four accessor methods, Speak(), and Sleep().

The Dog class inherits from Mammal, as indicated on line 29. Every Dog object has three member variables: itsAge, itsWeight, and itsBreed. Note that the class declaration for Dog does not include the member variables itsAge and itsWeight. Dog objects inherit these variables from the Mammal class, along with all of Mammal's methods *except* the copy operator and the constructors and destructor.

Private Versus Protected Class Members

You might have noticed that a new access keyword, protected, has been introduced on lines 24 and 45 of Listing 12.1. Previously, class data had been declared private. However, private members are not available to derived classes. You could make itsAge and itsWeight public, but that is not desirable. You don't want other classes accessing these data members directly.

What you want is a designation that says, "Make these visible to this class and to classes that derive from this class." That designation is protected. Protected data members and functions are fully visible to derived classes but are otherwise private.

12

There are, in total, three access specifiers: public, protected, and private. If a function has an object of your class, it can access all the public member data and functions. The member functions, in turn, can access all private data members and functions of their own class, and all protected data members and functions of any class from which they derive. Therefore, the function Dog::WagTail() can access the private data itsBreed and can access the protected data in the Mammal class.

Even if other classes are layered between Mammal and Dog (for example, DomesticAnimals), the Dog class is still able to access the protected members of Mammal, assuming that these other classes all use public inheritance. Private and protected inheritance are discussed on Day 15, "Advanced Inheritance."

Listing 12.2 demonstrates how to create objects of type Dog and access the data and functions of that type.

TYPE   **Listing 12.2. Using a derived object.**

```
1:      //Listing 12.2 Using a derived object
2:
3:      #include <iostream.h>
4:      enum BREED { YORKIE, CAIRN, DANDIE, SHETLAND, DOBERMAN, LAB };
5:
6:      class Mammal
7:      {
8:      public:
9:          // constructors
10:         Mammal():itsAge(2), itsWeight(5){}
11:         ~Mammal(){}
12:
13:         //accessors
14:         int GetAge()const { return itsAge; }
15:         void SetAge(int age) { itsAge = age; }
16:         int GetWeight() const { return itsWeight; }
17:         void SetWeight(int weight) { itsWeight = weight; }
18:
19:         //Other methods
20:         void Speak()const { cout << "Mammal sound!\n"; }
21:         void Sleep()const { cout << "shhh. I'm sleeping.\n"; }
22:
23:
24:     protected:
25:         int itsAge;
26:         int itsWeight;
27:     };
28:
29:     class Dog : public Mammal
30:     {
31:     public:
32:
33:         // Constructors
```

12

```
34:        Dog():itsBreed(YORKIE){}
35:        ~Dog(){}
36:
37:        // Accessors
38:        BREED GetBreed() const { return itsBreed; }
39:        void SetBreed(BREED breed) { itsBreed = breed; }
40:
41:        // Other methods
42:        void WagTail() { cout << "Tail wagging...\n"; }
43:        void BegForFood() { cout << "Begging for food...\n"; }
44:
45:    private:
46:        BREED itsBreed;
47:    };
48:
49:    void main()
50:    {
51:        Dog fido;
52:        fido.Speak();
53:        fido.WagTail();
54:        cout << "Fido is " << fido.GetAge() << " years old\n";
55:    }
```

OUTPUT

```
Mammal sound!
Tail wagging...
Fido is 2 years old
```

ANALYSIS
On lines 6 through 27 the Mammal class is declared (all of its functions are inline to save space here). On lines 29 through 47, the Dog class is declared as a derived class of Mammal. Thus, by these declarations, all Dogs have an age, a weight, and a breed.

On line 51, a Dog is declared, fido. fido inherits all the attributes of a Mammal, as well as all the attributes of a Dog. Thus, fido knows how to WagTail() but also knows how to Speak() and Sleep().

Constructors and Destructors

Dog objects are Mammal objects. This is the essence of the *inheritance*. When fido is created, his base constructor is called first, creating a Mammal. Then the Dog constructor is called, completing the construction of the Dog object. Because you gave fido no parameters, the default constructor is called in each case. fido doesn't exist until he is completely constructed, which means that both his Mammal part and his Dog part must be constructed. Thus, both constructors must be called.

When fido is destroyed, first the Dog destructor is called and then the destructor for the Mammal part of fido is called. Each destructor is given an opportunity to clean up after its own part of fido. Remember to clean up after your Dog! Listing 12.3 demonstrates this.

TYPE   Listing 12.3. Constructors and destructors called.

```
1:      //Listing 12.3 Constructors and destructors called.
2:
3:      #include <iostream.h>
4:      enum BREED { YORKIE, CAIRN, DANDIE, SHETLAND, DOBERMAN, LAB };
5:
6:      class Mammal
7:      {
8:      public:
9:          // constructors
10:         Mammal();
11:         ~Mammal();
12:
13:         //accessors
14:         int GetAge() const { return itsAge; }
15:         void SetAge(int age) { itsAge = age; }
16:         int GetWeight() const { return itsWeight; }
17:         void SetWeight(int weight) { itsWeight = weight; }
18:
19:         //Other methods
20:         void Speak() const { cout << "Mammal sound!\n"; }
21:         void Sleep() const { cout << "shhh. I'm sleeping.\n"; }
22:
23:
24:     protected:
25:         int itsAge;
26:         int itsWeight;
27:     };
28:
29:     class Dog : public Mammal
30:     {
31:     public:
32:
33:         // Constructors
34:         Dog();
35:         ~Dog();
36:
37:         // Accessors
38:         BREED GetBreed() const { return itsBreed; }
39:         void SetBreed(BREED breed) { itsBreed = breed; }
40:
41:         // Other methods
42:         void WagTail() { cout << "Tail wagging...\n"; }
43:         void BegForFood() { cout << "Begging for food...\n"; }
44:
45:     private:
46:         BREED itsBreed;
47:     };
48:
49:     Mammal::Mammal():
50:     itsAge(1),
51:     itsWeight(5)
52:     {
53:         cout << "Mammal constructor...\n";
54:     }
```

12

```
55:
56:      Mammal::~Mammal()
57:      {
58:          cout << "Mammal destructor...\n";
59:      }
60:
61:      Dog::Dog():
62:      itsBreed(YORKIE)
63:      {
64:          cout << "Dog constructor...\n";
65:      }
66:
67:      Dog::~Dog()
68:      {
69:          cout << "Dog destructor...\n";
70:      }
71:      void main()
72:      {
73:          Dog fido;
74:          fido.Speak();
75:          fido.WagTail();
76:          cout << "Fido is " << fido.GetAge() << " years old\n";
77:      }
```

OUTPUT
```
Mammal constructor...
Dog constructor...
Mammal sound!
Tail wagging...
Fido is 1 years old
Dog destructor...
Mammal destructor...
```

ANALYSIS   Listing 12.3 is just like Listing 12.2, except that the constructors and destructors now print to the screen when called. Mammal's constructor is called and then Dog's is called. At that point, the Dog fully exists, and its methods can be called. When fido goes out of scope, Dog's destructor is called, followed by a call to Mammal's destructor.

Passing Arguments to Base Constructors

It is possible that you'll want to overload the constructor of Mammal to take a specific age and that you'll want to overload the Dog constructor to take a breed. How do you get the age and weight parameters passed up to the right constructor in Mammal? What if Dogs want to initialize weight but Mammals don't?

Base class initialization can be performed during class initialization by writing the base class name, followed by the parameters expected by the base class. Listing 12.4 demonstrates this.

Listing 12.4. Overloading constructors in derived classes.

```
1:     //Listing 12.4 Overloading constructors in derived classes
2:
3:     #include <iostream.h>
4:     enum BREED { YORKIE, CAIRN, DANDIE, SHETLAND, DOBERMAN, LAB };
5:
6:     class Mammal
7:     {
8:     public:
9:         // constructors
10:        Mammal();
11:        Mammal(int age);
12:        ~Mammal();
13:
14:        //accessors
15:        int GetAge() const { return itsAge; }
16:        void SetAge(int age) { itsAge = age; }
17:        int GetWeight() const { return itsWeight; }
18:        void SetWeight(int weight) { itsWeight = weight; }
19:
20:        //Other methods
21:        void Speak() const { cout << "Mammal sound!\n"; }
22:        void Sleep() const { cout << "shhh. I'm sleeping.\n"; }
23:
24:
25:     protected:
26:        int itsAge;
27:        int itsWeight;
28:     };
29:
30:     class Dog : public Mammal
31:     {
32:     public:
33:
34:        // Constructors
35:        Dog();
36:        Dog(int age);
37:        Dog(int age, int weight);
38:        Dog(int age, BREED breed);
39:        Dog(int age, int weight, BREED breed);
40:        ~Dog();
41:
42:        // Accessors
43:        BREED GetBreed() const { return itsBreed; }
44:        void SetBreed(BREED breed) { itsBreed = breed; }
45:
46:        // Other methods
47:        void WagTail() { cout << "Tail wagging...\n"; }
48:        void BegForFood() { cout << "Begging for food...\n"; }
49:
50:     private:
51:        BREED itsBreed;
52:     };
53:
```

```
54:     Mammal::Mammal():
55:     itsAge(1),
56:     itsWeight(5)
57:     {
58:         cout << "Mammal constructor...\n";
59:     }
60:
61:     Mammal::Mammal(int age):
62:     itsAge(age),
63:     itsWeight(5)
64:     {
65:         cout << "Mammal(int) constructor...\n";
66:     }
67:
68:     Mammal::~Mammal()
69:     {
70:         cout << "Mammal destructor...\n";
71:     }
72:
73:     Dog::Dog():
74:     Mammal(),
75:     itsBreed(YORKIE)
76:     {
77:         cout << "Dog constructor...\n";
78:     }
79:
80:     Dog::Dog(int age):
81:     Mammal(age),
82:     itsBreed(YORKIE)
83:     {
84:         cout << "Dog(int) constructor...\n";
85:     }
86:
87:     Dog::Dog(int age, int weight):
88:     Mammal(age),
89:     itsBreed(YORKIE)
90:     {
91:         itsWeight = weight;
92:         cout << "Dog(int, int) constructor...\n";
93:     }
94:
95:     Dog::Dog(int age, int weight, BREED breed):
96:     Mammal(age),
97:     itsBreed(breed)
98:     {
99:         itsWeight = weight;
100:        cout << "Dog(int, int, BREED) constructor...\n";
101:    }
102:
103:    Dog::Dog(int age, BREED breed):
104:    Mammal(age),
105:    itsBreed(breed)
106:    {
107:        cout << "Dog(int, BREED) constructor...\n";
108:    }
```

continues

Listing 12.4. continued

```
109:
110:    Dog::~Dog()
111:    {
112:        cout << "Dog destructor...\n";
113:    }
114:    void main()
115:    {
116:        Dog fido;
117:        Dog rover(5);
118:        Dog buster(6,8);
119:        Dog yorkie (3,YORKIE);
120:        Dog dobbie (4,20,DOBERMAN);
121:        fido.Speak();
122:        rover.WagTail();
123:        cout << "Yorkie is " << yorkie.GetAge() << " years old\n";
124:        cout << "Dobbie weighs " << dobbie.GetWeight() << " pounds\n";
125:    }
```

NOTE

The output has been numbered so that each line can be referred to in this analysis.

```
1:  Mammal constructor...
2:  Dog constructor...
3:  Mammal(int) constructor...
4:  Dog(int) constructor...
5:  Mammal(int) constructor...
6:  Dog(int, int) constructor...
7:  Mammal(int) constructor...
8:  Dog(int, BREED) constructor....
9:  Mammal(int) constructor...
10: Dog(int, int, BREED) constructor...
11: Mammal sound!
12: Tail wagging...
13: Yorkie is 3 years old.
14: Dobbie weighs 20 pounds.
15: Mammal destructor...
16: Dog destructor...
17: Mammal destructor...
18: Dog destructor...
19: Mammal destructor...
20: Dog destructor...
21: Mammal destructor...
22: Dog destructor...
23: Mammal destructor...
```

ANALYSIS In Listing 12.4, Mammal's constructor has been overloaded on line 11 to take an integer—the Mammal's age. The implementation on lines 61 through 66 initializes itsAge with the value passed into the constructor and itsWeight with the value 5.

Dog has overloaded five constructors, on lines 35 through 39. The first is the default constructor. The second takes the age, which is the same parameter that the Mammal constructor takes. The third constructor takes both the age and the weight; the fourth takes the age and breed; and the fifth takes the age, weight, and breed.

Note that on line 74 Dog's default constructor calls Mammal's default constructor. Although it is not strictly necessary to do this, it serves as documentation that you *intended* to call the base constructor, which takes no parameters. The base constructor would be called in any case, but actually doing so makes your intentions explicit.

The implementation for the Dog constructor, which takes an integer, is on lines 80 through 85. In its initialization phase (lines 81 through 82), Dog initializes its base class, passing in the parameter, and then it initializes its breed.

Another Dog constructor is on lines 87 through 93. This one takes two parameters. Once again it initializes its base class by calling the appropriate constructor, but this time it also assigns weight to its base class's variable itsWeight. Note that you cannot assign to the base class variable in the initialization phase. Because Mammal does not have a constructor that takes this parameter, you must do this within the body of the Dog's constructor.

Walk through the remaining constructors to make sure you are comfortable with how they work. Note what is initialized and what must wait for the body of the constructor.

The first two lines of output represent the instantiation of fido, using the default constructor.

In the output, lines 3 and 4 represent the creation of rover. Lines 5 and 6 represent buster. Note that the Mammal constructor that is called is the constructor that takes one integer, but the Dog constructor is the constructor that takes two integers.

After all the objects are created, they are used and then go out of scope. As each object is destroyed, first the Dog destructor and then the Mammal destructor is called—five of each in total.

Overriding Functions

A Dog object has access to all the member functions in class Mammal, as well as to any member functions, such as WagTail(), that the declaration of the Dog class might add. It can also *override* a base class function. Overriding a function means changing the implementation of a base class function in a derived class. When you make an object of the derived class, the correct function is called.

When a derived class creates a function with the same return type and signature as a member function in the base class, but with a new implementation, it is said to be *overriding* that method.

When you override a function, it must agree in return type and in signature with the function in the base class. The signature is the function prototype other than the return type (that is, the name, the parameter list, and the keyword const if used).

NEW TERM The *signature* of a function is its name, as well as the number and type of its parameters. The signature does not include the return type.

Listing 12.5 illustrates what happens if the Dog class overrides the Speak() method in Mammal. To save room, the accessor functions have been left out of these classes.

TYPE

Listing 12.5. Overriding a base class method in a derived class.

```
1:     //Listing 12.5 Overriding a base class method in a derived class
2:
3:     #include <iostream.h>
4:     enum BREED { YORKIE, CAIRN, DANDIE, SHETLAND, DOBERMAN, LAB };
5:
6:     class Mammal
7:     {
8:     public:
9:         // constructors
10:        Mammal() { cout << "Mammal constructor...\n"; }
11:        ~Mammal() { cout << "Mammal destructor...\n"; }
12:
13:        //Other methods
14:        void Speak()const { cout << "Mammal sound!\n"; }
15:        void Sleep()const { cout << "shhh. I'm sleeping.\n"; }
16:
17:
18:    protected:
19:        int itsAge;
20:        int itsWeight;
21:    };
22:
23:    class Dog : public Mammal
24:    {
25:    public:
26:
27:        // Constructors
28:        Dog(){ cout << "Dog constructor...\n"; }
29:        ~Dog(){ cout << "Dog destructor...\n"; }
30:
31:        // Other methods
32:        void WagTail() { cout << "Tail wagging...\n"; }
33:        void BegForFood() { cout << "Begging for food...\n"; }
34:        void Speak()const { cout << "Woof!\n"; }
```

12

```
35:
36:     private:
37:         BREED itsBreed;
38:     };
39:
40:     void main()
41:     {
42:         Mammal bigAnimal;
43:         Dog fido;
44:         bigAnimal.Speak();
45:         fido.Speak();
46:     }
```

OUTPUT
```
Mammal constructor...
Mammal constructor...
Dog constructor...
Mammal sound!
Woof!
Dog destructor...
Mammal destructor...
Mammal destructor...
```

ANALYSIS   On line 34, the Dog class overrides the Speak() method, causing Dog objects to say Woof! when the Speak() method is called. On line 42, a Mammal object, bigAnimal, is created, causing the first line of output when the Mammal constructor is called. On line 43, a Dog object, fido, is created, causing the next two lines of output, where the Mammal constructor and then the Dog constructor are called.

On line 44, the Mammal object calls its Speak() method, and then on line 45, the Dog object calls its own Speak() method. The output reflects that the correct methods are called. Finally, the two objects go out of scope and the destructors are called.

Overloading Versus Overriding

These terms are similar and they do similar things. When you *overload* a method, you create more than one method with the same name, but with a different signature. When you *override* a method, you create a method in a derived class with the same name as a method in the base class—and the same signature.

Hiding the Base Class Method

In the previous listing, the Dog class's method Speak() hides the base class's method. This is just what you want, but it can have unexpected results. If Mammal has a method, Move(), which is overloaded, and Dog overrides that method, the Dog method hides all of the Mammal methods with that name.

If Mammal overloads Move() as three methods—one that takes no parameters, one that takes an integer, and one that takes an integer and a direction—and Dog overrides just the Move() method (which takes no parameters), it will not be easy to access the other two methods using a Dog object. Listing 12.6 illustrates this problem.

TYPE   **Listing 12.6. Hiding methods.**

```
1:      //Listing 12.6 Hiding methods
2:
3:      #include <iostream.h>
4:
5:      class Mammal
6:      {
7:      public:
8:          void Move() const { cout << "Mammal move one step\n"; }
9:          void Move(int distance) const { cout << "Mammal move "
   << distance <<" steps.\n"; }
10:     protected:
11:         int itsAge;
12:         int itsWeight;
13:     };
14:
15:     class Dog : public Mammal
16:     {
17:     public:
18:         void Move() const { cout << "Dog move 5 steps.\n"; }
19:     };        // You may receive a warning that you are hiding a function!
20:
21:     void main()
22:     {
23:         Mammal bigAnimal;
24:         Dog fido;
25:         bigAnimal.Move();
26:         bigAnimal.Move(2);
27:         fido.Move();
28:         // fido.Move(10);
29:     }
```

OUTPUT   Mammal move one step
Mammal move 2 steps
Dog move 5 steps

ANALYSIS   All of the extra methods and data have been removed from these classes. On lines 8 and 9, the Mammal class declares the overloaded Move() methods. On line 18, Dog overrides the version of Move() with no parameters. These are invoked on lines 25 through 27, and the output reflects this as executed.

Line 28, however, is commented out because it causes a compile-time error. Although the Dog class could have called the Move(int) method if it had not overridden the version of Move()

without parameters, now that it has done so, it must override both if it wants to use both. This is reminiscent of the rule that if you supply any constructor, the compiler no longer supplies a default constructor.

It is a common mistake to hide a base class method when you intend to override it, by forgetting to include the keyword const. const is part of the signature, and leaving it off changes the signature and hides the method rather than overriding it.

Calling the Base Method

If you have overridden the base method, it is still possible to call it by fully qualifying the name of the method. You do this by writing the base name, followed by two colons and then the method name—for example, `Mammal::Move()`.

It is possible to rewrite line 28 in Listing 12.6 so that it would compile, by writing the following:

```
28:     fido.Mammal::Move(10);
```

This calls the Mammal method explicitly. Listing 12.7 fully illustrates this idea.

TYPE

Listing 12.7. Calling a base method from an overridden method.

```
1:     //Listing 12.7 Calling base method from overridden method.
2:
3:     #include <iostream.h>
4:
5:     class Mammal
6:     {
7:     public:
8:        void Move() const { cout << "Mammal move one step\n"; }
9:        void Move(int distance) const { cout << "Mammal move "
    << distance << "_steps.\n"; }
10:    protected:
11:       int itsAge;
12:       int itsWeight;
13:    };
14:
15:    class Dog : public Mammal
16:    {
17:    public:
18:       void Move()const;
19:
20:    };
21:
22:    void Dog::Move() const
23:    {
```

continues

Listing 12.7. continued

```
24:        cout << "In dog move...\n";
25:        Mammal::Move(3);
26:    }
27
28:    void main()
29:    {
30:        Mammal bigAnimal;
31:        Dog fido;
32:        bigAnimal.Move(2);
33:        fido.Mammal::Move(6);
34:    }
```

OUTPUT   Mammal move 2 steps
            Mammal move 6 steps

ANALYSIS   On line 30, a `Mammal` called `bigAnimal` is created, and on line 31, a `Dog` called `fido` is created. The method call on line 32 invokes the `Move()` method of `Mammal`, which takes an `int`.

The programmer wanted to invoke `Move(int)` on the `Dog` object, but it had a problem. `Dog` overrides the `Move()` method, but does not overload it and does not provide a version that takes an `int`. This is solved by the explicit call to the base class `Move(int)` method on line 33.

Do	**Don't**

DO extend the functionality of tested classes by deriving.

DO change the behavior of certain functions in the derived class by overriding the base class methods.

DON'T hide a base class function by changing the function signature.

Virtual Methods

This lesson has emphasized the fact that a `Dog` object *is-a* `Mammal` object. So far, that has meant only that the `Dog` object has inherited the attributes (data) and capabilities (methods) of its base class. But the *is-a* relationship needs help because a `Dog` is not just a `Mammal`; it is a special kind of `Mammal` that moves and speaks differently than other `Mammal`s. It would be nice to have `Mammal` objects figure out the correct action to perform based on the particular kind of `Mammal` they are. In object-oriented terminology, this is called *polymorphism*. C++ provides *virtual functions* to implement polymorphism.

Polymorphism is the capability to ignore the details of derived objects and let the derived objects attend to the details when calling them with a base class pointer. C++ provides this capability with _virtual functions_. Polymorphism is one great advantage C++ has over many other object-oriented languages. In fact, many object-oriented programming purists would say that polymorphism is the essence of object-oriented programming.

C++ extends the _is-a_ relationship to enable pointers to base classes to be assigned to derived class objects. Thus, you can write the following:

```
Mammal* pMammal = new Dog;
```

This creates a new Dog object on the heap and returns a pointer to that object, which it assigns to a pointer to Mammal. This is fine, because a Dog _is-a_ Mammal. This is often referred to as _upcasting_ because inheritance diagrams are usually drawn with the base classes at the top and derived classes toward the bottom as you saw in Figure 12.1.

You can then use this pointer to invoke any method on Mammal. What you would like is for those methods that are overridden in Dog() to call the correct function. Virtual functions let you do that.

The _virtual_ Function

The syntax for a virtual function is similar to that of other functions, except you precede the return type in the function prototype.

Example

```
virtual void FunctionName();
```

 Listing 12.8 illustrates the difference between virtual and nonvirtual methods.

12

Listing 12.8. Using virtual methods.

```
1:    //Listing 12.8 Using virtual methods
2:
3:    #include <iostream.h>
4:
5:    class Mammal
6:    {
7:    public:
8:       Mammal():itsAge(1) { cout << "Mammal constructor...\n"; }
9:       ~Mammal() { cout << "Mammal destructor...\n"; }
10:      void Move() const { cout << "Mammal move one step\n"; }
11:      virtual void Speak() const { cout << "Mammal speak!\n"; }
12:   protected:
13:      int itsAge;
14:
```

continues

Listing 12.8. continued

```
15:    };
16:
17:    class Dog : public Mammal
18:    {
19:    public:
20:       Dog() { cout << "Dog Constructor...\n"; }
21:       ~Dog() { cout << "Dog destructor...\n"; }
22:       void WagTail() { cout << "Wagging Tail...\n"; }
23:       void Speak()const { cout << "Woof!\n"; }
24:       void Move()const { cout << "Dog moves 5 steps...\n"; }
25:    };
26:
27:    void main()
28:    {
29:
30:       Mammal *pDog = new Dog;
31:       pDog->Move();
32:       pDog->Speak();
33:
34:    }
```

OUTPUT

```
Mammal constructor...
Dog Constructor...
Mammal move one step
Woof!
```

ANALYSIS On line 11, Mammal is provided a virtual method—Speak(). The designer of this class thereby signals that she expects this class to eventually be another class's base type. The derived class will probably want to override this function.

On line 30, a pointer to Mammal is created, pDog, but it is assigned the address of a new Dog object. Because a Dog is a Mammal, this is a legal assignment. The pointer is then used to call the Move() function. Because the compiler knows pDog only to be a Mammal, it looks to the Mammal object to find the Move() method.

On line 32, the pointer then calls the Speak() method. Because Speak() is virtual, the Speak() method overridden in Dog is invoked.

This is almost magical. As far as the calling function knew, it had a Mammal pointer, but here a method on Dog is called. In fact, if you had an array of pointers to Mammal, each of which pointed to a subclass of Mammal, you could call each in turn, and the correct function would be called. Listing 12.9 illustrates this idea.

NOTE

This capability to call the right function dependent on the run-time type of the calling object is the essence of polymorphism. You could, for example, create many different types of windows, including dialog boxes, scrollable windows, and listboxes, and give them each a virtual draw() method. By creating a pointer to window and assigning dialog boxes and other derived types to that pointer, you can call draw() without regard to the actual run-time type of the object pointed to. The correct draw() function is called.

TYPE **Listing 12.9. Multiple virtual functions called in turn.**

```
1:      //Listing 12.9 Multiple virtual functions called in turn
2:
3:      #include <iostream.h>
4:
5:      class Mammal
6:      {
7:      public:
8:         Mammal():itsAge(1) {  }
9:         ~Mammal() { }
10:        virtual void Speak() const { cout << "Mammal speak!\n"; }
11:     protected:
12:        int itsAge;
13:     };
14:
15:     class Dog : public Mammal
16:     {
17:     public:
18:        void Speak()const { cout << "Woof!\n"; }
19:     };
20:
21:
22:     class Cat : public Mammal
23:     {
24:     public:
25:        void Speak()const { cout << "Meow!\n"; }
26:     };
27:
28:
29:     class Horse : public Mammal
30:     {
31:     public:
32:        void Speak()const { cout << "Winnie!\n"; }
33:     };
34:
35:     class Pig : public Mammal
36:     {
37:     public:
38:        void Speak()const { cout << "Oink!\n"; }
39:     };
40:
41:     void main()
42:     {
```

12

continues

Listing 12.9. continued

```
43:        Mammal* theArray[5];
44:        Mammal* ptr;
45:        int choice;
46:        for (int i = 0; i<5; i++)
47:        {
48:            cout << "(1)dog (2)cat (3)horse (4)pig: ";
49:            cin >> choice;
50:            switch (choice)
51:            {
52:                case 1: ptr = new Dog;
53:                break;
54:                case 2: ptr = new Cat;
55:                break;
56:                case 3: ptr = new Horse;
57:                break;
58:                case 4: ptr = new Pig;
59:                break;
60:                default: ptr = new Mammal;
61:                break;
62:            }
63:            theArray[i] = ptr;
64:        }
65:        for (i=0;i<5;i++)
66:            theArray[i]->Speak();
67:    }
```

OUTPUT

```
(1)dog (2)cat (3)horse (4)pig: 1
(1)dog (2)cat (3)horse (4)pig: 2
(1)dog (2)cat (3)horse (4)pig: 3
(1)dog (2)cat (3)horse (4)pig: 4
(1)dog (2)cat (3)horse (4)pig: 5
Woof!
Meow!
Winnie!
Oink!
Mammal Speak!
```

ANALYSIS This stripped-down program, which provides only the barest functionality to each class, illustrates virtual functions in their purest form. Four classes are declared, Dog, Cat, Horse, and Pig—all derived from Mammal.

On line 10, Mammal's Speak() function is declared to be virtual. On lines 18, 25, 32, and 38, the four derived classes override the implementation of Speak().

The user is prompted to pick which objects to create, and the pointers are added to the array on lines 46 through 63.

NOTE

Note that at compile time, it is impossible to know which objects will be created, and thus which Speak() methods will be invoked. The pointer ptr is bound to its object at run-time. This is called *dynamic binding*, or *run-time binding*, as opposed to *static binding*, or *compile-time binding*.

Overriding a virtual method supports polymorphism, while hiding it undermines polymorphism.

With this new knowledge and understanding of the power of polymorphism, you might wonder why it isn't just done by default without having to specify it with virtual functions. Well, there is a catch. The catch is that polymorphism adds some small overhead, which can affect the efficiency of your programs. That overhead is discussed again, later in this lesson and on Day 22.

You Can't Get There from Here

If the Dog object had a method, WagTail(), which is not in the Mammal, you could not use the pointer to Mammal to access that method (unless you cast it to be a pointer to Dog). Because WagTail() is not a virtual function and because it is not in a Mammal object, you can't get there without either a Dog object or a Dog pointer.

Although you can transform the Mammal pointer into a Dog pointer, there are usually far better and safer ways to call the WagTail() method. C++ frowns on explicit casts because they are error-prone. This subject is addressed in depth on Day 13, "Multiple Inheritance," on Day 19, "Templates," and again on Day 22, " Advanced C++ Features."

Slicing

Note that the virtual function magic only operates on pointers and references. Passing an object by value does not enable the virtual functions to be invoked. The problem encountered when you pass an object by value, expecting the virtual function to select the correct response, is called *data slicing*. Listing 12.10 illustrates this problem.

TYPE   **Listing 12.10. Data slicing when passing by value.**

```
1:     //Listing 12.10 Data slicing with passing by value
2:
3:     #include <iostream.h>
4:
5:
```

continues

Listing 12.10. continued

```
6:      class Mammal
7:      {
8:      public:
9:          Mammal():itsAge(1) {  }
10:         ~Mammal() { }
11:         virtual void Speak() const { cout << "Mammal speak!\n"; }
12:     protected:
13:         int itsAge;
14:     };
15:
16:     class Dog : public Mammal
17:     {
18:     public:
19:         void Speak()const { cout << "Woof!\n"; }
20:     };
21:
22:     class Cat : public Mammal
23:     {
24:     public:
25:         void Speak()const { cout << "Meow!\n"; }
26:     };
27:
28:      void ValueFunction (Mammal);
29:     void PtrFunction    (Mammal*);
30:     void RefFunction (Mammal&);
31:     void main()
32:     {
33:         Mammal* ptr=0;
34:         int choice;
35:         while (true)
36:         {
37:             bool fQuit = false;
38:             cout << "(1)dog (2)cat (0)Quit: ";
39:             cin >> choice;
40:             switch (choice)
41:             {
42:                 case 0: fQuit = true;
43:                 break;
44:                 case 1: ptr = new Dog;
45:                 break;
46:                 case 2: ptr = new Cat;
47:                 break;
48:                 default: ptr = new Mammal;
49:                 break;
50:             }
51:              if (fQuit)
52:                 break;
53:             PtrFunction(ptr);
54:             RefFunction(*ptr);
55:             ValueFunction(*ptr);
56:         }
57:     }
58:
```

12

```
59:    void ValueFunction (Mammal MammalValue)
60:    {
61:       MammalValue.Speak();
62:    }
63:
64:    void PtrFunction (Mammal * pMammal)
65:    {
66:       pMammal->Speak();
67:    }
68:
69:    void RefFunction (Mammal & rMammal)
70:    {
71:       rMammal.Speak();
72:    }
```

OUTPUT
```
 (1)dog (2)cat (0)Quit: 1
Woof
Woof
Mammal Speak!
(1)dog (2)cat (0)Quit: 2
Meow!
Meow!
Mammal Speak!
 (1)dog (2)cat (0)Quit: 0
```

ANALYSIS On lines 6 through 26, stripped-down versions of the Mammal, Dog, and Cat classes are declared. Three functions are declared—PtrFunction(), RefFunction(), and ValueFunction(). They take a pointer to a Mammal, a Mammal reference, and a Mammal object, respectively. All three functions then do the same thing; they call the Speak() method.

The user is prompted to choose a Dog or Cat, and based on the choice he makes, a pointer to the correct type is created on lines 44 through 49.

In the first line of the output, the user chooses Dog. The Dog object is created on the free store on line 44. The Dog is then passed as a pointer, as a reference, and by value to the three functions.

The pointer and references all invoke the virtual functions, and the Dog->Speak() member function is invoked. This is shown on the first two lines of output after the user's choice.

The dereferenced pointer, however, is passed by value. The function expects a Mammal object, so the compiler slices down the Dog object to just the Mammal part. At that point, the Mammal Speak() method is called, as reflected in the third line of output after the user's choice.

This experiment is then repeated for the Cat object, with similar results.

Virtual Destructors

It is legal and common to pass a pointer to a derived object when a pointer to a base object is expected. What happens when that pointer to a derived subject is deleted? If the destructor is virtual, as it should be, the right thing happens: The derived class's destructor is called. Because the derived class's destructor automatically invokes the base class's destructor, the entire object is properly destroyed.

The rule of thumb is this: If any of the functions in your class are virtual, the destructor should be as well. Consider the following possible function for ending all your programs that use the Dog and Mammal classes:

```
CleanUp(Mammal *pMammal)
{
    // Do some other cleanup stuff then:
    delete pMammal;
}
```

If the Mammal destructor is not a virtual function, the Dog destructor is never called from this function even if pMammal is pointing to a Dog object!

Virtual Copy Constructors

As previously stated, no constructor can be virtual. Nonetheless, there are times when your program desperately needs to be able to pass in a pointer to a base object and have a copy of the correct derived object created.

A common solution to this problem is to create a *clone* method in the base class and make that be virtual. The clone method creates a new object copy of the current class and returns that object. Because each derived class overrides the clone method, a copy of the derived class is created. Listing 12.11 illustrates how this is used.

TYPE **Listing 12.11. Virtual copy constructor.**

```
1:      //Listing 12. Virtual copy constructor
2:
3:      #include <iostream.h>
4:
5:      class Mammal
6:      {
7:      public:
8:          Mammal():itsAge(1) { cout << "Mammal constructor...\n"; }
9:          ~Mammal() { cout << "Mammal destructor...\n"; }
10:         Mammal (const Mammal & rhs);
11:         virtual void Speak() const { cout << "Mammal speak!\n"; }
12:         virtual Mammal* Clone() { return new Mammal(*this); }
➡ // virtual _constructor
13:         int GetAge()const { return itsAge; }
14:     protected:
15:         int itsAge;
16:     };
17:
```

```
18:    Mammal::Mammal (const Mammal & rhs):itsAge(rhs.GetAge())
19:    {
20:        cout << "Mammal Copy Constructor...\n";
21:    }
22:
23:    class Dog : public Mammal
24:    {
25:    public:
26:        Dog() { cout << "Dog constructor...\n"; }
27:        ~Dog() { cout << "Dog destructor...\n"; }
28:        Dog (const Dog & rhs);
29:        void Speak()const { cout << "Woof!\n"; }
30:        virtual Mammal* Clone() { return new Dog(*this); }
31:    };
32:
33:    Dog::Dog(const Dog & rhs):
34:    Mammal(rhs)
35:    {
36:        cout << "Dog copy constructor...\n";
37:    }
38:
39:    class Cat : public Mammal
40:    {
41:    public:
42:        Cat() { cout << "Cat constructor...\n"; }
43:        ~Cat() { cout << "Cat destructor...\n"; }
44:        Cat (const Cat &);
45:        void Speak()const { cout << "Meow!\n"; }
46:        virtual Mammal* Clone() { return new Cat(*this); }
47:    };
48:
49:    Cat::Cat(const Cat & rhs):
50:    Mammal(rhs)
51:    {
52:        cout << "Cat copy constructor...\n";
53:    }
54:
55:    enum ANIMALS { MAMMAL, DOG, CAT};
56:    const int NumAnimalTypes = 3;
57:    void main()
58:    {
59:        Mammal *theArray[NumAnimalTypes];
60:        Mammal* ptr;
61:        int choice;
62:        for (int i = 0; i<NumAnimalTypes; i++)
63:        {
64:            cout << "(1)dog (2)cat (3)Mammal: ";
65:            cin >> choice;
66:            switch (choice)
67:            {
68:                case DOG: ptr = new Dog;
69:                break;
70:                case CAT: ptr = new Cat;
71:                break;
```

continues

Listing 12.11. continued

```
72:                default: ptr = new Mammal;
73:                break;
74:            }
75:            theArray[i] = ptr;
76:        }
77:        Mammal *OtherArray[NumAnimalTypes];
78:        for (i=0;i<NumAnimalTypes;i++)
79:        {
80:            theArray[i]->Speak();
81:            OtherArray[i] = theArray[i]->Clone();
82:        }
83:        for (i=0;i<NumAnimalTypes;i++)
84:            OtherArray[i]->Speak();
85:    }
```

OUTPUT
```
1:  (1)dog (2)cat (3)Mammal: 1
2:  Mammal constructor...
3:  Dog Constructor...
4:  (1)dog (2)cat (3)Mammal: 2
5:  Mammal constructor...
6:  Cat constructor...
7:  (1)dog (2)cat (3)Mammal: 3
8:  Mammal constructor...
9:  Woof!
10: Mammal copy Constructor...
11: Dog copy constructor...
12: Meow!
13: Mammal copy Constructor...
14: Cat copy constructor...
15: Mammal speak!
16: Mammal copy Constructor...
17: Woof!
18: Meow!
19: Mammal speak!
```

ANALYSIS Listing 12.11 is very similar to the previous two listings, except that a new virtual method, Clone(), has been added to the Mammal class. This method returns a pointer to a new Mammal object by calling the copy constructor and passing in itself (*this) as a const reference.

Dog and Cat both override the Clone() method, initializing their data and passing in copies of themselves to their own copy constructors. Because Clone() is virtual, this effectively creates a virtual copy constructor, as shown on line 81.

The user is prompted to choose dogs, cats, or mammals, and these are created on lines 62 through 74. A pointer to each choice is stored in an array on line 75.

As the program iterates over the array, each object has its Speak() and its Clone() method called, in turn, on lines 80 and 81. The result of the Clone() call is a pointer to a copy of the object, which is then stored in a second array on line 81.

On line 1 of the output, the user is prompted and responds with 1, choosing to create a dog. The Mammal and Dog constructors are invoked. This is repeated for Cat and for Mammal on lines 4 through 8 of the constructor.

Line 9 of the constructor represents the call to Speak() on the first object, the Dog. The virtual Speak() method is called, and the correct version of Speak() is invoked. The Clone() function is then called; and, because this is also virtual, Dog's Clone method is invoked, causing the Mammal constructor and the Dog copy constructor to be called. Note that as part of the call to the Dog copy constructor, the Mammal copy constructor (but not the Mammal constructor) is called.

The same is repeated for Cat on lines 12 through 14, and then for Mammal on lines 15 and 16. Finally, the new array is iterated, and each of the new objects has Speak() invoked.

The Cost of Virtual Methods

Because objects with virtual methods must maintain a certain amount of information concerning the run-time type, they add some small overhead to your program. If you have a very small class, from which you do not expect to derive other classes, there might be no reason to have any virtual methods at all. On Day 22 you learn more details about exactly what the polymorphism overhead consists of.

After you declare *any* methods virtual, you've paid most of the price in efficiency. At that point, you'll want the destructor to be virtual, and the assumption is that all other methods probably will be virtual as well. Take a long hard look at any nonvirtual methods and be certain you understand why they are not virtual.

12

Do	Don't

DO use virtual methods when you expect to derive from a class.

DO use a virtual destructor if any methods are virtual.

DON'T mark the constructor as virtual.

Summary

Today you learned how derived classes inherit from base classes. This lesson discussed public inheritance and virtual functions. Classes inherit all the public and protected data and functions from their base classes.

Protected access is public to derived classes and private to all other objects. Even derived classes cannot access private data or functions in their base classes.

Constructors can be initialized before the body of the constructor. It is at this time that base constructors are invoked and parameters can be passed to the base class.

Functions in the base class can be overridden in the derived class. If the base class functions are virtual and if the object is accessed by pointer or reference, the derived class's functions are invoked based on the run-time type of the object pointed to.

Methods in the base class can be invoked by explicitly naming the function with the prefix of the base class name and two colons. For example, if Dog inherits from Mammal, Mammal's walk() method can be called with Mammal::Walk().

In classes with virtual methods, the destructor should almost always be made virtual. A virtual destructor ensures that the derived part of the object is freed when delete is called on the pointer. Constructors cannot be virtual. Virtual copy constructors can be effectively created by making a virtual member function that calls the copy constructor.

Q&A

Q Are inherited members and functions passed along to subsequent generations? If Dog derives from Mammal and Mammal derives from Animal, does Dog inherit Animal's functions and data?

A Yes. As derivation continues, derived classes inherit the sum of all the functions and data in all their base classes.

Q If, in the preceding question, Mammal overrides a function in Animal, does Dog get the original or the overridden function?

A If Dog inherits from Mammal, it gets the function in the state Mammal has it: the overridden function.

Q Can a derived class make a public base function private?

A Yes, and it remains private for all subsequent derivation.

Q Why not make all class functions virtual?

A There is overhead with the first virtual function in the creation of a v-table. After that, the overhead is trivial. Many C++ programmers feel that if one function is virtual, all others should be. Other programmers disagree, feeling that there should always be a reason for what you do.

Q Assume a function, SomeFunc(), is virtual in a base class and is also overloaded so as to take either an integer or two integers, and the derived class overrides the form taking one integer. What is called when a pointer to a derived object calls the two integer form?

12

A The overriding of the one int form hides the entire base class function, and thus you get a compile error complaining that the function requires only one int.

Quiz

1. What makes the polymorphism less efficient than compile-time binding?
2. What is a virtual destructor?
3. How do you show the declaration of a virtual constructor?
4. How can you create a virtual copy constructor?
5. How do you invoke a base member function from a derived class in which you've overridden that function?
6. How do you invoke a base member function from a derived class in which you have not overridden that function?
7. If a base class declares a function to be virtual, and a derived class does not use the term virtual when overriding that class, is it still virtual when inherited by a third-generation class?
8. What is the protected keyword used for?

Exercises

1. Show the declaration of a virtual function that takes an integer parameter and returns void.
2. Show the declaration of a class Square, which derives from Rectangle, which in turn derives from Shape.
3. If, in exercise 2, Shape takes no parameters, Rectangle takes two parameters (length and width), and Square takes only one parameter (length), show the constructor initialization for Square.
4. Write a virtual copy constructor for the class Square (in exercise 3).
5. **BUG BUSTERS:** What is wrong with this code snippet?
   ```
   void SomeFunction (Shape);
   Shape * pRect = new Rectangle;
   SomeFunction(*pRect);
   ```
6. **BUG BUSTERS:** What is wrong with this code snippet?
   ```
   class Shape()
   {
   public:
       Shape();
       virtual ~Shape();
       virtual Shape(const Shape&);
   };
   ```

12

Day 13

Multiple Inheritance

On Day 12, you learned how to write virtual functions in derived classes. This is the fundamental building block of polymorphism: the capability to bind specific, derived class objects to base class pointers and still invoke the correct methods at run-time. Today you learn

- [ ] What multiple inheritance is and how to use it.
- [ ] What virtual inheritance is.
- [ ] What abstract data types are.
- [ ] What pure virtual functions are.

Problems with Single Inheritance

Single inheritance has some limitations when you're attempting to model real-world situations. For instance, how can you show the inheritance tree that represents a dog as a mammal, which is an animal *and* a pet at the same time? What you want to show is how two different views of the object provide different sets of data and capabilities to the object. You can cuddle a dog because it is a pet, but you cannot (or would not attempt to) cuddle a tiger.

Tigers and dogs are both mammals, but they are not both pets. The inheritance required to represent that dogs are in both the mammal tree and the pet tree is *multiple inheritance*. Multiple inheritance can take two forms—one where all the attributes of the two classes are fully enclosed in the new derived class, as is the case for dogs, which are both fully pets and fully mammals; and partial inheritance, where only parts of one or all base classes are included.

Partial multiple inheritance is best illustrated with an example. Suppose you've been working with your animal classes for awhile and you've divided the class hierarchy into `Birds` and `Mammals`. The `Bird` class includes the member function `Fly()`. The `Mammal` class has been divided into a number of types of `Mammals`, including `Horse`. The `Horse` class includes the member functions `Whinny()` and `Gallop()`. Suddenly, you realize you need a `Pegasus` object—a cross between a `Horse` and a `Bird`. A `Pegasus` can `Fly()`, it can `Whinny()`, and it can `Gallop()`.

Figure 13.1 illustrates the multiple inheritance and partial multiple inheritance of these two examples.

Figure 13.1.

Types of multiple inheritance.

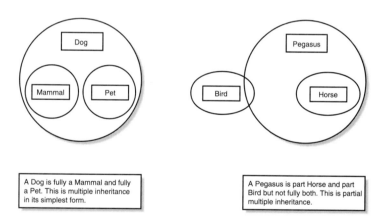

A Dog is fully a Mammal and fully a Pet. This is multiple inheritance in its simplest form.

A Pegasus is part Horse and part Bird but not fully both. This is partial multiple inheritance.

The type of inheritance where one object fully contains all the other multiple inheritance base types is easy. The partial kind, such as our Pegasus, is a little more tricky.

You can make `Pegasus` a `Bird`, but then it won't be able to `Whinny()` or `Gallop()`. You can make it a `Horse`, but then it won't be able to `Fly()`. So, good or bad, you decide to go with multiple inheritance to design the `Pegasus`.

NOTE This portion of the model breaks down, however, because you might decide that a `Pegasus` is not really a part `Bird`/part `Horse` object but rather a specialization of a horse. For the sake of illustration, though, let's stick with the idea with which we started: A Pegasus is a part Bird/part Horse object. Virtually every multiple inheritance design has tradeoffs such as this one—whether or not to repeat functionality in two types based on the real-world problem. Typically, your best bet is to stick with the model that most closely models the real world. In this lesson, you choose the more difficult form of multiple inheritance in order to point out some of the arguments for and against using multiple inheritance. In this lesson, you find out why some object-oriented programming experts think multiple inheritance is a bad idea and why others cling to it for dear life.

Your first solution is to copy the Fly() method into the Pegasus class and derive Pegasus from Horse. This works fine, at the cost of having the Fly() method in two places (Bird and Pegasus). If you change one, you must remember to change the other. Of course, a developer who comes along months or years later to maintain your code must also know to fix both places.

Soon, however, you have a new problem. You want to create a list of Horse objects and a list of Bird objects. You would like to be able to add your Pegasus objects to either list, but if a Pegasus is a Horse, you can't add it to a list of Birds.

You have a couple of potential solutions. You can rename the Horse method Gallop() to Move(), and then override Move() in your Pegasus object to do the work of Fly(). You would then override Move() in your other horses to do the work of Gallop(). Perhaps Pegasus could be clever enough to gallop short distances and fly longer distances.

```
Pegasus::Move(long distance)
{
     if (distance > veryFar)
          fly(distance);
     else
          gallop(distance);
}
```

This is a bit limiting. Perhaps one day, Pegasus will want to fly a short distance or gallop a long distance. Your next solution might be to move Fly() up into Horse, as illustrated in Listing 13.1. The problem is that most horses can't fly, so you have to make this method do nothing unless it is a Pegasus.

13

TYPE | Listing 13.1. If horses could fly....

```
1:      // Listing 13.1. If horses could fly...
2:      // Percolating Fly() up into Horse
3:
4:      #include <iostream.h>
5:
6:      class Horse
7:      {
8:      public:
9:          void Gallop(){ cout << "Galloping...\n"; }
10:         virtual void Fly() { cout << "Horses can't fly.\n" ; }
11:     private:
12:         int itsAge;
13:     };
14:
15:     class Pegasus : public Horse
16:     {
17:     public:
18:         void Fly() { cout << "I can fly! I can fly! I can fly!\n"; }
19:     };
20:
21:     const int NumberHorses = 5;
22:     void main()
23:     {
24:         Horse* Ranch[NumberHorses];
25:         Horse* pHorse;
26:         int choice;
27:         for (int i=0; i<NumberHorses; i++)
28:         {
29:             cout << "(1)Horse (2)Pegasus: ";
30:             cin >> choice;
31:             if (choice == 2)
32:                 pHorse = new Pegasus;
33:             else
34:                 pHorse = new Horse;
35:             Ranch[i] = pHorse;
36:         }
37:         cout << "\n";
38:         for (i=0; i<NumberHorses; i++)
39:         {
40:             Ranch[i]->Fly();
41:             delete Ranch[i];
42:         }
43:     }
```

OUTPUT

```
(1)Horse (2)Pegasus: 1
(1)Horse (2)Pegasus: 2
(1)Horse (2)Pegasus: 1
(1)Horse (2)Pegasus: 2
(1)Horse (2)Pegasus: 1

Horses can't fly.
I can fly! I can fly! I can fly!
```

13

```
Horses can't fly.
I can fly! I can fly! I can fly!
Horses can't fly.
```

 This program certainly works, though at the expense of the Horse class having a Fly() method. And, again, we're back to the problem of having a Fly() function in several places.

On line 10, the method Fly() is provided to Horse. In a real-world class, you might have it issue an error, or fail quietly. On line 18, the Pegasus class overrides the Fly() method to "do the right thing," represented here by printing a happy message.

The array of Horse pointers on line 24 is used to demonstrate that the correct Fly() method is called based on the run-time binding of the Horse or Pegasus object.

Percolating Upward

Putting the required function higher in the class hierarchy is a common solution to this problem, and results in many functions *percolating up* into the base class. The base class is then in grave danger of becoming a global namespace for all the functions that might be used by any of the derived classes. This can seriously undermine the class typing of C++ and can create a large and cumbersome base class.

In general, you want to percolate shared functionality up the hierarchy without migrating the interface of each class. This means that if two classes that share a common base class (for example, Horse and Bird both share Animal) have a function in common (both birds and horses eat, for example), you'll want to move that functionality up into the base class and create a virtual function.

What you'll want to avoid, however, is percolating an interface (such as Fly up where it doesn't belong), just so you can call that function only on some derived classes.

In situations such as this, you might be tempted to cast the pointer down to the derived type in order to call the correct function. This is referred to as *downcasting*. However, once you do that, you defeat the purpose and spirit of polymorphism, making it pointless. Worse than that, you increase the likelihood that one of your cast statements will introduce bugs or inhibit code updates.

Do	Don't

DO move functionality up the inheritance hierarchy.

DON'T move interface up the inheritance hierarchy.

13

> **DON'T** downcast pointers to base objects to derived objects! Later, on Day 15,
> "Advanced Inheritance," you see how this can be done if there is no other choice.
> Typically, the need to cast down is a sign of poor design.

To derive from more than the base class, you separate each base class by commas in the class
designation. Listing 13.2 illustrates how to declare Pegasus so that it derives from both Horses
and Birds. The program then adds Pegasus objects to both types of lists.

TYPE   **Listing 13.2. Multiple inheritance of Pegasus.**

```
1:      // Listing 13.2. Multiple inheritance.
2:      // Multiple Inheritance
3:
4:      #include <iostream.h>
5:
6:      class Horse
7:      {
8:      public:
9:          Horse() { cout << "Horse constructor... "; }
10:         virtual ~Horse() { cout << "Horse destructor... "; }
11:         virtual void Whinny() const { cout << "Whinny!... "; }
12:     private:
13:         int itsAge;
14:     };
15:
16:     class Bird
17:     {
18:     public:
19:         Bird() { cout << "Bird constructor... "; }
20:         virtual ~Bird() { cout << "Bird destructor... "; }
21:         virtual void Chirp() const { cout << "Chirp... ";  }
22:         virtual void Fly() const { cout
➥     << "I can fly! I can fly! I can fly! "; }
23:     private:
24:         int itsWeight;
25:     };
26:
27:     class Pegasus : public Horse, public Bird
28:     {
29:     public:
30:         void Chirp() const { Whinny(); }
31:         Pegasus() { cout << "Pegasus constructor... "; }
32:         ~Pegasus() { cout << "Pegasus destructor...  "; }
33:     };
34:
35:     const int MagicNumber = 2;
36:     void main()
37:     {
38:         Horse* Ranch[MagicNumber];
39:         Bird* Aviary[MagicNumber];
```

13

```
40:        Horse * pHorse;
41:        Bird * pBird;
42:        int choice;
43:        for (int i=0; i<MagicNumber; i++)
44:        {
45:           cout << "\n(1)Horse (2)Pegasus: ";
46:           cin >> choice;
47:           if (choice == 2)
48:              pHorse = new Pegasus;
49:           else
50:              pHorse = new Horse;
51:           Ranch[i] = pHorse;
52:        }
53:        for (i=0; i<MagicNumber; i++)
54:        {
55:           cout << "\n(1)Bird (2)Pegasus: ";
56:           cin >> choice;
57:           if (choice == 2)
58:              pBird = new Pegasus;
59:           else
60:              pBird = new Bird;
61:           Aviary[i] = pBird;
62:        }
63:
64:        cout << "\n";
65:        for (i=0; i<MagicNumber; i++)
66:        {
67:           cout << "\nRanch[" << i << "]: " ;
68:           Ranch[i]->Whinny();
69:           delete Ranch[i];
70:        }
71:
72:        for (i=0; i<MagicNumber; i++)
73:        {
74:           cout << "\nAviary[" << i << "]: " ;
75:           Aviary[i]->Chirp();
76:           Aviary[i]->Fly();
77:           delete Aviary[i];
78:        }
79:     }
```

OUTPUT

```
(1)Horse (2)Pegasus: 1
Horse constructor...
(1)Horse (2)Pegasus: 2
Horse constructor... Bird constructor... Pegasus constructor
(1)Bird (2)Pegasus: 1
Bird constructor...
(1)Bird (2)Pegasus: 2
Horse constructor... Bird constructor... Pegasus constructor

Ranch[0]: Whinny!... Horse destructor...
Ranch[1]: Whinny!... Pegasus destructor.. Bird destructor... Horse
destructor...
Aviary[0]: Chirp... I can fly! I can fly! I can fly! Bird destructor...
Aviary[1]: Whinny!... I can fly! I can fly! I can fly! Pegasus destructor...
➥ Bird destructor... Horse destructor...
```

13

ANALYSIS On lines 6 through 14, a Horse class is declared. The constructor and destructor print out a message, and the Whinny() method prints the word Whinny!

On lines 16 through 25, a Bird class is declared. In addition to its constructor and destructor, this class has two methods: Chirp() and Fly(), both of which print an identifying message. In a real program, these might, for example, activate the speaker or generate animated images.

Finally, on lines 27 through 33, the class Pegasus is declared. It derives both from Horse and from Bird. The Pegasus class overrides the Chirp() method to call the Whinny() method, which it inherits from Horse.

Two lists are created, a Ranch with pointers to Horse on line 38, and an Aviary with pointers to Bird on line 39. On lines 43 through 52, Horse and Pegasus objects are added to the Ranch. On lines 53 through 62, Bird and Pegasus objects are added to the Aviary.

Invocations of the virtual methods on both the Bird pointers and the Horse pointers do the right things for Pegasus objects. For example, on line 75, the members of the Aviary array are used to call Chirp() on the objects to which they point. The Bird class declares this to be a virtual method, so the right function is called for each object.

Note that each time a Pegasus object is created, the output reflects that both the Bird part and the Horse part of the Pegasus object are also created. When a Pegasus object is destroyed, the Bird and Horse parts are destroyed as well, thanks to the destructors being made virtual.

Declaring Multiple Inheritance

SYNTAX

Declare an object to inherit from more than one class by listing the base classes following the colon after the class name. Separate the base classes by commas.

Example 1:

```
class Pegasus : public Horse, public Bird
```

Example 2:

```
class Schnoodle : public Schnauzer, public Poodle
```

The Parts of a Multiple Inheritance Object

When the Pegasus object is created in memory, both of the base classes form part of the Pegasus object, as illustrated in Figure 13.2

A number of issues arise with objects with multiple base classes. For example, what happens if two base classes that happen to have the same name have virtual functions or data? How are multiple base class constructors initialized? What happens if multiple base classes derive from the same class? The next sections answer these questions and explore how you can put multiple inheritance to work.

Figure 13.2.
Objects with multiple inheritance.

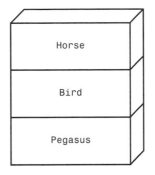

Constructors in Multiple Inheritance Objects

If Pegasus derives from both Horse and Bird and each of the base classes has constructors that take parameters, the Pegasus class initializes these constructors in turn. Listing 13.3 illustrates how this is done.

TYPE **Listing 13.3. Calling multiple constructors.**

```
1:    // Listing 13.3
2:    // Calling multiple constructors
3:    #include <iostream.h>
4:    typedef int HANDS;
5:    enum COLOR { Red, Green, Blue, Yellow, White, Black, Brown } ;
6:
7:
8:    class Horse
9:    {
10:   public:
11:      Horse(COLOR color, HANDS height);
12:      virtual ~Horse() { cout << "Horse destructor...\n"; }
13:      virtual void Whinny()const { cout << "Whinny!... "; }
14:      virtual HANDS GetHeight() const { return itsHeight; }
15:      virtual COLOR GetColor() const { return itsColor; }
16:   private:
17:      HANDS itsHeight;
18:      COLOR itsColor;
19:   };
20:
21:   Horse::Horse(COLOR color, HANDS height):
22:      itsColor(color),itsHeight(height)
23:   {
24:      cout << "Horse constructor...\n";
25:   }
26:
27:   class Bird
28:   {
29:   public:
```

continues

Listing 13.3. continued

```
30:        Bird(COLOR color, bool migrates);
31:        virtual ~Bird() {cout << "Bird destructor...\n";  }
32:        virtual void Chirp()const { cout << "Chirp... ";  }
33:        virtual void Fly()const { cout
➥   << "I can fly! I can fly! I can fly! "; }
34:        virtual COLOR GetColor()const { return itsColor; }
35:        virtual bool GetMigration() const { return itsMigration; }
36:
37:    private:
38:        COLOR itsColor;
39:        bool itsMigration;
40:    };
41:
42:    Bird::Bird(COLOR color, bool migrates):
43:        itsColor(color), itsMigration(migrates)
44:    {
45:        cout << "Bird constructor...\n";
46:    }
47:
48:    class Pegasus : public Horse, public Bird
49:    {
50:    public:
51:        void Chirp()const { Whinny(); }
52:        Pegasus(COLOR, HANDS, bool,long);
53:        ~Pegasus() {cout << "Pegasus destructor...\n";}
54:        virtual long GetNumberBelievers() const {
➥    return   itsNumberBelievers; }
55:
56:    private:
57:        long itsNumberBelievers;
58:    };
59:
60:    Pegasus::Pegasus(COLOR aColor, HANDS height,
➥    bool migrates, long NumBelieve):
61:    Horse(aColor, height),
62:    Bird(aColor, migrates),
63:    itsNumberBelievers(NumBelieve)
64:    {
65:        cout << "Pegasus constructor...\n";
66:    }
67:
68:    void main()
69:    {
70:        Pegasus *pPeg = new Pegasus(Red, 5, true, 10);
71:        pPeg->Fly();
72:        pPeg->Whinny();
73:        cout << "\nYour Pegasus is " << pPeg->GetHeight();
74:        cout << " hands tall and ";
75:        if (pPeg->GetMigration())
76:            cout << "it does migrate.";
77:        else
78:            cout << "it does not migrate.";
79:        cout << "\nA total of " << pPeg->GetNumberBelievers();
80:        cout << " people believe it exists.\n";
81:        delete pPeg;
82:    }
```

13

OUTPUT

```
Horse constructor...
Bird constructor...
Pegasus constructor...
I can fly! I can fly! I can fly! Whinny...
Your Pegasus is 5 hands tall and it does migrate.
A total of 10 people believe it exists.
Pegasus destructor...
Bird destructor...
Horse destructor...
```

ANALYSIS On lines 8 through 19, the Horse class is declared. The constructor takes two parameters; color uses the enumeration declared on line 5. The implementation of the constructor on lines 21 through 25 simply initializes the member variables and prints a message.

On lines 27 through 40, the Bird class is declared, and the implementation of its constructor is on lines 42 through 46. Again, the Bird class takes two parameters. Interestingly, the Horse constructor takes color (so that you can detect horses of different colors), and the Bird constructor takes the color of the feathers (so those of one feather can stick together). This leads to a problem when you want to ask the Pegasus for its color, which you'll see in the next example.

The Pegasus class itself is declared on lines 48 through 58, and its constructor is on lines 60 through 66. The initialization of the Pegasus object includes three statements. First, the Horse constructor is initialized with color and height. Then the Bird constructor is initialized with color and the Boolean. Finally, the Pegasus member variable itsNumberBelievers is initialized. After all that is accomplished, the body of the Pegasus constructor is called.

In the main() function, a Pegasus pointer is created and used to access the member functions of the base objects. On line 79, the Pegasus accessor GetNumberBelievers() is called, though the data member itsNumberBelievers could have been called directly.

Ambiguity Resolution

In Listing 13.3, both the Horse class and the Bird class have a method GetColor(). You may need to ask the Pegasus object to return its color, but you have a problem: the Pegasus class inherits from both Bird and Horse. They both have a color, and their methods for getting that color have the same names and signature. This creates an ambiguity for the compiler, which you must resolve.

If you simply write

```
COLOR currentColor = pPeg->GetColor();
```

you get a compiler error:

```
Member is ambiguous: 'Horse::GetColor' and 'Bird::GetColor'
```

13

You can resolve the ambiguity with an explicit call to the function you wish to invoke:

```
COLOR currentColor = pPeg->Horse::GetColor();
```

Anytime you need to resolve which class a member function or member data inherits from, you can fully qualify the call by prepending the class name to the base class data or function.

Note that if Pegasus were to override this function, then the problem would be moved, as it should be, into the Pegasus member function:

```
virtual COLOR GetColor()const { return Horse::itsColor; }
```

This hides the problem from clients of the Pegasus class and encapsulates within Pegasus the knowledge of which base class it wishes to inherit its color from. A client is still free to force the issue by writing the following:

```
COLOR currentColor = pPeg->Bird::GetColor();
```

Inheriting from a Shared Base Class

What happens if both Bird and Horse inherit from a common base class, such as Animal? Figure 13.3 illustrates what this looks like.

Figure 13.3.

Common base classes.

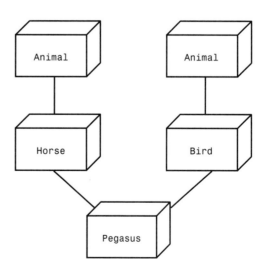

As you can see in Figure 13.3, two base class objects exist. When a function or data member is called in the shared base class, another ambiguity exists. For example, if Animal declares itsAge as a member variable and GetAge() as a member function, and you call pPeg->GetAge(), did you mean to call the GetAge() function you inherit from Animal by way of Horse, or by way of Bird? You must resolve this ambiguity as well, as illustrated in Listing 13.4.

TYPE **Listing 13.4. Common base classes.**

```
1:  // Listing 13.4
2:  // Common base classes
3:  #include <iostream.h>
4:
5:  typedef int HANDS;
6:  enum COLOR { Red, Green, Blue, Yellow, White, Black, Brown } ;
7:
8:
9:  class Animal        // common base to both horse and bird
10: {
11: public:
12:    Animal(int);
13:    virtual ~Animal() { cout << "Animal destructor...\n"; }
14:    virtual int GetAge() const { return itsAge; }
15:    virtual void SetAge(int age) { itsAge = age; }
16: private:
17:    int itsAge;
18: };
19:
20: Animal::Animal(int age):
21: itsAge(age)
22: {
23:    cout << "Animal constructor...\n";
24: }
25:
26: class Horse : public Animal
27: {
28: public:
29:    Horse(COLOR color, HANDS height, int age);
30:    virtual ~Horse() { cout << "Horse destructor...\n"; }
31:    virtual void Whinny()const { cout << "Whinny!... "; }
32:    virtual HANDS GetHeight() const { return itsHeight; }
33:    virtual COLOR GetColor() const { return itsColor; }
34: protected:
35:    HANDS itsHeight;
36:    COLOR itsColor;
37: };
38:
39: Horse::Horse(COLOR color, HANDS height, int age):
40:    Animal(age),
41:    itsColor(color),itsHeight(height)
42: {
43:    cout << "Horse constructor...\n";
44: }
45:
46: class Bird : public Animal
47: {
48: public:
49:    Bird(COLOR color, bool migrates, int age);
50:    virtual ~Bird() {cout << "Bird destructor...\n";  }
51:    virtual void Chirp()const { cout << "Chirp... ";  }
```

continues

13

Listing 13.4. continued

```
52:        virtual void Fly()const { cout
➡    << "I can fly! I can fly! I can fly! "; }
53:        virtual COLOR GetColor()const { return itsColor; }
54:        virtual bool GetMigration() const { return itsMigration; }
55:
56:    protected:
57:        COLOR itsColor;
58:        bool itsMigration;
59:    };
60:
61:    Bird::Bird(COLOR color, bool migrates, int age):
62:        Animal(age),
63:        itsColor(color), itsMigration(migrates)
64:    {
65:        cout << "Bird constructor...\n";
66:    }
67:
68:    class Pegasus : public Horse, public Bird
69:    {
70:    public:
71:        void Chirp()const { Whinny(); }
72:        Pegasus(COLOR, HANDS, bool, long, int);
73:        ~Pegasus() {cout << "Pegasus destructor...\n";}
74:        virtual long GetNumberBelievers() const {
➡    return   itsNumberBelievers; }
75:        virtual COLOR GetColor()const { return Horse::itsColor; }
76:        virtual int GetAge() const { return Horse::GetAge(); }
77:
78:    private:
79:        long itsNumberBelievers;
80:    };
81:
82:    Pegasus::Pegasus(
83:        COLOR aColor,
84:        HANDS height,
85:        bool migrates,
86:        long NumBelieve,
87:        int age):
88:    Horse(aColor, height,age),
89:    Bird(aColor, migrates,age),
90:    itsNumberBelievers(NumBelieve)
91:    {
92:        cout << "Pegasus constructor...\n";
93:    }
94:
95:    void main()
96:    {
97:        Pegasus *pPeg = new Pegasus(Red, 5, true, 10, 2);
98:        int age = pPeg->GetAge();
99:        cout << "This pegasus is " << age << " years old.\n";
100:       delete pPeg;
101:   }
```

```
 1:  Animal constructor...
 2:  Horse constructor...
 3:  Animal constructor...
 4:  Bird constructor...
 5:  Pegasus constructor...
 6:  This pegasus is 2 years old.
 7:  Pegasus destructor...
 8:  Bird destructor...
 9:  Animal destructor...
10:  Horse destructor...
11:  Animal destructor...
```

ANALYSIS This listing has a number of interesting features. The Animal class is declared on lines 9 through 18. Animal adds one member variable, itsAge and an accessor, SetAge().

On line 26, the Horse class is declared to derive from Animal. The Horse constructor now has a third parameter, age, which it passes to its base class, Animal. Note that the Horse class does *not* override GetAge(); it simply inherits it.

On line 46, the Bird class is declared to derive from Animal. Its constructor also takes an age and uses it to initialize its base class, Animal. It also inherits GetAge() without overriding it.

Pegasus inherits from both Bird and Animal, and therefore has two Animal classes in its inheritance chain. If you were to call GetAge() on a Pegasus object, you would have to disambiguate, or fully qualify, the method you want if Pegasus did not override the method.

This is solved on line 76 when the Pegasus object overrides GetAge() to do nothing more than to *chain up*—that is, to call the same method—in a base class.

NEW TERM *Chaining up* is done for two reasons: either to disambiguate which base class to call, as in this case, or to do some work and then let the function in the base class do some more work. At times, you may want to do work and then chain up, or chain up and then do the work when the base class function returns.

The Pegasus constructor takes five parameters: the creature's color, its height (in HANDS), whether or not it migrates, how many believe in it, and its age. The constructor initializes the Horse part of the Pegasus with the color, height, and age on line 88. It initializes the Bird part with color, whether it migrates, and age on line 89. Finally, it initializes itsNumberBelievers on line 90.

The call to the Horse constructor on line 88 invokes the implementation shown on line 39. The Horse constructor uses the age parameter to initialize the Animal part of the Horse part of the Pegasus. It then goes on to initialize the two member variables of Horse (itsColor and itsAge).

The call to the Bird constructor on line 89 invokes the implementation shown on line 61. Here too, the age parameter is used to initialize the Animal part of the Bird.

13

Note that the `color` parameter to the `Pegasus` is used to initialize member variables in both `Bird` and `Horse`. Note also that the `age` is used to initialize `itsAge` in the `Horse`'s base `Animal` and in the `Bird`'s base `Animal`.

Virtual Inheritance

In Listing 13.4, the `Pegasus` class goes to some lengths to disambiguate which of its `Animal` base classes it means to invoke. Most of the time, the decision as to which one to use is arbitrary—after all, the `Horse` and the `Bird` have exactly the same base class.

It is possible to tell C++ that you do not want two copies of the shared base class, as shown previously in Figure 13.3, but rather to have a single shared base class, as shown in Figure 13.4. Inheriting from a single base class is often referred to as *diamond inheritance*.

Figure 13.4.

A diamond inheritance.

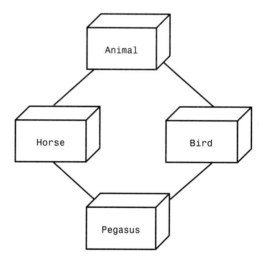

You accomplish this by making `Animal` a virtual base class of both `Horse` and `Bird`. The `Animal` class does not change at all. The `Horse` and `Bird` classes change only in their use of the term `virtual` in their declarations. `Pegasus`, however, changes substantially.

Normally, a class's constructor initializes only its own variables and its base class. However, virtually inherited base classes are an exception. They are initialized by their *most derived* class. Thus, `Animal` is initialized not by `Horse` and `Bird`, but by `Pegasus`. `Horse` and `Bird` have to initialize `Animal` in their constructors, but these initializations are ignored when a `Pegasus` object is created.

Listing 13.5 rewrites Listing 13.4 to take advantage of virtual derivation.

13

TYPE   **Listing 13.5. Illustrates use of virtual inheritance.**

```
1:    // Listing 13.5
2:    // Virtual inheritance
3:    #include <iostream.h>
4:
5:    typedef int HANDS;
6:    enum COLOR { Red, Green, Blue, Yellow, White, Black, Brown } ;
7:
8:
9:    class Animal        // common base to both horse and bird
10:   {
11:   public:
12:       Animal(int);
13:       virtual ~Animal() { cout << "Animal destructor...\n"; }
14:       virtual int GetAge() const { return itsAge; }
15:       virtual void SetAge(int age) { itsAge = age; }
16:   private:
17:       int itsAge;
18:   };
19:
20:   Animal::Animal(int age):
21:   itsAge(age)
22:   {
23:       cout << "Animal constructor...\n";
24:   }
25:
26:   class Horse : virtual public Animal
27:   {
28:   public:
29:       Horse(COLOR color, HANDS height, int age);
30:       virtual ~Horse() { cout << "Horse destructor...\n"; }
31:       virtual void Whinny()const { cout << "Whinny!... "; }
32:       virtual HANDS GetHeight() const { return itsHeight; }
33:       virtual COLOR GetColor() const { return itsColor; }
34:   protected:
35:       HANDS itsHeight;
36:       COLOR itsColor;
37:   };
38:
39:   Horse::Horse(COLOR color, HANDS height, int age):
40:       Animal(age),
41:       itsColor(color),itsHeight(height)
42:   {
43:       cout << "Horse constructor...\n";
44:   }
45:
46:   class Bird : virtual public Animal
47:   {
48:   public:
49:       Bird(COLOR color, bool migrates, int age);
50:       virtual ~Bird() {cout << "Bird destructor...\n";  }
51:       virtual void Chirp()const { cout << "Chirp... ";  }
52:       virtual void Fly()const { cout
➥      << "I can fly! I can fly! I can fly! "; }
```

continues

Listing 13.5. continued

```
53:          virtual COLOR GetColor()const { return itsColor; }
54:          virtual bool GetMigration() const { return itsMigration; }
55:
56:      protected:
57:          COLOR itsColor;
58:          bool itsMigration;
59:      };
60:
61:      Bird::Bird(COLOR color, bool migrates, int age):
62:          Animal(age),
63:          itsColor(color), itsMigration(migrates)
64:      {
65:          cout << "Bird constructor...\n";
66:      }
67:
68:      class Pegasus : public Horse, public Bird
69:      {
70:      public:
71:          void Chirp()const { Whinny(); }
72:          Pegasus(COLOR, HANDS, bool, long, int);
73:          ~Pegasus() {cout << "Pegasus destructor...\n";}
74:          virtual long GetNumberBelievers() const {
➥    return  itsNumberBelievers; }
75:          virtual COLOR GetColor()const { return Horse::itsColor; }
76:
77:      private:
78:          long itsNumberBelievers;
79:      };
80:
81:      Pegasus::Pegasus(
82:          COLOR aColor,
83:          HANDS height,
84:          bool migrates,
85:          long NumBelieve,
86:          int age):
87:      Horse(aColor, height,age),
88:      Bird(aColor, migrates,age),
89:      Animal(age*2),
90:      itsNumberBelievers(NumBelieve)
91:      {
92:          cout << "Pegasus constructor...\n";
93:      }
94:
95:      void main()
96:      {
97:          Pegasus *pPeg = new Pegasus(Red, 5, true, 10, 2);
98:          int age = pPeg->GetAge();
99:          cout << "This pegasus is " << age << " years old.\n";
100:         delete pPeg;
101:     }
```

13

Animal constructor...
Horse constructor...
Bird constructor...
Pegasus constructor...
This pegasus is 4 years old
Pegasus destructor...
Bird destructor...
Horse destructor...
Animal destructor...

 On line 26, Horse declares that it inherits *virtually* from Animal, and on line 46, Bird makes the same declaration. Note that the constructors for both Bird and Animal still initialize the Animal object.

Pegasus inherits from both Bird and Animal, and as the most derived object of Animal, Pegasus also initializes Animal. It is Pegasus's initialization that is performed by the Pegasus constructor, and the calls to Animal's constructor in Bird and Horse are ignored. You can see this because the value 2 is passed in, and Horse and Bird pass it along to Animal, but Pegasus doubles it. The result, 4, is reflected in the printout on line 99 and as shown in the output.

Pegasus no longer has to disambiguate the call to GetAge() and as a result, is free to simply inherit this function from Animal. Note that Pegasus must still disambiguate the call to GetColor() because this function is in both of its base classes and not in Animal.

Declaring Classes for Virtual Inheritance

To ensure that derived classes have only one instance of common base classes, declare the intermediate classes to inherit virtually from the base class.

Example 1:

```
class Horse : virtual public Animal
class Bird : virtual public Animal
class Pegasus : public Horse, public Bird
```

Example 2:

```
class Schnauzer : virtual public Dog
class Poodle : virtual public Dog
class Schnoodle : public Schnauzer, public Poodle
```

13

Problems with Multiple Inheritance

Although multiple inheritance offers a number of advantages over single inheritance, many C++ programmers are reluctant to use it. The problems they cite are that many compilers don't support it yet, that it makes debugging harder, and that nearly everything that can be done with multiple inheritance can be done without it.

These are valid concerns, and you should be on your guard against installing needless complexity into your programs. Some debuggers have a hard time with multiple inheritance, and some designs are needlessly made complex by using multiple inheritance when it is not needed.

Do	Don't

DO use multiple inheritance when a new class needs functions and features from more than one base class.

DO use virtual inheritance when the most derived classes must have only one instance of the shared base class.

DO initialize the shared base class from the most derived class when using virtual base classes.

DON'T use multiple inheritance when single inheritance will do.

Mixins and Capabilities Classes

One way to strike a middle ground between multiple inheritance and single inheritance is to use what are called *Mixins*. For example, you might have your `Horse` class derive from `Animal` and from `Displayable`. `Displayable` would just add a few methods for displaying any object on-screen.

NEW TERM   A Mixin, or *capability class*, is a class that adds functionality without adding much or any data.

Capability classes are mixed into a derived class like any other class might be, by declaring the derived class to inherit publicly from them. The only difference between a capability class and any other class is that the capability class has little or no data. This is an arbitrary distinction, of course, and is simply a shorthand way of noting that at times, all you want to do is mix in some additional capabilities without complicating the derived class. The streams class is one example of a capabilities class that can be extended easily to provide additional capabilities to new classes. Streams are covered in two other lessons—Day 16 and Bonus Day 23.

For some debuggers, this does make it easier to work with Mixins than with more complex multiple inheritance objects. There is also less likelihood of ambiguity in accessing the data in the other principal base class.

13

For example, if Horse derives from Animal and from Displayable, Displayable would have no data. Animal would be just as it always is, so all the data in Horse would derive from Animal, but the functions in Horse would derive from both.

The term Mixin comes from an ice-cream store in Sommerville, Massachusetts where candies and cakes were mixed into the basic ice-cream flavors. This seemed like a good metaphor to some of the object-oriented programmers who used to take a summer break there, especially while working with the object-oriented programming language SCOOPS.

Abstract Data Types

Often, you will create a hierarchy of classes together. For example, you might create a Shape class, and derive from that Rectangle and Circle. Shape is an abstract term for both Rectangles and Circles. You would not directly create any objects of type Shape, but Rectangles and Circles are Shapes. Shape is referred to as an *abstract class* or *abstract data type*.

Each of the derived classes will override the Draw() method, the GetArea() method Shape abstract class, and so on. Listing 13.6 illustrates a bare-bones implementation of the Shape class and its derived Circle and Rectangle classes.

TYPE   **Listing 13.6. Shape classes.**

```
1:     //Listing 13.6. Shape classes.
2:
3:     #include <iostream.h>
4:
5:
6:
7:     class Shape
8:     {
9:     public:
10:        Shape(){}
11:        ~Shape(){}
12:        virtual long GetArea() { return -1; } // error
13:        virtual long GetPerim() { return -1; }
14:        virtual void Draw() {}
15:    private:
16:    };
17:
18:    class Circle : public Shape
```

continues

Listing 13.6. continued

```
19:     {
20:     public:
21:             Circle(int radius):itsRadius(radius){}
22:             ~Circle(){}
23:             long GetArea() { return 3 * itsRadius * itsRadius; }
24:             long GetPerim() { return 9 * itsRadius; }
25:             void Draw();
26:     private:
27:         int itsRadius;
28:         int itsCircumference;
29:     };
30:
31:     void Circle::Draw()
32:     {
33:         cout << "Circle drawing routine here!\n";
34:     }
35:
36:
37:     class Rectangle : public Shape
38:     {
39:     public:
40:             Rectangle(int len, int width):
41:                 itsLength(len), itsWidth(width){}
42:             ~Rectangle(){}
43:             virtual long GetArea() { return itsLength * itsWidth; }
44:             virtual long GetPerim() {return 2*itsLength + 2*itsWidth; }
45:             virtual int GetLength() { return itsLength; }
46:             virtual int GetWidth() { return itsWidth; }
47:             virtual void Draw();
48:     private:
49:         int itsWidth;
50:         int itsLength;
51:     };
52:
53:     void Rectangle::Draw()
54:     {
55:         for (int i = 0; i<itsLength; i++)
56:         {
57:             for (int j = 0; j<itsWidth; j++)
58:                 cout << "x ";
59:
60:             cout << "\n";
61:         }
62:     }
63:
64:     class Square : public Rectangle
65:     {
66:     public:
67:             Square(int len);
68:             Square(int len, int width);
69:             ~Square(){}
70:             long GetPerim() {return 4 * GetLength();}
71:     };
72:
```

13

```
73:    Square::Square(int len):
74:        Rectangle(len,len)
75:    {}
76:
77:    Square::Square(int len, int width):
78:        Rectangle(len,width)
79:
80:    {
81:        if (GetLength() != GetWidth())
82:            cout << "Error, not a square... a Rectangle??\n";
83:    }
84:
85:    void main()
86:    {
87:        int choice;
88:        bool fQuit = false;
89:        Shape * sp;
90:
91:        while (true)
92:        {
93:            cout << "(1)Circle (2)Rectangle (3)Square (0)Quit: ";
94:            cin >> choice;
95:
96:            switch (choice)
97:            {
98:                case 1: sp = new Circle(5);
99:                break;
100:                case 2: sp = new Rectangle(4,6);
101:                break;
102:                case 3: sp = new Square(5);
103:                break;
104:                default: fQuit = true;
105:                break;
106:            }
107:            if (fQuit)
108:                break;
109:
110:            sp->Draw();
111:            cout << "\n";
112:        }
113:    }
```

OUTPUT

```
 (1)Circle (2)Rectangle (3)Square (0)Quit: 2
x x x x x x
x x x x x x
x x x x x x
x x x x x x
 (1)Circle (2)Rectangle (3)Square (0)Quit:3
x x x x x
x x x x x
x x x x x
x x x x x
x x x x x
 (1)Circle (2)Rectangle (3)Square (0)Quit:0
```

13

On lines 7 through 16, the Shape class is declared. The GetArea() and GetPerim() methods return an error value, and Draw() takes no action. After all, what does it mean to draw a shape? Only types of shapes (circles, rectangle, and so on) can be drawn; Shapes as an abstraction cannot be drawn.

Circle derives from Shape and overrides the three virtual methods. Note that there is no reason to add the word virtual, because that is part of their inheritance. However, there is no harm in doing so either, as shown in the Rectangle class on lines 43, 44, and 47. It is a good idea to include the term virtual as a reminder, a form of documentation.

Square derives from Rectangle, and it, too, overrides the GetPerim() method, inheriting the rest of the methods defined in Rectangle.

It is troubling, though, that a client might try to instantiate a Shape object, and it might be desirable to make that impossible. The Shape class exists only to provide an interface for the classes derived from it; as such it is an *abstract data type*, or ADT.

NEW TERM   An abstract data type represents a concept (such as shape) rather than an object (such as circle). In C++, an ADT is always the base class to other classes, and it is not valid to make an instance of an ADT.

Pure Virtual Functions

C++ supports the creation of abstract data types with *pure virtual functions*. A virtual function is made pure by initializing it with zero, as in:

```
virtual void Draw() = 0;
```

Any class with one or more pure virtual functions is an ADT, and it is illegal to instantiate an object of a class that is an ADT. Trying to do so causes a compile-time error. Putting a pure virtual function in your class signals two things to clients of your class:

- ☐ Don't make an object of this class derive from it.
- ☐ Make sure you override the pure virtual function.

Any class that derives from an ADT inherits the pure virtual function as pure, and therefore, must override every pure virtual function if it is expected to instantiate objects. Thus, if Rectangle inherits from Shape, and Shape has three pure virtual functions, Rectangle must override all three or it, too, becomes an ADT. Listing 13.7 rewrites the Shape class to be an abstract data type. To save space, the rest of Listing 13.6 is not reproduced here. Replace the declaration of Shape in Listing 13.6, lines 7 through 16, with the declaration of Shape in Listing 13.7 and run the program again.

TYPE **Listing 13.7. Abstract data types.**

```
1:   class Shape
2:   {
3:   public:
4:        Shape(){}
5:        ~Shape(){}
6:        virtual long GetArea() = 0; // error
7:        virtual long GetPerim()= 0;
8:        virtual void Draw() = 0;
9:   private:
10: };
```

OUTPUT
```
(1)Circle (2)Rectangle (3)Square (0)Quit:2
x x x x x x
x x x x x x
x x x x x x
x x x x x x
(1)Circle (2)Rectangle (3)Square (0)Quit:3
x x x x x
x x x x x
x x x x x
x x x x x
x x x x x
 (1)Circle (2)Rectangle (3)Square (0)Quit:0
```

ANALYSIS As you can see, the workings of the program are totally unaffected. The only difference is that it would now be impossible to make an object of class Shape.

Abstract Data Types

SYNTAX

Declare a class to be an abstract data type by including one or more pure virtual functions in the class declaration. Declare a pure virtual function by writing = 0 after the function declaration.

Example:

```
class Shape
{
     virtual void Draw() = 0;    // pure virtual
};
```

13

Implementing Pure Virtual Functions

Typically, the pure virtual functions in an abstract base class are never implemented. Because no objects of that type are ever created, there is no reason to provide implementations, and the ADT works purely as the definition of an interface to objects that derive from it.

It is possible, however, to provide an implementation to a pure virtual function. The function can then be called by objects *derived* from the ADT, perhaps to provide common functionality to all the overridden functions. Listing 13.8 reproduces Listing 13.6, this time with Shape as an ADT and with an implementation for the pure virtual function Draw(). The Circle class overrides Draw(), as it must, but it then chains up to the base class function for additional functionality.

In this example, the additional functionality is simply an additional message printed, but one can imagine that the base class provides a shared drawing mechanism, perhaps setting up a window that all derived classes can use.

TYPE   **Listing 13.8. Implementing pure virtual functions.**

```
1:      //Implementing pure virtual functions
2:
3:      #include <iostream.h>
4:
5:
6:
7:      class Shape
8:      {
9:      public:
10:        Shape(){}
11:        ~Shape(){}
12:        virtual long GetArea() = 0; // error
13:        virtual long GetPerim()= 0;
14:        virtual void Draw() = 0;
15:      private:
16:      };
17:
18:       void Shape::Draw()
19:      {
20:         cout << "Abstract drawing mechanism!\n";
21:      }
22:
23:      class Circle : public Shape
24:      {
25:      public:
26:            Circle(int radius):itsRadius(radius){}
27:            ~Circle(){}
28:            long GetArea() { return 3 * itsRadius * itsRadius; }
29:            long GetPerim() { return 9 * itsRadius; }
30:            void Draw();
31:      private:
32:        int itsRadius;
33:        int itsCircumference;
34:      };
35:
36:      void Circle::Draw()
37:      {
38:         cout << "Circle drawing routine here!\n";
39:         Shape::Draw();
```

```
40:     }
41:
42:
43:     class Rectangle : public Shape
44:     {
45:     public:
46:         Rectangle(int len, int width):
47:             itsLength(len), itsWidth(width){}
48:         ~Rectangle(){}
49:         long GetArea() { return itsLength * itsWidth; }
50:         long GetPerim() {return 2*itsLength + 2*itsWidth; }
51:         virtual int GetLength() { return itsLength; }
52:         virtual int GetWidth() { return itsWidth; }
53:         void Draw();
54:     private:
55:         int itsWidth;
56:         int itsLength;
57:     };
58:
59:     void Rectangle::Draw()
60:     {
61:         for (int i = 0; i<itsLength; i++)
62:         {
63:             for (int j = 0; j<itsWidth; j++)
64:                 cout << "x ";
65:
66:             cout << "\n";
67:         }
68:         Shape::Draw();
69:     }
70:
71:
72:     class Square : public Rectangle
73:     {
74:     public:
75:         Square(int len);
76:         Square(int len, int width);
77:         ~Square(){}
78:         long GetPerim() {return 4 * GetLength();}
79:     };
80:
81:     Square::Square(int len):
82:         Rectangle(len,len)
83:     {}
84:
85:     Square::Square(int len, int width):
86:         Rectangle(len,width)
87:
88:     {
89:         if (GetLength() != GetWidth())
90:             cout << "Error, not a square... a Rectangle??\n";
91:     }
92:
93:     void main()
94:     {
95:         int choice;
```

continues

Listing 13.8. continued

```
96:        bool fQuit = false;
97:        Shape * sp;
98:
99:        while (true)
100:        {
101:            cout << "(1)Circle (2)Rectangle (3)Square (0)Quit: ";
102:            cin >> choice;
103:
104:            switch (choice)
105:            {
106:                case 1: sp = new Circle(5);
107:                break;
108:                case 2: sp = new Rectangle(4,6);
109:                break;
110:                case 3: sp = new Square (5);
111:                break;
112:                default: fQuit = true;
113:                break;
114:            }
115:            if (fQuit)
116:                break;
117:
118:            sp->Draw();
119:            cout << "\n";
120:        }
121:    }
```

OUTPUT
```
    (1)Circle (2)Rectangle (3)Square (0)Quit: 2
x x x x x x
x x x x x x
x x x x x x
x x x x x x
Abstract drawing mechanism!
(1)Circle (2)Rectangle (3)Square (0)Quit:3
x x x x x
x x x x x
x x x x x
x x x x x
x x x x x
Abstract drawing mechanism!
  (1)Circle (2)Rectangle (3)Square (0)Quit:0
```

ANALYSIS On lines 7 through 16, the abstract data type Shape is declared, with all three of its accessor methods declared to be pure virtual. Note that this is not necessary. If any one is declared pure virtual, the class becomes an ADT.

The GetArea() and GetPerim() methods are not implemented, but Draw() is. Circle and Rectangle both override Draw(), and both chain up to the base method, taking advantage of shared functionality in the base class.

13

Complex Hierarchies of Abstraction

At times, you might derive ADTs from other ADTs. It might be that you want to make some of the derived pure virtual functions non-pure and leave others pure.

If you create the Animal class, you may make Eat(), Sleep(), Move(), and Reproduce() all as pure virtual functions. Perhaps from Animal, you derive Mammal and Fish.

On examination, you decide that every Mammal reproduces in the same way, and so you make Mammal::Reproduce() non-pure, but you leave Eat(), Sleep(), and Move() as pure virtual functions.

From Mammal you derive Dog, and Dog must override and implement the three remaining pure virtual functions so that you can make objects of type Dog.

What you've said, as class designer, is that no Animals or Mammals can be instantiated, but that all Mammals can inherit the provided Reproduce() method without overriding it.

Listing 13.9 illustrates this technique with a bare-bones implementation of these classes.

TYPE **Listing 13.9. Deriving ADTs from other ADTs.**

```
1:     // Listing 13.9
2:     // Deriving ADTs from other ADTs
3:     #include <iostream.h>
4:
5:     enum COLOR { Red, Green, Blue, Yellow, White, Black, Brown } ;
6:
7:
8:     class Animal        // common base to both horse and bird
9:     {
10:    public:
11:        Animal(int);
12:        virtual ~Animal() { cout << "Animal destructor...\n"; }
13:        virtual int GetAge() const { return itsAge; }
14:        virtual void SetAge(int age) { itsAge = age; }
15:        virtual void Sleep() const = 0;
16:        virtual void Eat() const = 0;
17:        virtual void Reproduce() const = 0;
18:        virtual void Move() const = 0;
19:        virtual void Speak() const = 0;
20:    private:
21:        int itsAge;
22:    };
23:
24:    Animal::Animal(int age):
25:    itsAge(age)
26:    {
27:        cout << "Animal constructor...\n";
28:    }
```

continues

Listing 13.9. continued

```
29:
30:    class Mammal : public Animal
31:    {
32:    public:
33:        Mammal(int age):Animal(age){ cout << "Mammal constructor...\n";}
34:        ~Mammal() { cout << "Mammal destructor...\n";}
35:        virtual void Reproduce() const { cout <<
➥   "Mammal reproduction depicted...\n"; }
36:    };
37:
38:    class Fish : public Animal
39:    {
40:    public:
41:        Fish(int age):Animal(age){ cout << "Fish constructor...\n";}
42:        virtual ~Fish() {cout << "Fish destructor...\n";  }
43:        virtual void Sleep() const { cout << "fish snoring...\n"; }
44:        virtual void Eat() const { cout << "fish feeding...\n"; }
45:        virtual void Reproduce() const { cout << "fish laying eggs...\n"; }
46:        virtual void Move() const { cout << "fish swimming...\n";    }
47:        virtual void Speak() const { }
48:
49:    };
50:
51:    class Horse : public Mammal
52:    {
53:    public:
54:        Horse(int age, COLOR color ):
55:            Mammal(age), itsColor(color) { cout << "Horse constructor...\n"; }
56:        virtual ~Horse() { cout << "Horse destructor...\n"; }
57:        virtual void Speak()const { cout << "Whinny!... \n"; }
58:        virtual COLOR GetItsColor() const { return itsColor; }
59:        virtual void Sleep() const { cout << "Horse snoring...\n"; }
60:        virtual void Eat() const { cout << "Horse feeding...\n"; }
61:        virtual void Move() const { cout << "Horse running...\n";}
62:
63:    protected:
64:        COLOR itsColor;
65:    };
66:
67:    class Dog : public Mammal
68:    {
69:    public:
70:        Dog(int age, COLOR color ):
71:            Mammal(age), itsColor(color) { cout << "Dog constructor...\n"; }
72:        virtual ~Dog() { cout << "Dog destructor...\n"; }
73:        virtual void Speak()const { cout << "Whoof!... \n"; }
74:        virtual void Sleep() const { cout << "Dog snoring...\n"; }
75:        virtual void Eat() const { cout << "Dog eating...\n"; }
76:        virtual void Move() const  { cout << "Dog running...\n"; }
77:        virtual void Reproduce() const { cout << "Dogs reproducing...\n"; }
78:
79:    protected:
80:        COLOR itsColor;
81:    };
```

13

```
82:
83:     void main()
84:     {
85:         Animal *pAnimal=0;
86:         int choice;
87:         bool fQuit = false;
88:
89:         while (true)
90:         {
91:             cout << "(1)Dog (2)Horse (3)Fish (0)Quit: ";
92:             cin >> choice;
93:
94:             switch (choice)
95:             {
96:                 case 1: pAnimal = new Dog(5,Brown);
97:                 break;
98:                 case 2: pAnimal = new Horse(4,Black);
99:                 break;
100:                case 3: pAnimal = new Fish (5);
101:                break;
102:                default: fQuit = true;
103:                break;
104:            }
105:            if (fQuit)
106:                break;
107:
108:            pAnimal->Speak();
109:            pAnimal->Eat();
110:            pAnimal->Reproduce();
111:            pAnimal->Move();
112:            pAnimal->Sleep();
113:            delete pAnimal;
114:            cout << "\n";
115:        }
116:
117:
118:
119:    }
```

OUTPUT

```
   (1)Dog (2)Horse (3)Fish (0)Quit: 1
Animal constructor...
Mammal constructor...
Dog constructor...
Whoof!...
Dog eating...
Dog reproducing....
Dog running...
Dog snoring...
Dog destructor...
Mammal destructor...
Animal destructor...
   (1)Dog (2)Horse (3)Bird (0)Quit: 0
```

13

ANALYSIS On lines 8 through 22, the abstract data type `Animal` is declared. `Animal` has non-pure virtual accessors for `itsAge`, and they are shared by all `Animal` objects. It has five pure virtual functions: `Sleep()`, `Eat()`, `Reproduce()`, `Move()`, and `Speak()`.

`Mammal` is derived from `Animal` and is declared on lines 30 through 36 and adds no data. It overrides `Reproduce()` however, providing a common form of reproduction for all mammals. `Fish` *must* override `Reproduce()`, because `Fish` derives directly from `Animal` and cannot take advantage of mammalian reproduction (and a good thing, too!).

`Mammal` classes no longer have to override the `Reproduce()` function, but they are free to do so if they choose, as `Dog` does on line 77. `Fish`, `Horse`, and `Dog` all override the remaining pure virtual functions, so that objects of their respective types can be instantiated.

In the body of the program, an `Animal` pointer is used to point to the various derived objects in turn. The virtual methods are invoked, and based on the run-time binding of the pointer, the correct method is called in the derived class.

It would be a compile-time error to try to instantiate an `Animal` or a `Mammal`, because both are abstract data types.

Which Types Are Abstract?

In one program, the class `Animal` is abstract; in another, it is not. What determines whether to make a class abstract or not?

The answer to this question is decided not by any real-world intrinsic factor, but by what makes sense in your program. If you are writing a program that depicts a farm or a zoo, you may want `Animal` to be an abstract data type, but `Dog` to be a class from which you can instantiate objects.

On the other hand, if you are making an animated kennel, you may want to keep `Dog` as an abstract data type and only instantiate types of dogs: retrievers, terriers, and so forth. The level of abstraction is a function of how finely you need to distinguish your types.

Do	Don't

DO use abstract data types to provide common functionality for a number of related classes.

DO override all pure virtual functions.

DO make pure virtual any function that must be overridden.

DON'T try to instantiate an object of an abstract data type.

13

Summary

Today you learned how to take advantage of multiple inheritance and polymorphism, two key features that few computer languages can boast. You learned how to avoid possible pitfalls that come with multiple inheritance. You learned how to build virtual classes and abstract classes that model real-world concepts and how to use those classes to enhance your programs. Today was a day that you moved into areas that fainter hearts would have skipped. Congratulations!

Q&A

Q What does percolating functionality upward mean?

A This refers to the idea of moving shared functionality upward into a common base class. If more than one class shares a function, it is desirable to find a common base class in which that function can be stored.

Q Is percolating upward always a good thing?

A The answer is yes, if you are percolating *shared* functionality upward; no, if all you are moving is *interface*. That is, if all the derived classes can't use the method, it is a mistake to move it up into a common base class. If you do, you'll have to switch on the run-time type of the object before deciding if you can invoke the function.

Q Why is switching on the run-time type of an object bad?

A With large programs, the switch statements become large and hard to maintain. The point of virtual functions is to let the virtual table, rather than the programmer, determine the run-time type of the object.

Q Why is casting bad?

A Casting isn't bad if it is done in a way that is type-safe. If a function is called that *knows* that the object *must* be of a particular type, casting to that type is fine. Casting can be used to undermine the strong type checking in C++, and that is what you want to avoid. If you are switching on the run-time type of the object and then casting a pointer, that may be a warning sign that something is wrong with your design.

Q Why not make all functions virtual?

A Virtual functions are supported by a virtual function table that incurs run-time overhead, both in the size of the program and in the performance of the program. If you have very small classes that you don't expect to subclass, you may not want to make any of the functions virtual.

13

Q When should the destructor be made virtual?

A Any time you think the class will be subclassed and a pointer to the base class will be used to access an object of the subclass. As a general rule of thumb, if you've made *any* functions in your class virtual, be sure to make the destructor virtual as well.

Q Why bother making an abstract data type—why not just make it non-abstract and avoid creating any objects of that type?

A The purpose of many of the conventions in C++ is to enlist the compiler in finding bugs so as to avoid run-time bugs in code that you give your customers. Making a class abstract, that is, giving it pure virtual functions, causes the compiler to flag any objects created of that abstract type as errors.

Quiz

1. What is a downcast?

2. What is partial multiple inheritance?

3. If both `DomesticAnimal` and `Mammal` classes derive from `Animal` and `Dog` is derived from `DomesticAnimal` and `Mammal`, how many `Animals` are created when you instantiate a `Dog`?

4. If `Horse` and `Bird` inherit from `Animal` using public virtual inheritance, do their constructors initialize the `Animal` constructor? If `Pegasus` inherits from both `Horse` and `Bird`, how does it initialize `Animal`'s constructor?

5. Declare a class, `vehicle`, and make it an abstract data type.

6. If a base class is an ADT, and it has three pure virtual functions, how many of these *must* be overridden in its derived classes?

Exercises

1. Show the declaration for a class, `JetPlane`, that inherits from `Rocket` and `Airplane`.

2. Show the declaration for `747`, which inherits from the `JetPlane` class described in exercise 1.

3. Write a program that derives `Car` and `Bus` from the class `Vehicle`. Make `Vehicle` an ADT with two pure virtual functions. Make `Car` and `Bus` not be ADTs.

4. Modify the program in exercise 3 so that `Car` is an ADT, and derive `SportsCar`, `Wagon`, and `Coupe` from `Car`. In the `Car` class, provide an implementation for one of the pure virtual functions in `Vehicle` and make it non-pure.

Day 14

Special Classes and Functions

C++ offers a number of ways to limit the scope and impact of variables and pointers. So far, you've seen how to create global variables, local function variables, pointers to variables, and class member variables. Today you learn

☐ What static member variables and static member functions are.

☐ How to use static member variables and static member functions.

☐ How to create and manipulate pointers to functions and pointers to member functions.

☐ How to work with arrays of pointers to functions.

Static Member Data

Until now, you have probably thought of the data in each object as unique to that object and not shared among objects in a class. For example, if you have five Cat objects, each has its own age, weight, and other data. The age of one does not affect the age of another.

There are times, however, when you'll want to keep track of a pool of data. For example, you might want to know how many objects for a specific class have been created in your program, and how many are still in existence. Static member variables are shared among all instances of a class. They are a compromise between global data, which is available to all parts of your program, and member data, which is usually available only to each object.

You can think of a static member as belonging to the class rather than to the object. Normal member data is one per object, but static members are one per class. Listing 14.1 declares a Cat object with a static data member, HowManyCats. This variable keeps track of how many Cat objects have been created. This is done by incrementing the static variable, HowManyCats, with each construction and decrementing it with each destruction.

TYPE   **Listing 14.1. Static member data.**

```
1:     //Listing 14.1 static data members
2:
3:     #include <iostream.h>
4:
5:     class Cat
6:     {
7:     public:
8:        Cat(int age):itsAge(age){HowManyCats++; }
9:        virtual ~Cat() { HowManyCats--; }
10:       virtual int GetAge() { return itsAge; }
11:       virtual void SetAge(int age) { itsAge = age; }
12:       static int HowManyCats;
13:
14:    private:
15:       int itsAge;
16:
17:    };
18:
19:    int Cat::HowManyCats = 0;
20:
21:    void main()
22:    {
23:       const int MaxCats = 5;
24:       Cat *CatHouse[MaxCats];
25:       for (int i = 0; i<MaxCats; i++)
26:          CatHouse[i] = new Cat(i);
27:
28:       for (i = 0; i<MaxCats; i++)
29:       {
30:          cout << "There are ";
31:          cout << Cat::HowManyCats;
32:          cout << " cats left!\n";
33:          cout << "Deleting the one which is ";
34:          cout << CatHouse[i]->GetAge();
35:          cout << " years old\n";
36:          delete CatHouse[i];
37:          CatHouse[i] = 0;
38:       }
39:    }
```

14

```
There are 5 cats left!
Deleting the one which is 0 years old
There are 4 cats left!
Deleting the one which is 1 years old
There are 3 cats left!
Deleting the one which is 2 years old
There are 2 cats left!
Deleting the one which is 3 years old
There are 1 cats left!
Deleting the one which is 4 years old
```

ANALYSIS On lines 5 to 17 the simplified class Cat is declared. On line 12 HowManyCats is declared to be a static member variable of type int.

The declaration of HowManyCats does not define an integer; no storage space is set aside. Unlike the nonstatic member variables, no storage space is set aside by instantiating a Cat object because the HowManyCats member variable is not *in* the object. Thus, on line 19 the variable is defined and initialized.

It is a common mistake to forget to define the static member variables of classes. Don't let this happen to you! Of course, if it does, the linker catches it with a helpful error message such as the following:

```
undefined symbol Cat::HowManyCats
```

You don't need to do this for itsAge because it is a nonstatic member variable and is defined each time you make a Cat object, which you do here on line 26.

The constructor for Cat increments the static member variable on line 8. The destructor decrements it on line 9. Thus, at any moment, HowManyCats has an accurate measure of how many Cat objects were created but not yet destroyed.

The driver program on lines 21 to 39 instantiates five Cats and puts them in an array. This calls five Cat constructors, and thus HowManyCats is incremented five times from its initial value of 0.

The program then loops through each of the five positions in the array and prints out the value of HowManyCats before deleting the current Cat pointer. The printout reflects that the starting value is five (after all, five are constructed), and that each time the loop is run, one fewer Cat remains.

Note that HowManyCats is public and is accessed directly by main(). There is no reason to expose this member variable in this way. It is preferable to make it private along with the other member variables and provide a public accessor method, as long as you can always access the data through an instance of Cat. On the other hand, if you would like to access this data directly without necessarily having a Cat object available, you have two options: Keep it public, as shown in Listing 14.2, or provide a static member function, as discussed later in this lesson.

14

TYPE   **Listing 14.2. Accessing static members without an object.**

```
1:      //Listing 14.2 static data members
2:
3:      #include <iostream.h>
4:
5:      class Cat
6:      {
7:      public:
8:          Cat(int age):itsAge(age){HowManyCats++; }
9:          virtual ~Cat() { HowManyCats--; }
10:         virtual int GetAge() { return itsAge; }
11:         virtual void SetAge(int age) { itsAge = age; }
12:         static int HowManyCats;
13:
14:     private:
15:         int itsAge;
16:
17:     };
18:
19:     int Cat::HowManyCats = 0;
20:
21:     void TelepathicFunction();
22:
23:     void main()
24:     {
25:         const int MaxCats = 5;
26:         Cat *CatHouse[MaxCats];
27:         for (int i = 0; i<MaxCats; i++)
28:         {
29:             CatHouse[i] = new Cat(i);
30:             TelepathicFunction();
31:         }
32:
33:         for ( i = 0; i<MaxCats; i++)
34:         {
35:             delete CatHouse[i];
36:             TelepathicFunction();
37:         }
38:     }
39:
40:     void TelepathicFunction()
41:     {
42:         cout << "There are " << Cat::HowManyCats << " cats alive!\n";
43:     }
```

OUTPUT
```
There are 1 cats alive!
There are 2 cats alive!
There are 3 cats alive!
There are 4 cats alive!
There are 5 cats alive!
There are 4 cats alive!
There are 3 cats alive!
There are 2 cats alive!
```

14

```
There are 1 cats alive!
There are 0 cats alive!
```

ANALYSIS Listing 14.2 is much like Listing 14.1 except for the addition of a new function, `TelepathicFunction()`. This function does not create a Cat object, nor does it take a Cat object as a parameter, yet it can access the HowManyCats member variable. Again, it is worth reemphasizing that this member variable is not in any particular object; it is in the class as a whole, and if public, it can be accessed by any function in the program.

The alternative to making this member variable public is to make it private. If you do, you can access it through a member function, but then you must have an object of that class available. Listing 14.3 shows this approach. The alternative, static member functions, is discussed immediately after the analysis of Listing 14.3.

TYPE

Listing 14.3. Accessing static members using nonstatic member functions.

```
1:      //Listing 14.3 private static data members
2:
3:      #include <iostream.h>
4:
5:      class Cat
6:      {
7:      public:
8:          Cat(int age):itsAge(age){HowManyCats++; }
9:          virtual ~Cat() { HowManyCats--; }
10:         virtual int GetAge() { return itsAge; }
11:         virtual void SetAge(int age) { itsAge = age; }
12:         virtual int GetHowMany() { return HowManyCats; }
13:
14:
15:     private:
16:         int itsAge;
17:         static int HowManyCats;
18:     };
19:
20:     int Cat::HowManyCats = 0;
21:
22:     void main()
23:     {
24:         const int MaxCats = 5;
25:         Cat *CatHouse[MaxCats];
26:         for (int i = 0; i<MaxCats; i++)
27:             CatHouse[i] = new Cat(i);
28:
29:         for (i = 0; i<MaxCats; i++)
30:         {
31:             cout << "There are ";
32:             cout << CatHouse[i]->GetHowMany();
33:             cout << " cats left!\n";
34:             cout << "Deleting the one which is ";
```

continues

14

Listing 14.3. continued

```
35:             cout << CatHouse[i]->GetAge()+2;
36:             cout << " years old\n";
37:             delete CatHouse[i];
38:             CatHouse[i] = 0;
39:         }
40:     }
```

OUTPUT
```
There are 5 cats left!
Deleting the one which is 2 years old
There are 4 cats left!
Deleting the one which is 3 years old
There are 3 cats left!
Deleting the one which is 4 years old
There are 2 cats left!
Deleting the one which is 5 years old
There are 1 cats left!
Deleting the one which is 6 years old
```

ANALYSIS On line 17 the static member variable HowManyCats is declared to have private access. Now you cannot access this variable from nonmember functions, such as TelepathicFunction from the previous listing.

Even though HowManyCats is static, it is still within the scope of the class. Any class function (such as GetHowMany()) can access it, just as member functions can access any member data. However, for a function to call GetHowMany(), it must have an object on which to call the function.

Do	Don't

DO use static member variables to share data among all instances of a class.

DO make static member variables protected or private if you want to restrict access to them.

DON'T use static member variables to store data for one object. Static member data is shared among all objects of its class.

Static Member Functions

Static member functions are like static member variables: They exist not in an object but in the scope of the class. They can therefore be called without having an object of that class, as illustrated in Listing 14.4.

TYPE **Listing 14.4. Static member functions.**

```
1:      //Listing 14.4 static data members
2:
3:      #include <iostream.h>
4:
5:      class Cat
6:      {
7:      public:
8:          Cat(int age):itsAge(age){HowManyCats++; }
9:          virtual ~Cat() { HowManyCats--; }
10:         virtual int GetAge() { return itsAge; }
11:         virtual void SetAge(int age) { itsAge = age; }
12:         static int GetHowMany() { return HowManyCats; }
13:     private:
14:         int itsAge;
15:         static int HowManyCats;
16:     };
17:
18:     int Cat::HowManyCats = 0;
19:
20:     void TelepathicFunction();
21:
22:     void main()
23:     {
24:         const int MaxCats = 5;
25:         Cat *CatHouse[MaxCats];
26:         for (int i = 0; i<MaxCats; i++)
27:         {
28:             CatHouse[i] = new Cat(i);
29:             TelepathicFunction();
30:         }
31:
32:         for ( i = 0; i<MaxCats; i++)
33:         {
34:             delete CatHouse[i];
35:             TelepathicFunction();
36:         }
37:     }
38:
39:     void TelepathicFunction()
40:     {
41:         cout << "There are " << Cat::GetHowMany() << " cats alive!\n";
42:     }
```

OUTPUT
```
There are 1 cats alive!
There are 2 cats alive!
There are 3 cats alive!
There are 4 cats alive!
There are 5 cats alive!
There are 4 cats alive!
There are 3 cats alive!
There are 2 cats alive!
There are 1 cats alive!
There are 0 cats alive!
```

14

The static member variable `HowManyCats` is declared to have private access on line 15 of the `Cat` declaration. The public accessor function, `GetHowMany()`, is declared to be both public and static on line 12.

Because `GetHowMany()` is public, it can be accessed by any function, and because it is static, there is no need to have an object of type `Cat` on which to call it. Thus, on line 41, the function `TelepathicFunction()` is able to access the public static accessor, even though it has no access to a `Cat` object. Of course, you could have called `GetHowMany()` on the `Cat` objects available in `main()`, just as with any other accessor functions.

 NOTE   Static member functions do not have a `this` pointer. For this reason, they cannot be declared `const` or `virtual`. Also, because member data variables are accessed in member functions using the `this` pointer, static member functions cannot access any nonstatic member variables!

Static Member Functions

SYNTAX

You can access static member functions by calling them on an object of the class just as you do any other member function, or you can call them without an object by fully qualifying the class and object name.

Example:

```
class Cat
{
public:
    static int GetHowMany() { return HowManyCats; }
private:
    static int HowManyCats;
};
    int Cat::HowManyCats = 0;
void main()
{
    int howMany;
    Cat theCat;                        // define a cat
    howMany = theCat.GetHowMany();     // access through an object
    howMany = Cat::GetHowMany();       // access without an object
}
```

Pointers to Functions

Just as an array name is a constant pointer to the first element of the array, a function name is a constant pointer to the function. It is possible to declare a pointer variable that points to a function and then invoke the function by using that pointer. This can be very useful; it enables you to create programs that decide which functions to invoke based on user input.

The only tricky part about function pointers is understanding the type of the object being pointed to. A pointer to int points to an integer variable, and a pointer to a function must point to a function of the appropriate return type and signature.

In the declaration

```
long (* funcPtr) (int);
```

funcPtr is declared to be a pointer (not the * in front of the name) pointing to a function that takes an integer parameter and returns a long. The parentheses around * funcPtr are necessary because the parentheses around int bind more tightly; they have higher precedence than the indirection operator (*). Without the first parentheses this declares a function that takes an integer and returns a pointer to a long. (Remember that spaces are meaningless here.)

Examine these two declarations:

```
long * Function (int);
long (* funcPtr) (int);
```

The first declaration, Function (), is a function taking an integer and returning a pointer to a variable of type long. The second, funcPtr, is a pointer to a function taking an integer and returning a variable of type long.

The declaration of a function pointer always includes the return type and the parentheses indicating the type of the parameters, if any. Listing 14.5 illustrates the declaration and use of function pointers.

TYPE Listing 14.5. Pointers to functions.

```
1:     // Listing 14.5 Using function pointers
2:
3:     #include <iostream.h>
4:
5:     void Square (int&,int&);
6:     void Cube (int&, int&);
7:     void Swap (int&, int &);
8:     void GetVals(int&, int&);
9:     void PrintVals(int, int);
10:
11:
12:    void main()
13:    {
14:        void (* pFunc) (int &, int &);
15:        bool fQuit = false;
16:
17:        int valOne=1, valTwo=2;
```

continues

14

Listing 14.5. continued

```
18:         int choice;
19:         while (fQuit == false)
20:         {
21:            cout << "(0)Quit (1)Change Values (2)Square (3)Cube (4)Swap: ";
22:            cin >> choice;
23:            switch (choice)
24:            {
25:               case 1: pFunc = GetVals; break;
26:               case 2: pFunc = Square; break;
27:               case 3: pFunc = Cube; break;
28:               case 4: pFunc = Swap; break;
29:               default : fQuit = true; break;
30:            }
31:
32:            if (fQuit)
33:               break;
34:
35:            PrintVals(valOne, valTwo);
36:            pFunc(valOne, valTwo);
37:            PrintVals(valOne, valTwo);
38:         }
39:      }
40:
41:      void PrintVals(int x, int y)
42:      {
43:         cout << "x: " << x << " y: " << y << endl;
44:      }
45:
46:      void Square (int & rX, int & rY)
47:      {
48:         rX *= rX;
49:         rY *= rY;
50:      }
51:
52:      void Cube (int & rX, int & rY)
53:      {
54:         int tmp;
55:
56:         tmp = rX;
57:         rX *= rX;
58:         rX = rX * tmp;
59:
60:         tmp = rY;
61:         rY *= rY;
62:         rY = rY * tmp;
63:      }
64:
65:      void Swap(int & rX, int & rY)
66:      {
67:         int temp;
68:         temp = rX;
69:         rX = rY;
70:         rY = temp;
71:      }
```

```
72:
73:    void GetVals (int & rValOne, int & rValTwo)
74:    {
75:       cout << "New value for ValOne: ";
76:       cin >> rValOne;
77:       cout << "New value for ValTwo: ";
78:       cin >> rValTwo;
79:    }
```

OUTPUT
```
  (0)Quit (1)Change Values (2)Square (3)Cube (4)Swap: 1
x: 1 y:2
New value for ValOne: 2
New value for ValTwo: 3
x: 2 y:3
(0)Quit (1)Change Values (2)Square (3)Cube (4)Swap: 3
x: 2 y:3
x: 8 y: 27
(0)Quit (1)Change Values (2)Square (3)Cube (4)Swap: 2
x: 8 y: 27
x:64 y:729
(0)Quit (1)Change Values (2)Square (3)Cube (4)Swap: 4
x:64 y:729
x:729 y:64
  (0)Quit (1)Change Values (2)Square (3)Cube (4)Swap: 0
```

ANALYSIS On lines 5 through 8, four functions are declared, each with the same return type and signature, returning void and taking two references to integers.

On line 14, pFunc is declared to be a pointer to a function that returns void and takes two integer reference parameters. Any of the previous functions can be pointed to by pFunc. The user is repeatedly offered the choice of which functions to invoke, and pFunc is assigned accordingly. On lines 35 and 36, the current value of the two integers is printed, the currently assigned function is invoked, and then the values are printed again.

Pointer to Function

SYNTAX

A pointer to function is invoked exactly like the functions to which it points, except that the function pointer name is used instead of the function name.

Assign a pointer to function to a specific function by assigning to the function name without the parentheses. The function name is a constant pointer to the function itself. Use the pointer to function just as you would the function name. The pointer to function must agree in return value and signature with the function to which you assign it.

Example:

```
long (*pFuncOne) (int, int);
long SomeFunction (int, int);
pFuncOne = SomeFunction;
pFuncOne(5,7);
```

14

Why Use Function Pointers?

You certainly could write the program in Listing 14.5 without function pointers, but the use of these pointers makes the intent and use of the program explicit: Pick a function from a list, and then invoke it.

Listing 14.6 uses the function prototypes and definitions from Listing 14.5, but the body of the program does not use a function pointer. Examine the differences between these two listings.

NOTE To compile this program, place lines 41 to 79 from Listing 14.5 immediately after line 55.

TYPE **Listing 14.6. Rewriting Listing 14.5 without the pointer to function.**

```
1:   // Listing 14.6 Without function pointers
2:
3:   #include <iostream.h>
4:
5:   void Square (int&,int&);
6:   void Cube (int&, int&);
7:   void Swap (int&, int &);
8:   void GetVals(int&, int&);
9:   void PrintVals(int, int);
10:
11:
12:  void main()
13:  {
14:     bool fQuit = false;
15:     int valOne=1, valTwo=2;
16:     int choice;
17:     while (fQuit == false)
18:     {
19:        cout << "(0)Quit (1)Change Values (2)Square (3)Cube (4)Swap: ";
20:        cin >> choice;
21:        switch (choice)
22:        {
23:           case 1:
24:              PrintVals(valOne, valTwo);
25:              GetVals(valOne, valTwo);
26:              PrintVals(valOne, valTwo);
27:              break;
28:
29:           case 2:
30:              PrintVals(valOne, valTwo);
31:              Square(valOne,valTwo);
```

14

```
32:                    PrintVals(valOne, valTwo);
33:                    break;
34:
35:                case 3:
36:                    PrintVals(valOne, valTwo);
37:                    Cube(valOne, valTwo);
38:                    PrintVals(valOne, valTwo);
39:                    break;
40:
41:                case 4:
42:                    PrintVals(valOne, valTwo);
43:                    Swap(valOne, valTwo);
44:                    PrintVals(valOne, valTwo);
45:                    break;
46:
47:                default :
48:                    fQuit = true;
49:                    break;
50:            }
51:
52:            if (fQuit)
53:                break;
54:        }
55:    }
```

OUTPUT

```
(0)Quit (1)Change Values (2)Square (3)Cube (4)Swap: 1
x: 1 y:2
New value for ValOne: 2
New value for ValTwo: 3
X: 2 y: 3
(0)Quit (1)Change Values (2)Square (3)Cube (4)Swap: 3
x: 2 y:3
x: 8 y: 27
(0)Quit (1)Change Values (2)Square (3)Cube (4)Swap: 2
x: 8 y: 27
x:64 y:729
(0)Quit (1)Change Values (2)Square (3)Cube (4)Swap: 4
x:64 y:729
x:729 y:64
 (0)Quit (1)Change Values (2)Square (3)Cube (4)Swap: 0
```

ANALYSIS The implementation of the functions has been left out because it is identical to that provided in Listing 14.5. As you can see, the output is unchanged, but the body of the program has expanded from 27 lines to 38. The calls to PrintVals() must be repeated for each case.

It was tempting to put PrintVals() at the top of the while loop and again at the bottom, rather than in each case statement. This would have called PrintVals() even for the exit case, however, and that was not part of the specification.

Setting aside the increased size of the code and the repeated calls to do the same thing, the overall clarity is somewhat diminished. This is an artificial case, however, created to show how

14

pointers to functions work. In real-world conditions the advantages are even clearer: Pointers to functions can eliminate duplicate code, clarify your program, and enable you to make tables of functions to call based on runtime conditions.

Callback Functions

Callback functions are functions that are called when a certain event occurs. Callback functions are often implemented using function pointers. For instance, you might have one class that monitors the activity of another class. You want a certain function to be called—for instance, InterpretEvent() when an event occurs. InterpretEvent() is a callback function. Callback functions are declared and used differently depending on your operating system and compiler.

Shorthand Invocation

The pointer to function does not need to be dereferenced, although you are free to do so. Therefore, if pFunc is a pointer to a function taking an integer and returning a variable of type long, and you assign pFunc to a matching function, you can invoke that function with either

```
pFunc(x);
```

or

```
(*pFunc)(x);
```

The two forms are identical. The former is just a shorthand version of the latter.

Arrays of Pointers to Functions

Just as you can declare an array of pointers to integers, you can declare an array of pointers to functions returning a specific value type and with a specific signature. Listing 14.7 again rewrites Listing 14.5, this time using an array to invoke all the choices at once.

NOTE

To compile this program, place lines 41 to 79 of Listing 14.5 immediately after line 38.

TYPE   Listing 14.7. Using an array of pointers to functions.

```
1:     // Listing 14.7 demonstrates use of an array of pointers to functions
2:
3:     #include <iostream.h>
4:
5:     void Square (int&,int&);
6:     void Cube (int&, int&);
7:     void Swap (int&, int &);
8:     void GetVals(int&, int&);
9:     void PrintVals(int, int);
10:
11:
12:    void main()
13:    {
14:        int valOne=1, valTwo=2;
15:        int choice;
16:        const MaxArray = 5;
17:        void (*pFuncArray[MaxArray])(int&, int&);
18:
19:        for (int i=0;i<MaxArray;i++)
20:        {
21:           cout << "(1)Change Values (2)Square (3)Cube (4)Swap: ";
22:           cin >> choice;
23:           switch (choice)
24:           {
25:              case 1:pFuncArray[i] = GetVals; break;
26:              case 2:pFuncArray[i] = Square; break;
27:              case 3:pFuncArray[i] = Cube; break;
28:              case 4:pFuncArray[i] = Swap; break;
29:              default:pFuncArray[i] = 0;
30:           }
31:        }
32:
33:        for (i=0;i<MaxArray; i++)
34:        {
35:           pFuncArray[i](valOne,valTwo);
36:           PrintVals(valOne,valTwo);
37:        }
38:    }
```

OUTPUT
```
(1)Change Values (2)Square (3)Cube (4)Swap: 1
(1)Change Values (2)Square (3)Cube (4)Swap: 2
(1)Change Values (2)Square (3)Cube (4)Swap: 3
(1)Change Values (2)Square (3)Cube (4)Swap: 4
(1)Change Values (2)Square (3)Cube (4)Swap: 2
New Value for ValOne: 2
New Value for ValTwo: 3
x: 2 y: 3
x: 4 y: 9
x: 64 y: 729
x: 729 y: 64
x: 531441 y:4096
```

14

Once again, the implementation of the functions has been left out to save space, but it is the same as in Listing 14.5. On line 17, the array pFuncArray is declared to be an array of five pointers to functions that return void and take two integer references.

On lines 19 to 31, the user is asked to pick the functions to invoke, and each member of the array is assigned the address of the appropriate function. On lines 33 to 37, each function is invoked in turn. The result is printed after each invocation.

Passing Pointers to Functions to Other Functions

The pointers to functions (and arrays of pointers to functions, for that matter) can be passed to other functions, which can take action and then call the right function using the pointer.

For example, you might improve Listing 14.5 by passing the chosen function pointer to another function (outside of main()), which prints the values, invokes the function, and then prints the values again. Listing 14.8 illustrates this variation.

NOTE

> To compile this program, place lines 46 to 79 of Listing 14.5 immediately after line 44.

 Listing 14.8. Passing pointers to functions as function arguments.

```
1:      // Listing 14.8 Without function pointers
2:
3:      #include <iostream.h>
4:
5:      void Square (int&,int&);
6:      void Cube (int&, int&);
7:      void Swap (int&, int &);
8:      void GetVals(int&, int&);
9:      void PrintVals(void (*)(int&, int&),int&, int&);
10:
11:
12:     void main()
13:     {
14:        int valOne=1, valTwo=2;
15:        int choice;
16:        bool fQuit = false;
17:
18:        void (*pFunc)(int&, int&);
19:
20:        while (fQuit == false)
21:        {
```

```
22:            cout << "(0)Quit (1)Change Values (2)Square (3)Cube (4)Swap: ";
23:            cin >> choice;
24:            switch (choice)
25:            {
26:                case 1:pFunc = GetVals; break;
27:                case 2:pFunc = Square; break;
28:                case 3:pFunc = Cube; break;
29:                case 4:pFunc = Swap; break;
30:                default:fQuit = true; break;
31:            }
32:            if (fQuit == true)
33:                break;
34:            PrintVals ( pFunc, valOne, valTwo);
35:        }
36:
37:    }
38:
39:    void PrintVals( void (*pFunc)(int&, int&),int& x, int& y)
40:    {
41:        cout << "x: " << x << " y: " << y << endl;
42:        pFunc(x,y);
43:        cout << "x: " << x << " y: " << y << endl;
44:    }
```

OUTPUT
```
    (0)Quit (1)Change Values (2)Square (3)Cube (4)Swap: 1
x: 1 y:2
New value for ValOne: 2
New value for ValTwo: 3
x: 2 y:3
(0)Quit (1)Change Values (2)Square (3)Cube (4)Swap: 3
x: 2 y:3
x: 8 y: 27
(0)Quit (1)Change Values (2)Square (3)Cube (4)Swap: 2
x: 8 y: 27
x:64 y:729
(0)Quit (1)Change Values (2)Square (3)Cube (4)Swap: 4
x:64 y:729
x:729 y:64
    (0)Quit (1)Change Values (2)Square (3)Cube (4)Swap: 0
```

ANALYSIS On line 18, pFunc is declared to be a pointer to a function returning void and taking two parameters, both integer references. On line 9, PrintVals is declared to be a function taking three parameters. The first is a pointer to a function that returns void but takes two integer reference parameters, and the second and third arguments to PrintVals are integer references. The user is again prompted for which functions to call; then, on line 34, PrintVals is called.

This is the kind of declaration that you use infrequently and probably look up in the book each time you need it, but it saves your program on those rare occasions when it is exactly the required construct.

14

Using *typedef* with Pointers to Functions

The construct void (*)(int&, int&) is cumbersome at best. You can use typedef to simplify this. Declare a type VPF as a pointer to a function returning void and taking two integer references. Listing 14.9 rewrites Listing 14.8 using this typedef statement.

TYPE

Listing 14.9. Using typedef to make pointers to functions more readable.

```
1:      // Listing 14.9. using typedef to make pointers to
2:      // functions more _readable
3:      #include <iostream.h>
4:
5:      void Square (int&,int&);
6:      void Cube (int&, int&);
7:      void Swap (int&, int &);
8:      void GetVals(int&, int&);
9:      typedef  void (*VPF) (int&, int&) ;
10:     void PrintVals(VPF,int&, int&);
11:
12:
13:     void main()
14:     {
15:         int valOne=1, valTwo=2;
16:         int choice;
17:         bool fQuit = false;
18:
19:         VPF pFunc;
20:
21:         while (fQuit == false)
22:         {
23:             cout << "(0)Quit (1)Change Values (2)Square (3)Cube (4)Swap: ";
24:             cin >> choice;
25:             switch (choice)
26:             {
27:                 case 1:pFunc = GetVals; break;
28:                 case 2:pFunc = Square; break;
29:                 case 3:pFunc = Cube; break;
30:                 case 4:pFunc = Swap; break;
31:                 default:fQuit = true; break;
32:             }
33:             if (fQuit == true)
34:                 break;
35:             PrintVals ( pFunc, valOne, valTwo);
36:         }
37:
38:     }
39:
40:     void PrintVals( VPF pFunc,int& x, int& y)
41:     {
42:         cout << "x: " << x << " y: " << y << endl;
43:         pFunc(x,y);
44:         cout << "x: " << x << " y: " << y << endl;
45:     }
```

14

OUTPUT
```
  (0)Quit (1)Change Values (2)Square (3)Cube (4)Swap: 1
x: 1 y:2
New value for ValOne: 2
New value for ValTwo: 3
x: 2 y:3
(0)Quit (1)Change Values (2)Square (3)Cube (4)Swap: 3
x: 2 y:3
x: 8 y: 27
(0)Quit (1)Change Values (2)Square (3)Cube (4)Swap: 2
x: 8 y: 27
x:64 y:729
(0)Quit (1)Change Values (2)Square (3)Cube (4)Swap: 4
x:64 y:729
x:729 y:64
  (0)Quit (1)Change Values (2)Square (3)Cube (4)Swap: 0
```

ANALYSIS
On line 9, typedef is used to declare VPF to be of the type of a function that returns void and takes two parameters, both integer references.

On line 10 the function PrintVals() is declared to take three parameters—a VPF and two integer references. On line 19, pFunc is now declared to be of type VPF.

When the type VPF is defined, all subsequent uses to declare pFunc and PrintVals() are much cleaner. The output is identical.

Pointers to Member Functions

Up to this point, all of the function pointers you've created have been for general, nonclass functions. It is also possible to create pointers to functions that are members of classes.

To create a pointer to member function, use the same syntax as with a pointer to function, but include the class name and the scoping operator (::). If pFunc points to a member function of the class Shape, which takes two integers and returns void, the declaration for pFunc is the following:

```
void (Shape::*pFunc) (int, int);
```

Pointers to member functions are used in exactly the same way as pointers to functions, except that they require an object of the correct class on which to invoke them. Listing 14.10 illustrates the use of pointers to member functions.

TYPE **Listing 14.10. Pointers to member functions.**

```
1:     //Listing 14.10 Pointers to member functions using virtual methods
2:
3:     #include <iostream.h>
4:
5:
```

continues

Listing 14.10. continued

```
6:      class Mammal
7:      {
8:      public:
9:         Mammal():itsAge(1) {  }
10:        ~Mammal() { }
11:        virtual void Speak() const = 0;
12:        virtual void Move() const = 0;
13:     protected:
14:        int itsAge;
15:     };
16:
17:     class Dog : public Mammal
18:     {
19:     public:
20:        void Speak()const { cout << "Woof!\n"; }
21:        void Move() const { cout << "Walking to heel...\n"; }
22:     };
23:
24:
25:     class Cat : public Mammal
26:     {
27:     public:
28:        void Speak()const { cout << "Meow!\n"; }
29:        void Move() const { cout << "slinking...\n"; }
30:     };
31:
32:
33:     class Horse : public Mammal
34:     {
35:     public:
36:        void Speak()const { cout << "Winnie!\n"; }
37:        void Move() const { cout << "Galloping...\n"; }
38:     };
39:
40:
41:     void main()
42:     {
43:        void (Mammal::*pFunc)() const =0;
44:        Mammal* ptr =0;
45:        int Animal;
46:        int Method;
47:        bool fQuit = false;
48:
49:        while (fQuit == false)
50:        {
51:           cout << "(0)Quit (1)dog (2)cat (3)horse: ";
52:           cin >> Animal;
53:           switch (Animal)
54:           {
55:              case 1: ptr = new Dog; break;
56:              case 2: ptr = new Cat; break;
57:              case 3: ptr = new Horse; break;
58:              default: fQuit = true; break;
59:           }
```

14

```
60:            if (fQuit)
61:                break;
62:
63:            cout << "(1)Speak  (2)Move: ";
64:            cin >> Method;
65:            switch (Method)
66:            {
67:                case 1: pFunc = Mammal::Speak; break;
68:                default: pFunc = Mammal::Move; break;
69:            }
70:
71:            (ptr->*pFunc)();
72:            delete ptr;
73:        }
74:    }
```

 OUTPUT
```
 (0)Quit (1)Dog (2)Cat (3)Horse: 1
(1)Speak (2)Move: 1
Woof!
(0)Quit (1)Dog (2)Cat (3)Horse: 2
(1)Speak (2)Move: 1
Meow!
(0)Quit (1)Dog (2)Cat (3)Horse: 3
(1)Speak (2)Move: 2
Galloping...
 (0)Quit (1)Dog (2)Cat (3)Horse: 0
```

ANALYSIS On lines 6 to 15, the abstract data type Mammal is declared, with two pure virtual methods—Speak() and Move(). Mammal is subclassed into Dog, Cat, and Horse, each of which overrides Speak() and Move().

The driver program in main() asks the user to choose which type of animal to create, and then a new subclass of Animal is created on the free store and assigned to ptr on lines 55 to 57.

The user is then prompted for which method to invoke, and that method is assigned to the pointer pFunc. On line 71 the chosen method is invoked by the object created by using the pointer ptr to access the object and pFunc to access the function.

Finally, on line 72, delete is called on the pointer ptr to return the memory set aside for the object to the free store. Note that there is no reason to call delete on pFunc because this is a pointer to code, not to an object on the free store. In fact, attempting to do so generates a compile-time error.

Arrays of Pointers to Member Functions

As with pointers to functions, pointers to member functions can be stored in an array. The array can be initialized with the addresses of various member functions, and these can be invoked by offsets into the array. Listing 14.11 illustrates this technique.

14

TYPE   **Listing 14.11. Array of pointers to member functions.**

```
1:      //Listing 14.11 Array of pointers to member functions
2:
3:      #include <iostream.h>
4:
5:
6:
7:      class Dog
8:      {
9:      public:
10:         void Speak()const { cout << "Woof!\n"; }
11:         void Move() const { cout << "Walking to heel...\n"; }
12:         void Eat() const { cout << "Gobbling food...\n"; }
13:         void Growl() const { cout << "Grrrrr\n"; }
14:         void Whimper() const { cout << "Whining noises...\n"; }
15:         void RollOver() const { cout << "Rolling over...\n"; }
16:         void PlayDead() const { cout
➥   << "Is this the end of Little Caeser?\n"; }
17:      };
18:
19:      typedef void (Dog::*PDF)()const ;
20:      void main()
21:      {
22:         const int MaxFuncs = 7;
23:         PDF DogFunctions[MaxFuncs] =
24:             {  Dog::Speak,
25:                Dog::Move,
26:                Dog::Eat,
27:                Dog::Growl,
28:                Dog::Whimper,
29:                Dog::RollOver,
30:                Dog::PlayDead };
31:
32:         Dog* pDog =0;
33:         int Method;
34:         bool fQuit = false;
35:
36:         while (!fQuit)
37:         {
38:             cout <<     "(0)Quit (1)Speak (2)Move (3)Eat (4)Growl";
39:             cout << " (5)Whimper (6)Roll Over (7)Play Dead: ";
40:             cin >> Method;
41:             if (Method == 0)
42:             {
43:                 fQuit = true;
44:                 break;
45:             }
46:             else
47:             {
48:                 pDog = new Dog;
49:                 (pDog->*DogFunctions[Method-1])();
50:                 delete pDog;
51:             }
52:         }
53:      }
```

14

OUTPUT

```
  (0)Quit (1)Speak (2)Move (3)Eat (4)Growl (5)Whimper
➥(6)Roll Over (7)Play Dead: 1
Woof!
(0)Quit (1)Speak (2)Move (3)Eat (4)Growl (5)Whimper
➥(6)Roll Over (7)Play Dead: 4
Grrrrr
(0)Quit (1)Speak (2)Move (3)Eat (4)Growl (5)Whimper
➥(6)Roll Over (7)Play Dead: 7
Is this the end of Little Caeser?
  (0)Quit (1)Speak (2)Move (3)Eat (4)Growl (5)Whimper
➥(6)Roll Over (7)Play Dead: 0
```

ANALYSIS

On lines 7 to 17, the class Dog is created, with seven member functions all sharing the same return type and signature. On line 19, a typedef declares PDF to be a pointer to a member function of Dog that takes no parameters and returns no values. That pointer is const, the return signature of the seven member functions of Dog.

On lines 23 to 30, the array DogFunctions is declared to hold seven such member functions, and it is initialized with the addresses of these functions.

On lines 38 and 39, the user is prompted to pick a method. Unless the user picks Quit, a new Dog is created on the heap, and then the correct method is invoked on the array on line 49.

Once again, this is a bit esoteric, but when you need a table built from member functions, it can make your program far easier to read and understand.

Do	Don't

DO invoke pointers to member functions on a specific object of a class.

DO use typedef to make pointer to member function declarations easier to read.

DON'T use pointer to member functions when there are simpler solutions.

Summary

Today you learned how to create static member variables in your class. Each class, rather than each object, has one instance of the static member variable. It is possible to access this member variable without an object of the class type by fully qualifying the name, assuming you've declared the static member to have public access.

Static member variables can be used as counters across instances of the class, and static member functions are part of the class in the same way as static member variables.

14

You also learned how to declare and use pointers to functions and pointers to member functions. You saw how to create arrays of these pointers and how to pass them to functions.

Pointers to functions and pointers to member functions can be used to create tables of functions that can be selected from at runtime. This adds flexibility to your program not easily achieved without these pointers.

Q&A

Q Why use static data when you can use global data?

A Static data is scoped to the class, and it is therefore available only through an object of the class, through an explicit and full call using the class name if the static data is public, or by using a static member function. Static data is typed to the class type, however, and the restricted access and strong typing makes static data safer than global data.

Q Why use static member functions when you can use global functions?

A Static member functions are scoped to the class and can be called only by using an object of the class or an explicit full specification (such as `ClassName::FunctionName()`).

Q Is it common to use many pointers to functions and pointers to member functions?

A No, these have their special uses but are not common constructs. Many complex and powerful programs have neither.

Quiz

1. Can static member variables be private?
2. Show the declaration for a static member variable.
3. Show the declaration for a static function pointer.
4. Show the declaration for a pointer to function returning `long` and taking an integer parameter.
5. Modify the pointer in question 4 so that it's a pointer to member function of class `Car`.
6. Show the declaration for an array of 10 pointers as defined in question 5.

Exercises

1. Write a short program declaring a class with one member variable and one static member variable. Have the constructor initialize the member variable and increment the static member variable. Have the destructor decrement the member variable.

2. Using the program from exercise 1, write a short driver program that makes three objects and then displays their member variables and the static member variable. Then destroy each object and show the effect on the static member variable.

3. Modify the program from exercise 2 to use a static member function to access the static member variable. Make the static member variable private.

4. Write a pointer to member function to access the nonstatic member data in the program in exercise 3, and use that pointer to print the value of that data.

5. Add two more member variables to the class from the preceding exercises. Add accessor functions that return data values, and give all the member functions the same return values and signatures. Use the pointer to member function to access these functions.

14

In Review

The Week in Review program for Week 2 brings together many of the skills you've acquired over the past fortnight and produces a powerful program.

This demonstration of linked lists utilizes virtual functions, pure virtual functions, function overriding, polymorphism, public inheritance, function overloading, forever loops, pointers, references, and more.

The goal of this program is to create a linked list. The nodes on the list are designed to hold parts, as might be used in a factory. While this is not the final form of this program, it does make a good demonstration of a fairly advanced data structure. The code list is 300 lines. Try to analyze the code on your own before reading the analysis that follows the output.

```
1:     // ****************************************************
2:     //
3:     // Title:        Week 2 in review
4:     //
5:     // File:         Week2
6:     //
7:     // Description:  Provide a linked list demonstration program
8:     //
9:     // Classes:  PART - holds part numbers and potentially other
10:    //                  information about parts
11:    //
12:    //            PartNode - acts as a node in a PartsList
13:    //
14:    //            PartsList - provides the mechanisms for a linked list of
➥parts
15:    //
16:    // Author:       Jesse Liberty (jl)
17:    //
18:    // Developed:    486/66 32mb RAM  MVC 1.5
19:    //
20:    // Target:       Platform independent
21:    //
22:    // Rev History:  9/94 - First release (jl)
23:    //
24:    //****************************************************
25:
26:    #include <iostream.h>
27:
28:    typedef unsigned long ULONG;
29:    typedef unsigned short USHORT;
30:
31:
32:    // **************** Part ************
33:
34:    // Abstract base class of parts
35:    class Part
36:    {
37:    public:
38:        Part():itsPartNumber(1) {}
39:        Part(ULONG PartNumber):itsPartNumber(PartNumber){}
40:        virtual ~Part(){};
41:        ULONG GetPartNumber() const { return itsPartNumber; }
42:        virtual void Display() const =0;  // must be overridden
43:    private:
44:        ULONG itsPartNumber;
45:    };
46:
47:    // implementation of pure virtual function so that
48:    // derived classes can chain up
49:    void Part::Display() const
50:    {
51:        cout << "\nPart Number: " << itsPartNumber << endl;
52:    }
53:
54:    // **************** Car Part ************
55:
```

```
56:     class CarPart : public Part
57:     {
58:     public:
59:         CarPart():itsModelYear(94){}
60:         CarPart(USHORT year, ULONG partNumber);
61:         virtual void Display() const { Part::Display(); cout
➥<< "Model Year: " << itsModelYear << endl;  }
62:     private:
63:         USHORT itsModelYear;
64:     };
65:
66:     CarPart::CarPart(USHORT year, ULONG partNumber):
67:         itsModelYear(year),
68:         Part(partNumber)
69:     {}
70:
71:
72:     // *************** AirPlane Part ************
73:
74:     class AirPlanePart : public Part
75:     {
76:     public:
77:         AirPlanePart():itsEngineNumber(1){};
78:         AirPlanePart(USHORT EngineNumber, ULONG PartNumber);
79:         virtual void Display() const{ Part::Display(); cout
➥ << "Engine No.: " << itsEngineNumber << endl;  }
80:     private:
81:         USHORT itsEngineNumber;
82:     };
83:
84:     AirPlanePart::AirPlanePart(USHORT EngineNumber, ULONG PartNumber):
85:         itsEngineNumber(EngineNumber),
86:         Part(PartNumber)
87:     {}
88:
89:     // *************** Part Node ************
90:     class PartNode
91:     {
92:     public:
93:         PartNode (Part*);
94:         ~PartNode();
95:         void SetNext(PartNode * node) { itsNext = node; }
96:         PartNode * GetNext() const;
97:         Part * GetPart() const;
98:     private:
99:         Part *itsPart;
100:        PartNode * itsNext;
101:    };
102:
103:    // PartNode Implementations...
104:
105:    PartNode::PartNode(Part* pPart):
106:    itsPart(pPart),
107:    itsNext(0)
108:    {}
109:
```

```
110:    PartNode::~PartNode()
111:    {
112:        delete itsPart;
113:        itsPart = 0;
114:        delete itsNext;
115:        itsNext = 0;
116:    }
117:
118:    // Returns NULL if no next PartNode
119:    PartNode * PartNode::GetNext() const
120:    {
121:            return itsNext;
122:    }
123:
124:    Part * PartNode::GetPart() const
125:    {
126:        if (itsPart)
127:            return itsPart;
128:        else
129:            return NULL; //error
130:    }
131:
132:    // *************** Part List ************
133:    class PartsList
134:    {
135:    public:
136:        PartsList();
137:        ~PartsList();
138:        // needs copy constructor and operator equals!
139:        Part*       Find(ULONG & position, ULONG PartNumber)  const;
140:        ULONG       GetCount() const { return itsCount; }
141:        Part*       GetFirst() const;
142:        static      PartsList& GetGlobalPartsList() {
➥       return  GlobalPartsList; }
143:        void        Insert(Part *);
144:        void        Iterate(void (Part::*f)()const) const;
145:        Part*       operator[](ULONG) const;
146:    private:
147:        PartNode * pHead;
148:        ULONG itsCount;
149:        static PartsList GlobalPartsList;
150:    };
151:
152:    PartsList PartsList::GlobalPartsList;
153:
154:    // Implementations for Lists...
155:
156:    PartsList::PartsList():
157:        pHead(0),
158:        itsCount(0)
159:        {}
160:
161:    PartsList::~PartsList()
162:    {
163:        delete pHead;
164:    }
```

```
165:
166:    Part*   PartsList::GetFirst() const
167:    {
168:       if (pHead)
169:          return pHead->GetPart();
170:       else
171:          return NULL;  // error catch here
172:    }
173:
174:    Part *  PartsList::operator[](ULONG offSet) const
175:    {
176:       PartNode* pNode = pHead;
177:
178:       if (!pHead)
179:          return NULL; // error catch here
180:
181:       if (offSet > itsCount)
182:          return NULL; // error
183:
184:       for (ULONG i=0;i<offSet; i++)
185:          pNode = pNode->GetNext();
186:
187:      return   pNode->GetPart();
188:    }
189:
190:    Part*   PartsList::Find(ULONG & position, ULONG PartNumber)  const
191:    {
192:       PartNode * pNode = 0;
193:       for (pNode = pHead, position = 0;
194:             pNode!=NULL;
195:             pNode = pNode->GetNext(), position++)
196:       {
197:          if (pNode->GetPart()->GetPartNumber() == PartNumber)
198:             break;
199:       }
200:       if (pNode == NULL)
201:          return NULL;
202:       else
203:          return pNode->GetPart();
204:    }
205:
206:    void PartsList::Iterate(void (Part::*func)()const) const
207:    {
208:       if (!pHead)
209:          return;
210:       PartNode* pNode = pHead;
211:       do
212:          (pNode->GetPart()->*func)();
213:       while (pNode = pNode->GetNext());
214:    }
215:
216:    void PartsList::Insert(Part* pPart)
217:    {
218:       PartNode * pNode = new PartNode(pPart);
219:       PartNode * pCurrent = pHead;
220:       PartNode * pNext = 0;
```

```
221:
222:        ULONG New =  pPart->GetPartNumber();
223:        ULONG Next = 0;
224:        itsCount++;
225:
226:        if (!pHead)
227:        {
228:            pHead = pNode;
229:            return;
230:        }
231:
232:        // if this one is smaller than head
233:        // this one is the new head
234:        if (pHead->GetPart()->GetPartNumber() > New)
235:        {
236:            pNode->SetNext(pHead);
237:            pHead = pNode;
238:            return;
239:        }
240:
241:        for (;;)
242:        {
243:            // if there is no next, append this new one
244:            if (!pCurrent->GetNext())
245:            {
246:                pCurrent->SetNext(pNode);
247:                return;
248:            }
249:
250:            // if this goes after this one and before the next
251:            // then insert it here, otherwise get the next
252:            pNext = pCurrent->GetNext();
253:            Next = pNext->GetPart()->GetPartNumber();
254:            if (Next > New)
255:            {
256:                pCurrent->SetNext(pNode);
257:                pNode->SetNext(pNext);
258:                return;
259:            }
260:            pCurrent = pNext;
261:        }
262:    }
263:
264:    void main()
265:    {
266:        PartsList pl = PartsList::GetGlobalPartsList();
267:        Part * pPart = 0;
268:        ULONG PartNumber;
269:        USHORT value;
270:        ULONG choice;
271:
272:        while (true)
273:        {
274:            cout << "(0)Quit (1)Car (2)Plane: ";
275:            cin >> choice;
276:
```

```
277:          if (!choice)
278:             break;
279:
280:          cout << "New PartNumber?: ";
281:          cin >>  PartNumber;
282:
283:          if (choice == 1)
284:          {
285:             cout << "Model Year?: ";
286:             cin >> value;
287:             pPart = new CarPart(value,PartNumber);
288:          }
289:          else
290:          {
291:             cout << "Engine Number?: ";
292:             cin >> value;
293:             pPart = new AirPlanePart(value,PartNumber);
294:          }
295:
296:          pl.Insert(pPart);
297:       }
298:       void (Part::*pFunc)()const = Part::Display;
299:       pl.Iterate(pFunc);
300:    }
```

OUTPUT

```
(0)Quit (1)Car (2)Plane: 1
New PartNumber?: 2837
Model Year? 90

  (0)Quit (1)Car (2)Plane: 2
New PartNumber?: 378
Engine Number?: 4930

  (0)Quit (1)Car (2)Plane: 1
New PartNumber?: 4499
Model Year? 94

  (0)Quit (1)Car (2)Plane: 1
New PartNumber?: 3000
Model Year? 93

  (0)Quit (1)Car (2)Plane: 0

Part Number: 378
Engine No. 4938

Part Number: 2837
Model Year: 90

Part Number: 3000
Model Year: 93

Part Number 4499
Model Year: 94
```

ANALYSIS   The Week 2 in Review program provides a linked list implementation for `Part` objects. A linked list is a dynamic data structure; that is, it is like an array, but it is sized to fit as objects are added and deleted.

This particular linked list is designed to hold objects of class `Part`, where `Part` is an abstract data type serving as a base class to any objects with a part number. In this example, `Part` has been subclassed into `CarPart` and `AirplanePart`.

Class `Part` is declared on lines 34 through 45 and consists of a part number and some accessors. Presumably, this class could be fleshed out to hold other important information about the parts, such as what components they are used in, how many are in stock, and so forth. `Part` is an abstract data type, enforced by the pure virtual function `Display()`.

Note that `Display()` does have an implementation, on lines 50 through 52. It is the designer's intention that derived classes will be forced to create their own `Display()` method, but may chain up to this method as well.

Two simple derived classes, `CarPart` and `AirPlanePart` are provided on lines 56 through 69 and 74 through 87, respectively. Each provides an overridden `Display()` method, which does in fact chain up to the base class `Display()` method.

The class `PartNode` serves as the interface between the `Part` class and the `PartList` class. It contains a pointer to a part and a pointer to the next node in the list. Its only methods are to get and set the next node in the list and to return the `Part` to which it points.

The intelligence of the list is, appropriately, in the class `PartsList`, whose declaration is on lines 133 through 150. The `PartsList` keeps a pointer to the first element in the list (`pHead`) and uses that to access all other methods by *walking the list*. Walking the list means asking each node in the list for the next node, until you reach a node whose next pointer is `NULL`.

This is only a partial implementation; a fully developed list would provide either greater access to its first and last nodes, or would provide an iterator object to allow clients to easily walk the list.

The `PartsList` nonetheless provides a number of interesting methods, which are listed in alphabetical order. This is often a good idea because it makes finding the functions easier.

`Find()` takes a `PartNumber` and a `ULONG`. If the part corresponding to the `PartNumber` is found, it returns a pointer to the `Part` and fills the `ULONG` with the position of that part in the list. If the `PartNumber` is not found, it returns `NULL` and the position is meaningless.

`GetCount()` returns the number of elements in the list. `PartsList` keeps this number as the member variable, `itsCount`. However, it could, of course, compute this number by walking the list.

`GetFirst()` returns a pointer to the first `Part` in the list or returns `NULL` if the list is empty.

GetGlobalPartsList() returns a reference to the static member variable GlobalPartsList. This is a static instance of this class; every program with a PartsList also has one GlobalPartsList, though of course, it is free to make other PartsLists as well. A full implementation of this idea would modify the constructor of Part to ensure that every part is created on the GlobalPartsList.

Insert takes a pointer to a Part, creates a PartNode for it, and adds it to the list, ordered by PartNumber.

Iterate takes a pointer to a member function of Part, which takes no parameters, returns void and is const. It calls that function for every Part object in the list. In the sample program, this is called on Display(), which is a virtual function, so the appropriate Display() method is called based on the run-time type of the Part object called.

Operator[] allows direct access to the Part at the offset provided. Rudimentary bounds checking is provided. If the list is empty or if the offset requested is greater than the size of the list, NULL (0) is returned as an error condition.

Note that in a real program these comments on the functions would be written into the class declaration.

The driver program is on lines 264 through 300. A pointer to PartsList is declared on line 266 and initialized with the GlobalPartsList. Note that the GlobalPartsList itself is initialized on line 152. This is necessary because the declaration of a static member variable does not define it; definition must be done outside the declaration of the class.

On lines 272 through 294, the user is repeatedly prompted to choose whether to enter a car part or an airplane part. Depending on the choice, the right value is requested, and the appropriate part is created. Once created, the part is inserted into the list on line 296.

The implementation for the Insert() method of PartsList is on lines 216 through 262. When the first part number is entered, 2837, a CarPart with that part number and the model year 90 is created and passed in to LinkedList::Insert().

On line 218, a new PartNode is created with that part, and the variable New is initialized with the part number. The PartsList's itsCount member variable is incremented on line 224.

On line 226, the test that pHead is NULL evaluates true. Since this is the first node, it *is* true that the PartsList's pHead pointer has 0. Thus, on line 228 pHead is set to point to the new node, and this function returns.

The user is prompted to enter a second part, and this time an AirPlane part with part number 378 and engine number 4938 is entered. Once again, PartsList::Insert() is called, and once again pNode is initialized with the new node. The static member variable itsCount is incremented to 2, and pHead is tested. Since pHead was assigned last time, it is no longer null, and the test fails.

On line 234, the part number held by pHead, 2837, is compared against the current part number, 378. Because the new one is smaller than the one held by pHead, the new one must become the new head pointer, and the test on line 234 is true.

On line 236, the new node is set to point to the node currently pointed to by pHead. Note that this does not point the new node to pHead itself, but rather to the node that pHead was pointing to! On line 237, pHead is set to point to the new node.

The third time through the loop, the user enters the part number 4499 for a Car with model year 94. The counter is incremented, and the number this time is *not* less than the number pointed to by pHead, so the for loop that begins on line 241 is entered.

The value pointed to by pHead is 378. The value pointed to by the second node is 2837. The current value is 4499. The pointer pCurrent points to the same node as pHead, and so it does have a next value; it points to the second node, and so the test on line 244 fails.

The pointer pCurrent is set to point to the next node, and the loop repeats. This time the test on line 145 succeeds; there is no next item, so the current node is told to point to the new node on line 246, and the insert is finished.

The fourth time through, the part number 3000 is entered. This proceeds just as the previous did, but this time when the current node is pointing to 2837 and the next node has 4499, the test on line 254 returns true, and the new node is inserted into position.

When the user finally presses 0, the test on line 277 evaluates true, and the while(true) loop breaks. On line 298, the member function Display() is assigned to the pointer to member function pFunc. In a real program, this would be assigned dynamically, based on the user's choice of method.

The pointer to member function is passed to the PartsList Iterate() method. On line 208, the Iterate() method ensures that the list is not empty. Then on lines 211 through 213, each Part on the list is called, using the pointer to member function. This calls the appropriate Display() method for the Part, as shown in the output.

WEEK

3

At A Glance

You have finished the second week of learning C++. By now, you should feel comfortable with some of the more advanced aspects of object-oriented programming, including encapsulation and polymorphism.

Where You Are Going

This week begins with a discussion of advanced inheritance. On Day 16, you learn about streams in depth, and on Day 17, you learn advanced tricks of the preprocessor. Day 18 is a departure—rather than focusing on the syntax of the language, you take a day out to learn ways to write programs that are easy to maintain, portable to other computer platforms, and ready for reuse. On Day 19, templates are introduced, and on Day 20, exceptions are explained. Day 21 covers some of the things you need to know for managing a large project using C++ in multiple files.

Day 15

Advanced Inheritance

So far, you have worked with single and multiple inheritance to create *is-a* relationships. Today you will learn

- [ ] What containment is and how to model it.
- [ ] What delegation is and how to model it.
- [ ] How to implement one class in terms of another.
- [ ] How to use private inheritance.

Containment

As you saw in previous examples, it is possible for the member data of a class to include objects of another class. C++ programmers say that the outer class *contains* the inner class. Thus, an Employee class might contain string objects (for the name of the employee) as well as integers (for the employee's salary), and so forth.

Listing 15.1 describes an incomplete but still useful String class. This listing does not produce any output. Instead it is used with later listings.

NOTE

> ANSI C++ defines a string.h file that already contains all the function-
> ality defined in Listing 15.1. If your compiler is fully ANSI compliant,
> you will not need this class, you will only need to include the string.h
> header file.

TYPE **Listing 15.1. The `String` class.**

```
1:      #include <iostream.h>
2:      #include <string.h>
3:
4:      class String
5:      {
6:         public:
7:             // constructors
8:             String();
9:              String(const char *const);
10:              String(const String &);
11:             ~String();
12:
13:             // overloaded operators
14:             char & operator[](int offset);
15:             char operator[](int offset) const;
16:             String operator+(const String&);
17:             void operator+=(const String&);
18:             String & operator= (const String &);
19:
20:             // General accessors
21:             int GetLen()const { return itsLen; }
22:             const char * GetString() const { return itsString; }
23:             // static int ConstructorCount;
24:
25:         private:
26:             String (int);          // private constructor
27:             char * itsString;
28:             unsigned short itsLen;
29:
30:      };
31:
32:      // default constructor creates string of 0 bytes
33:      String::String()
34:      {
35:         itsString = new char[1];
36:         itsString[0] = '\0';
37:         itsLen=0;
38:         // cout << "\tDefault string constructor\n";
39:         // ConstructorCount++;
40:      }
41:
42:      // private (helper) constructor, used only by
43:      // class methods for creating a new string of
44:      // required size.  Null filled.
```

15

```
45:     String::String(int len)
46:     {
47:        itsString = new char[len+1];
48:        for (int i = 0; i<=len; i++)
49:           itsString[1] = '\0';
50:        itsLen=len;
51:        // cout << "\tString(int) constructor\n";
52:        // ConstructorCount++;
53:     }
54:
55:     // Converts a character array to a String
56:     String::String(const char * const cString)
57:     {
58:        itsLen = strlen(cString);
59:        itsString = new char[itsLen+1];
60:        for (int i = 0; i<itsLen; i++)
61:           itsString[i] = cString[i];
62:        itsString[itsLen]='\0';
63:        // cout << "\tString(char*) constructor\n";
64:        // ConstructorCount++;
65:     }
66:
67:     // copy constructor
68:     String::String (const String & rhs)
69:     {
70:        itsLen=rhs.GetLen();
71:        itsString = new char[itsLen+1];
72:        for (int i = 0; i<itsLen;i++)
73:           itsString[i] = rhs[i];
74:        itsString[itsLen] = '\0';
75:        // cout << "\tString(String&) constructor\n";
76:        // ConstructorCount++;
77:     }
78:
79:     // destructor, frees allocated memory
80:     String::~String ()
81:     {
82:        delete [] itsString;
83:        itsLen = 0;
84:        // cout << "\tString destructor\n";
85:     }
86:
87:     // operator equals, frees existing memory
88:     // then copies string and size
89:     String& String::operator=(const String & rhs)
90:     {
91:        if (this == &rhs)
92:           return *this;
93:        delete [] itsString;
94:        itsLen=rhs.GetLen();
95:        itsString = new char[itsLen+1];
96:        for (int i = 0; i<itsLen;i++)
97:           itsString[i] = rhs[i];
98:        itsString[itsLen] = '\0';
99:        return *this;
```

continues

Listing 15.1. continued

```
100:        // cout << "\tString operator=\n";
101:     }
102:
103:     //non constant offset operator, returns
104:     // reference to character so it can be
105:     // changed!
106:     char & String::operator[](int offset)
107:     {
108:        if (offset > itsLen)
109:           return itsString[itsLen-1];
110:        else
111:           return itsString[offset];
112:     }
113:
114:     // constant offset operator for use
115:     // on const objects (see copy constructor!)
116:     char String::operator[](int offset) const
117:     {
118:        if (offset > itsLen)
119:           return itsString[itsLen-1];
120:        else
121:           return itsString[offset];
122:     }
123:
124:     // creates a new string by adding current
125:     // string to rhs
126:     String String::operator+(const String& rhs)
127:     {
128:        int  totalLen = itsLen + rhs.GetLen();
129:        String temp(totalLen);
130:        for (int i = 0; i<itsLen; i++)
131:           temp[i] = itsString[i];
132:        for (int j = 0; j<rhs.GetLen(); j++, i++)
133:           temp[i] = rhs[j];
134:        temp[totalLen]='\0';
135:        return temp;
136:     }
137:
138:     // changes current string, returns nothing
139:     void String::operator+=(const String& rhs)
140:     {
141:        unsigned short rhsLen = rhs.GetLen();
142:        unsigned short totalLen = itsLen + rhsLen;
143:        String  temp(totalLen);
144:        for (int i = 0; i<itsLen; i++)
145:           temp[i] = itsString[i];
146:        for (int j = 0; j<rhs.GetLen(); j++, i++)
147:           temp[i] = rhs[i-itsLen];
148:        temp[totalLen]='\0';
149:        *this = temp;
150:     }
151:
152:     // int String::ConstructorCount = 0;
```

OUTPUT   There is no output.

ANALYSIS   Listing 15.1 provides a `String` class much like the one used in Listing 11.12. The significant difference here is that the constructors and a few other functions have print statements to show their use, which are currently commented out. These are used in later examples.

On line 23 the static member variable `ConstructorCount` is declared, and on line 152 it is initialized. This variable is incremented in each string constructor. All of this is currently commented out; it is used in a later listing.

Listing 15.2 describes an `Employee` class that contains three string objects.

TYPE   **Listing 15.2. The `Employee` class and driver program.**

```
1:     class Employee
2:     {
3:
4:     public:
5:         Employee();
6:         Employee(char *, char *, char *, long);
7:         ~Employee();
8:         Employee(const Employee&);
9:         Employee & operator= (const Employee &);
10:
11:        const String & GetFirstName() const { return itsFirstName; }
12:        const String & GetLastName() const { return itsLastName; }
13:        const String & GetAddress() const { return itsAddress; }
14:        long GetSalary() const { return itsSalary; }
15:
16:        void SetFirstName(const String & fName) { itsFirstName = fName; }
17:        void SetLastName(const String & lName) { itsLastName = lName; }
18:        void SetAddress(const String & address) { itsAddress = address; }
19:        void SetSalary(long salary) { itsSalary = salary; }
20:     private:
21:        String     itsFirstName;
22:        String     itsLastName;
23:        String     itsAddress;
24:        long       itsSalary;
25:     };
26:
27:     Employee::Employee():
28:        itsFirstName(""),
29:        itsLastName(""),
30:        itsAddress(""),
31:        itsSalary(0)
32:     {}
33:
34:     Employee::Employee(char * firstName, char * lastName,
35:        char * address, long salary):
```

continues

Listing 15.2. continued

```
36:         itsFirstName(firstName),
37:         itsLastName(lastName),
38:         itsAddress(address),
39:         itsSalary(salary)
40:     {}
41:
42:     Employee::Employee(const Employee & rhs):
43:         itsFirstName(rhs.GetFirstName()),
44:         itsLastName(rhs.GetLastName()),
45:         itsAddress(rhs.GetAddress()),
46:         itsSalary(rhs.GetSalary())
47:     {}
48:
49:     Employee::~Employee() {}
50:
51:     Employee & Employee::operator= (const Employee & rhs)
52:     {
53:         if (this == &rhs)
54:             return *this;
55:
56:         itsFirstName = rhs.GetFirstName();
57:         itsLastName = rhs.GetLastName();
58:         itsAddress = rhs.GetAddress();
59:         itsSalary = rhs.GetSalary();
60:
61:         return *this;
62:     }
63:
64:     void main()
65:     {
66:         Employee Edie("Jane","Doe","1461 Shore Parkway", 20000);
67:         Edie.SetSalary(50000);
68:         String LastName("Levine");
69:         Edie.SetLastName(LastName);
70:         Edie.SetFirstName("Edythe");
71:
72:         cout << "Name: ";
73:         cout << Edie.GetFirstName().GetString();
74:         cout << " " << Edie.GetLastName().GetString();
75:         cout << ".\nAddress: ";
76:         cout << Edie.GetAddress().GetString();
77:         cout << ".\nSalary: " ;
78:         cout << Edie.GetSalary();
79:     }
```

NOTE If your compiler does not contain the string functionality of the code from Listing 15.1, place the Listing 15.1 code into a file called STRING.HPP. Any time you need the String class, you can include

15

Listing 15.1 by using #include. For example, at the top of Listing 15.2, add the line #include "String.hpp". This adds the String class to your program.

Name; Edythe Levine
Address: 1461 Shore Parkway
Salary: 50000

Listing 15.2 shows the Employee class, which contains three string objects: itsFirstName, itsLastName, and itsAddress.

On line 66 an employee object is created, and four values are passed in to initialize the employee object. On line 67 the Employee access function SetSalary() is called, with the constant value 50000. Note that in a real program this would either be a dynamic value (set at runtime) or a constant.

On line 68 a string is created and initialized using a C++ string constant. This string object is then used as an argument to SetLastName() on line 69.

On line 70 the Employee function SetFirstName() is called with yet another string constant. However, if you are paying close attention, you should notice that Employee does not have a function SetFirstName() that takes a character string as its argument; SetFirstName() requires a constant string reference.

The compiler resolves this because it knows how to make a string from a constant character string. It knows this because you told it how to do so on line 9 of Listing 15.1.

Accessing Members of the Contained Class

Employee objects do not have special access to the member variables of String. If the employee object Edie tries to access the member variable itsLen of its own itsFirstName member variable, it gets a compile-time error. This is not much of a burden, however. The accessor functions provide an interface for the String class, and the Employee class need not worry about the implementation details any more than it worries about how the integer variable, itsSalary, stores its information.

Filtering Access to Contained Members

Note that the String class provides the operator+. The designer of the Employee class has blocked access to the operator+ being called on employee objects by declaring that all the string accessors, such as GetFirstName(), return a constant reference. Because operator+ is not (and can't be) a const function (it changes the object that it is called on), attempting to write the following line causes a compile-time error:

```
String buffer = Edie.GetFirstName() + Edie.GetLastName();
```

GetFirstName() returns a constant String, and you can't call operator+ on a constant object.

To fix this, overload GetFirstName() to be non-const:

```
const String & GetFirstName() const { return itsFirstName; }
String & GetFirstName()  { return itsFirstName; }
```

Note that the return value is no longer const and that the member function itself is no longer const. Changing the return value is not sufficient to overload the function name; you must change the constancy of the function itself.

Cost of Containment

It is important to note that the user of an Employee class pays the price of each of those string objects each time one is constructed or a copy of the Employee is made.

Uncommenting the cout statements in Listing 15.1 (lines 38, 51, 63, 75, 84, and 100) reveals how often these are called. Listing 15.3 rewrites the driver program to add print statements indicating where in the program objects are being created:

NOTE

To compile this listing, complete the following steps:

1. Uncomment lines 38, 51, 63, 75, 84, and 100 in Listing 15.1.

2. Edit Listing 15.2. Remove lines 64 to 79 and substitute Listing 15.3.

3. Add #include string.hpp as previously noted.

Listing 15.3. Contained class constructors.

```
1:      void main()
2:      {
3:          cout << "Creating Edie...\n";
4:          Employee Edie("Jane","Doe","1461 Shore Parkway", 20000);
5:          Edie.SetSalary(20000);
6:          cout << "Calling SetFirstName with char *...\n";
7:          Edie.SetFirstName("Edythe");
8:          cout << "Creating temporary string LastName...\n";
9:          String LastName("Levine");
```

15

```
10:         Edie.SetLastName(LastName);
11:
12:         cout << "Name: ";
13:         cout << Edie.GetFirstName().GetString();
14:         cout << " " << Edie.GetLastName().GetString();
15:         cout << "\nAddress: ";
16:         cout << Edie.GetAddress().GetString();
17:         cout << "\nSalary: " ;
18:         cout << Edie.GetSalary();
19:         cout << endl;
20:     }
```

OUTPUT

```
1:   Creating Edie...
2:           String(char*) constructor
3:           String(char*) constructor
4:           String(char*) constructor
5:   Calling SetFirstName with char *...
6:           String(char*) constructor
7:           String destructor
8:   Creating temporary string LastName...
9:           String(char*) constructor
10:  Name: Edythe Levine
11:  Address: 1461 Shore Parkway
12:  Salary: 20000
13:          String destructor
14:          String destructor
15:          String destructor
16:          String destructor
```

ANALYSIS Listing 15.3 uses the same class declarations as Listings 15.1 and 15.2, but the cout statements have been uncommented. The output from Listing 15.3 has been numbered to make analysis easier.

On line 3 of Listing 15.3 the statement Creating Edie... is printed, as reflected on line 1 of the output. On line 4 an Employee object, Edie, is created with four parameters. The output reflects the constructor for String being called three times, as expected.

Line 6 prints an information statement, and then on line 7 is the statement Edie.SetFirstName("Edythe"). This statement causes a temporary string to be created from the character string "Edythe", as reflected on lines 6 and 7 of the output. Note that the temporary is destroyed immediately after it is used in the assignment statement.

On line 9 a string object is created in the body of the program. Here, the programmer is doing explicitly what the compiler did implicitly on the previous statement. This time you see the constructor on line 9 of the output, but no destructor. This object is not destroyed until it goes out of scope at the end of the function.

On lines 13 through 16, the strings in the employee object are destroyed as the employee object falls out of scope; the string LastName, created on line 9, is destroyed as well when it falls out of scope.

Copying by Value

Listing 15.3 illustrates how the creation of one employee object caused five string constructor calls. Listing 15.4 again rewrites the driver program. This time the print statements are not used, but the string static member variable ConstructorCount is uncommented and used.

Examination of Listing 15.1 shows that ConstructorCount is incremented each time a string constructor is called. The driver program in Listing 15.4 calls the print functions, passing in the Employee object first by reference and then by value. ConstructorCount keeps track of how many string objects are created when the employee is passed as a parameter.

> **NOTE**
>
> To compile this listing, complete the following steps:
>
> 1. Uncomment lines 23, 39, 52, 64, 76, and 152 in Listing 15.1.
>
> 2. Edit Listing 15.2. Remove lines 64 to 79 and substitute Listing 15.4.
>
> 3. Add #include string.hpp as previously noted.

TYPE   **Listing 15.4. Passing by value.**

```
1:      void PrintFunc(Employee);
2:      void rPrintFunc(const Employee&);
3:
4:      void main()
5:      {
6:          Employee Edie("Jane","Doe","1461 Shore Parkway", 20000);
7:          Edie.SetSalary(20000);
8:          Edie.SetFirstName("Edythe");
9:          String LastName("Levine");
10:         Edie.SetLastName(LastName);
11:
12:         cout << "Constructor count: " << String::ConstructorCount << endl;
13:         rPrintFunc(Edie);
14:         cout << "Constructor count: " << String::ConstructorCount << endl;
15:         PrintFunc(Edie);
16:         cout << "Constructor count: " << String::ConstructorCount << endl;
17:      }
18:      void PrintFunc (Employee Edie)
19:      {
20:
21:          cout << "Name: ";
22:          cout << Edie.GetFirstName().GetString();
23:          cout << " " << Edie.GetLastName().GetString();
24:          cout << ".\nAddress: ";
25:          cout << Edie.GetAddress().GetString();
26:          cout << ".\nSalary: " ;
```

```
27:          cout << Edie.GetSalary();
28:          cout << endl;
29:
30:     }
31:
32:     void rPrintFunc (const Employee& Edie)
33:     {
34:        cout << "Name: ";
35:        cout << Edie.GetFirstName().GetString();
36:        cout << " " << Edie.GetLastName().GetString();
37:        cout << "\nAddress: ";
38:        cout << Edie.GetAddress().GetString();
39:        cout << "\nSalary: " ;
40:        cout << Edie.GetSalary();
41:        cout << endl;
42:     }
```

OUTPUT

```
Constructor count: 5
Name: Edythe Levine
Address: 1461 Shore Parkway
Salary: 20000
Constructor count: 5
Name: Edythe Levine
Address: 1461 Shore Parkway
Salary: 20000
Constructor count: 8
```

ANALYSIS The output shows that five string objects were created as part of creating one employee object. When the employee object is passed to rPrintFunc() by reference, no additional employee objects are created, so no additional string objects are created. (They too are passed by reference.)

When, on line 15, the employee object is passed to PrintFunc() by value, a copy of the employee is created and three more string objects are created (by calls to the copy constructor).

Delegation Versus Implemented in Terms of

Sometimes one class needs to draw on some of the attributes of another class. For example, suppose you need to create a PartsCatalog class. The specification you've been given defines a PartsCatalog as a collection of parts; each part has a unique part number. The PartsCatalog does not enable duplicate entries, and does enable access by part number.

The listing for the Week in Review for Week 2 provides a linked list class. This linked list is well-tested and understood, and you should build on that technology when making your PartsCatalog, rather than inventing it from scratch.

You could create a new PartsCatalog class and have it contain a linked list. The PartsCatalog could delegate management of the linked list to its contained linked list object.

An alternative would be to make the PartsCatalog derive from LinkedList and thereby inherit the properties of a linked list. Remembering, however, that public inheritance provides an *is-a* relationship, you should question whether a PartsCatalog really *is a* type of linked list.

One way to answer the question of whether PartsCatalog is a linked list is to assume that LinkedList is the base and PartsCatalog is the derived class, and then to ask these other questions:

1. Is there anything in the base class that should not be in the derived? For example, does the linked list base class have functions that are inappropriate for the PartsCatalog class? If so, you probably don't want public inheritance.

2. Might the class you are creating have more than one of the base? For example, might a PartsCatalog need two linked lists in each object? If it might, you almost certainly want to use containment.

3. Do you need to inherit from the base class so that you can take advantage of virtual functions or access protected members? If so, you must use inheritance—public or private.

Based on the answers to these questions, you must choose between public inheritance (the *is-a* relationship) and either private inheritance or containment.

 Contained: An object declared as a member of another class is *contained* by that class.

Delegation: Using the attributes of a contained class to accomplish functions not otherwise available to the containing class.

Implemented in terms of: Building one class on the capabilities of another without using public inheritance.

Delegation

Why not derive PartsCatalog from LinkedList? The PartsCatalog isn't a linked list because linked lists are ordered collections and each member of the collection can repeat. The PartsCatalog has unique entries that are not ordered. The fifth member of the PartsCatalog is not part number 5.

It is certainly possible to inherit publicly from PartsList and then override Insert() and the offset operators ([ ]) to work in a special PartsList way instead of a generic LinkedList way, but then you change the essence of the PartsList class. Instead, you'll build a PartsCatalog that has no offset operator, does not enable duplicates, and defines the operator+ to combine two sets.

The first way to accomplish this is with containment. The PartsCatalog delegates list management to a contained LinkedList. Listing 15.5 illustrates this approach.

TYPE | **Listing 15.5. Delegating to a contained linked list.**

```
1:      #include <iostream.h>
2:
3:      typedef unsigned long ULONG;
4:      typedef unsigned short USHORT;
5:
6:
7:      // *************** Part ***********
8:
9:      // Abstract base class of parts
10:     class Part
11:     {
12:     public:
13:         Part():itsPartNumber(1) {}
14:         Part(ULONG PartNumber):itsPartNumber(PartNumber){}
15:         virtual ~Part(){};
16:         ULONG GetPartNumber() const { return itsPartNumber; }
17:         virtual void Display() const =0;  // must be overridden
18:     private:
19:         ULONG itsPartNumber;
20:     };
21:
22:     // implementation of pure virtual function so that
23:     // derived classes can chain up
24:     void Part::Display() const
25:     {
26:         cout << "\nPart Number: " << itsPartNumber << endl;
27:     }
28:
29:     // *************** Car Part ***********
30:
31:     class CarPart : public Part
32:     {
33:     public:
34:         CarPart():itsModelYear(94){}
35:         CarPart(USHORT year, ULONG partNumber);
36:         virtual void Display() const { Part::Display();
➥   cout << "Model Year: "  << itsModelYear << endl;   }
37:     private:
38:         USHORT itsModelYear;
39:     };
40:
41:     CarPart::CarPart(USHORT year, ULONG partNumber):
42:         itsModelYear(year),
43:         Part(partNumber)
44:     {}
45:
46:
```

continues

Listing 15.5. continued

```
47:     // **************** AirPlane Part ************
48:
49:     class AirPlanePart : public Part
50:     {
51:     public:
52:         AirPlanePart():itsEngineNumber(1){};
53:         AirPlanePart(USHORT EngineNumber, ULONG PartNumber);
54:         virtual void Display() const{ Part::Display();
➡           cout << "Engine No.: " << itsEngineNumber << endl;   }
55:     private:
56:         USHORT itsEngineNumber;
57:     };
58:
59:     AirPlanePart::AirPlanePart(USHORT EngineNumber, ULONG PartNumber):
60:         itsEngineNumber(EngineNumber),
61:         Part(PartNumber)
62:     {}
63:
64:     // **************** Part Node ************
65:     class PartNode
66:     {
67:     public:
68:         PartNode (Part*);
69:         ~PartNode();
70:         void SetNext(PartNode * node) { itsNext = node; }
71:         PartNode * GetNext() const;
72:         Part * GetPart() const;
73:     private:
74:         Part *itsPart;
75:         PartNode * itsNext;
76:     };
77: // >> Insert lines 103-130 from the Listing in Week 2 in Review
78:
79:     // **************** Part List ************
80:     class PartsList
81:     {
82:     public:
83:         PartsList();
84:         ~PartsList();
85:         // needs copy constructor and operator equals!
86:         void      Iterate(void (Part::*f)()const) const;
87:         Part*      Find(ULONG & position, ULONG PartNumber)  const;
88:         Part*     GetFirst() const;
89:         void       Insert(Part *);
90:         Part*     operator[](ULONG) const;
91:         ULONG     GetCount() const { return itsCount; }
92:         static     PartsList& GetGlobalPartsList() { return  GlobalPartsList; }
93:     private:
94:         PartNode * pHead;
95:         ULONG itsCount;
96:         static PartsList GlobalPartsList;
97:     };
98:
99:     PartsList PartsList::GlobalPartsList;
```

15

```
100:    // >> Insert lines 154-262 from Week 2 in Review Listing
101:    class PartsCatalog
102:    {
103:    public:
104:        void Insert(Part *);
105:        ULONG Exists(ULONG PartNumber);
106:        Part * Get(int PartNumber);
107:        operator+(const PartsCatalog &);
108:        void ShowAll() { thePartsList.Iterate(Part::Display); }
109:    private:
110:        PartsList thePartsList;
111:    };
112:
113:    void PartsCatalog::Insert(Part * newPart)
114:    {
115:        ULONG partNumber =  newPart->GetPartNumber();
116:        ULONG offset;
117:
118:        if (!thePartsList.Find(offset, partNumber))
119:
120:            thePartsList.Insert(newPart);
121:        else
122:        {
123:            cout << partNumber << " was the ";
124:            switch (offset)
125:            {
126:                case 0:  cout << "first "; break;
127:                case 1:  cout << "second "; break;
128:                case 2:  cout << "third "; break;
129:                default: cout << offset+1 << "th ";
130:            }
131:            cout << "entry. Rejected!\n";
132:        }
133:    }
134:
135:    ULONG PartsCatalog::Exists(ULONG PartNumber)
136:    {
137:        ULONG offset;
138:        thePartsList.Find(offset,PartNumber);
139:            return offset;
140:    }
141:
142:    Part * PartsCatalog::Get(int PartNumber)
143:    {
144:        ULONG offset;
145:        Part * thePart = thePartsList.Find(offset, PartNumber);
146:        return thePart;
147:    }
148:
149:    void main()
150:    {
151:        PartsCatalog pc;
152:        Part * pPart = 0;
153:        ULONG PartNumber;
154:        USHORT value;
155:        ULONG choice;
```

continues

Listing 15.5. continued

```
156:
157:        while (1)
158:        {
159:           cout << "(0)Quit (1)Car (2)Plane: ";
160:           cin >> choice;
161:
162:           if (!choice)
163:              break;
164:
165:           cout << "New PartNumber?: ";
166:           cin >>  PartNumber;
167:
168:           if (choice == 1)
169:           {
170:              cout << "Model Year?: ";
171:              cin >> value;
172:              pPart = new CarPart(value,PartNumber);
173:           }
174:           else
175:           {
176:              cout << "Engine Number?: ";
177:              cin >> value;
178:              pPart = new AirPlanePart(value,PartNumber);
179:           }
180:           pc.Insert(pPart);
181:        }
182:        pc.ShowAll();
183:    }
```

OUTPUT

```
 (0)Quit (1)Car (2)Plane:  1
New Part Number?: 1234
Model Year?: 94
 (0)Quit (1)Car (2)Plane:  1
New Part Number?: 4434
Model Year?: 93
 (0)Quit (1)Car (2)Plane:  1
New Part Number?: 1234
Model Year?: 94
1234 was the first entry. Rejected!
 (0)Quit (1)Car (2)Plane:  1
New Part Number?: 2345
Model Year?: 93
 (0)Quit (1)Car (2)Plane:  0

Part Number: 1234
Model Year: 94

Part Number: 2345
Model Year: 93

Part Number: 4434
Model Year: 93
```

ANALYSIS Listing 15.5 reproduces the interface to the Part, PartNode, and PartList classes from Week 2 in Review, but to save room it does not reproduce the implementation of the PartNode and PartList methods. Insert lines from the Week 2 in Review section where commented in the code.

A new class, PartsCatalog, is declared on lines 101 to 111. PartsCatalog has a PartsList as its data member, to which it delegates list management. Another way to say this is that the PartsCatalog is implemented in terms of this PartsList.

Note that clients of the PartsCatalog do not have access to the PartsList directly. The interface is through the PartsCatalog, and therefore the behavior of the PartsList is dramatically changed. For example, the PartsCatalog::Insert() method does not enable duplicate entries in the PartsList.

The implementation of PartsCatalog::Insert() starts on line 113. The Part that is passed in as a parameter is asked for the value of its itsPartNumber member variable. This value is fed to the PartsList's Find() method, and if no match is found, the number is inserted; otherwise, an informative error message is printed.

Note that PartsCatalog does the actual insert by calling Insert() on its member variable, pl, which is a PartsList. The mechanics of the actual insertion, the maintenance of the linked list, as well as searching and retrieving from the linked list, are maintained in the contained PartsList member of PartsCatalog. There is no reason for PartsCatalog to reproduce this code; it can take full advantage of the well-defined interface.

This is the essence of reusability within C++: PartsCatalog can reuse the PartsList code, and the designer of PartsCatalog is free to ignore the implementation details of PartsList. The interface to PartsList (that is, the class declaration) provides all the information needed by the designer of the PartsCatalog class.

Private Inheritance

If PartsCatalog needs access to the protected members of LinkedList (in this case there are none) or needs to override any of the LinkedList methods, PartsCatalog is forced to inherit from PartsList.

Because a PartsCatalog is not a PartsList object, and because you don't want to expose the entire set of functionality of PartsList to clients of PartsCatalog, you need to use private inheritance.

The first thing to know about private inheritance is that all of the base member variables and functions are treated as if they were declared to be private, regardless of their actual access level in the base. Thus, to any function that is not a member function of PartsCatalog, every function inherited from PartsList is inaccessible. This is critical. Private inheritance does not involve inheriting interface, just implementation.

To clients of the PartsCatalog class, the PartsList class is invisible. None of its interface is available; you can't call any of its methods. You can call PartsCatalog methods, however, and they can access all of LinkedLists because they are derived from LinkedLists.

The important thing here is that the PartsCatalog isn't a PartsList, as would have been implied by public inheritance. It is implemented in terms of a PartsList, just as containment would be. The private inheritance is just a convenience.

Listing 15.6 demonstrates the use of private inheritance by rewriting the PartsCatalog class as privately derived from PartsList.

NOTE

> To compile this program, copy lines 1 to 100 from Listing 15.5 to the top of this listing.

TYPE   **Listing 15.6. Private inheritance.**

```
1:  //listing 15.6 demonstrates private inheritance
2:  //rewrites PartsCatalog from listing 15.5
3:
4:  // >> Insert lines 1-100 of Listing 15.5 (including
5:  // the Week 2 in Review lines where noted) and see
6:  // attached notes on compiling
7:     class PartsCatalog : private PartsList
8:     {
9:     public:
10:        void Insert(Part *);
11:        ULONG Exists(ULONG PartNumber);
12:        Part * Get(int PartNumber);
13:        operator+(const PartsCatalog &);
14:        void ShowAll() { Iterate(Part::Display); }
15:     private:
16:     };
17:
18:     void PartsCatalog::Insert(Part * newPart)
19:     {
20:        ULONG partNumber =  newPart->GetPartNumber();
21:        ULONG offset;
22:
23:        if (!Find(offset, partNumber))
24:            PartsList::Insert(newPart);
25:        else
26:        {
27:           cout << partNumber << " was the ";
28:           switch (offset)
29:           {
```

```
30:             case 0:  cout << "first "; break;
31:             case 1:  cout << "second "; break;
32:             case 2:  cout << "third "; break;
33:             default: cout << offset+1 << "th ";
34:           }
35:         cout << "entry. Rejected!\n";
36:       }
37:    }
38:
39:    ULONG PartsCatalog::Exists(ULONG PartNumber)
40:    {
41:       ULONG offset;
42:       Find(offset,PartNumber);
43:       return offset;
44:    }
45:
46:    Part * PartsCatalog::Get(int PartNumber)
47:    {
48:       ULONG offset;
49:       return (Find(offset, PartNumber));
50:
51:    }
52:
53:    void main()
54:    {
55:       PartsCatalog pc;
56:       Part * pPart = 0;
57:       ULONG PartNumber;
58:       USHORT value;
59:       ULONG choice;
60:
61:       while (true)
62:       {
63:          cout << "(0)Quit (1)Car (2)Plane: ";
64:          cin >> choice;
65:
66:          if (!choice)
67:             break;
68:
69:          cout << "New PartNumber?: ";
70:          cin >>  PartNumber;
71:
72:          if (choice == 1)
73:          {
74:             cout << "Model Year?: ";
75:             cin >> value;
76:             pPart = new CarPart(value,PartNumber);
77:          }
78:          else
79:          {
80:             cout << "Engine Number?: ";
81:             cin >> value;
82:             pPart = new AirPlanePart(value,PartNumber);
83:          }
84:          pc.Insert(pPart);
85:       }
86:       pc.ShowAll();
87:    }
```

OUTPUT

```
  (0)Quit (1)Car (2)Plane:  1
New Part Number?: 1234
Model Year?: 94
  (0)Quit (1)Car (2)Plane:  1
New Part Number?: 4434
Model Year?: 93
  (0)Quit (1)Car (2)Plane:  1
New Part Number?: 1234
Model Year?: 94
1234 was the first entry. Rejected!
  (0)Quit (1)Car (2)Plane:  1
New Part Number?: 2345
Model Year?: 93
  (0)Quit (1)Car (2)Plane:  0

Part Number: 1234
Model Year: 94

Part Number: 2345
Model Year: 93

Part Number: 4434
Model Year: 93
```

ANALYSIS

Listing 15.6 shows only the changed interface to PartsCatalog and the rewritten driver program. The interfaces to the other classes are unchanged from Listing 15.5.

On line 7 of Listing 15.6, PartsCatalog is declared to derive privately from PartsList. The interface to PartsCatalog doesn't change from Listing 15.5, though of course it no longer needs an object of type PartsList as member data.

The PartsCatalog ShowAll() function calls PartsList Iterate() with the appropriate pointer to member function of class Part. ShowAll() acts as a public interface to Iterate(), providing the correct information but preventing client classes from calling Iterate() directly. Although PartsList might enable other functions to be passed to Iterate(), PartsCatalog does not.

The Insert() function has changed as well. Note, on line 23, that Find() is now called directly because it is inherited from the base class. The call on line 24 to Insert() must be fully qualified, of course, or it would endlessly recurse into itself.

In short, when methods of PartsCatalog want to call PartsList methods, they can do so directly. The only exception is when PartsCatalog has overridden the method and the PartsList version is needed, in which case the function name must be qualified fully.

Private inheritance allows the PartsCatalog to inherit what it can use, but still provide mediated access to Insert and other methods to which client classes should not have direct access.

15

DO inherit publicly when the derived object is a kind of the base class.

DO use containment when you want to delegate functionality to another class, but you don't need access to its protected members.

DO use private inheritance when you need to implement one class in terms of another, and you need access to the base class's protected members.

DON'T use private inheritance when you need to use more than one of the base class. You must use containment. For example, if `PartsCatalog` needed two `PartsLists`, you could not have used private inheritance.

DON'T use public inheritance when members of the base class should not be available to clients of the derived class.

Friend Classes

Sometimes you create classes together, as a set. For example, `PartNode` and `PartsList` were tightly coupled, and it would have been convenient if `PartsList` could have read `PartNode`'s `Part` pointer, `itsPart`, directly.

You wouldn't want to make `itsPart` public, or even protected, because this is an implementation detail of `PartNode` and you want to keep it private. You do want to expose it to `PartsList`, however.

If you want to expose your private member data or functions to another class, you must declare that class to be a *friend*. This extends the interface of your class to include the friend class.

After `PartsNode` declares `PartsList` to be a friend, all of `PartsNode`'s member data and functions are public as far as `PartsList` is concerned.

It is important to note that friendship cannot be transferred. Just because you are my friend and Joe is your friend doesn't mean Joe is *my* friend. Friendship is not inherited either. Again, just because you are my friend and I'm willing to share my secrets with you, that doesn't mean I'm willing to share my secrets with your children.

Finally, friendship is not commutative. Assigning `Class One` to be a friend of `Class Two` does not make `Class Two` a friend of `Class One`. Just because you are willing to tell me your secrets doesn't mean I am willing to tell you mine.

Listing 15.7 illustrates friendship by rewriting the example from Listing 15.5, making
PartsList a friend of PartNode. Note that this does not make PartNode a friend of PartsList.

NOTE

> To compile this program, insert lines 7 to 63 from Listing 15.5
> between lines 5 and 6.

TYPE   **Listing 15.7. An illustration of a friend class.**

```
1:      #include <iostream.h>
2:
3:      typedef unsigned long ULONG;
4:      typedef unsigned short USHORT;
5:
6: // >> Insert lines 7 to 63 from Listing 15.6
7:      class PartsList;
8:
9:      // *************** Part Node ***********
10:     class PartNode
11:     {
12:     public:
13:        friend class PartsList;
14:        PartNode (Part*);
15:        ~PartNode();
16:        void SetNext(PartNode * node) { itsNext = node; }
17:        PartNode * GetNext() const;
18:        Part * GetPart() const;
19:     private:
20:        Part *itsPart;
21:        PartNode * itsNext;
22:     };
23:     //>> Insert lines 103-130 from Week 2 in Review
24:     // *************** Part List ***********
25:     class PartsList
26:     {
27:     public:
28:        PartsList();
29:        ~PartsList();
30:        // needs copy constructor and operator equals!
31:        void      Iterate(void (Part::*f)()const) const;
32:        Part*     Find(ULONG & position, ULONG PartNumber)  const;
33:        Part*     GetFirst() const;
34:        void      Insert(Part *);
35:        Part*     operator[](ULONG) const;
36:        ULONG     GetCount() const { return itsCount; }
37:        static    PartsList& GetGlobalPartsList() { return  GlobalPartsList;}
38:     private:
39:        PartNode * pHead;
40:        ULONG itsCount;
41:        static PartsList GlobalPartsList;
42:     };
```

15

```
43:
44:     PartsList PartsList::GlobalPartsList;
45:
46:     // Implementations for Lists...
47:
48:     PartsList::PartsList():
49:         pHead(0),
50:         itsCount(0)
51:         {}
52:
53:     PartsList::~PartsList()
54:     {
55:         delete pHead;
56:     }
57:
58:     Part*   PartsList::GetFirst() const
59:     {
60:         if (pHead)
61:             return pHead->itsPart;
62:         else
63:             return NULL;   // error catch here
64:     }
65:
66:     Part *  PartsList::operator[](ULONG offSet) const
67:     {
68:         PartNode* pNode = pHead;
69:
70:         if (!pHead)
71:             return NULL; // error catch here
72:
73:         if (offSet > itsCount)
74:             return NULL; // error
75:
76:         for (ULONG i=0;i<offSet; i++)
77:             pNode = pNode->itsNext;
78:
79:       return   pNode->itsPart;
80:     }
81:
82:     Part*   PartsList::Find(ULONG & position, ULONG PartNumber)  const
83:     {
84:         PartNode * pNode = 0;
85:         for (pNode = pHead, position = 0;
86:             pNode!=NULL;
87:             pNode = pNode->itsNext, position++)
88:         {
89:             if (pNode->itsPart->GetPartNumber() == PartNumber)
90:                 break;
91:         }
92:         if (pNode == NULL)
93:             return NULL;
94:         else
95:             return pNode->itsPart;
96:     }
97:
```

continues

Listing 15.7. continued

```
98:     void PartsList::Iterate(void (Part::*func)()const) const
99:     {
100:        if (!pHead)
101:            return;
102:        PartNode* pNode = pHead;
103:        do
104:            (pNode->itsPart->*func)();
105:        while (pNode = pNode->itsNext);
106:    }
107:
108:    void PartsList::Insert(Part* pPart)
109:    {
110:        PartNode * pNode = new PartNode(pPart);
111:        PartNode * pCurrent = pHead;
112:        PartNode * pNext = 0;
113:
114:        ULONG New =  pPart->GetPartNumber();
115:        ULONG Next = 0;
116:        itsCount++;
117:
118:        if (!pHead)
119:        {
120:            pHead = pNode;
121:            return;
122:        }
123:
124:        // if this one is smaller than head
125:        // this one is the new head
126:        if (pHead->itsPart->GetPartNumber() > New)
127:        {
128:            pNode->itsNext = pHead;
129:            pHead = pNode;
130:            return;
131:        }
132:
133:        for (;;)
134:        {
135:            // if there is no next, append this new one
136:            if (!pCurrent->itsNext)
137:            {
138:                pCurrent->itsNext = pNode;
139:                return;
140:            }
141:
142:            // if this goes after this one and before the next
143:            // then insert it here, otherwise get the next
144:            pNext = pCurrent->itsNext;
145:            Next = pNext->itsPart->GetPartNumber();
146:            if (Next > New)
147:            {
148:                pCurrent->itsNext = pNode;
149:                pNode->itsNext = pNext;
150:                return;
151:            }
```

15

```
152:            pCurrent = pNext;
153:        }
154:    }
155:
156:    class PartsCatalog : private PartsList
157:    {
158:    public:
159:        void Insert(Part *);
160:        ULONG Exists(ULONG PartNumber);
161:        Part * Get(int PartNumber);
162:        operator+(const PartsCatalog &);
163:        void ShowAll() { Iterate(Part::Display); }
164:    private:
165:    };
166:
167:    void PartsCatalog::Insert(Part * newPart)
168:    {
169:        ULONG partNumber =  newPart->GetPartNumber();
170:        ULONG offset;
171:
172:        if (!Find(offset, partNumber))
173:            PartsList::Insert(newPart);
174:        else
175:        {
176:            cout << partNumber << " was the ";
177:            switch (offset)
178:            {
179:                case 0:  cout << "first "; break;
180:                case 1:  cout << "second "; break;
181:                case 2:  cout << "third "; break;
182:                default: cout << offset+1 << "th ";
183:            }
184:            cout << "entry. Rejected!\n";
185:        }
186:    }
187:
188:    ULONG PartsCatalog::Exists(ULONG PartNumber)
189:    {
190:        ULONG offset;
191:        Find(offset,PartNumber);
192:        return offset;
193:    }
194:
195:    Part * PartsCatalog::Get(int PartNumber)
196:    {
197:        ULONG offset;
198:        return (Find(offset, PartNumber));
199:
200:    }
201:
202:    void main()
203:    {
204:        PartsCatalog pc;
205:        Part * pPart = 0;
206:        ULONG PartNumber;
207:        USHORT value;
```

continues

Listing 15.7. continued

```
208:        ULONG choice;
209:
210:        while (true)
211:        {
212:            cout << "(0)Quit (1)Car (2)Plane: ";
213:            cin >> choice;
214:
215:            if (!choice)
216:                break;
217:
218:            cout << "New PartNumber?: ";
219:            cin >>  PartNumber;
220:
221:            if (choice == 1)
222:            {
223:                cout << "Model Year?: ";
224:                cin >> value;
225:                pPart = new CarPart(value,PartNumber);
226:            }
227:            else
228:            {
229:                cout << "Engine Number?: ";
230:                cin >> value;
231:                pPart = new AirPlanePart(value,PartNumber);
232:            }
233:            pc.Insert(pPart);
234:        }
235:        pc.ShowAll();
236:    }
```

OUTPUT
```
 (0)Quit (1)Car (2)Plane:  1
New Part Number?: 1234
Model Year?: 94
 (0)Quit (1)Car (2)Plane:  1
New Part Number?: 4434
Model Year?: 93
 (0)Quit (1)Car (2)Plane:  1
New Part Number?: 1234
Model Year?: 94
1234 was the first entry. Rejected!
 (0)Quit (1)Car (2)Plane:  1
New Part Number?: 2345
Model Year?: 93
 (0)Quit (1)Car (2)Plane:  0

Part Number: 1234
Model Year: 94

Part Number: 2345
Model Year: 93

Part Number: 4434
Model Year: 93
```

15

ANALYSIS Listing 15.7 shows only the changed interface to Listing 15.8—that is, the changes to PartNode and PartsList.

On line 13, the class PartsList is declared to be a friend to the PartNode class. Because PartsList has not yet been declared, the compiler complains that this type is not known. On line 7, the PartsList name is declared to the compiler without a full declaration of the class. This is known as a forward declaration and is how you say to the compiler, "I'm about to use the name PartsList; that's a class name and I'll declare it in just a moment, I promise."

This listing places the friend declaration in the public section, but this is not required; it can be put anywhere in the class declaration without changing the meaning of the statement. Because of this statement, all the private member data and functions are available to any member function of class PartsList.

On line 61, the implementation of the member function GetFirst() reflects this change. Rather than returning pHead->GetPart, this function now returns the otherwise private member data by writing pHead->itsPart. Similarly, the Insert() function now writes pNode->itsNext = pHead rather than writing pNode->SetNext(pHead).

Admittedly, these are trivial changes, and there is not a good enough reason to make PartsList a friend of PartNode. But they do serve to illustrate how the keyword friend works.

Declarations of friend classes should be used with extreme caution. If two classes are inextricably entwined and one must frequently access data in the other, there might be good reason to use this declaration. But use it sparingly; it is often just as easy to use the public accessor methods, and doing so enables you to change one class without having to recompile the other.

NOTE

> You will often hear novice C++ programmers complain that friend declarations undermine the encapsulation that is so important to object-oriented programming. Frankly, this is errant nonsense. The friend declaration makes the declared friend part of the class interface and is no more an undermining of encapsulation than is public derivation.

Friend Class

SYNTAX

Declare one class to be a friend of another by putting the word friend into the class granting the access rights. That is, I can declare you to be my friend, but you can't declare yourself to be my friend.

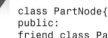

Example:

```
class PartNode{
public:
friend class PartList;   // declares PartList to be a friend of PartNode
};
```

friend Functions

At times, you will want to grant this level of access not to an entire class, but to only one or two functions of that class. You can do this by declaring the member functions of the other class to be friends, rather than declaring the entire class to be a friend. In fact, you can declare any function, whether or not it is a member function of another class, to be a friend function.

friend Functions and Operator Overloading

Listing 15.1 provided a `String` class that overrode the `operator+`. It also provided a constructor that took a constant character pointer, so that string objects could be created from C-style strings. This enabled you to create a string and add to it with a C-style string.

NOTE   C-style strings are null-terminated character arrays, such as `char myString[] = "Hello World.".`

What you could not do, however, was create a C-style string (a character string) and add to it using a string object, as shown in this example:

```
char cString[] = {"Hello"};
String sString(" World");
String sStringTwo = cString + sString;   //error!
```

C-style strings don't have an overloaded `operator+`. As discussed on Day 10, "Advanced Functions," when you say `cString + sString;`, you are really calling `cString.operator+(sString)`. Because you can't call `operator+()` on a C-style string, this causes a compile-time error.

You can solve this problem by declaring a friend function in `String`, which overloads `operator+` but takes two string objects. The C-style string is converted to a string object by the appropriate constructor, and then `operator+` is called using the two string objects.

| TYPE | **Listing 15.8. Friendly** operator+. |

```
1:    //Listing 15.8 - friendly operators
2:
3:    #include <iostream.h>
4:    #include <string.h>
5:
6:    // Rudimentary string class
7:    class String
8:    {
9:      public:
10:        // constructors
11:        String();
12:        String(const char *const);
13:        String(const String &);
14:        ~String();
15:
16:        // overloaded operators
17:        char & operator[](int offset);
18:        char operator[](int offset) const;
19:        String operator+(const String&);
20:        friend String operator+(const String&, const String&);
21:        void operator+=(const String&);
22:        String & operator= (const String &);
23:
24:        // General accessors
25:        int GetLen()const { return itsLen; }
26:        const char * GetString() const { return itsString; }
27:
28:      private:
29:        String (int);           // private constructor
30:        char * itsString;
31:        unsigned short itsLen;
32:    };
33: // >> Insert lines 32-122 from Listing 15.1
34:    // creates a new string by adding current
35:    // string to rhs
36:    String String::operator+(const String& rhs)
37:    {
38:      int  totalLen = itsLen + rhs.GetLen();
39:      String temp(totalLen);
40:      for (int i = 0; i<itsLen; i++)
41:        temp[i] = itsString[i];
42:      for (int j = 0; j<rhs.GetLen(); j++, i++)
43:        temp[i] = rhs[j];
44:      temp[totalLen]='\0';
45:      return temp;
46:    }
47:
48:    // creates a new string by adding
49:    // one string to another
50:    String operator+(const String& lhs, const String& rhs)
51:    {
```

continues

Listing 15.8. continued

```
52:          int  totalLen = lhs.GetLen() + rhs.GetLen();
53:          String temp(totalLen);
54:          for (int i = 0; i<lhs.GetLen(); i++)
55:              temp[i] = lhs[i];
56:          for (int j = 0; j<rhs.GetLen(); j++, i++)
57:              temp[i] = rhs[j];
58:          temp[totalLen]='\0';
59:          return temp;
60:      }
61: // >> Insert lines 138-152 from Listing 15.1
62:      void main()
63:      {
64:          String s1("String One ");
65:          String s2("String Two ");
66:          char *c1 = { "C-String One " } ;
67:          String s3;
68:          String s4;
69:          String s5;
70:
71:          cout << "s1: " << s1.GetString() << endl;
72:          cout << "s2: " << s2.GetString() << endl;
73:          cout << "c1: " << c1 << endl;
74:          s3 = s1 + s2;
75:          cout << "s3: " << s3.GetString() << endl;
76:          s4 = s1 + c1;
77:          cout << "s4: " << s4.GetString() << endl;
78:          s5 = c1 + s1;
79:          cout << "s5: " << s5.GetString() << endl;
80:      }
```

OUTPUT
```
s1: String One
s2: String Two
c1: C-String One
s3: String One String Two
s4: String One C-String One
s5: C-String One String One
```

ANALYSIS The implementation of all of the string methods except operator+ are unchanged from Listing 15.1, so they are left out of this listing. On line 20 a new operator+ is overloaded to take two constant string references and return a string, and this function is declared to be a friend.

Note that this operator+ is not a member function of this or any other class. It is declared within the declaration of the String class only so that it can be made a friend; but because it is declared, no other function prototype is needed.

The implementation of this operator+ is on lines 50 through 60. Note that it is similar to the earlier operator+, except that it takes two strings and accesses them both through their public accessor methods.

15

The driver program demonstrates the use of this function on line 78, where operator+ is now called on a C-style string!

Declaring *friend* Functions

Declare a function to be a friend by using the keyword friend and then the full specification of the function. Declaring a function to be a friend does not give the friend function access to the this pointer, but it does provide full access to all private and protected member data and functions.

Example:

```
class PartNode
{
friend void PartsList::Insert(Part *);   // make another class's member function
a _friend
friend int SomeFunction();               // make a global function a friend };
```

Overloading the Insertion Operator

You are finally ready to give your String class the capability to use cout like any other type. Until now, when you've wanted to print a string, you've been forced to write the following:

```
cout << theString.GetString();
```

What you would like to do is write this:

```
cout << theString;
```

To accomplish this, you must override operator<<(). On Day 16, "Streams," you see all the ins and outs (cins and couts?) of working with iostreams. For now, Listing 15.9 illustrates how operator<< can be overloaded using a friend function.

TYPE **Listing 15.9. Overloading operator<<().**

```
1:      #include <iostream.h>
2:      #include <string.h>
3:
4:      class String
5:      {
6:         public:
7:            // constructors
8:            String();
9:             String(const char *const);
10:            String(const String &);
11:            ~String();
12:
```

continues

Listing 15.9. continued

```
13:          // overloaded operators
14:          char & operator[](int offset);
15:          char operator[](int offset) const;
16:          String operator+(const String&);
17:          void operator+=(const String&);
18:          String & operator= (const String &);
19:          friend ostream& operator<<( ostream& theStream,String& theString);
20:          // General accessors
21:          int GetLen()const { return itsLen; }
22:          const char * GetString() const { return itsString; }
23:          // static int ConstructorCount;
24:
25:      private:
26:          String (int);          // private constructor
27:          char * itsString;
28:          unsigned short itsLen;
29:
30:      };
31:
32:      ostream& operator<<( ostream& theStream,String& theString)
33:      {
34:          theStream << theString.GetString();
35:          return theStream;
36:      }
37:      void main()
38:      {
39:          String theString("Hello world.");
40:          cout << theString;
41:      }
```

Hello world.

ANALYSIS To save space, the implementation of all of String's methods is left out, because they are unchanged from the previous examples.

On line 19, operator<< is declared to be a friend function that takes an ostream reference and a String reference and returns an ostream reference. Note that this is not a member function of String. It returns a reference to an ostream so that you can concatenate calls to operator<<, such as the following:

```
cout << "myAge: " << itsAge << " years.";
```

The implementation of this friend function is on lines 32 to 35. All this really does is hide the implementation details of feeding the string to the ostream, and that is just as it should be. You'll see more about overloading this operator and operator>> on Day 16.

Summary

Today you saw how to delegate functionality to a contained object. You also saw how to implement one class in terms of another by using either containment or private inheritance. Containment is restricted in that the new class does not have access to the protected members of the contained class, and it cannot override the member functions of the contained object. Containment is simpler to use than private inheritance and should be used when possible.

You also saw how to declare both `friend` functions and `friend` classes. Using a `friend` function, you saw how to overload the extraction operator to enable your new classes to use `cout` just as the built-in classes do.

Remember that public inheritance expresses *is-a*, containment expresses *has-a*, and private inheritance expresses *implemented in terms of.* The relationship *delegates to* can be expressed using either containment or private inheritance, although containment is more common.

Q&A

Q Why is it so important to distinguish between *is-a*, *has-a*, and *implemented in terms of*?

A The point of C++ is to implement well-designed, object-oriented programs. Keeping these relationships straight helps ensure that your design corresponds to the reality of what you are modeling. Furthermore, a well-understood design is more likely to be reflected in well-designed code.

Q Why is containment preferred over private inheritance?

A The challenge in modern programming is to cope with complexity. The more you can use objects as black boxes, the fewer details you have to worry about and the more complexity you can manage. Contained classes hide their details; private inheritance exposes the implementation details.

Q Why not make all classes friends of all the classes they use?

A Making one class a friend of another exposes the implementation details and reduces encapsulation. Ideally, you should keep as many of the details of each class hidden from all other classes as possible.

Q If a function is overloaded, do you need to declare each form of the function to be a friend?

A Yes. If you overload a function and declare it to be a friend of another class, you must declare `friend` for each form you want to grant this access to.

Quiz

1. How do you establish an *is-a* relationship?

2. How do you establish a *has-a* relationship?

3. What is the difference between containment and delegation?

4. What is the difference between delegation and *implemented in terms of*?

5. What is a `friend` function?

6. What is a `friend` class?

7. If `Dog` is a friend of `Boy`, is `Boy` a friend of `Dog`?

8. If `Dog` is a friend of `Boy` and `Terrier` derives from `Dog`, is `Terrier` a friend of `Boy`?

9. If `Dog` is a friend of `Boy` and `Boy` is a friend of `House`, is `Dog` a friend of `House`?

10. Where must the declaration of a friend function appear?

Exercises

1. Show the declaration of a class, `Animal`, that contains a data member that is a string object.

2. Show the declaration of a class `BoundedArray` that is an array.

3. Show the declaration of a class, `Set`, that is declared in terms of an array.

4. Modify Listing 15.9 to provide the `String` class with an `extraction operator (>>)`.

5. **BUG BUSTERS:** What is wrong with this program?

```
1:      #include <iostream.h>
2:
3:      class Animal;
4:
5:      void setValue(Animal& , int);
6:
7:
8:      class Animal
9:      {
10:     public:
11:         int GetWeight()const { return itsWeight; }
12:         int GetAge() const { return itsAge; }
13:     private:
14:         int itsWeight;
15:         int itsAge;
16:     };
17:
18:     void setValue(Animal& theAnimal, int theWeight)
19:     {
20:         friend class Animal;
21:         theAnimal.itsWeight = theWeight;
```

```
22:      }
23:
24:      void main()
25:      {
26:          Animal peppy;
27:          setValue(peppy,5);
28:      }
```

6. Fix the listing in exercise 5 so that it compiles.

7. **BUG BUSTERS:** What is wrong with this code?

```
1:       #include <iostream.h>
2:
3:       class Animal;
4:
5:       void setValue(Animal& , int);
6:       void setValue(Animal& ,int,int);
7:
8:       class Animal
9:       {
10:      friend void setValue(Animal& ,int);
11:      private:
12:          int itsWeight;
13:          int itsAge;
14:      };
15:
16:      void setValue(Animal& theAnimal, int theWeight)
17:      {
18:          theAnimal.itsWeight = theWeight;
19:      }
20:
21:
22:      void setValue(Animal& theAnimal, int theWeight, int theAge)
23:      {
24:          theAnimal.itsWeight = theWeight;
25:          theAnimal.itsAge = theAge;
26:      }
27:
28:      void main()
29:      {
30:          Animal peppy;
31:          setValue(peppy,5);
32:          setValue(peppy,7,9);
33:      }
```

8. Fix exercise 7 so that it compiles.

Day 16

Streams

Until now, you've been using cout to write to the screen and cin to read from the keyboard without a full understanding of how they work. Today, you learn

- ☐ What streams are and how they are used.
- ☐ How to manage input and output using streams.
- ☐ How to write to and read from files using streams.

Overview of Streams

C++ does not, as part of the language, define how data is written to the screen or to a file, nor how data is read into a program. These are clearly essential parts of working with C++, however, and the standard C++ library now includes the iostream library, which facilitates input and output (I/O).

The advantage of having the input and output kept apart from the language and handled in libraries is that it is easier to make the language *platform-independent*. That is, you can write C++ programs on a PC and then recompile and run them on a Sun Workstation. The compiler manufacturer just supplies the right library, and everything works. At least that's the theory.

NOTE

A library is a collection of .OBJ files that can be linked to your program to provide additional functionality. This is the most basic form of code reuse and has been around since ancient programmers chiseled 1s and 0s into the walls of caves.

Encapsulation

The iostream classes view the flow of data from your program to the screen as being a stream of data, one byte following another. If the destination of the stream is a file or the screen, the source is usually some part of your program. If the stream is reversed, the data can come from the keyboard or a disk file and be "poured" into your data variables.

One principal goal of streams is to encapsulate the problems of getting the data to and from the disk or the screen. After a stream is created, your program works with the stream and the stream sweats the details. Figure 16.1 illustrates this fundamental idea.

Figure 16.1.

Encapsulation through streams.

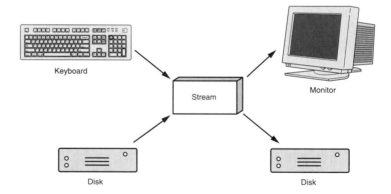

Buffering

Writing to the disk (and to a lesser extent the screen) is very "expensive." It takes a long time (relatively speaking) to write data to the disk or read data from the disk, and execution of the program is generally blocked by disk writes and reads. To solve this problem, streams provide *buffering*. Data is written into the stream, but it is not written back out to the disk immediately. Instead, the stream's buffer fills, and when it is full it writes to the disk all at once.

Picture water trickling into the top of a tank, and the tank gradually filling, but no water running out the bottom. Figure 16.2 illustrates this idea.

Figure 16.2.

Filling the buffer.

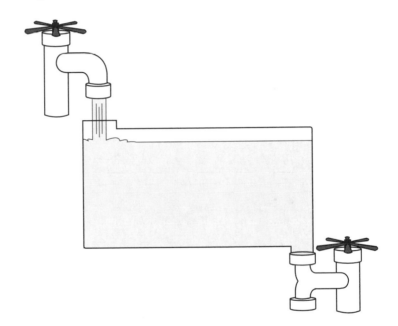

When the water (data) reaches the top, the valve opens and all the water flows out in a rush. Figure 16.3 illustrates this.

When the buffer is empty, the bottom valve closes, the top valve opens, and more water flows into the buffer tank. Figure 16.4 illustrates this.

Every once in a while you need to get the water out of the tank even before it is full. This is called *flushing* the buffer. See Figure 16.5.

Figure 16.3.
Emptying the buffer.

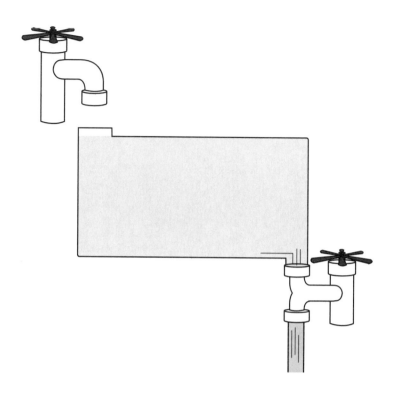

Figure 16.4.
Refilling the buffer.

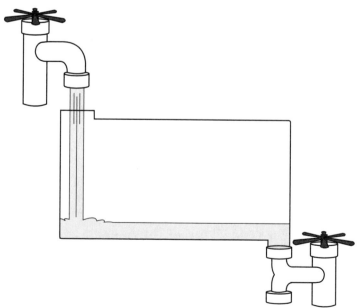

16

Figure 16.5.

Flushing a buffer.

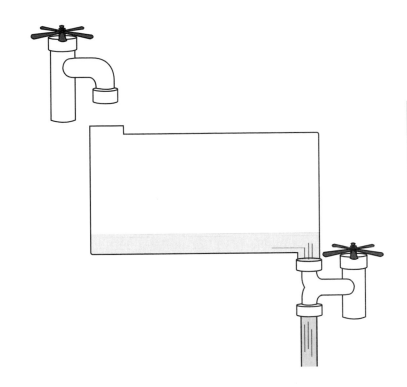

16

Streams and Buffers

As you might expect, C++ takes an object-oriented view toward implementing streams and buffers.

☐ The streambuf class manages the buffer, and its member functions provide the capability to fill, empty, flush, and otherwise manipulate the buffer.

☐ The ios class is the base class to the input and output stream classes. The ios class has a streambuf object as a member variable.

☐ The istream and ostream classes derive from the ios class and specialize input and output stream behavior, respectively.

☐ The iostream class is derived from both the istream and the ostream classes and provides input and output methods for writing to the screen.

☐ The fstream classes provide input and output from files.

Standard I/O Objects

When a C++ program that includes the iostream classes starts, four objects are created and initialized:

NOTE
> The iostream class library is added automatically to your program by the compiler. All you need to do to use these functions is to put the appropriate include statement at the top of your program listing.

- cin (pronounced "see-in") handles input from the standard input, the keyboard.
- cout (pronounced "see-out") handles output to the standard output, the screen.
- cerr (pronounced "see-err") handles unbuffered output to the standard error device, the screen. Because this is unbuffered, everything sent to cerr is written to the standard error device immediately, without waiting for the buffer to fill or for a flush command to be received.
- clog (pronounced "see-log") handles buffered error messages that are output to the standard error device, the screen. It is common for this to be *redirected* to a log file, as described in the following section.

Redirection

NEW TERM Each of the standard devices—input, output, and error—can be *redirected* to other devices. Standard error is often redirected to a file, and standard input and output can be *piped* to files using operating system commands.

Redirecting refers to sending output (or input) to a place different than the default. The redirection operators for DOS and UNIX are redirect input (<) and redirect output (>).

Piping refers to using the output of one program as the input of another.

DOS provides rudimentary redirection commands such as redirect output (>) and redirect input (<). UNIX provides more advanced redirection capabilities, but the general idea is the same: Take the output intended for the screen and write it to a file, or pipe it into another program. Alternatively, the input for a program can be extracted from a file rather than from the keyboard.

Redirection is more a function of the operating system than of the iostream libraries. C++ just provides access to the four standard devices; it is up to the user to redirect the devices to whatever alternatives are needed.

16

Input Using *cin*

The global object cin is responsible for input and is made available to your program when you include iostream.h. In previous examples, you used the overloaded extraction operator (>>) to put data into your program's variables. How does this work? The syntax, as you might remember, is the following:

```
int someVariable;
cout << "Enter a number: ";
cin >> someVariable;
```

The global object cout is discussed later today; for now, focus on the third line, cin >> someVariable;. What can you guess about cin?

Clearly it must be a global object, because you didn't define it in your own code. You know from previous operator experience that cin has overloaded the extraction operator (>>) and that the effect is to write whatever data cin has in its buffer into your local variable, someVariable.

What might not be immediately obvious is that cin has overloaded the extraction operator for a great variety of parameters, among them int&, short&, long&, double&, float&, char&, char*, and so forth. When you write cin >> someVariable;, the type of someVariable is assessed. In the previous example, someVariable is an integer, so the following function is called:

```
istream & operator>> (int &)
```

Note that because the parameter is passed by reference, the extraction operator is able to act on the original variable. Listing 16.1 illustrates the use of cin.

TYPE **Listing 16.1.** cin **handles different data types.**

```
1:      //Listing 16.1 -- character strings and cin
2:
3:      #include <iostream.h>
4:
5:      void main()
6:      {
7:          int myInt;
8:          long myLong;
9:          double myDouble;
10:         float myFloat;
11:         unsigned int myUnsigned;
12:
13:         cout << "int: ";
14:         cin >> myInt;
15:         cout << "Long: ";
16:         cin >> myLong;
```

continues

Listing 16.1. continued

```
17:          cout << "Double: ";
18:          cin >> myDouble;
19:          cout << "Float: ";
20:          cin >> myFloat;
21:          cout << "Unsigned: ";
22:          cin >> myUnsigned;
23:
24:          cout << "\n\nInt:\t" << myInt << endl;
25:          cout << "Long:\t" << myLong << endl;
26:          cout << "Double:\t" << myDouble << endl;
27:          cout << "Float:\t" << myFloat << endl;
28:          cout << "Unsigned:\t" << myUnsigned << endl;
29:     }
```

OUTPUT
```
int: 2
Long: 70000
Double: 987654321
Float: 3.33
Unsigned: 25

Int:        2
Long:       70000
Double:     9.87654e+08
Float:      3.33
Unsigned:   25
```

ANALYSIS
On lines 7 through 11, variables of various types are declared. On lines 13 through 22, the user is prompted to enter values for these variables, and the results are printed (using cout) on lines 24 through 28.

The output reflects that the variables were put into the right kinds of variables, and the program works as you intended.

Strings

cin can also handle character pointer (char*) arguments, so you can create a character buffer and use cin to fill it. For example, you can write this:

```
char YourName[50]
cout << "Enter your name: ";
cin >> YourName;
```

If you enter Jesse, the variable YourName is filled with the characters 'J', 'e', 's', 's', 'e', '\0'. The last character is the special null character; cin automatically ends the string with the null character, and you must have enough room in the buffer to allow for the entire string plus the null character. The null character signals "end of string" to the standard library functions discussed on Day 21, "Working with Multiple Files for Large Programs."

16

String Problems

After all this success with cin, you might be surprised when you try to enter a full name into a string. cin believes that white space is a separator. When it sees a space or a new line, it assumes the input for the parameter is complete, and in the case of strings it adds the null character right then and there. Listing 16.2 illustrates this problem.

TYPE **Listing 16.2. Trying to write more than one word to cin.**

```
1:    //Listing 16.2 - character strings and cin
2:
3:    #include <iostream.h>
4:
5:    void main()
6:    {
7:       char YourName[50];
8:       cout << "Your first name: ";
9:       cin >> YourName;
10:      cout << "Here it is: " << YourName << endl;
11:      cout << "Your entire name: ";
12:      cin >> YourName;
13:      cout << "Here it is: " << YourName << endl;
14:   }
```

OUTPUT
```
Your first name: Jesse
Here it is: Jesse
Your entire name: Jesse Liberty
Here it is: Jesse
```

ANALYSIS On line 7, a character array is created to hold the user's input. On line 8, the user is prompted to enter one name, and that name is stored properly as shown in the output.

On line 11, the user is again prompted, this time for a full name. cin reads the input, and when it sees the space between the names, it puts a NULL after the first word and terminates input. This is not exactly what was intended.

To understand why this works this way, examine Listing 16.3, which shows input for a number of fields.

TYPE **Listing 16.3. Multiple input.**

```
1:    //Listing 16.3 - character strings and cin
2:
3:    #include <iostream.h>
4:
5:    void main()
```

continues

Listing 16.3. continued

```
6:      {
7:          int myInt;
8:          long myLong;
9:          double myDouble;
10:         float myFloat;
11:         unsigned int myUnsigned;
12:         char myWord[50];
13:
14:         cout << "int: ";
15:         cin >> myInt;
16:         cout << "Long: ";
17:         cin >> myLong;
18:         cout << "Double: ";
19:         cin >> myDouble;
20:         cout << "Float: ";
21:         cin >> myFloat;
22:         cout << "Word: ";
23:         cin >> myWord;
24:         cout << "Unsigned: ";
25:         cin >> myUnsigned;
26:
27:         cout << "\n\nInt:\t" << myInt << endl;
28:         cout << "Long:\t" << myLong << endl;
29:         cout << "Double:\t" << myDouble << endl;
30:         cout << "Float:\t" << myFloat << endl;
31:         cout << "Word: \t" << myWord << endl;
32:         cout << "Unsigned:\t" << myUnsigned << endl;
33:
34:         cout << "\n\nInt, Long, Double, Float, Word, Unsigned: ";
35:         cin >> myInt >> myLong >> myDouble >> myFloat >> myWord >> myUnsigned;
36:
37:         cout << "\n\nInt:\t" << myInt << endl;
38:         cout << "Long:\t" << myLong << endl;
39:         cout << "Double:\t" << myDouble << endl;
40:         cout << "Float:\t" << myFloat << endl;
41:         cout << "Word: \t" << myWord << endl;
42:         cout << "Unsigned:\t" << myUnsigned << endl;
43:
44:
45:     }
```

OUTPUT

```
Int: 2
Long: 30303
Double: 393939397834
Float: 3.33
Word: Hello
Unsigned: 85

Int:        2
Long:       30303
Double      3.93939e+11
Float:      3.33
Word:       Hello
```

16

```
Unsigned: 85

Int, Long, Double, Float, Word, Unsigned: 3 304938 393847473 6.66 bye -2

Int:      3
Long:     304938
Double    3.93847e+08
Float:    6.66
Word:     bye
Unsigned: 65534
```

ANALYSIS Once again, a number of variables are created—this time including a char array. The user is prompted for input and the output is faithfully printed.

On line 34, the user is prompted for all the input at once, and then each "word" of input is assigned to the appropriate variable. It is in order to facilitate this kind of multiple assignment that cin must consider each word in the input to be the full input for each variable. If cin was to consider the entire input as part of one variable's input, this kind of concatenated input would be impossible.

Note that on line 35 the last object requested was an unsigned integer, but the user entered -2. Because cin believes it is writing to an unsigned integer, the bit pattern of -2 was evaluated as an unsigned integer, and when written out by cout the value 65534 was displayed. The unsigned value 65534 has the exact bit pattern of the signed value -2.

Later in this lesson, you see how to enter an entire string into a buffer, including multiple words. For now, the question arises, "How does the extraction operator manage this trick of concatenation?"

operator>> Returns a Reference to an *istream* Object

The return value of cin is a reference to an istream object. Because cin itself is an istream object, the return value of one extraction operation can be the input to the next extraction.

```
int VarOne, varTwo, varThree;
cout << "Enter three numbers: "
cin >> VarOne >> varTwo >> varThree;
```

When you write cin >> VarOne >> varTwo >> varThree;, the first extraction is evaluated (cin >> VarOne). The return value from this is another istream object, and that object's extraction operator gets the variable varTwo. It is as if you had written this:

```
((cin >> varOne) >> varTwo) >> varThree;
```

You'll see this technique repeated later when cout is discussed.

Other Member Functions of *cin*

In addition to overloading `operator>>`, `cin` has a number of other member functions. These are used when finer control over the input is required.

Single Character Input

The `operator>>` taking a character reference can be used to get a single character from the standard input. The member function `get()` can also be used to obtain a single character, and it can do so in two ways. `get()` can be used with no parameters, in which case the return value is used, or it can be used with a reference to a character.

Using *get()* with No Parameters

The first form of `get()` is without parameters. This returns the value of the character found, and returns `EOF` (end of file) if the end of the file is reached. `get()` with no parameters is not often used. It is not possible to concatenate this use of `get()` for multiple input, because the return value is not an `iostream` object. That is why the following doesn't work:

```
cin.get() >>myVarOne >> myVarTwo; //    illegal
```

The return value of (`cin.get() >> myVarOne`) is an integer, not an `iostream` object.

A common use of `get()` with no parameters is illustrated in Listing 16.4.

Listing 16.4. Using `get()` with no parameters.

```
1:      // Listing
2:      #include <iostream.h>
3:
4:      void main()
5:      {
6:         char ch;
7:         while ( (ch = cin.get()) != EOF)
8:         {
9:            cout << "ch: " << ch << endl;
10:        }
11:        cout << "\nDone!\n";
12:     }
```

NOTE   To exit this program, you must send the end of file from the keyboard. On DOS computers use Ctrl+Z; on UNIX units use Ctrl+D.

OUTPUT
```
Hello
ch: H
ch: e
ch: l
ch: l
ch: o
ch:

World
ch: W
ch: o
ch: r
ch: l
ch: d
ch:

(ctrl-z)
Done!
```

ANALYSIS On line 6 a local character variable is declared. The while loop assigns the input received from cin.get() to ch, and if it is not EOF, the string is printed out. This output is buffered until an end of line is read, however. When EOF is encountered (by pressing Ctrl+Z on a DOS machine or Ctrl+D on a UNIX machine), the loop exits.

Note that not every implementation of istream supports this version of get().

Using *get()* with a Character Reference Parameter

When a character is passed as input to get(), that character is filled with the next character in the input stream. The return value is an iostream object, so this form of get() can be concatenated, as illustrated in Listing 16.5.

TYPE **Listing 16.5 Using get() with parameters.**

```
1:     // Listing
2:     #include <iostream.h>
3:
4:     void main()
5:     {
6:         char a, b, c;
7:
8:         cout << "Enter three letters: ";
9:
10:        cin.get(a).get(b).get(c);
11:
12:        cout << "a: " << a << "\nb: " << b << "\nc: " << c << endl;
13:    }
```

OUTPUT

```
Enter three letters: one
a: o
b: n
c: e
```

ANALYSIS   On line 6 three character variables are created. On line 10, `cin.get()` is called three times, concatenated into one long series of `cin` objects (remember that each `get()` returns a `cin` object). First `cin.get(a)` is called. This puts the first letter into `a` and returns `cin` so that when it is done, `cin.get(b)` is called, putting the next letter into `b`. The end result is that `cin.get(c)` is called and the third letter is put in `c`.

Because `cin.get(a)` evaluates to `cin`, you could have written

```
cin.get(a) >> b;
```

In this form, `cin.get(a)` evaluates to `cin`, so the second phrase is `cin >> b;`.

Do   **Don't**

DO use the extraction operator (>>) when you need to skip over white space.

DO use `get()` with a character parameter when you need to examine every character, including white space.

DON'T use `get()` with no parameters at all; it is basically obsolete.

Getting Strings from Standard Input

The extraction operator (>>) can be used to fill a character array, as can the member functions `get()` and `getline()`.

The final form of `get()` takes three parameters. The first parameter is a pointer to a character array, the second parameter is the maximum number of characters to read plus one, and the third parameter is the termination character.

If you enter 20 as the second parameter, `get()` reads 19 characters and then null terminates the string, which it stores in the first parameter. The third parameter, the termination character, defaults to new line (`'\n'`). If a termination character is reached before the maximum number of characters is read, a null character is written and the termination character is left in the buffer.

Listing 16.6 illustrates the use of this form of `get()`.

16

TYPE **Listing 16.6. Using `get()` with a character array.**

```
1:     // Listing
2:     #include <iostream.h>
3:
4:     void main()
5:     {
6:         char stringOne[256];
7:         char stringTwo[256];
8:
9:         cout << "Enter string one: ";
10:        cin.get(stringOne,256);
11:        cout << "stringOne: " << stringOne << endl;
12:
13:        cout << "Enter string two: ";
14:        cin >> stringTwo;
15:        cout << "StringTwo: " << stringTwo << endl;
16:    }
```

OUTPUT
```
Enter string one: Now is the time
String One: Now is the time
Enter string two: For all good
String Two: For
```

ANALYSIS   On lines 6 and 7 two character arrays are created. On line 9 the user is prompted to
enter a string, and `cin.get()` is called on line 10. The first parameter is the buffer
to fill, and the second parameter is one more than the maximum number for `get()` to accept
(the extra position being given to NULL, `'\0'`). The defaulted third parameter is a new line.

The user enters `"Now is the time"`. Because the user ends the phrase with a new line, that
phrase is put into `stringOne`, followed by a terminating NULL.

The user is prompted for another string on line 13, and this time the extraction operator is
used. Because the extraction operator takes everything up to the first white space, the string
`For` with a terminating NULL is stored in the second string, which of course is not what was
intended.

Another way to solve this problem is to use `getline()`, as illustrated in Listing 16.7.

TYPE **Listing 16.7. Using `getline()`.**

```
1:     // Listing
2:     #include <iostream.h>
3:
4:     void main()
5:     {
6:         char stringOne[256];
7:         char stringTwo[256];
```

continues

16

Listing 16.7. continued

```
8:          char stringThree[256];
9:
10:         cout << "Enter string one: ";
11:         cin.getline(stringOne,256);
12:         cout << "stringOne: " << stringOne << endl;
13:
14:         cout << "Enter string two: ";
15:         cin >> stringTwo;
16:         cout << "stringTwo: " << stringTwo << endl;
17:
18:         cout << "Enter string three: ";
19:         cin.getline(stringThree,256);
20:         cout << "stringThree: " << stringThree << endl;
21:     }
```

OUTPUT
```
Enter string one: one two three
stringOne: one two three
Enter string two: four five six
String two: four
Enter string three: stringThree: five six
```

ANALYSIS This example warrants careful examination; there are some potential surprises. On lines 6 through 8, three character arrays are declared.

On line 10 the user is prompted to enter a string, and that string is read by getline(). Like get(), getline() takes a buffer and a maximum number of characters. Unlike get(), however, the terminating new line is read and thrown away. With get(), the terminating new line is not thrown away. It is left in the input buffer.

On line 14 the user is prompted again, and this time the extraction operator is used. The user enters four five six and the first word (four) is put in string two. The string Enter string three is then displayed, and getline() is called again. Because five six is still in the input buffer, it is immediately read up to the new line; getline() terminates and the string in stringThree is printed on line 20.

The user has no chance to enter string three, because the second getline() call is fulfilled by the string remaining in the input buffer after the call to the extraction operator on line 15.

SYNTAX

The extraction operator (>>) reads up to the first white space and puts the word into the character array.

The member function get() is overloaded. In one version, it takes no parameters and returns the value of the character it receives. In the second version, it takes a single character reference and returns the istream object by reference.

In the third and final version, get() takes a character array, a number of characters to get, and a termination character (which defaults to new line). This version of get() reads characters into the array until it gets to one fewer than its maximum number of characters or encounters the termination character, whichever comes first. If `get()` encounters the termination character, it leaves that character in the input buffer and stops reading characters.

The member function `getline()` also takes three parameters: the buffer to fill, one more than the maximum number of characters to get, and the termination character. It functions exactly like `get()` does with these parameters, except `getline()` throws away the terminating character.

Using *cin.ignore()*

At times you want to ignore the remaining characters on a line until you hit either end of line (EOL) or end of file (EOF). The member function `ignore()` serves this purpose. `ignore()` takes two parameters, the maximum number of characters to ignore, and the termination character. If you write `ignore(80, '\n')`, up to 80 characters are thrown away until a new line character is found. The new line is then thrown away and the `ignore()` statement ends. Listing 16.8 illustrates the use of `ignore()`.

Type   **Listing 16.8. Using** `ignore()`.

```
1:      // Listing
2:      #include <iostream.h>
3:
4:      void main()
5:      {
6:          char stringOne[255];
7:          char stringTwo[255];
8:
9:          cout << "Enter string one: ";
10:         cin.get(stringOne,255);
11:         cout << "String one" << stringOne << endl;
12:
13:         cout << "Enter string two: ";
14:         cin.getline(stringTwo,255);
15:         cout << "String two: " << stringTwo << endl;
16:
17:         cout << "\n\nNow try again...\n";
18:
19:         cout << "Enter string one: ";
20:         cin.get(stringOne,255);
21:         cout << "String one: " << stringOne<< endl;
22:
23:         cin.ignore(255,'\n');
24:
25:         cout << "Enter string two: ";
26:         cin.getline(stringTwo,255);
27:         cout << "String Two: " << stringTwo<< endl;
28:     }
```

OUTPUT
```
Enter string one: once upon a time
String one: once upon a time
Enter string two: String two:

Now try again...
Enter string one: once upon a time
String one: once upon a time
Enter string two: there was a
String two: there was a
```

ANALYSIS On lines 6 and 7 two character arrays are created. On line 9 the user is prompted for input and types Once upon a time, followed by Enter. On line 10, get() is used to read this string. get() fills stringOne and terminates on the new line, but leaves the new line character in the input buffer.

On line 13 the user is prompted again, but the getline() on line 14 reads the new line that is already in the buffer and terminates immediately, before the user can enter any input.

On line 19 the user is prompted again and puts in the same first line of input. This time, however, on line 23, ignore() is used to ignore the new line character. When the getline() call on line 26 is reached, the input buffer is empty, and the user can input the next line of the story.

peek() and putback()

The input object cin has two additional methods that can come in rather handy: peek(), which looks at but does not extract the next character, and putback(), which inserts a character into the input stream. Listing 16.9 illustrates how these might be used.

TYPE **Listing 16.9. Using peek() and putback().**

```
1:    // Listing
2:    #include <iostream.h>
3:
4:    void main()
5:    {
6:       char ch;
7:       cout << "enter a phrase: ";
8:       while ( cin.get(ch) )
9:       {
10:          if (ch == '!')
11:             cin.putback('$');
12:          else
13:             cout << ch;
14:          while (cin.peek() == '#')
15:             cin.ignore(1,'#');
16:       }
17:    }
```

Output

```
enter a phrase: Now!is#the!time#for!fun#!
Now$isthe$timefor$fun$
```

Analysis

On line 6 a character variable, `ch`, is declared; on line 7 the user is prompted to enter a phrase. The purpose of this program is to turn any exclamation marks (`!`) into dollar signs (`$`) and to remove any pound symbols (`#`).

The program loops as long as it is getting characters other than the end of file (remember that `cin.get()` returns `0` for end of file). If the current character is a dollar sign, it is thrown away and the `$` symbol is put back into the input buffer; it is read the next time through. If the current item is not an exclamation mark, it is printed. The next character is "peeked" at, and when pound symbols are found, they are removed.

This is not the most efficient way to do either of these things (and it won't find a pound symbol if it is the first character), but it does illustrate how these methods work. They are relatively obscure, so don't spend a lot of time worrying about when to use them. Put them into your bag of tricks; they'll come in handy sooner or later.

TIP

> `peek()` and `putback()` are typically used for parsing strings and other data, such as when writing a compiler.

Output with *cout*

You have used `cout` to write strings, integers, and other numeric data to the screen with the overloaded insertion operator (`<<`). It is also possible to format the data, aligning columns and writing the numeric data in decimal and hexadecimal. This section shows you how.

Flushing the Output

You've already seen that using `endl` flushes the output buffer. `Endl` calls `cout`'s member function `flush()`, which writes all of the data it is buffering. You can call the `flush()` method directly, either by calling the `flush()` member method or by writing the following:

```
cout << flush
```

This is convenient when you need to ensure that the output buffer is emptied and the contents are written to the screen.

Related Functions

Just as the extraction operator can be supplemented with get() and getline(), the insertion operator can be supplemented with put() and write().

The function put() is used to write a single character to the output device. Because put() returns an ostream reference, and because cout is an ostream object, you can concatenate put() just as you do the insertion operator. Listing 16.10 illustrates this idea.

TYPE **Listing 16.10. Using put().**

```
1:      // Listing
2:      #include <iostream.h>
3:
4:      void main()
5:      {
6:          cout.put('H').put('e').put('l').put('l').put('o').put('\n');
7:      }
```

OUTPUT Hello

ANALYSIS Line 6 is evaluated like this: cout.put('H') writes the letter H to the screen and returns the cout object. This leaves the following:

cout.put('e').put('l').put('l').put('o').put('\n');

The letter e is written, leaving cout.put('l').... This process repeats, with each letter being written and the cout object returned, until the final character ('\n') is written and the function returns.

The function write() works just like the insertion operator (<<), except that it takes a parameter that tells the function the maximum number of characters to write. Listing 16.11 illustrates its use.

TYPE **Listing 16.11. Using write().**

```
1:      // Listing
2:      #include <iostream.h>
3:      #include <string.h>
4:
5:      void main()
6:      {
7:          char One[] = "One if by land";
8:
9:
```

16

```
10:
11:        int fullLength = strlen(One);
12:        int tooShort = fullLength - 4;
13:        int tooLong = fullLength + 6;
14:
15:        cout.write(One,fullLength) << "\n";
16:        cout.write(One,tooShort) << "\n";
17:        cout.write(One,tooLong) << "\n";
18:    }
```

OUTPUT

```
One if by land
One if by
One if by land i?!
```

NOTE

> **Note:** The last line of output might look different on your computer.

ANALYSIS On lines 7, a phrase is created. On line 11 the integer fullLength is set to the length of the phrase, and tooShort is set to that length minus four, while tooLong is set to fullLength plus six.

On line 15, the phrase is printed using write(). The length is set to the actual length of the phrase, and the correct phrase is printed.

On line 16 the phrase is printed again, but it is four characters shorter than the full phrase, and that is reflected in the output.

On line 17 the phrase is printed again, but this time write() is instructed to write an extra six characters. After the phrase is written, the next six bytes of contiguous memory are written. The first extra byte is the null character at the end of phrase two; this is followed by the first five characters of phrase one.

Manipulators, Flags, and Formatting Instructions

The output stream maintains a number of state flags, determining which base (decimal or hexadecimal) to use, how wide to make the fields, and what character to use to fill in fields. A state flag is just a byte whose individual bits are each assigned a special meaning. Manipulating bits in this way is discussed on Day 21. Each of ostream's flags can be set using member functions and manipulators.

Using *cout.width()*

The default width of your output is just enough space to print the number, character, or string in the output buffer. You can change this by using width(). Because width() is a member function, it must be invoked with a cout object. It only changes the width of the very next output field and then immediately reverts to the default. Listing 16.12 illustrates its use.

TYPE **Listing 16.12. Adjusting the width of output.**

```
1:     // Listing
2:     #include <iostream.h>
3:
4:     void main()
5:     {
6:        cout << "Start >";
7:        cout.width(25);
8:        cout << 123 << "< End\n";
9:
10:       cout << "Start >";
11:       cout.width(25);
12:       cout << 123<< "< Next >";
13:       cout << 456 << "< End\n";
14:
15:       cout << "Start >";
16:       cout.width(4);
17:       cout << 123456 << "< End\n";
18:
19:
20:    }
```

OUTPUT
```
Start >                        123< End
Start >                        123< Next >456< End
Start >123456< End
```

ANALYSIS The first output, on lines 6 through 8, prints the number 123 within a field whose width is set to 25 on line 7. This is reflected in the first line of output.

The second line of output first prints the value 123 in the same field whose width is set to 25, and then prints the value 456. Note that 456 is printed in a field whose width is reset to be just large enough; as stated, the effect of width() lasts only as long as the very next output.

The final output reflects that setting a width smaller than the output is exactly like setting a width that is just large enough.

Setting the Fill Characters

Normally, cout fills the empty field created by a call to width() with spaces, as shown previously. At times you might want to fill the area with other characters, such as asterisks. To do this, you call fill() and pass in as a parameter the character you want used as a fill character. Listing 16.13 illustrates this.

TYPE **Listing 16.13. Using** fill()**.**

```
1:      // listing 16.3 fill()
2:
3:      #include <iostream.h>
4:
5:      void main()
6:      {
7:         cout << "Start >";
8:         cout.width(25);
9:         cout << 123 << "< End\n";
10:
11:
12:          cout << "Start >";
13:         cout.width(25);
14:         cout.fill('*');
15:         cout << 123 << "< End\n";
16:
17:      }
```

OUTPUT
```
Start >                      123< End
Start >*******************123< End
```

ANALYSIS Lines 7 through 9 repeat the functionality from the previous example. Lines 12 through 15 repeat this again; but this time, on line 14, the fill character is set to asterisks, as reflected in the output.

Set Flags

The iostream objects keep track of their state by using flags. You can set these flags by calling setf() and passing in one or another of the predefined enumerated constants.

NEW TERM Objects are said to have *state* when some or all of their data represents a *condition* that can change during the course of the program.

For example, you can set whether or not to show trailing zeros (so that 20.00 does not become truncated to 20). To turn trailing zeros on, call setf(ios::showpoint).

The enumerated constants are scoped to the iostream class (ios) and are therefore called with the full qualification ios::flagname, such as ios::showpoint.

You can turn the plus sign (+) on before positive numbers by using ios::showpos. You can change the alignment of the output by using ios::left, ios::right, or ios::internal.

Finally, you can set the base of the numbers for display by using ios::dec (decimal), ios::oct (octal—base eight), or ios::hex (hexadecimal—base sixteen). These flags can also be concatenated into the insertion operator. Listing 16.14 illustrates these settings. As a bonus, Listing 16.14 also introduces the setw manipulator, which sets the width but can be concatenated with the insertion operator.

TYPE   **Listing 16.14. Using setf.**

```
1:      // Listing
2:      #include <iostream.h>
3:      #include <iomanip.h>
4:
5:      void main()
6:      {
7:          const int number = 185;
8:          cout << "The number is " << number << endl;
9:
10:         cout << "The number is " << hex <<  number << endl;
11:
12:         cout.setf(ios::showbase);
13:         cout << "The number is " << hex <<  number << endl;
14:
15:         cout << "The number is " ;
16:         cout.width(10);
17:         cout << hex << number << endl;
18:
19:         cout << "The number is " ;
20:         cout.width(10);
21:         cout.setf(ios::left);
22:         cout << hex << number << endl;
23:
24:         cout << "The number is " ;
25:         cout.width(10);
26:         cout.setf(ios::internal);
27:         cout << hex << number << endl;
28:
29:         cout << "The number is:" << setw(10) << hex << number << endl;
30:
31:      }
```

16

```
The number is 185
The number is b9
The number is 0xb9
The number is              0xb9
The number is 0xb9
The number is 0x        b9
The number is 0x        b9
```

ANALYSIS On line 7 the constant int number is initialized to the value 185. This is displayed on line 8.

The value is displayed again on line 10, but this time the manipulator hex is concatenated, causing the value to be displayed in hexadecimal as b9. (b=11; 11×16=176+9=185).

On line 12 the flag showbase is set. This causes the prefix 0x to be added to all hexadecimal numbers, as reflected in the output.

On line 16 the width is set to 10, and the value is pushed to the extreme right. On line 20 the width is again set to 10, but this time the alignment is set to the left, and the number is again printed flush left.

On line 25, once again, the width is set to 10, but this time the alignment is internal. Thus the 0x is printed flush left, but the value b9 is printed flush right.

Finally, on line 29, the concatenation operator setw() is used to set the width to 10, and the value is printed again.

Streams Versus the *printf()* Function

Most C++ implementations also provide the standard C I/O libraries, including the printf() statement. Although printf() is in some ways easier to use than cout, it is far less desirable.

printf() does not provide type safety, so it is easy to inadvertently tell it to display an integer as if it was a character and vice versa. printf() also does not support classes, so it is not possible to teach it how to print your class data; you must feed each class member to printf() one by one.

On the other hand, printf() does make formatting much easier because you can put the formatting characters directly into the printf() statement. Because printf() has its uses and many programmers still make extensive use of it, this section briefly reviews its use.

To use printf(), be sure to include the STDIO.H header file. In its simplest form, printf() takes a formatting string as its first parameter and then a series of values as its remaining parameters.

The formatting string is a quoted string of text and conversion specifiers. All conversion specifiers must begin with the percent symbol (%). The common conversion specifiers are presented in Table 16.1.

Table 16.1. The common conversion specifiers.

Specifier	Used For
%s	strings
%d	integers
%l	long integer
%ld	long integers
%f	float
%%	% symbol

Each of the conversion specifiers can also provide a width statement and a precision statement, expressed as a float, where the digits to the left of the decimal are used for the total width and the digits to the right of the decimal provide the precision for floats. Thus, %5d is the specifier for a five-digit-wide integer, and %15.5f is the specifier for a 15-digit-wide float, of which the final five digits are dedicated to the decimal portion. Listing 16.15 illustrates various uses of printf().

TYPE **Listing 16.15. Printing with printf().**

```
1:    #include <stdio.h>
2:    void main()
3:    {
4:        printf("%s","hello world\n");
5:
6:        char *phrase = "Hello again!\n";
7:        printf("%s",phrase);
8:
9:        int x = 5;
10:       printf("%d\n",x);
11:
12:       char *phraseTwo = "Here's some values: ";
13:       char *phraseThree = " and also these: ";
14:       int y = 7, z = 35;
15:       long longVar = 98456;
16:       float floatVar =  8.8;
17:
18:       printf("%s %d %d %s %ld %f\n",phraseTwo,
              y,z,phraseThree,longVar,floatVar);
19:
```

```
20:        char *phraseFour = "Formatted: ";
21:        printf("%s %5d %10d   %10.5f\n",phraseFour,y,z,floatVar);
22:    }
```

```
hello world
Hello again!
5
Here's some values: 7 35 and also these: 98456 8.800000
Formatted:        7           35       8.800000
```

 The first `printf()` statement, on line 4, uses the standard form: the term `printf`, followed by a quoted string with a conversion specifier (in this case, `%s`), followed by a value to insert into the conversion specifier.

The `%s` indicates that this is a string, and the value for the string is, in this case, the quoted string `"hello world."`.

The second `printf()` statement is just like the first, but this time a `char` pointer is used instead of quoting the string right in place in the `printf()` statement.

The third `printf()`, on line 10, uses the integer conversion specifier, and for its value the integer variable `x`. The fourth `printf()` statement, on line 18, is more complex. Here six values are concatenated. Each conversion specifier is supplied, and then the values are provided, separated by commas.

Finally, on line 21, format specifications are used to specify width and precision. As you can see, all of this is somewhat easier than using manipulators.

As stated previously, however, the limitation here is that there is no type checking, and `printf()` cannot be declared a friend or member function of a class. If you want to print the various member data of a class, you must feed each accessor method to the `printf()` statement explicitly.

File Input and Output

Streams provide a uniform way to deal with data coming from the keyboard or the hard disk and going out to the screen or hard disk. In either case, you can use the insertion and extraction operators or the other related functions and manipulators. To open and close files, you create `ifstream` and `ofstream` objects as described in the next few sections.

ofstream

The particular objects used to read from or write to files are called `ofstream` objects. These are derived from the `iostream` objects you've been using so far.

To get started with writing to a file, you must first create an ofstream object and then associate that object with a particular file on your disk. To use ofstream objects, be sure to include fstream.h in your program.

NOTE

> Because fstream.h includes iostream.h, there is no need for you to include iostream explicitly.

Condition States

The iostream objects maintain flags that report on the state of your input and output. You can check each of these flags using the Boolean functions eof(), bad(), fail(), and good(). The function eof() returns true if the iostream object has encountered EOF, end of file. The function bad() returns true if you attempt an invalid operation. The function fail() returns true anytime bad() is true or an operation fails. Finally, the function good() returns true anytime all three of the other functions are false.

Opening Files for Input and Output

To open the file myfile.cpp with an ofstream object, declare an instance of an ofstream object and pass in the filename as a parameter:

```
ofstream fout("myfile.cpp");
```

Opening this file for input works exactly the same way, except it uses an ifstream object:

```
ifstream fin("myfile.cpp");
```

Note that fout and fin are names you assign; here fout has been used to reflect its similarity to cout, and fin has been used to reflect its similarity to cin.

One important file stream function that you need right away is close(). Every file stream object you create opens a file for either reading or writing (or both). It is important to close() the file after you finish reading or writing; this ensures that the file won't be corrupted and that the data you've written is flushed to the disk.

After the stream objects are associated with files, they can be used like any other stream objects. Listing 16.16 illustrates this.

16

TYPE   Listing 16.16. Opening files for read and write.

```
1:      #include <fstream.h>
2:      void main()
3:      {
4:          char fileName[80];
5:          char buffer[255];     // for user input
6:          cout << "File name: ";
7:          cin >> fileName;
8:
9:          ofstream fout(fileName);  // open for writing
10:         fout << "This line written directly to the file...\n";
11:         cout << "Enter text for the file: ";
12:         cin.ignore(1,'\n');   // ignore the new line after the file name
13:         cin.getline(buffer,255);  // get the user's input
14:         fout << buffer << "\n";   // and write it to the file
15:         fout.close();             // close the file, ready for reopen
16:
17:         ifstream fin(fileName);    // reopen for reading
18:         cout << "Here's the contents of the file:\n";
19:         char ch;
20:         while (fin.get(ch))
21:            cout << ch;
22:
23:         cout << "\n***End of file contents.***\n";
24:
25:         fin.close();              // always pays to be tidy
26:     }
```

16

OUTPUT

```
File name: test1
Enter text for the file: This text is written to the file!
Here's the contents of the file:
This line written directly to the file...
This text is written to the file!

***End of file contents.***
```

ANALYSIS   On line 4 a buffer is set aside for the filename, and on line 5 another buffer is set aside for user input. The user is prompted to enter a filename on line 6, and this response is written to the fileName buffer. On line 9 an ofstream object is created, fout, which is associated with the new filename. This opens the file; if the file already exists, its contents are thrown away.

On line 10 a string of text is written directly to the file. On line 11 the user is prompted for input. The new line character left over from the user's input of the filename is eaten on line 12, and the user's input is stored into buffer on line 13. That input is written to the file along with a new line character on line 14, and then the file is closed on line 15.

On line 17 the file is reopened, this time in input mode, and the contents are read one character at a time on lines 20 and 21.

Changing the Default Behavior of *ofstream* on Open

The default behavior upon opening a file is to create the file if it doesn't yet exist and to truncate the file (that is, delete all its contents) if it does exist. If you don't want this default behavior, you can explicitly provide a second argument to the constructor of your ofstream object.

Valid arguments include the following:

☐ ios::app appends to the end of existing files rather than truncating them.

☐ ios::ate places you at the end of the file, but you can write data anywhere in the file.

☐ ios::trunc is the default. It causes existing files to be truncated.

☐ ios::nocreate causes the open to fail if the file does not exist.

☐ ios::noreplace causes the open to fail if the file already exists.

Note that app is short for append; ate is short for at end; and trunc is short for truncate. Listing 16.17 illustrates using append by reopening the file from Listing 16.16 and appending to it.

TYPE   **Listing 16.17. Appending to the end of a file.**

```
1:      #include <fstream.h>
2:      int main()    // returns 1 on error
3:      {
4:          char fileName[80];
5:          char buffer[255];
6:          cout << "Please re-enter the file name: ";
7:          cin >> fileName;
8:
9:          ifstream fin(fileName);
10:         if (fin)                    // already exists?
11:         {
12:             cout << "Current file contents:\n";
13:             char ch;
14:             while (fin.get(ch))
15:                 cout << ch;
16:             cout << "\n***End of file contents.***\n";
17:         }
18:         fin.close();
19:
```

16

```
20:          cout << "\nOpening " << fileName << " in append mode...\n";
21:
22:          ofstream fout(fileName,ios::app);
23:          if (!fout)
24:          {
25:             cout << "Unable to open " << fileName << " for appending.\n";
26:             return(1);
27:          }
28:
29:          cout << "\nEnter text for the file: ";
30:          cin.ignore(1,'\n');
31:          cin.getline(buffer,255);
32:          fout << buffer << "\n";
33:          fout.close();
34:
35:          fin.open(fileName);   // reassign existing fin object!
36:          if (!fin)
37:          {
38:             cout << "Unable to open " << fileName << " for reading.\n";
39:             return(1);
40:          }
41:          cout << "\nHere's the contents of the file:\n";
42:          char ch;
43:          while (fin.get(ch))
44:             cout << ch;
45:          cout << "\n***End of file contents.***\n";
46:          fin.close();
47:          return 0;
48:       }
```

OUTPUT

```
Please re-enter the file name: test1
Current file contents:
This line written directly to the file...
This text is written to the file!

***End of file contents.***

Opening test1 in append mode...

Enter text for the file: More text for the file!

Here's the contents of the file:
This line written directly to the file...
This text is written to the file!
More text for the file!

***End of file contents.***
```

ANALYSIS The user is again prompted to enter the filename. This time an input file stream object is created on line 9. That open is tested on line 10, and if the file already exists, its contents are printed on lines 12 to 16. Note that if(fin) is synonymous with if (fin.good()).

The input file is then closed, and the same file is reopened, this time in append mode, on line 22. After this open (and every open), the file is tested to ensure that the file was opened properly. Note that if(!fout) is the same as testing if (fout.fail()). The user is then prompted to enter text, and the file is closed again on line 33.

Finally, as in Listing 16.16, the file is reopened in read mode; however, this time fin does not need to be redeclared. It is just reassigned to the same filename. Again the open is tested (on line 36), and if all is well, the contents of the file are printed to the screen and the file is closed for the final time.

Do	Don't

DO test each open of a file to ensure that it opened successfully.

DO reuse existing ifstream and ofstream objects.

DO close all fstream objects when you are done using them.

DON'T try to close or reassign cin or cout.

Binary Versus Text Files

Some operating systems, such as DOS, distinguish between text files and binary files. Text files store everything as text (as you might have guessed), so large numbers such as 54,325 are stored as a string of numerals ('5', '4', ',', '3', '2', '5'). This can be inefficient, but it has the advantage that the text can be read using simple type programs (such as the DOS program).

To help the file system distinguish between text and binary files, C++ provides the ios::binary flag. On many systems this flag is ignored, because all data is stored in binary format. On some rather prudish systems, the ios::binary flag is illegal and won't compile!

Binary files can store not only integers and strings, but entire data structures. You can write all the data at one time by using the write() method of fstream.

If you use write(), you can recover the data using read(). Each of these functions expects a pointer to character, however, so you must cast the address of your class to be a pointer to character.

The second argument to these functions is the number of characters to write, which you can determine using sizeof(). Note that what is being written is just the data, not the methods. What is recovered is just data. Listing 16.18 illustrates writing the contents of a class to a file.

16

TYPE **Listing 16.18. Writing a class to a file.**

```
1:     #include <fstream.h>
2:
3:     class Animal
4:     {
5:     public:
6:         Animal(int weight, long days):itsWeight(weight),
➡          itsNumberDaysAlive(days){}
7:         ~Animal(){}
8:
9:         int GetWeight()const { return itsWeight; }
10:        void SetWeight(int weight) { itsWeight = weight; }
11:
12:        long GetDaysAlive()const { return  itsNumberDaysAlive; }
13:        void SetDaysAlive(long days) { itsNumberDaysAlive = days; }
14:
15:    private:
16:        int itsWeight;
17:        long itsNumberDaysAlive;
18:    };
19:
20:    int main()   // returns 1 on error
21:    {
22:        // The file name:
23:        char fileName[80];
24:
25:        cout << "Please enter the file name: ";
26:        cin >> fileName;
27:        ofstream fout(fileName,ios::binary);
28:        if (!fout)
29:        {
30:            cout << "Unable to open " << fileName << " for writing.\n";
31:            return(1);
32:        }
33:
34:        Animal Bear(50,100);
35:        fout.write((char*) &Bear,sizeof Bear);
36:
37:        fout.close();
38:
39:        ifstream fin(fileName,ios::binary);
40:        if (!fin)
41:        {
42:            cout << "Unable to open " << fileName << " for reading.\n";
43:            return(1);
44:        }
45:
46:        Animal BearTwo(1,1);
47:
48:        cout << "BearTwo weight: " << BearTwo.GetWeight() << endl;
49:        cout << "BearTwo days: " << BearTwo.GetDaysAlive() << endl;
50:
51:        fin.read((char*) &BearTwo, sizeof BearTwo);
52:
```

continues

Listing 16.18. continued

```
53:        cout << "BearTwo weight: " << BearTwo.GetWeight() << endl;
54:        cout << "BearTwo days: " << BearTwo.GetDaysAlive() << endl;
55:        fin.close();
56:        return 0;
57:    }
```

OUTPUT

```
Please enter the file name: Animals
BearTwo weight: 1
BearTwo days: 1
BearTwo weight: 50
BearTwo days: 100
```

ANALYSIS   On lines 3 through 18, a stripped-down Animal class is declared. On lines 22 through 32, a file is created and opened for output in binary mode. An animal whose weight is 50 and who is 100 days old is created on line 34, and its data is written to the file on line 35.

The file is closed on line 37 and reopened for reading in binary mode on line 39. A second animal is created on line 46 whose weight is 1 and who is only one day old. The data from the file is read into the new animal object on line 51, wiping out the existing data and replacing it with the data from the file.

Command-Line Processing

Many operating systems, such as DOS and UNIX, enable the user to pass parameters to your program when the program starts. These are called command-line options, and they are typically separated by spaces on the command line. The following is an example:

```
SomeProgram Param1 Param2 Param3
```

These parameters are not passed to main() directly. Instead, every program's main() function is passed two parameters. The first is an integer count of the number of arguments on the command line. The program name itself is counted, so every program has at least one parameter. The example command line shown previously has four. (The name SomeProgram plus the three parameters makes a total of four command-line arguments.)

The second parameter passed to main() is an array of pointers to character strings. Because an array name is a constant pointer to the first element of the array, you can declare this argument to be a pointer to a pointer to char, a pointer to an array of char, or an array of arrays of char.

Typically, the first argument is called argc (argument count), but you can call it anything you like. The second argument is often called argv (argument vector), but again this is just a convention.

It is common to test argc to ensure that you've received the expected number of arguments, and to use argv to access the strings themselves. Note that argv[0] is the name of the program, and argv[1] is the first parameter to the program, represented as a string. If your program takes two numbers as arguments, you need to translate these numbers to strings. On Day 23 you learn how to use advanced streams functionality to convert strings to other forms. Listing 16.19 illustrates how to use the command-line arguments.

TYPE **Listing 16.19. Using command-line arguments.**

```
1:    #include <iostream.h>
2:    void main(int argc, char **argv)
3:    {
4:        cout << "Received " << argc << " arguments...\n";
5:        for (int i=0; i<argc; i++)
6:            cout << "argument " << i << ": " << argv[i] << endl;
7:    }
```

OUTPUT
```
TestProgram  Teach Yourself C++ In 21 Days
Received 7 arguments...
argumnet 0: TestProgram.exe
argument 1: Teach
argument 2: Yourself
argument 3: C++
argument 4: In
argument 5: 21
argument 6: Days
```

ANALYSIS The function main() declares two arguments: argc is an integer that contains the count of command-line arguments, and argv is a pointer to the array of strings. Each string in the array pointed to by argv is a command-line argument. Note that argv could just as easily have been declared as char *argv[] or char argv[][]. It is a matter of programming style how you declare argv; even though this program declared it as a pointer to a pointer, array offsets were still used to access the individual strings.

On line 4 argc is used to print the number of command-line arguments: seven in all, counting the program name itself.

On lines 5 and 6, each of the command-line arguments is printed, passing the null-terminated strings to cout by indexing into the array of strings.

A more common use of command-line arguments is illustrated by modifying Listing 16.18 to take the filename as a command-line argument. This listing does not include the class declaration, which is unchanged.

Listing 16.20. Using command-line arguments.

```
1:    #include <fstream.h>
2:    int main(int argc, char *argv[])    // returns 1 on error
3:    {
4:        if (argc != 2)
5:        {
6:            cout << "Usage: " << argv[0] << " <filename>" << endl;
7:            return(1);
8:        }
9:
10:       ofstream fout(argv[1],ios::binary);
11:       if (!fout)
12:       {
13:           cout << "Unable to open " << argv[1] << " for writing.\n";
14:           return(1);
15:       }
16:
17:       Animal Bear(50,100);
18:       fout.write((char*) &Bear,sizeof Bear);
19:
20:       fout.close();
21:
22:       ifstream fin(argv[1],ios::binary);
23:       if (!fin)
24:       {
25:           cout << "Unable to open " << argv[1] << " for reading.\n";
26:           return(1);
27:       }
28:
29:       Animal BearTwo(1,1);
30:
31:       cout << "BearTwo weight: " << BearTwo.GetWeight() << endl;
32:       cout << "BearTwo days: " << BearTwo.GetDaysAlive() << endl;
33:
34:       fin.read((char*) &BearTwo, sizeof BearTwo);
35:
36:       cout << "BearTwo weight: " << BearTwo.GetWeight() << endl;
37:       cout << "BearTwo days: " << BearTwo.GetDaysAlive() << endl;
38:       fin.close();
39:       return 0;
40:   }
```

OUTPUT
```
BearTwo weight: 1
BearTwo days: 1
BearTwo weight: 50
BearTwo days: 100
```

ANALYSIS   The declaration of the Animal class is the same as in Listing 16.18, so it is left out of this example. This time, however, rather than prompting the user for the filename, command-line arguments are used. On line 2, main() is declared to take two parameters: the count of the command-line arguments and a pointer to the array of command-line argument strings.

16

On lines 4 through 8, the program ensures that the expected number of arguments (exactly 2) is received. If the user fails to supply a single filename, an error message is printed:

```
Usage TestProgram <filename>
```

Then the program exits. Note that by using argv[0] rather than hard-coding a program name, you can compile this program to have any name and this usage statement works automatically.

On line 10 the program attempts to open the supplied filename for binary output. There is no reason to copy the filename into a local temporary buffer. It can be used directly by accessing argv[1].

This technique is repeated on line 22 when the same file is reopened for input, and it is used in the error condition statements when the files cannot be opened, on lines 13 and 25.

Summary

Today streams were introduced, and the global objects cout and cin were described. The goal of the istream and ostream objects is to encapsulate the work of writing to device drivers, and to buffer input and output.

There are four standard stream objects created in every program: cout, cin, cerr, and clog. Each of these can be redirected by many operating systems.

The istream object cin is used for input, and its most common use is with the overloaded extraction operator (>>). The ostream object cout is used for output, and its most common use is with the overloaded insertion operator (<<).

Each of these objects has a number of other member functions, such as get() and put(). Because the common forms of each of these methods returns a reference to a stream object, it is easy to concatenate each of these operators and functions.

The state of the stream objects can be changed by using manipulators. These can set the formatting and display characteristics and various other attributes of the stream objects.

File I/O can be accomplished by using the fstream classes, which derive from the stream classes. In addition to supporting the normal insertion and extraction operators, these objects also support read() and write() for storing and retrieving large binary objects.

Q&A

Q **How do you know when to use the insertion and extraction operators and when to use the other member functions of the `stream` classes?**

A In general, it is easier to use the insertion and extraction operators, and they are preferred when their behavior is what is needed. In unusual circumstances when these operators don't do the job (such as reading in a string of words), the other functions can be used.

Q **What is the difference between `cerr` and `clog`?**

A `cerr` is not buffered. Everything written to `cerr` is immediately written out. This is fine for errors written to the screen, but it might have too high a performance cost for writing logs to disk. `clog` buffers its output, and thus can be more efficient.

Q **Why were streams created if `printf()` works well?**

A `printf()` does not support the strong type system of C++, and it does not support user-defined classes.

Q **When would you ever use `putback()`?**

A You use it when one read operation is used to determine whether or not a character is valid, but a different read operation (perhaps by a different object) needs the character to be in the buffer. It is most often used when parsing a file; for example, the C++ compiler might use `putback()`.

Q **When would you use `ignore()`?**

A A common use of this is after using `get()`. Because `get()` leaves the terminating character in the buffer, it is not uncommon to immediately follow a call to `get()` with a call to `ignore(1,'\n');`. Once again, this is often used in parsing.

Q **My friends use `printf()` in their C++ programs. Can I?**

A Sure. You'll gain some convenience, but you'll pay by sacrificing type safety.

Quiz

1. What is the insertion operator, and what does it do?
2. What is the extraction operator, and what does it do?
3. What are the three forms of `cin.get()`, and what are their differences?
4. What is the difference between `cin.read()` and `cin.getline()`?
5. What is the default width for ouputing a long integer using the insertion operator?
6. What is the return value of the insertion operator?
7. What parameter does the constructor to an `ofstream` object take?
8. What does the `ios::ate` argument do?

Exercises

1. Write a program that writes to the four standard iostream objects: `cin`, `cout`, `cerr`, and `clog`.

2. Write a program that prompts the user to enter her full name and then displays it on the screen.

3. Rewrite Listing 16.9 to do the same thing it currently does, but without using `putback()` or `ignore()`.

4. Write a program that takes a filename as a parameter and opens the file for reading. Read every character of the file and display only the letters and punctuation to the screen. (Ignore all nonprinting characters.) Close the file and exit.

5. Write a program that displays its command-line arguments in reverse order and does not display the program name.

17

Day

The Preprocessor

Most of what you write in your source code files is C++. These are interpreted by the compiler and turned into your program. Before the compiler runs, however, the preprocessor runs; this provides an opportunity for *conditional compilation*. Today you will learn

☐ What conditional compilation is and how to manage it.

☐ How to write macros using the preprocessor.

☐ How to use the preprocessor to find bugs.

The Preprocessor and the Compiler

Every time you run your compiler, your preprocessor runs first. The preprocessor looks for preprocessor instructions, each of which begins with a pound symbol (#). The effect of each of these instructions is a change to the text of the source code. The result is a new source code file, a temporary file that you normally don't see, which you can instruct the compiler to save so that you can examine it.

The compiler does not read your original source code file; it reads the output of the preprocessor and compiles that file. You've seen the effect of this already with the `#include` directive. This instructs the preprocessor to find the file whose name follows the `#include` directive, and to write it into the intermediate file at that location. It's as if you had typed the entire file right into your source code, and by the time the compiler sees the source code, the included file is there.

Seeing the Intermediate Form

Just about every compiler has a switch that you can set either in the integrated development environment (IDE) or at the command line, which instructs the compiler to save the intermediate file. Check your compiler manual for the right switches to set for your compiler if you would like to examine this file.

Using *#define*

The `#define` command defines a string substitution. If you write

```
#define BIG 512
```

you have instructed the precompiler to substitute the string 512 wherever it sees the string BIG. This is not a string in the C++ sense. The characters 512 are substituted in your source code wherever the token BIG is seen. A token is a string of characters that can be used wherever a string, constant, or other set of letters might be used. Therefore, if you write

```
#define BIG 512
int myArray[BIG];
```

the intermediate file produced by the precompiler looks like this:

```
int myArray[512];
```

Note that the `#define` statement is gone. Precompiler statements are all removed from the intermediate file, and they do not appear in the final source code at all.

Using *#define* for Constants

One way to use `#define` is as a substitute for constants. This is almost never a good idea, however, because `#define` merely makes a string substitution and does no type checking. As explained in the section on constants, there are tremendous advantages to using the `const` keyword rather than `#define`.

Using *#define* for Tests

A second way to use #define is simply to declare that a particular character string is defined. You could write the following:

```
#define BIG
```

Later, you can test whether or not BIG has been defined and take action accordingly. The precompiler commands to test whether a string has been defined are #ifdef and #ifndef. Both of these must be followed by the command #endif before the block ends (before the next closing brace).

#ifdef evaluates true if the string it tests has been defined already. You can therefore write

```
#ifdef DEBUG
cout << "Debug defined";
#endif
```

When the precompiler reads the #ifdef, it checks a table that it has built to see whether you've defined DEBUG. If so, the #ifdef evaluates true, and everything to the next #else or #endif is written into the intermediate file for compiling. If it evaluates false, nothing between #ifdef DEBUG and #endif is written into the intermediate file, as though it had never been in the source code in the first place.

Note that #ifndef is the logical reverse of #ifdef. #ifndef evaluates true if the string has not been defined up to that point in the file.

The *#else* Precompiler Command

As you might imagine, the term #else can be inserted between either #ifdef or #ifndef and the closing #endif. Listing 17.1 illustrates how these terms are used.

TYPE **Listing 17.1. Using #define.**

```
1:      #define DemoVersion
2:      #define DOS_VERSION 5
3:      #include <iostream.h>
4:
5:
6:      void main()
7:      {
8:
9:      cout << "Checking on the definitions of DemoVersion, DOS_VERSION
➥and WINDOWS_VERSION...\n";
10:
11:     #ifdef DemoVersion
12:         cout << "DemoVersion defined.\n";
```

continues

Listing 17.1. continued

```
13:      #else
14:          cout << "DemoVersion not defined.\n";
15:      #endif
16:
17:      #ifndef DOS_VERSION
18:          cout << "DOS_VERSION not defined!\n";
19:      #else
20:          cout << "DOS_VERSION defined as: " << DOS_VERSION << endl;
21:      #endif
22:
23:      #ifdef WINDOWS_VERSION
24:          cout << "WINDOWS_VERSION defined!\n";
25:      #else
26:          cout << "WINDOWS_VERSION was not defined.\n";
27:      #endif
28:
29:       cout << "Done.\n";
30:      }
```

OUTPUT
```
Checking on the definitions of DemoVersion, DOS_VERSION and
WINDOWS_VERSION...
DemoVersion defined.
DOS_VERSION defined as: 5
WINDOWS_VERSION was not defined.
Done.
```

ANALYSIS On lines 1 and 2, DemoVersion and DOS_VERSION are defined, with DOS_VERSION defined with the string 5. On line 11 the definition of DemoVersion is tested, and because DemoVersion is defined (albeit with no value), the test is true and the string on line 12 is printed.

On line 17 is the test of whether DOS_VERSION is not defined. Because DOS_VERSION is defined, this test fails and execution jumps to line 20. Here the string 5 is substituted for the word DOS_VERSION, and this is seen by the compiler as follows:

```
cout << "DOS_VERSION defined as: " << 5 << endl;
```

Note that the first word DOS_VERSION is not substituted because it is in a quoted string. The second DOS_VERSION is substituted, however, and the compiler sees 5 as if you had typed 5 there.

Finally, on line 23 the program tests for WINDOWS_VERSION. Because you did not define WINDOWS_VERSION, the test fails and the message on line 26 is printed.

The *#error* Directive

For some large programs, compiling can be an extremely time-consuming process. Waiting for an entire compile to complete only to find that you forgot to define a variable or check the syntax of a single statement can be an annoyance. For instance, lines 17 through 19 of Listing 17.1 checked whether DOS_VERSION was defined. Suppose that you just forgot to define DOS_VERSION, and therefore to compile any further would just be a waste. You could change this section to something like the following:

```
#ifndef DOS_VERSION
// DOS_VERSION is required for this program, so if its not
➥ defined, compile no longer
#error "DOS_VERSION is not defined, not compiling any more!"
#else
// and so on as before ...
```

Now, if DOS_VERSION is not defined, the compiler stops at the error line and displays a message to that effect.

The *#pragma* Directive

The #pragma preprocessor directive provides a way to set preprocessor or compiler options and commands. The pragmas that your compiler or IDE recognizes are documented in your compiler/IDE documentation. If you use pragmas that your compiler does not recognize, the pragma line is ignored and docs not initiate an error. Options on most compilers provide for warnings on unrecognized pragmas.

An example of a common compiler pragma is one that provides for configuring data alignment. Data alignment is specific to your computer architecture and, therefore, specific to the compiler you use. Day 22 covers data alignment in more detail. It is mentioned here only as an example of the types of things for which the #pragma directive is used.

Inclusion and Inclusion Guards

A programmer creates projects with many different files. You will probably organize your directories so that each class has its own header file (.hpp) with the class declaration, and its own implementation file (.cpp) with the source code for the class methods.

Your main() function is in its own .cpp file, and all the .cpp files will be compiled into .obj files, which are linked together into a single program by the linker.

Because your programs use methods from many classes, many header files are included in each file. Also, header files often need to include one another. For example, the header file for a derived class's declaration must include the header file for its base class.

Imagine that the Animal class is declared in the file animal.hpp. The Dog class (which derives from Animal) must include the file animal.hpp in dog.hpp, or it is not able to derive from Animal. The Cat header also includes animal.hpp for the same reason. If you create a method that uses both a Cat and a Dog, you are in danger of including animal.hpp twice.

This generates a compile-time error, because it is not legal to declare a class (`Animal`) twice, even though the declarations are identical. You can solve this problem with *inclusion guards*. At the top of your ANIMAL header file you should write these lines:

```
#ifndef ANIMAL_HPP
#define ANIMAL_HPP
...                              // the whole file goes here
#endif
```

This says that if you haven't defined the term `ANIMAL_HPP`, go ahead and define it now. Between the `#define` statement and the closing `#endif` are the entire contents of the file.

The first time your program includes this file, it reads the first line and the test evaluates true; that is, you have not yet defined animal.hpp. Afterwards, the program goes ahead and defines animal.hpp, and then it includes the entire file.

The second time your program includes the animal.hpp file, it reads the first line and the test evaluates false; animal.hpp has been defined. It therefore skips to the next `#else` (there isn't one) or the next `#endif` (at the end of the file). It skips the entire contents of the file and the class is not declared twice.

The actual name of the defined symbol (animal.hpp) is not important, though it is customary to show the filename in all uppercase with the dot (.) changed to an underscore. This is purely convention, however.

Note

> It never hurts to use inclusion guards. They often save you hours of debugging time.

Defining on the Command Line

Almost all C++ compilers let you `#define` values either from the command line or from the integrated development environment (and usually both). For this reason, you can leave out lines 1 and 2 from Listing 17.1 and define `DemoVersion` and `BetaTestVersion` from the command line for some compilations, and not for others.

It is common to put in special debugging code surrounded by `#ifdef DEBUG` and `#endif`. This enables all of the debugging code to be easily removed from the source code when you compile the final version: Just don't define the term `DEBUG`.

Undefining

If you have a name defined and you want to turn it off from within your code, you can use `#undef`. This works as the antidote to `#define`. Listing 17.2 provides an illustration of its use.

TYPE **Listing 17.2. Using** `#undef`.

```
1:      #define DemoVersion
2:      #define DOS_VERSION 5
3:      #include <iostream.h>
4:
5:
6:      void main()
7:      {
8:
9:      cout << "Checking on the definitions of DemoVersion, DOS_VERSION and
➥WINDOWS_VERSION...\n";
10:
11:     #ifdef DemoVersion
12:         cout << "DemoVersion defined.\n";
13:     #else
14:         cout << "DemoVersion not defined.\n";
15:     #endif
16:
17:     #ifndef DOS_VERSION
18:         cout << "DOS_VERSION not defined!\n";
19:     #else
20:         cout << "DOS_VERSION defined as: " << DOS_VERSION << endl;
21:     #endif
22:
23:     #ifdef WINDOWS_VERSION
24:         cout << "WINDOWS_VERSION defined!\n";
25:     #else
26:         cout << "WINDOWS_VERSION was not defined.\n";
27:     #endif
28:
29:     #undef DOS_VERSION
30:
31:      #ifdef DemoVersion
32:         cout << "DemoVersion defined.\n";
33:     #else
34:         cout << "DemoVersion not defined.\n";
35:     #endif
36:
37:     #ifndef DOS_VERSION
38:         cout << "DOS_VERSION not defined!\n";
39:     #else
40:         cout << "DOS_VERSION defined as: " << DOS_VERSION << endl;
41:     #endif
42:
43:     #ifdef WINDOWS_VERSION
44:         cout << "WINDOWS_VERSION defined!\n";
45:     #else
46:         cout << "WINDOWS_VERSION was not defined.\n";
47:     #endif
48:
49:      cout << "Done.\n";
50:     }
```

OUTPUT

```
Checking on the definitions of DemoVersion, DOS_VERSION and
WINDOWS_VERSION...
DemoVersion defined.
DOS_VERSION defined as: 5
WINDOWS_VERSION was not defined.
DemoVersion defined.
DOS_VERSION not defined!
WINDOWS_VERSION was not defined.
Done.
```

ANALYSIS Listing 17.2 is the same as Listing 17.1 until line 29, when #undef DOS_VERSION is called. This removes the definition of the term DOS_VERSION without changing the other defined terms (in this case, DemoVersion). The rest of the listing just repeats the printouts. The tests for DemoVersion and WINDOWS_VERSION act as they did the first time, but the test for DOS_VERSION now evaluates true. In this second case, DOS_VERSION does not exist as a defined term.

Conditional Compilation

By combining #define or command line definitions with #ifdef, #else, and #ifndef, you can write one program that compiles different code depending on what is already #defined. This can be used to create one set of source code to compile on two different platforms, such as 16- or 32-bit operating systems.

Another common use of this technique is to conditionally compile in some code based on whether or not debug has been defined, as you'll see shortly.

Do	Don't

DO use conditional compilation when you need to create more than one version of your code at the same time.

DON'T let your conditions get too complex to manage.

DO use #undef as often as possible to avoid leaving stray definitions in your code.

DO use inclusion guards!

Macro Functions

The #define directive can also be used to create *macro functions*. A macro function is a symbol created using #define, which takes an argument much like a function does. The preprocessor substitutes the substitution string for whatever argument it is given. For example, you can define the macro TWICE as

```
#define TWICE(x) ( (x) * 2 )
```

and then in your code write the following:

```
TWICE(4)
```

The entire string TWICE(4) is removed and the value 8 is substituted! When the precompiler sees the 4, it substitutes ((4) * 2), which is then evaluated to 4 * 2, or 8.

A macro can have more than one parameter, and each parameter can be used repeatedly in the replacement text. Two common macros are MAX and MIN:

```
#define MAX(x,y) ( (x) > (y) ? (x) : (y) )
#define MIN(x,y) ( (x) < (y) ? (x) : (y) )
```

Note that in a macro function definition, the opening parenthesis for the parameter list must *immediately* follow the macro name, with no spaces. The preprocessor is not as forgiving of whitespace as is the compiler.

If you write

```
#define MAX (x,y) ( (x) > (y) ? (x) : (y) )
```

and then try to use MAX like so

```
int x = 5, y = 7, z;
z = MAX(x,y);
```

the intermediate code is as follows:

```
int x = 5, y = 7, z;
z = (x,y) ( (x) > (y) ? (x) : (y) ) (x,y)
```

A simple text substitution is done rather than invoking the macro function. The token MAX would have substituted (x,y) ((x) > (y) ? (x) : (y)) for it, followed by the (x,y) that followed MAX.

By removing the space between MAX and (x,y), however, the intermediate code becomes

```
int x = 5, y = 7, z;
z =7;
```

Why All the Parentheses?

You might be wondering why there are so many parentheses in many of the macros presented so far. The preprocessor does not demand that parentheses be placed around the arguments in the substitution string. The parentheses help you avoid unwanted side effects when you pass complicated values to a macro. For example, if you define MAX as

```
#define MAX (x,y) x > y ? x : y
```

and pass in the values 5 and 7, the macro works as intended. If you pass in a more complicated expression, you'll get unintended results, as shown in Listing 17.3.

TYPE **Listing 17.3. Using parentheses in macros.**

```
1:     // Listing 17.3 Macro Expansion
2:     #include <iostream.h>
3:
4:     #define CUBE(a) ( (a) * (a) * (a) )
5:     #define THREE(a) a * a * a
6:
7:     void main()
8:     {
9:        long x = 5;
10:       long y = CUBE(x);
11:       long z = THREE(x);
12:
13:       cout << "y: " << y << endl;
14:       cout << "z: " << z << endl;
15:
16:       long a = 5, b = 7;
17:       y = CUBE(a+b);
18:       z = THREE(a+b);
19:
20:       cout << "y: " << y << endl;
21:       cout << "z: " << z << endl;
22:    }
```

OUTPUT
```
y: 125
z: 125
y: 1728
z: 82
```

ANALYSIS On line 4 the macro CUBE is defined, with the argument x put into parentheses each time it is used. On line 5 the macro THREE is defined without the parentheses.

In the first use of these macros, the value 5 is given as the parameter, and both macros work fine. CUBE(5) expands to ((5) * (5) * (5)), which evaluates to 125, and THREE(5) expands to 5 * 5 * 5, which also evaluates to 125.

In the second use, on lines 16 through 18, the parameter is 5 + 7. In this case, CUBE(5+7) evaluates to

```
( (5+7) * (5+7) * (5+7) )
```

17

which evaluates to

```
( (12) * (12) * (12) )
```

which in turn evaluates to 1,728. THREE(5+7), however, evaluates to

```
5 + 7 * 5 + 7 * 5 + 7
```

Because multiplication has a higher precedence than addition, this becomes

```
5 + (7 * 5) + (7 * 5) + 7
```

which evaluates to

```
5 + (35) + (35) + 7
```

which finally evaluates to 82.

Macros Versus Functions and Templates

Macros suffer from four problems in C++. The first is that they can be confusing if they get large, because all macros must be defined on one line. You can extend that line by using the backslash character (\), but large macros quickly become difficult to manage.

The second problem is that macros are expanded in line each time they are used. This means that if a macro is used a dozen times, the substitution appears 12 times in your program, rather than once as a function call will. On the other hand, macros are usually faster than a function call because the overhead of a function call is avoided.

The fact that macros are expanded in line leads to the third problem, which is that the macro does not appear in the intermediate source code used by the compiler, and thus is unavailable in most debuggers. This makes debugging macros tricky.

The final problem, however, is the biggest: Macros are not type-safe. Although it is convenient that absolutely any argument can be used with a macro, this completely undermines the strong typing of C++ and so is anathema to C++ programmers. Templates overcome this problem, as you'll see on Day 19, "Templates."

Inline Functions

It is often possible to declare an inline function, rather than a macro. For example, Listing 17.4 creates a CUBE function, which accomplishes the same thing as the CUBE macro in Listing 17.3, but does so in a type-safe way.

Listing 17.4. Using inline rather than a macro.

```
1:      #include <iostream.h>
2:
3:      inline unsigned long Square(unsigned long a) { return a * a; }
4:      inline unsigned long Cube(unsigned long a) { return a * a * a; }
5:      void main()
6:      {
7:          unsigned long x=1 ;
8:
9:          for (;;)
10:         {
11:             cout << "Enter a number (0 to quit): ";
12:             cin >> x;
13:             if (x == 0)
14:                 break;
15:             cout << "You entered: " << x;
16:             cout << ".  Square(" << x << "): "  << Square(x) << ". Cube("
                         _<< x << "): " << Cube(x) << "." << endl;
17:         }
18:     }
```

```
Enter a number (0 to quit): 1
You entered: 1. Square(1): 1. Cube(1): 1.
Enter a number (0 to quit): 2
You entered: 2. Square(1): 4. Cube(1): 8.
Enter a number (0 to quit): 3
You entered: 3. Square(1): 9. Cube(1): 27.
Enter a number (0 to quit): 4
You entered: 4. Square(1): 16. Cube(1): 64.
Enter a number (0 to quit): 5
You entered: 5. Square(1): 25. Cube(1): 125.
Enter a number (0 to quit): 6
You entered: 6. Square(1): 36. Cube(1): 216.
Enter a number (0 to quit): 0
```

On lines 3 and 4, two inline functions are declared, Square() and Cube(). Each is declared to be inline, so like a macro function these are expanded in place for each call and there is no function call overhead.

As a reminder, expanded inline means that the content of the function is placed into the code wherever the function call is made (for example, on line 16). Because the function call is never made, there is no overhead of putting the return address and the parameters on the stack. If this sounds unfamiliar, please reread the section about function calls on Day 5, "Functions."

On line 16 the function Square is called, as is the function Cube. Again, because these are inline functions, it is exactly as if this line had been written:

```
16:         cout << ".  Square(" << x << "): "
➡           << x * x << ". Cube(" << x << "): "
➡           << x * x * x << "." << endl;
```

However, the macro replacements would have made it appear as one, long line.

String Manipulation

The preprocessor provides two special operators for manipulating strings in macros. The stringizing operator (#) substitutes a quoted string for whatever follows the stringizing operator. The concatenation operator bonds two strings together into one.

Stringizing

The stringizing operator (#) puts quotes around any characters following the operator, up to the next whitespace. If you write

```
#define WRITESTRING(x) cout << #x
```

and then call

```
WRITESTRING(This is a string);
```

the precompiler turns it into

```
cout << "This is a string";
```

Note that the string This is a string is put into quotes, as required by cout.

Concatenation

The concatenation operator enables you to combine more than one term into a new word. The new word is actually a *token*, which can be used as a class name, a variable name, an offset into an array, or anywhere else a series of letters might appear.

Assume for a moment that you have five functions, named fOnePrint, fTwoPrint, fThreePrint, fFourPrint, and fFivePrint. You can declare

```
#define fPRINT(x) f ## x ## Print
```

and then use it with fPRINT(Two) to generate fTwoPrint, and with fPRINT(Three) to generate fThreePrint.

At the conclusion of Week 2, a PartsList class was developed. This list could only handle objects of type List. Suppose that this list works well, and you want to be able to make lists of animals, cars, computers, and so on.

One approach is to create AnimalList, CarList, ComputerList, and so forth, cutting and pasting the code in place. This quickly becomes a nightmare because every change to one list must be written to all the others.

An alternative is to use macros and the concatenation operator. For example, you could define the following:

```
#define Listof(Type)  class Type##List \
{ \
public: \
Type##List(){} \
private:           \
int itsLength; \
};
```

This example is overly sparse, but the idea is to put in all the necessary methods and data. When you were ready to create an AnimalList, you would write the following:

```
Listof(Animal)
```

This would be turned into the declaration of the AnimalList class. There are some problems with this approach, all of which are covered in the detailed discussion of templates on Day 19.

Predefined Macros

Many compilers predefine a number of useful macros, including __DATE__, __TIME__, __LINE__, and __FILE__. Each of these names uses the two underscore characters to reduce the likelihood that the names conflict with names you've used in your program.

When the precompiler sees one of these macros, it makes the appropriate substitutions. For __DATE__, the current date is substituted. For __TIME__, the current time is substituted. __LINE__ and __FILE__ are replaced with the source code line number and filename respectively. You should note that this substitution is made when the source is precompiled, not when the program is run. If you ask the program to print __DATE__, you do not get the current date. Instead, you get the date that the program was compiled. These defined macros are very useful in debugging.

assert()

Many compilers offer an assert() macro. The assert() macro returns true if its parameter evaluates true and takes some kind of action if it evaluates false. Many compilers abort the program on an assert() that fails, and others throw an exception (see Day 20, "Exceptions and Error Handling").

One powerful feature of the assert() macro is that the preprocessor collapses it into no code at all if DEBUG is not defined. It is a great help during development, but when the final product ships, there is no performance penalty nor increase in the size of the executable version of the program.

Rather than depending on the compiler provided in assert(), you are free to write your own assert() macro. Listing 17.5 provides a simple assert() macro and shows its use.

TYPE | **Listing 17.5. A simple assert() macro.**

```
1:    // Listing 17.5 ASSERTS
2:    #define DEBUG
3:    #include <iostream.h>
4:
5:    #ifndef DEBUG
6:        #define ASSERT(x)
7:    #else
8:        #define ASSERT(x) \
9:                if (! (x)) \
10:               { \
11:                   cout << "ERROR!! Assert " << #x << " failed\n"; \
12:                   cout << " on line " << __LINE__  << "\n"; \
13:                   cout << " in file " << __FILE__ << "\n";  \
14:               }
15:    #endif
16:
17:
18:    void main()
19:    {
20:        int x = 5;
21:        cout << "First assert: \n";
22:        ASSERT(x==5);
23:        cout << "\nSecond assert: \n";
24:        ASSERT(x != 5);
25:        cout << "\nDone.\n";
26:    }
```

OUTPUT

```
First assert:

Second assert:
ERROR!! Assert x!=5 failed
on line 24
in file test1804.cpp
```

ANALYSIS On line 2 the term DEBUG is defined. Typically, this is done from the command line (or the IDE) at compile time so that you can turn it on and off at will. On lines 8 through 14, the assert() macro is defined. Typically, this is done in a header file, and that header (ASSERT.HPP) is included in all of your implementation files.

On line 5 the term DEBUG is tested. If it is not defined, assert() is defined to create no code at all. If DEBUG is defined, the functionality defined on lines 8 through 14 is applied.

The assert() itself is one long statement split across seven source code lines, as far as the precompiler is concerned. On line 9 the value passed in as a parameter is tested; if it evaluates false, the statements on lines 11 to 13 are invoked, printing an error message. If the value passed in evaluates true, no action is taken.

Debugging with *assert()*

When writing your program, you often know deep down in your soul that something is true: a function has a certain value, a pointer is valid, and so forth. It is the nature of bugs that what you know to be true might not be true under some conditions. For example, you know that a pointer is valid, yet the program crashes. assert() can help you find this type of bug, but only if you make it a regular practice to use assert()s liberally in your code. Every time you assign or are passed a pointer as a parameter or function return value, be sure to assert that the pointer is valid. Any time your code depends on a particular value being in a variable, assert() that it is true.

There is no penalty for frequent use of assert()s; they are removed from the code when you undefine debugging. They also provide good internal documentation, reminding the reader of what you believe is true at any given moment in the flow of the code.

assert() Versus Exceptions

On Day 20 you learn how to work with exceptions to handle error conditions. It is important to note that assert()s are not intended to handle run-time error conditions such as bad data, out of memory conditions, unable to open file, and so forth. assert()s are created to catch programming errors only. That is, if an assert() "fires," you know you have a bug in your code.

This is critical because when you ship your code to your customers, the assert()s are removed. You cannot depend on an assert() to handle a run-time problem because the assert() won't be there.

It is a common mistake to use assert() to test the return value from a memory assignment:

```
Animal *pCat = new Cat;
Assert(pCat);   // bad use of assert
pCat->SomeFunction();
```

This is a classic programming error; every time the programmer runs the program there is enough memory and the assert() never fires. After all, the programmer is running with lots of extra RAM to speed up the compiler, debugger, and so forth. The programmer then ships the executable, and when the poor user, who has less memory, reaches this part of the program, the call to new fails and returns null. The assert(), however, is no longer in the code and there is nothing to indicate that the pointer points to null. As soon as the statement pCat->SomeFunction() is reached, the program crashes.

Getting NULL back from a memory assignment is not a programming error, though it is an exceptional situation. Your program must be able to recover from this condition, if only by throwing an exception. Remember that the entire assert() statement is gone when debug is undefined. Exceptions are covered in detail on Day 20.

Side Effects

It is not uncommon to find that a bug appears only after the `assert()`s are removed. This is almost always due to the program unintentionally depending on side effects of things done in `assert()`s and other debug-only code. For example, if you write

```
ASSERT (x = 5)
```

when you mean to test whether `x == 5`, you create a particularly nasty bug.

Suppose that just prior to this `assert()`, you called a function that set x equal to zero. With this `assert()` you think you are testing whether x is equal to 5; in fact, you are setting x equal to 5. The test returns true because x = 5 not only sets x to 5, but it also returns the value 5, and because 5 is nonzero it evaluates as `TRUE`.

After you pass the `assert()` statement, x really is equal to 5 (you just set it!). Your program runs just fine, and you're ready to ship it, so you turn debugging off. Now the `assert()` disappears and you are no longer setting x to 5. Because x was set to zero just before this, it remains at zero and your program breaks.

In frustration, you turn debugging back on. Presto! The bug is gone. Once again, this is rather funny to watch but not to live through, so be very careful about side effects in debugging code. If you see a bug that only appears when debugging is turned off, take a look at your debugging code with an eye out for nasty side effects.

Class Invariants

Most classes have some conditions that should always be true whenever you are finished with a class member function. These class *invariants* are the *sine qua non* of your class. For example, it might be true that your `CIRCLE` object should never have a radius of zero, or that your `ANIMAL` should always have an age greater than zero and less than 100.

It can be very helpful to declare an `Invariants()` method that returns true only if each of these conditions is still true. You can then `Assert(Invariants())` at the start and completion of every class method. The exception is that your `Invariants()` do not expect to return true before your constructor runs or after your destructor ends. Listing 17.6 demonstrates the use of the `Invariants()` method in a trivial class.

Type **Listing 17.6. Using** `Invariants()`.

```
1:      #define DEBUG
2:      #define SHOW_INVARIANTS
3:      #include <iostream.h>
4:      #include <string.h>
```

continues

Listing 17.6. continued

```
5:
6:      #ifndef DEBUG
7:      #define ASSERT(x)
8:      #else
9:      #define ASSERT(x) \
10:                 if (! (x)) \
11:                 { \
12:                     cout << "ERROR!! Assert " << #x << " failed\n"; \
13:                     cout << " on line " << __LINE__ << "\n"; \
14:                     cout << " in file " << __FILE__ << "\n";  \
15:                 }
16:     #endif
17:
18:
19:
20:     class String
21:     {
22:        public:
23:            // constructors
24:            String();
25:            String(const char *const);
26:            String(const String &);
27:            ~String();
28:
29:            char & operator[](int offset);
30:            char operator[](int offset) const;
31:
32:            String & operator= (const String &);
33:            int GetLen()const { return itsLen; }
34:            const char * GetString() const { return itsString; }
35:            bool Invariants();
36:
37:        private:
38:            String (int);          // private constructor
39:            char * itsString;
40:            unsigned short itsLen;
41:     };
42:
43:     // default constructor creates string of 0 bytes
44:     String::String()
45:     {
46:         itsString = new char[1];
47:         itsString[0] = '\0';
48:         itsLen=0;
49:         ASSERT(Invariants());
50:     }
51:
52:     // private (helper) constructor, used only by
53:     // class methods for creating a new string of
54:     // required size.  Null filled.
55:     String::String(int len)
56:     {
57:         itsString = new char[len+1];
58:         for (int i = 0; i<=len; i++)
```

17

```
59:            itsString[1] = '\0';
60:        itsLen=len;
61:        ASSERT(Invariants());
62:    }
63:
64:    // Converts a character array to a String
65:    String::String(const char * const cString)
66:    {
67:        itsLen = strlen(cString);
68:        itsString = new char[itsLen+1];
69:        for (int i = 0; i<itsLen; i++)
70:            itsString[i] = cString[i];
71:        itsString[itsLen]='\0';
72:        ASSERT(Invariants());
73:    }
74:
75:    // copy constructor
76:    String::String (const String & rhs)
77:    {
78:        itsLen=rhs.GetLen();
79:        itsString = new char[itsLen+1];
80:        for (int i = 0; i<itsLen;i++)
81:            itsString[i] = rhs[i];
82:        itsString[itsLen] = '\0';
83:        ASSERT(Invariants());
84:    }
85:
86:    // destructor, frees allocated memory
87:    String::~String ()
88:    {
89:        ASSERT(Invariants());
90:        delete [] itsString;
91:        itsLen = 0;
92:    }
93:
94:    // operator equals, frees existing memory
95:    // then copies string and size
96:    String& String::operator=(const String & rhs)
97:    {
98:        ASSERT(Invariants());
99:        if (this == &rhs)
100:           return *this;
101:       delete [] itsString;
102:       itsLen=rhs.GetLen();
103:       itsString = new char[itsLen+1];
104:       for (int i = 0; i<itsLen;i++)
105:           itsString[i] = rhs[i];
106:       itsString[itsLen] = '\0';
107:       ASSERT(Invariants());
108:       return *this;
109:   }
110:
111:   //non constant offset operator, returns
112:   // reference to character so it can be
113:   // changed!
```

continues

Listing 17.6. continued

```
114:    char & String::operator[](int offset)
115:    {
116:       ASSERT(Invariants());
117:       if (offset > itsLen)
118:          return itsString[itsLen-1];
119:       else
120:          return itsString[offset];
121:       ASSERT(Invariants());
122:    }
123:
124:    // constant offset operator for use
125:    // on const objects (see copy constructor!)
126:    char String::operator[](int offset) const
127:    {
128:       ASSERT(Invariants());
129:       if (offset > itsLen)
130:          return itsString[itsLen-1];
131:       else
132:          return itsString[offset];
133:       ASSERT(Invariants());
134:    }
135:
136:
137:    bool String::Invariants()
138:    {
139:    #ifdef SHOW_INVARIANTS
140:       cout << " String OK ";
141:    #endif
142:        return ( (itsLen && itsString) || (!itsLen && !itsString) );
143:    }
144:
145:    class Animal
146:    {
147:    public:
148:       Animal():itsAge(1),itsName("John Q. Animal"){ASSERT(Invariants());}
149:       Animal(int, const String&);
150:       ~Animal(){}
151:       int GetAge() {  ASSERT(Invariants()); return itsAge;}
152:       void SetAge(int Age) { ASSERT(Invariants()); itsAge = Age;
                      _ASSERT(Invariants()); }
153:       String& GetName() { ASSERT(Invariants()); return itsName;  }
154:       void SetName(const String& name)
155:          { ASSERT(Invariants()); itsName = name; ASSERT(Invariants());}
156:       bool Invariants();
157:    private:
158:       int itsAge;
159:       String itsName;
160:    };
161:
162:    Animal::Animal(int age, const String& name):
163:    itsAge(age),
164:    itsName(name)
165:    {
166:       ASSERT(Invariants());
167:    }
```

17

```
168:
169:    bool Animal::Invariants()
170:    {
171:    #ifdef SHOW_INVARIANTS
172:        cout << " Animal OK ";
173:    #endif
174:        return (itsAge > 0 && itsName.GetLen());
175:    }
176:
177:    void main()
178:    {
179:        Animal sparky(5,"Sparky");
180:        cout << "\n" << sparky.GetName().GetString() << " is ";
181:        cout << sparky.GetAge() << " years old.";
182:        sparky.SetAge(8);
183:        cout << "\n" << sparky.GetName().GetString() << " is ";
184:        cout << sparky.GetAge() << " years old.";
185:    }
```

OUTPUT

```
String OK  String OK  String OK  String OK  String OK
➥ String OK String OK  _String OK
Animal OK  Animal OK
Sparky is  Animal OK  5 years old. Animal OK  Animal OK  Animal OK
Sparky is Animal OK 8 years old. String OK  String OK
```

ANALYSIS On lines 6 through 16 the assert() macro is defined. If DEBUG is defined, this writes out an error message when the assert() macro evaluates false.

On line 35 the String class member function Invariants() is declared; it is defined on lines 137 to 143. The constructor is declared on lines 44 to 50; and on line 49, after the object is fully constructed, Invariants() is called to confirm proper construction.

This pattern is repeated for the other constructors, and the destructor calls Invariants() only before it sets out to destroy the object. The remaining class functions call Invariants() before taking any action and then again before returning. This both affirms and validates a fundamental principal of C++: Member functions other than constructors and destructors should work on valid objects and should leave them in a valid state.

On line 155, the class Animal declares its own Invariants() method, implemented on lines 169 through 175. Note that on lines 151, 152, 153, and 155 inline functions can call the Invariants() method.

Printing Interim Values

In addition to asserting that something is true using the assert() macro, you might want to print the current value of pointers, variables, and strings. This can be very helpful for checking your assumptions about the progress of your program, and in locating off-by-one bugs in loops. Listing 17.7 illustrates this idea.

TYPE **Listing 17.7. Printing values in DEBUG mode.**

```
1:      // Listing 17.7
2:      #include <iostream.h>
3:      #define DEBUG
4:
5:      #ifndef DEBUG
6:      #define PRINT(x)
7:      #else
8:      #define PRINT(x) \
9:          cout << #x << ":\t" << x << endl;
10:     #endif
11:
12:
13:
14:     void main()
15:     {
16:         int x = 5;
17:         long y = 738981;
18:         PRINT(x);
19:         for (int i = 0; i < x; i++)
20:         {
21:             PRINT(i);
22:         }
23:
24:         PRINT (y);
25:         PRINT("Hi.");
26:         int *px = &x;
27:         PRINT(px);
28:         PRINT (*px);
29:     }
```

OUTPUT
```
x:          5
i:          0
i:          1
i:          2
i:          3
i:          4
y:          73898
"Hi.":      Hi.
px:         0x2100 (You may recieve a value other than 0x2100)
*px:        5
```

ANALYSIS The macro on lines 5 to 10 provides printing of the current value of the supplied parameter. Note that the first thing fed to cout is the stringized version of the parameter; that is, if you pass in x, cout receives x.

Next, cout receives the quoted string ":\t", which prints a colon and then a tab. Third, cout receives the value of the parameter (x) and then finally, endl, which writes a new line and flushes the buffer.

17

Debugging Levels

In large, complex projects, you might want more control than simply turning DEBUG on and off. You can define debug *levels* and test for them when deciding which macros to use and which to strip out.

To define a level, simply follow the #define DEBUG statement with a number. Although you can have any number of levels, a common system is to have four levels: HIGH, MEDIUM, LOW, and NONE. Listing 17.8 illustrates how this might be done, using the String and Animal classes from Listing 17.6. The definitions of the class methods other than Invariants() have been left out to save space, because they are unchanged from Listing 17.6.

NOTE

> To compile this code, copy lines 43 through 136 of Listing 17.6 and insert them between lines 64 and 65 of this listing.

17

TYPE **Listing 17.8. Levels of debugging.**

```
1:    enum LEVEL { NONE, LOW, MEDIUM, HIGH };
2:
3:
4:      #define DEBUGLEVEL MEDIUM
5:
6:      #include <iostream.h>
7:      #include <string.h>
8:
9:      #if DEBUGLEVEL < LOW   // must be medium or high
10:     #define ASSERT(x)
11:     #else
12:     #define ASSERT(x) \
13:                 if (! (x)) \
14:                 { \
15:                     cout << "ERROR!! Assert " << #x << " failed\n"; \
16:                     cout << " on line " << __LINE__  << "\n"; \
17:                     cout << " in file " << __FILE__ << "\n";  \
18:                 }
19:     #endif
20:
21:     #if DEBUGLEVEL < MEDIUM
22:     #define EVAL(x)
23:     #else
24:     #define EVAL(x) \
25:        cout << #x << ":\t" << x << endl;
26:     #endif
27:
```

continues

Listing 17.8. continued

```
28:    #if DEBUGLEVEL < HIGH
29:     #define PRINT(x)
30:     #else
31:     #define PRINT(x) \
32:       cout << x << endl;
33:     #endif
34:
35:
36:    class String
37:    {
38:       public:
39:           // constructors
40:           String();
41:           String(const char *const);
42:           String(const String &);
43:           ~String();
44:
45:           char & operator[](int offset);
46:           char operator[](int offset) const;
47:
48:           String & operator= (const String &);
49:           int GetLen()const { return itsLen; }
50:           const char * GetString() const { return itsString; }
51:           bool Invariants() const;
52:
53:       private:
54:           String (int);          // private constructor
55:           char * itsString;
56:           unsigned short itsLen;
57:    };
58:
59:    bool String::Invariants() const
60:    {
61:        PRINT("(String Invariants Checked)");
62:        return ( (itsLen && itsString) ¦¦ (!itsLen && !itsString) );
63:    }
64:
65:    class Animal
66:    {
67:    public:
68:       Animal():itsAge(1),itsName("John Q. Animal"){ASSERT(Invariants());}
69:       Animal(int, const String&);
70:       ~Animal(){}
71:       int GetAge() {  ASSERT(Invariants()); return itsAge;}
72:       void SetAge(int Age) { ASSERT(Invariants()); itsAge = Age;
                            _ASSERT(Invariants()); }
73:       String& GetName() { ASSERT(Invariants()); return itsName;  }
74:       void SetName(const String& name)
75:             { ASSERT(Invariants()); itsName = name; ASSERT(Invariants());}
76:       bool Invariants();
77:    private:
78:       int itsAge;
79:       String itsName;
80:    };
81:
```

17

```
82:    Animal::Animal(int age, const String& name):
83:    itsAge(age),
84:    itsName(name)
85:    {
86:        ASSERT(Invariants());
87:    }
88:
89:      bool Animal::Invariants()
90:      {
91:          PRINT("(Animal Invariants Checked)");
92:          return (itsAge > 0 && itsName.GetLen());
93:      }
94:
95:      void main()
96:      {
97:          const int AGE = 5;
98:          EVAL(AGE);
99:          Animal sparky(AGE,"Sparky");
100:           cout << "\n" << sparky.GetName().GetString() << " is ";
101:           cout << sparky.GetAge() << " years old.";
102:           sparky.SetAge(8);
103:           cout << "\n" << sparky.GetName().GetString() << " is ";
104:           cout << sparky.GetAge() << " years old.";
105:        }
```

OUTPUT

```
AGE:       5
  (String Invariants Checked)
  (String Invariants Checked)
  (String Invariants Checked)
  (String Invariants Checked)
  (String Invariants Checked)
  (String Invariants Checked)
  (String Invariants Checked)
  (String Invariants Checked)
  (Animal Invariants Checked)
  (String Invariants Checked)
  (Animal Invariants Checked)

Sparky is (Animal Invariants Checked)
5 Years old. (Animal Invariants Checked)
  (Animal Invariants Checked)
  (Animal Invariants Checked)

Sparky is (Animal Invariants Checked)
8 years old. (String Invariants Checked)
  (String Invariants Checked)

// run again with DEBUG = MEDIUM

AGE:       5
Sparky is 5 years old.
Sparky is 8 years old.
```

ANALYSIS On lines 9 to 19 the assert() macro is defined to be stripped if DEBUGLEVEL is less than LOW (that is DEBUGLEVEL is NONE). If any debugging is enabled, the assert() macro works. On line 21, EVAL is declared to be stripped if DEBUG is less than MEDIUM; if DEBUGLEVEL is NONE or LOW, EVAL is stripped.

On lines 28 to 33 the PRINT macro is declared to be stripped if DEBUGLEVEL is less than HIGH. PRINT is used only when DEBUGLEVEL is high, and you can eliminate this macro by setting DEBUGLEVEL to MEDIUM and still maintain your use of EVAL and of assert().

PRINT is used within the Invariants() methods to print an informative message. EVAL is used on line 98 to evaluate the current value of the constant integer AGE.

Do	Don't

DO use capitals for your macro names. This is a pervasive convention, and other programmers will be confused if you don't.

DON'T allow your macros to have side effects. Don't increment variables or assign values from within a macro.

DO surround all arguments with parentheses in macro functions.

Summary

Today you learned more details about working with the preprocessor. Each time you run the compiler, the preprocessor runs first and translates your preprocessor directives, such as #define and #ifdef.

The preprocessor does text substitution, although with the use of macros these can be somewhat complex. By using #ifdef, #else, and #ifndef you can accomplish conditional compilation, compiling in some statements under one set of conditions and in another set of statements under other conditions. This can assist in writing programs for more than one platform and is often used to conditionally include debugging information.

Macro functions provide complex text substitution based on arguments passed at compile time to the macro. It is important to put parentheses around every argument in the macro to ensure that the correct substitution takes place.

Macro functions, and the preprocessor in general, are less important in C++ than they were in C. C++ provides a number of language features, such as const variables and templates, which offer superior alternatives to the use of the preprocessor.

Q&A

Q If C++ offers better alternatives than the preprocessor, why is this option still available?

A First, C++ is backward-compatible with C, and all significant parts of C must be supported in C++. Second, there are some uses of the preprocessor that are still used frequently in C++, such as inclusion guards.

Q Why use macro functions when you can use a regular function?

A Macro functions are expanded inline and are used as a substitute for repeatedly typing the same commands with minor variations. Again, though, templates offer a better alternative.

Q How do you know when to use a macro instead of an inline function?

A Often it doesn't matter much, and you can use whichever is simpler. However, macros offer character substitution, stringizing, and concatenation. None of these are available with functions.

Q What is the alternative to using the preprocessor to print interim values during debugging?

A The best alternative is to use watch statements within a debugger. For information on watch statements, consult your compiler or debugger documentation.

Q How do you decide when to use an assert() and when to throw an exception?

A If the situation you're testing can be true without your having committed a programming error, use an exception. If the only reason for this situation to ever be true is a bug in your program, use an assert().

Quiz

1. What is an inclusion guard?
2. How do you instruct your compiler to print the contents of the intermediate file showing the effects of the preprocessor?
3. What is the difference between #define debug 0 and #undef debug?
4. Name four predefined macros.
5. Why can't you call invariants() as the first line of your constructor?

17

Exercises

1. Write the inclusion guard statements for the header file STRING.H.

2. Write an assert() macro that prints an error message and the file and line number if debug level is 2, prints just a message (without file and line number) if the level is 1, and does nothing if the level is 0.

3. Write a macro, DPrint, that tests whether debug is defined, and if it is prints the value passed in as a parameter.

4. Write a function that prints an error message. The function should print the line number and filename where the error occurred. Note that the line number and filename are passed into this function.

5. How would you call the preceding error function?

6. Write an assert() macro that uses the error function from exercise 4, and write a driver program that calls this assert() macro.

17

Day 18

Creating Reusable Code

C++ has spread like wildfire. Compilers are available for virtually any type of computer you can think of. At the same time, computer technology is growing by leaps. You are probably well aware of the fact that the personal computer you bought less than a year ago is already obsolete.

The only computer languages that will see success are those that can provide portability to new computer architectures. C++ can do that but you, the programmer, have to help. After all, as advanced as programming is, no one has found a way to make programs write themselves. Because you are still the vital link that determines how portable your programs can be, you need to keep some basic ideas in mind as you design and implement them. Here are some reuse and portability rules for writing better programs:

- [ ] Remember code reuse.
- [ ] Remember code maintenance.
- [ ] Remember code portability.

Remember Code Reuse

Reusability of code is a hot topic in the world of computer science. At one time, programs were designed with the assumption that the invention of interchangeable parts had no bearing on software design. It was assumed that each problem was a special case and that lessons and algorithms applied to one problem could not be implemented the same way for new problems. It was partially in reaction to that assumption that computer scientists gave birth to the object-oriented paradigm.

Humans stand out from other creatures in their ability to find solutions to current problems using similarities found in previously solved problems. For example, if you are given the challenge to design an aircraft navigation system, you'll probably choose to base your new design on a previous aircraft navigation system. The better your predecessor planned the previous system, the better off you are. Until you are well into the new project and committed to extending the life of a poor design, you might not realize that your predecessor went about her design thinking that no one else would ever need her code. Worse yet, your manager might not understand why you initially decided that your predecessor's code would work with little modification but now you are having problems making your schedules. Always make at least this one assumption: Somebody else will want to use your code later. The paragraphs that follow provide some pointers to help you design reusable code.

Avoid Literal Constants

There are times when it might seem quite reasonable to use a literal constant. Listing 18.1 is an example.

TYPE   **Listing 18.1. Literal constants.**

```
1:  // Determine the circumference of a circle
2:  void main()
3:  {
4:      double Radius, Circumf = 0.0;
5:      cout << "Enter the radius: ";
6:      cin >> Radius;
7:      // Apply the formula, 2(pi)(Radius)
8:      Circumf = 2 * (3.14 * Radius);
9:      cout << "The circumference is: "
10:          << Circumf << endl;
11: }
```

It is perfectly legitimate to assume that the value of pi never changes. However, it is not legitimate to assume that you never want to go to any greater accuracy than two decimal places. In a short program the problem is not so big. As your program increases in complexity and size, all the instances of pi might be hard to find. One alternative is to place all the constants in a header file that can be included in all the source files that need them. Later today you'll learn how to make use of how the system limits information so that you can specify pi to be accurate to the maximum level of accuracy for the platform on which your program is compiled.

Encapsulate the Details

The more the next programmer has to worry about the details inside your code, the longer it takes her to figure out how to use it. Encapsulation is the concept of hiding unimportant details about an object and only giving the details needed to make use of that object. It is a tenet of object-oriented design.

For example, if you wanted to create a way to track the C++ books you've read, you could create something like the following code:

```
#include "mybooks.h"
class CPlusPlusBook {
public:
    char Title[TitleLength];  // Book's title
    char Comments[BigBuffer]; // My thoughts
    bool ReadIt;              // Read it?
    CPlusPlusBook(void);
    ~CPlusPlusBook(void);
};
```

It is doubtful that you could come this far in this book and still do such a thing, but the example illustrates the point. The big problem with this code is that later you have to remember the values of `TitleLength` and `BigBuffer` whenever you enter information in the `Title` and `Comments` arrays. You also have to remember whether a false for `ReadIt` means that you have not read it, or whether it means that you decided you do not want to read it. A better approach is to keep the data private and use it only through access functions that return or set the data values. If you do that, you won't have to remember the details of how big an array is. In fact, you won't even have to remember that the information is in an array.

Comment on the Logic

Encapsulation goes a long way toward making it easy for others to later use your code without worrying about the internals. But what if someone needs to enhance your code with some new functionality that you had not anticipated? Imagine that those changes are required months after you thought the project was buried for good. Comments that explain the big-picture logic for a function are quite helpful.

Perhaps you really love to play tic-tac-toe. You can imagine how you might have trouble finding someone who likes the game as much as you to play, so you decide to write a program to be your opponent. You want your computer player to be the best tic-tac-toe player possible, so that a game is challenging enough to keep your interest. You might have a function like the one in Listing 18.2.

TYPE   **Listing 18.2. Tic-tac-toe move function.**

```
1:   Square ComputerChoice(void)
2:   { // Choose the square to move in next
3:       bool NotFound = true;
4:       MoveSquare MySquare = FirstSquare();
5:       while(NotFound) {
6:           if( !LegalSquare(MySquare) ) {
7:               MySquare = IllegalSquareConstant;
8:               break;
9:           }
10:          if( !Occupied(MySquare) )
11:              break;
12:      }
13:      return MySquare;
14: }
```

You won't play this opponent too long before you decide to update your code. The `if` tree logic makes it easy to add new strategies, but it makes it difficult to figure out what strategies you have already put in or in what order. A comment block at the top of the function could include the grand strategy and comments around the `if` statements could explain the tactical decisions your code is making. When you come back later, you would probably like to see something like the following:

```
// Function:  Square ComputerChoice(void)
// Purpose:   To pick a square for the next move
// Description: Cycle thru all the squares for
//     the best move by applying the following
//     algorithm:
//     1. Is the square legal? No=exit, yes=go to 2.
//     2. Does the square make 3 in a row for me?
//        No=try next square, on last square, go to 3.
//        Yes=Win!
//     3. Does the square block opponent?
//        No=try next square, last square go to 4.
//        Yes=Block
//     4. Does it give 2 in a row?
//        No=Try next square, take last square
//        Yes=take 2
```

Tic-tac-toe might not be the king of games, but applying this simple concept helps you to design the program correctly the first time and improve it later. It can also serve to make comments later in the code more explanatory without cluttering the view, such as in the following section of your new function:

18

```
// Logic step 3:
If( BlockingSquare(MySquare) )
    break;
```

The simple statement that refers to the block comments at the beginning of the function is much more helpful than several lines in the middle of a `while` loop would be.

Remember Code Maintenance

As with many of the things you are learning today, this has been touched on before. However, the importance of the subject begs possible repetition and reinforcement. Many programmers make the mistake of thinking that the big hurdle is to get the code working. It can sometimes seem that a schedule is the *only* hurdle to overcome. Some estimates on software maintenance say that the cost (as in programmer time) of a software project is less than 25 percent for the initial design and coding and more than 75 percent for maintaining that code after it is sent to market. Yet if you were to take a survey of professional programmers and ask them what part of their job they liked the least, many would say the maintenance phase of a project is the least enjoyable time to be in this business.

Planning for the maintenance phase early in the project is a lot like planning your tax withholdings early in the year. If you wait until April 15 to figure out whether your employer withheld enough, you might be very sorry. Maintenance won't go away, no matter how hard you try to ignore it. The sections that follow provide some guidelines that can help make your code easy to maintain.

The Power of Seven

A famous psychologist named George Miller discovered that there seems to be a limitation in the number of concepts a human can manage at one time. His findings were that seven concepts is the cognitive limit for humans. So what? So, break your functions down to manageable chunks of the larger algorithm. As a rule of thumb, make certain that no one function is responsible for more than seven basic tasks.

Document the Initial Code and Changes

Make dated notes in your code whenever you make a change. In fact, when you first write the code and put in the block comments at the top, always include a space marked for revision information. Simply having that comment section there reminds you to comment on changes every time you edit the code.

Most text editors that are worth their salt enable you to read in the contents of another file. Consider keeping a comment block template in a file so that every time you create a new function, you can read in the template and fill in the blanks.

Keep a notebook or an English text file that documents your thoughts as you write the code. You might think of something that you want to do to a function in another file while you're editing the main function file. Note those thoughts in your book so that you can come back to them later. It's amazing how remembering your train of thought from a previous day reminds you why certain changes were important. A historical record also keeps you from churning on ideas that you had thrown out before for some forgotten reason.

Develop a Consistent Coding Style

Earlier in this book, coding styles were mentioned, and they are discussed here in more detail. Knowing some of the more common styles helps you when you are working on programs that you did not write. Developing your own style and being consistent with it can help you remember what you did later and help others who have to read your programs.

Function, Variable, and Constant Name Styles

One popular coding style today comes from the practices of a Hungarian gentleman who was employed by Microsoft, Mr. Charles Simonyi. Mr. Simonyi is credited with starting the practice of naming variables with one or two letter prefixes that identified their type. This style has come to be known as Hungarian notation. Using Hungarian notation, you would know that the variables: `iValue`, `iCounter`, and `iWindows` are all integer variables. Table 18.1 lists some of the Hungarian notation prefixes and their meanings.

Table 18.1. Hungarian notation type prefixes.

Prefix	Meaning
a	Array
b	Boolean
by	Byte (unsigned `char`)
c	Character or count
dw	Double word
fn	Function
g	Global variable
h	Handle (system resource identifier)
i	Integer
m_	Member variable of a class
p	Pointer
l	Long

Prefix	Meaning
lp	Pointer to a long
s	String (or character array)
sz	Zero-terminated string

Because the notation was created for Microsoft applications on IBM-compatible personal computers, you might not recognize some of the types. The idea behind Hungarian notation is that you are less likely to assign inappropriate values to variables. For instance, you would not likely try to assign a bool value to a variable named iValue or szName. Hungarian notation was originally developed for C programming before C++, with its strong typing, became popular. Many C++ programmers still use the Hungarian notation. Hungarian notation is so popular that it has been extended to include other prefix specifications that tell more about the variable. If you are working on personal computer programs to run under the MS Windows environment, you might want to find a book that describes Hungarian notation in more detail.

Some programmers write variable names with a lowercase first letter and initial caps on all the successive words in multiword variable and function names—for instance, myVariableName or writeValues. This type of notation is often called camel notation because the capital letters give the appearance of camel humps. Others prefer to use underscore characters to separate words as in On_Off_Switch or Variable_Resistor.

Constant names are often written in all caps. It comes from C tradition where constants were always defined with the preprocessor #define directive. And, to be honest, it looks more UNCHANGEABLE than do Hungarian or camel notation variable names. One problem with this practice is that a lot of public domain code uses all caps only for #define constants but not for constants defined with const.

Because it is best to choose one style and stick with it, the bottom line question is, "Which style to should I choose?" The problem is that they are all a matter of personal taste. Another problem is that there may be outside factors that prevent you from choosing. It may be that your project requires all programmers to use a particular style. You decide to use a style you really don't like just to remain consistent with previous "legacy" code used in a project. It might seem to be such a minor thing that you wonder why I'm spending so much time on it. I cover this so that you can avoid the mistake of choosing one over another too quickly and then having to change your code when you change your mind.

Indentation Styles

Indentation is another area in which programmers have developed several methods. Of course, this practice assumes that you indent in some cases. Indenting can make the program readable where it would not be without it. It helps you identify the various subsections of your program so that you gain the big-picture view more quickly. Look at the following code snippet:

```
if(YouCanReadThis==true){
x=7;y=8;z=9;j=(x*y) + z;}
```

This compiles and runs, assuming you have the variables defined earlier in the program, but it's very difficult to read.

Indentation practices are identifiable in block statements. One style makes the surrounding brackets the same level of indentation as the statements they bracket, like the following:

```
if( TideIsHigh == true )
    {
    Waves = Surf;
    Surfer = Joe;
    Beach = Malibu;
    }
else
    {
    BummerDude();
    }
```

Another indentation style places the brackets at the level of the control statements that surround the block, like the following:

```
MyFavoriteFunction(void)
{
    cout << "Life's a beach."
            << endl;
}
```

A variation on this theme places the first bracket at the end of the control statement line:

```
while(Raining == true) {
    PlayComputerGames();
    ReadTeachYourself();
    PlayComputerGames();
}
```

Your text editor probably has options for what happens when you press the Tab key. For most word processing, tab stops are set to move the cursor over the distance of about eight spaces. As your programs become more complex, large tab values bounce embedded code blocks right off the screen. For your own sanity, set the tab stops to three or four spaces each.

Some programmers have their editor configured so that a tab character is entered when they press the Tab key. The tab character looks like a bunch of space characters, but it is still only one character. Other programmers configure their editor so that the tab character inserts three or four spaces. The difference might seem to matter little, but there are advantages and disadvantages to both practices. Making tabs as spaces causes your program to be indented the same no matter what editor you use later. If you use different editors, you probably like

18

the tabs-as-spaces method. The method that inserts tab characters instead of spaces makes it easy to change the indents simply by setting the tab stops in the editor.

Mixing the two tab practices in the same file messes up your indents worse than not indenting at all! If you change the setting, it only changes the code you type after the change and not the code you entered before. Be careful and decide which practice you want to use early in the development.

Another nice feature of some programming editors is the brace-matching feature. With this type of feature, the editor shows the matching brace whenever you type the closing brace. Some editors even apply the brace matching to parentheses. If your editor has it, use it. Some of the toughest compile-time errors are from mismatched brackets or parentheses.

Develop a Maintenance Strategy

Someday you might make a lot of changes to your program and end up breaking something that seemed unrelated. You want to go back to the previous version to retrace your steps but, alas, you overwrote the old version with the new version. What you need to do is one of the facets often referred to as *version control,* and there are a multitude of software packages out there to help you with version control. Probably the most well-known is the UNIX Source Code Control System (SCCS). Many version control packages today seem to model themselves after SCCS. The idea behind version control software is that at each stage of development (or anytime you like), you can check the current status of your project files into it as a snapshot of your project. Later, you check that version out and make changes, and then check the changes in. Rather than overwrite the old versions, the version control software simply keeps a record of the changes. You can request a copy of the project for any of the versions you have checked in.

Another question you might often ask yourself is, "what source files did I use to make this executable file?" The solution can be as simple as asking a sophisticated version control software program, or it could be something you plan to include in all of your source code files. You might decide to have a command line option for all your programs that displays the information for you. Go back to Day 17, "The Preprocessor," and scan the section on predefined macros again; then take a look at the program in Listing 18.3.

TYPE **Listing 18.3. The maintenance string encoding method.**

```
1:  // Listing 18.3 Encoded maintenance string
2:  #include<iostream.h>
3:
4:  void main(int argc, char **argv)
5:  {
```

continues

Listing 18.3. continued

```
6:      if( argc > 1 && argv[1][0] == 'M')
7:      {
8:          cout << "Compiled form of: "
9:                  << __FILE__ << " on: "
10:                 << __DATE__ << " at: "
11:                 << __TIME__ << endl;
12:     }
13:     else
14:     {
15:         cout << "Hello World!" << endl;
16:     }
17: }
```

OUTPUT

```
prog18_2<CR>
Hello World!
Prog18_2 M<CR>
Compiled form of: prog18_2.cpp on: Oct 28 1995 at: 11:13:56
```

ANALYSIS The only problem here is that this program only displays the source file that contains the main function; it does not display any of the other source files you included. With a little imagination, you might think of a way to tag all files with this information. The following is a handy trick. In each source code file, insert the following two lines outside any function or class definitions in that file:

```
#define TAGGIT static char __DOGTAG__[]= \
    "DogTag: "__FILE__ " "__DATE__" "
```

```
TAGGIT;
```

You can write a utility program that searches executable and/or object files for strings starting with the DogTag: identifier. The nifty thing is that every single source file has its own unique identifier string, so you could print out all the strings to see all the source files that were used to make the given executable or object file. If you end up using this method, just place the #define statement in a header file and include that header file in all your source code files followed by the TAGGIT macro call:

```
#include "identifiers.h"
```

```
TAGGIT;
```

Remember Code Portability

It's the typical programmer's nightmare story: Your group builds a function that seems to have a limited audience, and you expect to sell only a few copies. Instead, the program catches on and everybody wants a copy. Not only that, but they want copies for their UNIX machine at work, their Windows 95 computer at home, and their Macintosh at school. Now you have to figure out all the machine dependencies that are in your program and how in the world you can catch them all for every new platform.

One good approach is to try to isolate all those dependencies in one or two files and use preprocessor directives to select the code that should be compiled.

Adhere to the ANSI/ISO Standard

As with any standard, there are limitations to the level of compliance you can keep and still meet the efficiency demands of your design. For instance, many applications (such as graphics programs) are inherently hardware- or compiler-specific. Still, adhering to the standard as closely as possible limits the number of changes you have to make when moving your application to another platform.

Instead of relying on maximum and minimum values that depend on the computer architecture, use the standard header files for determining implementation details. The following sample code snippet is not portable.

```
// If the character c is in the char type range,
// save it
if( c > 0 && c < 256 )
    streamedFile << c;
```

Instead, a wiser programmer could use the maximum and minimum char values that are defined in the ANSI standard header file limits.h, like this:

```
// we need to know the limits for chars
#include <limits.h>
    // More code…
    if( c > c.min() && c < (c.max() + 1) )
        streamedFile << c;
```

Table 18.2 summarizes some of the constants defined for the implementation details of built-in data types.

Table 18.2. ANSI-defined constants.

Constant	Value/Use
digits	Precision digits (base radix)
digits10	Precision digits (base 10)
has_infinity	True if the type has a representation for infinity
infinity()	Representation of infinity (if has_infinity)
max()	Maximum value
min()	Minimum value

continues

Table 18.2. continued

Constant	Value/Use
max_exponent	Exponent maximum value (base 2)
max_exponent10	Exponent maximum value (base 10)
min_exponent	Exponent minimum value (base 2)
min_exponent10	Exponent minimum value (base 10)
radix	The base number of this type

Think Globally

Advanced communications developments around the globe, along with social developments, have opened the way for companies to team up with other companies overseas. This is particularly the case in development projects in which the product is to be sold in different countries. Having an insider in another country can decrease your time to market in that country and give you insight into customs or other issues that might affect your design, especially in the user interface design. Remember Day 4, "Expressions and Statements," when you first learned about the wchar_t type? The wchar_t is the type that is used to include the entire character set in a given geographical location as defined in clocale.h. Along with the wchar_t type are a collection of wide character and string functions built to work in the same way as their narrow character counterparts. For instance, the strcmp function for comparing char strings has a wchar_t counterpart called wstrcmp.

It is a good practice to isolate all the user interface strings that need to be translated to other human languages. Be sure to allow ample space in your string arrays because most languages require more characters than English does. The shorthand English often used for computer display to save space is sometimes referred to as *telegraph English* because it reads like a telegraph message. In telegraph messages you have to pay by the letter, so telegraph writers tend to abbreviate their language. Computer programmers have become accustomed to the same practice. The problem is that many languages other than English do not have the telegraph tradition. Certain implications are made that cannot be counted on in other languages. For instance, "Press Stop" makes perfect sense to someone accustomed to English as their first language; the "You" is implied. But that cannot be assumed about all the languages into which the code is going to be translated. If you find yourself in an international programming group, look for any of the many books available on the subject. Bonus Day 28, "What's Next?," contains information on some of the books you might find helpful. Digital Equipment Corporation has done relatively extensive studies in software internationalization and has published several books on the subject.

Do	**Don't**

DO use the wide character type wchar_t and the ANSI/ISO defined wide character string functions for international projects.

DO use comments that explain the logic behind what your program does.

DON'T use literal constants. Isolate the constant definitions in your programs so that they can be changed easily in one place.

DON'T use your own constants or values for maximum and minimum value checks. Use the ANSI/ISO defined functions and constants.

Summary

Today you learned about some of the things you need to keep in mind when writing your programs. You learned that there is often a good chance that your programs will be used by others, despite what you think when first writing them. You also learned the importance of planning to maintain your programs early in the development cycle. Finally, you learned some things to do to make your programs easily portable to other platforms. Keep in mind the three rules of code reuse:

- ☐ Remember code reuse.
- ☐ Remember code maintenance.
- ☐ Remember code portability.

Q&A

Q How do you write portable graphics programs?

A Because graphics programs are inherently machine dependent, it is difficult to make them portable. The ANSI/ISO draft standard does not define graphics programming standards as such. However, you can at least use the ANSI/ISO libraries for determining maximum, minimum, and precision values that you use in virtually any graphics program.

Q Should I always be concerned about all the subjects of this lesson?

A Yes and no. You should always be concerned about code maintenance because you will undoubtedly want to implement the same algorithms again. You should always be somewhat concerned about code reuse for the same reason. Portability is only a concern if there is a chance that your program needs to be ported to another platform. Be careful how you decide. Often, the programs you expect to have a short lifespan end up as a thorn in your side if you do not plan properly.

Q Are all C++ compilers ANSI/ISO compliant?

A Some might say that the idea of a standard would imply that if it is not standard-compliant, it is not C++. Realistically, however, compiler vendors could have some special circumstance for their inability to implement some feature documented in the standard. It's best to determine which standards are most important to you and shop the compilers with that criteria in hand.

Quiz

1. What is the most portable way to determine the maximum value that can be held in an `int` value?

2. Why should you avoid literal constants even for values that will never change?

3. What are some methods you might use to separate words in multiword variable names?

4. What advantage is there to setting your tab settings to enter spaces instead of tab characters?

5. Why is indentation important?

Exercises

1. Create variable names using Hungarian notation for each of the following:

   a. A pointer to an integer array.

   b. An integer.

   c. A zero-terminated string.

2. Write a `#define` directive that expands to uniquely identify the source file in which it is used.

3. Place the `#define` directive from exercise 2 inside an include file, and then rewrite the program in Listing 18.3 to print the identifier string you defined.

4. How might you best comment a function that performs a complex mathematical computation?

   a. Comment what it does.

   b. Comment how it does it.

   c. Write the formula in the comments.

   d. All of the above.

5. What should be the maximum number of tasks that any one function performs?

Day 19

Templates

On Day 17 you saw how to use macros to create various lists using the concatenation operator.

Today you will learn

- [ ] What templates are and how to use them.
- [ ] Why templates are a better alternative to macros.
- [ ] How to create class templates.
- [ ] How to create function templates.

What are Templates?

At the end of Week 2 you saw how to build a `PartsList` object and how to use that to create a `PartsCatalog`. If you want to build on the `PartsList` object to make a list of cats, you have a problem: `PartsList` only knows about parts.

To solve this problem, you can create a list base class and derive from it the `PartsList` and `CatsList` classes. You can then cut and paste much of the

PartsList class into the new CatsList declaration. Next week, when you want to make a list of Car objects, you will have to make a new class and again cut and paste.

Needless to say, this is not a satisfactory solution. Over time, the class and its derived classes have to be extended. Making sure that all the changes are propagated to all the related classes would be a nightmare.

On Day 17 one approach to parameterizing lists was briefly demonstrated—using macros and name concatenation. Although macros do save much of the cutting and pasting, they have one major disadvantage: Like everything else in the preprocessor, they are not type-safe.

Templates offer the preferred method of creating parameterized lists in C++. They are an integrated part of the language, they are type-safe, and they are very flexible.

Parameterized Types

Templates enable you to teach the compiler how to make a list of any type of thing, rather than creating a set of type-specific lists. A PartsList is a list of parts; a CatList is a list of cats. The only way in which they differ is the type of the thing on the list. With templates, the type of the thing on the list becomes a parameter to the definition of the class.

A common component of virtually all C++ libraries is an array class. As you saw with Lists, it is tedious and inefficient to create one array class for integers, another for doubles, and yet another for an array of Animals. Templates let you declare a parameterized array class, and then specify what type of object each *instance* of the array holds.

 The act of creating a specific type from a template is called *instantiation*, and the individual classes are called instances of the template.

 Parameterized templates provide you with the ability to create a general class and pass types as *parameters* to that class in order to build specific instances.

Template Definition

You declare a parameterized array object (a template for an array) by writing

```
1: template <class T>    // declare the template and the parameter
2: class Array           // the class being parameterized
3: {
4:     public:
5:         Array();
6:     // full class declaration here
7: };
```

The keyword template is used at the beginning of every declaration and definition of a template class. The parameters of the template are after the keyword template. The parameters are the things that change with each instance. For example, in the array template shown previously, the type of the objects stored in the array changes. One instance might store an array of integers, while another might store an array of Animals.

In this example, the keyword class is used, followed by the identifier T. The keyword class indicates that this parameter is a *type*. The identifier T is used throughout the rest of the template definition to refer to the parameterized type. One instance of this class substitutes int everywhere T appears, and another substitutes Cat.

To declare an int and a Cat instance of the parameterized array class, you would write

```
Array<int> anIntArray;
Array<Cat> aCatArray;
```

The object anIntArray is of the type *array of integers*; the object aCatArray is of the type *array of Cats*. You can now use the type Array<int> anywhere you would normally use a type—as the return value from a function, as a parameter to a function, and so forth. Listing 19.1 provides the full declaration of this stripped-down array template.

NOTE

Listing 19.1 is not a complete program!

TYPE **Listing 19.1. A template of an array class.**

```
1:      //Listing 19.1 A template of an array class
2:      #include <iostream.h>
3:      const int DefaultSize = 10;
4:
5:      template <class T>  // declare the template and the parameter
6:      class Array               // the class being parameterized
7:      {
8:      public:
9:          // constructors
10:         Array(int size = DefaultSize);
11:         Array(const Array &rhs);
12:         ~Array() { delete [] pType; }
13:
14:         // operators
15:         Array& operator=(const Array&);
16:         T& operator[](int offSet) { return pType[offSet]; }
17:
18:         // accessors
19:         int getSize() { return itsSize; }
20:
21:     private:
22:         T *pType;
23:         int  itsSize;
24:     };
```

19

OUTPUT There is no output. This is an incomplete program.

ANALYSIS The definition of the template begins on line 5 with the keyword `template` followed by the parameter. In this case, the parameter is identified to be a type by the keyword `class`, and the identifier `T` is used to represent the parameterized type.

From line 6 until the end of the template on line 24, the rest of the declaration is like any other class declaration. The only difference is that wherever the type of the object would normally appear, the identifier `T` is used instead. For example, `operator[]` is expected to return a reference to an object in the array, and in fact it is declared to return a reference to an object of type `T`.

When an instance of an integer array is declared, the `operator=` that is provided to that array returns a reference to an integer. When an instance of an `Animal` array is declared, the `operator=` provided to the `Animal` array returns a reference to an `Animal`.

Using the Name

Within the class declaration, the word `Array` can be used without further qualification. Elsewhere in the program, this class is referred to as `Array<T>`. For example, if you do not write the constructor within the class declaration, you must write

```
template <class T>
Array<T>::Array(int size):
itsSize = size
{
pType = new T[size];
for (int i = 0; i<size; i++)
pType[i] = 0;
}
```

The declaration on the first line of this code fragment is required to identify the type (`class` `T`). The template name is `Array<T>` and the function name is `Array(int size)`.

The remainder of the function is exactly the same as it would be for a nontemplate function. It is a common and preferred method to get the class and its functions working as a simple declaration before turning it into a template.

Implementing the Template

The full implementation of the template class array requires implementation of the copy constructor, `operator=`, and so forth. Listing 19.2 provides a simple driver program to exercise this template class.

NOTE

Some older compilers do not support templates. Templates are, however, part of the emerging C++ standard. All major compiler vendors have committed to supporting templates in their next release, if they have not already done so. If you have an older compiler, you won't be able to compile and run the exercises in this lesson. It's still a good idea to read through the entire lesson, however, and return to this material when you upgrade your compiler.

TYPE **Listing 19.2. The implementation of the template array.**

```
1:      #include <iostream.h>
2:
3:      const int DefaultSize = 10;
4:
5:      // declare a simple Animal class so that we can
6:      // create an array of animals
7:
8:      class Animal
9:      {
10:     public:
11:         Animal(int);
12:         Animal();
13:         ~Animal() {}
14:         int GetWeight() const { return itsWeight; }
15:         void Display() const { cout << itsWeight; }
16:     private:
17:         int itsWeight;
18:     };
19:
20:     Animal::Animal(int weight):
21:     itsWeight(weight)
22:     {}
23:
24:     Animal::Animal():
25:     itsWeight(0)
26:     {}
27:
28:
29:     template <class T>   // declare the template and the parameter
30:     class Array               // the class being parameterized
31:     {
32:     public:
33:         // constructors
34:         Array(int itsSize = DefaultSize);
35:         Array(const Array &rhs);
36:         ~Array() { delete [] pType; }
37:
```

continues

Listing 19.2. continued

```
38:         // operators
39:         Array& operator=(const Array&);
40:         T& operator[](int offSet) { return pType[offSet]; }
41:         const T& operator[](int offSet) const { return pType[offSet]; }
42:
43:         // accessors
44:         int GetSize() const { return itsSize; }
45:
46:     private:
47:         T *pType;
48:         int  itsSize;
49:     };
50:
51:     // implementations follow...
52:
53:     // implement the Constructor
54:     template <class T>
55:     Array<T>::Array(int size = DefaultSize):
56:     itsSize(size)
57:     {
58:         pType = new T[size];
59:         for (int i = 0; i<size; i++)
60:             pType[i] = 0;
61:     }
62:
63:     // copy constructor
64:     template <class T>
65:     Array<T>::Array(const Array &rhs)
66:     {
67:         itsSize = rhs.GetSize();
68:         pType = new T[itsSize];
69:         for (int i = 0; i<itsSize; i++)
70:             pType[i] = rhs[i];
71:     }
72:
73:     // operator=
74:     template <class T>
75:     Array<T>& Array<T>::operator=(const Array &rhs)
76:     {
77:         if (this == &rhs)
78:             return *this;
79:         delete [] pType;
80:         itsSize = rhs.GetSize();
81:         pType = new T[itsSize];
82:         for (int i = 0; i<itsSize; i++)
83:             pType[i] = rhs[i];
84:         return *this;
85:     }
86:
87:     // driver program
88:     void main()
89:     {
90:         Array<int> theArray;        // an array of integers
91:         Array<Animal> theZoo;       // an array of Animals
92:         Animal *pAnimal;
```

19

```
93:
94:        // fill the arrays
95:        for (int i = 0; i < theArray.GetSize(); i++)
96:        {
97:           theArray[i] = i*2;
98:           pAnimal = new Animal(i*3);
99:           theZoo[i] = *pAnimal;
100:       }
101:
102:       // print the contents of the arrays
103:       for (int j = 0; j < theArray.GetSize(); j++)
104:       {
105:          cout << "theArray[" << j << "]:\t" << theArray[j] << "\t\t";
106:          cout << "theZoo[" << j << "]:\t";
107:          theZoo[j].Display();
108:          cout << endl;
109:       }
110:
111:       // return the allocated memory before the arrays are destroyed.
112:       for (int k = 0; k < theArray.GetSize(); k++)
113:          delete &theZoo[k];
114:    }
```

OUTPUT

```
theArray[0]:     0        theZoo[0]:     0
theArray[1]:     2        theZoo[1]:     3
theArray[2]:     4        theZoo[2]:     6
theArray[3]:     6        theZoo[3]:     9
theArray[4]:     8        theZoo[4]:     12
theArray[5]:     10       theZoo[5]:     15
theArray[6]:     12       theZoo[6]:     18
theArray[7]:     14       theZoo[7]:     21
theArray[8]:     16       theZoo[8]:     24
theArray[9]:     18       theZoo[9]:     27
```

ANALYSIS Lines 8 through 26 provide a stripped-down Animal class, created here so that there are objects of a user-defined type to add to the array.

Line 29 declares that what follows is a template, and that the parameter to the template is a type designated as T. The Array class has two constructors as shown, the first of which takes a size and defaults to the constant integer DefaultSize.

The assignment and offset operators are declared, with the latter declaring both a const and a non-const variant. The only accessor provided is GetSize(), which returns the size of the array.

One can certainly imagine a fuller interface, and for any serious Array program, what has been supplied here would be inadequate. At a minimum, operators to remove elements, to expand the array, to pack the array, and so forth, are required.

The private data consists of the size of the array and a pointer to the actual in-memory array of objects.

19

Template Functions

If you want to pass an array object to a function, you must pass a particular *instance* of the array, and not a template. In other words, if SomeFunction() takes an integer array as a parameter, you can write the following:

```
void SomeFunction(Array<int>&);     // ok
```

But you cannot write

```
void SomeFunction(Array<T>&);     // error!
```

because there is no way to know what a T& is. You also cannot write

```
void SomeFunction(Array &);       // error!
```

because there is no class Array, only the template and the instances.

The more general, and preferred, approach is to declare a function template.

```
template <class T>
void MyTemplateFunction(Array<T>&);     // ok
```

Here the function MyTemplateFunction() is declared to be a template function by the declaration on the top line. Note that template functions can have any name, just as other functions can.

Template functions can also take instances of the template, in addition to the parameterized form. The following is an example:

```
template <class T>
void MyOtherFunction(Array<T>&, Array<int>&);     // ok
```

Note that this function takes two arrays: a parameterized Array and an Array of integers. The former can be an array of any object, but the latter is always an array of integers.

Templates and Friends

Template classes can declare three types of friends:

1. A nontemplate friend class or function.
2. A general template friend class or function.
3. A type-specific template friend class or function.

Nontemplate Friend Classes and Functions

It is possible to declare any class or function to be a friend to your template class. Each instance of the class treats the friend properly, as if the declaration of friendship had been made in that particular instance. Listing 19.3 adds a trivial friend function, Intrude(), to the template definition of the Array class, and the driver program invokes Intrude(). Because it is a friend, Intrude() can then access the private data of the Array. Because this is not a template function, it can only be called on Arrays of int.

NOTE

> To compile the program in Listing 19.3, copy lines 1 through 26 of Listing 19.2 and insert them after line 1 where indicated by the comment. Also copy lines 51 through 86 of Listing 19.2 and insert them after line 37 where indicated by the comment.

TYPE **Listing 19.3. A nontemplate friend function.**

```
1:    // Listing 19.3 - Type specific friend functions in templates
2:    // >> Insert lines 1-26 of Listing 19.2 here.
3:    template <class T>  // declare the template and the parameter
4:    class Array          // the class being parameterized
5:    {
6:    public:
7:        // constructors
8:        Array(int itsSize = DefaultSize);
9:        Array(const Array &rhs);
10:       ~Array() { delete [] pType; }
11:
12:       // operators
13:       Array& operator=(const Array&);
14:       T& operator[](int offSet) { return pType[offSet]; }
15:       const T& operator[](int offSet) const { return pType[offSet]; }
16:
17:       // accessors
18:       int GetSize() const { return itsSize; }
19:
20:       // friend function
21:       friend void Intrude(Array<int>);
22:
23:    private:
24:        T *pType;
25:        int  itsSize;
26:    };
27:
```

continues

Listing 19.3. continued

```
28:          // friend function. Not a template, can only be used
29:          // with int arrays! Intrudes into private data.
30:          void Intrude(Array<int> theArray)
31:          {
32:           cout << "\n*** Intrude ***\n";
33:           for (int i = 0; i < theArray.itsSize; i++)
34:              cout << "i: " <<    theArray.pType[i] << endl;
35:           cout << "\n";
36:          }
37:      // >> Insert lines 51-86 of Listing 19.2 here.
38:      // driver program
39:      int main()
40:      {
41:          Array<int> theArray;        // an array of integers
42:          Array<Animal> theZoo;       // an array of Animals
43:          Animal *pAnimal;
44:
45:          // fill the arrays
46:          for (int i = 0; i < theArray.GetSize(); i++)
47:          {
48:             theArray[i] = i*2;
49:             pAnimal = new Animal(i*3);
50:             theZoo[i] = *pAnimal;
51:          }
52:
53:          // print the contents of the arrays
54:          for (int j = 0; j < theArray.GetSize(); j++)
55:          {
56:             cout << "theZoo[" << j << "]:\t";
57:             theZoo[j].Display();
58:             cout << endl;
59:          }
60:          cout << "Now use the friend function to find"
61:              << " members of Array<int>";
62:           Intrude(theArray);
63:          // return the allocated memory before the arrays are destroyed.
64:          for (int k = 0; k < theArray.GetSize(); k++)
65:             delete &theZoo[j];
66:
67:          cout << "\n\nDone.\n";
68:          return 0;
69:       }
```

```
theZoo[0]:        0
theZoo[1]:        3
theZoo[2]:        6
theZoo[3]:        9
theZoo[4]:        12
theZoo[5]:        15
theZoo[6]:        18
theZoo[7]:        21
theZoo[8]:        24
theZoo[9]:        27
```

Now use the friend function to find the members of Array<int>.

```
*** Intrude ***
i: 0
i: 2
i: 4
i: 6
i: 8
i: 10
i: 12
i: 14
i: 16
i: 18
```

ANALYSIS The declaration of the array template has been extended to include the friend function Intrude(). This declares that every instance of an array considers Intrude() to be a friend function. Intrude() has access to the private member data and functions of the array instance.

On line 33 Intrude() accesses itsSize directly, and on line 34 it accesses pType directly. The trivial use of these members was unnecessary because the array class provides public accessors for this data, but it serves to demonstrate how friend functions can be declared with templates.

General Template Friend Class or Function

It would be helpful to add a display operator to the Array class. One approach would be to declare a display operator for each possible type of Array, but this undermines the whole point of having made Array a template.

What is needed is an insertion operator that works for any possible type of Array.

```
ostream& operator<< (ostream& Array<T>&);
```

To make this work, you need to declare operator<< to be a template function.

```
template <class T> ostream& operator<< (ostream&, Array<T>&)
```

Now that operator<< is a template function, you only need to provide an implementation. Listing 19.4 shows the Array template extended to include this declaration and provides the implementation for the operator<<.

NOTE To compile Listing 19.4, copy lines 51 through 86 of Listing 19.2 and insert them after line 36 where indicated by the comment.

TYPE **Listing 19.4. Implementing an** ostream **operator.**

```
1:      #include <iostream.h>
2:
3:      const int DefaultSize = 10;
4:
5:      template <class T>  // declare the template and the parameter
6:      class Array              // the class being parameterized
7:      {
8:      public:
9:          // constructors
10:         Array(int itsSize = DefaultSize);
11:         Array(const Array &rhs);
12:         ~Array() { delete [] pType; }
13:
14:         // operators
15:         Array& operator=(const Array&);
16:         T& operator[](int offSet) { return pType[offSet]; }
17:         const T& operator[](int offSet) const { return pType[offSet]; }
18:
19:         // accessors
20:         int GetSize() const { return itsSize; }
21:
22:        template <class T> friend ostream& operator<< (ostream&, Array<T>&);
23:
24:     private:
25:         T *pType;
26:         int  itsSize;
27:     };
28:
29:     template <class T>
30:     ostream& operator<< (ostream& output, Array<T>& theArray)
31:     {
32:         for (int i = 0; i<theArray.GetSize(); i++)
33:             output << "[" << i << "] " << theArray[i] << endl;
34:     }
35:
36:     // >> Insert lines 51-86 of Listing 19.2 here.
37:     void main()
38:     {
39:         bool Stop = FALSE;        // flag for looping
40:         int offset, value;
41:         Array<int> theArray;
42:
43:         while (!Stop)
44:         {
45:             cout << "Enter an offset (0-9) and a value. (-1 to stop): " ;
46:             cin >> offset >> value;
47:
48:             if (offset < 0)
49:                 break;
50:
51:             if (offset > 9)
52:             {
53:                 cout << "***Please use values between 0 and 9.***\n";
54:                 continue;
```

```
55:            }
56:
57:            theArray[offset] = value;
58:        }
59:
60:        cout << "\nHere's the entire array:\n";
61:        cout << theArray << endl;
62:    }
```

```
Enter an offset (0-9) and a value. (-1 to stop): 1 10
Enter an offset (0-9) and a value. (-1 to stop): 2 20
Enter an offset (0-9) and a value. (-1 to stop): 3 30
Enter an offset (0-9) and a value. (-1 to stop): 4 40
Enter an offset (0-9) and a value. (-1 to stop): 5 50
Enter an offset (0-9) and a value. (-1 to stop): 6 60
Enter an offset (0-9) and a value. (-1 to stop): 7 70
Enter an offset (0-9) and a value. (-1 to stop): 8 80
Enter an offset (0-9) and a value. (-1 to stop): 9 90
Enter an offset (0-9) and a value. (-1 to stop): 10 10
***Please use values between 0 and 9. ***
Enter an offset (0-9) and a value. (-1 to stop): -1 -1

Here's the entire array:
 [0] 0
 [1] 10
 [2] 20
 [3] 30
 [4] 40
 [5] 50
 [6] G0
 [7] 70
 [8] 80
 [9] 90
```

ANALYSIS On line 22 the function template operator<<() is declared to be a friend of the Array class template. Because operator<<() is implemented as a template function, every instance of this parameterized array type automatically has an operator<<(). The implementation for this operator starts on line 29. Every member of an array is called in turn. This only works if there is an operator<< defined for every type of object stored in the array.

A Type-Specific Template Friend Class or Function

Although the insertion operator shown in Listing 19.4 works, it is still not quite what is needed. Because the declaration of the friend operator on line 22 declares a template, it works for any instance of Array and any insertion operator taking an array of any type.

The insertion operator template shown in Listing 19.4 makes all instances of the insertion operator<< a friend of any instance of Array, whether the instance of the insertion operator is an integer, an Animal, or a Car. It makes no sense, however, for an Animal insertion operator to be a friend to the insertion operator for an integer Array.

The insertion operator for an Array of int needs to be a friend to the Array of int class. The insertion operator of an Array of Animals needs to be a friend to the Array of Animals instance.

To accomplish this, modify the declaration of the insertion operator on line 22 of Listing 19.4, and remove the words template <class T>. That is, change line 22 to read as follows:

```
friend ostream& operator<< (ostream&, Array<T>&);
```

This uses the type (T) declared in the template of Array, meaning that the operator<< for an integer only works with an array of integers.

Using Template Items

You can treat template items as you would any other type. You can pass them as parameters, either by reference or by value, and you can return them as the return values of functions, also by value or by reference. Listing 19.5 demonstrates how to pass template objects.

TYPE

Listing 19.5. Passing template objects to and from functions.

```
1:     #include <iostream.h>
2:
3:     const int DefaultSize = 10;
4:
5:     // A trivial class for adding to arrays
6:     class Animal
7:     {
8:     public:
9:     // constructors
10:         Animal(int);
11:         Animal();
12:         ~Animal();
13:
14:         // accessors
15:         int GetWeight() const { return itsWeight; }
16:         void SetWeight(int theWeight) { itsWeight = theWeight; }
17:
18:          // friend operators
19:         friend ostream& operator<< (ostream&, const Animal&);
20:
21:     private:
22:         int itsWeight;
23:     };
24:
25:     // extraction operator for printing animals
26:     ostream& operator<< (ostream& theStream, const Animal& theAnimal)
27:     {
28:     theStream << theAnimal.GetWeight();
29:     return theStream;
30:     }
```

19

```
31:
32:    Animal::Animal(int weight):
33:    itsWeight(weight)
34:    {
35:        // cout << "Animal(int)\n";
36:    }
37:
38:    Animal::Animal():
39:    itsWeight(0)
40:    {
41:        // cout << "Animal()\n";
42:    }
43:
44:    Animal::~Animal()
45:    {
46:        // cout << "Destroyed an animal...\n";
47:    }
48:
49:    template <class T>  // declare the template and the parameter
50:    class Array            // the class being parameterized
51:    {
52:    public:
53:        Array(int itsSize = DefaultSize);
54:        Array(const Array &rhs);
55:        ~Array() { delete [] pType; }
56:
57:        Array& operator=(const Array&);
58:        T& operator[](int offSet) { return pType[offSet]; }
59:        const T& operator[](int offSet) const { return pType[offSet]; }
60:        int GetSize() const { return itsSize; }
61:
62:        // friend function
63:      friend ostream& operator<< (ostream&, const Array<T>&);
64:
65:    private:
66:        T *pType;
67:        int  itsSize;
68:    };
69:
70:    template <class T>
71:    ostream& operator<< (ostream& output, const Array<T>& theArray)
72:    {
73:        for (int i = 0; i<theArray.GetSize(); i++)
74:            output << "[" << i << "] " << theArray[i] << endl;
75:        return output;
76:    }
77:
78:    void IntFillFunction(Array<int>& theArray);
79:    void AnimalFillFunction(Array<Animal>& theArray);
80:
81:
82:    void main()
83:    {
84:        Array<int> intArray;
85:        Array<Animal> animalArray;
```

continues

19

Listing 19.5. continued

```
86:          IntFillFunction(intArray);
87:          AnimalFillFunction(animalArray);
88:          cout << "intArray...\n" << intArray;
89:          cout << "\nanimalArray...\n" << animalArray << endl;
90:      }
91:
92:      void IntFillFunction(Array<int>& theArray)
93:      {
94:          bool Stop = false;
95:          int offset, value;
96:          while (!Stop)
97:          {
98:              cout << "Enter an offset (0-9) and a value. (-1 to stop): " ;
99:              cin >> offset >> value;
100:             if (offset < 0)
101:                 break;
102:             if (offset > 9)
103:             {
104:                 cout << "***Please use values between 0 and 9.***\n";
105:                 continue;
106:             }
107:             theArray[offset] = value;
108:         }
109:     }
110:
111:
112:     void AnimalFillFunction(Array<Animal>& theArray)
113:     {
114:         Animal * pAnimal;
115:         for (int i = 0; i<theArray.GetSize(); i++)
116:         {
117:             pAnimal = new Animal;
118:             pAnimal->SetWeight(i*100);
119:             theArray[i] = *pAnimal;
120:             delete pAnimal;  // a copy was put in the array
121:         }
122:     }
```

OUTPUT
```
Enter an offset (0-9) and a value. (-1 to stop): 1 10
Enter an offset (0-9) and a value. (-1 to stop): 2 20
Enter an offset (0-9) and a value. (-1 to stop): 3 30
Enter an offset (0-9) and a value. (-1 to stop): 4 40
Enter an offset (0-9) and a value. (-1 to stop): 5 50
Enter an offset (0-9) and a value. (-1 to stop): 6 60
Enter an offset (0-9) and a value. (-1 to stop): 7 70
Enter an offset (0-9) and a value. (-1 to stop): 8 80
Enter an offset (0-9) and a value. (-1 to stop): 9 90
Enter an offset (0-9) and a value. (-1 to stop): 10 10
***Please use values between 0 and 9. ***
Enter an offset (0-9) and a value. (-1 to stop): -1 -1
```

```
intArray:...
 [0] 0
 [1] 10
 [2] 20
 [3] 30
 [4] 40
 [5] 50
 [6] 60
 [7] 70
 [8] 80
 [9] 90

animalArray:...
 [0] 0
 [1] 100
 [2] 200
 [3] 300
 [4] 400
 [5] 500
 [6] 600
 [7] 700
 [8] 800
 [9] 900
```

ANALYSIS Most of the Array class implementation is left out to save space. The Animal class is declared on lines 6 through 23. Although this is a stripped-down and simplified class, it does provide its own insertion operator (<<) to enable the printing of Animals. Printing simply prints the current weight of the Animal.

Note that Animal has a default constructor. This is necessary because when you add an object to an array, the object's default constructor is used to create the object. This creates some difficulties, as you'll see.

On line 78 the function IntFillFunction() is declared. The prototype indicates that this function takes an integer array. Note that this is not a template function. IntFillFunction() expects only one type of an array—an integer array. Similarly, on line 79 AnimalFillFunction() is declared to take an Array of Animal.

The implementations for these functions are different from one another because filling an array of integers does not have to be accomplished in the same way as filling an array of Animals.

Specialized Functions

If you uncomment the print statements in Animal's constructors and destructor in Listing 19.5, you'll find that there are unanticipated extra constructions and destructions of Animals.

When an object is added to an array, the object's default constructor is called. The Array constructor, however, goes on to assign 0 to the value of each member of the array, as shown on lines 59 and 60 of Listing 19.2.

When you write someAnimal = (Animal) 0; you call the default operator= for Animal. This causes a temporary Animal object to be created, using the constructor, which takes an integer (zero). That temporary is used as the right side of the equals (=) operator and is then destroyed.

This is an unfortunate waste of time because the Animal object was already properly initialized. Unfortunately, you can't remove this line because integers are not automatically initialized to value 0. The solution is to teach the template not to use this constructor for Animals, and to use a special Animal constructor instead.

You can provide an explicit implementation for the Animal class, as indicated in Listing 19.6.

TYPE **Listing 19.6. Specializing template implementations.**

```
1:     #include <iostream.h>
2:
3:     const int DefaultSize = 3;
4:
5:     // A trivial class for adding to arrays
6:       class Animal
7:       {
8:       public:
9:           // constructors
10:          Animal(int);
11:          Animal();
12:          ~Animal();
13:
14:          // accessors
15:          int GetWeight() const { return itsWeight; }
16:          void SetWeight(int theWeight) { itsWeight = theWeight; }
17:
18:          // friend operators
19:          friend ostream& operator<< (ostream&, const Animal&);
20:
21:      private:
22:          int itsWeight;
23:      };
24:
25:       // extraction operator for printing animals
26:      ostream& operator<< (ostream& theStream, const Animal& theAnimal)
27:      {
28:        theStream << theAnimal.GetWeight();
29:        return theStream;
30:      }
31:
32:      Animal::Animal(int weight):
33:      itsWeight(weight)
34:      {
35:         cout << "animal(int) ";
36:      }
37:
38:      Animal::Animal():
39:      itsWeight(0)
```

```
40:     {
41:        cout << "animal() ";
42:     }
43:
44:     Animal::~Animal()
45:     {
46:       cout << "Destroyed an animal...";
47:     }
48:
49:  template <class T>  // declare the template and the parameter
50:  class Array              // the class being parameterized
51:  {
52:  public:
53:      // constructors
54:      Array(int itsSize = DefaultSize);
55:      Array(const Array &rhs);
56:      ~Array() { delete [] pType; }
57:
58:      // operators
59:      Array& operator=(const Array&);
60:      T& operator[](int offSet) { return pType[offSet]; }
61:      const T& operator[](int offSet) const { return pType[offSet]; }
62:
63:      // accessors
64:      int GetSize() const { return itsSize; }
65:
66:      // friend function
67:     friend ostream& operator<< (ostream&, const Array<T>&);
68:
69:  private:
70:      T *pType;
71:      int  itsSize;
72:  };
73:
74:  template <class T>
75:  Array<T>::Array(int size = DefaultSize):
76:  itsSize(size)
77:  {
78:      pType = new T[size];
79:      for (int i = 0; i<size; i++)
80:        pType[i] = (T)0;
81:  }
82:
83:  template <class T>
84:  Array<T>& Array<T>::operator=(const Array &rhs)
85:  {
86:      if (this == &rhs)
87:         return *this;
88:      delete [] pType;
89:      itsSize = rhs.GetSize();
90:      pType = new T[itsSize];
91:      for (int i = 0; i<itsSize; i++)
92:         pType[i] = rhs[i];
93:  }
94:
```

continues

Listing 19.6. continued

```
95:     template <class T>
96:     Array<T>::Array(const Array &rhs)
97:     {
98:         itsSize = rhs.GetSize();
99:         pType = new T[itsSize];
100:        for (int i = 0; i<itsSize; i++)
101:            pType[i] = rhs[i];
102:    }
103:
104:
105:    template <class T>
106:    ostream& operator<< (ostream& output, const Array<T>& theArray)
107:    {
108:        for (int i = 0; i<theArray.GetSize(); i++)
109:            output << "[" << i << "] " << theArray[i] << endl;
110:        return output;
111:    }
112:
113:
114:    Array<Animal>::Array(int AnimalArraySize):
115:    itsSize(AnimalArraySize)
116:    {
117:        pType = new T[AnimalArraySize];
118:    }
119:
120:
121:    void IntFillFunction(Array<int>& theArray);
122:    void AnimalFillFunction(Array<Animal>& theArray);
123:
124:
125:    void main()
126:    {
127:        Array<int> intArray;
128:        Array<Animal> animalArray;
129:        IntFillFunction(intArray);
130:        AnimalFillFunction(animalArray);
131:        cout << "intArray...\n" << intArray;
132:        cout << "\nanimalArray...\n" << animalArray << endl;
133:    }
134:
135:    void IntFillFunction(Array<int>& theArray)
136:    {
137:        bool Stop = false;
138:        int offset, value;
139:        while (!Stop)
140:        {
141:            cout << "Enter an offset (0-9) and a value. (-1 to stop): " ;
142:            cin >> offset >> value;
143:            if (offset < 0)
144:                break;
145:            if (offset > 9)
146:            {
147:                cout << "***Please use values between 0 and 9.***\n";
148:                continue;
```

```
149:            }
150:            theArray[offset] = value;
151:        }
152:    }
153:
154:
155:    void AnimalFillFunction(Array<Animal>& theArray)
156:    {
157:        Animal * pAnimal;
158:        for (int i = 0; i<theArray.GetSize(); i++)
159:        {
160:            pAnimal = new Animal(i*10);
161:            theArray[i] = *pAnimal;
162:            delete pAnimal;
163:        }
164:    }
```

NOTE

Line numbers have been added to the output to make analysis easier. Line numbers will not appear in your output.

OUTPUT

```
1:  animal() animal() animal()
2:  Enter an offset (0-9) and a value. (-1 to stop): 0 0
3:  Enter an offset (0-9) and a value. (-1 to stop): 1 1
4:  Enter an offset (0-9) and a value. (-1 to stop): 2 2
5:  Enter an offset (0-9) and a value. (-1 to stop): 3 3
6:  animal(int)
7:  Destroyed an animal...
8:  animal(int)
9:  Destroyed an animal...
10: animal(int)
11: Destroyed an animal...
12: initArray...
13: [0] 0
14: [1] 1
15: [2] 2
16:
17: animal array...
18: [0] 0
19: [1] 10
20: [2] 20
21:
22: Destroyed an animal...
23: Destroyed an animal...
24: Destroyed an animal...
25:
<<< Second run >>>

26: animal() animal() animal()
27: animal(int)  Destroyed an animal...
28: animal(int)  Destroyed an animal...
29: animal(int)  Destroyed an animal...
```

19

```
30: Enter an offset (0-9) and a value. (-1 to stop): 0 0
31: Enter an offset (0-9) and a value. (-1 to stop): 1 1
32: Enter an offset (0-9) and a value. (-1 to stop): 2 2
33: Enter an offset (0-9) and a value. (-1 to stop): 3 3
34: animal(int)
35: Destroyed an animal...
36: animal(int)
37: Destroyed an animal...
38: animal(int)
39: Destroyed an animal...
40: initArray...
41: [0] 0
42: [1] 1
43: [2] 2
44:
45: animal array...
46: [0] 0
47: [1] 10
48: [2] 20
49:
50: Destroyed an animal...
51: Destroyed an animal...
52: Destroyed an animal...
```

ANALYSIS   Listing 19.6 reproduces both classes in their entirety so that you can see the creation and destruction of temporary `Animal` objects. The value of `DefaultSize` has been reduced to 3 to simplify the output.

The `Animal` constructors and destructors on lines 32 through 47 each print a statement indicating when they are called.

On lines 77 through 81, the template behavior of an `Array` constructor is declared. On lines 114 through 118, the specialized constructor for an `Array` of `Animals` is demonstrated. Note that in this special constructor, the default constructor is allowed to set the initial value for each animal, and no explicit assignment is made.

The first time that this program is run, the first set of output is shown. Line 1 of the output shows the three default constructors called by creating the array. The user enters four numbers, and these are placed in the integer array.

Execution jumps to `AnimalFillFunction()`. Here a temporary animal is created on the heap on line 160, and its value is used to modify the `Animal` object in the array on line 161. On line 162 the temporary `Animal` is destroyed. This is repeated for each member of the array and is reflected in the output on lines 6 through 11.

At the end of the program, the arrays are destroyed. When their destructors are called, all their objects are destroyed as well. This is reflected in the output on lines 22 through 24.

For the second set of output (lines 26 through 52), the special implementation of the array of character constructor, shown on lines 114 through 118 of the program, is commented out.

When the program is run again, the template constructor (shown on lines 74 through 81 of the program) is run when the Animal array is constructed.

This causes temporary Animal objects to be called for each member of the array on lines 79 and 80 of the program, and is reflected in the output on lines 26 to 29 of the output.

In all other respects the output for the two runs is identical, as you would expect.

Static Members and Templates

A template can declare static data members. Each instantiation of the template then has its own set of static data, one per class type. That is, if you add a static member to the Array class (for example, a counter of how many arrays have been created) you have one such member per type: one for all the arrays of Animals, and another for all the arrays of integers. Listing 19.7 adds a static member and a static function to the Array class.

TYPE

Listing 19.7. Using static member data and functions with templates.

```
1:     #include <iostream.h>
2:
3:     template <class T>  // declare the template and the parameter
4:     class Array           // the class being parameterized
5:     {
6:     public:
7:         // constructors
8:         Array(int itsSize = DefaultSize);
9:         Array(const Array &rhs);
10:        ~Array() { delete [] pType;   itsNumberArrays--; }
11:
12:        // operators
13:        Array& operator=(const Array&);
14:        T& operator[](int offSet) { return pType[offSet]; }
15:        const T& operator[](int offSet) const { return pType[offSet]; }
16:
17:        // accessors
18:        int GetSize() const { return itsSize; }
19:        static int GetNumberArrays() { return itsNumberArrays; }
20:
21:        // friend function
22:      friend ostream& operator<< (ostream&, const Array<T>&);
23:
24:     private:
25:         T *pType;
26:         int  itsSize;
27:         static int itsNumberArrays;
28:     };
29:
```

continues

Listing 19.7. continued

```
30:    template <class T>
31:       int Array<T>::itsNumberArrays = 0;
32:
33:    template <class T>
34:    Array<T>::Array(int size = DefaultSize):
35:    itsSize(size)
36:    {
37:       pType = new T[size];
38:       for (int i = 0; i<size; i++)
39:         pType[i] = (T)0;
40:       itsNumberArrays++;
41:    }
42:
43:    template <class T>
44:    Array<T>& Array<T>::operator=(const Array &rhs)
45:    {
46:       if (this == &rhs)
47:          return *this;
48:       delete [] pType;
49:       itsSize = rhs.GetSize();
50:       pType = new T[itsSize];
51:       for (int i = 0; i<itsSize; i++)
52:          pType[i] = rhs[i];
53:    }
54:
55:    template <class T>
56:    Array<T>::Array(const Array &rhs)
57:    {
58:       itsSize = rhs.GetSize();
59:       pType = new T[itsSize];
60:       for (int i = 0; i<itsSize; i++)
61:          pType[i] = rhs[i];
62:       itsNumberArrays++;
63:    }
64:
65:
66:    template <class T>
67:    ostream& operator<< (ostream& output, const Array<T>& theArray)
68:    {
69:       for (int i = 0; i<theArray.GetSize(); i++)
70:          output << "[" << i << "] " << theArray[i] << endl;
71:       return output;
72:    }
73:
74:
75:    Array<Animal>::Array(int AnimalArraySize):
76:    itsSize(AnimalArraySize)
77:    {
78:       pType = new T[AnimalArraySize];
79:       itsNumberArrays++;
80:    }
81:
82:    void main()
83:    {
84:
```

```
85:        cout << Array<int>::GetNumberArrays() << " integer arrays\n";
86:        cout << Array<Animal>::GetNumberArrays() << " animal arrays\n\n";
87:
88:        Array<int> intArray;
89:        Array<Animal> animalArray;
90:
91:        cout << intArray.GetNumberArrays() << " integer arrays\n";
92:        cout << animalArray.GetNumberArrays() << " animal arrays\n\n";
93:
94:        Array<int> *pIntArray = new Array<int>;
95:
96:        cout << Array<int>::GetNumberArrays() << " integer arrays\n";
97:        cout << Array<Animal>::GetNumberArrays() << " animal arrays\n\n";
98:
99:        delete pIntArray;
100:
101:        cout << Array<int>::GetNumberArrays() << " integer arrays\n";
102:        cout << Array<Animal>::GetNumberArrays() << " animal arrays\n\n";
103:    }
```

OUTPUT

```
0 integer array
0 animal arrays

1 integer array
1 animal arrays

2 integer array
1 animal arrays

1 integer array
1 animal arrays
```

The declaration of the Animal class has been left out to save space. The Array class has added the static variable itsNumberArrays on line 27, and because this data is private, the static public accessor GetNumberArrays() was added on line 19.

Initialization of the static data is accomplished with a full template qualification, as shown on lines 30 and 31. The constructors of Array and the destructor are each modified to keep track of how many arrays exist at any moment.

Accessing the static members is exactly like accessing the static members of any class: You can do so with an existing object, as shown on lines 91 and 92, or by using the full class specification, as shown on lines 85 and 86. Note that you must use a specific type of array when accessing the static data. There is one variable for each type.

The Standard Template Library

You might wonder why somebody has not already created a set of templates for arrays and other complex data types. Wonder no more, because somebody has! ANSI/ISO describes a standard template library (STL), which must be included in any C++ implementation that wants to advertise ANSI compliance. Within the C++ STL are templates for data collection types (or *data structures*) such as arrays, lists, and trees. In addition, the STL provides templates for common algorithms and iterators. Later, on Bonus Day 25, you will learn more about advanced data structures.

The STL is created to be consistent in its design across all components. After you master one component, you should find the rest similar and easy to learn. Table 19.1 is a summary of the STL component structure.

Table 19.1. STL structure.

Component Type	Purpose
Adaptors	Provides component adaptation for a different interface
Algorithms	Provides a collection of basic processing algorithms
Containers	Provides data structure management
Iterators	Provides functions for iterating through a container
Function Objects	Provides encapsulating functions in an object so that they can be used by other components

This book cannot do complete justice to the STL in this limited space. Any time you spend getting to know the STL is well worth your effort. The STL and some good documentation are available through the Internet. See the World Wide Web pages listed in Bonus Day 28 for more details.

Do	Don't

DO use statics with templates as needed.

DO specialize template behavior by overriding template functions by type.

DO use the parameters to template functions to narrow their instances to be type-safe.

Summary

Today you learned how to create and use templates. Templates are a built-in facility of C++ used to create parameterized types: types that change their behavior based on parameters passed in at creation. They are a way to reuse code safely and effectively.

The definition of the template determines the parameterized type. Each instance of the template is an actual object, which can be used like any other object—as a parameter to a function, as a return value, and so forth.

Template classes can declare three types of friend functions: nontemplate, general template, and type-specific template. A template can declare static data members, in which case each instance of the template has its own set of static data.

If you need to specialize behavior for some template functions based on the actual type, you can override a template function with a particular type. This works for member functions as well.

Q&A

Q Why use templates when macros will do?

A Templates are type-safe and built into the language.

Q What is the difference between the parameterized type of a template function and the parameters to a normal function?

A A regular function (nontemplate) takes parameters on which it can take action. A template function enables you to parameterize the type of a particular parameter to the function. That is, you can pass an Array of Type to a function, and then have the Type determined by the template instance.

Q Why bother with templates when macros will work?

A All the usual reasons apply here: Templates are an integrated part of the language; macros are not. Templates are type-safe, and macros are not.

Q When do you use templates and when do you use inheritance?

A Use templates when all the behavior or virtually all of the behavior is unchanged, except in regard to the type of the item on which your class acts. If you find yourself copying a class and changing only the type of one or more of its members, it might be time to consider using a template.

Q When do you use general template friend classes?

A When every instance, regardless of type, should be a friend to this class or function.

Q When do you use type-specific template friend classes or functions?

A When you want to establish a one-to-one relationship between two classes. For example, Array<int> should match iterator<int> but not iterator<Animal>.

19

Quiz

1. What is the difference between a template and a macro?
2. What is the difference between the parameter in a template and the parameter in a function?
3. What is the difference between a type-specific template friend class and a general template friend class?
4. Is it possible to provide special behavior for one instance of a template but not for other instances?
5. How many static variables are created if you put one static member into a template class definition?

Exercises

1. Create a template based on this list class:
```
class List
{
private:

public:
        List():head(0),tail(0),theCount(0) {}
        virtual ~List();

        void insert( int value );
        void append( int value );
        int is_present( int value ) const;
        int is_empty() const { return head == 0; }
        int count() const { return theCount; }
private:
        class ListCell
        {
        public:
                ListCell(int value, ListCell *cell = 0):val(value),next(cell){}
                int val;
                ListCell *next;
        };
        ListCell *head;
        ListCell *tail;
        int theCount;
};
```
2. Write the implementation for the List class (nontemplate) version.
3. Write the template version of the implementations.
4. Declare three list objects: a list of strings, a list of Cats, and a list of ints.

5. **BUG BUSTERS:** What is wrong with the following code? (Assume that the List template is defined and Cat is the class defined earlier in the book.)

```
List<Cat> Cat_List;
Cat Felix;
CatList.append( Felix );
cout << "Felix is " <<
        ( Cat_List.is_present( Felix ) ) ? "" : "not " << "present\n";
```

HINT (this is tough): What makes Cat different from int?

6. Declare friend operator == for List.

7. Implement friend operator == for List.

8. Does operator== have the same problem as in Exercise 5?

9. Implement a template function for swap, which exchanges two variables.

19

Day **20**

Exceptions and Error Handling

The code you've seen in this book was created for illustration purposes. It has not dealt with errors, so that you would not be distracted from the central issues being presented. Real-world programs must take error conditions into consideration.

Today you will learn

- ☐ What exceptions are.
- ☐ How exceptions are used and what issues they raise.
- ☐ How to build exception hierarchies.
- ☐ How exceptions fit into an overall error-handling approach.
- ☐ What a debugger is.

Bugs, Errors, Mistakes, and Code Rot

All programs have bugs. The bigger the program, the more bugs it has. Many of those bugs actually "get out the door" and into final released software. The fact that this is true does not make it okay; making robust, bug-free programs is the number one priority of anyone serious about programming.

The single biggest problem in the software industry is buggy, unstable code. The biggest expense in many major programming efforts is testing and fixing. The person who solves the problem of producing good, solid, bulletproof programs at low cost and on time will revolutionize the software industry.

There are a number of bug categories that can trouble a program, and two are more common than most. The first is poor logic: The program does just what you asked, but you haven't thought through the algorithms properly. The second is syntactic: You used the wrong idiom, function, or structure.

Research and real-world experience show that the later in the development process you find a problem, the more it costs to fix it. The least expensive problems or bugs are the ones you manage to avoid creating. The next cheapest are those that the compiler spots. The C++ standards force compilers to put a lot of energy into making more and more bugs show up at compile time.

Bugs that get compiled but are caught at the first test—those that crash *every time*—are less expensive to find and fix than those that only crash once in a while.

A bigger problem than logic or syntactic bugs is unnecessary fragility: Your program works just fine if the user enters a number when you ask for one, but it crashes if the user enters letters. Other programs crash if they run out of memory, if the floppy disk is left out of the drive, or if the modem drops the line.

To combat this kind of fragility, programmers strive to make their programs *bulletproof*. A bulletproof program is one that can handle anything that comes up at runtime, from bizarre user input to running out of memory.

NOTE

> It is important to distinguish between *bugs*, which arise because the programmer made a mistake in syntax; *logic errors*, which arise because the programmer misunderstood the problem or how to solve it; and *exceptions*, which arise because of unusual but predictable problems such as running out of resources (memory or disk space).

20

Exceptions

Programmers use powerful compilers and sprinkle their code with asserts, as discussed on Day 17, to catch programming errors. They use design reviews and exhaustive testing to find logic errors.

Exceptions are different, however. You can't eliminate exceptional circumstances; you can only prepare for them. Your users *will* cause your program to run out of memory from time to time, and the only question is what to do. Your choices are limited to these:

1. Crash the program.
2. Inform the user and exit gracefully.
3. Inform the user and enable the user to try to recover and continue.
4. Take corrective action and continue without disturbing the user.

Although it is not necessary or even desirable for every program you write to automatically and silently recover from all exceptional circumstances, it is clear that the program must do better than crashing.

C++ exception handling provides a type-safe, integrated method for coping with the predictable but unusual conditions that arise while running a program.

A Word About Code Rot

Code rot is a well-proven phenomenon. Code rot is what happens when code deteriorates due to being neglected. Perfectly well-written, fully debugged code develops new and bizarre behavior six months after you release it, and there isn't much you can do to stop it. What you *can* do, of course, is write programs so that when you fix the spoilage, you can quickly and easily identify where the problems are.

NOTE

Code rot is somewhat of a programmer's joke used to explain how bug-free code suddenly becomes unreliable. It does, however, teach an important lesson. Programs are enormously complex, and bugs, errors, and mistakes can hide for a long time before turning up. Protect yourself by writing easy-to-maintain code.

Quick identification of problems requires your code to be commented even if you don't expect anyone else to ever look at it. Six months after you deliver your code, you'll read it with the eyes of a total stranger, bewildered that anyone could write such convoluted and twisty code and expect anything but disaster.

Preparing for Exceptions With C++

In C++, an *exception* is an object that is passed from the area of code where a problem occurs to the part of the code that is going to handle the problem. The passing of an exception object up the chain of control is called "throwing an exception." The type of exception determines which area of code handles the problem, and the contents of the object that is thrown, if any, can be used to provide feedback to the user.

The basic idea behind exceptions is fairly straightforward:

- ☐ The actual allocation of resources (for example, the allocation of memory or the locking of a file) is usually done at a very low level in the program.

- ☐ The logic of what to do when an operation fails, when memory cannot be allocated, or when a file cannot be locked is usually high in the program, with the code for interacting with the user.

- ☐ Exceptions provide an express path from the code that allocates resources to the code that can handle the error condition. If there are intervening layers of functions, they are given an opportunity to clean up memory allocations, but they are not required to include code whose only purpose is to pass along the error condition.

How Exceptions Are Used

try blocks are created to surround areas of code that might have a problem, as in the following example:

```
try
{
SomeDangerousFunction();
}
```

catch blocks handle the exceptions thrown in the try block, as in the following example:

```
try
{
SomeDangerousFunction();
}
// Catch any OutOfMemory exceptions thrown
// by SomeDangerousFunction()
catch(OutOfMemory)
{
// take some actions
}
// Catch any FileNotFound exceptions thrown
// by SomeDangerousFunction()
catch(FileNotFound)
{
// take other action
}
```

The basic steps in using exceptions are as follows:

1. Identify those areas of the program in which you begin an operation that might raise an exception, and put them in try blocks.
2. Create catch blocks to catch the exceptions if they are thrown, and to clean up allocated memory and inform the user as appropriate. Listing 20.1 illustrates the use of both try blocks and catch blocks.

Exceptions are objects used to transmit information about a problem.

A *try block* is a block surrounded by braces in which an exception can be thrown.

A *catch block* is the block immediately following a try block in which exceptions are handled.

When an exception is *thrown* (or *raised*) control transfers to the catch block immediately following the current try block.

In order to document all the exceptions that your functions might throw, you can include an exception specification in a parenthetical listing with the function declaration. For instance, instead of simply declaring the function definition like

```
void SomeThrowingFunction();
```

you would declare it like this:

```
void SomeThrowingFunction() throw(InExc, OutExc, AnExc);
```

If your function throws an exception other than one of those listed in the exception specification, an unexpected() exception is thrown. This topic is discussed in more detail later in this chapter.

NOTE

Some older compilers do not support exceptions. Exceptions are, however, part of the emerging C++ standard. All major compiler vendors have committed to supporting exceptions in their next release, if they have not already done so. If you have an older compiler, you won't be able to compile and run the exercises in this lesson. It's still a good idea to read through the entire lesson, however, and return to this material when you upgrade your compiler.

20

Some of the newer compilers still do not support the exception specification on the function prototype line. If your compiler complains when
you compile the code in this chapter, remove the "throw(…)" exception specification.

TYPE | **Listing 20.1. Raising an exception.**

```
1:   #include <iostream.h>
2:
3:   const int DefaultSize = 10;
4:
5:   class Array
6:   {
7:   public:
8:       // constructors
9:       Array(int Size = DefaultSize);
10:      Array(const Array &rhs);
11:      ~Array() { delete [] pType;}
12:
13:      // operators
14:      Array& operator=(const Array&);
15:      int& operator[](int offSet) throw(xBoundary);
16:      const int& operator[](int offSet) throw(xBoundary) const;
17:
18:      // accessors
19:      int GetitsSize() const { return itsSize; }
20:
21:      // friend function
22:     friend ostream& operator<< (ostream&, const Array&);
23:
24:      class xBoundary {};  // define the exception class
25:  private:
26:      int *pType;
27:      int  itsSize;
28:  };
29:
30:
31:  Array::Array(int size):
32:  itsSize(size)
33:  {
34:     pType = new int[size];
35:     for (int i = 0; i<size; i++)
36:       pType[i] = 0;
37:  }
38:
39:
40:  Array& Array::operator=(const Array &rhs)
41:  {
42:     if (this == &rhs)
43:        return *this;
44:     delete [] pType;
```

```
45:        itsSize = rhs.GetitsSize();
46:        pType = new int[itsSize];
47:        for (int i = 0; i<itsSize; i++)
48:            pType[i] = rhs[i];
49:    }
50:
51:    Array::Array(const Array &rhs)
52:    {
53:        itsSize = rhs.GetitsSize();
54:        pType = new int[itsSize];
55:        for (int i = 0; i<itsSize; i++)
56:            pType[i] = rhs[i];
57:    }
58:
59:
60:    int& Array::operator[](int offSet)
61:    {
62:        int size = GetitsSize();
63:        if (offSet >= 0 && offSet < GetitsSize())
64:            return pType[offSet];
65:        throw xBoundary();
66:    }
67:
68:
69:    const int& Array::operator[](int offSet) const
70:    {
71:        int mysize = GetitsSize();
72:        if (offSet >= 0 && offSet < GetitsSize())
73:            return pType[offSet];
74:        throw xBoundary();
75:    }
76:
77:    ostream& operator<< (ostream& output, const Array& theArray)
78:    {
79:        for (int i = 0; i<theArray.GetitsSize(); i++)
80:            output << "[" << i << "] " << theArray[i] << endl;
81:        return output;
82:    }
83:
84:    void main()
85:    {
86:        Array intArray(20);
87:        try
88:        {
89:            for (int j = 0; j< 100; j++)
90:            {
91:                intArray[j] = j;
92:                cout << "intArray[" << j << "] okay..." << endl;
93:            }
94:        }
95:        catch (Array::xBoundary)
96:        {
97:            cout << "Unable to process your input!\n";
98:        }
99:        cout << "Done.\n";
99:    }
```

OUTPUT
```
intArray[0] okay...
intArray[1] okay...
intArray[2] okay...
intArray[3] okay...
intArray[4] okay...
intArray[5] okay...
intArray[6] okay...
intArray[7] okay...
intArray[8] okay...
intArray[9] okay...
intArray[10] okay...
intArray[11] okay...
intArray[12] okay...
intArray[13] okay...
intArray[14] okay...
intArray[15] okay...
intArray[16] okay...
intArray[17] okay...
intArray[18] okay...
intArray[19] okay...
Unable to process your input!
Done.
```

ANALYSIS

Listing 20.1 presents a somewhat stripped-down Array class, based on the template developed on Day 19. On line 24 a new class is contained within the declaration of the Array: boundary.

This new class is not in any way distinguished as an exception class. It is just a class like any other. This particular class is incredibly simple: It has no data and no methods. Nonetheless, it is a valid class in every way.

In fact, it is incorrect to say that it has no methods because the compiler automatically assigns it a default constructor, destructor, copy constructor, and the copy operator (operator equals). In other words, it actually has four class functions, but no data.

Note that declaring the exception class within Array serves only to couple the two classes together. As discussed on Day 15, Array has no special access to xBoundary, nor does xBoundary have preferential access to the members of Array.

On lines 60 through 66 and 69 through 75, the offset operators are modified to examine the offset requested and, if it is out of range, to throw the xBoundary class as an exception. The parentheses are required to distinguish between this call to the xBoundary constructor and the use of an enumerated constant.

On line 87 the keyword try begins a try block that ends on line 94. Within that try block, 100 integers are added to the array that was declared on line 86.

On line 95 the catch block to catch xBoundary exceptions is declared.

In the driver program on lines 84 through 89, a try block is created in which each member of the array is initialized. When j (line 89) is incremented to 20, the member at offset 20 is accessed. This causes the test on line 63 to fail, and `operator[]` raises an `xBoundary` exception on line 65.

Program control switches to the `catch` block on line 95 and the exception is caught or handled by the case on the same line, which prints an error message. Program flow drops through to the end of the `catch` block on line 98.

try Blocks

A try block is a set of statements that begins with the word `try`; it is followed by an opening brace and ends with a closing brace.

Example:

```
try
{
Function();
};
```

catch Blocks

A catch block is a series of statements, each of which begins with the word `catch`, followed by an exception type in parentheses and an opening brace, and ending with a closing brace.

Example:

```
try
{
Function();
};
catch (OutOfMemory)
{
// take action
}
```

Using *try* Blocks and *catch* Blocks

Figuring out where to put your try blocks is not a trivial matter: It is not always obvious which actions might raise an exception. The next question is where to catch the exception. It might be that you'll want to throw all memory exceptions where the memory is allocated, but you'll want to catch the exceptions high in the program, where you deal with the user interface.

When attempting to determine try block locations, look to where you allocate memory or use resources. Other things to look for are out-of-bounds errors, illegal input, attempts at illegal math operations, and uninitialized pointers.

Catching Exceptions

Here's how it works: When an exception is thrown, the call stack is examined. The call stack is the list of function calls created when one part of the program invokes another function.

The call stack tracks the execution path. If main() calls the function Animal::GetFavoriteFood(), and GetFavoriteFood() calls Animal::LookupPreferences(), which in turn calls fstream::operator>>(), all of these are on the call stack. A recursive function might be on the call stack many times.

The exception is passed up the call stack to each enclosing block. As the stack is "unwound," the destructors for local objects on the stack are invoked, and the objects are destroyed.

After each try block are one or more catch statements. If the exception matches one of the catch statements, it is handled when that statement is executed. If it doesn't match any, the unwinding of the stack continues.

If the exception reaches all the way to the beginning of the program (main()) and is still not caught, a built-in handler is called that terminates the program.

It is important to note that the exception unwinding of the stack is a one-way street. As it progresses, the stack is unwound and objects on the stack are destroyed. There is no going back; once the exception is handled, the program continues after the try block of the catch statement that handled the exception.

That is why, in Listing 20.1, execution continues on line 99, the first line after the try block of the catch statement that handled the xBoundary exception. Remember that when an exception is raised, program flow continues after the catch block, *not* after the point where the exception was thrown.

More Than One *catch* Specification

It is possible for more than one condition to cause an exception. In this case, the catch statements can be lined up one after another, much like the conditions in a switch statement. The equivalent to the default statement is the "catch everything" statement indicated by catch(...). Listing 20.2 illustrates multiple exception conditions.

TYPE   **Listing 20.2. Multiple exceptions.**

```
1:      #include <iostream.h>
2:
3:      const int DefaultSize = 10;
4:      class Array
5:      {
6:      public:
```

```
7:          // constructors
8:          Array(int Size = DefaultSize) throw(xZero,
9:              xTooBig, xTooSmall, xNegative);
10:         Array(const Array &rhs);
11:         ~Array() { delete [] pType;}
12:
13:         // operators
14:         Array& operator=(const Array&);
15:         int& operator[](int offSet);
16:         const int& operator[](int offSet) const;
17:
18:         // accessors
19:         int GetitsSize() const { return itsSize; }
20:
21:         // friend function
22:        friend ostream& operator<< (ostream&, const Array&);
23:
24:       // define the exception classes
25:         class xBoundary {};
26:         class xTooBig {};
27:         class xTooSmall{};
28:         class xZero {};
29:         class xNegative {};
30:     private:
31:         int *pType;
32:         int  itsSize;
33:     };
34:
35:
36:     Array::Array(int size):
37:     itsSize(size)
38:     {
39:         if (size == 0)
40:             throw xZero();
41:         if (size < 10)
42:             throw xTooSmall();
43:         if (size > 30000)
44:             throw xTooBig();
45:         if (size < 1)
46:             throw xNegative();
47:
48:         pType = new int[size];
49:         for (int i = 0; i<size; i++)
50:           pType[i] = 0;
51:     }
52:
53:
54:
55:     void main()
56:     {
57:
58:         try
59:         {
60:             Array intArray(0);
61:             for (int j = 0; j< 100; j++)
62:             {
```

continues

Listing 20.2. continued

```
63:                 intArray[j] = j;
64:                 cout << "intArray[" << j << "] okay..." << endl;
65:             }
66:         }
67:         catch (Array::xBoundary)
68:         {
69:             cout << "Unable to process your input!\n";
70:         }
71:         catch (Array::xTooBig)
72:         {
73:             cout << "This array is too big..." << endl;
74:         }
75:         catch (Array::xTooSmall)
76:         {
77:             cout << "This array is too small..." << endl;
78:         }
79:         catch (Array::xZero)
80:         {
81:             cout << "You asked for an array of zero objects!" << endl;
82:         }
83:         catch (...)
84:         {
85:             cout << "Something went wrong, but I've no idea what!" << endl;
86:         }
87:         cout << "Done.\n";
88:     }
```

OUTPUT
You asked for an array of zero objects!
Done.

ANALYSIS   The implementation of all of Array's methods, except for its constructor, have been left out because they are unchanged from Listing 20.1.

Four new classes are created in lines 26 through 29: xTooBig, xTooSmall, xZero, and xNegative. In the constructor, on lines 36 through 51, the size passed to the constructor is examined. If it's too big, too small, negative, or zero, an exception is thrown.

The try block is changed to include catch statements for each condition other than negative, which is caught by the "catch everything" statement (catch(...)) shown on line 83.

Try this with a number of values for the size of the array. Then try putting in -5. You might have expected xNegative to be called, but the order of the tests in the constructor prevented this: size < 10 was evaluated before size < 1. To fix this, swap lines 41 and 42 with lines 45 and 46 and recompile.

Exception Hierarchies

Exceptions are classes, and as such they can be derived from. It might be advantageous to create a class xSize, and to derive from it xZero, xTooSmall, xTooBig, and xNegative. Some functions might just catch xSize errors, while other functions might catch the specific type of xSize error. Listing 20.3 illustrates this idea.

TYPE **Listing 20.3. Class hierarchies and exceptions.**

```
1:     #include <iostream.h>
2:
3:     const int DefaultSize = 10;
4:     class Array
5:     {
6:     public:
7:         // constructors
8:         Array(int Size = DefaultSize) throw(xZero,
9:             xTooBig, xTooSmall, xNegative);
10:        Array(const Array &rhs);
11:        ~Array() { delete [] pType;}
12:
13:        // operators
14:        Array& operator=(const Array&);
15:        int& operator[](int offSet);
16:        const int& operator[](int offSet) const;
17:
18:        // accessors
19:        int GetitsSize() const { return itsSize; }
20:
21:        // friend function
22:       friend ostream& operator<< (ostream&, const Array&);
23:
24:      // define the exception classes
25:        class xBoundary {};
26:        class xSize {};
27:        class xTooBig : public xSize {};
28:        class xTooSmall : public xSize {};
29:        class xZero  : public xTooSmall {};
30:        class xNegative  : public xSize {};
31:    private:
32:        int *pType;
33:        int  itsSize;
34:    };
35:
36:
37:    Array::Array(int size):
38:    itsSize(size)
39:    {
40:        if (size == 0)
41:            throw xZero();
```

continues

Listing 20.3. continued

```
42:        if (size > 30000)
43:            throw xTooBig();
44:        if (size <1)
45:            throw xNegative();
46:        if (size < 10)
47:            throw xTooSmall();
48:
49:        pType = new int[size];
50:        for (int i = 0; i<size; i++)
51:          pType[i] = 0;
52:    }
```

OUTPUT This array is too small...
Done.

  This listing leaves out the implementation of the array functions because they are unchanged, and it leaves out main() because it is identical to that in Listing 20.2.

The significant change is on lines 26 through 30, where the class hierarchy is established. Classes xTooBig, xTooSmall, and xNegative are derived from xSize, and xZero is derived from xTooSmall.

The Array is created with size zero—but what's this? The wrong exception appears to be caught! Examine the catch block carefully, however, and you find that it looks for an exception of type xTooSmall *before* it looks for an exception of type xZero. Because an xZero object is thrown and an xZero object *is* an xTooSmall object, it is caught by the handler for xTooSmall. After it is handled, the exception is *not* passed on to the other handlers, so the handler for xZero is never called.

The solution to this problem is to carefully order the handlers so that the most specific handlers come first and the less specific handlers come later. In this particular example, switching the placement of the two handlers, xZero and xTooSmall, fixes the problem.

Data in Exceptions and Naming Exception Objects

To respond properly to an error, you often need to know more than just what type the exception was. Exception classes are like any other classes. You are free to provide data, initialize that data in the constructor, and read that data at any time. Listing 20.4 illustrates how to do this.

Type

Listing 20.4. Getting data out of an exception object.

```
1:     #include <iostream.h>
2:
3:     const int DefaultSize = 10;
4:     class Array
5:     {
6:     public:
7:         // constructors
8:         Array(int Size = DefaultSize) throw(xZero,
9:             xTooBig, xTooSmall, xNegative);
10:        Array(const Array &rhs);
11:        ~Array() { delete [] pType;}
12:
13:        // operators
14:        Array& operator=(const Array&);
15:        int& operator[](int offSet);
16:        const int& operator[](int offSet) const;
17:
18:        // accessors
19:        int GetitsSize() const { return itsSize; }
20:
21:        // friend function
22:       friend ostream& operator<< (ostream&, const Array&);
23:
24:      // define the exception classes
25:        class xBoundary {};
26:        class xSize
27:        {
28:        public:
29:            xSize(int size):itsSize(size) {}
30:            ~xSize(){}
31:            int GetSize() { return itsSize; }
32:        private:
33:            int itsSize;
34:        };
35:
36:        class xTooBig : public xSize
37:        {
38:        public:
39:            xTooBig(int size):xSize(size){}
40:        };
41:
42:        class xTooSmall : public xSize
43:        {
44:        public:
45:            xTooSmall(int size):xSize(size){}
46:        };
47:
48:        class xZero  : public xTooSmall
49:        {
50:        public:
51:            xZero(int size):xTooSmall(size){}
52:        };
53:
```

continues

20

Listing 20.4. continued

```
54:        class xNegative : public xSize
55:        {
56:        public:
57:            xNegative(int size):xSize(size){}
58:        };
59:
60:    private:
61:        int *pType;
62:        int  itsSize;
63:    };
64:
65:
66:    Array::Array(int size):
67:    itsSize(size)
68:    {
69:        if (size == 0)
70:            throw xZero(size);
71:        if (size > 30000)
72:            throw xTooBig(size);
73:        if (size <1)
74:            throw xNegative(size);
75:        if (size < 10)
76:            throw xTooSmall(size);
77:
78:        pType = new int[size];
79:        for (int i = 0; i<size; i++)
80:          pType[i] = 0;
81:    }
82:
83:
84:    void main()
85:    {
86:
87:        try
88:        {
89:            Array intArray(9);
90:            for (int j = 0; j< 100; j++)
91:            {
92:                intArray[j] = j;
93:                cout << "intArray[" << j << "] okay..." << endl;
94:            }
95:        }
96:        catch (Array::xBoundary)
97:        {
98:            cout << "Unable to process your input!\n";
99:        }
100:        catch (Array::xZero theException)
101:        {
102:            cout << "You asked for an array of zero objects!" << endl;
103:            cout << "Received " << theException.GetSize() << endl;
104:        }
105:        catch (Array::xTooBig theException)
106:        {
107:            cout << "This array is too big..." << endl;
108:            cout << "Received " << theException.GetSize() << endl;
```

```
109:      }
110:      catch (Array::xTooSmall theException)
111:      {
112:          cout << "This array is too small..." << endl;
113:          cout << "Received " << theException.GetSize() << endl;
114:      }
115:      catch (...)
116:      {
117:          cout << "Something went wrong, but I've no idea what!" << endl;
118:      }
119:      cout << "Done.\n";
120:  }
```

OUTPUT

```
This array is too small...
Received 9
Done.
```

ANALYSIS The declaration of xSize has been modified to include an itsSize member variable on line 33, and a GetSize() member function on line 31. Additionally, a constructor has been added that takes an integer and initializes the member variable, as shown on line 29.

The derived classes declare a constructor that does nothing but initialize the base class. No other functions were declared, in part to save space in the listing.

The catch statements on lines 100 to 118 are modified to name the exception that they catch, theException, and to use this object to access the data stored in itsSize.

NOTE Keep in mind that if you are constructing an exception, it is because an exception has been raised: Something has gone wrong and your exception should be careful not to re-create the same problem. In other words, if you are creating an OutOfMemory exception, you probably don't want to allocate memory in its constructor.

It is time-consuming and likely to generate errors if you have each of these catch statements individually print the appropriate message. This job belongs to the object, which knows what type of object it is and what value it received. Listing 20.5 takes a more object-oriented approach to this problem, using virtual functions so that each exception "does the right thing."

20

Listing 20.5. Passing by reference and using virtual functions in exceptions.

```
1:    #include <iostream.h>
2:
3:    const int DefaultSize = 10;
4:    class Array
5:    {
6:    public:
7:        // constructors
8:        Array(int Size = DefaultSize) throw(xZero,
9:            xTooBig, xTooSmall, xNegative);
10:       Array(const Array &rhs);
11:       ~Array() { delete [] pType;}
12:
13:       // operators
14:       Array& operator=(const Array&);
15:       int& operator[](int offSet);
16:       const int& operator[](int offSet) const;
17:
18:       // accessors
19:       int GetitsSize() const { return itsSize; }
20:
21:       // friend function
22:     friend ostream& operator<< (ostream&, const Array&);
23:
24:     // define the exception classes
25:       class xBoundary {};
26:       class xSize
27:       {
28:       public:
29:          xSize(int size):itsSize(size) {}
30:          ~xSize(){}
31:          virtual int GetSize() { return itsSize; }
32:          virtual void PrintError() { cout <<
33:              "Size error. Received: " << itsSize << endl; }
34:       protected:
35:          int itsSize;
36:       };
37:       class xTooBig : public xSize
38:       {
39:       public:
40:          xTooBig(int size):xSize(size){}
41:          virtual void PrintError() { cout << "Too big! Received: " <<
42:                          _xSize::itsSize << endl; }
43:       };
44:       class xTooSmall : public xSize
45:       {
46:       public:
47:          xTooSmall(int size):xSize(size){}
48:          virtual void PrintError() { cout << "Too small! Received: " <<
49:                          _xSize::itsSize << endl; }
50:       };
```

20

```
51:          class xZero   : public xTooSmall
52:          {
53:          public:
54:             xZero(int size):xTooSmall(size){}
55:             virtual void PrintError() { cout << "Zero!!. Received: " <<
                                _xSize::itsSize << endl; }
56:          };
57:
58:          class xNegative : public xSize
59:          {
60:          public:
61:             xNegative(int size):xSize(size){}
62:             virtual void PrintError() { cout << "Negative! Received: " <<
                                _xSize::itsSize << endl; }
63:          };
64:
65:      private:
66:         int *pType;
67:         int  itsSize;
68:      };
69:
70:      Array::Array(int size):
71:      itsSize(size)
72:      {
73:         if (size == 0)
74:            throw xZero(size);
75:         if (size > 30000)
76:            throw xTooBig(size);
77:         if (size <1)
78:            throw xNegative(size);
79:         if (size < 10)
80:            throw xTooSmall(size);
81:
82:         pType = new int[size];
83:         for (int i = 0; i<size; i++)
84:            pType[i] = 0;
85:      }
86:
87:      void main()
88:      {
89:
90:         try
91:         {
92:            Array intArray(9);
93:            for (int j = 0; j< 100; j++)
94:            {
95:               intArray[j] = j;
96:               cout << "intArray[" << j << "] okay..." << endl;
97:            }
98:         }
99:         catch (Array::xBoundary)
100:        {
101:           cout << "Unable to process your input!\n";
102:        }
103:        catch (Array::xSize& theException)
104:        {
```

continues

Listing 20.5. continued

```
105:            theException.PrintError();
106:        }
107:        catch (...)
108:        {
109:            cout << "Something went wrong, but I've no idea what!" << endl;
110:        }
111:        cout << "Done.\n";
112:    }
```

OUTPUT
Too small! Received 9
Done.

ANALYSIS Listing 20.5 declares a virtual method in the xSize class, PrintError(), which prints an error message and the actual size of the class. This is overridden in each of the derived classes.

On line 103 the exception object is declared to be a reference. When PrintError() is called with a reference to an object, polymorphism causes the correct version of PrintError() to be invoked. The code is cleaner, easier to understand, and easier to maintain.

Exceptions and Templates

When creating exceptions to work with templates, you have a choice: You can create an exception for each instance of the template, or you can use exception classes declared outside of the template declaration. Listing 20.6 illustrates both approaches.

TYPE ## Listing 20.6. Using exceptions with templates.

```
1:    #include <iostream.h>
2:
3:    const int DefaultSize = 10;
4:    class xBoundary {};
5:    template <class T>
6:    class Array
7:    {
8:    public:
9:        // constructors
10:        Array(int Size = DefaultSize) throw(xZero,
11:            xTooBig, xTooSmall, xNegative);
12:        Array(const Array &rhs);
13:        ~Array() { delete [] pType;}
14:
15:        // operators
16:        Array& operator=(const Array<T>&);
17:        T& operator[](int offSet) throw(xBoundary);
18:        const T& operator[](int offSet) throw(xBoundary) const;
```

```
19:
20:        // accessors
21:        int GetitsSize() const { return itsSize; }
22:
23:        // friend function
24:      friend ostream& operator<< (ostream&, const Array<T>&);
25:
26:     // define the exception classes
27:
28:        class xSize {};
29:
30:    private:
31:        int *pType;
32:        int  itsSize;
33:    };
34:
35:    template <class T>
36:    Array<T>::Array(int size):
37:    itsSize(size)
38:    {
39:        if (size <10 || size > 30000)
40:            throw xSize();
41:        pType = new T[size];
42:        for (int i = 0; i<size; i++)
43:          pType[i] = 0;
44:    }
45:
46:    template <class T>
47:    Array<T>& Array<T>::operator=(const Array<T> &rhs)
48:    {
49:        if (this == &rhs)
50:            return *this;
51:        delete [] pType;
52:        itsSize = rhs.GetitsSize();
53:        pType = new T[itsSize];
54:        for (int i = 0; i<itsSize; i++)
55:            pType[i] = rhs[i];
56:    }
57:    template <class T>
58:    Array<T>::Array(const Array<T> &rhs)
59:    {
60:        itsSize = rhs.GetitsSize();
61:        pType = new T[itsSize];
62:        for (int i = 0; i<itsSize; i++)
63:            pType[i] = rhs[i];
64:    }
65:
66:    template <class T>
67:    T& Array<T>::operator[](int offSet)
68:    {
69:        int size = GetitsSize();
70:        if (offSet >= 0 && offSet < GetitsSize())
71:            return pType[offSet];
72:        throw xBoundary();
73:    }
74:
```

continues

Listing 20.6. continued

```
75:     template <class T>
76:     const T& Array<T>::operator[](int offSet) const
77:     {
78:         int mysize = GetitsSize();
79:         if (offSet >= 0 && offSet < GetitsSize())
80:             return pType[offSet];
81:         throw xBoundary();
82:     }
83:
84:     template <class T>
85:     ostream& operator<< (ostream& output, const Array<T>& theArray)
86:     {
87:         for (int i = 0; i<theArray.GetitsSize(); i++)
88:             output << "[" << i << "] " << theArray[i] << endl;
89:         return output;
90:     }
91:
92:
93:     void main()
94:     {
95:
96:         try
97:         {
98:             Array<int> intArray(9);
99:             for (int j = 0; j< 100; j++)
100:            {
101:                intArray[j] = j;
102:                cout << "intArray[" << j << "] okay..." << endl;
103:            }
104:        }
105:        catch (xBoundary)
106:        {
107:            cout << "Unable to process your input!\n";
108:        }
109:        catch (Array<int>::xSize)
110:        {
111:            cout << "Bad Size!\n";
112:        }
113:
114:        cout << "Done.\n";
115:    }
```

OUTPUT
```
Bad Size!
Done.
```

ANALYSIS The first exception, xBoundary, is declared outside the template definition on line 4. The second exception, xSize, is declared from within the definition of the template.

The exception xBoundary is not tied to the template class, but it can be used like any other class. xSize is tied to the template and must be called based on the instantiated Array. You

20

can see the difference in the syntax for the two catch statements. Line 105 shows `catch (xBoundary)`, but line 109 shows `catch (Array<int>::xSize)`. The latter is tied to the instantiation of an integer `Array`.

Exceptions Without Errors

When C++ programmers get together for a virtual beer in the cyberspace bar after work, talk often turns to whether exceptions should be used for routine conditions. Some maintain that by their nature exceptions should be reserved for those predictable but exceptional circumstances (hence the name!) that a programmer must anticipate, which are not part of the routine processing of the code.

Others point out that exceptions offer a powerful and clean way to return through many layers of function calls without danger of memory leaks. A frequent example is this: The user requests an action in a GUI environment. The part of the code that catches the request must call a member function on a dialog manager, which in turn calls code that processes the request, which calls code that decides which dialog box to use, which in turn calls code to put up the dialog box, which finally calls code that processes the user's input. If the user presses Cancel, the code must return to the very first calling method where the original request was handled.

One approach to this problem is to put a `try` block around the original call and catch `CancelDialog` as an exception, which can be raised by the handler for the Cancel button. This is safe and effective, but pressing Cancel is a routine circumstance, not an exceptional one.

This frequently becomes something of a religious argument, but there is a reasonable way to decide the question: Does use of exceptions in this way make the code easier or harder to understand? Are there fewer risks of errors and memory leaks or more? Will it be harder or easier to maintain this code? These decisions, like so many others, require an analysis of the trade-offs. There is no obvious right answer.

Bugs and Debugging

You saw on Day 17 how to use asserts to trap runtime bugs during the testing phase, and today you saw how to use exceptions to trap runtime problems. There is one more powerful weapon you'll want to add to your arsenal as you attack bugs: the debugger.

Nearly all modern development environments include one or more high-powered debuggers. The essential idea of using a debugger is this: You run the debugger, which loads your source code, and then you run your program from within the debugger. This enables you to see each instruction in your program as it executes and examine your variables as they change during the life of your program.

20

All compilers let you compile with or without symbols. Compiling with symbols tells the compiler to create the necessary mapping between your source code and the generated program; the debugger uses this to point to the line of source code that corresponds to the next action in the program.

Full-screen symbolic debuggers make this chore a delight. When you load your debugger, it reads through all your source code and shows the code in a window. You can step over function calls or direct the debugger to step into the function, line by line.

With most debuggers, you can switch between the source code and the output to see the results of each executed statement. More powerfully, you can examine the current state of each variable; you can look at complex data structures and examine the value of member data within classes. You also can look at the actual values in memory of various pointers and other memory locations. You can execute several types of control within a debugger that include setting breakpoints, setting watch points, examining memory, and looking at the assembler code.

Breakpoints

Breakpoints are instructions to the debugger that when a particular line of code is ready to be executed, the program should stop. This enables you to run your program unimpeded until the line in question is reached. Breakpoints help you analyze the current condition of variables just before and after a critical line of code.

Watch Points

It is possible to tell the debugger to show you the value of a particular variable, or to break when a particular variable is read or written to. Watch points enable you to set these conditions, and at times to even modify the value of a variable while the program is running.

Examining Memory

At times it is important to see the actual values held in memory. Modern debuggers can show values in the form of the actual variable; that is, strings can be shown as characters, longs as numbers rather than as four bytes, and so forth. Sophisticated C++ debuggers can even show complete classes, providing the current value of all the member variables, including the this pointer.

Assembler

Although reading through the source can be all that is required to find a bug, when all else fails it is possible to instruct the debugger to show you the actual assembly code generated for each line of your source code. You can examine the memory registers and flags, and generally delve as deep into the inner workings of your program as required.

Learn to use your debugger. It can be the most powerful weapon in your holy war against bugs. Runtime bugs are the hardest to find and squash, and a powerful debugger can make it possible, if not easy, to find nearly all of them.

Summary

Today you learned how to create and use exceptions. Exceptions are objects that can be created and thrown at points in the program where the executing code cannot handle the error or other exceptional condition. Other parts of the program, higher in the call stack, implement catch blocks that catch the exception and take appropriate action.

Exceptions are normal user-created objects, and as such they can be passed by value or by reference. They can contain data and methods, and the catch block can use that data to decide how to deal with the exception.

It is possible to create multiple catch blocks, but when an exception matches a catch block's signature, it is considered to be handled and is not given to the subsequent catch blocks. It is important to order the catch blocks appropriately so that more specific catch blocks have first chance and more general catch blocks handle those not otherwise handled.

This lesson also examined some of the fundamentals of symbolic debuggers, including using watch points, breakpoints, and so forth. These tools can help you zero in on the part of your program that is causing the error and let you see the value of variables as they change during the course of the program's execution.

Q&A

Q Why bother with raising exceptions? Why not handle the error right where it happens?

A Often the same error can be generated in a number of different parts of the code. Exceptions let you centralize the handling of errors. Additionally, the part of the code that generates the error might not be the best place to determine *how* to handle the error.

20

Q Why generate an object? Why not just pass an error code?

A Objects are more flexible and powerful than error codes. They can convey more information, and the constructor/destructor mechanisms can be used for the creation and removal of resources that might be required to properly handle the exceptional condition.

Q Why not use exceptions for nonerror conditions? Isn't it convenient to be able to express-train back to previous areas of the code, even when nonexceptional conditions exist?

A Yes, some C++ programmers use exceptions for just that purpose. The danger is that exceptions might create memory leaks as the stack is unwound and some objects are inadvertently left in the free store. With careful programming techniques and a good compiler, this can usually be avoided. Otherwise, it is a matter of personal aesthetics; some programmers feel that by their nature exceptions should not be used for routine conditions.

Q Does an exception have to be caught in the same place where the `try` block created the exception?

A No, it is possible to catch an exception anywhere in the call stack. As the stack is unwound, the exception is passed up the stack until it is handled.

Q Why use a debugger when you can use `cout` with conditional (`#ifdef debug`) compiling?

A The debugger provides a much more powerful mechanism for stepping through your code and watching values change, without having to clutter your code with thousands of debugging statements.

Quiz

1. What is an exception?
2. What is a `try` block?
3. What is a `catch` statement?
4. What information can an exception contain?
5. When are exception objects created?
6. Should you pass exceptions by value or by reference?
7. Will a `catch` statement catch a derived exception if it is looking for the base class?
8. If there are two `catch` statements, one for base and one for derived, which should come first?
9. What does `catch(...)` mean?
10. What is a breakpoint?

Exercises

1. Create a try block, a catch statement, and a simple exception.

2. Modify the answer from exercise 1, put data into the exception along with an accessor function, and use it in the catch block.

3. Modify the class from exercise 2 to be a hierarchy of exceptions. Modify the catch block to use the derived objects and the base objects.

4. Modify the program from exercise 3 to have three levels of function calls.

5. **BUG BUSTERS:** What is wrong with the following code?

```
class xOutOfMemory
{
public:
    xOutOfMemory( const String& message ) : itsMsg( message ){}
    ~xOutOfMemory(){}
    virtual const String& Message(){ return itsMsg;}
private:
    String itsMsg;          // assume you are using the string class as
            _previously defined
}

main()
{
    try {
        char *var = new char;
        if ( var == 0 )
            throw xOutOfMemory();
    }
    catch( xOutOfMemory& theException )
    {
        cout <<  theException.Message() << "\n";
    }
}
```

20

Day 21

Working With Multiple Files for Large Programs

To this point, most of the programs you've done have been contained in one, or at most, two files. In the real world, however, there are tremendous advantages to dividing your programs into multiple files. For instance, finding the correct class definition in a monster file that contains 10 or 20 class definitions can be a nightmare. Even if you remember all the class names and your text editor search mechanisms are cutting edge, it's still faster to look through a single file dedicated to a single class.

Searching files isn't as bad as compiling them. There is nothing quite as frustrating as compiling a huge file and then noticing you should have typed a 7 instead of a 6. It isn't unusual for a compile of a big project to take several minutes. I've even heard horror stories of projects that take hours to build! If you break the project down into multiple files and compile and link only the files that have changed since the last time you linked, your life will be a lot less frustrating.

But you still think multiple files just make things more difficult for you to remember what has and has not been compiled since the last link. You think that you'll be hopping from one file to the next just to change a variable name wherever it was used in your program. To ease your concerns, I don't know of any compilers that do not come with some sort of tracking mechanism to track what files need to be recompiled. Tradition has identified such a tool as a *make* tool. Some systems still call the command for that tool make. The other problem— tracking down every instance of a variable—is not that much of a hindrance. If you follow the design guidelines for object-oriented design, there will be very few times that you have to skip across multiple files for changes.

One final pitch: If you are a member of a team of programmers working on a project, how will you decide who works on a given source file without overwriting each other's work? This issue emphasizes the importance of how you break up the project files, which this lesson covers in detail.

Basic Concepts

As a rule of thumb, always place function prototypes, #define macros and constants, typedef statements, and class declarations in header files (traditionally, with a .h filename extension). Put the function and class definitions into source files (with a .cpp or similar extension). Although it isn't absolutely necessary, naming files similarly makes things easier. For instance, a header file and matching implementation file might be named, myclass.h and myclass.cpp respectively. That's the convention used in this book, and there is good reason for it. This method makes things easier to find, especially because other C++ programmers understand that tradition and expect your files to be divided that way.

Header Files

Let's look at a large project and think about how it might be divided. Imagine that your company has won a contract to build an employee payroll application. You and the other programmers on the team decide the following classes are needed for this application:

1. Employee
2. Hourly and Salary employees derived from Employee
3. PartTime employees derived from Hourly employees
4. PayPeriod, which specifies all the things related to a pay period

Of course, there would probably be more classes. Knowing this much alone, however, you can start to fill out the skeletons for the required files as in the following examples:

```
// File: Employ.h

#ifndef (EMPL_INC)
#define EMPL_INC

#include "projhdr.h" // More on this include file later

class Employee {
    // Details to follow
};

#endif

// File: Hourly.h

#ifndef (HOURLY_INC)
#define HOURLY_INC

#include "Employ.h"

class Hourly : public Employee {
    // Details to follow

    static list<Employee> EmployeeList;
};

class PartTime : public Hourly {
    // Details to follow
};

#endif

// File: Salary.h

#ifndef (SALARY_INC)
#define SALARY_INC

#include "Employ.h"

class Salary : public Employee {
    // Details to follow
};

#endif

// File: PayPrd.h

#ifndef (PAYPERIOD_INC)
#define PAYPERIOD_INC

#include "projhdr.h"

#include "Hourly.h"
#include "Salary.h"
```

21

```
class PayPeriod {
};

#endif
```

It might not seem like much, but you already know the basic *include tree* telling which files are needed where, which classes are needed, and who needs them. Now you can send individual programmers or programmer teams off to work on individual header files. As the project progresses, the header files get enough flesh on them for everybody to use. If your design is good, all any programmer needs to know about your class are the public (and, possibly, protected) member functions. If you need to know how to do anything with an Hourly employee, all you need is the Hourly.h file to tell you the function call parameter types and return values. In the meantime, the Hourly employee programmer team can implement all the public member functions without having to hold your hand.

Precompiled Header Files

Notice the line near the top that includes the file named projhdr.h. As the comment promises, there is more to that line than meets the eye. Many times on a project, you find that all the programmers are including the same subset of header files. Each time you compile your file, the compiler compiles those header files as well, whether they have changed or not. Most compilers today have become robust enough to precompile header files into one object file. In addition, they usually have an option that enables you to specify a *master header file* to contain the include lines common to your project. This master header file also compiles all of the include lines into one precompiled header file that you specify. The header file projhdr.h in the Employee listings might look like this:

```
// File: projhdr.h, project header file
// To be a precompiled header

#include<iostream.h>
#include<stdlib.h>
#include<math.h>
// Possibly more header files to include...
```

To force it to be a precompiled header, you need a source file like the following:

```
// File: projhdr.cpp, precompiled header source
#include "projhdr.h"
```

If projhdr is identified as a precompiled header file, compiling projhdr.cpp creates the precompiled header, and all the files that include projhdr.h include a group of header files that are already compiled. This speeds the compiles a great deal when you find yourself using a lot of include statements over and over again.

Variable Names and Function Prototypes

One common practice among programmers is to place only the parameter types without variable names in the function prototype statements. For example, the header file might look like the following:

```
// File: novars.h

void Printit(char *);
int AddThem(int, int);
double AddThem(double, double);
```

This can save you some time when you are changing variable names in the implementation file:

```
// File: novars.cpp

#include "novars.h"

void Printit(char *strValue)
{
    cout << strValue << endl;
}

int AddThem(int Low, int Delta)
{
    return(Low + Delta);
}

double AddThem(double CurrValue, double PrevValue)
{
    double Change = CurrValue - PrevValue;
    return(Change);
}
```

Implementation Files and Variable Scope

Some particularly sinister bugs are due to global variables in multiple files. That's another one of the reasons that the use of global variables should be limited. Still, you can't control the actions of other programmers who code things that you inherit, and you might find yourself in a situation where the most obvious approach to the problem is a global variable. Let's try an example. Assume you have three files as in Listing 21.1.

TYPE **Listing 21.1. Global variable scope in multiple files.**

21

```
1.1: // File1.cpp
1.2: #include<iostream.H>
1.3:
```

continues

Listing 21.1. continued

```
1.4: int MyGlobalVar;
1.5:
1.6: void fileTwoFt();
1.7: int addFunction(int);
1.8:
1.9: void main()
1.10:{
1.11:    int passedVar =12;
1.12:
1.13:    MyGlobalVar = 0x007; // Some really cool number
1.14:
1.15:    fileTwoFt();
1.16:
1.17:    int LocalVar = addFunction(passedVar);
1.18:
1.19:    cout << "MyGlobalVar back in main: "
1.20:         << MyGlobalVar << endl;
1.21:}

2.1: // File2.cpp
2.2: #include<iostream.h>
2.3:
2.4: extern int MyGlobalVar;
2.5: void fileTwoFt()
2.6: {
2.7:    cout << "MyGlobalVar in File 2: "
2.8:         << MyGlobalVar << endl;
2.9:}

3.1: // File3.cpp
3.2: #include<stdlib.h>
3.3: #include<iostream.h>
3.4: extern int MyGlobalVar;
3.5: static int OnlyInThisFile;
3.6: int addFunction(int Number)
3.7: {
3.8:    MyGlobalVar += Number;
3.9:    srand(static_cast<unsigned>(MyGlobalVar));
3.10:   OnlyInThisFile = rand();
3.11:   cout << "MyGlobalVar after add in File 3: "
3.12:        << MyGlobalVar << endl;
3.13:
3.14:   cout << "OnlyInThisFile is only available"
3.15:        << " in file 3: "
3.16:        << OnlyInThisFile << endl;
3.17:   return(MyGlobalVar);
3.18:}
```

OUTPUT

```
MyGlobalVar in File 2: 7
MyGlobalVar after add in File 3: 19
OnlyInThisFile is only available in file 3: 100
MyGlobalVar back in main: 19
```

ANALYSIS   On line 1.4 (file 1, line 4) `MyGlobalVar` is declared as a global integer value. It can be seen by all the functions in all the files of your program (with a catch, which is discussed soon). Lines 1.11 and 1.13 initialize the integer variables and pass control to `fileTwoFt()`, which is defined in `File2.cpp`.

In file 2, line 2.4, there is a new keyword, `extern`, and `MyGlobalVar` is declared again. The `extern` keyword makes a difference, though, because it basically tells the compiler, "Don't set aside memory for this `int` because the memory is already set aside in another file to be linked with this one." Had you not used the `extern` keyword, the compiler would complain about referencing an undeclared variable on line 2.8. If you had left the `extern` keyword out and declared it as `int MyGlobalVar` again in this file, the linker would complain about multiple definitions of `MyGlobalVar`.

After printing the message in `fileTwoFt()`, control returns to the main function, which calls `addFunction()`, defined in `File3.cpp`, with the `passVar` value. Again, you have to declare `MyGlobalVar` with `extern` on line 3.4. On line 3.5 there is a new use for `static` that has not yet been mentioned. When used in this way (as a global variable), it indicates that the variable is global only within the file, following the place where it is declared. It is not visible to any of the functions defined in the other two files, and it is not visible to any functions that might be defined before it in `File3.cpp`. This is a key thing to remember when you're trying to limit the scope of global variables and control their use.

After printing a couple of appropriate messages, `addFunction()` returns control to `main` where the final message is printed.

Interdependency of Variables Between Files

All of this might give you a false sense of security about returning to global variables to avoid passing them around between functions. Before you decide to dump all the warnings about globals out the window, you might want to consider some things. Look at Listing 21.2 and see whether you can tell what the output for these files should be.

TYPE   **Listing 21.2. Interdependency bugs.**

```
//File1.cpp

int ClassesPlusOne = 1; // Global counter


// File2.cpp
#include<iostream.h>

extern int ClassesPlusOne;
```

continues

21

Listing 21.2. continued

```
class MyGlobalClass {
public:
        MyGlobalClass() {
                ClassesPlusOne++;
                cout << "There are now " <<
                        << (ClassesPlusOne - 1)
                        << "MyGlobalClass objects!"
                        << endl;
        }

};
MyGlobalClass AGlobalObject;
```

OUTPUT These files are not complete and do not compile, so there is no output.

ANALYSIS In `File1.cpp` there is a single line declaration of a global `int` variable. In `File2.cpp` there is a simple class definition and an instantiation of an object of that class. The class depends on the global variable in `File1.cpp`, and it appears as though there should be no problems. But there is a problem: It compiles fine and runs as expected on one platform, but gives odd results on another. There is no control over the order in which global variables are initialized. If the code in `File2.cpp` is executed first, `ClassesPlusOne` is not initialized when `AGlobalObject` is instantiated! This is another reason to avoid global variables.

If you absolutely have to program something like Listing 21.2 and you really can't see any other way around it, fear not. A clever group of programmers have developed a method to fix this problem. Place all the globals inside a dummy class and initialize them by instantiating an object of that class. Listing 21.3 illustrates this technique.

TYPE **Listing 21.3. Safe initialization of globals.**

```
//projdep.h

extern int ClassesPlusOne;
extern int MyGlobalVar;

class MyGlobalClass {
private:
    static int counter;
public:
    MyGlobalClass() {
        // We want to initialize only the first time
        counter++;
        if(counter < 2)
        {
```

```
                    ClassesPlusOne = 1;
                    MyGlobalVar = 7;
                }
        }
};

static MyGlobalClass ASingleClassObject;

// projdep.cpp

#include "projdep.h"
int MyGlobalClass::counter = 0;

int MyGlobalVar;
int ClassesPlusOne;


// File2.cpp, same as before except for
// an additional include line
#include<iostream.h>

#include "projdep.h"

extern int ClassesPlusOne;

class MyGlobalClass {
public:
        MyGlobalClass() {
                ClassesPlusOne++;
                cout << "There are now " <<
                        << (ClassesPlusOne - 1)
                        << "MyGlobalClass objects!"
                        << endl;
        }

};
MyGlobalClass AGlobalObject;
```

OUTPUT These files still do not compile, but they now work predictably when completed with other functions.

ANALYSIS This time, all the global data is initialized inside a new class provided for that purpose inside a new header file. The last line of the header file, `static MyGlobalClass ASingleClassObject;`, creates a single instance of this class in each file where `projdep.h` is included. In addition, the dummy class constructor makes certain that the variables are initialized only once by using the `counter` static member variable.

21

More About *extern*

Because there is a lot of legacy C code out there that many companies have invested in, you might find it a pain to have to rewrite that code in C++. Unfortunately, simply including C code in your program can cause problems due to "name mangling" performed by your C++ compiler. The compiler mangles (alters) function names to enable it to keep track of all the possible overloaded versions of functions. If you include a C program function, you don't want the compiler to mangle its name—but how can you prevent it? You have the same problem when linking object files for any other language. The ANSI/ISO standard provides an answer by overloading the extern keyword as a linkage specifier. ANSI currently specifies two types of linkage, C (no name mangling) or C++ (allow name mangling). The following could be used to ensure C linkage to prevent a function name from being mangled:

```
// single-line version to indicate a single
// function to have C linkage:
extern "C" int SomeCFuntion(char *Str, int X);

// block version for multiple functions
extern "C" {
    float CSqrt(float Sqrd);
    int SomeCFunction(char *Str, int X);
}
```

Although the ANSI/ISO standard only specifies C and C++ linkage, it does not preclude compiler vendors from providing linkage specifiers for other languages as well.

Hiding Variables and Global Scope Resolution

Just as it is possible to identify a particular class member with a scope resolution operator, you can also use them to identify hidden global variables. Listing 21.4 is an example of various scope resolution mechanisms and global variable hiding.

TYPE   **Listing 21.4. Scope resolution operators.**

```
1: // Listing 21.4,  family.cpp
2: #include<iostream.h>
3: #include<string.h>
4:
5: class family {
6: public:
7:     char sirName[15];
8:     int familySize;
9:     static double avgSize;
10:    family(char *n, int s) {
```

```
11:        strcpy(sirName, n);
12:        familySize = s;
13:    }
14:};
15:// The average for all families in this program:
16:double family::avgSize = 0;
17:
18:double avgSize = 3.5; // National average
19:
20:void main()
21:{
22:    family Hord("Hord", 6);
23:    family Clinton("Clinton", 3);
24:    double avgSize;
25:    // What is the average of our two families?
26:    family::avgSize =
27:        (Hord.familySize + Clinton.familySize)
28:        / 2;
29:
30:    avgSize =              // 2-family to national comparison
31:        (family::avgSize // family average
32:        - ::avgSize);     // national avg
33:
34:    if( avgSize > 0 )
35:    {
36:        // The two-family average is above the
37:        // national average
38:        cout << "Average is above average."
39:            << endl;
40:    }
41:    else
42:    {
43:        cout << "Aver. is = or < average size."
44:            << endl;
45:    }
46:}
```

OUTPUT Average is above average.

ANALYSIS Because this is confusing enough already, I limited everything to one file in this example. The quirks of this example are equally pertinent to multiple file examples. The one thing you need to notice here is that there are three variables named avgSize. One is a static member variable of the family class (line 9), one is a global variable (line 18), and one is a local variable in main (line 30). If the example seems unrealistic, imagine that you want to keep track of the average size of all the families that your program knows about and be able to compare the program average with the average size of families in the nation. The static member variable keeps track of the average for all families, the global variable contains the national average, and the main function variable provides a temporary variable for the comparison.

21

On lines 22 and 23, two families were created to track and initialize the two-family average on line 26. Without the family:: qualifier on line 26, the local avgSize is initialized instead. The local variable hides the global avgSize. On lines 30 to 32, the national avgSize (notice how the scope resolution operator, ::, is used) is subtracted from the Hord/Clinton family avgSize to set the comparison avgSize. Again, any references to avgSize inside main that do not include some sort of scope resolution refer to the local avgSize. The if statement starting on line 34 determines whether the family avgSize is greater than the national (global) avgSize and prints an appropriate message.

Avoiding Multiple Declarations

There is one last consideration concerning the use of static and global variables in multiple file development. Listing 21.5 is an example of a possible header file. Can you see the possible problem that this might cause when you include this file in more than one source code file of your program?

TYPE   **Listing 21.5. Multiple declaration error.**

```
// Listing 21.5, simple.h

class SimpleClass {
private:
   static int SimpleCount;
public:
   SimpleClass() { SimpleCount++; }
   ~SimpleClass() {}
   static void ShowCount() {
      cout << SimpleCount << endl;
   }
};

int SimpleClass::SimpleCount = 0;
```

OUTPUT   This contains only a class definition, so there is no output.

ANALYSIS   Because this is such a simple and short class, it might seem unnecessary to have a separate implementation file. But there is an error waiting to happen, and a novice programmer might spend a long time trying to figure it out. If you include this file in just one source file, there are no problems. If your project grows to multiple source files and more than one of them includes this SimpleClass header file, your compiler starts to cry about multiple declarations and you'll wonder what you changed to cause it. To avoid that problem, always create a separate source file to implement the class if there are any initialization requirements. Afterwards, compile that source file and link it with the rest of your source files. In the SimpleClass example, the implementation file would just have an include line to include the SimpleClass header file and the static variable intitializer statement.

Do	**Don't**

DO modularize your program development into separately compiled files to speed development.

DO avoid using the same name for variables in your program. If you need to, use scope resolution operators to specify between variables.

DON'T overuse global variables. In fact, use them only when not using them makes no sense or makes the program confusing.

DO use precompiled header files to speed compilation.

DO separate class declaration and definition into separate files to avoid multiple definition errors.

Summary

Today you learned not only how to divide a project into multiple files, but why it is necessary to do so. You also learned more about variable scope rules and how they pertain to multiple file projects. You learned yet another purpose for static and you learned the dual meaning of extern.

Q&A

Q What is the variable scope of a static variable declared at the file level?

A It has the scope (or is visible) for all the functions that follow it in that file.

Q Does a variable declared with extern cause the compiler to set aside a memory location for that variable?

A No. The purpose of extern, in this case, is to indicate that a variable by that name and of that type exists, but not to set aside storage for it.

21

Q Why would you ever name multiple variables with the same name?

A Normally, you would avoid doing this. If, however, the real-world problem matches the concept, it might make sense to do so.

Quiz

1. How does dividing your project into multiple files speed project builds?
2. What is the difference in scope between a global variable and a global variable declared with `static`?
3. What is the difference between `extern` used to declare a variable and `extern` to indicate a linkage type?
4. Why is it a good idea to place static member variable initialization in a separate file from the class header file?
5. What is a precompiled header?

Exercises

1. Write a program that has a global variable named `Global` and, in a separate file, a function with a local variable named `Global`. Show scope resolution.
2. Write a program that has a main function, a user-defined class with a static member variable, and a variable printing function, each in its own file.
3. Write two function prototypes named `sqrt`—one taking a complex and returning a complex, and one taking a `double` and returning a `double`. Write the code necessary to make the `double` version link with C linkage and the complex version link with C++ linkage.
4. **BUG BUSTERS:** What is wrong with this program?

```
1:      #include <iostream.h>
2:
3:      int JamesBond 0x007;
3:      void main()
4:      {
5:        int JamesBond = 0x005;
6:        cout << (JamesBond + JamesBond)
7:              << endl;
8:      }
```

5. **BUG BUSTERS:** What is wrong with this program?

```
1:      #include <iostream.h>
2:
```

```
3:    char *SomeFunct()
4:    {
5:        return(Goldfinger);
6:    }
7:
8:    static char *Goldfinger ="Goldfinger";
9:
10:   void main()
11:   {
12:       cout << "Here is Goldfinger:"
13:            << SomeFunct() << endl;
14:   }
```

6. Delete the static keyword in line 8 of exercise 5. Does it work now? Why?

21

In Review

The following program brings together many of the advanced techniques you've learned during the past three weeks of hard work. Week 3 in Review provides a template-based, linked list with exception handling. Examine it in detail; if you understand it fully, you *are* a C++ programmer.

WARNING

If your compiler does not support templates, or if your compiler does not support try and catch, you will not be able to compile or run this listing.

```
1:      // ****************************************************
2:      //
3:      // Title:        Week 3 in review
4:      //
5:      // File:         Week3
6:      //
7:      // Description:  Provide a template-based linked list
8:      //                   demonstration program with exception handling
9:      //
10:     // Classes:      PART - holds part numbers and potentially other
11:     //                   information about parts. This will be the
12:     //                   example class for the list to hold
13:     //                   Note use of operator<< to print the
14:     //                   information about a part based on its
15:     //                   run time type.
16:     //
17:     //               Node - acts as a node in a List
18:     //
19:     //               List - template based list which provides the
20:     //                   mechanisms for a linked list
21:     //
22:     //
23:     // Author:       Jesse Liberty (jl)
24:     //
25:     // Developed:    486/66 32mb RAM  MVC 1.5
26:     //
27:     // Target:       Platform independent
28:     //
29:     // Rev History:  9/94 - First release (jl)
30:     // ****************************************************
31:
32:     #include <iostream.h>
33:
34:     typedef unsigned long ULONG;
35:     typedef unsigned short USHORT;
36:
37:     // exception classes
38:     class Exception {};
39:     class OutOfMemory : public Exception{};
40:     class NullNode : public Exception{};
41:     class EmptyList : public Exception {};
42:     class BoundsError : public Exception {};
43:
44:
45:     // *************** Part ************
46:     // Abstract base class of parts
47:     class Part
48:     {
49:     public:
50:         Part():itsObjectNumber(1) {}
51:         Part(ULONG ObjectNumber):itsObjectNumber(ObjectNumber){}
52:         virtual ~Part(){};
53:         ULONG GetObjectNumber() const { return itsObjectNumber; }
54:         virtual void Display() const =0;  // must be overridden
55:
```

```
56:     private:
57:         ULONG itsObjectNumber;
58:     };
59:
60:     // implementation of pure virtual function so that
61:     // derived classes can chain up
62:     void Part::Display() const
63:     {
64:         cout << "\nPart Number: " << itsObjectNumber << endl;
65:     }
66:
67:     // this one operator<< will be called for all part objects.
68:     // It need not be a friend as it does not access private data
69:     // It calls Display() which uses the required polymorphism
70:     // We'd like to be able to override this based on the real type
71:     // of thePart, but C++ does not support contravariance
72:     ostream& operator<<( ostream& theStream,Part& thePart)
73:     {
74:         thePart.Display();  // virtual contravariance!
75:         return theStream;
76:     }
77:
78:     // **************** Car Part ************
79:     class CarPart : public Part
80:     {
81:     public:
82:         CarPart():itsModelYear(94){}
83:         CarPart(USHORT year, ULONG partNumber);
84:         USHORT GetModelYear() const { return itsModelYear; }
85:         virtual void Display() const;
86:     private:
87:         USHORT itsModelYear;
88:     };
89:
90:     CarPart::CarPart(USHORT year, ULONG partNumber):
91:         itsModelYear(year),
92:         Part(partNumber)
93:     {}
94:
95:     void CarPart::Display() const
96:     {
97:         Part::Display();
98:         cout << "Model Year: " << itsModelYear << endl;
99:     }
100:
101:    // *************** AirPlane Part ************
102:    class AirPlanePart : public Part
103:    {
104:    public:
105:        AirPlanePart():itsEngineNumber(1){};
106:        AirPlanePart(USHORT EngineNumber, ULONG PartNumber);
107:        virtual void Display() const;
108:        USHORT GetEngineNumber()const { return itsEngineNumber; }
109:    private:
110:        USHORT itsEngineNumber;
111:    };
```

```
112:
113:    AirPlanePart::AirPlanePart(USHORT EngineNumber, ULONG PartNumber):
114:        itsEngineNumber(EngineNumber),
115:        Part(PartNumber)
116:    {}
117:
118:    void AirPlanePart::Display() const
119:    {
120:        Part::Display();
121:        cout << "Engine No.: " << itsEngineNumber << endl;
122:    }
123:
124:    // forward declaration of class List
125:    template <class T>
126:    class List;
127:
128:    // ***************  Node ***********
129:    // Generic node, can be added to a list
130:    // **********************************
131:
132:    template <class T>
133:    class Node
134:    {
135:    public:
136:        friend class List<T>;
137:        Node (T*);
138:        ~Node();
139:        void SetNext(Node * node) { itsNext = node; }
140:        Node * GetNext() const;
141:        T * GetObject() const;
142:    private:
143:        T* itsObject;
144:        Node * itsNext;
145:    };
146:
147:    // Node Implementations...
148:
149:    template <class T>
150:    Node<T>::Node(T* pOjbect):
151:    itsObject(pOjbect),
152:    itsNext(0)
153:    {}
154:
155:    template <class T>
156:    Node<T>::~Node()
157:    {
158:        delete itsObject;
159:        itsObject = 0;
160:        delete itsNext;
161:        itsNext = 0;
162:    }
163:
164:    // Returns NULL if no next Node
165:    template <class T>
166:    Node<T> * Node<T>::GetNext() const
167:    {
```

```
168:          return itsNext;
169:     }
170:
171:     template <class T>
172:     T * Node<T>::GetObject() const
173:     {
174:        if (itsObject)
175:           return itsObject;
176:        else
177:           throw NullNode();
178:     }
179:
180:     // *************** List ************
181:     // Generic list template
182:     // Works with any numbered object
183:     // ********************************
184:     template <class T>
185:     class List
186:     {
187:     public:
188:        List();
189:        ~List();
190:
191:        void     Iterate(void (T::*f)()const) const;
192:        T*         Find(ULONG & position, ULONG ObjectNumber)  const;
193:        T*       GetFirst() const;
194:        void       Insert(T *);
195:        T*       operator[](ULONG) const;
196:        ULONG    GetCount() const { return itsCount; }
197:     private:
198:        Node<T> * pHead;
199:        ULONG itsCount;
200:     };
201:
202:     // Implementations for Lists...
203:     template <class T>
204:     List<T>::List():
205:        pHead(0),
206:        itsCount(0)
207:        {}
208:
209:     template <class T>
210:     List<T>::~List()
211:     {
212:        delete pHead;
213:     }
214:
215:     template <class T>
216:     T*    List<T>::GetFirst() const
217:     {
218:        if (pHead)
219:           return pHead->itsObject;
220:        else
221:           throw EmptyList();
222:     }
223:
```

```
224:     template <class T>
225:     T *  List<T>::operator[](ULONG offSet) const
226:     {
227:         Node<T>* pNode = pHead;
228:
229:         if (!pHead)
230:             throw EmptyList();
231:
232:         if (offSet > itsCount)
233:             throw BoundsError();
234:
235:         for (ULONG i=0;i<offSet; i++)
236:             pNode = pNode->itsNext;
237:
238:        return    pNode->itsObject;
239:     }
240:
241:     // find a given object in list based on its unique number (id)
242:     template <class T>
243:     T*    List<T>::Find(ULONG & position, ULONG ObjectNumber)  const
244:     {
245:         Node<T> * pNode = 0;
246:         for (pNode = pHead, position = 0;
247:                 pNode!=NULL;
248:                 pNode = pNode->itsNext, position++)
249:         {
250:             if (pNode->itsObject->GetObjectNumber() == ObjectNumber)
251:                 break;
252:         }
253:         if (pNode == NULL)
254:             return NULL;
255:         else
256:             return pNode->itsObject;
257:     }
258:
259:     // call function for every object in list
260:     template <class T>
261:     void List<T>::Iterate(void (T::*func)()const) const
262:     {
263:         if (!pHead)
264:             return;
265:         Node<T>* pNode = pHead;
266:         do
267:             (pNode->itsObject->*func)();
268:         while (pNode = pNode->itsNext);
269:     }
270:
271:     // insert if the number of the object is unique
272:     template <class T>
273:     void List<T>::Insert(T* pObject)
274:     {
275:         Node<T> * pNode = new Node<T>(pObject);
276:         Node<T> * pCurrent = pHead;
277:         Node<T> * pNext = 0;
278:
279:         ULONG New =  pObject->GetObjectNumber();
280:         ULONG Next = 0;
```

```
281:        itsCount++;
282:
283:        if (!pHead)
284:        {
285:            pHead = pNode;
286:            return;
287:        }
288:
289:        // if this one is smaller than head
290:        // this one is the new head
291:        if (pHead->itsObject->GetObjectNumber() > New)
292:        {
293:            pNode->itsNext = pHead;
294:            pHead = pNode;
295:            return;
296:        }
297:
298:        for (;;)
299:        {
300:            // if there is no next, append this new one
301:            if (!pCurrent->itsNext)
302:            {
303:                pCurrent->itsNext = pNode;
304:                return;
305:            }
306:
307:            // if this goes after this one and before the next
308:            // then insert it here, otherwise get the next
309:            pNext = pCurrent->itsNext;
310:            Next = pNext->itsObject->GetObjectNumber();
311:            if (Next > New)
312:            {
313:                pCurrent->itsNext = pNode;
314:                pNode->itsNext = pNext;
315:                return;
316:            }
317:            pCurrent = pNext;
318:        }
319:    }
320:
321:
322:    int main()
323:    {
324:        List<Part> theList;
325:        int choice;
326:        ULONG ObjectNumber;
327:        USHORT value;
328:        Part * pPart;
329:        while (true)
330:        {
331:            cout << "(0)Quit (1)Car (2)Plane: ";
332:            cin >> choice;
333:
334:            if (!choice)
335:                break;
336:
```

```
337:            cout << "New ObjectNumber?: ";
338:            cin >>  ObjectNumber;
339:
340:            if (choice == 1)
341:            {
342:               cout << "Model Year?: ";
343:               cin >> value;
344:               try
345:               {
346:                  pPart = new CarPart(value,ObjectNumber);
347:               }
348:               catch (OutOfMemory)
349:               {
350:                  cout << "Not enough memory; Exiting..." << endl;
351:                  return 1;
352:               }
353:            }
354:            else
355:            {
356:               cout << "Engine Number?: ";
357:               cin >> value;
358:               try
359:               {
360:                  pPart = new AirPlanePart(value,ObjectNumber);
361:               }
362:               catch (OutOfMemory)
363:               {
364:                  cout << "Not enough memory; Exiting..." << endl;
365:                  return 1;
366:               }
367:            }
368:            try
369:            {
370:               theList.Insert(pPart);
371:            }
372:            catch (NullNode)
373:            {
374:               cout << "The list is broken, and the node is null!" << endl;
375:               return 1;
376:            }
377:            catch (EmptyList)
378:            {
379:               cout << "The list is empty!" << endl;
380:               return 1;
381:            }
382:         }
383:         try
384:         {
385:            for (int i = 0; i < theList.GetCount(); i++ )
386:               cout << *(theList[i]);
387:         }
388:         catch (NullNode)
389:         {
390:            cout << "The list is broken, and the node is null!" << endl;
391:            return 1;
392:         }
393:         catch (EmptyList)
```

```
394:            {
395:                cout << "The list is empty!" << endl;
396:                return 1;
397:            }
398:            catch (BoundsError)
399:            {
400:                cout << "Tried to read beyond the end of the list!" << endl;
401:                return 1;
402:            }
403:    return 0;
404:    }
```

OUTPUT

```
    (0)Quit (1)Car (2)Plane: 1
New PartNumber?: 2837
Model Year? 90

    (0)Quit (1)Car (2)Plane: 2
New PartNumber?: 378
Engine Number?: 4938

    (0)Quit (1)Car (2)Plane: 1
New PartNumber?: 4499
Model Year? 94

    (0)Quit (1)Car (2)Plane: 1
New PartNumber?: 3000
Model Year? 93

    (0)Quit (1)Car (2)Plane: 0

Part Number: 378
Engine No. 4938

Part Number: 2837
Model Year: 90

Part Number: 3000
Model Year: 93

Part Number 4499
Model Year: 94
```

ANALYSIS The Week 3 in Review listing modifies the program provided in Week 2 to add templates, ostream processing, and exception handling. The output is identical.

On lines 37 through 42, a number of exception classes are declared. In the somewhat primitive exception handling provided by this program, no data or methods are required of these exceptions; they serve as flags to the catch statements, which print out a very simple warning and then exit. A more robust program might pass these exceptions by reference and then extract context or other data from the exception objects in an attempt to recover from the problem.

On line 45, the abstract base class `Part` is declared exactly as it was in Week 2. The only interesting change here is in the *non-class member* `operator<<()`, which is declared on lines 72 through 76. Note that this is neither a member of `Part` nor a friend of `Part`; it simply takes a `Part` reference as one of its arguments.

You might want to have `operator<<` take a `CarPart` and an `AirPlanePart` in the hope that the correct `operator<<` would be called, based on whether a car part or an airplane part is passed. Because the program passes a pointer to a part, however, and not a pointer to a car part or an airplane part, C++ would have to call the right function based on the real type of one of the arguments to the function. This is called *contravariance* and is not supported in C++.

There are only two ways to achieve polymorphism in C++: function polymorphism and virtual functions. Function polymorphism won't work here because in every case, you are matching the same signature—the one taking a reference to a `Part`.

Virtual functions won't work here because `operator<<` is not a member function of `Part`. You can't make `operator<<` a member function of `Part` because you want to invoke

```
cout << thePart
```

This means that the actual call would be to `cout.operator<<(Part&)`, and `cout` does not have a version of `operator<<` that takes a `Part` reference!

To get around this limitation, the Week 3 program uses just one `operator<<`, taking a reference to a `Part`. This then calls `Display()`, which *is* a virtual member function, and thus the right version is called.

On lines 132 through 145, `Node` is defined as a template. It serves the same function as `Node` did in the Week 2 review program, but this version of `Node` is *not* tied to a `Part` object. It can, in fact, be the node for any type of object.

Note that if you try to get the object from the `Node` and there is no object, this is considered an exception, and the exception is thrown on line 177.

On lines 180 through 200, a generic `List` class template is defined. This `List` class can hold nodes of any objects that have unique identification numbers, and it keeps them sorted in ascending order. Each of the list functions checks for exceptional circumstances and throws the appropriate exceptions as required.

On lines 322 through 404, the driver program creates a list of two types of `Part` objects, and then prints out the values of the objects in the list by using the standard streams mechanism.

WEEK 4

Bonus Week At A Glance

Bravo! In just 21 days, you've taught yourself how to program in the hottest computer language in the industry. Take a few minutes to reflect and give yourself a well-deserved pat on the back before reading any further.

The Bonus Week contains additional information that can help you hone your C++ skills to a razor finish. This last week is not essential for you to become a serious C++ programmer, but you will find it rewarding.

On Bonus Day 22, "Advanced C++ Features," you learn to use a collection of specialized ANSI C++ tools that many programmers don't even realize exist. These are tools that are not essential for every C++ programmer to know but are indispensable in many circumstances.

22

23

24

25

26

27

28

Bonus Day 23, "More About Streams," covers some of the more advanced streams programming techniques. After completing this lesson, you will have all you need to create new manipulators for the stream classes you learned to create on Day 16. You also learn a great deal about other streams programming techniques that space would not allow us to cover on Day 16.

On Bonus Day 24, "Object-Oriented Design," you learn more about this important subject. Without object-oriented design techniques, C++ is "just another C" with few advantages over its predecessor. This lesson helps you think in a way that builds on the object-oriented design paradigm.

Bonus Days 25 and 26, "Data Structures" and "Simple Sorting and Searching Algorithms," respectively, introduce you to the inner sanctum of computer science. On these two days you learn how to solve several common categories of problems.

"Common Mistakes and Basic Debugging," on Bonus Day 27, is designed to help you avoid some of the common mistakes that many beginning programmers make. Not all errors can be avoided, but with this lesson, you should more quickly recognize many errors by category and more quickly find the solutions.

The final day of the bonus week, "What's Next?," gives you some insight on where to turn when you run into a question that this book doesn't seem to answer. It also provides the resources you need to further improve your C++ programming skills.

Day **22**

Advanced C++ Features

In previous lessons you learned about some of the advantages of reusable code. You also learned about polymorphism using virtual functions. In this lesson, you will learn about writing libraries of C++ programs and classes that other programmers can use in their programs. These libraries are like software components that others can plug in and use without change in their programs.

This lesson also discusses the internals of how a computer performs polymorphism calls with the correct virtual functions.

You will also examine the idea of Run-Time Type Identification (RTTI) and casting, which is a method for changing the type or const status of an object. As stated previously, a need for RTTI and/or casting can be a sign of poor design, but there are rare occasions where it maps more directly to the real world. Anytime something maps directly to the real world, it is usually a sign of good design. ANSI/ISO C++ provides a way to safely perform RTTI and casting types, or const status.

Lastly, data alignment is discussed. Understanding data alignment can help you increase program performance for size in memory, speed, or both.

Namespaces and Class Libraries

One of the payoffs of object-oriented design is the capability to design self-contained software objects, called *libraries*. These libraries, such as the C++ standard libraries, provide all the functionality needed to use the objects they define. Because of their encapsulated design, libraries can be used in a variety of applications. For example, a complex math library contains all the functionality needed for complex math and can be used for physics applications or business applications.

Some companies are even now designing and building C++ libraries for profit. Libraries can be highly specialized or generic, as long as they provide all the basic functionality required for a given class of objects. Maybe there is a need for a particular set of C++ class libraries for the types of applications you design. The following sections introduce you to some of the basic concepts you need in order to design and implement class libraries.

Namespaces

You might have already started to wonder about what would happen if you chose to name a class by the same name that somebody else in your project had chosen. Maybe you have seen the problem of picking a name that was already used in a header file that you included. Library programmers have dealt with this problem for some time. Some library programmers give long complicated names to their classes so that their names don't clash with names that an application programmer might use. This has been called a *namespace* problem because you cannot have multiple class names in the same space. The namespace problem is particularly nasty in the global data area, which cuts across file boundaries. ANSI C++ provides a built-in way around the namespace problem with a `namespace` construct.

The `namespace` construct is similar to a class definition, except that it does not have the closing semicolon. Listing 22.1 is an example of how to use the namespace construct:

Listing 22.1. The namespace construct.

```
1:      namespace MyMammalClasses {
2:          // A collection of mammals
3:          class Dog {
4:          public:
5:            Dog(int itsAge);
6:            ~Dog();
7:            Stick fetch();
8:            // Other Dog declarations
9:          };
10:         class Cat {
11:         public:
12:           Cat(int Lives = 9);
```

```
13:          ~Cat();
14:          Rodent play();
15:          // Other Cat declarations
16:        };
17:      class Horse {
18:      public:
19:        Horse(Hands Height);
20:        ~Horse();
21:        void prance();
22:        // Other Horse declarations
23:        };
24:    }
```

References to items in the namespace are similar to the references made to classes:

```
// Use MyMammalClasses in SomeFunction()

void SomeFunction()
{
    MyMammalClasses::Cat Felix;        // Scope resolution of namespace
    MyMammalClasses::Horse Beauty(9);
    Rodent Mouse;
    Mouse = Felix.play();
    Beauty.prance();
}
```

This can get pretty tedious if you use these classes often. Fortunately, ANSI/ISO C++ provides a way to make the scope resolution automatic with the using keyword.

```
// Use MyMammalClasses in SomeFunction(), the easy way

void SomeFunction()
{
    using namespace MyMammalClass; // Scope is MyMammals if not otherwise stated
    Cat Felix;                     // Ah, much simpler and easier to understand
    Horse Beauty(9);
    Rodent Mouse;
    Mouse = Felix.play();
    Beauty.prance();
}
```

Of course, the using keyword can defeat the idea behind namespaces when two namespaces clash. If that happens, the problem doesn't show up at the using keyword line; it appears at the point of conflict:

```
namespace PetFunctions {
    // A collection of functions for keeping track of multiple pets
    char *RandomNamer();
    // And so on
}
namespace FamilyFunctions {
    // A collection of functions for keeping track of a growing family
    char *RandomNamer();
    // And so on
}
```

```
void main()
{
    const int NameSize = 10;
    using namespace PetFunctions;
    using namespace FamilyFunctions; // No problems here
    char CatsName[NameSize];
  // More useful code…
    strcpy(CatsName, RandomNamer());          // Oops, which RandomNamer() func-
tion?
}
```

This program does not compile, so there is no output.

To resolve the scope resolution, you can also directly identify the desired scope for the ambiguous line or with the using keyword:

```
// Same namespaces as previous listing
void main()
{
    const int NameSize = 10;
    using PetFunctions::RandomNamer;
            // This is the default RandomNamer() to be called
    using namespace FamilyFunctions; // No problems here
    char CatsName[NameSize];
    char SonsName[NameSize];
  // More useful code…
    strcpy(CatsName, RandomNamer());
            // Now this is OK, it refers to the pet Name()
    // To get the Family RandomNamer(), we have to use scope resolution
    strcpy(SonsName,
            FamilyFunctions::RandomNamer());
}
```

Again, this program doesn't compile, so there is no output.

Class Library Design

A library in C and C++ is a special-case object file linked with the object files created from your source code. A class library is a C++ library that contains all the functionality of a class of objects. For example, the iostream library is a class library that contains all the functionality required for input/output on your computer. You notify the compiler that you want to link with a particular library by identifying the library header file in an include statement, as in #include <iostream.h>.

Here is the basic procedure to create and use a class library:

1. Create the C++ header file that contains the function and class prototypes for the class.

2. Create the source file that contains the function definitions for the class.

3. Compile the source file to create an object file.

4. Use the compiler library tool to convert the object file to a library file.

Let's use an example to get a concrete grasp on this procedure. Listing 22.2 is a simple Dog classes header file.

Listing 22.2. The Dog class header.

```
1:     // Listing 22.2 DOG.H, A header file that contains
2:     // some Dog classes that illustrates my bias
3:
4:     #ifndef _DOG_BREEDS_INC_
5:     #define _DOG_BREEDS_INC_
6:
7:     namespace DogBreeds {
8:
9:     enum dogSize { Small, Medium, Large };
10:
11:    class Dog { // The base class
12:    private:
13:        int itsAge;
14:        dogSize itsSize;
15:    public:
16:        Dog(int Age);
17:        virtual ~Dog();
18:        virtual void Speak();
19:        void SetSize(dogSize Sz);
20:    };
21:
22:    class GreatDane : public Dog { // A GreatDane is a Dog
23:    public:
24:        GreatDane(int Age);
25:        ~GreatDane();
26:        void Speak();
27:    };
28:
29:    class ToyPoodle : public Dog { // Arguably, a ToyPoodle is also a Dog
30:    public:
31:        ToyPoodle(int Age);
32:        ~ToyPoodle();
33:        void Speak();
34:    };
35:
36:    }
37:    #endif
```

Listing 22.3 is the source file that eventually becomes the library.

Listing 22.3. A library source file.

```
 1:     // Listing 22.3 The Dog library source file
 2:     #include<iostream.h>
 3:     #include "Dog.h"
 4:
 5:     namespace DogBreeds {
 6:
 7:     Dog::Dog(int Age) { itsAge = Age; }
 8:     Dog::~Dog() {
 9:         cout << "Putting a Dog to sleep."
10:             << endl;
11:     }
12:     void Dog::Speak() {
13:         cout << "Rough!" << endl;
14:     }
15:     void Dog::SetSize(dogSize Sz) {
16:         itsSize = Sz;
17:     }
18:
19:     GreatDane::GreatDane(int Age)   : Dog(Age) {
20:         SetSize(Large);
21:     }
22:     GreatDane::~GreatDane() {
23:         cout << "Poor fellow." << endl;
24:     }
25:     void GreatDane::Speak() {
26:         cout << "ROUGH! ROUGH! ROUGH!" << endl;
27:     }
28:
29:     ToyPoodle::ToyPoodle(int Age) : Dog(Age) {
30:         SetSize(Small);
31:     }
32:     ToyPoodle::~ToyPoodle() {
33:         cout << "Good ridance!" << endl;
34:     }
35:
36:     void ToyPoodle::Speak() {
37:         cout << "yip-yip-yip-yip!" << endl;
38:     }
39:
40:     } // End of namespace DogBreeds
```

Refer to your compiler or IDE documentation to compile this source file to create an object file. Then consult your compiler or IDE documentation to convert the object file to a library file. After you've created the library file, you are effectively done and you can share this library file with others. Before you do, though, test the library by creating a program that uses it, as in the example in Listing 22.4.

Listing 22.4. A program that uses a library.

```
1:      // Listing 22.4 DOGGIE.CPP, A program that uses the // DogBreeds library
2:      #include "dogs.h"
3:
4:      void main()
5:      {
6:          using namespace DogBreeds;
7:          GreatDane Natasha(3);
8:          ToyPoodle Fluffy(2);
9:          Natasha.Speak();
10:         Fluffy.Speak();
11:     }
```

Compile and link this program with the DogBreeds library file and see whether it works.

How Polymorphism Works

If you are the curious type, you might wonder how compiler vendors implemented polymorphism. Polymorphism, as you probably recall, is the capability to make the correct virtual function call based on the data type of an object at run-time. Remember that polymorphism comes into play only when you pass a base-type pointer that points to a derived class. For instance, if you were to use the Dogs class library that you created in the previous section, you might have a code fragment that looks something like the following:

```
1:      #include "Dogs.h"
2:      // Assuming we have the following:
3:      using namespace DogBreeds;
4:
5:      void SpeakCommand(Dog *ptrDog) {
6:          ptrDog->Speak();
7:      }
8:
9:      void main()
10:     {
11:         // Create a Dog pointer and assign a ToyPoodle to it
12:         Dog *pDog = new ToyPoodle(3);
13:         // Command the Dog to speak, polymorphically
14:         SpeakCommand(pDog); // ToyPoodle::Speak() called
15:     }
```

You might envision a chunk of memory that looks something like Figure 22.1 when you think of the ToyPoodle Dog object you created.

Figure 22.1.
The hierarchy of
`ToyPoodle`.

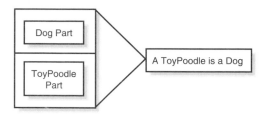

How do you picture the call to the `ToyPoodle::Speak()` function rather than the `Dog::Speak()` function? The way compilers handle finding the correct function call at run-time is through a pointer added to the class, which points to the correct functions for the derived types. Figure 22.2 illustrates the way that's done. A v-pointer (virtual pointer) is added to the object and initialized to point to a v-table. The v-table contains pointers to the appropriate functions for that object.

Figure 22.2.
*Finding the correct
virtual function.*

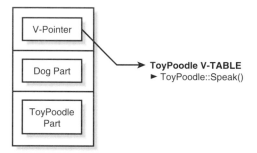

Whenever the object is called with a member function, the v-table (pointed to by the v-pointer) is checked and the pointer to the correct function is found. Back on Day 12, "Inheritance," you learned how the base function could only be invoked by calling it directly with the scope qualifier, `Dog::Speak()` in this case. The call to a derived class member function from a base type pointer is referred to as polymorphism or, sometimes, *upcasting*. *Downcasting* is the act of casting the type from a base class to one of its derived classes. Typically, downcasting is a sign that you have design problems; in fact, it is almost impossible to downcast using the features you have learned about C++ so far. Downcasting also defeats the purpose behind polymorphism, which effectively does the downcast through virtual functions. In the next section you learn some of the built-in tools for accessing and changing type information, including a mechanism for downcasting.

Casting and Run-Time Type Identification

Although a need to cast an object to a new type is often a sign of poor design, there are occasionally circumstances when you have little choice. For instance, you might be building on a previous application that did not use an object-oriented approach. Or, perhaps the new C++ code you are adding must convert objects to built-in C types for low-level hardware calls.

Some conversions are implicit (as are automatic enum type to int conversions), but others must be explicit to circumvent the strong type checking of of C++. To meet the need for casting while still maintaining some level of type safety, ANSI/ISO C++ provides improved casting mechanisms through type information template functions. In addition, C++ provides a means to determine type information from an object. Be cautious in using these mechanisms.

There is a danger of overusing the run-time type identification tools. If you find yourself using them often, it could be a sign that you do not quite understand the intent behind data abstraction and information hiding. Using RTTI tools can make your code less portable and hard to update. For that reason alone, it should be avoided if at all possible.

Another thing to keep in mind is that the RTTI and casting functions are primarily designed to work with polymorphic types. This means that the results with nonpolymorphic types can sometimes be hard to determine.

Table 22.1 summarizes the C++ casting and run-time type identification (RTTI) mechanisms.

Table 22.1. Cast and RTTI functions.

Function	Use
const_cast	Casting away const or volatile
dynamic_cast	Downcasting to a derived type
static_cast	Safe, well-defined casting
reinterpret_cast	Casting to a completely different meaning
typeinfo	Determine type information of an object

Each of these is discussed with limited detail in the sections that follow.

Const Cast

Consider the following code fragment:

```
const double pi = 3.14;
double *ptrPI = &pi;
  // Error, cannot assign a non-const pointer to a const value
```

Ignoring for a moment the poor design indicated by the need to do this, there is a way to do what you want here and make the change obvious. You can use the const_cast function to change the variable from const to non-const (called casting away const-ness):

```
const double pi = 3.14;
double *ptrPI = const_cast<double*>(&pi);
   // Lets the compiler know that you coded this on
   // purpose and that you know what you're doing
```

const_cast can also be used to convert a volatile variable to non-volatile. However, it cannot be used to convert from one type to another type at the same time:

```
long *ptrlPI = const_cast<long*>(&pi); // illegal!
```

Dynamic Cast

When you want to downcast from a pointer or reference to a base type to the derived equivalent, use the dynamic_cast function. This concept is the opposite of the automatic casting performed in a virtual function call.

The dynamic cast is the most useful in the entire repertoire of RTTI functions. I know, it's more bias, but I feel that it is worthwhile to spend more time in this section discussing it.

One example given in many C++ books is the idea of identifying different objects with different colors, depending on their types. You might add a member variable that contains the color for that object, but that might get confusing and distract future programmers from the "important" members of the class. The dynamic_cast function, to be safe, returns a null-pointer value if the cast is unsuccessful.

Listing 22.5 illustrates the use of dynamic_cast to identify and treat objects differently depending on their derived type.

TYPE

Listing 22.5. An example of using dynamic_cast.

```
 1: #include <iostream.h>
 2: #include <time.h>
 3: #include <string.h>
 4: #include <stdlib.h>
 5:
 6: const int MaxNameLength = 60;
 7:
 8: // A rather intelligent party goer who can comment
 9: // appropriately on the music it hears.
10:
11: class MusicCD {
12: public:
13:     MusicCD() { /* ... */ }
14:     virtual ~MusicCD() { /* ... */ }
15: };
16:
17: class CountryCD : public MusicCD {
```

22

```
18: private:
19:     char *ArtistName;
20: public:
21:     CountryCD(char *Name = "Unknown") {
22:       ArtistName = new char[MaxNameLength];
23:     strcpy(ArtistName, Name);
24:       cout << "Howdy!" << endl;
25:     }
26:     ~CountryCD() {
27:         cout << "'Night Y'all!"
28:             ,   << endl;
29:     }
30: };
31:
32: class ClassicalCD : public MusicCD {
33: private:
34:     char *Composer;
35: public:
36:     ClassicalCD(char *Name = "Unknown") {
37:         Composer = new char[MaxNameLength];
38:      strcpy(Composer, Name);
39:         cout << "Greetings." << endl;
40:     }
41:     ~ClassicalCD() {
42:         cout << "Good evening." << endl;
43:     }
44: };
45:
46: void main()
47: {
48:     int ClassicsCount = 0;
49:     int CountryCount = 0;
50:     MusicCD *SomeCDs[5];
51:     time_t currTime;
52:
53:     // Seed the random number gen in preparation
54:     // of creating some random CDs
55:     srand( static_cast<unsigned>(time(&currTime)) );
56:     cout << "Let's listen to some CDs." << endl;
57:     for(int i=0; i<5; i++)
58:     {
59:       if( (rand() % 2) )
60:           SomeCDs[i] = new CountryCD;
61:       else
62:           SomeCDs[i] = new ClassicalCD;
63:     }
64:     for(int j=0; j<5; j++)
65:     {
66:         CountryCD *ptrMusic = dynamic_cast<CountryCD *>(SomeCDs[j]);
67:
68:         // Make an appropriate comment:
69:         if( ptrMusic )
70:         {
71:             // If we could cast it to Country
72:             CountryCount++;
```

continues

Listing 22.5. continued

```
73:            cout << "That sure is purdy!" << endl;
74:        }
75:        else
76:        {
77:            // Must be classical music
78:            ClassicsCount++;
79:            cout << "That was lovely." << endl;
80:        }
81:    }
82:
83:    cout << "That was: "
84:        << ClassicsCount << " classical and "
85:        << CountryCount << " country CDs."
86:        << endl;
87:    // Cleanup:
88:    for(int  k=0; k<5; k++)
89:        delete SomeCDs[k];
90: }
```

OUTPUT
```
Let's listen to some CDs.
Greetings.
Howdy!
Howdy!
Greetings.
Howdy!
That was lovely.
That sure is purdy!
That sure is purdy!
That was lovely.
That sure is purdy!
That was 2 classical and 3 country CDs.
Good evening.
'Night Y'all!
'Night Y'all!
Good evening.
'Night Y'all!
```

NOTE

> Actually, because the CD creations are random, your output will be different each time you run the program.

ANALYSIS On line 55 we use a static_cast to cast the return type from srand(). The static_cast will be explained shortly. On lines 57 through 63, CDs are created and placed in the SomeCDs MusicCD pointer array. If a random number is not divisible by 2 (a remainder is given in the modulus divide step), a CountryCD is created. Otherwise, a ClassicalCD is created.

Line 66 attempts to cast the MusicCD pointer given at the current array pointer to a CountryCD pointer with the dynamic_cast function.

In lines 69 through 73, if the cast was a success (ptrMusic is pointing at a CountryCD), a comment is made appropriately for country music and the country music CD counter (CountryCounter) is incremented.

In lines 77 through 79, if the pointer could not be cast to a CountryCD type, it must be a ClassicalCD, so an appropriate comment is made for that and the ClassicalCounter is incremented.

Line 83 prints out the count for each type of MusicCD you've heard. Finally, at lines 88 and 89, memory is cleaned up by deleting all the MusicCD object pointers.

Static Cast

The static_cast function is used for "safe" casts that are well-defined or even automatic to begin with. This includes explicit casting in place of implicit (automatic) conversions, narrowing (data-loss) conversion casting, casting from void* types, and substituting for dynamic_cast in class hierarchy determination. The best way to explain each conversion type is through an example, as given in Listing 22.6.

TYPE **Listing 22.6. An example using static_cast.**

```
1:    #include<iostream.h>
2:    class Base {
3:        /* ... */
4:    };
5:
6:    class First : public Base {
7:    private:
8:        int BaseNumber;
9:    public:
10:        First() { BaseNumber = 1; }
11:        // ...
12:    };
13:
14:    void SomeFunction(int i) {
15:        cout << i << endl;
16:    }
17:
18:    void main()
19:    {
20:        int someInt = 0xFF;
21:        char someChar = 'C';
22:        void *ptrVoid;
23:
24:        // Automatic conversions that do
25:        // not require a cast since there is no
26:        //data loss
```

continues

Listing 22.6. continued

```
27:        someInt = someChar; // OK, no problem
28:        someInt = static_cast<int>(someChar);
29:        // Much clearer and obvious
30:
31:        // Conversions that narrow:
32:        someChar = someInt; // Compiler warning
33:        someChar = static_cast<char>(someInt); // no errors or warnings
34:
35:        // Conversions where dynamic_cast would be
36:        // preferred but static_cast works and where
37:        // a cast is not necessarily required but
38:        // helpful to make the meaning clear
39:        First FirstBase;
40:        Base *ptrBase1 = &FirstBase; // This works fine
41:        Base *ptrBase2 =
42:            static_cast<Base*>(&FirstBase); // More obvious
43:        First *ptrFirst =
44:            static_cast<First*>(ptrBase1);
45:        if( ptrFirst )
46:            cout << "Made it to first." << endl;
47:
48:        SomeFunction(someChar); // Automatic
49:        SomeFunction(static_cast<int>(someChar)); // Clearer
50:
51:        // Dangerous but legal conversion from void
52:        float *ptrFloat =
53:            static_cast<float*>(ptrVoid);
54:}
```

OUTPUT | Made it to first.

ANALYSIS | Lines 1 through 16 are simply definitions of a base class, a derived class, and a function that takes an int. In main, lines 24 through 33 are some conversion examples that are either perfectly safe or only slightly dangerous in their narrowing. static_cast makes the meaning clear and leaves a reminder that you intended to perform the cast.

Reinterpret Cast

If dynamic_cast was sandpaper, const_cast was a wood file, and static_cast was a belt sander, then reinterpret_cast would be a sledgehammer. Sure, it gets rid of some rough edges, but the sledgehammer is difficult to control and even makes it very difficult to predict the outcome of your efforts. I hesitate to mention it at all, but there are instances where a less drastic cast might not be sufficient for the drastic conversions required to mess with the underlying bit patterns of an object. Because it is so dangerous, I'm not even going to provide

22

an example here. When you're a serious bit-twiddling programmer, you can look it up in the ANSI/ISO standard and figure it out if you're convinced you need it. In the meantime, you can live without it. Trust me.

Type Info

There might come a time when you have to determine the type of an object or you want to get type information without really needing to cast. The typeid function and related member functions provide several tools for making that kind of determination.

Table 22.2 lists some of the member functions, or *overloaded operators*, provided with typeid.

Table 22.2. The typeid operators and functions.

Function	Use
==	Two types are identical as in
	typeid(7) == typeid(int);
!=	The two types are not identical:
	typeid(33.333) != typeid(int);
before()	Object Y is a descendant of object X:
	typeid(InstanceX).before(typeID(InstanceY));
name()	Get the name of the object's class:
	cout << "MyDog is a " << typeid(MyDog);

Explicit Constructors

Often, the way you build your classes can give the impression that you want an automatic conversion to be performed inside a function call. Consider the following:

```
class MyClass {
   char *AString;
public:
   MyClass(const *strString)
   {
       AString = new char(strString);
   }
   ~MyClass(){}
};

void SomeFunction(MyClass Variable)
{
   //
```

```
}
main()
{
   // Implicit type conversion:
   SomeFunction("This is a test");
}
```

In this example, the call to SomeFunction expects a MyClass object but gets a char string. Because there is a MyClass constructor that takes a char string, the compiler invokes the constructor with This is a test and goes happily on its way. But what if you made a mistake and really didn't want the automatic conversion to take place? What if the constructor for MyClass also had some side-effects, and you want to prevent anybody from calling it without explicitly doing so?

You can force a constructor to be called only if it is explicitly called with the keyword explicit, as in the following example:

```
class MyClass {
   char *AString;
public:
   explicit MyClass(const *strString) {
      AString = new char(strString);
   }
   ~MyClass(){}
};

void SomeFunction(MyClass Variable) {
  //
}

main() {
   // Now, the following causes a compiler error
   SomeFunction("This is a test");

   // But, this way works:
   SomeFunction(MyClass("This is a test"));
}
```

Use explicit anytime you want to make certain that the constructor is used explicitly, such as if the constructor has side-effects.

Data Alignment and Assembly Language

Sometimes, despite your best efforts, you need to understand the internal architecture of the computer platform when you are writing applications. Usually, this relates to the need to tweak the efficiency of a time-critical loop in your application. There are two major tools programmers use to improve efficiency that are related to the underlying computer architecture: data alignment and assembly language calls.

Packing Data by Understanding Data Alignment

Data alignment refers to the storage width your computer uses to store data in structs and unions. This is best understood with an example. Consider the following code snippet:

```
struct EmployeeInfo {
    int Age;                    // Voluntary info
    char SecurityClearance;
    // T=Top Secret, S=Secret, C=Confidential, U=Unclassified
    int SalaryGrade;            // Salary grade (pay) level
};
```

How much space does this use in memory? You might think it's the value of (2 * sizeof(int)) + sizeof(char), but your assumption would probably fail in practice.

Computers prefer to align things in memory in chunks that are multiples of its stack push and pop sizes. In other words, if the computer is built with a 16-bit architecture (it pushes and pops things from the stack in multiples of 16 bits), and then it stores structs in 16-bit blocks of memory. For instance, imagine looking at a stack of cubbyholes in memory, each being 16 bits (or 2 bytes wide). If an int takes 4 bytes of storage and a char takes 1 byte of storage in your computer, you have the situation illustrated in Figure 22.3.

Figure 22.3.

A data alignment illustration.

Age	Age
Age	Age
SecurityClearance	- -
SalaryGrade	SalaryGrade
SalaryGrade	SalaryGrade

So the space taken is actually 10 bytes and not 9 bytes, as your formula would have determined. Over a few small structures, the memory alignment is not a serious concern. However, if your computer has limited memory (as most computers do) and you have to store a lot of Employee data structs, memory usage becomes more critical. Most compilers enable you to alter the data alignment for your program. Most provide this capability through the #pragma preprocessor directive. Check your compiler documentation for details.

Spiking with Assembly Language

Assembly language is the low-level language that directly manipulates memory locations and registers in your computer to perform tasks. As you learned earlier, C++ provides some of this low-level functionality, but there are times when you want to make certain that something is compiled using a particular set of assembly language instructions.

ANSI/ISO C++ includes the asm keyword to enable you to enclose assembly language instructions right in your program. The syntax for using asm depends on your compiler, so see your compiler or IDE documentation for instructions on using asm.

Do	Don't

DO use class libraries for classes you might be using often or classes you want to share with others.

DO use RTTI functions only with polymorphic types and avoid their use for nonpolymorphic types.

DO use explicit constructors when there are unexpected side-effects in the constructor.

DON'T use RTTI if there is any sensible way to avoid it in your design.

Summary

Today you learned about some very powerful tools. You also learned, as is the case with any power tools, that you have to be careful not to misuse them. This is especially true in the case of the RTTI and casting functions.

In addition to RTTI and casting, you learned how to create and use class libraries and how to take advantage of the assembly language routines. You also learned something about data alignment and the impact it can have on your programs.

Controlling the use of constructors with explicit to prevent implicit calls was discussed in detail.

Several other covered topics provided you with the information you need in order to better understand and utilize the low-level features of C++ and your computer. Those included a description of how polymorphism works, a description of data alignment, and an introduction to the asm keyword.

If you keep these things in mind and use them wisely while tempering them with experience, you can leave the realm of novice and push into expert C++ programming.

Q&A

Q What advantage do class libraries provide?

A They hide the implementation details and compile more quickly.

Q What is a namespace conflict?

A A namespace conflict occurs when two or more names in the same compilation set are the same. Such a conflict can occur when there is more than one class or variable with the same name in your program.

Q What keyword would you use to identify assembly language code in your program?

A Use asm to identify assembly language code.

Quiz

1. What C++ mechanism can you use to limit the possibility of a namespace conflict?

2. What is a v-pointer?

3. A class library and an object file are

   a. identical to each other

   b. similar

   c. opposites

4. What is data alignment?

5. Why is static_cast preferred over reinterpret_cast?

6. What would be the result of the following?

```
#include <iostream.h>
class ADog {
//…
};
void main()
{
   ADog Fido;
   cout << "Fido is a "
        << typeid(Fido).name()
        << endl;
}
```

Exercises

1. Alter the following code where commented so that the final cout statement prints the correct number of Peppers ready to be picked.

```cpp
#include <iostream.h>
#include <time.h>
#include <stdlib.h>

class Veggie {
};

class Peppers : public Veggie {
  //…
};

class Celery : public Veggie {
  //…
};

class Spinach : public Veggie {
  //…
};

main()
{
    Veggie *Garden[100];
    int ModDiv = 3;
    int Remainder = 0;
    int PepperCount = 0;

    srand(
      static_cast<unsigned>(time()));

    for(int j=0; j<100; j++)
    {
        Remainder = rand() % ModDiv;
        switch (Remainder) {
          case 2: Garden[j] = new Spinach;
                  break;
          case 1: Garden[j] = new Celery;
                  break;
          default: Garden[j] = new Peppers;
        }
    }

    // Place code here to increment
    // each counter for each type

    cout << PepperCount
        << "Peppers for Peter to pick."
        << endl;
}
```

22

2. Look up the data alignment information for your compiler and determine whether it provides a way to change the setting.

3. **BUG BUSTERS:** What is wrong with this code?

```
#include <iostream.h>
namespace CharliesFunctions {
    void FunctionOne() { /*…*/ }
    void FunctionTwo() { /*…*/ }
}

void main()
{
    cout << "Calling Charlie's Functions"
        << endl;
    FunctionOne();
    FunctionTwo();
}
```

4. **BUG BUSTERS:** The programmer expected Calls to be 1 in the following code but instead got 2. What's wrong with this code, and what could be done to prevent the same problem for others who use the SomeClass class?

```
#include<iostream.h>

static int Calls = 0;

class SomeClass {
private:
    int X;
public:
    SomeClass(int I) {
        ++Calls;
        X = I;
    }
};

MyFunction(SomeClass AnObject) {
    Calls++;
}

void main()
{
    int MyInt;
    MyFunction(MyInt);
    cout << "Made " << Calls
        << " calls to MyFunction"
        << endl;
}
```

Day 23

More About Streams

On Day 16, "Streams," you learned the basics about streams. In this lesson you will begin to see the full potential of streams for more complex input and output.

If you are an experienced C programmer, you probably wondered whether Day 16 showed all that streams had to offer and why you would give up the functionality of sscanf and printf for something so simple in capabilities. Today your questions will be answered.

The Streams Hierarchy

Figure 23.1 illustrates the relationship of the built-in stream classes. The ios class is the base class and the other classes are derived from the class above them in the hierarchy.

Figure 23.1.

The streams hierarchy.

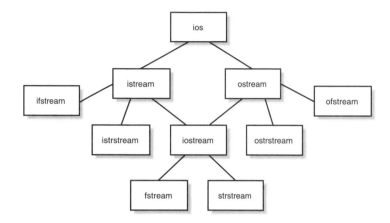

Some of the stream classes are new to you, but don't be concerned; you'll understand them all by the end of the day.

Using *istrstream*

Although the `iostream` and `fstream` classes provide the functions necessary for console and file input/output, the `strstream` classes provide the necessary functions for memory-based string streams. The string streams enable you to manipulate strings for input or output within memory. Manipulating strings in memory is more efficient than manipulating input or output one character or one line at a time.

With the member function, `str()`, you can get a pointer to the string buffer and treat the value as you would any character string. Listing 23.1 is a simple program that uses the `istrstream` class and the `str()` member function.

TYPE   **Listing 23.1. The `istrstream` class and `str()`.**

```
 1:  #include<strstrea.h>
 2: #include<iomanip.h>
 3:  float markUp(float, float);
 4:
 5:  void main()
 6:  {
 7:    istrstream inputStream("0.02 14.95 29.95   25486 3");
 8:    int numItems;
 9:    float Perc;
10:    float priceGasoline;
11:    float priceOilChange;
12:    float priceCar;
13:
```

23

```
14:     inputStream >> Perc
15:                 >> priceGasoline
16:                 >> priceOilChange
17:                 >> priceCar
18:                 >> numItems;
19:
20:     cout.setf(ios::fixed, ios::floatfield);
21:     cout << setprecision(2);
22:
23:     cout << "An oil change is: $"
24:          << markUp(priceOilChange, Perc) << endl;
25:
26:     cout << "A fillup is: $"
27:          << markUp(priceGasoline, Perc) << endl;
28:
29:     cout << "The cost of the car is: $"
30:          << markUp(priceCar, Perc) << endl;
31:
32:     cout << "There are " << numItems
33:          << " total items." << endl;
34:
35:     cout << "The input stream contains: "
36:          << endl << inputStream.str() << endl;
37: }
38:
39: float markUp(float V, float PMarkup)
40: {
41:     return(V + (V * PMarkup));
42: }
```

OUTPUT

```
An oil change is: $30.55
A fillup is: $15.25
The cost of the car is: $25995.72
There are 3 total items.
The input stream contains:
0.02 14.95 29.95  25486 3
```

ANALYSIS   This is a program to output the price of various items after a modest markup price is added. The base prices and number of items are stored in a istrstream and parsed for computation and output.

The include file strstrea.h on line 1 is required for string streams, and because strstream is derived from iostream, you need not specifically include iostream.h. On line 2 the iomanip.h file is included so that you can use the precision manipulators for floating point value outputs.

On line 7 the istrstream object is created. Lines 14 through 18 parse the stream contents into the appropriate variable types. Lines 20 and 21 set the floating point output to fixed and the precision to two digits after the decimal. If fixed was not set first, the precision value of 2 would be interpreted as two digits to the left of the decimal, and the decimal portions would be truncated.

Lines 23 through 36 output the markup values for each item followed by the total number of items stored in the `istrstream` object. The last output is the character string value of the `istrstream` object using the `str()` member function.

Using *ostrstream*

The `ostrstream` class differs from the `istrstream` class in one way. `ostrstream` size can be allocated automatically, while `istrstream` size cannot. To allocate a new `ostrstream` size, a new block of memory might have to be allocated each time more characters are added to the object. However, when the `str()` member function is used to obtain a character pointer, the current `ostrstream` object stream buffer is frozen. If it were not frozen and you attempted to use the pointer returned by `str()` later in the program, the results would be undefined.

The `strstream` classes also have an additional manipulator, `ends`, which inserts an end-of-string null terminator in the stream. Unlike string pointers, string streams do not automatically add the null terminator to string constants. Instead, the `ends` manipulator is used to add the string terminator.

To unfreeze the stream buffer, you need to call the `streambuf` member function `freeze()` with a `0` argument. The `streambuf` is accessed with the `rdbuf()` member function, which returns a pointer to the `streambuf`. Because the `rdbuf()` member function returns a pointer to the `streambuf`, it is also an efficient method to use for dumping the `streambuf` contents to another stream, such as the `cout` stream. Listing 23.2 illustrates `ostrstream` freezing and `streambuf` access.

TYPE   **Listing 23.2. Freezing the `ostrstream`.**

```
 1:
 2:  // Listing 23.2. ostrstream allocation and freeze
 3:  #include<strstrea.h>
 4:
 5:  void main()
 6:  {
 7:    ostrstream oStr;
 8:    char *ptrStr;
 9:
10:    oStr << "Four score and seven years ago " << ends;
11:    ptrStr = oStr.str(); // Freezes oStr
12:
13:    // cannot add to the stream while it's frozen
14:    // so, use the pointer and then unfreeze the stream
15:
16:    cout << ptrStr << endl;
17:
18:    // unfreeze the streambuffer
19:    oStr.rdbuf()->freeze(0);
20:
```

23

```
21:     oStr.seekp(-1, ios::end); // back up from end
22:     oStr << "our fathers set forth\n";
23:     oStr << "on this continent a new nation."
24:          << ends;
25:     cout << oStr.rdbuf() << endl;
26: }
```

OUTPUT

```
Four score and seven years ago
Four score and seven years ago our fathers set forth
on this continent a new nation.
```

ANALYSIS Line 10 inserts the first string, followed by the ends string terminator. Line 11 uses the str() member function to get the buffer pointer and assign it to a character pointer for later use. If you were now to add to the stream, it could force reallocation and the character pointer would be invalid. For that reason, str() freezes the buffer and prevents reallocation and strstream destructor calls.

Before you can add to the stream again, you have to unfreeze it using the streambuf freeze member function. To do that, you get the streambuf pointer with rdbuf() and unfreeze it on line 19. The seekp member function provides the capability to place the character put pointer. Currently, it is at the ends marker inserted previously. So, the statement on line 21 backs up the pointer one from the end to allow more characters to be added.

Finally, with all of the characters added, line 25 accesses the streambuf pointer with rdbuf() and outputs its contents to cout.

Remember that if you do not unfreeze a frozen ostrstream object, the object's destructor is not called automatically. When that happens, use delete to deallocate the streambuf space.

Stream Position

The streambuf has certain position tracking mechanisms in output and input streams. For instance, all streams must know the next character to be output when in an output stream or the next character to be input from an input stream. These are often referred to as the *put* and *get* positions, respectively.

For an input/output stream, there must be both a put and a get position for the stream at the same time, and the get and put positions may or may not be the same character position. To keep track of the stream positions, the streambuf uses three constants: ios::beg, ios::curr, and ios::end, which stand for beginning (first), current, and end (last) character positions in the stream. The put(), get(), and other such member functions automatically adjust the current position by the number of characters read or written. If you want to adjust the position at random rather than sequentially, you must use seekg() and seekp() for the get and put positions. In Listing 23.2 you saw how to use seekp() to adjust the put position from the end of the stream. To determine the current stream position, use tellg() and tellp().

If the end of a stream is reached, the badbit (the ios failure indicator) is set and the fail() member function returns true. If you want to clear the failure indication flag, use the clear() member function. Each of these is used later in this lesson.

Format Specification Flags

On Day 16 you learned about some of the stream class format flags. By using setf() and unsetf(), you can change the values of those flags.

Table 23.1 summarizes the on/off flags.

Table 23.1. The `ios` on/off flags.

Format Flag	Purpose
ios::boolalpha	Inserts alphabetic form of bool value in stream.
ios::dec	Converts to decimal (base 10).
ios::fixed	Convert floating point to fixed notation.
ios::hex	Converts to hexadecimal.
ios::internal	Fills between leading base symbol or sign indicator.
ios::left	Adds fill characters after a value.
ios::oct	Converts to octal.
ios::right	Adds fill characters before a value.
ios::scientific	Formats floating point in scientific notation.
ios::showbase	Generates a base prefix for numbers.
ios::showpoint	Always shows decimal point, even if right of decimal is zero.
ios::showpos	Always shows + sign for positive values.
ios::skipws	Skips whitespace on input.
ios::stdio	Flushes streambuf after each extraction.
ios::unitbuf	Flushes streambuf after each insertion.
ios::uppercase	Uses uppercase for hexadecimal numbers.

Creating Manipulators and Custom Stream Operators

Not only can you overload the << and >> operators, but you can also create new manipulators for changing the output. Creating a manipulator that does not take arguments (such as the endl manipulator) is pretty straightforward. Manipulators that accept arguments are a little tricky. Both are discussed here.

A manipulator must return a stream reference to be used with the stream operators. Listing 23.3 shows how to create a simple manipulator that requires no arguments.

TYPE **Listing 23.3. A simple manipulator example.**

```
1:   // Listing 23.3. A simple manipulator example
2:
3:   #include<iostream.h>
4:
5:   // A new manipulator for tabs:
6:
7:   ostream& tab(ostream& aStream)
8:   {
9:      return( aStream << '\t' );
10:  }
11:
12:  void main()
13:  {
14:     cout << "A" << tab << "few"
15:          << tab << "tab" << tab
16:          << "-" << tab << "separated"
17:          << tab << "words" << endl;
18:  }
```

OUTPUT A   few   tab   -   separated   words

ANALYSIS Lines 7 through 10 define a simple manipulator that inserts a tab in a stream. Lines 12 through 18 are the main function, which has a single statement that uses the tab manipulator in a stream.

There is more than one way to implement a manipulator that takes arguments, but probably the easiest is through what's called an *effector class*. The theory behind this method is to create a special class for the manipulator and include an overridden form of the stream operator. Listing 23.4 demonstrates the effector method of manipulator creation.

TYPE **Listing 23.4. An advanced manipulator example.**

```
1:   // Listing 23.4. Advanced manipulator example
2:
3:   #include<iostream.h>
4:   #include<limits.h>
5:   #include<iomanip.h>
```

continues

Listing 23.4. continued

```
6:
7:
8:   class binaryForm {
9:   public:
10:    char itsSpace;
11:    unsigned long itsValue;
12:    binaryForm(unsigned long aVal, bool Spaced = false)
13:    {
14:      if(Spaced)
15:        itsSpace = ' ';
16:      else
17:        itsSpace = 0;
18:
19:      itsValue = aVal;
20:    }
21:
22:    ~binaryForm() {}
23:
24:    friend ostream &operator<<(ostream &theStream, binaryForm &binary);
25:   };
26:
27:   ostream &operator<<(ostream &theStream, binaryForm &binary)
28:   {
29:     // initialize the high bit
30:     unsigned long HighBits = ~(binary.itsValue.max() >> 1);
31:
32:     while(HighBits)
33:     {
34:       for(int i=0; i<4; i++)
35:       {
36:         if( (binary.itsValue & HighBits) )
37:           theStream << 1;
38:         else
39:           theStream << 0;
40:
41:         HighBits >>= 1;
42:       }
43:
44:       if(binary.itsSpace)
45:         theStream << ' ';
46:
47:     }
48:
49:     return( theStream );
50:   }
51:
52:   void main()
53:   {
54:     unsigned long ABigOne = 0x1ABCDEF9;
55:     unsigned long ASmallOne = 0xA;
56:
57:     cout << setfill('*') << setw(30) << '*'
58:          << endl;
59:
```

23

```
60:    cout << "ABigOne in spaced format:"
61:         << endl << binaryForm(ABigOne, true)
62:         << endl << setw(30) << '*'
63:         << endl << "ASmallOne without spaces:"
64:         << endl << binaryForm(ASmallOne)
65:         << endl;
66:  }
```

BD 23

OUTPUT

```
******************************
ABigOne in spaced format:
0001 1010 1011 1100 1101 1110 1111 1001
******************************
ASmallOne without spaces:
00000000000000000000000000001010
```

ANALYSIS The output you see depends on the unsigned long max() value for your computer. You might need to go back and take a look at Day 18, "Creating Reusable Code," for details on max().

The goal of the binaryForm manipulator is to insert the binary value of a number in the stream. A default argument determines whether or not to make the output more readable with spacing to separate sets of four bits. Lines 8 through 50 declare and define the binaryForm class to be used as a manipulator. The binaryForm constructor takes one or two values. The first value is the number to be inserted in binary form, and the second value is an indicator for whether or not to separate the binary in groups of four. The second argument has a default value of false so that the number is not spaced.

The operator<< is overloaded and declared as a friend function for binaryForm. On line 30 the high bit is set so that subsequent shifts move this bit through each of the binary bit positions of the unsigned long type when a number is to be put into the stream. The >> operator for binaryForm shifts the HighBits to the right one bit at a time and determines whether the input value has that bit set. If space is set, every fourth bit insertion adds a space to the stream.

The main function, lines 52 through 66, declares two unsigned long values and outputs their binary form. For one of the numbers, the binary form with spaces is used; for the other, the default (no spaces) is used. Notice the setfill() and setw() functions. Setfill() sets the character to be used for filling field widths, and setw() sets the field width.

Multiple Streams

Now that you are nearly a streams expert, let's put everything you've learned about streams together in a program.

Listing 23.5 is a program that uses various stream types and manipulators to perform a number of I/O functions.

TYPE | **Listing 23.5. A multiple streams program.**

```
 1:   // Listing 23.5. Multiple streams example
 2:
 3:   #include<strstrea.h>
 4:   #include<fstream.h>
 5:   #include<iomanip.h>
 6:
 7:   // a tab spacing manipulator
 8:   ostream& tab(ostream& aStream)
 9:   {
10:     return( aStream << '\t' );
11:   }
12:
13:   class Point {
14:     // A simple cartesian point class
15:   private:
16:     float x;
17:     float y;
18:   public:
19:     float xOffSet() { return( x ); }
20:     float yOffSet() { return( y ); }
21:     friend istream &operator>>( istream &aStream, Point &P );
22:     friend ostream &operator<<( ostream &aStream, Point P );
23:   };
24:
25:   istream &operator>>( istream &aStream, Point &P )
26:   {
27:     aStream >> P.x >> P.y;
28:
29:     return( aStream );
30:   }
31:
32:   ostream &operator<<( ostream &aStream, Point P )
33:   {
34:     aStream << P.x << ' ' << P.y;
35:
36:     return( aStream );
37:   }
38:
39:   class Line {
40:     // A simple line class
41:   private:
42:     Point P1;
43:     Point P2;
44:   public:
45:     float Slope();
46:     friend istream &operator>>( istream &aStream, Line &L );
47:     friend ostream &operator<<( ostream &aStream, Line L );
48:   };
49:
50:   float Line::Slope()
51:   {
52:     float theSlope;
53:
```

```
54:     theSlope = (P1.yOffSet() - P2.yOffSet() ) /
55:            (P1.xOffSet() - P2.xOffSet() );
56:
57:     return( theSlope );
58:  }
59:
60:  istream &operator>>( istream &aStream, Line &L )
61:  {
62:     aStream >> L.P1 >> L.P2;
63:
64:     return( aStream );
65:  }
66:
67:  ostream &operator<<( ostream &aStream, Line L )
68:  {
69:     aStream << L.P1 << tab << L.P2;
70:
71:     return( aStream );
72:  }
73:
74:  void main()
75:  {
76:     const int Big = 256;
77:     char flname[Big];
78:     ostrstream outStream;
79:     ofstream savefile;
80:     ifstream infile;
81:
82:     Point First, Second;
83:     Line slopedLine;
84:
85:     cout << tab << "Slope Computer!" << endl;
86:
87:     cout << "Enter x and y offsets for first point:"
88:            << endl;
89:
90:     cin >> First;
91:     cin.ignore();
92:
93:     cout << "Enter x and y for the second point:"
94:            << endl;
95:
96:     cin >> Second;
97:     cin.ignore();
98:
99:
100:    // Open the save file and save the points
101:    cout << "Enter a file name for the save file: ";
102:    cin.getline(flname, Big);
103:    istrstream fileName(flname);
104:
105:    savefile.open(fileName.str(), ios::app);
106:    outStream << First << tab << Second
107:               << endl << ends;
108:
```

BD
23

continues

Listing 23.5. continued

```
109:      savefile << outStream.str();  // save them
110:      outStream.rdbuf()->freeze(0); // unfreeze
111:
112:      savefile.close();
113:
114:      // re-open and read the saved values for computation
115:      infile.open(fileName.str(), ios::in);
116:
117:      cout.setf(ios::fixed);
118:      cout.precision(2);
119:
120:      infile >> slopedLine;
121:      cout << tab << "Slopes of all saved lines."
122:           << endl;
123:
124:      do
125:      {
126:        cout << endl << "Slope="
127:             << slopedLine.Slope();
128:
129:        infile >> slopedLine;
130:
131:      } while(! infile.fail() );
132:
133:      cout << endl;
134:
135:      infile.clear();
136:
137:      infile.seekg(0, ios::beg);
138:
139:      cout << "The line(s) again: " << endl;
140:
141:      infile >> slopedLine;
142:
143:      do
144:      {
145:        cout << slopedLine << endl;
146:        infile >> slopedLine;
147:
148:      } while(! infile.fail() );
149:  }
```

OUTPUT
```
Slope Computer!
Enter x and y offsets for first point:
3.45 6.78
Enter x and y for the second point:
4.56 22.23
Enter a file name for the save file: myline.txt
        Slopes of all saved lines.

Slope=13.92
The line(s) again:
3.45 6.78        4.56 22.23
```

23

ANALYSIS Lines 7 through 11 are the tab manipulator that you created previously. Lines 13 through 37 declare and define a class for storing and retrieving Points. A Line is really nothing more than two Points and has a slope, so in the interest of space, the constructor and destructor are not included in this listing. The Line class is defined in lines 39 through 72 and is roughly equivalent to a Point class in the stream operation.

The main function reads two points from cin, stores the points to a file (from a filename supplied through cin), reads all the stored lines in the file, and computes the slope of each line. Each time you run the program and enter the same filename, it appends your entries to the file so that old entries are not overwritten.

Do	Don't

DO include stream operators and necessary manipulators with your classes.

DON'T forget to free ostrstream memory that has been frozen either with the freeze() member function or with delete.

Summary

In this lesson you learned some tricks of the trade for working with streams. You saw how streams can represent data not just in the form of console and file I/O, but also within memory using the strstream classes. You also learned how to clear a failed I/O stream with the clear() member function and how to unfreeze a frozen streambuf with freeze(0).

Q&A

Q What is an effector?

A An effector is a special class that enables you to create stream manipulators that take arguments.

Q What is the purpose of seekp()?

A The seekp() member function nonsequentially moves the put position.

Q What is a frozen output stream?

A A stream is frozen when its streambuf is accessed with the str() member function. When an output stream is frozen, automatic memory allocation cannot take place.

Quiz

1. True or False: The `tellg()` function indicates the number of bytes in a stream.
2. What is the member function, `setfill()`, used for?
3. Where is the put position after the statement `seekp(0, ios::end);` is executed?
4. What does the statement `setf(ios::boolalpha)` do?

Exercises

1. Write a program that uses `seekg()` and `tellg()` to determine the size of a file (in characters).
2. Write a program that subtracts 3 from each of the `int` values in the following object: `istrstream theStr("1 2 3 4");`.
3. Write a manipulator called `doubleline` that places two newline characters in the stream.

Day 24

Object-Oriented Design

In today's lesson you will gain the knowledge to begin learning object-oriented design (OOD) techniques. I should emphasize the word *begin* in that first statement. This lesson is not an exhaustive study on OOD, and it is essential that you read further on the subject and draw your own conclusions about it.

What OOD Is Not

You can only fully understand the impact of OOD if you understand an alternative approach. It often helps to clarify what something is when you understand what it is not.

When I was first exposed to programming, the accepted design technique was known as *structured programming*. Knowing nothing more than the name of the design technique, it might seem like a perfectly valid concept. After all, shouldn't all programs have a structure?

In its day, structured programming was quite an innovation, and many of the tenets of that technique influenced OOD techniques. So, at the risk of boring you, I think it's important to gain a quick overview of structured programming as it was accepted in its maturity.

Structured Programming

As you've probably guessed by now, structured design is not just about giving programs structure. The idea of structure with respect to this design paradigm is to view a program as one big, fluid procedure. The procedure is the forefront of the program. Every real-world problem is first changed into a procedure that logically progresses to the desired result. The big procedure is then broken down into small pieces, but each piece is still just another procedure that solves a portion of the big procedure problem.

When this approach is used to solve a problem, all real-world problems are first converted into computer problems. In other words, a programmer must think like the computers of a few years ago that could only perform one step in a set of instructions at a time. Such a computer sees everything as step-by-step instructions, so that's what must be created—a collection of step-by-step instructions.

Structured Programming Drawbacks

In an approach like this, all the parts become like tangled spaghetti. It becomes more and more difficult to control which procedures have access to which data. A new programmer might come on board and not know that one part of the program should not touch a particular variable because changing that one variable has horrible side effects on the whole. There is, however, no built-in mechanism to stop a new programmer from making dangerous changes. In an attempt to solve the problem, structured design emphasized the need to decouple the parts as much as possible, limiting the number of procedures that accessed data to a controllable few. This was an attempt at encapsulation, but it couldn't go far enough. Instead, it meant that procedures that acted on the data had to know more details about the data that they acted upon—which is anathema to the theory of encapsulation.

When you use this design approach on a large problem, you often start by drawing diagrams that represent the data flowing through various procedures, and you break the procedures into functional groups. Programmers are assigned functional groups of procedures. As the problem solving techniques change with the problem understanding, those changes trickle down into the various functional areas. The changes are often spread throughout the various parts of the program. After all, all the procedure groups are just smaller functional parts of the whole, so it only makes sense that they are all intertwined in solving the big problem.

It is unfortunate that structured programming had so many problems. It did provide many solutions that previous design methods did not. Modularization was a big step in the structured programming approach. Structured programming also helped formulate the need for encapsulation and the concept of simplifying a problem with another level of indirection. The computer languages of the 1970s and 1980s were more complex than most of their predecessors, and structured design techniques helped programmers understand the complexity and put it to work in their favor.

24

It is difficult to pinpoint exactly when an alternative to structured design first became apparent. There were, I think, several parallel developments that led to the OOD model. One of those developments was primarily in the area of artificial intelligence circles, where the concepts of *active data* and *data-driven models* started to take form. Another development came in the area of simulation, where the structured design techniques could not readily describe the problems of simulating real-world situations. Both of these approaches emphasized the need for an object view over a procedural view of a problem. Out of that need came what is now called the object-oriented design approach.

OOD Steps

There are many thoughts on the steps in the OOD process. The steps detailed here are based on the Booch model, named for Grady Booch, the person who first formalized these steps. Volumes have been written on the Booch model, and this lesson alone cannot give you the full picture. Provided here are some of the basic ideas and concepts that can help you make productive use of this technique right away.

Formalizing the OOD steps with the small programs in this book might seem to have little value. However, OOD is particularly useful for large, complex software projects. To succeed with OOD in a large project, you really should understand the steps and some of the ways to implement them. These steps can be performed concurrently or in series, but they can be boiled down to the following logical elements:

1. Describe the problem and identify the real-world objects.
2. Identify the methods or activities that define the objects.
3. Identify and establish object visibility.
4. Establish the interface.
5. Implement the object classes.
6. Maintain or iterate the design.

Each of these steps is detailed in the sections that follow.

Identify the Objects

There are many ways to do this, but I recommend the method described by Grady Booch in his books on software engineering. First, put the problem into words and write them down. This is very similar to the planning phase of previous software design methods, but there is a difference in the purpose. Not only does this focus your design goals, it gives you the keys to identify the objects involved in the problem. Objects in a problem are represented by nouns in your written description.

For example, let's use this method to design a stereo system emulator. I'll start by describing the problem:

A stereo system can contain a CD player, a tape player, and a radio. It is used to play music CDs, to play cassette tapes, and to tune in to radio stations. All of these are controlled through mechanical control knobs on the system.

Perhaps the description should be more detailed, but this is something to start with. Nouns that represent objects are identified: stereo system, players, radio tuner, CDs, cassette tapes, radio stations/frequencies, and controls. A player is a base type of CD player and tape player—an abstract class. Another abstract class implied by the player abstraction is the media being played; tapes and CDs are two types of recording media. Another abstract type implied here is a *control* because both digital and analog control types are necessary in the frequency tuning control and bass level control, respectively.

Adjectives often represent or describe data members within the objects. For instance, the system might have interchangeable parts such as a high-quality tape player aimed at music distributors. Or, perhaps the domestic consumer model must have FM and AM radio frequency capability, while an international model also includes short-wave band capability. Adjectives describe the objects.

One good thing to do at this point is buy a packet of index cards, using one card to represent each class as you identify it. Then, add to the card as you progress through the remaining steps. If you can't fit all the things for a single class on that index card, there is a good chance that the class is too complicated and needs to be broken down into simpler pieces. Also, after you write down the class names on the cards, stick them on a white board or a big sheet of paper so that you can build on the model and keep the classes in front of you.

Identify the Methods

The second step is to identify the methods. What can the objects do, or what are the operations that make the objects what they are? Methods are often identified by verbs. Some of the verbs in the description are *play*, *tune*, and *adjust*. Perhaps you notice that *tuning* is just another word for the more abstract term, *adjust*, so you stick with just *play* and *adjust* for now. Perhaps you see other methods. If so, add to the description to formalize the thought and focus your goals.

As you identify the methods, write the method names down on their representative cards. Then, draw lines on the white board or paper to connect the objects that are acted upon by the methods. For instance, if you have a cassette tape object, a player object, and a play method in the player object, draw a line from the play method to the cassette tape class card.

Establish the Visibility

In this step, the things in objects that other objects need to know about must be identified. For instance, does the tape player need to know when the radio is playing? If the player needs to automatically record the radio at certain times, additional radio must be provided. Fortunately, you can start simply. If you follow the OOD model, adding functions won't break other parts of the program.

In the previous step of identifying methods, operations that the objects could perform were identified. In this step, parts of the object that should be visible to other objects are identified. For instance, other objects probably need to know the current volume setting of the radio tuner or media player. This implies that a method is needed to access those items and come up with some accessor methods for the classes. Write the accessor methods on the index cards. The accessor implies the type of data the methods access later on.

Look for natural boundaries in the real world that imply where visibility should be limited. For instance, a nuclear power plant simulator might have access boundaries between primary and secondary coolant systems.

Establish the Interface

Now you have almost complete descriptions of classes on index cards pasted up on a white board. The next step is to determine how all those parts interact to make the stereo system.

The interface is the group of activities that tie the objects to the outside world. In this case, these are primarily represented in the control class. The control class somehow gets commands from a user and sends messages to the stereo components to perform those choices. Because this interface should be as simple as possible, you decide to have one volume control.

The controller class might need to know which component is currently active to adjust the volume for that component. You might decide that this is a bad idea, so you add a speaker class and have the control adjust the speaker volume without knowing which component is giving the speaker its volume. However, there could be a good reason that the controller should know which component is active. Maybe the controller might someday detect radio commercials and reduce the volume—in which case it needs to know when the radio is the active component.

Humans need some sort of feedback as they make adjustments. Perhaps a lighted level indicator for the volume should be considered. It might need a red-line area for levels that endanger the speakers and a component selector switch.

BD
24

In any event, you see how each step in the design uncovers more thoughts on the earlier step and helps you fine-tune the concept as you go. That's one of the strengths of OOD. Each step clarifies (without complicating) the design.

Implement the Objects

All the previous steps could be done in rough pseudocode that can easily be spilled into header files for each object. Now you can take those header files, flesh out each method, and determine how the contained objects should be represented. You might decide that the volume setting in a player object should be an integer and the tuner setting should be a float.

Perhaps you notice that the play method requires knowledge of the current volume and equalizer settings, or maybe you were able to isolate those things so that it doesn't need to know. You can still add functions as required. You might see that no other objects need certain functions you've included, so you can move them to the private or protected sections of the class.

Maintain or Iterate the Design

Every project I've worked on has evolved over the course of the design. The older software design techniques stressed a need for up-front planning to avoid later changes during the process. Of course, programmers found out the hard way that they could not fully understand a problem and how to solve it until they began trying to solve it. The act of solving a problem often defines for us how it is to be solved. Don't fear change during the design. If the objects you've designed appear to be wrong, add to them to make them right.

If you create methods that you find you are never using, don't throw them out. Save the methods you don't use. Their presence probably implies that they will be needed at some time. You'll find that, in most cases, you won't be able to reuse classes without change in other projects. You can usually reuse those classes simply by adding to them. As you add to them, you make them more useful in the original program.

Maintenance should no longer be a strategy of holding ground. Instead maintenance can be a strategy of new conquests. As you maintain and tune the current project classes, try to determine whether the current changes prevent class reuse in other projects. If your design is a good one, the changes should not affect the reuse of current classes for future projects. You might want to keep the current class as is and derive a new class from it to be specific to the current program.

Other OOD Descriptions

By no means is the Booch model the only formalized OOD technique. The Booch method is probably the most common, but it might not fit your particular project as well as some others. The company you work for might have adopted another method as the standard.

Some other popular OOD techniques are the object modeling technique (OMT) and the responsibility-driven design (RDD) technique. These methods are similar to the Booch technique in that they follow the OOD model but differ in the underlying conceptual view of the problem. Many books are available on each of these techniques, and you might find it helpful to eventually become familiar with them both.

When Not to Use OOD

There are OOD purists who will be very angry at me for saying that there are times when you would not use OOD techniques. Such times are few and far between, but they definitely exist.

If the program you are writing is definitely not going to be used more than once and it is going to be small, I do not recommend using OOD. If you think you might be able to use the classes you create in future programs, you have to weigh the current need with the future needs or desires. For instance, I once had the need for a collection of simple command-line math programs. There was no need to create a complex math class for those functions. The straightforward C-like approach meant the programs would be about five lines of code each. Creating special classes in such a case would have been a waste of time.

Low-level or time-critical applications can at times be inappropriate for OOD techniques as well. Abstract classes (virtual function calls) add some overhead. In most cases, that overhead is hardly noticeable, but there are times when you want to squeeze every possible machine instruction or memory location and that virtual table might be too much to stomach. Imagine, for instance, a program that monitors a premature baby's heartbeat, where every split second can decide life or death. In such a system, you need to weigh the efficiency question against the related OOD benefits (such as, maintainability and greater code solidity). Such a system must have time-critical portions that should not be hampered even with virtual function lookup time.

On the other hand, there are times when OOD should be the only choice. In particular, complex systems and systems with maintenance cycles always benefit from OOD techniques. Simple projects often become complex projects, so they too benefit from OOD strengths that make upgrading easier.

BD
24

Always weigh the benefits of OOD. If your sole concern is schedule and you think the OOD approach takes longer, in most cases you are wrong. It has been my experience that the OOD approach always requires less time, except in the very quick single-use projects discussed previously. Do not assume that OOD takes longer even for your first attempt. I have yet to hear one horror story about how OOD made a project late. If I heard such a story, I would be pretty safe to assume that OOD was just the scapegoat and another reason was behind the project's delay.

Do	Don't

DO read about other OOD techniques and become an expert in at least one.

DON'T assume that every project you work on will benefit equally from OOD.

DO get on with coding as soon as possible and refine the initial design as you go.

DO look for natural boundaries that hint at where classes should and should not interact.

Summary

Today the basics that underpin software design were discussed. This knowledge is what identifies you as a software engineer and not just a hacker. Without a solid understanding of these techniques, you cannot fully appreciate the power of C++. You learned that OOD differs in many ways from previous design paradigms but, at the same time, enhances and expands upon the good ideas that previous design paradigms introduced. OOD brings the design closer to the code and gives you the ability to code and design at the same time like never before.

You learned about maintainability in the OOD world, and how OOD has changed maintainability from a phase of boring bug tracing to new heights in design.

You also learned that the OOD paradigm comes in several forms and that there is no one OOD model that is better than another. Each has strengths that can depend upon the problem to be solved.

24

Q&A

Q Is the Booch model the only OOD model?

A No, but it is probably the most well-known model for OOD.

Q Are there times when OOD techniques are not appropriate?

A Yes, but it is safest to err on the side of OOD rather than make the mistake of thinking OOD will delay schedules.

Quiz

1. True or False: The object modeling and responsibility-driven design techniques are not based on OOD methods.
2. Using the Booch model, in which phase would you establish the visibility between classes?
3. True or False: The OOD model stresses up-front planning for understanding the problem more than previous design methods.
4. True or False: The OOD model does not require structure in program design.

**BD
24**

Exercises

1. Use the first step of the Booch OOD technique to identify the objects required to bake a cake.
2. Identify the methods in exercise 1.
3. Do you see any natural boundaries that separate or imply visibility in exercises 1 and 2?

Day 25

Data Structures

The term *data structures* refers to the way a programmer views and treats a collection of data. It has nothing to do with how the data is actually stored in memory, but it has everything to do with how that data is accessed and manipulated. Arrays are contiguous memory locations containing data items and are exceptions to this view. Choosing the correct view of a collection of data can make a world of difference in how efficiently your program deals with that data.

Looking Back at Arrays

Back on Day 11, you learned how to use arrays to build simple linked lists. Most complex data structures are built on the concept of arrays at their core, but it is in how the data is accessed and manipulated that the differences come into play. On Day 19, you learned how templates could be used to create complex data structures so that the details of the structure do not distract you from their purpose.

Today you will learn how a few simple data structures work and how you can put them to use. With today's knowledge, you will be ready to put the lessons of earlier days to work. You might find it helpful to review the linked list example from Day 11 as you work on this lesson.

Queues and Stacks

Of all data structures, queues and stacks are most like arrays. A queue is a method of storing data so that the first item stored is the first item retrieved. A stack is the opposite: The last item stored is the first item retrieved. Queues are sometimes called *first in first out* (FIFO, pronounced "Fy-foe") buffers, and stacks are often referred to as *last in first out* (LIFO, pronounced "Ly-foe") buffers. In both structures, you keep track of the next available memory slot and next item to be removed with pointers.

Inserting items into a queue or a stack is referred to as *pushing* items. Removing items is referred to as *popping* items from the queue or stack.

A Simple Queue Example

Figure 25.1 illustrates the concept of a queue. In this example, you're storing `ints`, but a queue can be used to store any data type.

The queue starts out empty with a pointer to the first slot (`ptrFirst`) and a pointer to the next available slot (`ptrNext`). Because the queue is empty, both pointers are pointing to the same slot.

At the first push, the next available slot pointer is moved to the point of the next empty slot. The first pointer continues to point at the first slot, which now contains the new item. Each push increments `ptrNext` and keeps `ptrFirst` assigned to the first item pushed into the queue. Each pop leaves `ptrNext` pointing to the next empty slot and increments `ptrFirst` to point to the next oldest item in the list.

Listing 25.1 is a simple queue class that uses an array as the queue. To keep things simple, `ptrNext` and `ptrFirst` are not actually implemented as pointers but as array index values instead. This is not necessarily the most efficient way to implement a queue, but it is the simplest to understand.

25

Figure 25.1.

How a queue works.

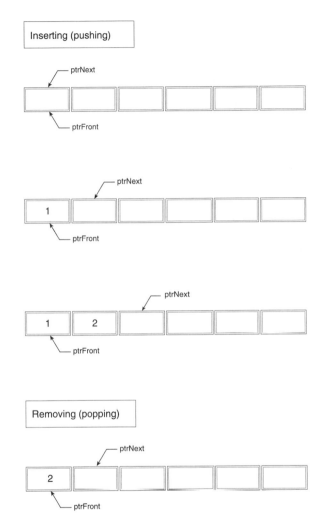

Inserting (pushing)

Removing (popping)

TYPE | **Listing 25.1. A simple queue example.**

```
1:    // Listing 25.1, Using a Simple Queue class
2:
3:    #include<iostream.h>
4:
5:    // A simple integer storage queue
6:
7:    class IntQueue {
8:    private:
9:        int ptrNext;
```

continues

Listing 25.1. continued

```
10:          int ptrFirst;
11:          enum { QSIZE = 256 };
12:          int theQueue[QSIZE];
13:      public:
14:          IntQueue();
15:          ~IntQueue();
16:
17:          bool Push(int);
18:          bool Pop(int &);
19:
20:          bool IsEmpty();
21:          bool IsFull();
22:      };
23:
24:      IntQueue::IntQueue(){
25:
26:          ptrNext = ptrFirst = 0;
27:
28:          for(int i=0; i<QSIZE; i++)
29:              theQueue[i] = 0;
30:      }
31:
32:      IntQueue::~IntQueue(){}
33:
34:      bool IntQueue::Push(int anInt){
35:
36:          if( IsFull() )
37:              return(false);
38:
39:          theQueue[ptrNext] = anInt;
40:          ptrNext++;
41:
42:          return(true);
43:      }
44:
45:      bool IntQueue::Pop(int &firstInt){
46:
47:          if( IsEmpty() )
48:              return(false);
49:
50:          firstInt = theQueue[ptrFirst];
51:          ptrFirst++;
52:
53:          return(true);
54:      }
55:
56:      bool IntQueue::IsEmpty(){
57:          return( ptrNext == ptrFirst);
58:      }
59:
60:      bool IntQueue::IsFull(){
61:          return( QSIZE == ptrNext );
62:      }
```

25

```
63:
64:    void main()
65:    {
66:
67:        IntQueue OurQueue;
68:        int Value;
69:
70:        while( !OurQueue.IsFull() )
71:        {
72:            cout << "Enter an integer value or a 0 to quit: ";
73:            cin >> Value;
74:            cin.ignore(); // ignore <CR>
75:
76:            if( 0 == Value )
77:                break;
78:
79:            OurQueue.Push(Value);
80:        }
81:
82:        cout << "The ints in order:" << endl;
83:
84:        while(! OurQueue.IsEmpty() )
85:            if( OurQueue.Pop(Value) )
86:                cout << Value << endl;
87:    }
```

OUTPUT

```
Enter an integer value or a 0 to quit: 10
Enter an integer value or a 0 to quit: 9
Enter an integer value or a 0 to quit: 8
Enter an integer value or a 0 to quit: 7
Enter an integer value or a 0 to quit: 6
Enter an integer value or a 0 to quit: 0
The ints in order:
10
9
8
7
6
```

BD
25

ANALYSIS Lines 7 to 62 define a simple queue class. In the constructor, the index values for first and next are both set to 0 on line 26. All the values in the queue are initialized to 0 as well. The Push function (lines 36 to 40) simply inserts the incoming item if the queue is not full and increments the ptrNext index so that it is ready for the next insert.

The Pop member function checks to make sure the queue is not empty and then assigns the reference variable with the value that ptrFirst points to and increments ptrFirst. This is where the class is inappropriate for any serious implementation, because ptrFirst and ptrNext could eventually reach the full mark even if the queue is not full. Because the purpose here is to keep things simple, the ptrNext and ptrFirst increment values are shifted instead of shifting the entire array contents as items are inserted or removed.

IsEmpty and IsFull are simple in their checks to indicate whether the queue is empty or full.

Inside main, at lines 70 to 79, integers can be entered until the queue is full or until a 0 is entered. In lines 84 to 86, the queue is emptied and displayed one item at a time with Pop.

There is a way around your queue's space weakness besides shifting the contents. Shifting the contents works, but—depending on the size of the queue—it can be costly to do so. One alternative is a circular queue.

A Circular Queue

A circular queue is a special form of a queue that, in implementation, resembles what would happen if you curled the end of a regular queue to connect with the head. Instead of reaching a full mark, the next pointer starts back at the beginning again. The first pointer follows the next pointer around the circle with each pop. The only thing similar to full in a circular queue is when the next pointer travels all the way around and threatens to bump into the first pointer. Figure 25.2 illustrates a circular queue.

Figure 25.2.

How a circular queue works.

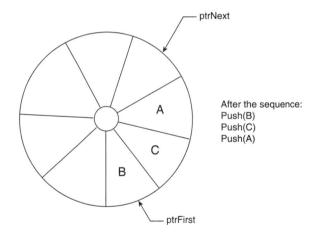

After the sequence:
Push(B)
Push(C)
Push(A)

A Simple Stack Example

A stack is simply the opposite of a queue. Items are removed in the opposite direction that they are inserted. Figure 25.3 illustrates how a stack works.

Implementing a stack is even easier than implementing a queue. To push items on the stack, copy the item into the stack and increment the next pointer.

25

Figure 25.3.

How a stack works.

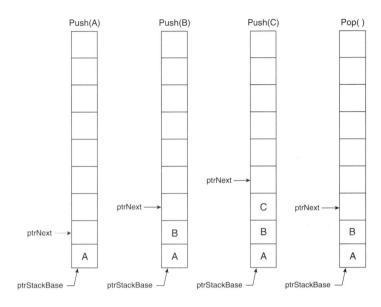

To pop items from the stack, simply decrement the next pointer and pop the item to which it points. The base pointer, which points at the very first slot (or, *base slot*) always remains where it is. If next and base are equal, the stack is empty. If next is equal to the stack size, the stack is full.

Stack implementation is discussed in an exercise at the end of this lesson.

Trees

Trees, in computer science terminology, are just another way to view stored data. The confusing hurdle to overcome is that computer science trees are upside down. In other words, the root of the tree is at the top and the branches are at the bottom. Each portion of the tree that contains data is called a node. In addition to a data item, each node contains pointers to other nodes. Each node can point to any number of other nodes to build complex trees. A company organization chart is a tree, as illustrated in Figure 25.4.

Trees are particularly well-suited for storing and retrieving sorted data. The most common tree type is a binary tree. A binary tree is a tree in which no node points to more than two nodes below it. In addition, a binary tree sorts data as it is entered into the tree by moving data greater than the root toward the right and data less than the root to the left. For example, Figure 25.5 illustrates how data is arranged if the data being stored is integers in the order, G, D, C, I, E, W.

BD
25

Figure 25.4.

An organization chart is a tree.

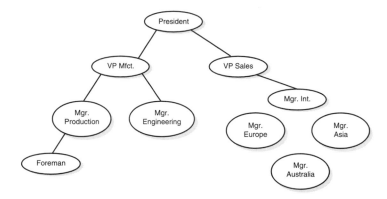

Figure 25.5.

A binary tree example.

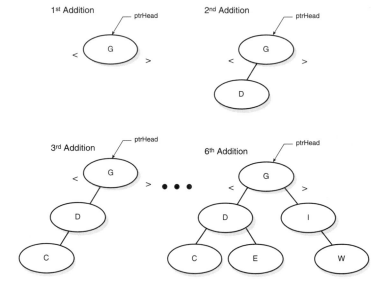

When G is added, there are no nodes, so G becomes the root node. D is added, compared to G, found less than G, and attached to the left of G. C is added and found less than G; then it falls through to the left, is found less than D, and is attached to the left of D. I is found greater than G and attached to the right of G. E is less than G but greater than D, so it is attached to the right of D. Finally, W is greater than G and greater than I, so it is attached to the right of I.

It does not seem quite as confusing if you try not to think of the entire tree at once. Concentrate on one node at a time. When a node starts out, it has two pointers, one to the right (greater side) and one to the left (lesser side). If both pointers are assigned, the new nodes trickle down to fill unassigned slots. If a comparison finds the new node greater, the new node trickles to the right. If it is less, it trickles to the left.

25

There are three ways to move through a binary tree: in-order traversal, post-order traversal, and pre-order traversal.

In-order traversal is the method of visiting each node in the tree using the following algorithm: visit the left node, the current node, and then the right node. Using the example of Figure 25.5, in-order traversal visits the nodes in the sequence, C, D, E, G, I, W. In other words, in-order traversal visits the nodes in sorted order.

Post-order traversal visits the left node, the right node, and then the current node. In Figure 25.5, post-order traversal is in the sequence C, E, D, W, I, G—or, reverse-sorted order.

Pre-order traversal visits the current node, the left node, and then the right node. Pre-order produces the sequence G, D, C, E, I, W.

If you think of binary tree in a recursive fashion, it helps you understand how the traversal methods work. Each node has either 0, 1, or 2 subtrees attached to it. The post-order and in-order traversals visit the subtrees first, and then the root. The pre-order visits the root and then each subtree.

Listing 25.2 is a simple binary tree implementation used to store int values. To save space, only an in-order tree traversal function is implemented. The other tree traversal methods are similar.

BD 25

TYPE **Listing 25.2. A simple binary tree example.**

```
 1:    // Listing 25.2, Binary tree example
 2:    // Binary Tree Header File section:
 3:
 4:    #include<iostream.h>
 5:
 6:
 7:    #ifndef NULL
 8:    #define NULL (0)
 9:    #endif
10:
11:    ////////
12:     // A tree node is a node for a binary tree
13:
14:    class TreeNode {
15:    protected:
16:       TreeNode *ptrRight;
17:       TreeNode *ptrLeft;
18:       int itsData;
19:    public:
20:       TreeNode(int Data);
21:       TreeNode();
22:       virtual ~TreeNode();
23:
24:       bool Data(int Data);
```

continues

Listing 25.2. continued

```
25:
26:        int Data();
27:
28:        TreeNode *Add(int Data);
29:
30:        TreeNode *&RightNode();
31:
32:        TreeNode *&LeftNode();
33:
34:        bool Right(TreeNode *&pRight);
35:
36:        bool Left(TreeNode *&pLeft);
37:
38:
39:
40:    };
41:
42:    ////////
43:    // A Binary Tree is simply a TreeNode with 0
44:    //              or more children
45:
46:    class BinaryTree : public TreeNode {
47:    private:
48:        static TreeNode *ptrHead;
49:    public:
50:        BinaryTree(int Data);
51:        BinaryTree(TreeNode *tNode);
52:        BinaryTree();
53:        ~BinaryTree() { }
54:
55:        static TreeNode *Head() { return( ptrHead ); }
56:
57:
58:
59:        // Tree Traversal
60:
61:        bool InOrderPrint(TreeNode *tNode=ptrHead);
62:
63:        // Adding nodes
64:        bool Add(int Data, TreeNode *&Root = ptrHead,
65:                bool NoDuplicates = true);
66:        // Searching
67:
68:        TreeNode *Find(int KeyData, TreeNode *tNode=ptrHead);
69:    };
70:
71:    // TreeNode and BinaryTree Class
72:    // Implementation file section:
73:
74:    TreeNode::TreeNode(int Data) {
75:        itsData = Data;
76:        ptrRight = ptrLeft = NULL;
77:    }
78:
```

25

```
79:     TreeNode::TreeNode() {
80:         ptrRight = NULL;
81:         ptrLeft = NULL;
82:     }
83:
84:     TreeNode::~TreeNode() {
85:
86:
87:         delete ptrRight;
88:
89:
90:         delete ptrLeft;
91:
92:     }
93:
94:     bool TreeNode::Data(int Data) {
95:         itsData = Data;
96:         return(true);
97:     }
98:
99:     int TreeNode::Data() {
100:        return(itsData);
101:    }
102:
103:    TreeNode *TreeNode::Add(int Data)
104:    {
105:        if(Data < itsData)
106:        {
107:            ptrLeft = new TreeNode(Data);
108:            return( ptrLeft );
109:        }
110:        else
111:        {
112:            ptrRight = new TreeNode(Data);
113:            return( ptrRight );
114:        }
115:    }
116:
117:    TreeNode *&TreeNode::RightNode() {
118:        return(ptrRight);
119:    }
120:
121:    TreeNode *&TreeNode::LeftNode() {
122:        return(ptrLeft);
123:    }
124:
125:    bool TreeNode::Right(TreeNode *&pRight)
126:    {
127:        ptrRight = pRight;
128:        return(true);
129:    }
130:
131:    bool TreeNode::Left(TreeNode *&pLeft)
132:    {
133:        ptrLeft = pLeft;
```

continues

Listing 25.2. continued

```
134:        return(true);
135:    }
136:
137:    /////////
138:    // The BinaryTree implementation section:
139:
140:    TreeNode *BinaryTree::ptrHead = NULL;
141:
142:    BinaryTree::BinaryTree(int Data) {
143:        ptrHead = this;
144:        ptrHead->Data(Data);
145:    }
146:
147:    BinaryTree::BinaryTree() {
148:        ptrHead = this;
149:        ptrHead->Data(0);
150:    }
151:
152:
153:
154:        // Tree Traversal
155:
156:    bool BinaryTree::InOrderPrint(TreeNode *tNode) {
157:
158:        if( tNode )
159:        {
160:            InOrderPrint( tNode->LeftNode() );
161:            cout << tNode->Data() << endl;
162:            InOrderPrint( tNode->RightNode() );
163:        }
164:        return(true);
165:
166:    }
167:
168:        // Adding nodes
169:
170:    bool BinaryTree::Add(int Data, TreeNode *&Root, bool NoDuplicates) {
171:
172:        if( NoDuplicates && Find(Data, Root) )
173:        {
174:            return(false);
175:        }
176:        else
177:        {
178:            // Add to the right tree if greater else add to
179:            // the left tree
180:            if( 0 == Root->Data() )
181:            {
182:                Root->Data(Data);
183:                return( true );
184:            }
185:
186:            if( Data > Root->Data() )
187:            {
```

25

```
188:                    if( Root->RightNode() )
189:                        Add(Data, Root->RightNode(), NoDuplicates);
190:                    else
191:                    {
192:                        Root->Add(Data);
193:                    }
194:                }
195:                else
196:                {
197:                    if( Root->LeftNode() )
198:                        Add(Data, Root->LeftNode(), NoDuplicates);
199:                    else
200:                    {
201:                        Root->Add(Data);
202:                    }
203:                }
204:            }
205:
206:        return( true );
207:    }
208:
209:        // Searching
210:
211:    TreeNode *BinaryTree::Find(int KeyData, TreeNode *tNode) {
212:
213:        // pre-order search
214:        if( (NULL == tNode) || (KeyData == tNode->Data()) )
215:            return( tNode );
216:
217:        if( KeyData < tNode->Data() )
218:            return( Find(KeyData, tNode->LeftNode()) );
219:        else
220:            return( Find(KeyData, tNode->RightNode()) );
221:    }
222:
223:        // Main function file section:
224:
225:    void main()
226:    {
227:        BinaryTree *ATree = new BinaryTree;
228:        int Value = 0;
229:
230:        while( true )
231:        {
232:            cout << "Enter a zero to quit or any integer: ";
233:
234:            cin >> Value;
235:            cin.ignore();
236:
237:            if( 0 == Value )
238:                break;
239:
240:            ATree->Add(Value);
241:        }
242:
```

continues

Listing 25.2. continued

```
243:          cout << "Enter an integer to find: ";
244:          cin >> Value;
245:          cin.ignore();
246:
247:          TreeNode *TNode = ATree->Find(Value);
248:
249:          if( TNode )
250:             cout << "Found: " << TNode->Data() << endl;
251:          else
252:             cout << "Not found." << endl;
253:
254:          ATree->InOrderPrint();
255:
256:          delete ATree;
257:      }
```

OUTPUT

```
Enter a zero to quit or any integer: 8
Enter a zero to quit or any integer: 7
Enter a zero to quit or any integer: 10
Enter a zero to quit or any integer: 25
Enter a zero to quit or any integer: 45
Enter a zero to quit or any integer: 2
Enter a zero to quit or any integer: 1
Enter a zero to quit or any integer: 0
Enter an integer to find: 25
Found: 25
1
2
7
8
10
25
45
```

ANALYSIS   Many compilers define the pointer NULL, but lines 7 to 9 provide the definition just in case yours doesn't. Whenever a pointer needs to be initialized, it is initialized to NULL in this program.

This might appear intimidating, but when taken a few lines at a time it's very simple. Just imagine a single TreeNode with a slot for data (an int, in this example) and two pointers for TreeNodes to the left and right. A BinaryTree can be represented by its root TreeNode, which is kept in the variable ptrHead.

TreeNode is very simple, so let's cut to the chase and dig into the BinaryTree. The BinaryTree constructors (lines 142 to 150) initialize the ptrHead TreeNode and the data it contains.

25

Lines 154 to 166 provide an in-order traversal function, which prints the ints in order. The tree is identified by its root TreeNode, which is ptrHead passed as a default argument. If ptrHead is NULL (meaning that the tree is empty or doesn't exist), it simply returns without doing anything. The next step (line 156) is to traverse the left subtree in order, which is represented by the TreeNode attached to the left of tNode. This recursive call keeps looping through the left TreeNode pointers until it reaches a NULL back at the function entry test, and then it unwinds with each successive answer at line 161. After the left subtree and the root are traversed, InOrderPrint starts recursively on the right subtree. Whenever you work with trees, remember the basic traversal rules for a single node and then implement them recursively. In-order is simply left, current, right. That's exactly what you find here.

Adding a TreeNode to a BinaryTree is a little confusing unless you can, again, simplify the problem to adding to a single TreeNode. To add a TreeNode to a BinaryTree, follow these steps:

1. If the root TreeNode is empty or NULL, simply add at the root location.
2. If the data to add is greater than the root TreeNode data, you should do one of two things: If the right TreeNode is NULL, attach new node to the right. Or, add to the right subtree represented by the right pointer (restart at 1 with the new right tree root).
3. If the data to add is less than the root TreeNode, add to the left subtree as described for the right in step 2.

This example also verifies that repeats are not entered. Look at lines 172 to 175. The test checks to see whether duplicate entries should be prevented (the default) and, if so, checks to see whether the new entry can be found in the current tree. If the data is not in the tree, control continues in the else part at lines 180 to 184 where the logic is followed as described earlier in step 1.

Lines 186 to 194 mechanize step 2 of the TreeNode addition logic, and lines 195 to 204 follow the logic of step 3. If no TreeNode is added, as is the case on a duplicate, false is returned. If a TreeNode is added, true is returned.

You might have noticed that there is no TreeNode deletion in this class. Deleting TreeNodes is a bit complicated. As you get used to programming, you should study trees further, but for now, pretend you don't want to delete any TreeNodes.

Lines 211 to 221 are a function for finding a TreeNode that contains a particular data item. It uses pre-order traversal (current, left, right) to search the tree and returns a pointer to the TreeNode that contains the data.

The main function (lines 225 to 257) simply creates an instance of a tree, enables you to enter some integers, and stores them. Lastly, it asks for an integer to search the tree for, returns its result, and uses the InOrderPrint function to print the data in order.

BD 25

Do	**Don't**

DO use data structures to simplify your program data storage.

DO choose structures that represent the real-world data.

DON'T attempt to force data into a complicated structure if you don't need to. More complex data structures can make your program hard to follow and prone to bugs.

Summary

Today you entered the world of the computer scientist. No longer are you a simple hacker trying to force everything into huge arrays that consume memory and time. Now you have the tools to write some pretty serious applications with large data structures.

You can write your own robust versions of the data structures in this lesson to create bulletproof applications. But before you get too far, you probably wonder why nobody ever did template versions of these structures. The Standard Template Library (STL) provides exactly what you have in mind, along with a large collection of algorithms. You can still go about writing that robust `BinaryTree` class as an exercise in understanding how data structures work, but you can use the STL to speed serious development.

This lesson is not an exhaustive reference. If you want to learn more, there are plenty of great books that can provide a lot of detail on the subject. Day 28 provides several listings of books for further study.

Q&A

Q **What is the first item out of a queue on the first `Pop()`?**

A The first item out is the first one that was pushed into the queue.

Q **What kind of queue would you use if you were going to do a lot of additions and removals in your program?**

A A circular queue is best because the memory is less likely to be exhausted in the multiple operations.

25

Q **Why would access time normally be quicker from a binary tree than from a queue, stack, or simple array if large quantities of data are stored?**

A Searching a queue, stack, or simple array requires looking at each item in the order in which it appears in the structure. Searching a binary tree narrows the search to an ordered process through the data, using comparisons to the current data.

Quiz

1. In what order does a pre-order traversal visit the nodes of a binary tree?
2. Are binary trees a kind of contiguous memory structure?
3. How is a binary tree like a single tree node?
4. Why are binary tree traversals often recursive?

Exercises

1. Alter Listing 25.1 to implement a simple stack class.
2. Alter the code from exercise 1 to store character values instead of `ints`.
3. Alter the `InOrderPrint` function in Listing 25.2 to do a post-order print instead.

BD
25

Day 26

Simple Sorting and Searching

Once the realm of artificial intelligence, sorting and searching algorithms have forced their way into virtually every type of application. Don't be intimidated, though; you won't find this any more difficult than other subjects covered to date. The fact that you've made it this far says that you are a cut above the many learners who give up at the first sign of difficulty.

You have used many of the concepts that you'll learn today since you were a child, before you had formalized your system of logic. Some of the concepts might seem so rooted in common sense that you wonder why you hadn't thought of them before.

Sorting and searching are the building blocks of many application types. Perhaps nothing in computer science can have as great an impact on efficiency as choosing the right sorting or searching methods. Sort routines are built into the standard libraries, but their general-purpose nature makes them less efficient for complex data types. In addition, if you understand the strengths and weaknesses of sorting and searching algorithms in detail, you are better able to choose the right one for your application.

Because searching algorithms often require the data to be sorted, sorting is covered in detail first. Sorting and searching are forever bound together as a team. Always remember that the number of lines of code or the complexity of the algorithm do not indicate the efficiency of an algorithm. Sometimes the simplest approach is the quickest solution, and other times the more complex method is necessary for useful results.

Sorting

Sorting is the process of taking an unordered data set, typically an array, and placing the data in ascending or descending order. The methods humans use to sort information can be placed into three categories:

1. Swap or exchange sorts
2. Insertion sorts
3. Selection sorts

First, you'll look at the theory behind each sorting type and then you'll see some examples of these sorting methods. To understand each of the sort methods, imagine that you have a string of different sized beads. To make things simple, imagine that you can snap the beads on and off the string at any point you like.

To use the exchange sort method, start at the left end of the string and compare the left two beads. If bead 1 is larger than bead 2, swap the beads. Compare bead 2 and bead 3 the same way, and then bead 3 with bead 4, and so on. When you reach the right side, start back at the left and repeat the process. If you go through the entire string without having to make a swap, you are done. Computer scientists call this a *bubble sort* because the larger beads appear to bubble across the string to reach their places.

When sorting your imaginary necklace with a selection sort, you select the smallest bead from the string, remove it, and place it at the far left end of the string. Start at the second bead, and find the smallest bead between the second and last bead and move it to the left end. Keep removing the smallest remaining bead and placing it to the left until there are no further beads to the right of the last bead you place. The string is sorted, and you're done.

The insertion sort progresses like this: Take the first bead from the string and place it on the string in the place where it belongs with respect to its size. Take the next bead and do the same. When you place the final bead, the sort is complete, and the beads are in order, largest to smallest.

The following sections cover each of the general sorting categories with a representative sort routine and then discuss a sorting algorithm that is typically more efficient than the general sorts.

The Bubble Sort

The bubble sort is the easiest sort to code and is relatively efficient for small data sets. This is the workhorse of sorting algorithms. It is typically the first (and the easiest) one programmers learn to use. Listing 26.1 implements a simple variation on the bubble sort.

TYPE **Listing 26.1. A bubble sort example.**

```
1:   // Listing 26.1. A Bubble Sort example
2:
3:   #include <iostream.h>
4:   #include <stdlib.h>
5:   #include <time.h>
6:
7:   int BubbleSort(int MyIntegers[], int arraySize);
8:
9:   int BubbleSort(int MyIntegers[], int arraySize)
10:  {
11:     int tmpInt, i, j;
12:
13:     // Just for kicks, keep track of the swap count
14:     int swaps = 0;
15:
16:     for(i=0; i<arraySize; i++)
17:     {
18:       for(j=0; j<arraySize; j++)
19:       {
20:         // If the left one is larger, then swap
21:         if( MyIntegers[i] < MyIntegers[j] )
22:         {
23:           swaps++;
24:           // Save the first one before swap
25:           tmpInt = MyIntegers[i];
26:
27:           MyIntegers[i] = MyIntegers[j];
28:           MyIntegers[j] = tmpInt;
29:         }
30:       }
31:     }
32:
33:     return( swaps );
34:  }
35:
36:  void main()
37:  {
38:     const int Big = 500;
39:
40:     int SomeIntegers[Big];
41:     int howMany = 0;
42:     int i, numSwaps;
43:
44:     time_t timer = time(0);
```

continues

Listing 26.1. continued

```
45:     srand(static_cast<unsigned>(timer));
46:
47:     cout << "Enter a number between 1 and "
48:         << Big << ": ";
49:
50:     cin >> howMany;
51:     cin.ignore();
52:
53:     cout << "Building an array of "
54:         << howMany << " ints" << endl;
55:
56:     for(i=0; i<howMany; i++)
57:       SomeIntegers[i] = rand() % Big;
58:
59:
60:     cout << endl
61:         << "\tThe ints before sort:" << endl;
62:
63:     for(i=0; i<howMany; i++)
64:     {
65:       if( (i % 20) == 0)
66:         cout << SomeIntegers[i] << endl;
67:       else
68:         cout << SomeIntegers[i] << ' ';
69:     }
70:
71:
72:     numSwaps =
73:       BubbleSort(SomeIntegers, howMany);
74:
75:     cout << endl
76:         << "\tand after sort:" << endl;
77:
78:     for(i=0; i<howMany; i++)
79:     {
80:       if( (i % 20) == 0)
81:         cout << SomeIntegers[i] << endl;
82:       else
83:         cout << SomeIntegers[i] << ' ';
84:     }
85:
86:     cout << endl << endl << numSwaps
87:         << " swaps were required." << endl;
88: }
```

OUTPUT

```
Enter a number between 1 and 500: 25
Building an array of 25 ints

        The ints before sort:
10
401 419 494 220 87 334 472 364 70 37 305 474 369 8 282 207 57 444 53 389
409 111 441 175
```

26

```
        and after sort:
8
10 37 53 57 70 87 111 175 207 220 282 305 334 364 369 389 401 409 419 441
444 472 474 494

163 swaps were required.
```

ANALYSIS This bubble sort compares the first value with the second, the first with the third, the first with the fourth, and so on until it reaches the end. After comparing the first with each of the other values, it performs the same comparison on each with the second, and so on. Let's look more closely.

The main function is a simple loop for filling an array with random numbers. The sort is called on line 73 with the array and sizeSomeIntegers.

All the sorts in this lesson keep track of the number of swaps performed so that you can compare them against each other. Obviously, the fewer swaps a sort must perform, the more efficient the algorithm.

The outer loop of the bubble sort, starting at line 16, increments through the array slot to be compared. The loop, starting on line 18, increments through the items in the array, comparing each with the item identified by the outer loop. If the outer loop item is greater than the inner loop item, the two are swapped. To swap them, the first item in the tmpInt variable on line 25 is saved. On lines 27 and 28, you perform the swap. Inside this swap bracket, the number of swaps in the swaps variable are incremented. The last pass compares the last array item with all other array items and then exits the loops and returns the swaps count.

The remainder of the sort program listings in this lesson use a nearly identical main function; the only difference is the sort function name, which is changed on line 73. In the interest of brevity and clarity, the main function listing is not repeated in the other sort program listings.

The weakness in the bubble sort is that all the comparisons take place even if the array is sorted after the first pass. That's not so bad for a small array, but imagine that you pass an array of 500 items that only has one item out of place. This is one reason the bubble sort isn't recommended for large arrays.

The bubble sort is said to be an *n-square* sort because the sort time is a function of the square of the number of items in the array. An n-square sort is the most inefficient kind of sort.

In order to judge the efficiencies of the various sorts, certain formulae are used to describe the sort behavior. One formula in this book details the worst-case number of exchanges that a sort must make. For instance, the bubble sort, at its worst case, requires

$$1.5 * (n^2 - n)$$

exchanges. To determine the worst case for a given array, insert the number of items in the array for n. For example, an array of 20 items requires an average 1.5 * (400 - 20), or 570

BD 26

exchanges. Try some different numbers and see how quickly the average exchanges rise with the number of array items.

The Selection Sort

The selection efficiency ratings are slightly better than the bubble sort on average. Worst-case exchanges for the selection sort are

$$n^2 / 4 + 3 * (n-1)$$

When worked out for an array of 20 items, this equals 157 worst-case swaps.

TYPE   **Listing 26.2. A selection sort example.**

```
 1:  // Listing 26.2. A Selection Sort example
 2:
 3:  #include <iostream.h>
 4:  #include <stdlib.h>
 5:  #include <time.h>
 6:
 7:  SelectionSort(int MyIntegers[], int arraySize);
 8:
 9:  SelectionSort(int MyIntegers[], int arraySize)
10:  {
11:    int SelectedSlot, InSlot, tmpInt, i;
12:    int swaps = 0;
13:
14:    for(InSlot = 0; InSlot<arraySize; InSlot++)
15:    {
16:      // Save
17:
18:      SelectedSlot = InSlot;
19:
20:      tmpInt = MyIntegers[InSlot];
21:
22:      for(i=InSlot+1; i<arraySize; i++)
23:      {
24:        // Select the smallest in the remainder
25:
26:      if(MyIntegers[i]<MyIntegers[SelectedSlot] )
27:        {
28:          SelectedSlot = i;
29:          swaps++;
30:        }
31:      }
32:
33:      --MyIntegers[InSlot]=MyIntegers[SelectedSlot];
34:      MyIntegers[SelectedSlot] = tmpInt;
35:    }
36:    return( swaps );
37:  }
```

26

```
38:
39:  void main()
40:  {
41:      // Same as Listing 26.1 until the sort
42:      // is called:
43:    numSwaps =
44:      SelectionSort(SomeIntegers, howMany);
45:      // The remainder is the same as
46:      // Listing 26.1.
47:  }
```

```
Enter a number between 1 and 500: 25
Building an array of 25 ints

        The ints before sort:
323
340 236 74 51 151 67 45 324 54 399 194 249 494 291 88 221 165 180 373 92
284 298 38 150
        and after sort:
38
45 51 54 67 74 88 92 150 151 165 180 194 221 236 249 284 291 298 323 324
340 373 399 494

48 swaps were required.
```

ANALYSIS   The main function here is identical to the one used in Listing 26.1 except for the name of the sort function.

The outer loop, starting on line 14, increments the slot where the next value is to be inserted. Line 22 starts an inner loop that increments through the remaining items of the array looking for a value that is one smaller than the current insertion slot value. If a smaller value is found, the index to that slot is saved in SelectedSlot and swaps is incremented to indicate that a swap is needed.

A swap could be done each time it hits a smaller item, but it seems more efficient to only change the index and perform the swap outside the loop at lines 33 and 34. This method saves several steps. To swap each time a smaller value is found requires performing the swap more often. However, swaps is incremented even if the swap is not performed inside the loop. Incrementing swaps in this way shows what the absolute worst-case swaps could be.

The selection sort is an efficiency improvement over the bubble sort, but it is still a sort with an n^2 proportion. The insertion sort is similar in efficiency and is not detailed here so that more time can be devoted to more efficient sorts.

The Shell Sort

The shell sort is a cross between the selection sort and the insertion sort. Imagine that you have a row of shells in front of you, each with a number painted on its underside. Using the shell sort, you would lift the first shell and a shell that is about half the total away from the first (let's say the tenth from the first in a row of 22 shells). If the tenth shell is smaller than the first shell, then swap them. Now lift the second shell and compare it to the tenth shell from the second. If the eleventh (tenth from the second) is smaller, swap the eleventh and second. Continue until you have reached the last shell that can be compared with the 10-shell gap. Go back to the first shell, and this time compare it with the ninth shell from the first; then go through the row in the same manner as you did with a 10-shell gap. On the next pass, decrease the gap to eight, and then seven, and so on.

The shell sort was not named for the analogy used to describe it. It was named after the gentleman who invented it, Donald Shell. Although it might seem amazing that it actually works, it not only works but it is more efficient than any of the sort algorithms covered so far.

The math for the shell sort is a bit complicated, but the sort is in proportion to $n^{1.2}$ rather than n^2 as in the other sorts discussed so far. Just in case that seems insignificant, look at Table 26.1, which shows various numbers raised to the 1.2 power compared to the same number squared.

Table 26.1. Comparing n^2 to $n^{1.2}$ sorts.

n	n^2	$n^{1.2}$
2	4	2.3
10	100	15.8
100	10000	251.2

As you can see, the difference can be quite substantial, especially as n grows larger. Listing 26.3 is an example of how to implement a shell sort.

TYPE   **Listing 26.3. A shell sort example.**

```
1:  // Listing 26.3. A Shell Sort example
2:
3:  #include <iostream.h>
4:  #include <stdlib.h>
5:  #include <time.h>
6:
7:  ShellSort(int MyIntegers[], int arraySize);
8:
9:  ShellSort(int MyIntegers[], int arraySize)
10: {
11:    int Gap, tmpInt, i;
12:    int swaps = 0;
13:    bool swappedTwo;
14:
```

26

```
15:     Gap = arraySize/2;
16:
17:     do { // As long as we can divide Gap/2
18:        do { // As long as we've swapped
19:          swappedTwo = false;
20:
21:          for(i = 0; i<arraySize - Gap; i++)
22:          {
23:             if( MyIntegers[i] > MyIntegers[i + Gap] )
24:             {
25:
26:                tmpInt = MyIntegers[i];
27:                MyIntegers[i] = MyIntegers[i + Gap];
28:                MyIntegers[i + Gap] = tmpInt;
29:
30:                swaps++;
31:                swappedTwo = true;
32:             }
33:          }
34:
35:        } while( swappedTwo );
36:     } while( Gap = Gap/2 );
37:     return( swaps );
38: }
39: void main()
40: {
41:     // Same as Listing 26.1 until the sort
42:     // is called:
43:     numSwaps =
44:       ShellSort(SomeIntegers, howMany);
45:     // The remainder is the same as
46:     // Listing 26.1.
47: }
```

BD 26

OUTPUT
```
Enter a number between 1 and 500: 25
Building an array of 25 ints
        The ints before sort:
178
86 5 280 257 309 467 21 260 128 193 444 486 159 260 223 221 200 221 41
303
133 39 133 68
        and after sort:
5
21 39 41 68 86 128 133 133 159 178 193 200 221 221 223 257 260 260 280
303
309 444 467 486
66 swaps were required.
```

ANALYSIS Again, main is changed only at the line where the sort is called.

In the shell sort, you need to know when you have made an entire array traversal without the need to swap any values. So, on line 19 a bool value is initialized, swappedTwo, which does the swap tracking. On line 15 the first Gap value is initialized, indicating how far apart the first round of comparisons are.

Lines 17 and 18 are the beginning of a nested do-while loop pair. The inner loop exits only after going through the entire array using the Gap increment without performing a swap (based on the value of swappedTwo). As soon as the inner loop is exited the first time, the outer loop divides Gap by 2 and reenters the inner loop with the new Gap value. The outer loop is exited only after the inner loop is exited (no swaps), and the Gap cannot be divided further (Gap is less than 2).

The Quick Sort

The math for a quick sort is also somewhat complicated, so I won't bore you with the details—just the bottom line. The number of exchanges works out to be as follows:

```
n/6 log n
```

So, for an array of 100 items, the quick sort requires an average of 200 exchanges. Compare that to the exponential growth of the simpler searches, and you should realize why the quick sort is the best sort known to date.

Listing 26.4 is a quick sort example. Notice that this is the only place where the main function changes. In the quick sort, the last item index is passed instead of the size of the array, so the howMany that yields the last item index is decremented.

TYPE **Listing 26.4. A quick sort example.**

```
 1:  // Listing 26.4. A Quick Sort example
 2:
 3:  #include <iostream.h>
 4:  #include <stdlib.h>
 5:  #include <time.h>
 6:
 7:  int QuickSort(int MyIntegers[],
 8:          int iLast, int iFirst = 0);
 9:  int QuickSort(int MyIntegers[], int iLast, int iFirst)
10:  {
11:     static int swaps = 0;
12:
13:     int tmpInt, iLow, iHigh, valueSeparator;
14:
15:     iLow = iFirst;
16:     iHigh = iLast;
17:     valueSeparator = MyIntegers[ (iFirst + iLast) / 2 ];
18:
19:     do {
20:       while( MyIntegers[iLow] < valueSeparator )
21:         iLow++;
22:
```

```
23:        while( MyIntegers[iHigh] > valueSeparator )
24:          iHigh--;
25:
26:        if( iLow <= iHigh )
27:        {
28:          swaps++;
29:
30:          tmpInt = MyIntegers[iLow];
31:          MyIntegers[iLow++] = MyIntegers[iHigh];
32:          MyIntegers[iHigh--] = tmpInt;
33:        }
34:      } while( iLow <= iHigh);
35:
36:      if( iFirst < iHigh )
37:        QuickSort(MyIntegers, iHigh, iFirst);
38:
39:      if( iLow < iLast )
40:        QuickSort(MyIntegers, iLast, iLow);
41:
42:      return( swaps );
43:    }
44:
45:    void main()
46:    {
47:        // Same as Listing 26.1 until the sort
48:        // is called. Notice that howMany is
49:        // for the quick sort on the first call:
50:      numSwaps =
51:        QuickSort(SomeIntegers, howMany - 1);
52:        // The remainder is the same as
53:        // Listing 26.1.
54:    }
```

OUTPUT

```
Enter a number between 1 and 500: 25
Building an array of 25 ints

        The ints before sort:
381
415 59 304 137 459 193 380 396 428 246 465 52 319 360 301 231 162 10 422
199 104 438 7 154
        and after sort:
7
10 52 59 104 137 154 162 193 199 231 246 301 304 319 360 380 381 396 415
422 428 438 459

32 swaps were required.
```

ANALYSIS The main function here needs a slight modification. Other than that modification, it is essentially the same as in Listing 26.1.

Sorting Disk Files

Sorting files is really beyond the scope of this book. Array sorting is something every programmer needs eventually, but only a few require file sorting skills. I do want to let you in on a secret that I found out the hard way. The secret is that the methods for sorting files are sometimes similar to the methods for sorting arrays but most often are not.

A sort that is often employed for files is called the *merge sort*, a variation on the quick sort. In a merge sort, the file is divided in half and the two halves are merged back in order over and over again until the file is sorted.

If you need to sort a file and cannot (or don't want to), first place the file contents in an array for sorting; then look for a book that covers the subject in some detail or ask a more experienced programmer for help. On Bonus Day 28 you will find a list of resources for further reading, and some of those have information on file sorting.

Searching

Searching is the act of scanning an array for a particular value. The most efficient search algorithms are for data that is sorted. If that wasn't obvious before, think about how much fun it would be to search the New York City yellow pages without listings that are sorted alphabetically. If you can figure out a way to search unsorted data as efficiently as sorted data, you will be rich beyond your wildest dreams. Because it hasn't been done yet, most programmers sort the data before searching.

The catch is that sorting can make the data useless in some cases. For instance, you wouldn't sort the characters in an editor to simplify the search for a user, because the user wants to find the data in context, not in an ordered sequence. For that reason, both search types are covered, beginning with the more difficult—a straightforward search through an unordered array.

The Straightforward String Search

Probably the first search application you'll need to implement is a simple string search. The straightforward string search is the simplest, but for the most part, most inefficient method for searching strings. However, the theory behind it is one that you need for searching unordered arrays of other data types.

In the straightforward string search (SFS), you start with the array of characters to be searched and the portion of the string to search for, which is called the *key*. Suppose you wanted to search the previous paragraph for the first place that the word *search* occurs in that paragraph. You would start by looking at the first character in the paragraph and comparing it to the *s* in *search*. You keep incrementing through the paragraph until you find an *s* to match the first letter in the key. Then you check the next letter in the paragraph to see whether it matches the second letter, *e*, of the key. If it does, you take the next letter and compare it to *a*, and so on. If you hit a mismatch, you start scanning again from the point of the mismatch, looking for an *s* again.

Listing 26.5 is an example of the SFS searching a string and returning the index where the key begins in the string.

TYPE | **Listing 26.5. An SFS example.**

```
1:   // Listing 26.5. A Straight Forward String Search example
2:
3:   #include <iostream.h>
4:
5:   char *SearchString(char *StrToSearch, const char *StrToFind);
6:
7:   char *SearchString(char *StrToSearch, const char *StrToFind)
8:   {
9:      int i, j, Slot;
10:
11:     for(i=0; StrToSearch[i]; i++)
12:     {
13:        for(j = i, Slot = 0; StrToSearch[j] == StrToFind[Slot]; j++, Slot++)
14:        {
15:           if(! StrToFind[Slot + 1])
16:           {
17:              return(StrToSearch + i);
18:           }
19:        }
20:     }
21:
22:     cout << "Nope, not that one!" << endl;
23:     return('\0');
24:
25:  }
26:
27:  void main()
28:  {
29:     const int NameLength = 100;
30:     char *Handsome = "Mark Hord";
31:
32:     char Guess[NameLength];
33:
34:     cout << "I'm thinking of a very handsome gentleman."
35:          << endl
36:          << "Guess who? ";
37:
38:     cin.getline(Guess, NameLength);
39:
40:     if(! SearchString(Handsome, Guess) )
41:     {
```

continues

BD
26

Listing 26.5. continued

```
42:      do
43:      {
44:        cout << "Try again: ";
45:        cin.getline(Guess, NameLength);
46:
47:      } while(! SearchString(Handsome, Guess) );
48:    }
49:
50:    cout << "\rThat's the one!" << endl;
51: }
```

OUTPUT
```
I'm thinking of a very handsome gentleman.
Guess who? Jesse Liberty
Nope, not that one!
Try again: Elvis Presley
Nope, not that one!
Try again: Mark Hord
That's the one!
```

ANALYSIS The main function simply creates a cute string and keeps looping until a substring of that string is entered.

The SearchString function starts on line 7. It returns the substring from the point of the SearchString match to the end of the string to be searched. If there is no match, it returns a null string—that is, a 0.

The outer loop, starting at line 11, increments through the string to be searched until it reaches the null terminator in that string. The inner loop keeps looping as long as the strings match and as long as the null terminator is not reached. It returns the string pointer if the null terminator of the key string is reached inside the matching loop.

If both loops reach the null terminators without a match, the null terminator character is returned to indicate that no match was found.

The Binary Search

The binary search is the most commonly used search. It is one that people use every day but seldom think about. So, in a sense, it is easy to understand. The downside of this search is that the data has to be sorted to make it possible.

The binary search is a divide-and-conquer method similar to searching the phone book. If you were looking for a devilishly handsome fellow named Mark Hord, you would plop the phone book open about halfway, and you might end up in the names that start with K. You know that H comes before K, so you take the left half of the book and open it about half way to the names that start with C. You know that H is somewhere in your right hand, so you divide the portion in your right hand about halfway. With each division, you are eliminating half of the remaining portion of the book and narrowing the amount you have left to search. If you keep dividing the book with this method, you eventually narrow the choices down to just two or three names, and then down to just one—mine.

Listing 26.6 illustrates a binary search on an array of integers.

TYPE **Listing 26.6. A binary search example.**

```
1:  // Listing 26.6. A Binary Search example
2:
3:  #include <iostream.h>
4:
5:  int BinarySearch(int MyInts[], int arraySize, int iKey);
6:
7:  int BinarySearch(int MyInts[], int arraySize, int iKey)
8:  {
9:    bool Found = false; // found the value?
10:   int iHigh = arraySize, iLow = 0, iMiddle;
11:
12:   iMiddle = (iHigh + iLow) / 2; // half way
13:
14:   while( (iHigh >= iLow) )
15:   {
16:     if( iKey == MyInts[iMiddle] )
17:     {
18:       Found = true;  // Found it, break out to exit
19:       break;
20:     }
21:
22:     if( iKey > MyInts[iMiddle] )
23:     {
24:       // String we're looking for is bigger
25:
26:       iLow - iMiddle   1;
27:     }
28:     else
29:     {
30:       // else the string is lower
31:
32:       iHigh = iMiddle + 1;
33:     }
34:
35:     iMiddle = (iHigh + iLow) / 2;
36:   }
37:
38:   if( Found ) // If we found it, return its idex
39:     return( iMiddle );
40:   else
41:     return( -1 );
42:
43: }
```

continues

Listing 26.6. continued

```
44:
45:   void main()
46:   {
47:     const int Big = 500;
48:
49:     int SomeIntegers[Big];
50:     int howMany = 0;
51:     int i, IntToFind, Slot;
52:
53:     cout << "Enter a number between 1 and "
54:          << Big << ": ";
55:
56:     cin >> howMany;
57:     cin.ignore();
58:
59:     cout << "Building an array of "
60:          << howMany << " ints" << endl;
61:
62:     for(i=0; i<howMany; i++)
63:       SomeIntegers[i] = i;
64:
65:
66:     cout << endl
67:          << "\tEnter an int between 1 and "
68:          << howMany << " to search for: " ;
69:
70:     cin >> IntToFind;
71:
72:     Slot = BinarySearch(SomeIntegers, howMany, IntToFind);
73:
74:     if(0 > Slot)
75:       cout << "Not found." << endl;
76:     else
77:       cout << "Found in slot: "
78:            << Slot << endl;
79:   }
```

OUTPUT
```
Enter a number between 1 and 500: 300
Building an array of 300 ints

        Enter an int between 1 and 300 to search for: 50
Found in slot: 50
```

ANALYSIS The main function creates an integer array with the number of integers you request in order.

BinarySearch is given the array, the size of the array, and the integer you're looking for. It returns the index to the array item that contains that value.

26

Inside BinarySearch, on line 9, variables are declared for incrementing through the array and for determining when the value has been found. The search loop continues for as long as the iHigh is greater than or equal to iLow starting at line 14. If the middle item is the one being searched for (line 16), the break jumps out of the while loop and drops down to where the middle item slot number is returned.

If the middle item is greater than the one being looked for (line 22), the search is narrowed to the upper portion of the array by setting iLow to one less than iMiddle.

If the middle item is smaller than the one being looked for, the search is narrowed to the lower portion of the array by setting iHigh to one above iMiddle.

The last step in the loop, line 35, sets iMiddle to the middle of the narrowed array. The loop continues until the value is found or until iLow and iHigh pass each other at the middle. After the loop exits, BinarySearch returns the slot number or -1 to indicate it was not found.

Do	Don't

DO become familiar with the idea behind each of the sorting and searching methods.

DO choose the algorithm by the size and mix of the data set when possible.

DON'T assume that the simplest method with the fewest lines of code is always the most efficient.

BD
26

Summary

As with many topics in computer science, there are many methods for doing the same job, and the method you choose often depends on the objects you want to manipulate. There are many more sort and search algorithms. Volumes have been written on the subject. Today you scratched the surface and came out with tools that you need to sort or search virtually any collection of data. You also learned which method is most efficient for that data.

Q&A

Q Why is the bubble sort inefficient?

A The bubble sort is inefficient because, on average, it must perform more exchanges to sort an array than other sorts.

Q Which sort is most efficient in most cases?

A The quick sort.

Quiz

1. True or False: The shell sort is an *n-square* sort.

2. A binary search:

   a. Repeatedly divides the array in half until only the match or nothing is left.

   b. Selects items one at a time from the array until it finds the match or reaches the end.

   c. Searches from both sides of the array, alternating between high and low array slots until the middle is reached.

3. The quick sort:

   a. Selects an item from the array, compares it with the current lowest item, and then swaps the current lowest with the lowest in the remainder.

   b. Recursively executes on smaller and smaller subarrays until it breaks the main array down into single-item subarrays for sorting.

   c. Calculates a gap value, which it uses as an average of the array values, and sorts using that average as the midpoint in the array.

4. The shell sort:

   a. Repeatedly divides the array and merges it back together in increasing order with each repetition.

   b. Sorts disk file contents in a command shell.

   c. Calculates a gap value, sorts the array items separated by that gap, and decrements the gap with each iteration.

Exercises

1. Alter the bubble sort program in Listing 26.1 to sort a character array entered by a user.

2. Which sort is identified by an execution time proportional to $n^{1.2}$?

26

3. The execution time of an n^2 sort:

    a. Doubles with each increment in array size.

    b. Increases exponentially with each increment in array size.

    c. Increases by a power of 2 with each increment in array size.

4. **BUG BUSTERS:** Assuming that you use the quick sort from Listing 26.4, what is wrong with this QuickSort function call?

```
for(int I=0; I<10; I++)
  Array[I] = rand() % 15;

QuickSort(Array, 10);
```

Day 27

Common Mistakes and Basic Debugging

Compared to some of the other lessons you've made it through, this one is a breeze. It is not so much a scholastic study as it is a collection of anecdotes. These anecdotes might not prevent you from making mistakes in your programs, but they should help you recognize certain types of mistakes more quickly. The more programming experience you gain, the more useful this lesson is as a reference tool.

Class Explosion

I am a strong believer in object-oriented models and the concept of closely mapping the solution to the real-world problem. There is, however, a subtle danger in the real-world mapping concept.

I enjoy the initial design phase of building basic classes. Sometimes, I get carried away and don't want to stop. I keep thinking of new base and derived classes to add to the program and, before long, I have more classes than I can understand.

The class explosion doesn't clarify the situation; it makes it harder to understand how they all relate.

Consider the example in Listing 27.1.

TYPE | **Listing 27.1. Music class example.**

```
1:
2:   #include <String.h>
3:   #include <iostream.h>
4:   #include <time.h>
5:
6:   enum LifeLength { SHORT, LONG, VERY_LONG, FOREVER};
7:   enum Quality { POOR, FAIR, GOOD, EXCELLANT};
8:   enum Age {NEW = 100, WORN = 200, OLD = 300, ANCIENT = 350};
9:
10:  struct TemperatureRange {   // A temperature range
11:    char tempUnits; // C or F
12:    int low, high;
13:  };
14:
15:
16:  class MusicMedium {
17:  protected:
18:    LifeLength itsLifeSpan;
19:    Quality itsSoundQuality;
20:    time_t LastCleaning;
21:    // Keep track of the number of plays to determine how worn it is:
22:    int Plays;
23:    TemperatureRange StorageTemp;
24:  public:
25:    virtual LifeLength LifeSpan() { return(itsLifeSpan); }
26:    virtual Quality SoundQuality() { return(itsSoundQuality); }
27:    virtual bool Clean()=0;
28:    virtual bool Store()=0;
29:    virtual bool Play()=0;
30:    virtual void TemperatureRange() = 0; // Print the storage temp range
31:  };
32:
33:
34:  class Cassette : public MusicMedium {
35:  private:
36:  public:
37:    Cassette();
38:    Cassette(String);
39:    ~Cassette();
40:
41:    bool Clean(){return true;} // Can't clean a Cassette so do nothing
42:    bool Store();   // Ensure temperature etc
43:
44:    bool Play() {
45:    ++Plays;
46:    if(Plays > ANCIENT)
47:    {
```

27

```
48:       itsSoundQuality = POOR;
49:       cout <<
50:        "Whoa! That cassette is ancient, time to replace it!"
51:        << endl;
52:     }
53:     else if(Plays > OLD)
54:     {
55:        itsSoundQuality = FAIR;
56:        cout <<
57:        "It would be a real good time to replace this with a CD now."
58:         << endl;
59:     }
60:     return true;
61:     }
62:
63:  };
64:
65:  class CD : public MusicMedium {
66:  private:
67:  public:
68:    CD();
69:    CD(String);
70:    ~CD();
71:
72:    bool Clean(){return true;}
73:    bool Store();
74:    bool Play();
75:
76:  };
77:
78:  class Record : public MusicMedium {
79:  private:
80:    bool Scratched;
81:  public:
82:    Record();
83:    Record(String);
84:    ~Record();
85:
86:    bool Clean(){return true;}
87:    bool Store();
88:    bool Play();
89:
90:  };
91:
92:  class EightTrack : public MusicMedium {
93:  private:
94:  public:
95:    EightTrack() { cout << "Are you serious?!" << endl;}
96:    EightTrack(String) { cout << "I hope it was free!" << endl; }
97:    ~EightTrack(){}
98:
99:
100:    bool Clean(){return false;} // Can't clean 8-tracks
101:    bool Store();
102:    bool Play();
103:  };
```

NOTE
> You might encounter a problem with this code because `String` is a class that is defined in the ANSI String.h file, but not yet by VC++ in the String.h file. To make it compile, replace `String` with `int` for now.

ANALYSIS This listing is a basic collection of classes that track and maintain a music collection. All music is on some type of recording medium, whether it be tape, compact disc, or vinyl record. You young kids might not know what I'm talking about, so you'll have to trust me on the vinyl and 8-track parts.

So far, things seem pretty straightforward. But, if you're like me, you appreciate many different kinds of music. You might see the real-world model as more complex, so you decide to extend it. Perhaps you decide to make some new classes for different kinds of music: rock, classical, country, and rap. Then it makes sense to create classes derived from the medium classes and music type classes. You might end up with something like this:

```
class CountryCD : public countryMusic, public CD {
  //
};
```

Imagine that you write all of these things and go on vacation for a few weeks, or imagine that you have to come back years from now to add some small functionality that the original didn't need. You have to look through the code and figure out where that new functionality belongs. Worse yet, imagine that your boss originally assigned you to write a simple set of classes that could be used to clean and play various music media. He assumes it should take you a week, but you've committed yourself to a month's worth of work to flesh out all the derived classes you've invented. The structure is no longer as simple as your boss is expecting.

Avoid this problem by not spending too much time in the design phase. Let the design phase blend into the coding phase so that you add functionality as you need it. This seems counterintuitive to most people, especially people who have experience from structured programming days. Classes evolve, and if you follow the object-oriented approach, evolution is something you plan for. The index card rule (keeping all class declarations on a single index card) is a good one to keep in mind.

You should also remember to keep your eye on the big picture and personify the objects. If your application is going to be a stereo system controller, try to think like a stereo. A stereo doesn't care about the kind of music on a medium; it only cares about the kind of medium (tape, CD, vinyl, and so on). A turntable doesn't care what artist is on a record; it only cares if the record is scratched and if it's clean. I might think a rap CD should be played so softly that nobody can hear it, but a CD player doesn't care.

Boundary Violations and Off-by-One Errors

Boundary violations and off-by-one errors are common mistakes for programmers in almost all computer languages. You see this bug most often in relation to an array increment, such as in Listing 27.2.

TYPE **Listing 27.2. An off-by-one error.**

```
#include <iostream.h>
void main()
{
  char *cArray[3] = { "OK", "Fine", "Never reached" };
  for(int i=0; i<=3; i++)
    cout << cArray[i] << endl;
    // cArray[3] is not displayed
}
```

Generally speaking, you won't make this error in the same way shown here. The problem usually appears when the final item number of the array is computed and there is an off-by-one error in your computation.

A problem similar to the off-by-one problem is a violation of a boundary condition. This most often shows up with an array where the final index is computed with an index greater than the size of the array. Look over Listing 27.3, and see whether you can guess the potential problem. In fact, don't even try to run this one!

TYPE **Listing 27.3. A boundary violation example.**

```
1:    // Listing 27.3 Boundary error bug
2:
3:    #include <iostream.h>
4:
5:    class SomeClass {
6:    private:
7:      int SomeArray[5];
8:      int *Ptr;
9:    public:
10:     SomeClass(int *Value) {
11:        Ptr = Value;
12:        for(int i=0; i<5; i++)
```

**BD
27**

continues

Listing 27.3. continued

```
13:            SomeArray[i] = 0;
14:        }
15:        ~SomeClass(){}
16:        void ShowSome() {
17:          for(int i=0; i<5; i++)
18:            cout << SomeArray[i] << endl;
19:          cout << "(*Ptr) is " << (*Ptr) << endl;
20:        }
21:        void SetSome(int HowMany, int NewVal) {
22:          for(int i=0; i<HowMany; i++)
23:            SomeArray[i] = NewVal;
24:        }
25:    };
26:
27:    void main()
28:    {
29:      int anInt = 20;
30:      SomeClass Boundary(&anInt);
31:      Boundary.ShowSome();
32:      Boundary.SetSome(6, 1000);
33:      Boundary.ShowSome();
34:    }
```

OUTPUT Output varies depending on your operating system. In fact, this program could cause your entire system to come down!

ANALYSIS Do you see what happened to Ptr? In the SetSome method, it should have been left alone, but the off-by-one error caused Ptr to be overwritten because it followed the array in memory. When it was overwritten, it no longer contained a pointer to the integer in main; it contained the address 1000, which (odds are) is probably not the same.

Increment and Decrement Errors

Increment and decrement errors are common for new C++ programmers and can cause some of the most bizarre run-time problems. The most common problem for new programmers is understanding the difference between post-decrement/increment and pre-decrement/increment. This problem was discussed on Day 4, "Expressions and Statements" (see Listing 4.3 for more detail). This problem is so common that it bears repeating.

Pointer Problems

Pointers can be confusing for even the most experienced programmer. There are two basic categories of pointer problems: The first is misunderstanding the pointer and indirection operators; the second is using an invalid pointer. These problems were touched upon in the discussion of pointers and the new operator. C++ provides an advantage over C in the pointer/ indirection operator confusion. Listing 27.4 illustrates the pointer indirection confusion.

TYPE   **Listing 27.4. Pointer bugs.**

```
int *MyInt = 3; // Declare an int pointer
                // and assign it to 3.
int *OurInt;    // Declare a pointer but
                // don't initialize it.
*OurInt = 0x007; // Assign hex 7 to the address
                // of OurInt - danger!
cout << OurInt; // Outputs what memory location
                // 0x007 points to! Good chance
                // that this will crash.
```

Bracket or Parenthesis Mismatch

Mismatched brackets or parentheses are minor glitches that can really throw a compiler for a loop. Depending on your compiler, this mistake often shows up as a screen full of error messages that have nothing to do with the problem. Listing 27.5 is an example of a mismatched bracket problem.

TYPE   **Listing 27.5. A bracket mismatch problem.**

```
#include <iostream.h>
void Printit();
void main()
{
  Printit();

void Printit()
{
   cout << "It" << endl;
}
```

BD 27

At least one compiler I know of complains with a message referring to nested function definitions. A nested function definition is a function definition inside a function. When the compiler sees the first bracket in main, it doesn't know that the function definition for main is complete until it sees the closing bracket for main. That's why it thinks that Printit is a function definition nested inside main.

Many text editors provide ways to identify matching brackets and parentheses. One popular editor temporarily bounces back to the open parenthesis or bracket when you type its closing match. If you get used to that behavior, you can see immediately when you've made this mistake. Other editors have a built-in command that enables you to search for the matching brackets or parentheses and check the file at any time during the writing.

Test and Assignment Confusion

I think test and assignment confusion, (X = 1) as opposed to (X == 1), is probably the most common and the most confusing of errors. Because it is so common, many other languages alleviate this problem with a separate operator for assignment and equality testing. But, in C++ as in C, an alternative way around the problem must be found. One coding style that many programmers have adopted is to put the constant value first:

```
if( false == Success ) // instead of (Success == false)
```

The idea is that `false` can never be assigned a value, so the compiler flags the mistake with an error:

```
if( false = Success) // causes a compile-time error
```

If you adopt this style, stick with it in all your code. It is the opposite of the way most people think, but once you grasp the concept you can see the advantages and recognize it in other programs.

Debugging Tips

Your debugging methods will develop over time, affected in part by your personality and skill set. The following are some basic concepts that should help you along that road:

- ☐ Compile as you program rather than attempting to complete everything before you first compile. This helps you find bugs early and limits the number of errors you have to track down when you're close to the deadline.

- ☐ Use cout to display current variable values. I often have cout statements in my code bracketed inside a conditional debugging code gate. That way, I can see what's happening as it happens at critical points in the code.

- ☐ Test as you compile. Incremental testing gives you confidence on earlier tested code and helps you narrow problems to the most likely area—the new code. If you're certain that one function works and you add a new function and start seeing bugs, there is a good chance that the problem is in the new function.

- ☐ Get to know the debugging tools available to you. They're different, depending on your compiler environment, but most provide the same basic functionality. One useful thing is the capability to step through the program one statement at a time. In fact, it wouldn't hurt to step through all of your programs at least once.

☐ Make use of assert() to catch bugs early on.

Asking for Help

No matter how much time you spend debugging, there are always new problems that you cannot anticipate. There comes a time when you need help on some bug. Most programmers I know believe that the only dumb question is the unasked question. There are a few unpleasant people in this profession, just as there are in any profession. Don't let them prevent you from asking for help. If you can't get help from one of them, don't hesitate to ask somebody else.

In the next lesson, you'll find detailed information on places to get help and how to expand your knowledge of C++. Ask a friend or look at the next section if you can't solve a problem. Remember that you should always spend time trying to figure out a problem on your own before you turn to someone else. If you don't try to solve a problem on your own, some people might think that you want them to write the program for you.

Do	Don't

DO ask for help after trying to solve a problem on your own.

DON'T hesitate to use cout or your debugging tools to display current program states.

DO use your debugging tools to step through the programs you write even if there appear to be no bugs.

**BD
27**

Summary

Today, basic programming concepts were covered. To help you create bulletproof programs, many topics were discussed that help you develop your debugging style and make your programming time more efficient. You might want to refer back to this lesson occasionally as you become more experienced. Programming, like mathematics, can only be fully understood by doing it. And, in the doing, you become more adept at understanding basic concepts that seemed confusing before.

Q&A

Q **What is an off-by-one error, and when does it most often occur?**

A An off-by-one error is an error in incrementing through a set of values where the computation is off by one. This error is most common when incrementing through an array in which the final index is computed incorrectly.

Q **What is class explosion and how can it be avoided?**

A Class explosion is getting too detailed in mapping the real-world objects to C++ classes. Try to limit the time you spend in the design phase and extend the design as the need becomes apparent.

Quiz

1. **BUG BUSTERS:** What sort of error does the following program contain?

```cpp
#include <iostream.h>
void main()
{
    int i;
    const int Size = 10;
    char aString[Size];

    for(i=0; i<Size+1; i++)
        cin >> aString[i];
}
```

2. **BUG BUSTERS:** What's wrong with the following program?

```cpp
#include <iostream.h>
void main()
{
    int It;
    cout << "Enter a number: ";
    cin >> It;
    if( It = 1)
    {
        cout << "One" << endl;
    }
    else
    {
        cout << "Not one." << endl;
    }
}
```

Exercises

1. Fix the program from Quiz question 2, and do it in a way that avoids the problem in the future.

2. What error is identifiable by compiler messages that refer to `nested function definitions`?

3. Is it best to finish all the code and compile just once or to compile a piece at a time?

BD
27

Day 28

What's Next?

Congratulations! You have nearly completed a full four-week intensive introduction to C++. Although you should now have a solid understanding of C++, remember that there is always more to learn, especially in modern programming. This lesson fills in some missing details and then sets the course for continued study.

Today you will learn

- [ ] What the standard libraries are.
- [ ] How to manipulate individual bits and use them as flags.
- [ ] Further steps that you can take to use C++ effectively.

The Standard Libraries

Over time, the C programming language has gained a larger and larger set of standard header files included with all standard C compilers. When C++ was created, those libraries were used in the first C++ compilers as well. It soon became apparent that C libraries could be replaced with template-based libraries in C++. Those template libraries have only recently become part of the draft standard.

Many of the programs you wrote in this course used some of the older C libraries, although the streams libraries were an exception. The C libraries are included with C++ compilers in order to provide as much backward compatibility as possible. As the ANSI/ISO standard evolves and more compiler vendors come on board, the C libraries will probably become obsolete.

Table 28.1 summarizes the C++ libraries.

Table 28.1. C++ libraries.

Library Category	Description
Language Support	Built-in functions for the language, including limits and exceptions.
Diagnostics	Functionality for error codes and exceptions.
General Utilities	A collection of miscellaneous components that are used by many other C++ libraries.
Strings	A string class.
Localization	Internationalization support.
Containers	A collection of template-based data structures.
Iterators	A collection of iterators for data structures and algorithms in template form.
Algorithms	Template-based algorithms collection.
Numerics	A collection of resources for performing common numerical tasks.
Input/Output	The streams (which have already been discussed in detail).

To use a library, you typically include a header file in your source code, much as you did by writing #include <iostreams.h> in many of the examples in this book. The angle brackets around the filename signal to the compiler to look in the directory where you keep the header files for your compiler's standard libraries.

28

There are dozens of libraries, covering everything from file manipulation, to setting the date and time, to math functions. Today, you will review just a few of the most popular functions and classes in the standard library that have not yet been covered. In addition to the C++ libraries, many of the C libraries are still included in the latest version of the ANSI/ISO standard.

With the latest draft of the ANSI/ISO C++ standard, most of the libraries are now template-based libraries that provide functionality for all of the built-in data types.

Many of these libraries were not finalized at this writing, so they were not used extensively in this book. Standard C libraries were used instead. In addition, the standard C++ libraries (as opposed to the standard C libraries) are contained within the `namespace std` (an abbreviation for "standard"). This was not mentioned earlier because no compilers have yet implemented the libraries in a separate namespace. In the future, you need to use the `using` keyword for `namespace std`, as described on Day 22, "Coding Styles and Idioms."

The following sections cover some of the common libraries in more detail.

String

The most popular library is almost certainly the string library. This library provides `char` and `wchar_t` string classes that have the same level of functionality as the built-in data types. For instance, the string class provides comparison operators, a `length()` member function, and overloaded math operators. The string class is similar to the string class you created on Day 11.

Localization Library

This library is extremely important for internationalizing software. It provides special character manipulations, conversions, time and money formats, and locale-specific information. Many of the functions of the localization library have replaced the `stdlib.h` character functions. In the future, you may need to use the `locale.h` file for some functions such as replacing `toupper()` with `do_upper()`.

Containers, Iterators, and Algorithms

These libraries constitute the bulk of what has come to be known as the Standard Template Library (STL), mentioned in previous lessons. These libraries provide for all the data structures (containers) discussed on Day 25 ("Data Structures"), and all the algorithms of Day 26 ("Simple Sorting and Searching Algorithms"). Iterators are simply the mechanisms used to step through the items in a container or the steps of an algorithm. One STL function you will find especially useful is the quick sort template in the algorithms library. Listing 28.1 illustrates its use.

TYPE **Listing 28.1. The algorithms library sort.**

```
1:// Listing 28.1. Using the algorithm sort and containers
2:#include<vector.h>
3:#include<algorithm.h>
4:#include<iostream.h>
5:
6:void main()
7:{
8:   vector<int> MyVector;
9:
10:   do
11:   {
12:     cout << "Enter an integer: ";
13:     cin >> anInt;
14:     MyVector.push_front(anInt);
15:
16:   } while( anInt != 0 );
17:
18:   sort(MyVector.beg(), MyVector.end(), int);
19:}
```

Bit Fields and Bitset

Sometimes every byte counts, and saving six or eight bytes in a class can add up to a substantial memory or performance savings. If your class or structure has a series of Boolean variables, or variables that can have only a small number of possible values, you might save room by using bit fields.

Using the standard C++ data types, the smallest type you can use in your class is a type char, which is one byte. More often, you'll end up using an int, which is two or more (often four) bytes. By using bit fields, you can store eight binary values in a char and 32 values in a long.

Here's how bit fields work: Bit fields are named and accessed like any class member. Their type is always declared to be unsigned int. After the bit field name, write a colon followed by a number. The number tells the compiler how many bits to assign to this variable. If you write 1, the bit represents either the value 0 or 1. If you write 2, the bit can represent 0, 1, 2, or 3—a total of four values. A three-bit field can represent eight values, and so forth. Appendix C reviews binary numbers.

This has all been simplified with the new C++ libraries. Now, you can use the bitset templates provided in bitset.h to create virtually any type or size bitfield. The bitset provides much of the capability that other built-in types have, just as the strings library does for strings.

Numerics Library

Almost every programmer needs a complex number type at some time. In the past, programmers built their own, and everybody's was different. Now the numerics library provides programmers with complex number classes, polar and trigonometric functions, array math functions, and more.

BD 28

Next Steps

You've spent four long, hard weeks working at C++, and you are now a competent C++ programmer, but you are by no means finished. There is much more to learn, and many more books to read as you move from novice C++ programmer to expert.

The following sections recommend a number of specific books, colored by my personal experience and opinions. There are dozens of books on each of these topics, so you might want to get other opinions before purchasing them.

Sharpening Your Skills

One of the greatest things about the information superhighway is the availability of help. There are a lot of experts out there. Don't hesitate to ask for opinions on a piece of your code. Who knows? You might just find a new way of doing something and help others with your ideas. Other types of help are discussed in the following paragraphs.

Other Great Books

It seems that every time I make a trip to the bookstore there is a new shelf of C++ books. Although Jesse and I together could not read even half of the books available, we've still read quite a few, and the following are some of our favorites.

Books on C++

Meyers, Scott. *Effective C++* (ISBN: 0-201-56364-9). Addison-Wesley Publishing, 1993.

Eckel, Bruce. *Thinking in C++* (ISBN: 0-13-917709-4). Prentice Hall, Inc., 1995.

Books on Software Engineering

If you are serious about object-oriented programming and design, be sure to pick up a good book on the subject. This book only scratches the surface of this complex topic, and either of the following books are a valuable addition to your library:

Booch, Grady. *Object-Oriented Analysis and Design with Applications*, 2nd Edition (ISBN: 0-8053-5340-2). The Benjamin/Cummings Publishing Company, Inc., 1994.

Rumbaugh, et al. *Object-Oriented Modeling and Design* (ISBN: 0-13-629841-9). Prentice Hall, Inc., 1991.

Writing Solid Code

A number of books have recently been published about writing high-quality code. These three are highly recommended:

McConnel, Steve. *Code Complete* (ISBN: 1-55615-484-4). Microsoft Press, 1993.

Maguire, Steve. *Writing Solid Code* (ISBN: 1-55615-551-4). Microsoft Press, 1993.

Thielen, David. *No Bugs! Delivering Error-Free Code in C and C++* (ISBN: 0-201-60890-1). Addison-Wesley Publishing, 1992.

Internationalizing Software

This is a subject that is becoming more and more important, and there are several good books on the subject. Here is one I've seen that is quite popular:

Taylor, Dave. *Global Software: Developing Applications for the International Market* (ISBN: 0-387-797706-6). Springer Verlog, 1992.

Magazines

Reading all of these books and more is vitally important, and going online gives you day-to-day access to other C++ programmers, but there is one more thing you can do to strengthen your skills: Subscribe to a good magazine on C++ programming. The following magazines are good places to start.

C++ Report from SIGS Publications, P.O. Box 2031, Langhorne, PA 19047-9700.

Dr. Dobb's Journal from Miller Freeman, Inc., 600 Harrison St., San Francisco, CA 94107.

Internet and the World Wide Web

The Internet and the World Wide Web (WWW) are rapidly becoming the resource of choice for virtually any need. You can search news groups or Web sites with the keyword c++, the name of your operating system, or programming to find an exhaustive list. In fact, most programming magazines now have a WWW site where you can download listings from their articles, talk to authors, and so on. Here are some of the resources I use regularly on the Internet:

comp.std.c++: A newsgroup for discussing the ANSI/ISO C++ standard.

comp.lang.c++: A newsgroup for discussing C++ programming.

http://info.desy.de/user/projects/C++.html: A WWW site that contains links to almost anything you could imagine related to C++.

Electronic Mail

Jesse and I would both like to hear from you if you have comments or questions about this book. The best way to reach either of us is through e-mail:

Jesse Liberty: jliberty@zdi.ziff.com

Mark Hord: pajtim@cybercomm.net

Do	Don't

DO look at other books. There is much to learn and no single book can teach you everything you need to know.

DON'T just read code! The best way to learn C++ is to write C++ programs.

DO subscribe to a good C++ magazine and join a good C++ user group.

DO write if you have questions or comments.

Summary

Today you saw how some of the standard libraries, shipped with your C++ compiler, can be used to manage routine tasks.

Q&A

Q Why are the standard C libraries included with C++ compilers, and when would you use them?

A They are included for backwards-compatibility with C. They are not type-safe, and they don't work well with user-created classes, so their use is limited.

Q When would you use bit structures rather than simply using integers?

A When the size of the object is crucial. If you are working with limited memory or with communications software, you might find that the savings offered by these structures is essential to the success of your product.

Q What is the very next thing to read?

A Tough question. If you want to review the fundamentals, read one of the other primers. If you want to hone C++, run out and get Scott Meyer's *Effective C++* or Bruce Eckel's *Thinking in C++*. If you want to expand your object-oriented skills, read one of the recommended books on object-oriented analysis and design.

Q Is that it?

A Yes! You've learned ANSI/ISO C++. But, also no. Ten years ago it was possible for one person to learn all there was to know about microcomputers, or at least to feel pretty confident that he was close. Today it is out of the question: You can't possibly catch up, and even as you try, the industry is changing. Be sure to keep reading, and stay in touch with the resources that keep you up with the latest changes: magazines and online services.

Quiz

1. What library provides the built-in type operations for character strings?
2. What does the algorithms library provide?
3. What library should be used to replace the character manipulation functions of the `stdlib.h` C library such as `toupper()`?
4. What is a bitset class?

APPENDIX

A

Operator Precedence

It is important to understand that operators *have* a precedence, but it is not essential to memorize the precedence.

 Precedence is the order in which a program performs the operations in a formula. If one operator has precedence over another operator, it is evaluated first.

Higher precedence operators "bind tighter" than lower precedence operators, and they are evaluated first. The *lower* the rank in the following chart, the *higher* the precedence.

Table A.1. C++ operator precedence.

Rank	Operator	Meaning	Associativity
1	::	Scope resolution	None
	::	Global	None
	[ ]	Array subscript	Left to right
	( )	Function call	Left to right
	( )	Conversion	Innermost first
	.	Member selection (object)	Left to right
	->	Member selection (pointer)	Left to right
2	++	Postfix increment	None
	--	Postfix decrement	None
	new	Allocate object	None
	delete	Deallocate object	None
	delete[ ]	Deallocate object	None
	++	Prefix increment	None
	--	Prefix decrement	None
	*	Dereference	None
	&	Address-of	None
	+	Unary plus	None
	-	Arithmetic negation (unary)	None
	!	Logical NOT	None
	~	Bitwise complement	None
	sizeof	Size of object	None
	sizeof ( )	Size of type	None
	typeid( )	type name	None
	(*type*)	Type cast (conversion)	Right to left

Rank	Operator	Meaning	Associativity
	`const_cast`	Type cast (conversion)	None
	`dynamic_cast`	Type cast (conversion)	None
	`reinterpret_cast`	Type cast (conversion)	None
	`static_cast`	Type cast (conversion)	None
	`.*`	Apply pointer to class member (objects)	Left to right
	`->*`	Dereference pointer to class member	Left to right
3	`*`	Multiplication	Left to right
	`/`	Division	Left to right
	`%`	Remainder (modulus)	Left to right
4	`+`	Addition	Left to right
	`-`	Subtraction	Left to right
5	`<<`	Left shift	Left to right
	`>>`	Right shift	Left to right
6	`<`	Less than	Left to right
	`>`	Greater than	Left to right
	`<=`	Less than or equal to	Left to right
	`>=`	Greater than or equal to	Left to right
7	`==`	Equality	Left to right
	`!=`	Inequality	Left to right
8	`&`	Bitwise AND	Left to right
9	`^`	Bitwise exclusive OR	Left to right
10	`¦`	Bitwise OR	Left to right
11	`&&`	Logical AND	Left to right
12	`¦¦`	Logical OR	Left to right
13	`e1?e2:e3`	Conditional	Right to left
14	`=`	Assignment	Right to left
	`*=`	Multiplication assignment	Right to left
	`/=`	Division assignment	Right to left

continues

Table A.1. continued

Rank	Operator	Meaning	Associativity
	%=	Modulus assignment	Right to left
	+=	Addition assignment	Right to left
	-=	Subtraction assignment	Right to left
	<<=	Left-shift assignment	Right to left
	>>=	Right-shift assignment	Right to left
	&=	Bitwise AND assignment	Right to left
	¦=	Bitwise inclusive OR assignment	Right to left
	^=	Bitwise exclusive OR assignment	Right to left
15	,	Comma	Left to right

APPENDIX

B

C++ Keywords

Keywords are reserved to the compiler for use by the language. You cannot define a class, variable, or function that has any of these keywords as its name. The current ANSI C++ keywords (including alternative tokens) are listed in Table B.1.

Table B.1. Keywords and alternative tokens.

asm	enum	protected	typedef
auto	explicit	public	typeid
bool	extern	register	typename
break	false	reinterpret_cast	union
case	float	return	unsigned
catch	for	short	using
char	friend	signed	virtual
class	goto	sizeof	void
const	if	static	volatile
const_cast	inline	static_cast	wchar_t
continue	int	struct	while
default	long	switch	xor
delete	mutable	template	xor_eq
do	namespace	this	
double	new	throw	
dynamic_cast	operator	true	
else	private	try	
and	bitor	not_eq	
and_eq	compl	or	
bitand	not	or_eq	

APPENDIX

C

Binary and Hexadecimal

You learned the fundamentals of arithmetic so long ago that it is difficult to imagine what it would be like without that knowledge. When you look at the number 145, you instantly see "one hundred and forty-five" without much reflection.

Understanding binary and hexadecimal requires that you reexamine the number 145 and see it not as a number, but as a code for a number.

Start small: examine the relationship between the number three and "3." The *numeral* 3 is a squiggle on a piece of paper; the number three is an idea. The numeral is used to represent the number. This distinction can be made clear by realizing that three, 3, |||, III, and *** can all be used to represent the same idea of three.

In base 10 (decimal) math, you use the numerals 0, 1, 2, 3, 4, 5, 6, 7, 8, 9 to represent all numbers. How is the number ten represented?

One can imagine that we would have evolved a strategy of using the letter A to represent ten; or we might have used IIIIIIIII to represent that idea. The Romans used X. The Arabic system, which we use, makes use of *position* in conjunction with numerals to represent values. The first (right most) column is used for ones, and the next column is used for tens. Therefore, the number fifteen is represented as 15 (read that one-five)—that is, 1 ten and 5 ones.

Certain rules emerge, from which you can make some generalizations:

- ☐ Base 10 uses the digits 0–9.
- ☐ The columns are powers of ten: ones, tens, hundreds, and so on.
- ☐ If the third column is 100, the largest number you can make with two columns is 99. More generally, with n columns you can represent 0 to (10^n-1). Therefore, with three columns, you can represent 0 to (10^3-1) or 0–999.

Other Bases

It is not a coincidence that we use base 10; we have 10 fingers. However, one can imagine a different base. Using the rules found in base 10, you can describe base 8:

- ☐ The digits used in base 8 are 0–7.
- ☐ The columns are powers of 8: ones, eights, sixty-fourths, and so on.
- ☐ With n columns you can represent 0 to 8^n-1.

To distinguish numbers written in each base, write the base as a subscript next to the number. The number fifteen in base 10 would be written as 15_{10} and read as "one-five, base ten."

Thus, to represent the number 15_{10} in base 8, you would write 17_8. This is read "one-seven, base eight." Note that it can also be read "fifteen" because that is the number it continues to represent.

Why 17? The 1 means one eight, and the 7 means seven ones. One eight plus seven ones equals fifteen. Consider fifteen asterisks:

```
*****     *****
*****
```

The natural tendency is to make two groups: a group of ten asterisks and another of five. This would be represented in decimal as 15 (1 ten and 5 ones). You can also group the asterisks as

```
****        *******
****
```

That is, eight asterisks and seven. That would be represented in base eight as 17_8. That is, one eight and seven ones.

Around the Bases

You can represent the number fifteen in base ten as 15, in base nine as 16_9, in base 8 as 17_8, and in base 7 as 21_7. Why 21_7? In base 7 there is no numeral larger than 6. In order to represent fifteen, you need two sevens and one 1.

How do you generalize the process? To convert a base 10 number to base 7, think about the columns: in base 7 they are ones, sevens, forty-nines, three-hundred forty-threes, and so forth. Why these columns? They represent 7^0, 7^1, 7^2, 7^3, and so forth. Create a table for yourself using the following format:

The first row represents the column number. The second row represents the power of 7. The third row represents the weighted value of each number in that row.

4	3	2	1
7^3	7^2	7^1	7^0
343	49	7	1

To convert from a decimal value to base 7, here is the procedure: examine the number and decide which column to use first. If the number is 200, for example, you know that column 4 (343) is 0 and you don't have to worry about it.

To find out how many 49s there are, divide 200 by 49. The answer is 4 with a remainder of 4, so put the answer (4) in column 3 and examine the remainder: 4. There are no sevens in 4, so put a zero in the sevens column. There are 4 ones in 4, so put a 4 in the ones column. The answer is 404_7.

To convert the number 968 to base 6:

5	4	3	2	1
6^4	6^3	6^2	6^1	6^0
1,296	216	36	6	1

There are no 1,296s in 968, so column 5 has 0. Dividing 968 by 216 yields 4 with a remainder of 104. Column 4 is 4. Dividing 104 by 36 yields 2 with a remainder of 32. Column 3 is 2. Dividing 32 by 6 yields 5 with a remainder of 2. The answer therefore is $4,252_6$, as illustrated in the following table.

5	4	3	2	1
6^4	6^3	6^2	6^1	6^0
1,296	216	36	6	1
0	4	2	5	2

There is a shortcut when converting from one base to another base (such as 6 to base 10). You can multiply and add the totals:

$$4 \times 216 = 864$$
$$2 \times 36 = 72$$
$$5 \times 6 = 30$$
$$2 \times 1 = 2$$
$$968$$

Binary

Base 2 is the ultimate extension of this idea. There are only two digits: 0 and 1. The columns are:

Col:	8	7	6	5	4	3	2	1
Power:	2^7	2^6	2^5	2^4	2^3	2^2	2^1	2^0
Value:	128	64	32	16	8	4	2	1

To convert the number 88 to base 2, you follow the same procedure: there are no 128s, so column 8 is 0.

There is one 64 in 88, so column 7 is 1, and 24 is the remainder. There are no 32s in 24, so column 6 is 0.

There is 1 sixteen in 24, so column 5 is 1. The remainder is 8. There is one 8 in 8, and so column 4 is 1. There is no remainder, so the rest of the columns are 0.

0	1	0	1	1	0	0	0

To test this answer, convert it back:

```
1 * 64 =  64
0 * 32 =   0
1 * 16 =  16
1 *  8 =   8
0 *  4 =   0
0 *  2 =   0
0 *  1 =   0
          88
```

Why Base 2?

The power of base 2 is that it corresponds so cleanly to what a computer needs to represent. Computers do not really know anything at all about letters, numerals, instructions or programs. At their core they are just circuitry, and at a given juncture, there either is a lot of power or there is very little.

To keep the logic clean, engineers do not treat this as a relative scale: "a little power, some power, more power, lots of power, tons of power," but rather as a binary scale: "enough power or not enough power." Rather than saying even enough or not enough, they simplify it down to "yes or no." Yes or no, or TRUE or FALSE, can be represented as 1 or 0. By convention, 1 means TRUE or Yes, but that is just a convention; it could just as easily have meant false or no.

Once you make this great leap of intuition, the power of binary becomes clear: with ones and zeroes, you can represent the fundamental truth of every circuit: There is power or there isn't. All a computer ever knows is "Is you is, or is you ain't?" Is you is = 1; is you ain't = 0.

Bits, Bytes, and Nibbles

Once the decision is made to represent truth and falsehood with 1s and 0s, BInary digiTS (or BITS) become very important. Since early computers could send eight bits at a time, it was natural to start writing code using eight-bit numbers, called bytes.

NOTE

> Half a byte (four bits) is called a nibble!

With eight binary digits, you can represent up to 256 different values. Why? Examine the columns: If all eight bits are set to 1, the value is 255. If none is set (all the bits are clear or zero) the value is 0. The range of 0–255 is 256 possible states.

What's a KB?

It turns out that 2^{10} (1024) is roughly equal to 10^3 (1,000). This coincidence was too good to miss, so computer scientists started referring to 2^{10} bytes as 1KB or 1 kilobyte, based on the scientific prefix of kilo for thousand.

Similarly, 1024×1024 (1,048,576) is close enough to one million to receive the designation 1MB or 1 megabyte, and 1024 megabytes is called 1 gigabyte (giga implies thousand-million or billion.)

Binary Numbers

Computers use patterns of 1s and 0s to encode everything they do. Machine instructions are encoded as a series of 1s and 0s and interpreted by the fundamental circuitry. Arbitrary sets of 1s and 0s can be translated back into numbers by computer scientists, but it would be a mistake to think that these numbers have intrinsic meaning.

For example, the Intel 80x86 chip set interprets the bit pattern 1001 0101 as an instruction. You certainly can translate this into decimal (149), but that number, per se, has no meaning.

Sometimes the numbers are instructions, sometimes they are values, and sometimes they are codes. One important standardized code set is ASCII. In ASCII, every letter and punctuation mark is given a seven-digit binary representation. For example, the lowercase letter a is represented by 0110 0001. This is *not* a number, though you can translate it to the number 97 (64 + 32 + 1). It is in this sense that people say that the letter a is represented by 97 in ASCII; but the truth is that the binary representation of 97, 01100001, is the encoding of the letter a, and the decimal value 97 is a human convenience.

Hexadecimal

Because binary numbers are difficult to read, a simpler way to represent the same values is often desirable. Translating from binary to base 10 involves a fair bit of manipulation of numbers, but it turns out that translating from base 2 to base 16 is very simple because there is a very good shortcut.

To understand this, first you must understand base 16, known as hexadecimal. In base 16, there are sixteen numerals: 0, 1, 2, 3, 4, 5, 6, 7, 8, 9, A, B, C, D, E, F. The last six are arbitrary; the letters A to F were chosen because they are easy to represent on a keyboard. The columns in hexadecimal are:

4	3	2	1
16^3	16^2	16^1	16^0
4,096	256	16	1

To translate from hexadecimal to decimal, you can multiply. Thus the number F8C represents:

```
F * 256 = 15 * 256 = 3840
8 * 16  =            128
C * 1 = 12 * 1 =      12
                    3980
```

Translating the number FC to binary is best done by translating first to base 10, and then to binary:

```
F * 16 = 15 * 16 =  240
C * 1 = 12 * 1 =     12
                    252
```

Converting 252_{10} to binary requires the chart:

Col:	9	8	7	6	5	4	3	2	1
Power:	2^8	2^7	2^6	2^5	2^4	2^3	2^2	2^1	2^0
Value:	256	128	64	32	16	8	4	2	1

```
There are no 256's.
1 128 leaves 124
1 64 leaves 60
1 32 leaves 28
1 16 leaves 12
1 8 leaves 4
1 4 leaves 0
0
0
1   1   1   1   1   1   0   0
```

Thus, the answer in binary is 1111 1100.

Now, it turns out that if you treat this binary number as two sets of four digits, you can do a magical transformation.

The right set is 1100. In decimal, that is 12 or in hexadecimal it is C.

The left set is 1111, which in base 10 is 15, or in hex is F.

Thus you have:

```
1111 1100
F    C
```

Putting the two hex numbers together is FC, which is the real value of 1111 1100. This shortcut always works. You can take any binary number of any length, and reduce it to sets of four, translate each set of four to hex, and put the hex numbers together to get the result in hex. Here's a much larger number:

```
1011 0001 1101 0111
```

The columns are 1, 2, 4, 8, 16, 32, 64, 128, 256, 512, 1024, 2048, 4096, 8192, 16384, and 32768.

```
1 x 1   =              1
1 x 2=                 2
1 x 4   =              4
0 x 8   =              0

1 x 16  =             16
0 x 32  =              0
1 x 64  =             64
1 x 128 =            128

1 x 256 =            256
0 x 512 =              0
0 x 1024 =             0
0 x 2048 =             0

1 x 4096 =        4,096
1 x 8192 =        8,192
0 x 16384 =           0
1 x 32768 =      32,768
Total:           45,527
```

Converting this to hexadecimal requires a chart with the hexadecimal values.

```
65535   4096   256   16  1
```

There are no 65,535s in 45,527 so the first column is 4096. There are eleven 4096's (45,056), with a remainder of 471. There is one 256 in 471 with a remainder of 215. There are thirteen 16s (208) in 215 with a remainder of seven. Thus the hexadecimal number is B1D7.

Checking the math:

```
B (11) * 4096 =       45,056
1 * 256 =                256
D (13) * 16 =            208
7 * 1 =                    7
Total                 45,527
```

The shortcut version would be to take the original binary number, 1011000111010111, and break it into groups of four: 1011 0001 1101 0111. Each of the four is then evaluated as a hexadecimal number:

```
1011 =
1 x 1 =              1
```

```
1 x 2 =          2
0 x 4 =          0
1 x 8 =          8
Total           11
Hex:             B

0001 =
1 x 1 =          1
0 x 2 =          0
0 x 4 =          0
0 * 8 =          0
Total            1
Hex:             1

1101 =
1 x 1 =          1
0 x 2 =          0
1 x 4 =          4
1 x 8 =          8
Total           13
Hex =            D

0111 =
0 x 1 =          1
1 x 2 =          2
1 x 4 =          4
0 x 8 =          0
Total            7
Hex:             7

Total Hex:   B1D7
```

APPENDIX

D

Answers

Day 1

Quiz

1. What is the difference between an interpreter and a compiler?

   Interpreters read through source code and translate a program, turning the programmer's code, or program instructions, directly into actions. Compilers translate source code into an executable program that can be run at a later time.

2. How do you compile the source code with your compiler?

   Every compiler is different. Be sure to check the documentation that came with your compiler.

3. What does the linker do?

   The linker's job is to tie together your compiled code with the libraries supplied by your compiler vendor and other sources. The linker lets you build your program in "pieces" and then link together the pieces into one big program.

4. What are the steps in the computer program development cycle?

   Edit source code, compile, link, test, repeat.

Exercises

1. Initializes two integer variables and then prints out their sum.
2. See your compiler manual for details on compiling and linking.
3. You must put a # symbol before the word `include` on the first line.
4. This program prints the words `Hello World` to the screen, followed by a new line (carriage return).

Day 2

Quiz

1. What is the difference between the compiler and the preprocessor?

   Each time you run your compiler, the preprocessor runs first. It reads through your source code and includes the files you've asked for and performs other housekeeping chores. The preprocessor is discussed in detail on Day 18.

2. Why is the function `main()` special?

   `main()` is called automatically, each time your program is executed.

3. What are the two types of comments, and how do they differ?

C++-style comments are two slashes (//) and they comment out any text until the end of the line. C-style comments come in pairs (/* */), and everything between the matching pairs is commented out. You must be careful to ensure you have matched pairs.

4. Can comments be nested?

Yes, C++-style comments can be nested within C-style comments. You can, in fact, nest C-style comments within C++-style comments, as long as you remember that the C++-style comments end at the end of the line.

5. Can comments be longer than one line?

C-style comments can. If you want to extend C++-style comments to a second line, you must put another set of double slashes (//).

Exercises

1. Write a program that writes I love C++ to the screen.

```
1: #include <iostream.h>
2:
3: void main()
4: {
5:     cout << "I love C++\n";
6: }
```

2. Write the smallest program that can be compiled, linked, and run.

```
void main(){}
```

3. **BUG BUSTERS:** Enter this program and compile it. Why does it fail? How can you fix it?

```
1: #include <iostream.h>
2: void main()
3: {
4:     cout << Is there a bug here?";
5: }
```

Line 4 is missing an opening quote for the string.

4. Fix the bug in Exercise 3 and recompile, link, and run it.

```
1: #include <iostream.h>
2: void main()
3: {
4:     cout << "Is there a bug here?";
5: }
```

Day 3

Quiz

1. What is the difference between an integral variable and a floating-point variable?

   Integer variables are whole numbers; floating-point variables are "reals" and have a "floating" decimal point. Floating-point numbers can be represented using a mantissa and exponent.

2. What are the differences between an unsigned short int and a long int?

   The keyword unsigned means that the integer holds only positive numbers. On most computers, short integers are two bytes and long integers are four.

3. What are the advantages of using a symbolic constant rather than a literal?

   A symbolic constant explains itself; the name of the constant tells what it is for. Also, symbolic constants can be redefined at one location in the source code, rather than the programmer having to edit the code everywhere the literal is used.

4. What are the advantages of using the const keyword rather than #define?

   const variables are "typed," and thus the compiler can check for errors in how they are used. Also, they survive the preprocessor, and therefore, the name is available in the debugger.

5. What makes for a good or bad variable name?

   A good variable name tells you what the variable represents; a bad variable name has no information. myAge and PeopleOnTheBus are good variable names, but xjk and prndl are probably less useful.

6. Given this enum, what is the value of BLUE?

   ```
   enum COLOR { WHITE, BLACK = 100, RED, BLUE, GREEN = 300 };
   ```

   BLUE equals 102

7. Which of the following variable names are good, which are bad, and which are invalid?

   a. Age

      Good

   b. !ex

      Not legal

   c. R79J

      Legal, but a bad choice since it isn't very descriptive.

d. `TotalIncome`

Good

e. `__Invalid`

Not legal

Exercises

1. What would be the correct variable type in which to store the following information?

    a. Your age.

    Unsigned short integer.

    b. The area of your backyard.

    Unsigned long integer or unsigned float.

    c. The number of stars in the galaxy.

    Unsigned double.

    d. The average rainfall for the month of January.

    Unsigned short integer.

2. Create good variable names for this information.

    a. `myAge`

    b. `backYardArea`

    c. `StarsInGalaxy`

    d. `averageJanRainFall`

3. Declare a constant for pi as 3.14159.

    ```
    const float Pi = 3.14159;
    ```

4. Declare a `float` variable and initialize it using your pi constant.

    ```
    float myPi = Pi;
    ```

Day 4

Quiz

1. What is an expression?

    Any statement that returns a value.

2. Is `x = 5 + 7` an expression? What is its value?

    Yes, `12`.

3. What is the value of 201 / 4?

   50.

4. What is the value of 201 % 4?

   1.

5. If myAge, a, and b are all int variables, what are their values after the following is run:

   ```
   myAge = 39;
   a = myAge++;
   b = ++myAge;
   ```

   myAge: 41, a: 39, b: 41.

6. What is the value of 8+2*3?

   14.

7. What is the difference between if(x = 3) and if(x == 3)?

   The first one assigns 3 to x and returns true. The second one tests whether x is equal to 3; it returns true if the value of x is equal to 3 and false if it is not.

8. Do the following values evaluate to true or false?

   a. 0

   b. 1

   c. -1

   d.x = 0

   e.x == 0 // assume that x has the value of 0

   a.false; b.true; c.true; d.true; e.true

Exercises

1. Write a single if statement that examines two integer variables and changes the larger to the smaller, using only one else clause.

   ```
   if (x > y)
       x = y;
   else              // y > x ¦¦ y == x
       y = x;
   ```

2. Examine the following program. Imagine entering three numbers, and write what output you expect.

   ```
   1:    #include <iostream.h>
   2:    void main()
   3:    {
   4:         int a, b, c;
   ```

```
5:           cout << "Please enter three numbers\n";
6:           cout << "a: ";
7:           cin >> a;
8:           cout << "\nb: ";
9:           cin >> b;
10:          cout << "\nc: ";
11:          cin >> c;
12:
13:          if (c == (a-b))
14:               cout << "a: ";
15:               cout << a;
16:               cout << " minus b: ";
17:               cout << b;
18:               cout << " equals c: ";
19:               cout << c << endl;
20:               if(c > 5)
21:                    cout << "and it is > 5!" << endl;
22:          else
23:               cout << "a-b does not equal c: " << endl;
24:  }
```

3. Enter the program from Exercise 2; compile, link, and run it. Enter the numbers 20, 10, and 50. Did you get the output you expected? Why not?

```
Please enter three numbers
a: 20

b: 10

c: 50
20 minus b: 10 equals c: 50
and it is > 5!
```

There should be an opening bracket after line 13 and a closing bracket after line 21 to open and close the first if block.

4. Examine this program and anticipate the output:

```
1:    #include <iostream.h>
2:    void main()
3:    {
4:        int a = 1, b = 1, c;
5:        if (c = (a-b))
6:            cout << "The value of c is: " << c;
7:    }
```

5. Enter, compile, link, and run the program from Exercise 4. What is the output? Why?

Because line 5 is assigning the value of a-b to c, the value of the assignment is a (1) minus b (1), or 0. Because 0 is evaluated as false, the if fails and nothing is printed.

D

Day 5

Quiz

1. What are the differences between the function prototype and the function definition?

   The function prototype declares the function; the definition defines it. The prototype ends with a semicolon; the definition need not. The declaration can include the keyword `inline` and default values for the parameters; the definition cannot. The declaration need not include names for the parameters; the definition must.

2. Do the names of parameters have to agree in the prototype, definition, and call to the function?

   No; all parameters are identified by position, not name.

3. If a function doesn't return a value, how do you declare the function?

   Declare the function to return `void`.

4. If you don't declare a return value, what type of return value is assumed?

   Any function that does not explicitly declare a return type returns `int`.

5. What is a local variable?

   A local variable is a variable passed into or declared within a block, typically a function. It is visible only within the block.

6. What is scope?

   Scope refers to the visibility and lifetime of local and global variables. Scope is usually established by a set of braces.

7. What is recursion?

   Recursion generally refers to the capability of a function to call itself.

8. When should you use global variables?

   Global variables are typically used when many functions need access to the same data. Global variables are very rare in C++; once you know how to create static class variables, you will almost never create global variables.

9. What is function overloading?

   Function overloading is the capability to write more than one function with the same name, distinguished by the number or type of the parameters.

10. Are different return types alone enough for the compiler to distinguish overloaded functions?

No. Overloaded functions must differ in parameter type, parameter order, or parameter count.

Exercises

1. Write the prototype for a function named Perimeter that returns an unsigned long int and takes two parameters, both unsigned short ints.

```
unsigned long int Perimeter(unsigned short int, unsigned short int);
```

2. Write the definition of the function Perimeter as described in Exercise 1. The two parameters represent the length and width of a rectangle and have the function return the perimeter (twice the length plus twice the width).

```
unsigned long int Perimeter(unsigned short int length, unsigned short int
width)
{
    return 2*length + 2*width;
}
```

3. **BUG BUSTERS:** What is wrong with the function?

```
#include <iostream.h>
void myFunc(unsigned short int x);
void main()
{
    unsigned short int x, y;
    y = myFunc(x);
    cout << "x: " << x << " y: " << y << "\n";
}

void myFunc(unsigned short int x)
{
    return (4*x);
}
```

The function is declared to return void, and it cannot return a value.

4. **BUG BUSTERS:** What is wrong with the function?

```
#include <iostream.h>
int myFunc(unsigned short int x);
void main()
{
    unsigned short int x, y;
    y = myFunc(x);
    cout << "x: " << x << " y: " << y << "\n";
}

int myFunc(unsigned short int x);
{
    return (4*x);
}
```

This function would be fine, but there is a semicolon at the end of the function definition's header.

5. Write a function that takes two `unsigned short int` arguments and returns the result of dividing the first by the second. Do not do the division if the second number is 0, but do return -1.

```
short int Divider(unsigned short int valOne, unsigned short int valTwo)
{
    if (valTwo == 0)
        return -1;
    else
        return valOne / valTwo;
}
```

6. Write a program that asks the user for two numbers and calls the function you wrote in Exercise 5. Print the answer, or print an error message if you get -1.

```
#include <iostream.h>
typedef unsigned short int USHORT;
typedef unsigned long int ULONG;
short int Divider(unsigned short int valone,unsigned short into valtwo);
void main()
{
    USHORT one, two;
    short int answer;
    cout << "Enter two numbers.\n Number one: ";
    cin >> one;
    cout << "Number two: ";
    cin >> two;
    answer = Divider(one, two);
    if (answer > -1)
        cout << "Answer: " << answer;
    else
        cout << "Error, can't divide by zero!";
}
```

7. Write a program that asks for a number and a power. Write a recursive function that takes the number to the power. Thus, if the number is 2 and the power is 4, the function returns 16.

```
#include <iostream.h>
typedef unsigned long ULONG
typedef unsigned short USHORT
ULONG GetPower(USHORT n, USHORT power);
void main()
{
    USHORT number, power;
    ULONG answer;
    cout << "Enter a number: ";
    cin >> number;
    cout << "To what power? ";
    cin >> power;
    answer = GetPower(number,power);
    cout << number << " to the " << power << "th power is " << answer <<
endl;
}
```

```
ULONG GetPower(USHORT n, USHORT power)
{
    if(power == 1)
     return n;
    else
        return (n * GetPower(n,power-1));
}
```

Day 6

Quiz

1. What is the dot operator, and what is it used for?

   The dot operator is the period (.). It is used to access the members of the class.

2. Which sets aside memory—declaration or definition?

   Definitions of variables set aside memory. Declarations of classes don't set aside memory.

3. Is the declaration of a class its interface or its implementation?

   The declaration of a class is its interface; it tells clients of the class how to interact with the class. The implementation of the class is the set of member functions stored—usually in a related .cpp file.

4. What is the difference between public and private data members?

   Public data members can be accessed by clients of the class. Private data members can be accessed only by member functions of the class.

5. Can member functions be private?

   Yes. Both member functions and member data can be private.

6. Can member data be public?

   Although member data can be public, it is good programming practice to make it private and to provide public accessor functions to the data.

7. If you declare two Cat objects, can they have different values in their itsAge member data?

   Yes. Each object of a class has its own data members.

8. Do class declarations end with a semicolon? Do class method definitions?

   Declarations end with a semicolon after the closing brace; function definitions do not.

9. What would the header for a Cat function, Meow, that takes no parameters and returns void look like?

The header for a Cat function, Meow(), that takes no parameters and returns void looks like this:

```
void Cat::Meow()
```

10. What function is called to initialize a class?

The constructor is called to initialize a class.

Exercises

1. Write the code that declares a class called Employee with these data members: Age, YearsOfService, and Salary.

```
class Employee
{
    int Age;
    int YearsOfService;
    int Salary;
};
```

2. Rewrite the Employee class to make the data members private and provide public accessor methods to get and set each of the data members.

```
class Employee
{
public:
    int GetAge() const;
    void SetAge(int age);
    int GetYearsOfService()const;
    void SetYearsOfService(int years);
    int GetSalary()const;
    void SetSalary(int salary);

private:
    int Age;
    int YearsOfService;
    int Salary;
};
```

3. Write a program with the Employee class that makes two Employees, sets the Age, YearsOfService, and Salary, and prints their values.

```
main()
{
    Employee John;
    Employee Sally;
    John.SetAge(30);
    John.SetYearsOfService(5);
    John.SetSalary(50000);

    Sally.SetAge(32);
    Sally.SetYearsOfService(8);
    Sally.SetSalary(40000);
```

```
    cout << "At AcmeSexist company, John and Sally have the same job.\n";
    cout << "John is " << John.GetAge() << " years old and he has been
with";
    cout << "the firm for " << John.GetYearsOfService << " years.\n";
    cout << "John earns $" << John.GetSalary << " per year.\n\n";
    cout << "Sally, on the other hand is " << Sally.GetAge() << " years old
and has";
    cout << "been with the company " << Sally.GetYearsOfService;
    cout << " years. Yet Sally only makes $" << Sally.GetSalary();
    cout << " per year!  Something here is unfair.";
}
```

4. Continuing from Exercise 3, provide a method of Employee that reports how many thousands of dollars the employee earns, rounded to the nearest 1,000.

```
float Employee:GetRoundedThousands()const
{
    return Salary % 1000;
}
```

5. Change the Employee class so that you can initialize Age, YearsOfService, and Salary when you create the employee.

```
class Employee
{
public:

    Employee(int Age, int YearsOfService, int Salary);
    int GetAge()const;
    void SetAge(int age);
    int GetYearsOfService()const;
    void SetYearsOfService(int years);
    int GetSalary()const;
    void SetSalary(int salary);

private:
    int Age;
    int YearsOfService;
    int Salary;
};
```

6. **BUG BUSTERS:** What is wrong with the following declaration?

```
class Square
{
public:
    int Side;
};
```

Class declarations must end with a semicolon.

7. **BUG BUSTERS:** Why isn't the following class declaration very useful?

```
class Cat
{
    int GetAge()const;
private:
    int itsAge;
};
```

The accessor GetAge() is private. Remember: All class members are private unless you say otherwise.

8. **BUG BUSTERS:** What three bugs in this code will the compiler find?

```
class  TV
{
public:
    void SetStation(int Station);
    int GetStation() const;
private:
    int itsStation;
};

main()
{
    TV myTV;
    myTV.itsStation = 9;
    TV.SetStation(10);
    TV myOtherTv(2);
}
```

You can't access itsStation directly. It is private.

You can't call SetStation() on the class. You can call SetStation() only on objects.

You can't initialize itsStation because there is no matching constructor.

Day 7

Quiz

1. How do you initialize more than one variable in a for loop?

   Separate the initializations with commas, such as

   ```
   for (x = 0, y = 10; x < 100; x++, y++).
   ```

2. Why is goto avoided?

   goto jumps in any direction to any arbitrary line of code. This makes for source code that is difficult to understand and therefore, difficult to maintain.

3. Is it possible to write a for loop with a body that is never executed?

   Yes; if the condition is false after the initialization, the body of the for loop never executes. Here's an example:

   ```
   for (int x = 100; x < 100; x++)
   ```

4. Is it possible to nest while loops within for loops?

   Yes, any loop may be nested within any other loop.

5. Is it possible to create a loop that never ends? Give an example.

Yes. Following are examples for both a `for` loop and a `while` loop:

```
for(;;)
{
    // This for loop never ends!
}
while(1)
{
    // This while loop never ends!
}
```

6. What happens if you create a loop that never ends?

Your program "hangs," and you usually must reboot the computer.

Exercises

1. What is the value of x when the `for` loop completes?

```
for (int x = 0; x < 100; x++)
```

```
100
```

2. Write a nested `for` loop which prints a 10×10 pattern of 0s.

```
for (int i = 0; i< 10; i++)
{
    for ( int j = 0; j< 10; j++)
        cout << "0";
    cout << "\n";
}
```

3. Write a `for` statement to count from 100 to 200 by twos.

```
for (int x = 100; x<=200; x+=2)
```

4. Write a `while` loop to count from 100 to 200 by twos.

```
int x = 100;
while (x < 200)
    x+= 2;
```

5. Write a do...while loop to count from 100 to 200 by twos.

```
int x = 100;
do
{
    x+=2;
} while (x < 200);
```

6. **BUG BUSTERS:** What is wrong with this code?

```
int counter = 0;
while (counter < 10)
{
    cout << "counter: " << counter;
    counter++;
}
```

`counter` is never incremented, and the `while` loop will never terminate.

D

7. **BUG BUSTERS:** What is wrong with this code?

```
for (int counter = 0; counter < 10; counter++);
    cout << counter << "\n";
```

There is a semicolon after the loop, and the loop does nothing. The programmer may have intended this, but if counter is supposed to print each value, it doesn't.

8. **BUG BUSTERS:** What is wrong with this code?

```
int counter = 100;
while (counter < 10)
{
    cout << "counter now: " << counter;
    counter--;
}
```

counter is initialized to 100, but the test condition tests to see if it is less than 10; the test will always be false, and the while body will never be executed. If line 1 were changed to int counter = 5; the loop would not terminate until it had counted down past the smallest possible int and turned over to the largest int. Since int is signed by default, this is probably not what was intended either.

9. **BUG BUSTERS:** What is wrong with this code?

```
cout << "Enter a number between 0 and 5: ";
cin >> theNumber;
switch (theNumber)
{
    case 0:
        doZero();
    case 1:              // fall through
    case 2:              // fall through
    case 3:              // fall through
    case 4:              // fall through
    case 5:
        doOneToFive();
        break;
    default:
        doDefault();
        break;
}
```

Case 0 probably needs a break statement. If not, it should be documented with a comment.

Day 8

Quiz

1. What operator is used to determine the address of a variable?

   The address of operator (&) is used to determine the address of any variable.

2. What operator is used to find the value stored at an address held in a pointer?

The dereference operator (*) is used to access the value at an address in a pointer.

3. What is a pointer?

A pointer is a variable that holds the address of another variable.

4. What is the difference between the address stored in a pointer and the value at that address?

The address stored in the pointer is simply a number that identifies a location in memory. The value is stored at the address that the pointer holds. Remember that your address is not your home; it is an identifier that points to your home.

5. What is the difference between the indirection operator and the address of operator?

The indirection operator returns the value at the address stored in a pointer. The address of operator (&) returns the memory address of the variable.

6. What is the difference between const int * ptrOne and int * const ptrTwo?

The const int * ptrOne declares that ptrOne is a pointer to a constant integer. The integer itself cannot be changed using this pointer.

The int * const ptrTwo declares that ptrTwo is a constant pointer to integer. Once it is initialized, this pointer cannot be reassigned.

Exercises

1. What do these declarations do?

    a. `int * pOne;`

    b. `int vTwo;`

    c. `int * pThree = &vTwo;`

a. `int * pOne;` declares a pointer to an integer.

b. `int vTwo;` declares an integer variable.

c. `int * pThree = &vTwo;` declares a pointer to an integer and initializes it with the address of another variable.

2. If you have an unsigned short variable named yourAge, how would you declare a pointer to manipulate yourAge?

`unsigned short *pAge = &yourAge;`

3. Assign the value 50 to the variable yourAge by using the pointer that you declared in Exercise 2.

`*pAge = 50;`

4. Write a small program that declares an integer and a pointer to integer. Assign the address of the integer to the pointer. Use the pointer to set a value in the integer variable.

```
int theInteger;
int *pInteger = &theInteger;
*pInteger = 5;
```

5. **BUG BUSTERS:** What is wrong with this code?

```
#include <iostream.h>
void main()
{
    int *pInt;
    *pInt = 9;
    cout << "The value at pInt: " << *pInt;
}
```

pInt should be initialized. More important, because it is not initialized and is not assigned the address of any memory, it points to a random place in memory. Assigning 9 to that random place is a dangerous bug.

6. **BUG BUSTERS:** What is wrong with this code?

```
void main()
{
    int SomeVariable = 5;
    cout << "SomeVariable: " << SomeVariable << "\n";
    int *pVar = & SomeVariable;
    pVar = 9;
    cout << "SomeVariable: " << *pVar << "\n";
}
```

Presumably, the programmer meant to assign 9 to the value at pVar. Unfortunately, 9 was assigned to be the value of pVar because the indirection operator (*) was left off. This will lead to disaster if pVar is used to assign a value.

Day 9

Quiz

1. What is the difference between a reference and a pointer?

A reference is an alias, and a pointer is a variable that holds an address. References cannot be null and cannot be assigned to.

2. When must you use a pointer rather than a reference?

When you may need to reassign what is pointed to, or when the pointer may be null.

3. What does new return if there is insufficient memory to make your new object?

A null pointer (0).

4. What is a constant reference?

This is a shorthand way of saying a reference to a constant object.

5. What is the difference between passing *by* reference and passing *a* reference?

Passing *by* reference means not making a local copy. It can be accomplished by passing a reference or by passing a pointer.

Exercises

1. Write a program that declares an int, a reference to an int, and a pointer to an int. Use the pointer and the reference to manipulate the value in the int.

```
void main()
{
int varOne;
int& rVar = varOne;
int* pVar = &varOne;
rVar = 5;
*pVar = 7;
}
```

2. Write a program that declares a constant pointer to a constant integer. Initialize the pointer to an integer variable, varOne. Assign 6 to varOne. Use the pointer to assign 7 to varOne. Create a second integer variable, varTwo. Reassign the pointer to varTwo.

```
void main()
{
    int varOne;
    const int * const pVar = &varOne;
    varOne = 6;
    *pVar = 7;
    int varTwo;
    pVar = &varTwo;
}
```

3. Compile the program in Exercise 2. What produces errors? What produces warnings?

You can't assign a value to a constant object, and you can't reassign a constant pointer.

4. Write a program that produces a stray pointer.

```
void main()
{
int * pVar;
*pVar = 9;
}
```

5. Fix the program from Exercise 4.

```
void main()
{
int VarOne;
```

```
int * pVar = &varOne;
*pVar = 9;
}
```

6. Write a program that produces a memory leak.

```
int FuncOne();
void main()
{
    int localVar = FunOne();
    cout << "the value of localVar is: " << localVar;
}

int FuncOne()
{
    int * pVar = new int (5);
    return *pVar;
}
```

7. Fix the program from Exercise 6.

```
void FuncOne();
void main()
{
    FuncOne();
}

void FuncOne()
{
    int * pVar = new int (5);
    cout << "the value of *pVar is: " << *pVar ;
}
```

8. **BUG BUSTERS:** What is wrong with this program?

```
1:      #include <iostream.h>
2:
3:      class CAT
4:      {
5:          public:
6:              CAT(int age) { itsAge = age; }
7:              ~CAT(){}
8:              int GetAge() const { return itsAge;}
9:          private:
10:             int itsAge;
11:     };
12:
13:     CAT & MakeCat(int age);
14:     void main()
15:     {
16:         int age = 7;
17:         CAT Boots = MakeCat(age);
18:         cout << "Boots is " << Boots.GetAge() << " years old\n";
19:     }
20:
21:     CAT & MakeCat(int age)
22:     {
23:         CAT * pCat = new CAT(age);
24:         return *pCat;
25:     }
```

MakeCat returns a reference to the CAT created on the free store. There is no way to free that memory, and this produces a memory leak.

9. Fix the program from Exercise 8.

```
1:    #include <iostream.h>
2:
3:    class CAT
4:    {
5:       public:
6:          CAT(int age) { itsAge = age; }
7:          ~CAT(){}
8:          int GetAge() const { return itsAge;}
9:       private:
10:          int itsAge;
11:    };
12:
13:    CAT * MakeCat(int age);
14:    void main()
15:    {
16:       int age = 7;
17:       CAT * Boots = MakeCat(age);
18:       cout << "Boots is " << Boots->GetAge() << " years old\n";
19:       delete Boots;
20:    }
21:
22:    CAT * MakeCat(int age)
23:    {
24:       return new CAT(age);
25:    }
```

Day 10

Quiz

1. When you overload member functions, in what ways must they differ?

   Overloaded member functions are functions in a class that share a name, but that differ in the number or type of their parameters.

2. What is the difference between a declaration and a definition?

   A definition sets aside memory, but a declaration does not. Almost all declarations *are* definitions; the major exceptions are class declarations, function prototypes, and typedef statements.

3. When is the copy constructor called?

   Whenever a temporary copy of an object is created. This happens every time an object is passed by value.

D

4. When is the destructor called?

The destructor is called each time an object is destroyed, either because it goes out of scope or because you call `delete` on a pointer pointing to it.

5. How does the copy constructor differ from the assignment operator (=)?

The assignment operator acts on an existing object; the copy constructor creates a new one.

6. What is the `this` pointer?

The `this` pointer is a hidden parameter in every member function that points to the object itself.

7. How do you differentiate between overloading the prefix and postfix increments?

The prefix operator takes no parameters. The postfix operator takes a single `int` parameter that is used as a signal to the compiler that this is the postfix variant.

8. Can you overload the `operator+` for short integers?

No, you cannot overload any operator for built-in types.

9. Is it legal in C++ to overload `operator++` so that it decrements a value in your class?

It is legal, but it is a bad idea. Operators should be overloaded in a way that is likely to be readily understood by anyone reading your code.

10. What return value must a conversion operator have in its declaration?

None. Like constructors and destructors, it has no return value.

Exercises

1. Write a `SimpleCircle` class declaration (only) with one member variable: `itsRadius`. Include a default constructor, a destructor, and accessor methods for radius.

```
class SimpleCircle
{
public:
    SimpleCircle();
    ~SimpleCircle();
    void SetRadius(int);
    int GetRadius();
private:
    int itsRadius;
};
```

2. Using the class you created in Exercise 1, write the implementation of the default constructor, initializing `itsRadius` with the value 5.

```
SimpleCircle::SimpleCircle():
itsRadius(5)
{}
```

3. Using the same class, add a second constructor that takes a value as its parameter and assigns that value to itsRadius.

```
SimpleCircle::SimpleCircle(int radius):
itsRadius(radius)
{}
```

4. Create a prefix and postfix increment operator for your SimpleCircle class that increments itsRadius.

```
SimpleCircle SimpleCircle::operator++()
{
    itsRadius++;
    return *this;
}

SimpleCircle SimpleCircle::operator++ (int)
{
    itsRadius++;
    return *this;
}
```

5. Change SimpleCircle to store itsRadius on the free store, and fix the existing methods.

```
class SimpleCircle
{
public:
    SimpleCircle();
    SimpleCircle(int);
    ~SimpleCircle();
    void SetRadius(int);
    int GetRadius();
    SimpleCircle operator++();
    SimpleCircle operator++(int);
private:
    int *itsRadius;
};


SimpleCircle::SimpleCircle()
{itsRadius = new int(5);}

SimpleCircle::SimpleCircle(int radius)
{itsRadius = new int(radius);}

SimpleCircle SimpleCircle::operator++()
{
    (*itsRadius)++;
    return *this;
}

SimpleCircle SimpleCircle::operator++ (int)
{
    (*itsRadius)++;
    return *this;
}
```

6. Provide a copy constructor for SimpleCircle.

```
SimpleCircle::SimpleCircle(const SimpleCircle & rhs)
{
    int val = rhs.GetRadius();
    itsRadius = new int(val);
}
```

7. Provide an operator= for SimpleCircle.

```
SimpleCircle& SimpleCircle::operator=(const SimpleCircle & rhs)
{
    if (this == &rhs)
        return *this;
    *itsRadius = rhs.GetRadius();
}
```

8. Write a program that creates two SimpleCircle objects. Use the default constructor on one and instantiate the other with the value 9. Call increment on each and then print their values. Finally, assign the second to the first and print its values.

```
#include <iostream.h>

class SimpleCircle
{
public:
        // constructors
    SimpleCircle();
    SimpleCircle(int);
    SimpleCircle(const SimpleCircle &);
    ~SimpleCircle() {}

// accessor functions
    void SetRadius(int);
    int GetRadius()const;

// operators
    SimpleCircle operator++();
    SimpleCircle operator++(int);
    SimpleCircle& operator=(const SimpleCircle &);

private:
    int *itsRadius;
};


SimpleCircle::SimpleCircle()
{itsRadius = new int(5);}

SimpleCircle::SimpleCircle(int radius)
{itsRadius = new int(radius);}

SimpleCircle::SimpleCircle(const SimpleCircle & rhs)
{
    int val = rhs.GetRadius();
    itsRadius = new int(val);
```

```
}
SimpleCircle& SimpleCircle::operator=(const SimpleCircle & rhs)
{
    if (this == &rhs)
        return *this;
    *itsRadius = rhs.GetRadius();
    return *this;
}

SimpleCircle SimpleCircle::operator++()
{
    (*itsRadius)++;
    return *this;
}

SimpleCircle SimpleCircle::operator++ (int)
{
    (*itsRadius)++;
    return *this;
}
int SimpleCircle::GetRadius() const
{
    return *itsRadius;
}
void main()
{
    SimpleCircle CircleOne, CircleTwo(9);
    CircleOne++;
    ++CircleTwo;
    cout << "CircleOne: " << CircleOne.GetRadius() << endl;
    cout << "CircleTwo: " << CircleTwo.GetRadius() << endl;
    CircleOne = CircleTwo;
    cout << "CircleOne: " << CircleOne.GetRadius() << endl;
    cout << "CircleTwo: " << CircleTwo.GetRadius() << endl;
}
```

9. **BUG BUSTERS:** What is wrong with this implementation of the assignment operator?

```
SQUARE SQUARE ::operator=(const SQUARE & rhs)
{
    itsSide = new int;
    *itsSide = rhs.GetSide();
    return *this;
}
```

You must check to see whether rhs equals this, or the call to a = a crashes your program.

10. **BUG BUSTERS:** What is wrong with this implementation of operator+?

```
VeryShort  VeryShort::operator+ (const VeryShort& rhs)
{
    itsVal += rhs.GetItsVal();
    return *this;
}
```

This operator+ is changing the value in one of the operands rather than creating a new VeryShort object with the sum. The right way to do this is as follows:

```
VeryShort  VeryShort::operator+ (const VeryShort& rhs)
{
    return VeryShort(itsVal + rhs.GetItsVal();
}
```

Day 11

Quiz

1. What are the first and last elements in SomeArray[25]?

   SomeArray[0] and SomeArray[24].

2. How do you declare a multidimensional array?

   Write a set of subscripts for each dimension. For example, SomeArray[2][3][2] is a three-dimensional array. The first dimension has two elements; the second has three; and the third has two.

3. Initialize the members of the array in Question 2.

   SomeArray[2][3][2] = { { {1,2},{3,4},{5,6} } , { {7,8},{9,10},{11,12} } };

4. How many elements are in the array SomeArray[10][5][20]?

   $10 \times 5 \times 20 = 1,000$

5. What is the maximum number of elements that you can add to a linked list?

   There is no fixed maximum. It depends on how much memory you have available.

6. Can you use subscript notation on a linked list?

   You can use subscript notation on a linked list only by writing your own class to contain the linked list and by overloading the subscript operator.

7. What is the last character in the string "Brad is a nice guy."?

   The null character.

Exercises

1. Declare a two-dimensional array that represents a tic-tac-toe game board.

   int GameBoard[3][3];

2. Write the code that initializes all the elements in the array you created in Exercise 1 to the value 0.

   int GameBoard[3][3] = { {0,0,0},{0,0,0},{0,0,0} };

3. Write the declaration for a Node class that holds unsigned short integers.

```
class Node
{
public:
    Node ();
    Node (int);
    ~Node();
    void SetNext(Node * node) { itsNext = node; }
    Node * GetNext() const { return itsNext; }
    int GetVal() const { return itsVal; }
    void Insert(Node *);
    void Display();
private:
    int itsVal;
    Node * itsNext;
};
```

4. **BUG BUSTERS:** What is wrong with this code fragment?

```
unsigned short SomeArray[5][4];
for (int i = 0; i<4; i++)
    for (int j = 0; j<5; j++)
        SomeArray[i][j] = i+j;
```

The array is five elements by four elements, but the code initializes 4×5.

5. **BUG BUSTERS:** What is wrong with this code fragment?

```
unsigned short SomeArray[5][4];
for (int i = 0; i<=5; i++)
    for (int j = 0; j<=4; j++)
        SomeArray[i][j] = 0;
```

You wanted to write i<5, but you wrote i<=5 instead. The code will run when i ==
5 and j == 4, but there is no such element as SomeArray[5][4].

Day 12

Quiz

1. What makes the polymorphism less efficient than compile-time binding?

   Polymorphism requires a small overhead for each class that contains virtual
   functions and all classes derived from those classes.

2. What is a virtual destructor?

   A destructor of any class can be declared to be virtual. When the pointer is deleted,
   the run-time type of the object is assessed, and the correct derived destructor
   invoked.

3. How do you show the declaration of a virtual constructor?

   There are no virtual constructors.

4. How can you create a virtual copy constructor?

You can do this by creating a virtual method in your class, which itself calls the copy constructor.

5. How do you invoke a base member function from a derived class in which you've overridden that function?

```
Base::FunctionName();
```

6. How do you invoke a base member function from a derived class in which you have not overridden that function?

```
FunctionName();
```

7. If a base class declares a function to be virtual, and a derived class does not use the term virtual when overriding that class, is it still virtual when inherited by a third-generation class?

Yes, the virtualness is inherited and *cannot* be turned off.

8. What is the protected keyword used for?

protected members are accessible to the member functions of derived objects.

Exercises

1. Show the declaration of a virtual function taking an integer parameter and returning void.

```
virtual void SomeFunction(int);
```

2. Show the declaration of a class Square that derives from Rectangle, which in turn derives from Shape.

```
class Square : public Rectangle
{};
```

3. If, in Exercise 2, Shape takes no parameters, Rectangle takes two (length and width), but Square takes only one (length), show the constructor initialization for Square.

```
Square::Square(int length):
    Rectangle(length, length){}
```

4. Write a virtual copy constructor for the class Square (in Exercise 3).

```
Square& Square::Clone()
{ return new Square(*this); }
```

5. **BUG BUSTERS:** What is wrong with this code snippet?

```
void SomeFunction (Shape);
Shape * pRect = new Rectangle;
SomeFunction(*pRect);
```

Perhaps nothing. SomeFunction expects a Shape object. You've passed it a Rectangle "sliced" down to a Shape. As long as you don't need any of the Rectangle parts, this is fine. If you do need the `Rectangle` parts, you'll need to change `SomeFunction` to take a pointer or a reference to a `Shape`.

6. **BUG BUSTERS:** What is wrong with this code snippet?

```
class Shape()
{
public:
    Shape();
    virtual ~Shape();
    virtual Shape(const Shape&);
};
```

You can't declare a copy constructor to be virtual.

Day 13

Quiz

1. What is a down cast?

   A down cast (also called "casting down") is a declaration that a pointer to a base class is to be treated as a pointer to a derived class.

2. What is partial multiple inheritance?

   Partial multiple inheritance is when a class derives part of the base class but not all. Partial multiple inheritance can often lead to problems and is one reason many computer scientists frown on the use of multiple inheritance.

3. If both `DomesticAnimal` and `Mammal` classes derive from `Animal`, and `Dog` is derived from `DomesticAnimal` and `Mammal`, how many `Animals` are created when you instantiate a `Dog`?

   If neither class inherits using the keyword `virtual`, two `Animals` are created, one for `Mammal` and one for `DomesticAnimal`. If the keyword `virtual` is used for both classes, only one shared `Animal` is created.

4. If `Horse` and `Bird` inherit virtual public from `Animal`, do their constructors initialize the `Animal` constructor? If `Pegasus` inherits from both `Horse` and `Bird`, how does it initialize `Animal`'s constructor?

   Both `Horse` and `Bird` initialize their base class, `Animal`, in their constructors. `Pegasus` does so as well, and when a `Pegasus` is created, the `Horse` and `Bird` initializations of `Animal` are ignored.

5. Declare a class, `Vehicle`, and make it an abstract data type.

```
class Vehicle
{
    virtual void Move() = 0;
}
```

6. If a base class is an ADT, and it has three pure virtual functions, how many of these must be overridden in its derived classes?

None must be overridden unless you want to make the class nonabstract, in which case, all three must be overridden.

Exercises

1. Show the declaration for a class `JetPlane` that inherits from `Rocket` and `Airplane`.

```
class JetPlane : public Rocket, public Airplane
```

2. Show the declaration for `747` that inherits from the `JetPlane` class described in Exercise 1.

```
class 747 : public JetPlane
```

3. Write a program that derives `Car` and `Bus` from the class `Vehicle`. Make `Vehicle` an ADT with two pure virtual functions. Make `Car` and `Bus` not be ADTs.

```
class Vehicle
{
    virtual void Move() = 0;
    virtual void Haul() = 0;
};

class Car : public Vehicle
{
    virtual void Move();
    virtual void Haul();
};

class Bus : public Vehicle
{
    virtual void Move();
    virtual void Haul();
};
```

4. Modify the program in Exercise 3 so that `Car` is an ADT, and derive `SportsCar`, `Wagon`, and `Coupe` from `Car`. In the `Car` class, provide an implementation for one of the pure virtual functions in `Vehicle` and make it nonpure.

```
class Vehicle
{
    virtual void Move() = 0;
    virtual void Haul() = 0;
};

class Car : public Vehicle
{
    virtual void Move();
};
```

```
class Bus : public Vehicle
{
    virtual void Move();
    virtual void Haul();
};

class SportsCar : public Car
{
    virtual void Haul();
};

class Wagon : public Car
{
    virtual void Haul();
};

class Coupe : public Car
{
    virtual void Haul();
};
```

Day 14

Quiz

1. Can static member variables be private?

   Yes, they are member variables and their access can be controlled as any other variable. If they are private, they can be accessed only by using member functions or, more commonly, by using static member functions.

2. Show the declaration for a static member variable.

   ```
   static int itsStatic;
   ```

3. Show the declaration for a static function pointer.

   ```
   static int SomeFunction();
   ```

4. Show the declaration for a pointer to a function returning long and taking an integer parameter.

   ```
   long (* function)(int);
   ```

5. Modify the pointer in Exercise 4 to be a pointer to a member function of class Car.

   ```
   long (* Car::function)(int);
   ```

6. Show the declaration for an array of 10 pointers as defined in Question 5.

   ```
   (long (* Car::function)(int) theArray [10];
   ```

Exercises

1. Write a short program declaring a class with one member variable and one static member variable. Have the constructor initialize the member variable and increment the static member variable. Have the destructor decrement the member variable.

```
1:      class myClass
2:      {
3:      public:
4:          myClass();
5:          ~myClass();
6:      private:
7:          int itsMember;
8:          static int itsStatic;
9:      };
10:
11:     myClass::myClass():
12:       itsMember(1)
13:     {
14:         itsStatic++;
15:     }
16:
17:     myClass::~myClass()
18:     {
19:         itsStatic--;
20:     }
21:
22:     int myClass::itsStatic = 0;
23:
24:     void main()
25:     {}
```

2. Using the program from Exercise 1, write a short driver program that makes three objects and then displays their member variables and the static member variable. Then destroy each object and show the effect on the static member variable.

```
1:      #include <iostream.h>
2:
3:      class myClass
4:      {
5:      public:
6:          myClass();
7:          ~myClass();
8:          void ShowMember();
9:          void ShowStatic();
10:     private:
11:         int itsMember;
12:         static int itsStatic;
13:     };
14:
15:     myClass::myClass():
16:       itsMember(1)
17:     {
18:         itsStatic++;
```

```
19:    }
20:
21:    myClass::~myClass()
22:    {
23:       itsStatic--;
24:       cout << "In destructor. ItsStatic: " << itsStatic << endl;
25:    }
26:
27:    void myClass::ShowMember()
28:    {
29:       cout << "itsMember: " << itsMember << endl;
30:    }
31:
32:    void myClass::ShowStatic()
33:    {
34:       cout << "itsStatic: " << itsStatic << endl;
35:    }
36:    int myClass::itsStatic = 0;
37:
38:    void main()
39:    {
40:       myClass obj1;
41:       obj1.ShowMember();
42:       obj1.ShowStatic();
43:
44:       myClass obj2;
45:       obj2.ShowMember();
46:       obj2.ShowStatic();
47:
48:       myClass obj3;
49:       obj3.ShowMember();
50:       obj3.ShowStatic();
51:    }
```

3. Modify the program from Exercise 2 to use a static member function to access the static member variable. Make the static member variable private.

```
1:     #include <iostream.h>
2:
3:     class myClass
4:     {
5:     public:
6:        myClass();
7:        ~myClass();
8:        void ShowMember();
9:        static int GetStatic();
10:    private:
11:       int itsMember;
12:       static int itsStatic;
13:    };
14:
15:    myClass::myClass():
16:     itsMember(1)
17:    {
18:       itsStatic++;
19:    }
20:
```

```
21:    myClass::~myClass()
22:    {
23:        itsStatic--;
24:        cout << "In destructor. ItsStatic: " << itsStatic << endl;
25:    }
26:
27:    void myClass::ShowMember()
28:    {
29:        cout << "itsMember: " << itsMember << endl;
30:    }
31:
32:    int myClass::itsStatic = 0;
33:
34:    int myClass::GetStatic()
35:    {
36:        return itsStatic;
37:    }
38:
39:    void main()
40:    {
41:        myClass obj1;
42:        obj1.ShowMember();
43:        cout << "Static: " << myClass::GetStatic() << endl;
44:
45:        myClass obj2;
46:        obj2.ShowMember();
47:        cout << "Static: " << myClass::GetStatic() << endl;
48:
49:        myClass obj3;
50:        obj3.ShowMember();
51:        cout << "Static: " << myClass::GetStatic() << endl;
52:    }
```

4. Write a pointer to a member function to access the nonstatic member data in the program in Exercise 3 and use that pointer to print the value of that data.

```
1:     #include <iostream.h>
2:
3:     class myClass
4:     {
5:     public:
6:         myClass();
7:         ~myClass();
8:         void ShowMember();
9:         static int GetStatic();
10:    private:
11:        int itsMember;
12:        static int itsStatic;
13:    };
14:
15:    myClass::myClass():
16:      itsMember(1)
17:    {
18:        itsStatic++;
19:    }
20:
21:    myClass::~myClass()
```

```
22:    {
23:        itsStatic--;
24:        cout << "In destructor. ItsStatic: " << itsStatic << endl;
25:    }
26:
27:    void myClass::ShowMember()
28:    {
29:        cout << "itsMember: " << itsMember << endl;
30:    }
31:
32:    int myClass::itsStatic = 0;
33:
34:    int myClass::GetStatic()
35:    {
36:        return itsStatic;
37:    }
38:
39:    void main()
40:    {
41:        void (myClass::*PMF) ();
42:
43:        PMF=myClass::ShowMember;
44:
45:        myClass obj1;
46:        (obj1.*PMF)();
47:        cout << "Static: " << myClass::GetStatic() << endl;
48:
49:        myClass obj2;
50:        (obj2.*PMF)();
51:        cout << "Static: " << myClass::GetStatic() << endl;
52:
53:        myClass obj3;
54:        (obj3.*PMF)();
55:        cout << "Static: " << myClass::GetStatic() << endl;
56:    }
```

5. Add two more member variables to the class from the previous questions. Add accessor functions that return data values and give all the member functions the same return values and signatures. Use the pointer to a member function to access these functions.

```
1:     #include <iostream.h>
2:
3:     class myClass
4:     {
5:     public:
6:         myClass();
7:         ~myClass();
8:         void ShowMember();
9:         void ShowSecond();
10:        void ShowThird();
11:        static int GetStatic();
12:    private:
13:        int itsMember;
14:        int itsSecond;
15:        int itsThird;
```

```
16:        static int itsStatic;
17:    };
18:
19:    myClass::myClass():
20:     itsMember(1),
21:     itsSecond(2),
22:     itsThird(3)
23:    {
24:        itsStatic++;
25:    }
26:
27:    myClass::~myClass()
28:    {
29:        itsStatic--;
30:        cout << "In destructor. ItsStatic: " << itsStatic << endl;
31:    }
32:
33:    void myClass::ShowMember()
34:    {
35:        cout << "itsMember: " << itsMember << endl;
36:    }
37:
38:    void myClass::ShowSecond()
39:    {
40:        cout << "itsSecond: " << itsSecond << endl;
41:    }
42:
43:    void myClass::ShowThird()
44:    {
45:        cout << "itsThird: " << itsThird << endl;
46:    }
47:    int myClass::itsStatic = 0;
48:
49:    int myClass::GetStatic()
50:    {
51:        return itsStatic;
52:    }
53:
54:    void main()
55:    {
56:        void (myClass::*PMF) ();
57:
58:        myClass obj1;
59:        PMF=myClass::ShowMember;
60:        (obj1.*PMF)();
61:        PMF=myClass::ShowSecond;
62:        (obj1.*PMF)();
63:        PMF=myClass::ShowThird;
64:        (obj1.*PMF)();
65:        cout << "Static: " << myClass::GetStatic() << endl;
66:
67:        myClass obj2;
68:        PMF=myClass::ShowMember;
69:        (obj2.*PMF)();
70:        PMF=myClass::ShowSecond;
71:        (obj2.*PMF)();
```

```
72:          PMF=myClass::ShowThird;
73:          (obj2.*PMF)();
74:          cout << "Static: " << myClass::GetStatic() << endl;
75:
76:          myClass obj3;
77:          PMF=myClass::ShowMember;
78:          (obj3.*PMF)();
79:          PMF=myClass::ShowSecond;
80:          (obj3.*PMF)();
81:          PMF=myClass::ShowThird;
82:          (obj3.*PMF)();
83:          cout << "Static: " << myClass::GetStatic() << endl;
84:      }
```

Day 15

Quiz

1. How do you establish an is-a relationship?

   With public inheritance.

2. How do you establish a has-a relationship?

   With containment; that is, one class has a member that is an object of another type.

3. What is the difference between containment and delegation?

   Containment describes the idea of one class having a data member that is an object of another type. Delegation expresses the idea that one class uses another class to accomplish a task or goal. Delegation is usually accomplished by containment.

4. What is the difference between delegation and "implemented in terms of?"

   Delegation expresses the idea that one class uses another class to accomplish a task or goal. "Implemented in terms of" expresses the idea of inheriting implementation from another class.

5. What is a friend function?

   A friend function is a function declared to have access to the protected and private members of your class.

6. What is a friend class?

   A friend class is a class declared so that all of its member functions are friend functions of your class.

7. If Dog is a friend of Boy, is Boy a friend of Dog?

   No, friendship is not commutative.

8. If Dog is a friend of Boy, and Terrier derives from Dog, is Terrier a friend of Boy?

   No, friendship is not inherited.

D

9. If Dog is a friend of Boy, and Boy is a friend of House, is Dog a friend of House?

No, friendship is not associative.

10. Where must the declaration of a friend function appear?

Anywhere within the class declaration. It makes no difference whether you put the declaration within the public, protected, or private access areas.

Exercises

1. Show the declaration of a class, Animal, that contains a data member that is a string object.

```
class Animal:
{
private:
   String itsName;
};
```

2. Show the declaration of a class BoundedArray that is an array.

```
class boundedArray : public Array
{
//...
}
```

3. Show the declaration of a class Set that is declared in terms of an array.

```
class Set : private Array
{
// ...
}
```

4. Modify Listing 15.9 to provide the String class with an extraction operator (>>).

```
1:          #include <iostream.h>
2:          #include <string.h>
3:
4:          class String
5:          {
6:             public:
7:                 // constructors
8:                 String();
9:                  String(const char *const);
10:                 String(const String &);
11:                 ~String();
12:
13:                 // overloaded operators
14:                 char & operator[](int offset);
15:                 char operator[](int offset) const;
16:                 String operator+(const String&);
17:                 void operator+=(const String&);
18:                 String & operator= (const String &);
19:                 friend ostream& operator<<( ostream&
                                    _theStream,String& theString);
20:                 friend istream& operator>>( istream&
                                    _theStream,String& theString);
```

```
21:              // General accessors
22:              int GetLen()const { return itsLen; }
23:              const char * GetString() const { return itsString; }
24:              // static int ConstructorCount;
25:
26:          private:
27:              String (int);          // private constructor
28:              char * itsString;
29:              unsigned short itsLen;
30:
31:          };
32:
33:      ostream& operator<<( ostream& theStream,String& theString)
34:      {
35:          theStream << theString.GetString();
36:          return theStream;
37:      }
38:
39:      istream& operator>>( istream& theStream,String& theString)
40:      {
41:          theStream >> theString.GetString();
42:          return theStream;
43:      }
44:
45:      void main()
46:      {
47:          String theString("Hello world.");
48:          cout << theString;
49:      }
```

5. **BUG BUSTERS:** What is wrong with this program?

```
1:      #include <iostream.h>
2:
3:      class Animal;
4:
5:      void setValue(Animal& , int);
6:
7:
8:      class Animal
9:      {
10:     public:
11:         int GetWeight()const { return itsWeight; }
12:         int GetAge() const { return itsAge; }
13:     private:
14:         int itsWeight;
15:         int itsAge;
16:     };
17:
18:     void setValue(Animal& theAnimal, int theWeight)
19:     {
20:         friend class Animal;
21:         theAnimal.itsWeight = theWeight;
22:     }
23:
24:     void main()
25:     {
```

```
26:        Animal peppy;
27:        setValue(peppy,5);
28:     }
```

You can't put the friend declaration into the function. You must declare the function to be a friend in the class.

6. Fix the listing in Exercise 5 so it compiles.

```
1:      #include <iostream.h>
2:
3:      class Animal;
4:
5:      void setValue(Animal& , int);
6:
7:
8:      class Animal
9:      {
10:     public:
11:        friend void setValue(Animal&, int);
12:        int GetWeight()const { return itsWeight; }
13:        int GetAge() const { return itsAge; }
14:     private:
15:        int itsWeight;
16:        int itsAge;
17:     };
18:
19:     void setValue(Animal& theAnimal, int theWeight)
20:     {
21:        theAnimal.itsWeight = theWeight;
22:     }
23:
24:     void main()
25:     {
26:        Animal peppy;
27:        setValue(peppy, 5);
28:     }
```

7. **BUG BUSTERS:** What is wrong with this code?

```
1:      #include <iostream.h>
2:
3:      class Animal;
4:
5:      void setValue(Animal&, int);
6:      void setValue(Animal&, int, int);
7:
8:      class Animal
9:      {
10:     friend void setValue(Animal&, int); // here's the change!
11:     private:
12:        int itsWeight;
13:        int itsAge;
14:     };
15:
16:     void setValue(Animal& theAnimal, int theWeight)
17:     {
18:         theAnimal.itsWeight = theWeight;
```

```
19:      }
20:
21:
22:      void setValue(Animal& theAnimal, int theWeight, int theAge)
23:      {
24:          theAnimal.itsWeight = theWeight;
25:          theAnimal.itsAge = theAge;
26:      }
27:
28:      void main()
29:      {
30:          Animal peppy;
31:          setValue(peppy, 5);
32:          setValue(peppy, 7, 9);
33:      }
```

The function setValue(Animal&, int) was declared to be a friend, but the
overloaded function setValue(Animal&, int, int) was not declared to be a friend.

8. Fix Exercise 7 so that it compiles.

```
1:       #include <iostream.h>
2:
3:       class Animal;
4:
5:       void setValue(Animal& , int);
6:       void setValue(Animal& ,int,int); // here's the change!
7:
8:       class Animal
9:       {
10:      friend void setValue(Animal& ,int);
11:      friend void setValue(Animal& ,int,int);
12:      private:
13:          int itsWeight;
14:          int itsAge;
15:      };
16:
17:      void setValue(Animal& theAnimal, int theWeight)
18:      {
19:          theAnimal.itsWeight = theWeight;
20:      }
21:
22:
23:      void setValue(Animal& theAnimal, int theWeight, int theAge)
24:      {
25:          theAnimal.itsWeight = theWeight;
26:          theAnimal.itsAge = theAge;
27:      }
28:
29:      void main()
30:      {
31:          Animal peppy;
32:          setValue(peppy,5);
33:          setValue(peppy,7,9);
34:      }
```

Day 16

Quiz

1. What is the insertion operator, and what does it do?

   The insertion operator (<<) is a member operator of the ostream object and is used for writing to the output device.

2. What is the extraction operator, and what does it do?

   The extraction operator (>>) is a member operator of the istream object and is used for writing to your program's variables.

3. What are the three forms of cin.get(), and what are the differences between them?

   The first form of get() is without parameters. This returns the value of the character found and returns EOF (end of file) if the end of the file is reached.

   The second form of get() takes a character reference as its parameter; that character is filled with the next character in the input stream. The return value is an iostream object.

   The third form of get() takes an array, a maximum number of characters to get, and a terminating character. This form of get() fills the array with up to one fewer characters than the maximum (appending null), unless it reads the terminating character, in which case it immediately writes a null and leaves the terminating character in the buffer.

4. What is the difference between cin.read() and cin.getline()?

   cin.read() is used for reading binary data structures.

   getline() is used to read from the istream's buffer.

5. What is the default width for outputting a long integer using the insertion operator?

   Wide enough to display the entire number.

6. What is the return value of the insertion operator?

   A reference to an istream object.

7. What parameter does the constructor to an ofstream object take?

   The filename to be opened.

8. What does the ios::ate argument do?

   ios::ate places you at the end of the file, but you can write data anywhere in the file.

Exercises

1. Write a program that writes to the four standard `iostream` objects: `cin`, `cout`, `cerr`, and `clog`.

```
1:      #include <iostream.h>
2:      void main()
3:      {
4:          int x;
5:          cout << "Enter a number: ";
6:          cin >> x;
7:          cout << "You entered: " << x << endl;
8:          cerr << "Uh oh, this to cerr!" << endl;
9:          clog << "Uh oh, this to clog!" << endl;
10:     }
```

2. Write a program that prompts the user to enter her full name and then displays it on the screen.

```
1:      #include <iostream.h>
2:      void main()
3:      {
4:          char name[80];
5:          cout << "Enter your full name: ";
6:          cin.getline(name,80);
7:          cout << "\nYou entered: " << name << endl;
8:      }
```

3. Rewrite Listing 16.9 to do the same thing, but without using `putback()` or `ignore()`.

```
1:      // Listing
2:      #include <iostream.h>
3:
4:      void main()
5:      {
6:          char ch;
7:          cout << "enter a phrase: ";
8:          while ( cin.get(ch) )
9:          {
10:             switch (ch)
11:             {
12:                case '!':
13:                    cout << '$';
14:                    break;
15:                case '#':
16:                    break;
17:                default:
18:                    cout << ch;
19:                    break;
20:             }
21:         }
22:     }
```

4. Write a program that takes a filename as a parameter and opens the file for reading. Read every character of the file and display only the letters and punctuation to the screen. (Ignore all nonprinting characters.) Then close the file and exit.

```
1:      #include <fstream.h>
2:      enum BOOL { FALSE, TRUE };
3:
4:      int main(int argc, char**argv)    // returns 1
on error
5:      {
6:
7:          if (argc != 2)
8:          {
9:              cout << "Usage: argv[0] <infile>\n";
10:             return(1);
11:         }
12:
13:     // open the input stream
14:         ifstream fin (argv[1],ios::binary);
15:         if (!fin)
16:         {
17:             cout << "Unable to open " << argv[1] <<
" for reading.\n";
18:             return(1);
19:         }
20:
21:         char ch;
22:         while ( fin.get(ch))
23:             if ((ch > 32 && ch < 127) || ch == '\n'
|| ch == '\t')
24:                 cout << ch;
25:         fin.close();
26:     }
```

5. Write a program that displays its commandline arguments in reverse order and does not display the program name.

```
1:      #include <fstream.h>
2:
3:      int main(int argc, char**argv)    // returns 1
on error
4:      {
5:          for (int ctr = argc; ctr ; ctr--)
6:              cout << argv[ctr] << " ";
7:      }
```

Day 17

Quiz

1. What is an inclusion guard?

Inclusion guards are used to protect a header file from being included in a program more than once.

2. How do you instruct your compiler to print the contents of the intermediate file showing the effects of the preprocessor?

This quiz question must be answered by you, depending on the compiler you are using.

3. What is the difference between #define debug 0 and #undef debug?

#define debug 0 defines the term debug to equal 0 (zero). Everywhere the word debug is found, the character 0 will be substituted. #undef debug removes any definition of debug; when the word debug is found in the file, it will be left unchanged.

4. Name four predefined macros.

__DATE__ __TIME__ __FILE__ __LINE__

5. Why can't you call invariants() as the first line of your constructor?

The job of your constructor is to create the object; the class invariants cannot and should not exist before the object is fully created, and so any meaningful use of invariants() returns false until the constructor is finished.

Exercises

1. Write the inclusion guard statements for the header file STRING.H.

```
#ifndef STRING_H
#define STRING_H
...
#endif
```

2. Write an assert() macro that prints an error message and the file and line number if debug level is 2; just a message (without file and line number) if the level is 1; and does nothing if the level is 0.

```
1:     #include <iostream.h>
2:
3:     #ifndef DEBUG
4:     #define ASSERT(x)
5:     #elif DEBUG == 1
6:     #define ASSERT(x) \
7:             if (! (x)) \
8:             { \
9:                cout << "ERROR!! Assert " <<
   ➥#x << " failed\n"; \
10:            }
11:    #elif DEBUG == 2
12:    #define ASSERT(x) \
13:            if (! (x) ) \
14:            { \
15:               cout << "ERROR!! Assert " <<
   ➥#x << " failed\n"; \
16:               cout << " on line " <<
   ➥__LINE__ << "\n"; \
```

```
17:                              cout << " in file " <<
➥ __FILE__ << "\n";  \
18:                         }
19:      #endif
```

3. Write a macro DPrint that tests if debug is defined, and if it is, prints the value passed in as a parameter.

```
#ifndef DEBUG
#define DPRINT(string)
#else
#define DPRINT(STRING) cout << #STRING ;
#endif
```

4. Write a function that prints an error message. The function should print the line number and filename where the error occurred. Note that the line number and filename are passed in to this function.

```
1:      #include <iostream.h>
2:
3:       void ErrorFunc(
4:          int LineNumber,
5:          const char * FileName)
6:      {
7:          cout << "An error occurred in file ";
8:           cout << FileName;
9:           cout << " at line ";
10:          cout << LineNumber << endl;
11:      }
```

5. How would you call the preceding error function?

```
1:      // driver program to exercise ErrorFunc
2:      void main()
3:      {
4:          cout << "An error occurs on next line!";
5:          ErrorFunc(__LINE__, __FILE__);
6:      }
```

Note that the __LINE__ macro and the __FILE__ macro are used at the point of the error, and not in the error function. If you used them in the error function, they would report the line and file for the error function itself.

6. Write an assert() macro that uses the error function from Exercise 4, and write a driver program that calls this assert() macro.

```
1:      #include <iostream.h>
2:
3:      #define DEBUG // turn error handling on
4:
5:      #ifndef DEBUG
6:      #define ASSERT(x)
7:      #else
8:      #define ASSERT(X) \
9:          if (! (X)) \
10:         {  \
11:             ErrorFunc(__LINE__, __FILE__); \
12:         }
```

```
13:      #endif
14:
15:      void ErrorFunc(int LineNumber, const char * FileName)
16:      {
17:           cout << "An error occurred in file ";
18:           cout << FileName;
19:           cout << " at line ";
20:           cout << LineNumber << endl;
21:      }
22:
23:      // driver program to exercise ErrorFunc
24:      void main()
25:      {
26:         int x = 5;
27:         ASSERT(x >= 5);   // no error
28:         x = 3;
29:         ASSERT(x >= 5); // error!
30:      }
```

Note that in this case, the __LINE__ and __FILE__ macros can be called in the
assert() macro and still give the correct line (line 29). This is because the assert()
macro is expanded in place—where it is called. Thus, this program is evaluated
exactly as if main() were written as

```
1:      // driver program to exercise ErrorFunc
2:      void main()
3:      {
4:         int x = 5;
5:         if (! (x >= 5)) {ErrorFunc(__LINE__, __FILE__);}
6:         x = 3;
7:         if (! (x >= 5)) {ErrorFunc(__LINE__, __FILE__);}
8:      }
```

Day 18

Quiz

1. What is the most portable way to determine the maximum value that can be held
   in an int value?

   With the limits.h max() function for the int type.

2. Why should you avoid literal constants even for values that never change?

   You never know when your needs may change in precision or space.

3. What are some methods you might use to separate words in multiword variable
   names?

   Underscore characters and initial capitalization.

4. What advantage is there to setting your tab settings to enter spaces instead of tab characters?

Spaces instead of tabs make the indentation the same no matter what text editor you use.

5. Why is indentation important?

A consistent indentation style makes the code more readable and therefore easier to maintain.

Exercises

1. Create variable names using Hungarian notation for each of the following:

   a. A pointer to an integer array.

   ```
   piaTheArray
   ```

   b. An integer.

   ```
   iTheInteger
   ```

   c. A zero-terminated string.

   ```
   szString
   ```

2. Write a #define directive that expands to uniquely identify the source file in which it is used.

   ```
   #define THISFILE const char here[]="Striny:" FILE_
   ```

3. Place the #define directive from Question 2 inside an include file, then rewrite the program in Listing 18.3 to print the identifier string you defined.

   ```
   1:
   2:  #include<iostream.h>
   3:  #include "marker.h"
   4:  void main(int argc, char **argv)
   5:  {
   6:      if( argc > 1 && argv[1][0] == 'M' )
   7:      {
   8:          cout << here;
   9:      }
   10:     else
   11:     {
   12:         cout << "Hello World!" << endl;
   13:     }
   14: }
   ```

4. How might you best comment a function that performs a complex mathematical computation?

   a. Comment what it does.

   b. Comment how it does it.

   c. Write the formula in the comments.

   d. All the above.

5. What should be the maximum number of tasks any one function performs?

   As a rule of thumb, make certain that no one function is responsible for more than seven basic tasks.

Day 19

Quiz

1. What is the difference between a template and a macro?

   Templates are built into the C++ language and are type-safe. Macros are implemented by the preprocessor and are not type-safe.

2. What is the difference between the parameter in a template and the parameter in a function?

   The parameter to the template creates an instance of the template for each type. If you create six template instances, six different classes or functions are created. The parameters to the function change the behavior or data of the function, but only one function is created.

3. What is the difference between a type-specific template friend class and a general template friend class?

   The general template friend function creates one function for every type of the parameterized class; the type-specific function creates a type-specific instance for each instance of the parameterized class.

4. Is it possible to provide special behavior for one instance of a template but not for other instances?

   Yes, create a specialized function for the particular instance. In addition to creating `Array<t>::SomeFunction()`, also create `Array<int>::SomeFunction()` to change the behavior for integer arrays.

5. How many static variables are created if you put one static member into a template class definition?

One for each instance of the class.

Exercises

1. Create a template based on this `List` class:

```
class List
{
private:

public:
    List():head(0),tail(0),theCount(0) {}
    virtual ~List();

    void insert( int value );
    void append( int value );
    int is_present( int value ) const;
    int is_empty() const { return head == 0; }
    int count() const { return theCount; }
private:
    class ListCell
    {
    public:
        ListCell(int value, ListCell *cell = 0):val(value),next(cell){}
        int val;
        ListCell *next;
    };
    ListCell *head;
    ListCell *tail;
    int theCount;
};
```

The following is one way to implement this template:

```
template <class Type>
class List
{

public:
    List():head(0),tail(0),theCount(0) { }
    virtual ~List();

    void insert( Type value );
    void append( Type value );
    int is_present( Type value ) const;
    int is_empty() const { return head == 0; }
    int count() const { return theCount; }

private:
    class ListCell
    {
```

```
public:
     ListCell(Type value, ListCell *cell = 0):val(value),next(cell){}
     Type val;
     ListCell *next;
};

ListCell *head;
ListCell *tail;
int theCount;
};
```

2. Write the implementation for the List class (non-template) version.

```
void List::insert(int value)
{
     ListCell *pt = new ListCell( value, head );
     assert (pt != 0);

     // this line added to handle tail
     if ( head == 0 ) tail = pt;

     head = pt;
     theCount++;
}

void List::append( int value )
{
     ListCell *pt = new ListCell( value );
     if ( head == 0 )
          head = pt;
     else
          tail->next = pt;

     tail = pt;
     theCount++;
}

int List::is_present( int value ) const
{
     if ( head == 0 ) return 0;
     if ( head->val == value || tail->val == value )
          return 1;

     ListCell *pt = head->next;
     for (; pt != tail; pt = pt->next)
          if ( pt->val == value )
               return 1;

     return 0;
}
```

3. Write the template version of the implementations.

```
template <class Type>
List<Type>::~List()
{
     ListCell *pt = head;
```

```
        while ( pt )
        {
            ListCell *tmp = pt;
            pt = pt->next;
            delete tmp;
        }
        head = tail = 0;
}

template <class Type>
void List<Type>::insert(Type value)
{
    ListCell *pt = new ListCell( value, head );
    assert (pt != 0);

    // this line added to handle tail
    if ( head == 0 ) tail = pt;

    head = pt;
    theCount++;
}

template <class Type>
void List<Type>::append( Type value )
{
    ListCell *pt = new ListCell( value );
    if ( head == 0 )
        head = pt;
    else
        tail->next = pt;

    tail = pt;
    theCount++;
}

template <class Type>
int List<Type>::is_present( Type value ) const
{
    if ( head == 0 ) return 0;
    if ( head->val == value || tail->val == value )
        return 1;

    ListCell *pt = head->next;
    for (; pt != tail; pt = pt->next)
        if ( pt->val == value )
            return 1;

    return 0;
}
```

4. Declare three List objects: a list of strings, a list of Cats, and a list of ints.

```
List<String> string_list;
List<Cat> Cat_List;
List<int> int_List;
```

5. **BUG BUSTERS:** What is wrong with the following code? (Assume the List template is defined and Cat is the class defined on Day 6.)

```
List<Cat> Cat_List;
Cat Felix;
CatList.append( Felix );
cout << "Felix is " <<
     ( Cat_List.is_present( Felix ) ) ? "" : "not " << "present\n";
```

HINT (this is tough): What makes Cat different from int?

Cat doesn't have operator == defined; all operations that compare the values in the List cells, such as is_present, will result in compiler errors. To reduce the chance of this, put copious comments before the template definition, stating what operations must be defined for the instantiation to compile.

6. Declare friend operator== for List. friend int operator==(const Type& lhs, const Type& rhs);

7. Implement friend operator == for List.

```
template <class Type>
int List<Type>::operator==( const Type& lhs, const Type& rhs )
{
     // compare lengths first
     if ( lhs.theCount != rhs.theCount )
          return 0;     // lengths differ

     ListCell *lh = lhs.head;
     ListCell *rh = rhs.head;

     for(; lh != 0; lh = lh.next, rh = rh.next )
          if ( lh.value != rh.value )
               return 0;

     return 1;          // if they don't differ, they must match
}
```

8. Does operator== have the same problem as in Exercise 5?

Yes, because comparing the array involves comparing the elements; operator!= must be defined for the elements, as well.

9. Implement a template function for swap that exchanges two variables.

```
// template swap:
// must have assignment and the copy constructor defined for the Type.
template <class Type>
void swap( Type& lhs, Type& rhs)
{
     Type temp( lhs );
     lhs = rhs;
     rhs = temp;
}
```

D

Day 20

Quiz

1. What is an exception?

   An exception is an object that is created as a result of invoking the keyword throw. It is used to signal an exceptional condition and is passed up the call stack to the first catch statement that handles its type.

2. What is a try block?

   A try block is a set of statements that might generate an exception.

3. What is a catch statement?

   A catch statement has a signature of the type of exception it handles. It follows a try block and acts as the receiver of exceptions raised within the try block.

4. What information can an exception contain?

   An exception is an object and can contain any information that can be defined within a user-created class.

5. When are exception objects created?

   Exception objects are created when you invoke the keyword throw.

6. Should you pass exceptions by value or by reference?

   In general, exceptions should be passed by reference. If you don't intend to modify the contents of the exception object, you should pass a const reference.

7. Will a catch statement catch a derived exception if it is looking for the base class?

   Yes, if you pass the exception by reference.

8. If there are two catch statements, one for base and one for derived, which should come first?

   catch statements are examined in the order they appear in the source code. The first catch statement whose signature matches the exception is used.

9. What does catch(...) mean?

   catch(...) catches any exception of any type.

10. What is a breakpoint?

    A breakpoint is a place in the code where the debugger stops execution.

Exercises

1. Create a try block, a catch statement, and a simple exception.

```cpp
#include <iostream.h>
class OutOfMemory {};
void main()
{

    try
    {
        int *myInt = new int;
        if (myInt == 0)
            throw OutOfMemory();
    }
    catch (OutOfMemory)
    {
        cout << "Unable to allocate memory!\n";
    }
}
```

2. Modify the answer from Exercise 1, put data into the exception along with an accessor function, and use it in the catch block.

```cpp
#include <iostream.h>
#include <stdio.h>
#include <string.h>
class OutOfMemory
{
public:
    OutOfMemory(char *);
    char* GetString() { return itsString; }
private:
    char* itsString;
};

OutOfMemory::OutOfMemory(char * theType)
{
    itsString = new char[80];
    char warning[] = "Out Of Memory! Can't allocate room for: ";
    strncpy(itsString,warning,60);
    strncat(itsString,theType,19);
}

void main()
{

    try
    {
        int *myInt = new int;
        if (myInt == 0)
            throw OutOfMemory("int");
    }
    catch (OutOfMemory& theException)
    {
        cout << theException.GetString();
    }
}
```

D

3. Modify the class from Exercise 2 to be a hierarchy of exceptions. Modify the catch block to use the derived objects and the base objects.

```
1:      #include <iostream.h>
2:
3:      // Abstract exception data type
4:      class Exception
5:      {
6:      public:
7:          Exception(){}
8:          virtual ~Exception(){}
9:          virtual void PrintError() = 0;
10:     };
11:
12:     // Derived class to handle memory problems.
13:     // Note no allocation of memory in this class!
14:     class OutOfMemory : public Exception
15:     {
16:     public:
17:         OutOfMemory(){}
18:         ~OutOfMemory(){}
19:         virtual void PrintError();
20:     private:
21:     };
22:
23:     void OutOfMemory::PrintError()
24:     {
25:         cout << "Out of Memory!!\n";
26:     }
27:
28:     // Derived class to handle bad numbers
29:     class RangeError : public Exception
30:     {
31:     public:
32:         RangeError(unsigned long number){badNumber = number;}
33:         ~RangeError(){}
34:         virtual void PrintError();
35:         virtual unsigned long GetNumber() { return badNumber; }
36:         virtual void SetNumber(unsigned long number) {badNumber = num
➡ber;}
37:     private:
38:         unsigned long badNumber;
39:     };
40:
41:     void RangeError::PrintError()
42:     {
43:         cout << "Number out of range. You used " << GetNumber() <<
➡"!!\n";
44:     }
45:
46:     void MyFunction();   // func. prototype
47:
48:     void main()
49:     {
50:         try
51:         {
```

```
52:            MyFunction();
53:        }
54:        // Only one catch required, use virtual functions to do the
55:        // right thing.
56:        catch (Exception& theException)
57:        {
58:            theException.PrintError();
59:        }
60:    }
61:
62:    void MyFunction()
63:    {
64:        unsigned int *myInt = new unsigned int;
65:        long testNumber;
66:        if (myInt == 0)
67:            throw OutOfMemory();
68:
69:        cout << "Enter an int: ";
70:        cin >> testNumber;
71:        // this weird test should be replaced by a series
72:        // of tests to complain about bad user input
73:        if (testNumber > 3768 || testNumber < 0)
74:            throw RangeError(testNumber);
75:
76:        *myInt = testNumber;
77:        cout << "Ok. myInt: " << *myInt;
78:        delete myInt;
79:    }
```

4. Modify the program from Exercise 3 to have three levels of function calls.

```
1:     #include <iostream.h>
2:
3:     // Abstract exception data type
4:     class Exception
5:     {
6:     public:
7:         Exception(){}
8:         virtual ~Exception(){}
9:         virtual void PrintError() = 0;
10:    };
11:
12:    // Derived class to handle memory problems.
13:    // Note no allocation of memory in this class!
14:    class OutOfMemory : public Exception
15:    {
16:    public:
17:        OutOfMemory(){}
18:        ~OutOfMemory(){}
19:        virtual void PrintError();
20:    private:
21:    };
22:
23:    void OutOfMemory::PrintError()
24:    {
25:        cout << "Out of Memory!!\n";
26:    }
```

```
27:
28:     // Derived class to handle bad numbers
29:     class RangeError : public Exception
30:     {
31:     public:
32:        RangeError(unsigned long number){badNumber = number;}
33:        ~RangeError(){}
34:        virtual void PrintError();
35:        virtual unsigned long GetNumber() { return badNumber; }
36:        virtual void SetNumber(unsigned long number) {badNumber = num
➡ber;}
37:     private:
38:        unsigned long badNumber;
39:     };
40:
41:     void RangeError::PrintError()
42:     {
43:        cout << "Number out of range. You used " << GetNumber() <<
➡"!!\n";
44:     }
45:
46:     // func. prototypes
47:     void MyFunction();
48:     unsigned int * FunctionTwo();
49:     void FunctionThree(unsigned int *);
50:
51:     void main()
52:     {
53:        try
54:        {
55:           MyFunction();
56:        }
57:        // Only one catch required, use virtual functions to do the
58:        // right thing.
59:        catch (Exception& theException)
60:        {
61:           theException.PrintError();
62:        }
63:     }
64:
65:  unsigned int * FunctionTwo()
66:  {
67:     unsigned int *myInt = new unsigned int;
68:     if (myInt == 0)
69:        throw OutOfMemory();
70:     return myInt;
71:  }
72:
73:
74:   void MyFunction()
75:   {
76:        unsigned int *myInt = FunctionTwo();
77:
```

```
78:            FunctionThree(myInt);
79:            cout << "Ok. myInt: " << *myInt;
80:            delete myInt;
81:    }
82:
83:    void FunctionThree(unsigned int *ptr)
84:    {
85:            long testNumber;
86:            cout << "Enter an int: ";
87:            cin >> testNumber;
88:            // this weird test should be replaced by a series
89:            // of tests to complain about bad user input
90:            if (testNumber > 3768 || testNumber < 0)
91:                    throw RangeError(testNumber);
92:            *ptr = testNumber;
93:    }
```

5. **BUG BUSTERS:** What is wrong with the following code?

```
#include "stringc.h"          // our string class

class xOutOfMemory
{
public:
      xOutOfMemory( const String& where ) : location( where ){}
      ~xOutOfMemory(){}
      virtual String where(){ return location; }
private:
      String location;
}

main()
{
      try {
            char *var = new char;
            if ( var == 0 )
                  throw xOutOfMemory();
      }
      catch( xOutOfMemory& theException )
      {
            cout << "Out of memory at " << theException.location() << "\n";
      }
}
```

In the process of handling an "out of memory" condition, a string object is created by the constructor of xOutOfMemory. This exception can only be raised when the program is out of memory, and so this allocation must fail.

It is possible that trying to create this string will raise the same exception, creating an infinite loop until the program crashes. If this string is really required, you can allocate the space in a static buffer before beginning the program, and then use it as needed when the exception is thrown.

Day 21

Quiz

1. How does dividing your project into multiple files speed project builds?

   By dividing the project into multiple source files, you can compile and link only the files that are changed, and as a result, compiling takes less time.

2. What is the difference in scope between a global variable and a global variable declared with `static`?

   The `static` variable only has scope of all the functions that follow it in that file, the normal global variable has scope of all the source files where it is declared and where it is identified with `extern`.

3. What is the difference between `extern` used to declare a variable and `extern` to indicate a linkage type?

   When `extern` is used to declare a variable, it simply means that the variable exists somewhere in one of the compilation units. When used for linkage, it indicates that the function names should not be mangled for linkage.

4. Why is it a good idea to place `static` member variable initialization in a separate file from the class header file?

   Placing them in a separate file that is included only once in the compile process avoids compiler errors that would occur with the multiple `includes` of the header file.

5. What is a precompiled header?

   A precompiled header is a special header file that contains a collection of `include` statements for a project and is compiled by itself.

Exercises

1. Write a program that has a global variable named `Global` and, in a separate file, a function with a local variable named `Global`. Show scope resolution.

```
// First file
int Global = 5;
void SomeFunction();
main()
{
    SomeFunction();
}

// Second file
#include<iostream.h>
```

```
    extern int Global;

    void SomeFunction();

    void SomeFunction()
    {
        int Global = 7;
        cout << "The global Global: "
            << ::Global << endl;
        cout << "Local Global: "
            << Global << endl;
    }
```

2. Write a program that has a main function, a user-defined class with a static member variable, and a variable printing function, each in its own file.

```
    // mainf.cpp, the main file
    #include "classy.h"

    void Show(Classy cObj);

    void main()
    {
        Classy Object;
        Show(Object);
    }

    // show.cpp, the variable printing function
    #include<iostream.h>
    #include "classy.h"

    void Show(Classy cObj)
    {
        cout << cObj.SeeIt() << endl;
    }

    // classy.h, the header file for classy

    class Classy {
        static int cCounter;
    public:
        Classy(){ cCounter++; }
        ~Classy(){}
        static int SeeIt() { return(cCounter);}
    };

    // classy.cpp, the classy implementation
    #include "classy.h"
    int Classy::cCounter = 0;
```

3. Write two function prototypes named sqrt—one taking a complex and returning a complex, and one taking a double and returning a double. Write the code necessary to make the double version link with C linkage and the complex version link with C++ linkage.

```
    complex sqrt(complex); // C++ linkage (default)
    extern "C"  double sqrt(double); // C linkage
```

4. **BUG BUSTERS:** What is wrong with this program?

```
1:      #include <iostream.h>
2:
3:      int JamesBond 0x007;
3:      void main()
4:      {
5:         int JamesBond = 0x005;
6:         cout << (JamesBond + JamesBond)
7:               << endl;
8:      }
```

The JamesBond variable on line 5 hides the global JamesBond variable on line 3.

5. **BUG BUSTERS:** What is wrong with this program?

```
1:      #include <iostream.h>
2:
3:      char *SomeFunct()
4:      {
5:          return(Goldfinger);
6:      }
7:
8:      static char *Goldfinger ="Goldfinger";
9:
10:     void main()
11:     {
12:         cout << "Here is Goldfinger: "
13:               << SomeFunct() << endl;
14:     }
```

Goldfinger is not in scope inside SomeFunct(), only inside main() and any functions that follow main().

6. Delete the static keyword in line 8 of exercise 5. Does it work now? Why?

Deleting static makes the program work because it gives Goldfinger global file scope.

Day 22

Quiz

1. What C++ mechanism can you use to limit the possibility of a name space conflict?

Use the namespace directive.

2. What is a v-pointer?

A v-pointer (virtual pointer) is a pointer that the compiler places inside a class when that class has one or more virtual functions. The v-pointer points to a table that contains the pointers to the virtual functions in that class.

3. A class library and an object file are which of the following:

   a. Identical to each other

   b. Similar

   c. Opposites

   b. Similar

4. What is data alignment?

   Data alignment is the way an operating system allocates storage to store and retrieve variables. Common alignment is on 16-bit and 32-bit boundaries.

5. Why is static_cast preferred over reinterpret_cast?

   static_cast is safer because it does not force illegal casts.

6. What would be the result of the following?

```
#include <iostream.h>
class ADog {
//...
};
void main()
{
    ADog Fido;
    cout << "Fido is a "
         << typeid(Fido).name()
         << endl;
}
```

   This program displays the data type of the object Fido: Fido is a ADog.

Exercises

1. Alter the following code where commented so that the final cout statement prints the correct number of Peppers ready to be picked.

```
#include <iostream.h>
#include <time.h>
#include <stdlib.h>

class Veggie {
};

class Peppers : public Veggie {
   //...
};

class Celery : public Veggie {
   //...
};

class Spinach : public Veggie {
   //...
};
```

```
main()
{
    Veggie *Garden[100];
    int ModDiv = 3;
    int Remainder = 0;
    int PepperCount = 0;

    srand(
      static_cast<unsigned>(time()));

    for(int j=0; j<100; j++)
    {
        Remainder = rand() % ModDiv;
        switch (Remainder) {
          case 2: Garden[j] = new Spinach;
                  break;
          case 1: Garden[j] = new Celery;
                  break;
          default: Garden[j] = new Peppers;
        }
    }

    // Place code here to increment
    // counter for Peppers:
    for(int j=0; j<100; j++)
    {
        Pepper *pPepper =
            dynamic_cast<Pepper*>(Garden[j]);

        if(pPepper) PepperCount++;
    }
    // End of Pepper counter code

    cout << PepperCount
         << "Peppers for Peter to pick."
         << endl;
}
```

3. Look up the data alignment information for your compiler and determine if it provides a way to change the setting.

4. **BUG BUSTERS:** What is wrong with this code?

```
#include <iostream.h>
namespace CharliesFunctions {
    void FunctionOne() { /*…*/ }
    void FunctionTwo() { /*…*/ }
}

void main()
{
    cout << "Calling Charlie's Functions"
         << endl;
    FunctionOne();
    FunctionTwo();
}
```

The main function requires the using `CharliesFunctions` directive before it can use the functions inside that namespace.

5. **BUG BUSTERS:** The programmer expected `Calls` to be 1 in the following code but instead got 2. What's wrong with this code and what could be done to prevent the same problem for others who use the `SomeClass` class?

```cpp
#include<iostream.h>

static int Calls = 0;

class SomeClass {
private:
    int X;
public:
    SomeClass(int I) {
        ++Calls;
        X = I;
    }
};

MyFunction(SomeClass AnObject) {
    Calls++;
}

void main()
{
    int MyInt;
    MyFunction(MyInt);
    cout << "Made " << Calls
        << " calls to MyFunction"
        << endl;
}
```

The function `MyFunction` expects a variable of `SomeClass` type. When it receives an `int` instead, it searches for and finds a constructor it can use to create a `SomeClass` type from the `int`. The constructor also increments the `Calls` global variable. There are actually a couple of ways to solve the problem but the one most obvious would be to prevent automatic constructor calls by declaring the `SomeClass` constructor with the qualifier, `explicit` as follows:

```cpp
explicit SomeClass(int I) {…
```

Day 23

Quiz

1. True or False. The `tellg()` function indicates the number of bytes in a stream.

   False. The `tellg()` function indicates the current get position.

2. What is the member function, `setfill()`, used for?

   It sets the character that fills unused field characters.

3. Where is the put position after the statement, `seekp(0, ios::end);` is executed?

At the end of the stream.

4. What does the statement, `setf(ios::boolalpha)`, do?

It causes the alphabetic version of Boolean values (`true` or `false`) to be inserted in the stream.

Exercises

1. Write a program that uses `seekg()` and `tellg()` to determine the size of a file (in characters).

```
 1:// Listing D.23.1
 2:
 3:#include<fstream.h>
 4:
 5:void main()
 6:{
 7:   const int Size = 50;
 8:   char flname[Size];
 9:   streampos lastChar = 0;
10:
11:   cout << "Enter a filename: ";
12:
13:   cin.getline(flname, Size);
14:
15:   ifstream fl(flname, ios::nocreate | ios::in);
16:
17:   if(fl)
18:   {
19:      fl.seekg(0, ios::end);
20:      lastChar = fl.tellg();
21:   }
22:
23:   cout << lastChar << endl;
24:}
```

2. Write a program that subtracts three from each of the `int` values in the following object: `istrstream theStr("1 2 3 4");`.

```
 1:// Listing D.23.2
 2:#include<strstrea.h>
 3:
 4:void main()
 5:{
 6:   istrstream theStr("1 2 3 4");
 7:   int iValue;
 8:
 9:   while( true )
10:   {
11:      theStr >> iValue;
12:
13:      if( theStr.fail() )
14:         break;
```

```
15:
16:    cout << ( iValue - 3 )
17:       << endl;
18:  }
19:}
```

3. Write a manipulator called `doubleline` that places two newline characters in the stream.

```
ostream& doubleline(ostream& aStream)
{
  return( aStream << '\n' << '\n');
}
```

Day 24

Quiz

1. True or False. The object modeling and responsibility-driven design techniques are not based in OOD methods.

   False.

2. Using the Booch model, in which phase would you establish the visibility between classes?

   In the establish visibility step.

3. True or False. The OOD model stresses up-front planning for understanding the problem more than previous design methods.

   False. Previous models required a complete understanding of the problem before coding could start. The Booch OOD design method allows the design to change during the design as opposed to before the design.

4. True or False. The OOD model does not require structure in program design.

   False.

Exercises

1. Use the first step of the Booch OOD technique to identify the objects required to bake a cake.

   To bake a cake, preheat the oven to the appropriate temperature, mix the ingredients, pour them into a greased pan, and bake for the appropriate time. (Your response may vary depending on your knowledge of the problem.)

2. Identify the methods in Exercise 1.

   Yours may vary again but here are a few: `Oven::Preheat`, `pan::grease`, `ingredients::Mix`.

3. Do you see any natural boundaries that separate or imply visibility in Exercises 1 and 2?

Pan and oven have nothing really to do with each other relevant to the problem space. You may see others as well.

Day 25

Quiz

1. In what order does a pre-order traversal visit the nodes of a binary tree?

Current, left, right.

2. Are binary trees a kind of contiguous memory structure?

No. Although the data structures may be represented as a contiguous section of memory internally, they are not necessarily represented that way. Data structures are simply a different method of storing and retrieving data.

3. How is a binary tree like a single tree node?

A binary tree is nothing more than a tree node, referred to as the "root" node, which has zero to two tree nodes (or, subtrees) attached to it.

4. Why are binary tree traversals often recursive?

The answer to this one is related to the answer to Question 3. If the tree is represented as a root node, then each subtree is as well.

Exercises

1. Alter Listing 25.1 to implement a simple stack class.

The only real change needed is in the way the Pop function works. Other than that, only variable names need to change to indicate more accurately the data structure.

```
1: // Listing 25.1, Using a Simple Stack class
2:
3:#include<iostream.h>
4:
5:// A simple integer storage queue
6:
7:class IntStack {
8:private:
9:    int ptrNext;
10:    int ptrBase;
11:    enum { SSIZE = 256 };
12:    int theStack[SSIZE];
13:public:
```

```
14:     IntStack();
15:     ~IntStack();
16:
17:     bool Push(int);
18:     bool Pop(int &);
19:
20:     bool IsEmpty();
21:     bool IsFull();
22:};
23:
24:IntStack::IntStack(){
25:
26:     ptrNext = ptrBase = 0;
27:
28:     for(int i=0; i<SSIZE; i++)
29:         theStack[i] = 0;
30:}
31:
32:IntStack::~IntStack(){}
33:
34:bool IntStack::Push(int anInt){
35:
36:     if( IsFull() )
37:         return(false);
38:
39:     theStack[ptrNext] = anInt;
40:     ptrNext++;
41:
42:     return(true);
43:}
44:
45:bool IntStack::Pop(int &firstInt){
46:
47:     if( IsEmpty() )
48:         return(false);
49:
50:     ptrNext--;
51:     firstInt = theStack[ptrNext];
52:
53:     return(true);
54:}
55:
56:bool IntStack::IsEmpty(){
57:     return( ptrNext == ptrBase);
58:}
59:
60:bool IntStack::IsFull(){
61:     return( SSIZE == ptrNext );
62:}
63:
64:void main()
65:{
66:
67:     IntStack OurStack;
68:     int Value;
69:
```

D

```
70:    while( !OurStack.IsFull() )
71:    {
72:        cout << "Enter an integer value or a 0 to quit: ";
73:        cin >> Value;
74:        cin.ignore(); // ignore <CR>
75:
76:        if( 0 == Value )
77:            break;
78:
79:        OurStack.Push(Value);
80:    }
81:
82:    cout << "The ints in reverse order:" << endl;
83:
84:    while(! OurStack.IsEmpty() )
85:        if( OurStack.Pop(Value) )
86:            cout << Value << endl;
87:}
```

2. Alter the code from Exercise 1 to store character values instead of `ints`.

This one is so simple I didn't bother to include the code here. Just do a global replace of `int` with `char` (except for the two `ptr` variables). The idea of this exercise is to get you to look through the code in more detail and see how easy it would be to implement it using templates.

3. Alter the `InOrderPrint` function in Listing 25.2 to do a post order print instead.

```
bool BinaryTree::PostOrderPrint(TreeNode *tNode) {

    if( tNode )
    {
        PostOrderPrint( tNode->LeftNode() );
        PostOrderPrint( tNode->RightNode() );
        cout << tNode->Data() << endl;
    }
    return(true);
}
```

Day 26

Quiz

1. True or False. The shell sort is an n-square sort.
   False.

2. A binary search does which of the following:
   a. Repeatedly divides the array in half until only the match or nothing is left.
   b. Selects items one at a time from the array until it finds the match or reaches the end.

  c. Searches from both sides of the array, alternating between high and low array slots until the middle is reached.

a. Repeatedly divides the array.

3. The quick sort does which of the following:

  a. Selects items one at a time from the array and compares each with the current lowest and then swaps the current lowest with the lowest in the remainder.

  b. Recursively executes on smaller and smaller sub-arrays until it breaks the main array down into single-item sub-arrays for sorting.

  c. Calculates a gap value, which it uses as an average of the array values, and sorts using that average as the mid-point in the array.

b. Recursively executes on smaller and smaller portions of the array.

4. The shell sort does which of the following:

  a. Repeatedly divides the array and merges it back together in increasing order with each repetition.

  b. Sorts disk file contents in a command shell.

  c. Calculates a gap value, sorts the array items separated by that gap, and decrements the gap with each iteration.

c. Calculates the gap and sorts using that gap, then decrements the gap with each iteration.

Exercises

1. Alter the bubble sort program in Listing 26.1 to sort a character array entered by a user.

```
1:int BubbleSort(char MyChars[], int arraySize)
2:{
3:   int i, j;
4:   char tmpChar;
5:
6:   // Just for kicks, keep track of the swap count
7:   int swaps = 0;
8:
9:   for(i=0; i<arraySize; i++)
10:  {
11:    for(j=0; j<arraySize; j++)
12:    {
13:      // If the left one is larger, then swap
14:      if( MyChars[i] < MyChars[j] )
15:      {
16:        swaps++;
17:        // Save the first one before swap
18:        tmpChar = MyChars[i];
```

```
19:
20:          MyChars[i] = MyChars[j];
21:          MyChars[j] = tmpChar;
22:       }
23:    }
24: }
25:
26: return( swaps );
27:}
```

2. Which sort is identified by an execution time proportional to n^1.2?

   Shell sort.

3. The execution time of an n^2 sort does which of these:

   a. Doubles with each increment in array size.

   b. Increases exponentially with each increment in array size.

   c. Increases by a power of two with each increment in array size.

   b. Increases exponentially.

4. **BUG BUSTERS:** Assuming we use the quick sort from Listing 26.4, what is wrong with this QuickSort function call?

   ```
   for(int I=0; I<10; I++)
     Array[I] = rand() % 15;

   QuickSort(Array, 10);
   ```

   The quicksort takes the last element number, not the size of the array. The statement should be: QuickSort(Array, 9);

Day 27

Quiz

1. **BUG BUSTERS:** What sort of error does the following program contain?

   ```
   #include <iostream.h>
   void main()
   {
      int i;
      const int Size = 10;
      char aString[Size];

      for(i=0; i<Size+1; i++)
        cin >> aString[i];
   }
   ```

   This program has an off-by-one error in the last for loop.

2. **BUG BUSTERS:** What's wrong with the following program?

```cpp
#include <iostream.h>
void main()
{
  int It;
  cout << "Enter a number: ";
  cin >> It;
  if( It = 1)
  {
     cout << "One" << endl;
  }
  else
  {
     cout << "Not one." << endl;
  }
}
```

The test in the if statement is an assignment instead of a test.

Exercises

1. Fix the program in Quiz Question 2 and do it in a way that avoids the problem in the future.

```cpp
#include <iostream.h>
void main()
{
  int It;
  cout << "Enter a number: ";
  cin >> It;
  if( 1 == It )
  {
     cout << "One" << endl;
  }
  else
  {
     cout << "Not one." << endl;
  }
}
```

2. What error is identifiable by compiler messages that refer to "nested function definitions?"

   Unbalanced or a forgotten closing brace often generates this error.

3. Is it best to finish all the code and compile just once or to compile a piece at a time?

   You will find your development is much faster if you compile a little at a time.

Day 28

Quiz

1. What library provides the built-in type operations for character strings?

   The strings library contained in strings.h.

2. What does the algorithms library provide?

   It provides a collection of algorithms, such as sorting and searching algorithms.

3. What library should be used to replace the character manipulation functions of the stdlib.h C library, such as `toupper()`?

   The locale library in locale.h.

4. What is a `bitset` class?

   A special bit field class that provides many of the built-in data type capabilities for bit fields.

INDEX

Add to Your Sams Library Today with the Best Books for Programming, Operating Systems, and New Technologies

The easiest way to order is to pick up the phone and call
1-800-428-5331
between 9:00 a.m. and 5:00 p.m. EST.
For faster service please have your credit card available.

ISBN	Quantity	Description of Item	Unit Cost	Total Cost
0-672-30874-6		Visual C++ 4 Unleashed (Book/CD)	$49.99	
0-672-30795-2		Teach Yourself Visual C++ 4 in 21 Days (Book/CD)	$35.00	
0-672-30791-X		Peter Norton's Complete Windows 95 Guide	$29.99	
0-672-30762-6		32-Bit Windows Programming (Book/CD)	$39.99	
0-672-30602-6		Programming Windows 95 Unleashed (Book/CD)	$49.99	
0-672-30474-0		Windows 95 Unleashed (Book/CD)	$35.00	
0-672-30611-5		Your Windows 95 Consultant	$19.99	
0-672-30462-7		Teach Yourself MFC in 21 Days	$29.99	
0-672-30568-2		Teach Yourself OLE Programming in 21 Days (Book/CD)	$39.99	
0-672-30655-7		Developing Your Own 32-Bit Operating System (Book/CD)	$49.99	
0-672-30593-3		Develop a Professional Visual C++ Application in 21 Days (Book/CD)	$35.00	
❏ 3 ½" Disk		Shipping and Handling: See information below.		
❏ 5 ¼" Disk		TOTAL		

Shipping and Handling: $4.00 for the first book, and $1.75 for each additional book. Floppy disk: add $1.75 for shipping and handling. If you need to have it NOW, we can ship product to you in 24 hours for an additional charge of approximately $18.00, and you will receive your item overnight or in two days. Overseas shipping and handling adds $2.00 per book and $8.00 for up to three disks. Prices subject to change. Call for availability and pricing information on latest editions.

201 W. 103rd Street, Indianapolis, Indiana 46290

1-800-428-5331 — Orders   1-800-835-3202 — FAX   1-800-858-7674 — Customer Service

Book ISBN 0-672-30887-6